The Professional Practice
of Architectural
Working Drawings

The Professional Practice of Architectural Working Drawings

FOURTH EDITION

Osamu A. Wakita, Hon. AIA
Professor of Architecture

Nagy R. Bakhoum, Architect
Principal, Obelisk Architects, Inc.

Richard M. Linde, AIA Architect
Richard M. Linde & Associates, Inc.

WILEY

JOHN WILEY & SONS, INC.

Chapter 4: (Top) Courtesy of WePower LLC; (Bottom) Floralis Generica, Courtesy of WikiArquitectura.

Chapter 11: (Left) J. P. Getty Museum; (Right) Crystals at City Center, Las Vegas, NV.

Chapter 13: (Left) Cerritos Library, Cerritos, CA; (Right) J. P. Getty Museum.

For general information about our other products and services, please contact our Customer Care Department within the United States at (800) 762-2974, outside the United States at (317) 572-3993 or fax (317) 572-4002.

Wiley publishes in a variety of print and electronic formats and by print-on-demand. Some material included with standard print versions of this book may not be included in e-books or in print-on-demand. If this book refers to media such as a CD or DVD that is not included in the version you purchased, you may download this material at http://booksupport.wiley.com. For more information about Wiley products, visit www.wiley.com.

Library of Congress Cataloging-in-Publication Data:

Wakita, Osamu A.
    The professional practice of architectural working drawings/
Osamu A. Wakita, Nagy R. Bakhoum, Richard M. Linde. — 4th ed.
        p.   cm.
    Includes index.
    ISBN 978-0-470-61815-8 (cloth); ISBN 978-1-118-08415-1
(ebk); ISBN 978-1-118-08416-8 (ebk); ISBN 978-1-118-08654-4
(ebk); ISBN 978-1-118-08661-2; ISBN 978-1-118-08662-9 (ebk)
    1. Architecture—Designs and plans—Working   drawings.
    I. Bakhoum, Nagy R.   II.   Linde, Richard M. III. Title.
NA2713.W34 2011
720.28'4—dc22

                                                    2011006423

Printed in the United States of America

10 9 8 7 6

CONTENTS

Preface   **xiii**

PART I   PROFESSIONAL FOUNDATIONS   1

Chapter 1   **The Office**   **3**

The Physical Office   4

Office Practice and How It May Be Structured   4

Resource Library   6

Professional Organizations   7

Architect/Client Relationship   7

Implementation of the Construction Documents   12

Building   13

Influence of Building Information Modeling on Building Design   14

Chapter 2   **Standards and Techniques, Metrification, Hand Drafting, and Computer-aided Drafting**   **17**

Introduction to Standards and Techniques   18

Drawing Practice   18

Lettering   20

Architectural Drafting   26

Reproduction Methods   26

Office Standards   30

Metrics   35

Hand Drawing   44

Kinds of Drafting Equipment   44

Selecting and Using Drafting Pencils   48

Computer Drafting   49

Office Standards   49

A Game within a Game   67

Power of the CAD Drafter   69

Disadvantages of a Computer   72

Advantages of a Computer   73

Future of CAD   75

Conclusion   78

Chapter 3   BIM, Revit, and Human Concerns   79

Introduction   80

Human Considerations   80

Americans with Disabilities Act (ADA)   80

Building Information Modeling (BIM)   89

Chapter 4   Sustainable/Green Architecture   107

Environmental and Human Considerations   108

Sustainable Architecture   108

Lateral Influences   109

Energy Conservation   110

Sound   112

Snow   115

Fire and Smoke   116

Temperature   119

Deterioration   120

Drainage/Rainfall   121

Underground Gas Control   123

Water Table   123

Frost Line/Frost Depth   123

Termites and Termite Treatment   125

Energy Sources   126

Future of Energy Sources   132

Chapter 5   **Construction Materials and Methods**   **135**

     Building Materials   136

     Wood Floor Systems   136

     Wood Wall Systems   142

     Wood Roof Systems   144

     Concrete   149

     Steel Floor System   155

     Steel Stud Wall Framing System   156

     Steel Decking Roof System   157

     Light Steel Roof Framing System   157

     Masonry Wall System   157

     Composite Systems and Combinations of Materials   159

     Material Selections   161

     Wood as a Material   162

     Concrete as a Material   166

     Steel as a Material   169

     Masonry as a Material   174

Chapter 6   **Initial Preparation Phase for Construction Documents**   **177**

     Working Guidelines for Preparing Construction Documents   178

     Making the Transition from Schematic Drawings to Construction Documents   180

     Building Code Requirements   180

     Primary Materials Analysis   181

     Selecting the Primary Structural System   182

     Requirements of Consultants   182

     Regional Considerations   183

     Energy Conservation   185

     Interrelationship of Drawings   186

     Project Management   186

     Office Procedure and Planning Strategy   186

     Tracking a Set of Working Drawings   188

     Format/Cartoon   190

Project Book   191

Numbers—Legal, Job, Task   192

Drawing Sequence   197

Delivery Methods   208

PART II   DOCUMENT EVOLUTION   217

Chapter 7   Site and Grading Plan   219

Site Analysis   220

Site Analysis Applied   222

The Topography Map   225

The Soils and Geology Map   225

The Site Plan   227

The Grading Plan   231

The Site and Grading Plan   234

The Drainage Plan   241

The Erosion and Sediment Control Plans   245

The Utility Plan   245

The Circulation Plan   246

The Landscape, Irrigation, and Drainage Plans   246

The Site Improvement Plan: An Overview   247

Size and Location   250

Chapter 8   Floor Plan   253

Types of Floor Plans   254

Symbols   268

Other Floor-plan Considerations   273

Drawing a Floor Plan with a Computer   277

Chapter 9   Foundation and Roof Plans, Floor and Roof Framing Systems   287

Foundation Introduction   288

Types of Foundations   288

Examples   295

Summary of Typical Conventions for Foundation Plan   300

Exterior and Interior Walls   304

A Steel Structure   305

Roof Plans and Framing Systems   308

Framing with Different Materials   333

Floor Framing   337

Chapter 10   **Building Sections**   **347**

Building Sections Defined   348

Drawing a Building Section   348

Types of Building Sections   351

Drafting a Building Section   356

Drafting a Building Section of a Residence   356

Chapter 11   **Exterior and Interior Elevations**   **365**

Introduction to Exterior Elevations   366

Drawing Doors and Windows   372

Material Designations   374

Notes   375

Dotted Lines   377

Controlling Factors   380

Drafting an Exterior Elevation   383

Weatherproofing   385

Drawing an Elevation with and without a Model   387

Exterior Elevation Using BIM/Revit   389

Interior Elevations   390

Dimensions and Intersections   394

Drafting an Interior Elevation: Examples   394

Computers and Interior Elevations   395

Evolution of a Set of Interior Elevations   396

Interior Elevations Using BIM/Revit   397

Chapter 12   **Schedules: Door, Window, and Finish**   **403**

Schedules Defined   404

Tabulated Schedules: Doors and Windows   404

Pictorial Schedules: Doors and Windows   405

Choosing a Tabulated or Pictorial Schedule   406

Interior Finish Schedules   406

Additional Schedules   408

Schedules as They Relate to Structural Entities   408

CAD-Generated and Computer-Drafted Schedules   409

Schedule Templates   410

Schedules Using BIM or Revit   411

Chapter 13   **Architectural Details and Vertical Links (Stairs/Elevators)**   **421**

The Purpose of Architectural Details   422

Freehand Detail Sketches   422

Using Details in Construction Documents   422

Hard-Line (Hand-Drafted and CAD)   428

Footing Detail   430

Window Detail   432

Fireplace   436

Stair Design and Vertical Links   443

Mechanical Vertical Links   447

Detailing in BIM/Revit   451

Tenant Improvement Details   452

PART III   **CASE STUDIES**   **459**

Chapter 14   **Construction Documents for a One-story, Conventional Wood-framed Residence**   **461**

Conceptual Design   462

Design and Schematic Drawings   463

Evolution of the Working Drawings   467

Site Plan, Vicinity Map, Roof Plan, and Notes   467

Jadyn Residence Site Plan   471

Jadyn Residence Floor Plan   473

Jadyn Residence Roof Plan   480

Jadyn Residence Building Sections 480

Jadyn Residence Exterior Elevations 486

Jadyn Residence Foundation Plan 491

Framing a Residence 494

Jadyn Residence Roof Framing Plan 498

Jadyn Residence Interior Elevations 498

Set Check 502

Chapter 15 **Construction Documents for a Two-story, Wood-framed Residence with Basement** **507**

Schematic Design for Blu Residence 508

Site Plan 511

First-Floor Plan 513

Second-Floor Plan 514

Roof Plan 518

Blu Residence Building Sections 518

Blu Residence Building Elevations 522

Foundation Plan: Slab and Raised Wood 529

Blu Residence Foundation Plan: Raised Wood 534

Framing Plan 537

Support Drawings for Blu Residence 541

Chapter 16 **Conceptual Design and Construction Documents for a Steel and Masonry Building (Theater)** **549**

Introduction 550

Conceptual Design: Site and Client Requirements 550

Design Development Punch List 550

Initial Schematic Studies 550

Site Plan 554

Foundation Plan 556

Ground-Floor Plan 557

Partial Floor Plan and Interior Elevations 560

Exterior Elevations 560

Building Sections 564

        Roof Plan   575

        Roof Framing Plan   577

Chapter 17   **Madison Steel Building**   **597**

        Introduction   598

        The Madison Office Building   598

        Floor-plan Design Development Phase   603

        Summary   625

Chapter 18   **Tenant Improvements**   **627**

        Tenant Improvement Introduction   628

        Existing Buildings   628

        Existing Floor Level—Building A   628

        Development of Working Drawings—Building B   630

        Working Drawings   642

        Index   **653**

Appendix A   **Survey of Regional Differences available online at www.wiley.com/go/wakita**

Appendix B   **A Uniform System for Architectural Working Drawing available online at www.wiley.com/go/wakita**

Abbreviations available online at www.wiley.com/go/wakita

PowerPoint presentations available online at www.wiley.com/go/wakita

PREFACE

The purpose of this book is to teach techniques, attitudes, computer-aided drafting (CAD), and BIM via Revit, as well as the fundamental concepts of architectural working drawings. With the introduction of BIM, and its vehicle Revit, the profession has changed radically, as has the education of architectural drafters. In the past, employees concentrated on drafting; now we must return our focus to architecture. BIM requires our new legions of designers, drafters, and architects to know more about the process of architecture and building components than ever before. The profession of architecture has changed from 20% design and 80% working drawings to 80% constructing a three-dimensional (3-D) model and 20% working drawings. With Revit, when the design development phase of a project is complete, the working drawings are all but complete as well. The projects become front loaded and require a person working in the parametric form in 3-D to have full knowledge of structure, engineering, design, and site grading, to mention just a few of the necessary areas. There is a new approach to the process of creating working drawings: that of a fully parametric system where the software is integrated to aid in the process of drafting. The focus of developing drawings is shifted from the computer to the individual.

Every chapter has been revised with current information. The text is intended to strongly encourage drafters to go beyond the two-dimensional AutoCAD system and start thinking in 3-D, even if they still work in 2-D. It is both critical and essential to move out of your comfort zone to explore the programs that offer a more cohesive system of drafting, namely Revit. Within these chapters, you will find the method required to produce working drawings to a national standard.

The Professional Practice of Architectural Working Drawings, 4th edition, has three divisions. Part I, "Professional Foundations," consists of Chapters 1 through 6 and is designed to introduce such topics as LEED, BIM, Revit, energy use, and green and sustainable architecture. The first third of the book thus investigates the field of architecture and takes a close look at how offices work.

Part II, "Document Evolution," Chapters 7–13, reflects the attitudes and concerns covered in Part I, while establishing a professional approach toward the national standards for architectural drawings. It also covers how to communicate the architect's ideas into a series of dialogues among the architect, client, and contractor. Architectural words are defined as they are introduced in the text. An integration of chapters was developed to educate our pre-architectural pupil/readers to think three dimensionally, so that the process becomes a reality.

Part III, "Case Studies," includes two new case studies completed in AutoCAD, intended to further demonstrate working drawings for both a one-story and a two-story wood-framed residence. Drawings are broken down from the fundamental stages to completion. Two additional chapters exemplify the drawings of more complex commercial buildings for study, but are developed with the use of BIM and Revit. Last is a commercial tenant improvement project, which exemplifies a typical buildout of an established architectural space, such as a storefront or high-rise building.

As educators, we recognize the need to create a document for the future challenge, giving our young students a greater depth of understanding. If a prospective or new employee has good prior knowledge of the inner workings of architecture, an office will be able to teach technique in a short period of time. To that end, every chapter has been rewritten and reorganized to include a wealth of information on how drawings must be performed. All this is done with an eye toward how people learn. Education and architecture can and must be done in the same manner. It is imperative to perceive architecture holistically—as more than its parts—because the whole is indeed greater than the sum of its parts.

■ ACKNOWLEDGMENTS

Tony Micu, AIA, President of the South Bay Chapter of the AIA, for kick-starting our move toward BIM and Revit.

Cynthia Wakita, for her timeless and unceasing research and permissions work.

Wendy Ortiz, who performed half of the new drawings, corrections, and revised drawings.

Carol Peterson, for working behind-the-scenes research.

Natalie K. Bakhoum, for her unwavering support in this new venture.

Tamara Fofonka-Jelenic, for her significant efforts on both the text and the images.

Ana M. Girala-Tye, for developing, organizing, and illustrating new images for the text.

Margaret Cummins, fourth-edition senior editor, for her help in guiding us through yet another edition.

Lauren Poplawski, for providing technical information in response from Wiley.

Donna Conte, senior production editor, for her work on this fourth edition.

Dedication

*This book is dedicated to our families, to students of
architecture, and to the memory of Richard Linde,
Jakob Wakita, and Giichi and Nobue Wakita.*

PART

I

Professional Foundations

The information contained in Chapters 1 through 6 is intended to establish the fundamentals for those practicing in the field of architecture. These chapters will shape your understanding of an office, the practice, the stages, and the drawings of architecture. The concept of a good foundation applies to both structures and individuals: without a solid foundation, failure is imminent. On this basis, the groundwork for architecture—the office and specific aspects of construction documents—will be the rock on which these chapters are founded.

Chapter 1   The Office
Chapter 2   Standards and Techniques, Metrification, Hand Drafting, and Computer-aided Drafting
Chapter 3   BIM, Revit, and Human Concerns
Chapter 4   Sustainable/Green Architecture
Chapter 5   Construction Materials and Methods
Chapter 6   Initial Preparation Phase for Construction Documents

THE OFFICE

■ THE PHYSICAL OFFICE

The physical plant of the architectural office has begun to take on a new look. The firm that once worked only in a local community now has a global reach. Where proximity once limited the opportunity for a client to access global talent, the computer, transportation, and communications technology allow for interviews based on architectural ability rather than proximity. It is no longer necessary to select an architect in one's immediate community, because technology allows for virtual meetings around the globe.

It is not one firm, but many that may construct drawings in a collaborative effort based on the ebb and flow of the size of the project. The result is that any firm, of any size, can join another to achieve an assigned task. Today, *network* does more than just describe a system of communication; it also describes the architect's role. An individual may work on a drawing halfway around the world, while at the project location it is the middle of the night. **Redlines**, or corrected drawings, can be marked up electronically and sent via email for the next work shift, resulting in two times the production in half the normal time. An architecture firm that specializes in design can partner with another firm that specializes in construction documents.

Architecture is a small crafts industry in which most offices employ one to four people. A home office may also be part of the office structure. A single drafter may be hired by two or more firms, in which case the office becomes a docking station for electronic project information, such as construction documents. Because digital images can be rapidly moved electronically, one need not live within the city or even the country where the project will be sited; one can send documents across the world instantly. In the traditional architectural firm, an architect in a firm leads the project and distributes the work among the staff within the firm. When a workload jam arises, the architect may hire a subcontractor to aid in development of the required drawings.

■ OFFICE PRACTICE AND HOW IT MAY BE STRUCTURED

The Firm

The way in which an architectural firm is structured, and the office practices it employs, depend on the magnitude and type of its projects, the number of personnel, and the philosophies the architects hold with regard to office practice procedures. Normally, the architect or architects are the owners and/or principals of the practice.

Although a small firm will differ from a medium, large, or extra-large firm, many of the functions will be the same. In all firms, a licensed architect will oversee staff as a direct supervisor. In each firm, services such as **programming** (determining the objectives of the project), **space planning** (the layout of the furnishings and fixtures), feasibility studies, site analysis, coordination, scheduling, and architectural design will be provided according to the firm's contract with the client. As a firm's size increases, one major factor does change: that of documentation of directives and communications. Of course, it is imperative for a firm of any size to track its work and communications with clients. However, as the firm size increases, the documentation becomes critical; as larger project teams mobilize to perform tasks, any lack of documentation can result in reworking projects and significant loss of revenue.

In general, an architectural office can be separated into three main departments: the administration department, the design department, and the production department. The principal or principals oversee all three departments in addition to their other duties.

Administration Department

The administration department handles all communications between the architectural firm and its clients on items such as contracts, fee schedules, billing for services, and similar matters. This department handles all secretarial duties, including all written correspondence, payment of operating costs, accounting procedures, paying salaries, marketing, and maintaining project records relating to individual project costs and procedures. This department may also handle **human resources** (HR) functions, including management of the firm's staff.

Under the purview of administration, many firms also include a marketing department. Tasks for this department might include development and maintenance of a web site, creation and dissemination of publication materials, assembly of competition entries, and development of promotional materials. Marketing is used to focus a firm on a particular area of work and take advantage of opportunities that may arise for a specific project type that the firm prefers or in which it specializes.

Design Department

The design department is normally headed by a principal architect and/or an associate architect. This person or persons meets with the client to determine the requirements of a project, the economics of the project, and the anticipated time frame for completing the construction documents. These initial concerns determine the program for the project. The head or heads of this department delegate various work phases of a project to other staff members. The number of staff members depends on the size of the practice and the magnitude of the projects. Staff members may be assigned to teams or groups in their area of expertise for specific projects. A team takes a project from the initial schematic design concept, through design development, to the completed construction drawings and specifications. These stages may include model building, renderings, coordination among all consulting engineers to meet their individual job requirements, job billing, and reproduction responsibilities. The leader of a project and of the design team staff is designated the *project architect*. A project architect's responsibilities are to develop a "game plan" for a specific project, which will include:

1. Design studies, philosophy, and concept
2. Initial structural considerations
3. Exterior and interior materials
4. Municipality and building code requirements
5. Architectural committee reviews
6. Building equipment requirements, **LEED** (Leadership in Energy and Environmental Design)
7. Manufacturing resources
8. Selection of required engineering consultants (soils/ geology, structural, mechanical, etc.)
9. Planned man-hours, time sheets, and billing dates
10. Office standards for the representation of items on the working drawings, such as symbols, wall delineations, and other graphic depictions

Production Department

The production department, under the supervision of a project architect, prepares all the phases for a set of completed construction drawings. Working drawings may be produced by a senior drafter, intermediate drafter, or junior drafter under the supervision of a licensed architect. These staff members and the project architect or job captain work as a team to make the transition from the approved preliminary drawings to the completion and implementation of the working drawings. The transition from the approved preliminary drawings to the development of the working drawings is elaborated in Part II of this book. Other chapters provide step-by-step procedures on how different sections of the working drawings are developed: the site and grading plan, foundation plan, floor plan, building sections, exterior elevations, roof and framing plans, interior elevations, architectural details, and schedules. During the process and completion of the various sections, the project architect and/or job captain constantly reviews the drawings for clarity, accuracy, and craftsmanship of detail-

ing, and ensures that the drawings reflect all required revisions. Drawings are either created with the use of a **computer-aided drafting** (CAD) system or are drawn manually using conventional instruments. A suggested organizational chart for the practice of architecture is depicted in Figure 1.1.

The Architect

An *architect* is an individual licensed by the state in which he or she practices architecture. An architect can be licensed in multiple states and practice from multiple offices. In most cases, the architect has a college education consisting of an undergraduate four- or five-year degree or a six- to seven-year graduate program at an accredited university. For a university to become accredited, the **National Architectural Accrediting Board** (NAAB) must certify that university for its merit in education. In addition to the formal education, a three-year **apprenticeship** or on-the-job training by skilled practitioners in the field is required. In some situations, an **internship** (experience in an architectural office during one's course of education) may also be counted toward the apprenticeship period. The **Architecture Registration Examination** (ARE)—testing that rivals the bar exam for lawyers in difficulty—must be taken after completion of one's education; the ARE is administered by the **National Council of Architectural Registration Boards** (NCARB). Programs such as the **Intern Development Program** (IDP) are instrumental in aiding candidates for licensing, because they allow candidates to obtain experience in the diverse areas that are required to run and supervise an architectural firm. Once a license is obtained, the holder is required to pursue continuing education.

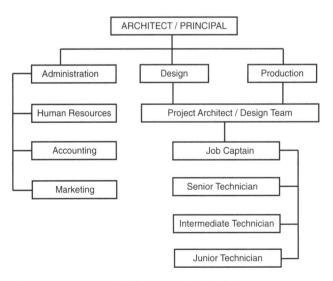

Figure 1.1 Suggested office organizational chart.

■ RESOURCE LIBRARY

Research

To find and detail all the equipment that is required for a structure (plumbing, hardware, finishes, and so forth), it is necessary to have access to the various manufacturing resources for specific products. The most widely used product information source is the Internet. Electronic access allows architects and engineers to survey the resources available and select the equipment that will best enable the function of a building. Such equipment may be available from a myriad of different manufacturers, and range from conveying systems to window and doors and the like. Samples can be included in a firm's in-house library. Most of the literature found in electronic form is based on the *MasterFormat*, an organizational system widely used in the construction industry. These particular systems use the major divisions shown in Figure 1.2.

Research via Computer

One can now electronically research anything from hardware to framing anchors, engineered lumber products to composite building products. You are limited only by your ability to navigate through the vast sea of information available through the Internet and your ability to retrieve the information necessary to satisfy and enhance completion of the working drawings. Digital drawings can also be obtained, making it unnecessary

MasterFormat GROUPS, SUBGROUPS, AND DIVISIONS

PROCUREMENT AND CONTRACTING REQUIREMENTS GROUP
Division 00 – Procurement and Contracting
      Requirements
    Introductory Information
    Procurement Requirements
    Contracting Requirements

SPECIFICATIONS GROUP

GENERAL REQUIREMENTS SUBGROUP
Division 01 – General Requirements

FACILITY CONSTRUCTION SUBGROUP
Division 02 – Existing Conditions
Division 03 – Concrete
Division 04 – Masonry
Division 05 – Metals
Division 06 – Wood, Plastics, and Composites
Division 07 – Thermal and Moisture Protection
Division 08 – Openings
Division 09 – Finishes
Division 10 – Specialties
Division 11 – Equipment
Division 12 – Furnishings
Division 13 – Special Construction
Division 14 – Conveying Equipment
Division 15 – Reserved for Future Expansion
Division 16 – Reserved for Future Expansion
Division 17 – Reserved for Future Expansion
Division 18 – Reserved for Future Expansion
Division 19 – Reserved for Future Expansion

FACILITY SERVICES SUBGROUP
Division 20 – Reserved for Future Expansion
Division 21 – Fire Suppression

Division 22 – Plumbing
Division 23 – Heating, Ventilating, and Air-
      Conditioning (HVAC)
Division 24 – Reserved for Future Expansion
Division 25 – Integrated Automation
Division 26 – Electrical
Division 27 – Communications
Division 28 – Electronic Safety and Security
Division 29 – Reserved for Future Expansion

SITE AND INFRASTRUCTURE SUBGROUP
Division 30 – Reserved for Future Expansion
Division 31 – Earthwork
Division 32 – Exterior Improvements
Division 33 – Utilities
Division 34 – Transportation
Division 35 – Waterway and Marine
      Construction
Division 36 – Reserved for Future Expansion
Division 37 – Reserved for Future Expansion
Division 38 – Reserved for Future Expansion
Division 39 – Reserved for Future Expansion

PROCESS EQUIPMENT SUBGROUP
Division 40 – Process Integration
Division 41 – Material Processing and Handling
      Equipment
Division 42 – Process Heating, Cooling, and
      Drying Equipment
Division 43 – Process Gas and Liquid Handling,
      Purification, and Storage
      Equipment
Division 44 – Pollution and Waste Control
      Equipment
Division 45 – Industry-Specific Manufacturing
      Equipment
Division 46 – Water and Wastewater Equipment
Division 47 – Reserved for Future Expansion
Division 48 – Electrical Power Generation
Division 49 – Reserved for Future Expansion

Figure 1.2 *MasterFormat* division numbers and titles. (The Groups, Subgroups and Divisions used in this textbook are from *MasterFormat*™ 2010 published by The Construction Specifications Institute (CSI) and Construction Specifications Canada (CSC), and is used with permission from CSI. For those interested in a more in-depth explanation of *MasterFormat*™ 2010 and its use in the construction industry visit www.cisnet.org/masterformat or contact: The Construction Specifications Institute, 110 South Union Street, Suite 100, Alexandria, VA 22314; 800-689-2900; 703-684–0300; www.csinet.org)

to draw configurations for products such as window profiles, stair rails, and so on. Caution must be taken when you utilize Internet details, though; we suggest that you do not simply copy them, because use of a copy makes you liable for the result or outcome of use of the detail. Always verify the accuracy and appropriateness of a detail before you adopt it as your own.

Manufacturers' Literature

A wealth of product information is available directly from manufacturers, in the form of brochures, pamphlets, catalogs, manuals, and hardbound books. Actual samples of their products may also be obtained. The information available may include:

1. Advantages of a particular product over others
2. How the system works or is assembled
3. Necessary engineering
4. Detailed drawings
5. Special design features
6. Colors, textures, and patterns
7. Safety tests
8. Dimensioning
9. Installation procedures

Adapt this information to your particular needs in your geographical location.

Other Reference Sources

Retail sources such as major book publishers produce architectural reference books. Many art supply and drafting supply stores also carry reference materials. Public libraries may have a variety of professional reference materials, including books, journals, and trade magazines. Colleges and universities offering architecture courses usually have a wealth of architectural resource materials. An example of a highly technical resource is the *AIA Architectural Graphics Standards* published by John Wiley & Sons. This book is found in almost all architectural offices. In addition, the **American Institute of Architects** (AIA) publishes standards and guidelines for architects to utilize as well.

■ PROFESSIONAL ORGANIZATIONS

Professional organizations can be an asset to the business performance and office functions of an architectural firm. The AIA is an example of a professional organization that will provide members with recommended documents, including client/architect contractual agreements, client/contractor agreements, and many others. The AIA also provides recommended guidelines relative to fee schedules and disbursements, construction documents, building specifications, and construction observation procedures and documentation.

Ethical procedures and office practice methods are recommended and defined as part of the many documents available from the AIA.

It is recommended that associate architects and employees at the various technical levels become involved with a professional organization for a number of reasons, but primarily to stay aware of current technical information and activities within the architectural profession. The AIA also offers programs and directions for those in an internship phase of their careers. Student associate member programs available through the AIA provide an overall view of the architectural profession.

Other professional organizations for students of architecture can be found through students' colleges and universities.

■ ARCHITECT/CLIENT RELATIONSHIP

Working Relationship

The relationship between the architect and the client will vary. In general, the relationship for a specific building project and the responsibilities and procedures necessary to accomplish the goals of the project will be initiated with the selection of the architect. After the architect is selected, the architect and the client enter into a contract, which defines the services to be performed and the responsibilities of the architect and the client. Many states require architects to use a written contract when providing professional services.

After the contractual agreement is signed and a retainer fee is received, the architect reviews the building site and confers with the client to determine the goals of the building project. After establishing the project goals, there will be meetings with the governing agencies, such as the planning department, the building department, and architectural committees. The primary goal of the architectural team at this point is to initiate the preliminary planning and design phases.

Most architectural contracts and agreements include provisions for the architect and the consulting engineers to observe construction of the project during the various building stages. It is a standard practice for the architects to visit the site, determine if the construction is progressing correctly, and report their findings.

Schematic Design and Reviews

The next step in the architect/client relationship is the architect's presentation of the **schematic design** (SD) for the project. After the client's initial review of the planning and design for the project, some revisions and alterations may be made to the design. In this case, the drawings are revised and presented again to the client for his or her approval. After the client approves the schematic design, the architect consults with and presents the schematic drawings to the various governing agencies, such as the planning department, for their review and comments. Any revisions and alterations that may be required by any of the agencies are executed and again reviewed by the client, and approved. The schematic drawings are often used to estimate the initial construction costs, which

are also submitted for client review and approval. Using BIM or Revit, it is possible to provide the client with a more accurate estimate of cost, because these programs incorporate the materials and methods of construction in the drafting process.

In the SD phase, a conceptual site plan and floor plan of the building areas are reviewed for the building orientation and the preservation of existing landscaping elements such as trees, topography, and other site conditions. Figure 1.3 shows an example of a conceptual site and building plan. The client for this project desires

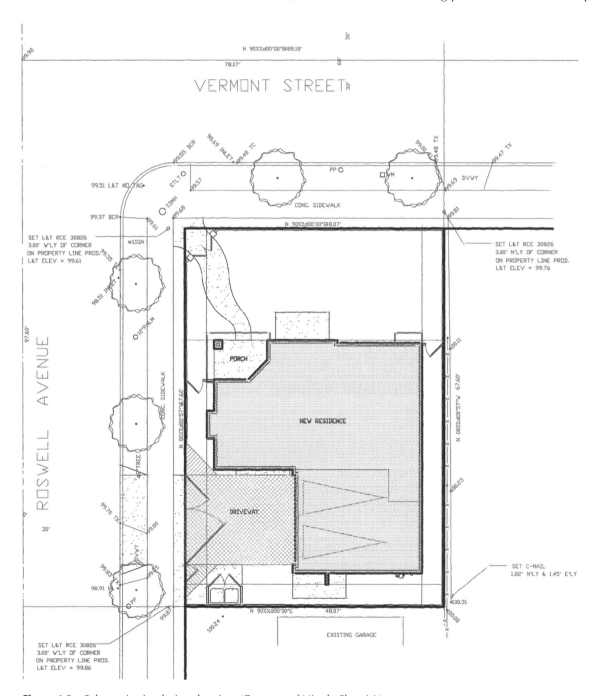

Figure 1.3   Schematic site design drawing. (Courtesy of Nicole Shweiri.)

to build a three-bedroom residence. The site, which is located in a beach community, is a small property. The lot is located on a corner where side and front-yard setbacks use most of the lot area and the garage must be additionally set back to allow for a driveway with visibility.

Wind direction, sun orientation, rainfall, flow of water on the site, and the most feasible automobile access to the site are considered (among other factors), and a schematic study is presented. From this initial schematic study, a preliminary floor plan is established, which shows the room orientations and their relationships to one another. Such a preliminary drawing is depicted in Figure 1.4. A second-floor level preliminary plan is studied as it relates to the first-floor plan and the room orientation, as shown in Figure 1.5. Finally, a roof plan is designed to facilitate the use of a roof deck and roof garden; this preliminary study is illustrated in Figure 1.6. The studies of the exterior elevations evolved utilizing an asphalt shingle roof material, with a shallow pitched

roof, and exterior walls of wood siding. After the client has approved the preliminary floor plans, the exterior elevations are presented to the client in preliminary form for approval, and to the governmental agencies for their preliminary approvals. The North and West elevations are depicted in Figures 1.7 and 1.8. These preliminary drawings and designs are examples of the architect's studies that may be presented to a client for his or her approval prior to implementation of the design development and construction drawings.

Design Development

After these numerous reviews of the schematic design, further development and refinement are required. This improved-drawing design phase is termed **design development** (DD) and represents a more definite solution to the program and the intended building outcome. A

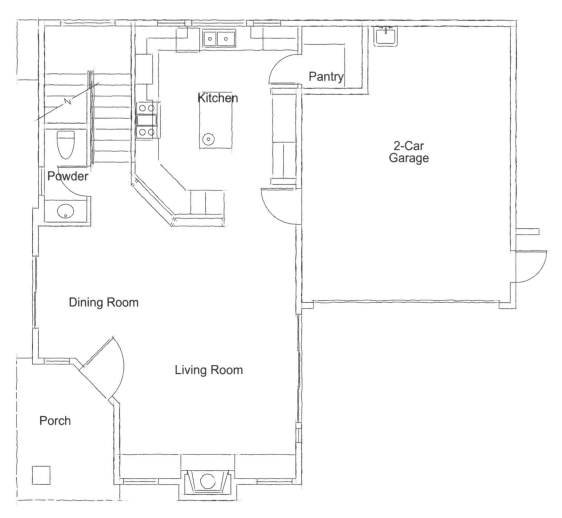

Figure 1.4 First-floor plan schematic design. (Courtesy of Nicole Shweiri.)

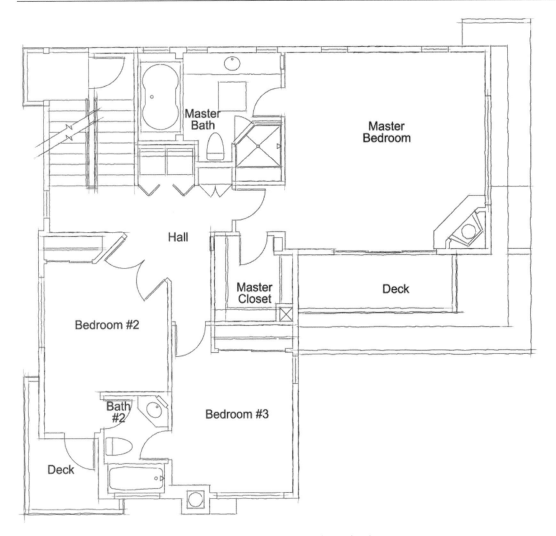

Figure 1.5   Second-floor plan schematic design. (Courtesy of Nicole Shweiri.)

primary area of refinement is materiality for the proposed project. During SD, a project may include all the rooms and a resolved floor-plan layout required for the client, but during DD the specific materials to be used in construction of the project will be determined. Small refinements would also be included in DD, such as where the specific fixtures in a kitchen would be located; this is in contrast to schematic design, in which you would just know where the kitchen is located relative to the adjacent rooms. As is the case for schematic design, after several reviews the architect will have the client sign off on the revised plans and budget for the project and move on to the next phase of work.

With a program like Revit, it is often difficult to determine when DD ends and the next phase begins, because Revit includes so much specific data (such as material type and construction methods) that is front-loaded into the computer. In Revit, even at SD a 3-D drawing of the design has already been developed and can be viewed after a limited amount of data is entered.

Materials and Specifications

There will be many conferences between the architect and the client during the design development phase to select and determine items such as exterior and interior wall finishes, ceiling finishes, flooring, plumbing fixtures, hardware design, type of masonry, roofing materials, and so on. During these conferences, the selections of building equipment and systems are also determined and reviewed. The equipment selection may include such items as types of windows and doors and the manufacturer, elevator type and manufacturer, mechanical system, electrical fixtures, and so on. Refer to Chapter 5 for related information on some of the aforementioned items; for others, search the Internet.

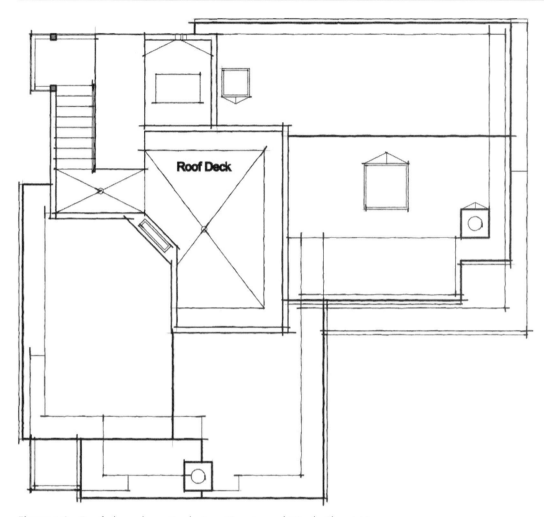

Figure 1.6 Roof plan schematic design. (Courtesy of Nicole Shweiri.)

Figure 1.7 North elevation schematic design. (Courtesy of Nicole Shweiri.)

Figure 1.8 West elevation schematic design. (Courtesy of Nicole Shweiri.)

■ IMPLEMENTATION OF THE CONSTRUCTION DOCUMENTS

Construction Documents

After the client and the various governing agencies involved approve the schematic designs and design development for a project, the architect's office initiates the construction drawing phase for the construction of the project.

During the **construction document** (CD) phase, architects determine which consulting engineers are required on a specific project. The engineers may be employed directly by the architect, or they may have their own private practices. These consultants may include soils and geological engineers, structural engineers, mechanical engineers, electrical engineers, and civil engineers. Other consultants may include landscape architects, interior designers, LEED consultants, and cost estimators. Periodic conferences with the client are recommended during this phase to attain approvals on the various phases of the construction drawings. These phases or stages may include lighting layout and electrical designs, cabinetry, reflected ceiling, and many other features for which client review and approval are needed.

Upon completion of the construction drawings and specifications, which are now termed *construction documents*, the architect and/or client may submit the CDs to financing institutions for building loans, to various construction firms for building cost proposals, and to governing agencies for their final approvals. Finally, the architectural firm will submit the construction documents to the local planning and building department to obtain the required building permits.

Bidding and Negotiating

Once the CDs have been developed, plans are put out to bid. For public projects, such as schools or state and federal buildings, an unlimited number of bidders can propose a price for completing the work. On private projects, the clients may choose who may bid and how many bidders they would like for the job. Often as many as four or five contractors will bid a job, allowing for a high, mid, and low bid and the opportunity to eliminate an unqualified bid or a bidder that has not met the bid submission deadline.

Negotiation of bids can occur for a project on which a specific price or timeline must be met. A single contractor may be asked to propose a budget and make revisions to replace expensive items or omit items from a project. The result of bid negotiations, ideally, is a modified contract document that will meet the budget and/or time requirements.

Construction Administration

When the construction firm has been selected and construction has commenced, the architect and consulting engineers, according to their agreement in the contract, observe the various phases of construction. This phase in the architecture contract is termed **construction administration** (CA). At this point, the architect's role may change to one that is more field active. These periodic observations generally correspond to the construction phases, such as field-visiting construction of the foundation, framing, and so forth. Following their observations, the architect and consulting engineers provide written reports to the client and contractor describing their observations, along with any recommendations or alterations they deem necessary for the success of the project. Performing site visits, making field revisions and clarifications, and responding to **requests for information** (RFI) enhance opportunities for better design, budget, and schedule results.

At the completion of the project, the architect and consultants make a final inspection of the construction of the building and prepare a *punch list*. This punch list, which is in written form, includes graphics indicating to the client and construction firm any revisions, reports, or alterations the architect or consultant deems pertinent and reasonable for a successful building project. After the construction firm makes the revisions, the architect and the consultants again inspect the project. If acceptable, a final notice of approval is sent to the client and the construction firm.

■ BUILDING

Building Codes

The purpose of building codes is to safeguard life, health, and the public welfare. Building codes are continually being revised to incorporate additional regulations based on tests or conditions caused by catastrophic events, such as hurricanes, earthquakes, and fires. In most cases, the governing building codes are similar in organization and context.

The requirements of various agencies and codes are of paramount influence in the design and detailing of today's structures. A great number of codes govern and regulate the many elements that are integrated into the construction of a building. The major codes that are used in the design and detailing of buildings are the building code, mechanical code, electrical code, fire code, energy code, and accessibility design criteria for compliance with the **Americans with Disabilities Act** (ADA).

Procedures for Use of Building Codes

STEP I. *Building use and occupancy.* The first step is to classify the building use and to determine the occupancy group for the building. When the occupancy classification has been determined, the building is assigned a group designation letter, which determines the description of the occupancy and the group it falls under.

STEP II. *Fire-rated wall assemblies.* Most codes provide a chapter on acceptable fire-resistive standards for assemblies, so that the architect is able to select an assembly that satisfies his or her specific condition. For example, a one-hour fire-rated wall is constructed with 2″ × 4″ wood stud partition with 5/8″ type "X" gypsum wallboard on both sides.

STEP III. *Building location on the site.* The location of the building on the site and the clearances to the property lines and other structures on the site determine the fire-resistant construction of the exterior walls. The openings are based on the distances from the property lines and other structures.

STEP IV. *Allowable floor areas.* The next step is to determine the proposed and allowable floor areas of the building based on the occupancy group, such as theater or assembly room, and the type of construction.

STEP V. *Height and the number of stories or floors in the building.* The architect computes the maximum height of the building and determines the number of stories and/or floors. The maximum number of stories and the height of the building are determined by the building occupancy and the type of construction.

Code Influence on Building Design

An example of code-related design requirements is provided by a site plan for a proposed two-story office building. The architect desires that all four sides of the building have windows. To satisfy this design factor, the minimum building setback from the property line will be a minimum ten feet for openings in exterior walls. Figure 1.9 depicts the proposed site plan for the two-story office building, showing property line setbacks satisfying one design requirement.

As the design program is developed, it is helpful to provide code-required assemblies in graphic form as a visual means for reviewing what is required for the various elements of the office building. An example of such a graphic aid appears in Figure 1.10. Building codes specify the wall assemblies that meet the fire-resistive requirements for the various elements of the building type selected.

Exit Requirements. Another very important part of a building code is the chapter dealing with egress requirements. This chapter sets forth the number of required exits for a specific occupancy use, based on an occupant load factor. The occupant load will depend on the use of the building. In the case of a two-story building that is designed for office use, the occupant load factor is 1 person per 100 square feet. To determine the number of exits required, the 100 square-foot occupant load factor is divided into the office floor area of 10,000 square feet. The resulting occupant factor of 100 exceeds the factor of 30, therefore requiring a minimum of two exits.

The next step in the design program is to plan the location of the required exits, required stairs, and an acceptable *egress travel* (the path to a required exit).

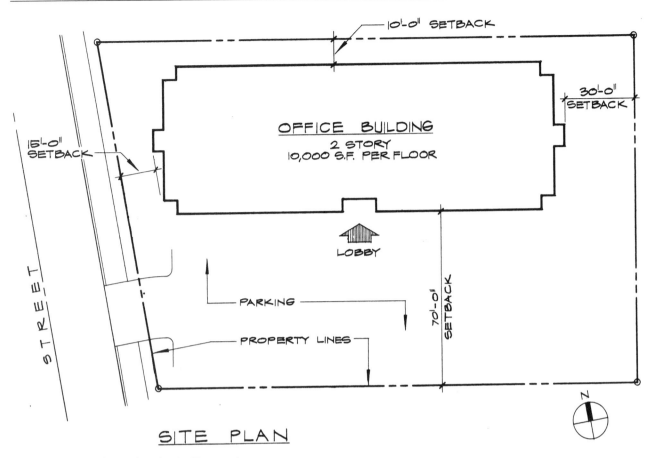

SITE PLAN

Figure 1.9   Site plan with setbacks illustrated.

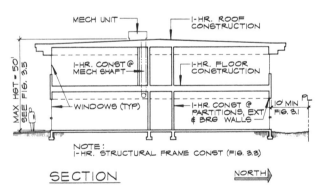

SECTION   NORTH

Figure 1.10   Graphic building section with fire-rated assembly.

Building codes regulate the maximum distance between required exits, the minimum width of exit corridors, and the entire design of required exit stairways. Figure 1.11 depicts the second-level floor plan of the proposed office building, illustrating an acceptable method for the planning of required exits and stair locations. An acceptable egress travel will terminate at the first-floor level, exiting outside the structure to a public right-of-way. A public right-of-way may be a sidewalk, street, alley, or other passage. On the first-level floor plan, illustrated in

Figure 1.12, the egress travel path terminates outside the building through an exit corridor at the east and west walls of the building.

■ INFLUENCE OF BUILDING INFORMATION MODELING ON BUILDING DESIGN

For centuries, architects have embraced new methods, new materials, and new technologies. This embrace accelerates the evolution of the field of architecture and shapes our built environment. **Building information modeling** (BIM) is such a technology, and it is setting new precedents in the world of architecture as we know it. Offering the drafter increased accuracy, productivity, collaboration, and organization—all while reducing repetition—BIM is a process of drafting in which almost every detail of a building assembly is included from its fundamental parts. For example, details such as stud, sheathing, building paper, lath, plaster, and gypsum are included to define a specific wall type. Where earlier programs established two lines to represent a wall, BIM identifies the entire wall with specificity.

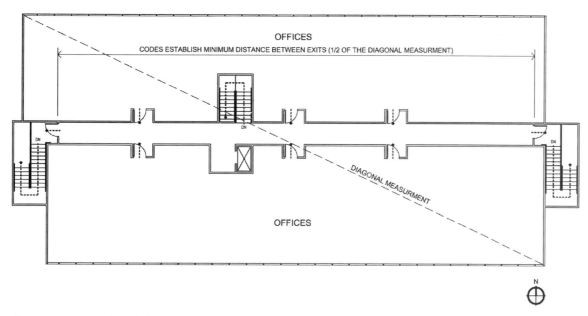

Figure 1.11   Second-level floor plan.

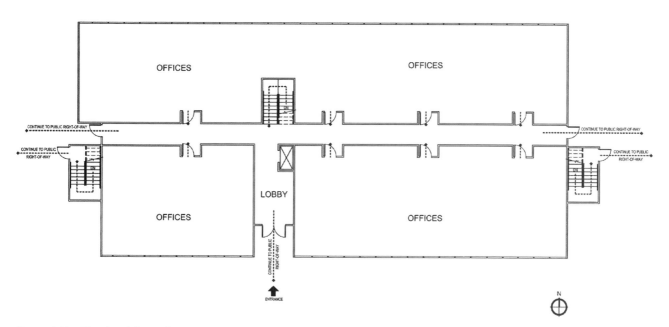

Figure 1.12   First-level floor plan.

Programs such as Revit by Autodesk are designed to increase productivity in all phases of drawing documentation. Its primary advantage is its ability to produce drawings that are generated by defining floor, wall, and roof types. In addition, Revit will develop schedules, identify doors and windows from the placement, and determine door and window sizes and types. Finish schedules are also established by using information on floor, wall, and roof materials. Revit will even go further in developing sections, elevations, and details.

Although it is not magic, it is amazing how such a program can aid in development of a construction set of drawings. This advantage is further enhanced by its process capability to modify all the plans, schedules, and elevations to reflect the changes when modifications are made. A standard drafting program would require a technician to modify all the plans based on his or her own experience. Of course the program is not perfect, but it does include a conflict detection element to aid in the process. Simply put, one can develop a more accurate, thorough, and coordinated set of drawings with the aid of Revit or other BIM technologies.

chapter

2

STANDARDS AND TECHNIQUES, METRIFICATION, HAND DRAFTING, AND COMPUTER-AIDED DRAFTING

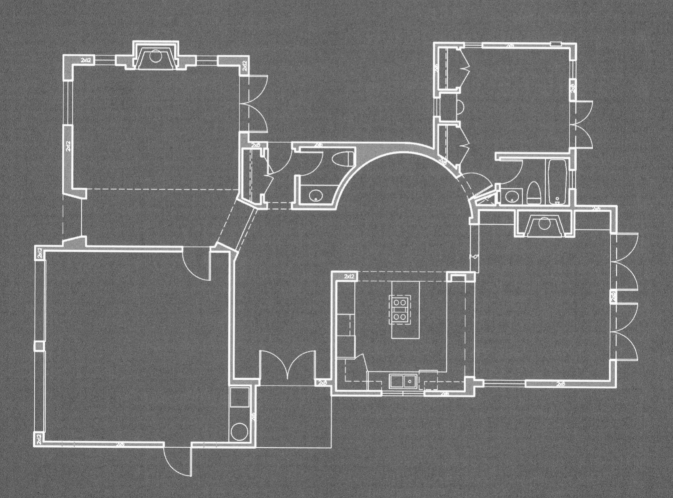

■ INTRODUCTION TO STANDARDS AND TECHNIQUES

This chapter covers four points:

1. Understanding the vocabulary of our profession
2. Metrification
3. Hand drafting
4. Computer-assisted drafting (CAD, AutoCAD)

Chapters 3 and 4 discuss the third phase of the evolution of drafting, BIM via Revit language, and its implications and impact on architecture.

Learning architecture is similar to learning a new language. First you must build vocabulary, assemble the words in a prescribed order, and punctuate to show the real intent of the phrase. The language of architecture is made up of lines with certain densities and conventions used nationally to denote a particular item, such as a door and its swing, an electrical symbol, and structural components. Standards have evolved to ensure and enhance comprehensibility of drawings; notations that follow the prescribed form are easily and quickly understood, thereby saving time and reducing the possibility of error. Architecture in the far past has been a local thing, but in the recent past our endeavors have expanded to a national and even global level.

The process of architecture is forever changing, from hand drafting to computer drafting to the newest BIM, as explained in Chapter 1, and the use of such programs as Revit to process BIM. Nevertheless, the language of architecture remains constant.

■ DRAWING PRACTICE

The actual practice of drawing must follow standards. Standards are prescribed to the drafter, for both manual and computer drafting, and have become the foundation for the translation of drawings from design drawings to construction documents.

With the possible exception of lettering, the following descriptions of line quality, material designation, profiling, dimensioning, and so forth, are for enhancement of the images (drawings) that we are preparing, and as such are not applicable to manual drafting.

Lines and Line Quality

Basically, lines can be broken down into three types: light, medium, and dark. Each of these types can be broken down further by variation of pressure and lead.

Light Lines. The lightest lines used are usually the guidelines drawn to help with lettering height. These lines should be only barely visible and should completely disappear when a print is made. See Figure 2.1A. At the darker end of the light line spectrum are lines for door swings or other less significant objects.

Medium Lines. Medium-weight lines are used for dimension lines and extension leaders. Leaders and break lines also use medium-weight lines. See Figure 2.1B. They can also be used for such nonstructural components as bath fixtures or cabinets.

Medium-Dark Lines. Medium to dark (darkest of this group) lines are used to describe objects (object lines) and for centerlines. Medium to slight dark lines are used for hidden or dashed lines. See Figure 2.1C.

Dark Lines. The darkest lines are used to profile objects, for border lines if they are not predrawn on the vellum, and for cutting plane lines. See Figure 2.1D. Walls or structural components of a building would be at the lighter end of the spectrum of dark lines.

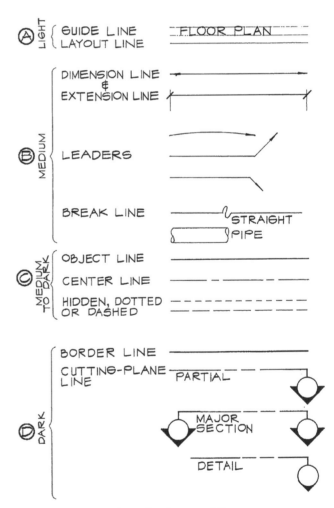

Figure 2.1 Vocabulary of architectural lines.

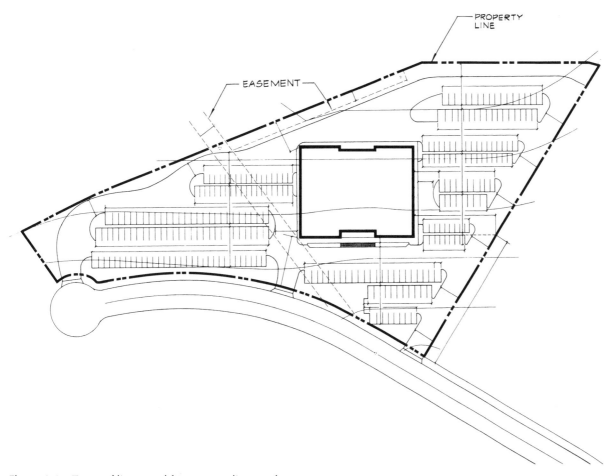

Figure 2.2 Types of lines used for property lines and easements.

Choosing Line Quality. Line quality depends on the use of that particular line. An intense line is used to profile and emphasize, an intermediate line is used to show elements such as walls and structural members, and a light line is used for elements such as dimensioning and door swings.

Another way to vary line quality is to increase the width of the line. A thicker line can represent the walls on a floor plan, the outline of a building on a site plan, or the outline of a roof on a roof plan. For line-quality examples and uses, see Figure 2.2, which shows a sample of the types of lines used to indicate property lines and easements.

Hidden or Dotted Lines. Hidden or dotted lines are used to indicate objects hidden from view. Solid objects covered by earth, such as foundations, can be indicated with hidden lines. This type of line can also depict future structures, items that are not in the contract, public utilities locations, easements, a wheelchair turning radius, or the direction of sliding doors and windows. Such lines are often used to delineate walls that are to be removed or demolished.

A floor plan will often show the roof outline, or a balcony above, or a change in ceiling height with a dotted line. On a site plan, dotted lines indicate the existing grades on the site (see Chapter 7).

Arrowheads. Different types of arrowheads are used in dimensioning. These are shown in Figure 2.3. The top one is used architecturally more for leaders than for dimension lines. The second one, with the tick mark, is the arrowhead most prevalently used in our field. The

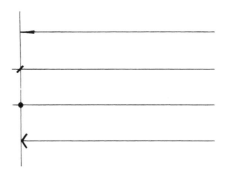

Figure 2.3 Types of arrowheads used in dimensioning.

dot is used in conjunction with the tick mark when you are dimensioning two systems. For example, the dot can be used to locate the center of steel columns, and the tick mark can be used to dimension the secondary structure within a building built of wood. The final wide arrowhead is used as a design arrowhead in many offices.

Material Designation Lines. Material designation lines are used to indicate the building material used. See Figure 2.4 for a sample of tapered or light-dark lines. (This device saves time; complete lines take longer to draw.) Also note the cross-hatched lines between the parallel lines that represent the wall thickness on Figure 2.5. These diagonal lines represent masonry.

Profiling

Architectural profiling is the process of taking the most important features of a drawing and outlining them. Figure 2.6 shows four applications of this concept.

Figure 2.4. Tapered lines.

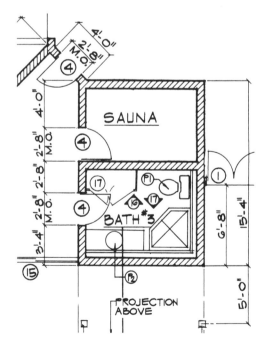

Figure 2.5 Lines representing masonry.

Example A illustrates the darkening of the lines that represent the walls of a floor plan. The dimension lines or extension lines are drawn as medium-weight lines not only to contrast with the walls, but also to allow the walls of the particular floor plan to stand out.

In example B, a footing detail is profiled. Because the concrete work is important here, its outline is drawn darker than any other part of the detail.

Example C shows the top portion (**head**) of a window. The light lines at the bottom of the detail represent the side (**jamb**) of the window. Note how the head section is outlined and the interior parts plus the sides of the walls are drawn lightly.

Example D represents another form of profiling, called **pouché**, which enhances the profile technique by using shading. The technique of using shading is limited to design drawings; in construction documents, pouché on a wall indicates a bearing wall, or a new wall in an addition or alteration. This shading can be done by pencil shading or by lines. Example B also uses this principle: In this instance, the dots and triangles that represent concrete in section are placed along the perimeter (near the profiled line) in greater quantity than toward the center.

In a section drawing, the items most often profiled are cut by the cutting plane line. A footing detail, for example, is nothing more than a theoretical knife (a cutting plane) cutting through the wall of the structure. The portion most often cut is the concrete, so it is profiled.

On an elevation, the main outline of the structure should be darkened. See Figure 2.7. This type of profiling is used to simplify the illusion of the elevation to show that the structure is basically an L-shape structure and that one portion does actually project forward.

In the plan view, often the outline of the main structure is heavily outlined (profiled) in order to make the main area stand out more than any other feature of the property. See Figure 2.8 for a finished plan and elevation that have been properly profiled.

■ LETTERING

Importance of Hand Lettering

Being able to hand letter well becomes very important when correcting drawings. This is especially true when correcting computer-generated construction documents. Take, for example, a computer-generated roof framing plan. Let us say the CAD drafter mislabeled a rafter on the plan and posted a 2 × 4 rafter at 12″ on center as a note, whereas in reality the rafter should have been a 2 × 6 rafter at 16″ center to center. For some strange reason, errors of this kind are usually discovered only after the document is printed and during the reproduction of multiple field copies. At this point, it takes a

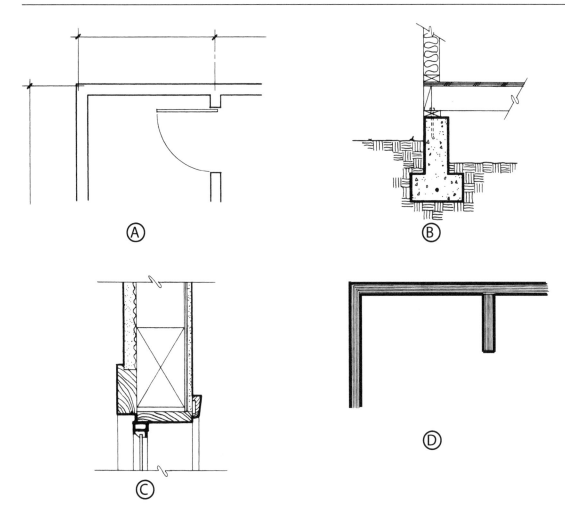

Figure 2.6 Profiling.

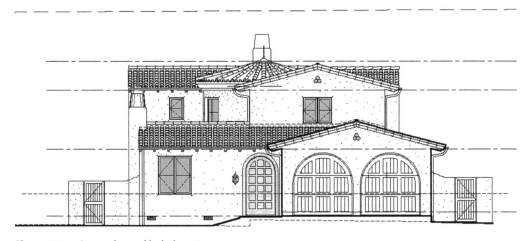

Figure 2.7 Correctly profiled elevation.

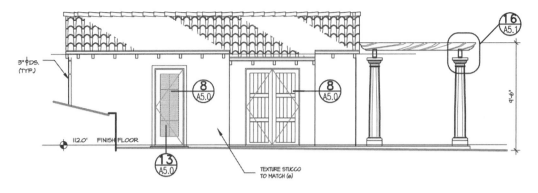

SOUTH / EAST ELEVATION

SCALE: 1/4" = 1'-0"

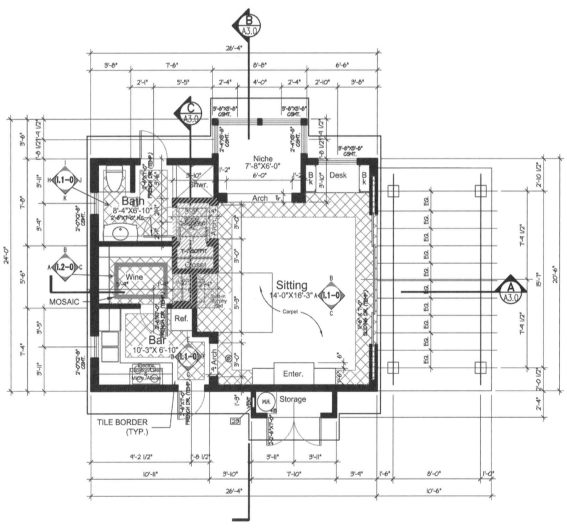

FLOOR PLAN @ POOLHOUSE

SCALE: 1/4" = 1'-0"

Figure 2.8   Correctly profiled plan and elevation.

time-consuming effort to locate the drawing in the computer's memory, correct it, and replot the drawing, not to mention the cost of supplies. Had the note been printed in an architectural font, it would be a simple matter to erase the error and re-letter it by hand on the already printed document. This would be a five-minute task. For this reason, it makes sense not only to use an architectural font on computer-generated drawings for dimensions, notes, and call-outs that may change, but also to master hand lettering and manual drafting as well.

Architectural lettering differs somewhat from the Gothic type letters developed by C. W. Reinhardt about eighty-plus years ago and now called *mechanical lettering*. Architectural lettering has evolved from a series of influences, including the demand for speed. We must not, however, interpret speed to mean or allow sloppiness.

Another influence on architectural lettering was style. The architecturally drafted plan was in essence an idea or concept on paper, a creative endeavor. Thus, the lines and the lettering took on a characteristic style of their own. In many firms, stylized lettering serves to identify the individual draftsperson. However, most firms attempt to create a uniform style of lettering that is used by the entire staff. Stylizing must not be confused with overdecoration. Lettering that looks like a new alphabet cannot be justified in the name of stylization.

Basic Rules for Lettering and Numbering

Following are a few simple rules for lettering and numbering:

1. Master mechanical lettering before attempting architectural lettering or any type of stylization. A drafter who cannot letter well in mechanical drafting has less chance of developing good architectural letters.
2. Learn to letter with vertical strokes first. Sloping letters may be easier to master, but most architectural offices prefer vertical lettering. It is easier to change from vertical to sloping letters than the reverse. See Figure 2.9.
3. Practice words, phrases, and numbers—not just individual letters. Copy a phrase from this book, for example.
4. The shape of a letter should not be changed. The proportion of the letter may be slightly altered, but one should never destroy the letter's original image. Although the middle example "W" in Figure 2.10 is in a style used for speed, it can be misconstrued as an "I" and a "V."
5. Changing the proportions of letters changes their visual effect. See Figure 2.11.
6. Certain strokes can be emphasized so that one letter is not mistaken for another. This also forces the draftsperson to be more definitive in the formation of individual strokes. The strokes emphasized should be those most important to that letter; for example, a "B" differs from an "R" by the rounded lower right stroke, and an "L" from an "I" by the horizontal bottom stroke extending to the right only. The beginning or end of these strokes can be emphasized by bearing down on the pencil to ensure a good reprint of that portion. See Figure 2.12.
7. Maintain all uppercase lettering. Do not pick up the bad habit of mixing upper- and lowercase letters.
8. Maintain proper spacing between letters and do not leave space within the letter that is not properly there. See Figure 2.13.
9. Consistency produces good lettering. If vertical lines are used, they must all be parallel. A slight variation produces poor lettering. Even round letters such as "O" have a center through which imaginary vertical strokes should go. See Figure 2.14.

Figure 2.9   Comparison between vertical and sloping lettering.

Figure 2.10   Overworking architectural letters.

Figure 2.11 Changing letter proportions to produce architectural effect.

Figure 2.12   Emphasis on certain strokes.

Figure 2.13   Spaces incorrectly left within letters.

Figure 2.14   Producing consistency.

10. Second only to the letter itself in importance is spacing. Good spacing protects good letter formation. Poor spacing destroys even the best lettering. See Figure 2.15.
11. Always use guidelines. Let your letters touch the top and bottom guideline but not extend beyond it. See Figure 2.16.

Using Guidelines

Although a purist might frown on the practice, a guideline or straightedge can be used in lettering to speed up the learning process. Horizontal lines are easier for a beginner than vertical lines, and shapes appear better formed when all of the vertical strokes are perfectly perpendicular and parallel to each other. Curved and round strokes are done without the aid of an instrument. Placing lined paper under the vellum is also a good trick to use, as is using grid vellum.

After drawing the guidelines, place a parallel about 2 or 3 inches. Relocate the straightedge below the lines. Place the triangle to the left of the area to be lettered, with the vertical portion of the triangle on the right side. See Figure 2.17. "Eyeball" the spacing of the letter. Position your pencil as if you were ready to make the

EXAMPLE:

PLYWOOD   P LY WO OD

   (Good)   (Poor)

Figure 2.15 Importance of good spacing.

PLYWOOD   PLYWOOD

   (Poor)   (Good)

Figure 2.16 Full use of guidelines.

Figure 2.17 Pencil placement for vertical lettering.

vertical line without the triangle. Before you make the vertical stroke, slide the triangle over against the pencil and make the stroke. See Figures 2.18 and 2.19. Draw nonvertical lines freehand. See Figure 2.20.

Using a straightedge helps build your skills. Eventually, you should discontinue its use as practice improves your lettering skills.

Figure 2.18 Placing the triangle against the pencil.

Figure 2.19 Drawing the vertical stroke.

Figure 2.20 Completing the letter.

Drafting Conventions and Dimensions

Using Net and Nominal Sizing. Many architectural offices have adopted the practice of separating the **net size** and the **nominal size** of lumber in their notations. The *net size* is the size of the actual piece of wood drawn and used. The *nominal size* (call-out size) is used to describe or order a piece of lumber. For example, the nominal size of a "two by four" is 2 × 4, but the net or actual size is 1½" × 3½". The distinction between the two sizes is accomplished by the use of inch (") marks. Figure 2.21A would be very confusing because the nominal size is listed but inch marks are used. Compare this notation with that of Figure 2.21B. The 16" o.c. (on center) is to be translated as precisely 16 inches, whereas the 2 × 4 is used to indicate nominal size.

Dimensions. Dimensions in feet are normally expressed by a small mark to the upper right of a number ('), and inches by two small marks (") in the same location. To separate feet from inches, a dash is used. See Figure 2.22. The dash in this type of dimensions becomes very important because it prevents dimensions from being misread and adds to clarity. If space for dimensions is restricted, an acceptable abbreviated form can be used. This is illustrated in Figure 2.23. The inches are raised and underlined to separate them from the feet notation.

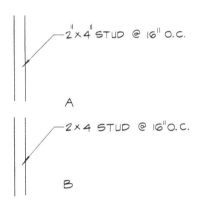

Figure 2.21 Net and nominal notation.

Figure 2.22 Expressing feet and inches.

Figure 2.23 Dimensions in a restricted area.

Placement of Dimensions. Dimension lines can be broken to show the numerical value, but it is faster simply to put numerical values above the lines. See Figure 2.24. When dimension lines run vertically, place the numbers above the dimension line as viewed from the right. See Figure 2.25.

Not all dimension lines, however, are horizontal or vertical. Often dimension lines are angled, and this can cause problems when you position the numerical value. Figure 2.26 suggests a possible location for such values.

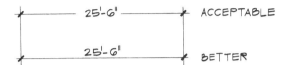

Figure 2.24 Placement of dimensions above or between dimension lines.

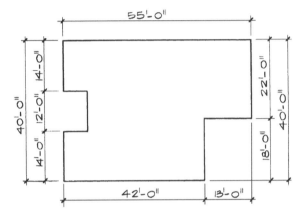

Figure 2.25 Dimensions read from bottom and from the right.

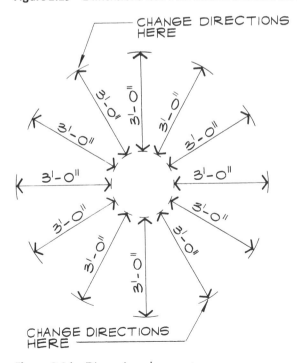

Figure 2.26 Dimension placement.

■ ARCHITECTURAL DRAFTING

The architectural version of **orthographic projection** is an object projected at 90° as you view the object, as shown in Figure 2.27. The top view (as viewed from a helicopter) is now called the *plan*, and the views all the way around from all four sides are referred to as **elevations**. Each of these elevations has a special name, as will be discussed in the chapter on exterior and interior elevations (Chapter 11).

In brief, a top view of the total property is called the **site** or **plot plan**. A horizontal section (drawn as if the structure were cut horizontally, the top portion removed, and the exposed interior viewed from above) is simply called a **plan**. There are many types of plans: **floor plans**, **electrical plans** (showing electrical features), **framing plans** (showing how a floor, ceiling, or roof is assembled), and **foundation plans**, to mention just a few.

A vertical cut through a structure is called a **cross-section** or a **longitudinal section**, depending on the direction of the cut. The cross-section is a cut taken through the short end of a structure. As of the turn of the century (and for some architects), the architectural term for cross-section, longitude section transverse, has been replaced with the term **building section**.

■ REPRODUCTION METHODS

The Blueprint Process

In the first half of the last century, the prevalent method of reproduction was the blueprint. **Blueprints** have a blue background and white lines. Bond paper was coated with light-sensitive chemicals, much like photographic film. The original, drawn on a translucent medium such as vellum, was placed over the paper and exposed to light. The light bleached out the chemicals except where they were screened off by lines. The paper was then dipped in a developing solution that reacted with those sections not exposed to the light. The print was then washed and dried. As you can imagine, this process was time-consuming. However, the lay public still uses the term *blueprint* to describe or refer to a copy of a drawing used in the building industry, even though these copies are now dark lines on a white background, most often made on a plain-paper copier.

Plain-Paper Copiers

Types and Sizes.   A variety of plain-paper copiers are now on the open market for sale or lease. Some machines

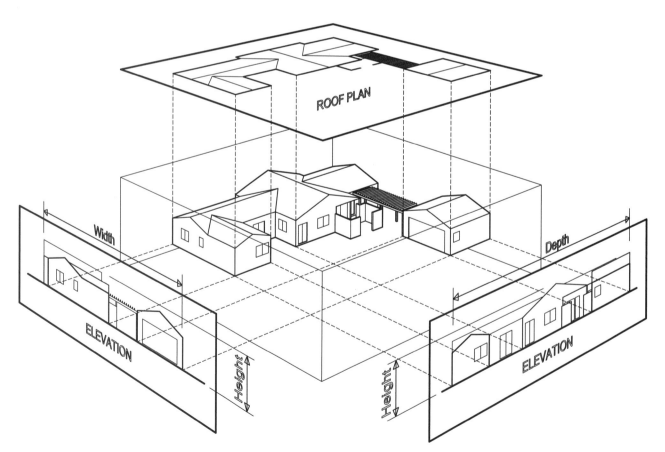

Figure 2.27 A multiview drawing of a structure.

can enlarge as well as reduce. Some copiers do not copy the original to its exact size; instead, they change the size slightly and often in only one direction. Plain-paper copiers usually use the standard paper formats of 8½″ × 11″ and 8½″ × 14″. The larger copiers can take copy widths up to 54″, and length is unlimited, because these machines accept roll stock. Paper copiers can reproduce on bond paper, vellum, or acetate.

Appliques. Most adhesive films for plain-paper copiers have two sheets: one sheet of adhesive film and a backing sheet or carrier. Because the adhesive film has a sticky substance on one side, the carrier is a nonstick material. Standard decals or appliques can be made with adhesive film for things like symbols, title block information, and even construction notes.

Computer

The new CAD systems are often combined with a printer or a plotter. A plotter can be used to reproduce a drawing and/or recreate a secondary original that can use the previously mentioned reproduction methods. The advantage is that you can change the size and scale of the reproduction instantly.

Because the industry is moving toward wireless units, both manufacturers and the computer industry are producing printers and plotters that can potentially be programmed directly to and from the computer. This promises to produce a flexibility heretofore unknown in the office to produce either single or multiple sets instantaneously.

Shortcut Procedures

Freehand Drawing. One of the best shortcuts you can learn is freehand drawing. Most of the preliminary design procedures and conceptual design details in this book were done freehand. You still should use a scale to maintain accuracy, and adhere to the drafting vocabulary of lines and techniques. Freehand skill is useful in field situations, for informal office communications, and for communications with contractors, building department officials, and clients.

Photography and Drafting. Photography plays a large part in architectural drafting. The older photographic method was used to produce a *photostat*. This technique is rapidly being replaced by the photo mechanical transfer (PMT) system. In this process, there is no real negative. Rather, there is an intermediate paper negative that takes about 30 seconds to make; the image is then transferred from this throwaway master to a positive.

Still, the best—and the most versatile—process is regular camera photography. The only limit to the size of print is the equipment itself, and 36″ × 42″ negatives are now available. Because negatives can be spliced together, the final limit is restricted only by the size of the positive paper available. Uses of photography are described later in this chapter.

Reprodrafting. Reprodrafting is a term used to describe a number of approaches to improving or revising drafted material in a way that takes advantage of photographic or photocopying processes. These approaches have spawned a number of new terms, including eraser drafting, paste-up drafting, photo-drafting, overlay drafting, pen drafting, and scissors drafting. Reprodrafting, then, actually consists of many processes.

Restoration refers to the process of taking a photograph of an old original or an old print and, by repairing the negative, producing a new master.

Composite drafting is the photographic process of making a single drawing from many, or of taking parts of other drawings to make a new drawing.

Paste-up drafting simply refers to the process of pasting pieces onto a single master sheet, and then photographing and reproducing the master. The lines on the negative made by edges of the pieces can be eliminated by a photo retoucher.

Scissors drafting takes an existing drawing and eliminates undesirable or corrected portions by cutting them out before the paste-up process. **Eraser drafting** is similar, but the unwanted portions are simply erased. In both cases, the original is never touched. A good copy on good quality paper is produced first. The copy must be printed in a way that allows easy erasure.

Photo-drafting, as the name indicates, uses both drafting and photography. It begins with a photograph of any drawing, such as a plan, elevation, or detail. The drawing is printed on a matte-surfaced film and additional information is drafted onto it. Photo-drafting is an ideal method for dealing with historical restoration drawings.

Other Shortcut Methods

Using Standardized Sheets. Standardized sheets are useful if all the jobs an office takes are similar or if the office specializes in a particular building type that calls for the same information each time.

A Simple Shortcut: Manual Drafting. Make a copy of all the early stages of the different parts of a building. See Figure 2.28. The final drawing is shown in Figure 2.29. If there are no significant changes, tape the drawing to a piece of bond paper, copy it onto the vellum, and

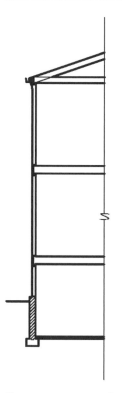

Figure 2.28 Save all earlier stages.

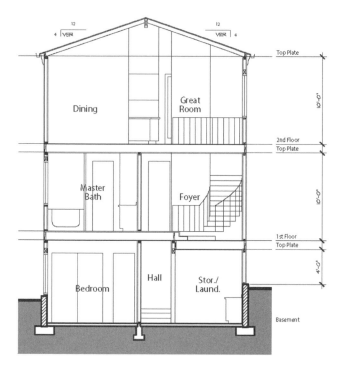

Section A-A   SCALE: 1/4" = 1'-0"

Figure 2.29 Using tracers.

then finish the process. If, for example, the **pitch** (roof slope) is different, then simply cut out the roof portion, tape it to a sheet of bond paper, and print onto vellum. Manually correct the new roof pitch and proceed to finish the process.

A Much-Needed Survival Skill

Let us first set up a hypothetical problem and then apply a much-needed drafting skill:

Your task as a junior drafter in the office is to produce a workable floor plan and site plan that have been sent to you in a reduced format. The scale is unknown and is similar to that in Figure 2.30.

The solution is to enlarge the drawing back to its original scale of ⅛" = 1'-0" for the site plan and ¼" = 1'-0" for the basement floor plan and print it on a 24" × 36" sheet of paper.

Manual Drafting Solution.

Step I. *Establish a measurable datum.* For the site plan, it is a matter of taking one of the known measurements, such as the 70' property line shown on Figure 2.30. Redraw this measurement on a separate piece of paper at ⅛" = 1'-0" scale. We will call this our *datum line.* See Figure 2.31.

Step II. *Enlarge on the copier.* Enlarge the 70' property line on the site plan to match the datum line. Do it based on an eyeball estimate.

Step III. *Compare the enlargement to the datum line.* Unless you are extremely lucky, the 70' property line will not exactly match the datum line, so make either another enlargement or a reduction.

Step IV. *Adjust the enlargement.* You may find, as you get within 1%, that the 1% enlargement is just a bit too large. Try reducing the drawing by a small percentage, such as 5%, and then enlarge the drawing by 6%.

This enlargement calculation can also be done by a simple math ratio. Measure the N.T.S. (not to scale) 70' line. Say it measures 56', with ⅛" being the desired scale: 70'/56' × 100 = 125% enlargement.

Using a Computer. To achieve the enlargement using a computer, the first thing to do is to scan the image into the computer. Isolate one corner of the line to be used. Zoom in on this corner for maximum accuracy. Locate the center of the corner.

Next, go to the scale command and scale the datum line with reference. When you type in the reference length, the drawing will automatically resize.

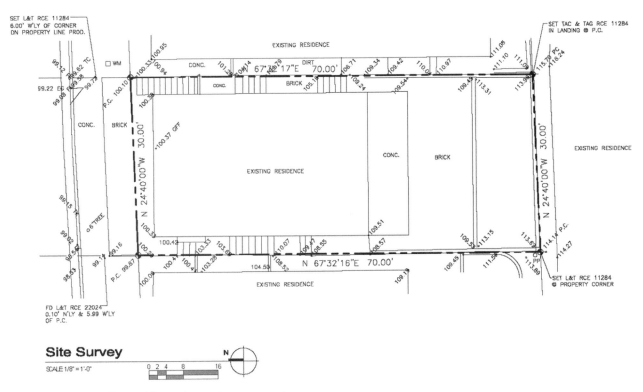

Figure 2.30 Site plan and floor plan (unknown scale).

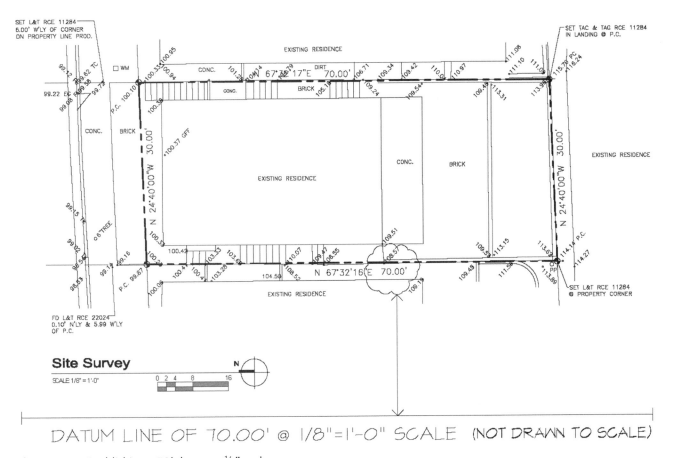

Figure 2.31 Establishing a 70' datum at ⅛" scale.

■ OFFICE STANDARDS

Sheet Size

The drawing sheet size varies from office to office depending on the type of work performed, size of the job, and the system of drafting used in the office. The most common sheet sizes are 24″ × 36″, 30″ × 42″, and 36″ × 48″.

When sheets are used horizontally, they are usually bound on the left side. Because of this, the border is larger on the left side. A typical border line is ⅜″ to ½″ around the three sides and 1″ to 1½″ on the left side.

Title blocks can run the full height of the right side rather than simply filling a square in the bottom right corner, as in mechanical drafting. The long title band contains such information as sheet number, client's name or project title, name of firm, name or title of the drawing, person drafting, scale, date, and revision dates. The title block sheets are usually preprinted, but can be applied to sheets in the form of decals or appliques.

This location of the title block allows you to leave a rectangular area for drawing purposes, whereas a title block in the lower right corner produces an L-shaped drawing area. (Even when drawing on a large sheet, take care to draft so that you use the sheet to its fullest.)

Many offices establish a sheet module. Here is an example of this method with a 24″ × 36″ sheet:

Binding side	1½″ border
Other 3 sides	½″ border
Title block	1½″

This leaves a drawing area of 23″ by 32½″. The vertical 23″ distance can be divided into four equal parts, while the horizontal 32½″ can be divided into eight equal parts. This provides 32 spaces 4¹⁄₁₆″ wide by 5¾″ high. This office procedure may be followed so that each sheet has a consistent appearance. Whether the sheet is full of details or a combination of a plan and details and/or notes, the module gives you parameters within which to work. You should draft from the right side of the sheet so that any blank spaces remaining are toward the inside (on the binding side).

Lettering Height

The height of lettering depends on the type of reproduction used. If you use normal diazo methods, use the following standards as a rule of thumb:

Main titles under drawings	¼″ maximum
Subtitles	³⁄₁₆″
Normal lettering	³⁄₃₂″–⅛″
Sheet number in title block	½″–1″

Increase these sizes when you are reducing drawings. For example, increase normal lettering from ³⁄₃₂″ to ⅛″ or ³⁄₁₆″, depending on the reduction ratio.

Lettering

One of the most important office standards to which a drafter must subscribe is lettering. Many offices use a combination of uppercase and lowercase letters for the main titles, such as for room names. Certain fonts, such as Helvetica and Garamond, are very popular. When selecting a font, be sure to find one based on a simple stroking system so as not to impede the printing process. There can be a marked difference in the printing or plotting time for different fonts, especially when the text is very long, as in general notes, framing notes, or energy notes.

The height of the letters is also very important for legibility. Lettering that is ⅛″ or ³⁄₃₂″ tall is very readable. Using letters ¼″ tall (maximum) for main titles produces enough contrast between notes and titles to enhance the construction documents.

In general, we suggest an architectural font. It speeds up the correction process. See "Importance of Hand Lettering" discussed earlier in this chapter.

A problem caused by the infusion of electronic equipment into our field is the difficulty in maintaining the lettering size on drawings that are electronically reduced either on a plain-paper copier or digitally on a computer.

Scale of Drawings

The scale selected should be the largest practical scale based on the size of the structure and the drawing space available. The following are the sizes most commonly used by offices, with the most desirable size being underlined where there is a choice.

Site Plan: ⅛″ = 1′-0″ for small sites. Drawings are provided by a civil engineer and scales are expressed in engineering terms such as 1″ = 10′, 1″ = 20′, etc.

Floor Plan: ¼″ = 1′-0″, ⅛″ or ¹⁄₁₆″ = 1′-0″ for larger structures.

Exterior Elevations: Same as the floor plan.

Building Sections: ¼″ = 1′-0″; ½″ = 1′-0″ for smaller projects.

Interior Elevations: ¼″ = 1′-0″, ⅜″ = 1′-0″, ½″ = 1′-0″.

Architectural Details: ½″ = 1′-0″ to 3″ = 1′-0″, depending on the size of the object being drawn or the amount of information that must be shown. Footing detail: ¾″ = 1′-0″ or 1″ = 1′-0″. Eave details: 1½″ = 1′-0″. Wall sections: typically ¾″ = 1′-0″.

Materials in Section

Figure 2.32 shows the various methods used throughout the United States to represent different materials in section. These conventions were developed by the Committee on Office Practice, American Institute of Architects (National), and published in *Architectural Graphic Standards*.

Clearly, there is standardization and there are variations. For example, all groups agree on the method of representing brick in section, yet there is a great deal of variation in the way concrete block is represented in section. The last figure shows specialty items from a variety of sources.

Graphic Symbols

The symbols in Figure 2.33 are the most common and acceptable, to judge by the frequency with which the architectural offices surveyed use them. This list can be and should be expanded by each office to include those symbols generally used in its practice and not indicated here.

Abbreviations

Suggested abbreviations compiled by Task Force #1, National Committee on Office Practice, American Institute of Architects, and published in the AIA *Journal*, can be found in Appendix C on the web site www.wiley.com/go/wakita.

Dimensioning

Dimensioning is the act of incorporating numerical values into a drawing as a means of sizing various components and also locating parts of a building. This is accomplished on dimension lines, in notes, and by reference to other drawings or details.

Grouping Dimensions. Group dimensions whenever possible, in order to provide continuity. This takes planning. Try running a print of the drawing in question and dimension it on this check print first. This will allow you to identify dimensions and decide how they can be effectively grouped.

Maintaining a Dimension Standard. The most important dimensions dictate subsequent dimensions. For example, if a wall is dimensioned to the center of the wall first, all subsequent dimensions using this wall as a reference point should be dimensioned at its center.

Size Dimensions and Location Dimensions. The two basic kinds of dimensions are size and location.

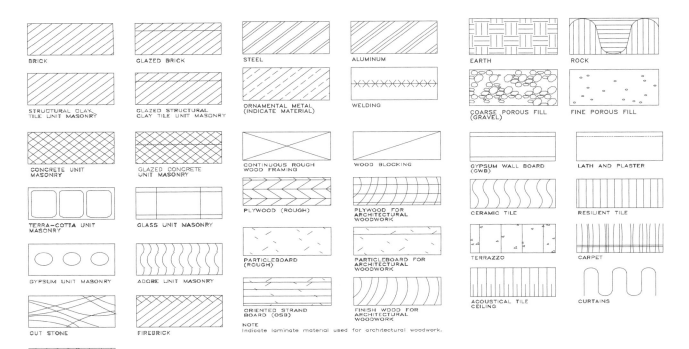

Figure 2.32 Graphic symbols for materials in section. (Copyright 2000, Architectural Graphic Standards CD-ROM, John Wiley & Sons Inc., Hoboken, NJ.)

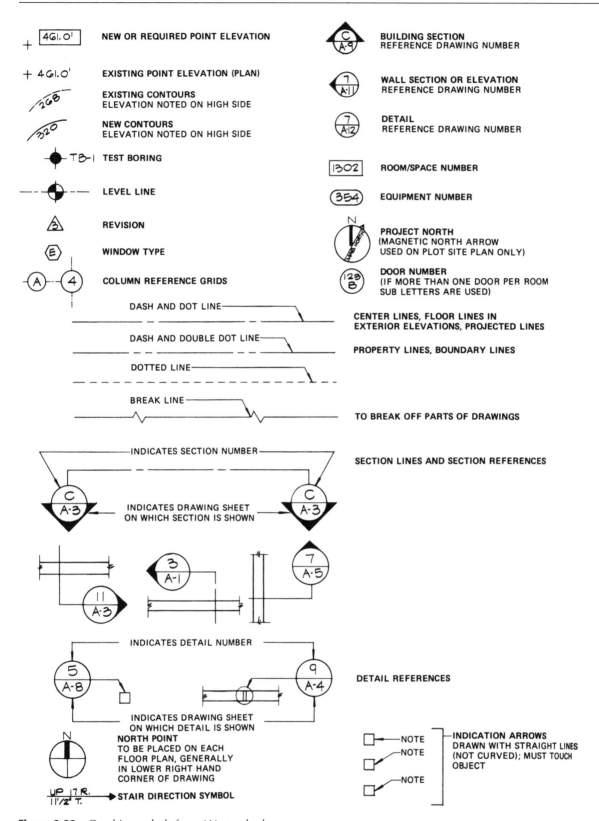

Figure 2.33 Graphic symbols from AIA standards.

See Figure 2.34. Size dimensions indicate overall size. Location dimensions deal with the actual placement of an object or structure, such as a wall, a window, or a planter.

The Dimensional Reference System. The **dimensional reference system** is based on a three-dimensional axis. See Figure 2.35. Critical planes are located by a series of reference bubbles and used as **planes of reference**. Figure 2.36 shows a box; reference bubbles describe the three planes of height, width, and depth. Now examine this box sliced in two directions, as shown in Figures 2.37 and 2.38. The first slice produces a **horizontal control plane**, and the second a **vertical control plane**.

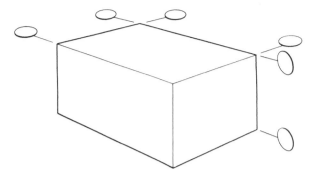

Figure 2.36   Three principal planes using dimensional reference system.

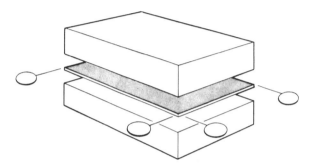

Figure 2.37   Horizontal control plane.

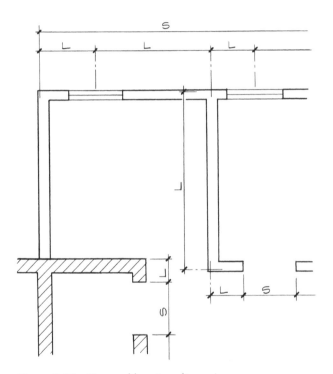

Figure 2.34   Size and location dimensions.

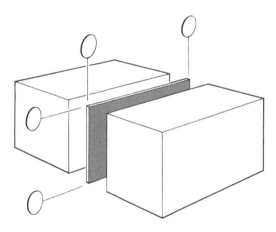

Figure 2.38   Vertical control plane.

The shaded area in Figure 2.39 represents a horizontal plane at a critical point on the structure, such as the floor line. The shaded area on Figure 2.40 represents a vertical plane at a critical point of the structure, such as the location of a series of columns or beams. There is a definite relationship between the vertical control plane and the horizontal control plane. Compare the plan and the section shown in Figure 2.41. The section is a vertical cut as in Figure 2.40 and the plan is a horizontal cut as in Figure 2.39. The two vertical and one horizontal reference bubbles on Figure 2.39 are an attempt to show this relationship.

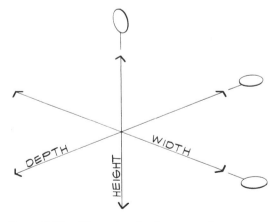

Figure 2.35   Dimensional reference system.

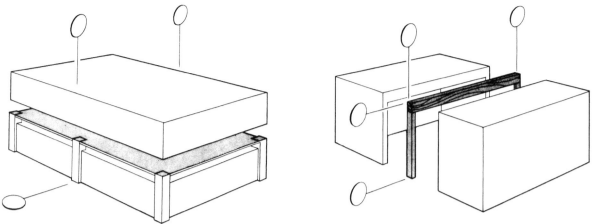

Figure 2.39   Horizontal plane.

Figure 2.40   Vertical plane.

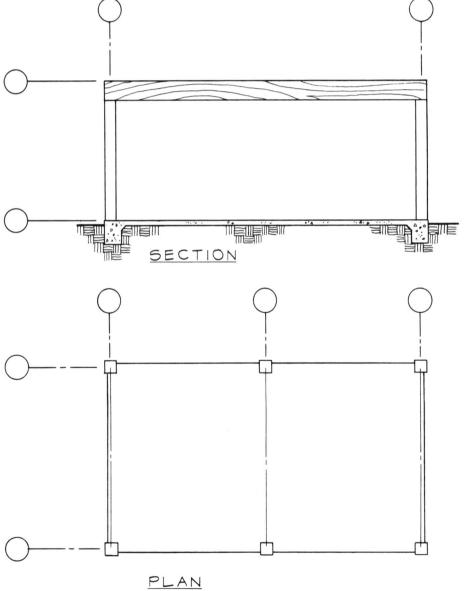

SECTION

PLAN

Figure 2.41   Section and plan.

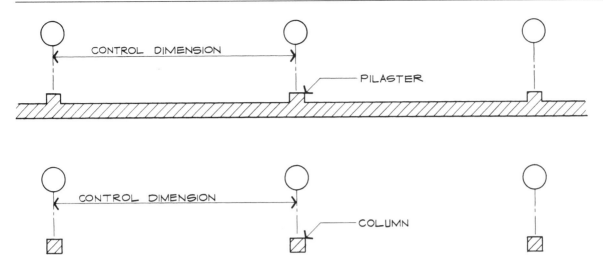

Figure 2.42 Axial control planes.

Types of Planes. There are two types of planes. The first is the **axial plane**, which goes through the center of critical structural items as shown in Figure 2.42. Note how the columns are dimensioned to the center. When **pilasters** (widening of a masonry wall for support) are used, they become a good location for control dimensions, as they support the structural members above.

The second type of plane is called a **boundary control plane**. See Figure 2.43. In this case, columns and walls are not dimensioned to the center; instead, their boundaries are dimensioned. Figure 2.44 shows examples of columns and walls located in the **neutral zone**. These neutral zones are especially valuable in dealing with the vertical dimensions of a section and with elevations. See Figure 2.45. A neutral zone is established between the ceiling and the floor above. The floor-to-ceiling heights can be established to allow the structural, mechanical, and electrical consultants to perform their work. Once that dimension is established, the neutral zone and floor-to-floor dimensions follow. See Figure 2.46 for a practical application for the **vertical control dimension** and **control zone** (another term for neutral zone).

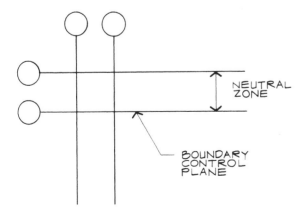

Figure 2.43 Boundary control planes.

■ METRICS

Why is metrics so important for students and professionals in architecture? With this information one can work internationally. So often we see European architects designing structures in our country, but we too have reciprocal opportunities. At any level, knowing the metrics helps broaden the scope of your employment.

A meter comprises ten decimeters which, in turn, each comprise ten centimeters. The smallest unit of conversion is the millimeter. Ten meters make a decameter, ten times that is a hectometer, and ten times that is a kilometer. Here is a chart showing these values:

kilometer	= 1,000 meters	km
*hectometer	= 100 meters	hm
*decameter	= 10 meters	dam
meter		m
*decimeter	= 1/10 meter	dm
centimeter	= 1/100 meter	cm
millimeter	= 1/1000 meter	mm

*Seldom used in modern drawings.

For architectural drafting, the millimeter, centimeter, and meter are the most desirable and most commonly used units.

Notation Method

Locate the decimal point in the center of the line of numerical value rather than close to the bottom of the line. For example, 304.65 is best written 304·65. However, the original notation is acceptable.

Commas are not used. Rather, spaces are left to denote where commas would have been. For example, 10·34674 meters would be written 10.346 74 meters,

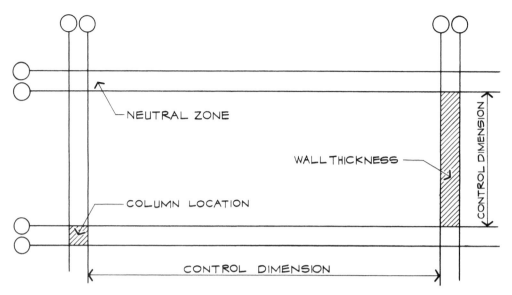

Figure 2.44 Column location in a neutral zone.

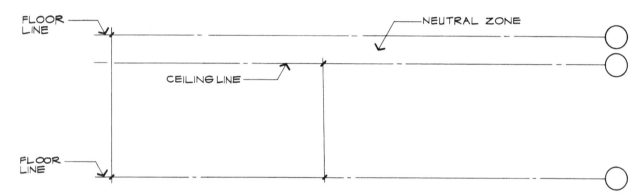

Figure 2.45 Neutral zone in a vertical dimension.

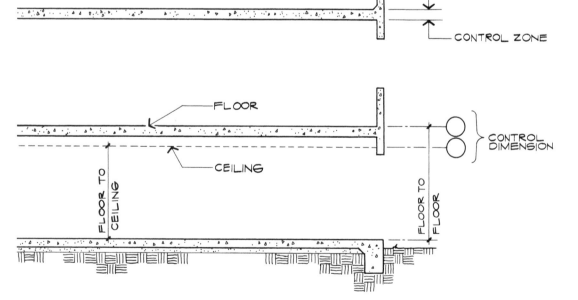

Figure 2.46 Vertical control dimension.

and 506,473·21 meters would be written as 506 473.21 meters. Our computers are not normally programmed to put the period in the center, so normal periods are used in their place. In addition, a space is left between 3 digits.

Abbreviations of metric units do not have special plural forms. For example, fifty centimeters is written 50 cm, *not* 50 cms. Note also the space between the number and the letters. It should read 50, space, abbreviation for centimeter(s): 50 cm.

Once a standard, such as "all measurements shall be in meters," is established for a set of drawings, it need not be noted on each drawing. A 4 by 8 sheet of plywood should be called out not as 1.219 2 m × 2.438 4 m plywood but rather as 1.219 2 × 2.438 4 plywood. However, if a size is in a measure other than meters, this should be noted.

English Equivalents

Here is a quick reference chart for converting linear measurements into metrics:

Length:

inches	× 2·54	= centimeters (cm)
feet	× 0·304 8	= meters (m)
yards	× 0·914 4	= meters (m)
miles	× 1·609 34	= kilometers (km)

General Conversion Rules

Using the equivalent values just given, you can convert by multiplication. For example, 16 inches is:

inches × 2·54 = cm
16 in. × 2·54 = 40·64 cm

To convert 25 feet into metric measurements:

feet   × 0·304 8 = m
25 ft   × 0·304 8 = 7.62 m

To convert 5 yards into meters:

yards   × 0·914 4 = m
75 yd × 0·914 4 = 68.58 m

Unit Change

To convert 17 feet 8 inches, follow this procedure:

17 ft × 0·304 8 = 5·181 6 m
8 in. × 2·54   = 20·32 cm

In this example, conversion of feet results in meters, and conversion of inches results in centimeters. You cannot add these quantities unless you convert them to the same unit of measurement. Do this simply by moving the

decimal point. In this example, if meters are desired, simply move the decimal point of the centimeter unit two units to the left: 20·32 cm are equal to ·203 2 m. Thus,

17 ft	=	5·181 6 m
8 in.	=	·203 2 m
		5·384 8 m

Actual versus Nominal

Presently, lumber uses an odd system of notation. When a piece of lumber is drawn, it is drafted to its actual size (net size). In the notes describing this particular piece of wood, it is called out in its nominal size (call-out size). For example, a 2 × 4 piece of wood is drawn at 1½″ × 3½″, but on the note pointing to this piece it is still called a 2 × 4.

Therefore, when converting to metric, the 1½″ × 3½″ size must be converted and drawn to the actual size. There is no set procedure for the call-out. Some drawings convert the 2 × 4 size metrically and note this piece of wood with the 1½″ × 3½″ size converted. A sample note might read as follows:

·038 1 × ·088 9 (net) STUD

Using Two Standards

Because metrics have only recently begun to be used in the American architectural profession, we are not yet geared to note things metrically. Lumber, reinforcing, glass, and other materials are still ordered in the English system. Their sizes, weights, and shapes are also still described using the English-system terms.

There are three approaches to this situation. First, we can note only those things we have control over in metrics, such as the size of a room, the width of a footing, and so on, while noting 2 × 4 studs, #4 reinforcing bars, ½″ anchor bolts, and the like, according to the manufacturers' nomenclature (until they change to the metric system).

A second method is dual notation. This system requires dimensions, notes, and all call-outs to be recorded twice. For example, a 35′-6″ dimension would have the metric value of 10·820 4 written directly below it.

The third and final method is to approach everything metrically. This may not be the best way in an office going through a transition, but it is the best student method because you will eventually be asked to work totally in metrics.

Conversion of Drafting

If we are to convert everything to metrics, there are three procedures to consider. First is that of "holding" certain dimension notes and call-outs. If, for example, we are dealing with a #4 rebar (which is a steel reinforcing bar ½″ in size) and the manufacturer has not changed to metrics, we must convert the ½″ by multiplying ½″ × 2·54 and note the rebar as:

1·27 cm rebar
or
0·127 rebar

The second procedure requires "rounding off." See Figure 2.47. In this figure, the scale on the top is an enlarged one that you are accustomed to seeing. The scale directly below is in the same enlarged proportion but in metric units. The numbers in this scale are in centimeters. Notice that 2·54 centimeters equal an inch. Notice also that one centimeter is less than ½ inch. Initially, this is a hard proportion to relate to for anyone making the transition. Also note that half a centimeter (0·5 cm) is smaller than ¼ inch and that one millimeter (one-tenth of a centimeter) is less than ¹/₁₆ of an inch.

Now compare this knowledge with an actual number. Assume that you wish to dig a trench 12 inches wide for a footing.

12 inches = (12 × 2·54) = 30·48 cm

Hence, there are 30+ units less than ½ inch in size that we can measure. The .4 is less than ³/₁₆″, which is very difficult to measure and impossible for a worker to deal with on the job. This is the point at which we should begin to round off.

The final number (0·08) is even worse. It amounts to just a little more than ¹/₃₂ of an inch—a measurement that a draftsperson would have difficulty even reading on the scale, and that the person digging the trench would have to ignore. The final rounded-off value should be 31·0 cm or 0·31. This trench is about ³/₁₆ inches wider than the desired 12 inches but is something the people out in the field can measure with their metric scales.

The third conversion procedure requires judgment about whether to increase or decrease. Certain measure-

ments must be increased in the rounding-off process; the trench discussed previously is a good example. If we round this number off to 30·0 cm or 0·30, the measurement is less than 12 inches. If the 12-inch requirement had been imposed by the local code, you would have thus violated the code. Had it been set at 12 inches for structural reasons, the building could be deemed unsafe. Another example is a planned opening for a piece of equipment. Rounding off to the smaller number might result in the equipment not fitting.

Another kind of danger lies in *exceeding* a required maximum. For example, the note for an anchor bolt reads:

½″ × 10″; to anchor bolt embedded 7″ into concrete 6′-0″ o.c. and 12″ from corners

The spacing of 6′-0″ on center is used to maintain a minimum number of anchor bolts per unit of length. If we increase the distance between bolts, we exceed the required spacing, and (as stated in the note) reduce the number of bolts per unit of length below the minimum required.

The second and third processes are called **soft conversion**; that is, an English measurement is converted directly into a metric equivalent and then rounded off to a workable metric value. In contrast, in a **hard conversion**, the total approach is changed. It is not just a numerical conversion but a change of medium as well. If bricks are the medium, for example, the procedure would be to subscribe to a brick that was sized metrically and dimension accordingly.

Listed below are some of the recommended rounding-off sizes:

¹/₈″	=	3·2 mm	1¾″	=	44·0 mm
¼″	=	6·4 mm	2″	=	50·0 mm
³/₈″	=	9·5 mm	2½″	=	63·0 mm
½″	=	12·7 mm	3″	=	75·0 mm
⁵/₈″	=	16·0 mm	4″	=	100·0 mm
¾″	=	19·0 mm	6″	=	150·0 mm
⁷/₈″	=	22·0 mm	8″	=	200·0 mm
1″	=	25·0 mm	10″	=	250·0 mm
1¼″	=	32·0 mm	12″	=	300·0 mm
1½″	=	38·0 mm			

Zero is used to avoid error in metrics. For example, .8 is written 0.8 or 0·8.

When other conversions are needed, round off fractions to the nearest 5 mm, inches to the nearest 25 mm, and feet to the nearest 0·1 meter.

Metric Scale

The metric scale is used in the same way as the architectural scales. It reduces a drawing to a selected

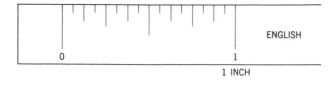

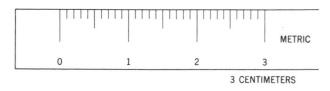

Figure 2.47 Comparison of English and metric scales.

proportion. You can purchase scales with the following metric divisions.

1:5	1:50
1:10	1:75
1:20	1:100
1:25	1:125
1:33⅓	1:200
1:40	

Although these proportions may not make sense initially, let us take one example and see what they mean. The 1:10 scale indicates that we are taking a known measurement (a meter) and making it ten times smaller. See Figure 2.48. In other words, if you visualize a meter (39·37 inches) and squeeze it until it is only one-tenth of its original size, you have a 1:10 ratio scale. Everything you draw is then one-tenth of its original size.

This also applies to any other scale. A 1:50 scale means that the original meter has been reduced to one-fiftieth of its original length. Figures 2.49 and 2.50 show the visual appearance of the 1:50, 1:10, 1:20, and 1:100 proportions, as they might be seen on an actual scale. Notice how the meter is to be located so that you can translate decimeters and centimeters. To measure 12 inches or 30·48 cm (0·3048 m) on a 1:10 scale, see Figure 2.51.

If you find it difficult to transfer a drawing scaled in inches and feet to a metric drawing, the following chart should help.

1:10 is approximately 1″ = 1′-0″ (1:12)
1:20 is approximately ½″ = 1′-0″ (1:24)
1:50 is approximately ¼″ = 1′-0″ (1:48)
1:100 is approximately ⅛″ = 1′-0″ (1:96)

Of the four scales in this chart, the 1:50 and 1:100 come closest to being exact conversions.

Drawing Sheet Size

When the total conversion to metrics takes place, the change will affect not only the drawing but also the sheet size of the drawing paper. Listed are some of the typical sizes used internationally. They are expressed in millimeters (mm).

841 × 1189	105 × 148
594 × 841	74 × 105
420 × 594	52 × 74
297 × 420	37 × 52
210 × 297	26 × 37
148 × 210	

A spot check of the various paper companies that sell reproduction paper as well as drawing paper shows that

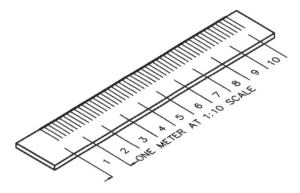

Figure 2.48 Pictorial of reduced metric scale.

Figure 2.49 How to read an actual scale—1:50 and 1:10.

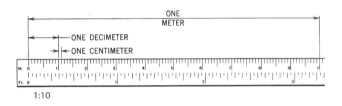

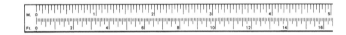

Figure 2.50 How to read an actual scale—1:20 and 1:100.

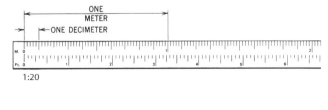

Figure 2.51 One foot equivalent in metric.

metrically sized paper is already being used for overseas work.

Possible Sizes

Because the various manufacturers have not converted to a uniform size, it is difficult to predict the final evolution of the various building materials. The following lists contain suggested sizes and those used by other countries.

Wood (in mm)

38 × 75	44 × 75	50 × 75	63 × 150
38 × 100	44 × 100	50 × 100	63 × 175
38 × 150	44 × 150	50 × 125	63 × 200
38 × 175	44 × 175	50 × 150	63 × 225
38 × 200	44 × 200	50 × 175	
38 × 225	44 × 225	50 × 200	75 × 200
		50 × 300	75 × 300

Brick (in mm)

300 × 100 × 100	200 × 100 × 100
200 × 100 × 75	200 × 200 × 100

Gypsum Lath (in mm)

9·5   12·7 or 12·00

Miscellaneous

12 mm diameter for rebar
3 mm for sheet glass
25 mm for sheathing

Modules

As indicated in Figure 2.52, the standard **module** in metrics is 100 mm. Groups of this standard 100-mm module are called a *multi-module*. When you select the multi-module, you should consider quantities such as 600 mm, 800 mm, 1,200 mm, 1,800 mm, and 2,400 mm. All of these numbers are divisible in a way that allows you flexibility. For example, the 600-mm multi-module is divisible by 2, 3, 4, and 5. The result of this division gives numbers such as 200, 300, 120, and 150. All of these are numbers for which building materials may be available. This is especially true of masonry units. Most of the sizes listed in the "Possible Sizes" section work evenly into a 600-mm module. See Figure 2.53.

Metrics and Computers

Using computers in the metrification process is relatively simple, because all of the symbols and conventions remain the same. Line weights, color, and layers also remain the same. In other words, the language remains the same. The only difference is the ruler used to make the changes. Thus, the unit of measurement changes.

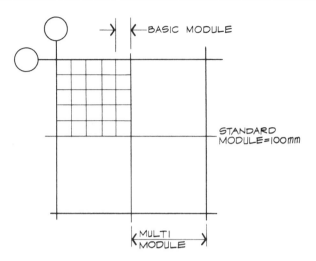

Figure 2.52   Standard module.

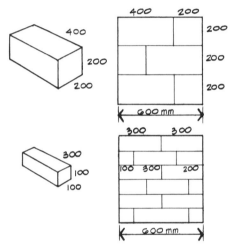

Figure 2.53   Brick and block dimensions.

Structures do not change in size. When we changed from feet and inches to the decimal equivalents, what was being measured did not change, only the instrument used to measure it. This means you must first deal with four things on the computer:

A. Settings
B. Grids and Snap
C. Scale
D. Scaling Factors

Setting the preferences or changing the settings is simple. Set the computer to metric rather than architectural. Decide to draw in meters, centimeters, or millimeters. Because of the size of structures, the plans, elevations, and sections are usually drawn in meters, whereas details are often drawn in millimeters and centimeters, but seldom in decimeters.

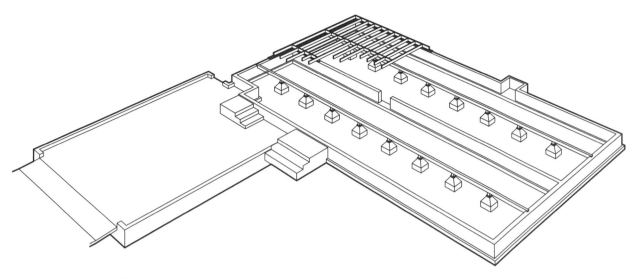

Figure 2.54 Pictorial of pier and girder system.

Structures are drawn full size and in model space. Because a scale must be attached when plotting, the CAD drafter must be aware of the typical scales and scale factors for the scale being used.

Desired drawings are often drawn freehand by the office manager, then translated by the CAD drafter. In the case of a foundation plan, the office manager or structural engineer can decide the number of piers, size of girder, and location of access openings, to mention just a few of the items that must be sized and spaced. Figure 2.54 shows a pictorial diagram of a desired foundation plan.

If the drawing has been sketched by the office manager and all of the sizes are listed in metric, the CAD drafter need only draw, dimension, and annotate the plan. As mentioned previously, this is called a *hard conversion* (see Figure 2.55). The soft conversion is a bit more cumbersome, because a soft conversion requires a thorough knowledge of the structure and the forces at work.

An effective CAD drafter who is asked to perform a soft conversion should be able to:

A. Perform simple conversions of wood members.
B. Round off to the nearest desirable measurement based on the work crew's tolerances in the field, while maintaining the strength of the member.
C. Review proportion of lumber and space available in which to work.
D. Select comparable sizes of lumber and rebar based on the available sizes in a particular region. A sampling of sizes available in Europe was listed earlier in the "Possible Sizes" section.
E. Check the proportion of the metric wood member.
F. Compute the cross-sectioned area of lumber (or steel) by existing charts and compare this cross-sectioned area in the English system against the metric measurements.
G. Select a scale.

A. *Conversion:* Although it is not the intent to engineer foundation plans, a CAD drafter should be able to convert from the English system (feet and inches) to the metric system. Consider the hypothetical situation shown in Figure 2.56.

The two measurements we will deal with are the 2×6 floor joist at 16″ o.c. and the 4′-6″ pier spacing.

Pier Spacing

$$4\text{-}6'' \quad = \quad 4' \times 12'' \text{ per foot} \quad = \quad 48''$$
$$\underline{6''}$$
$$54'' \text{ total}$$

B. *Rounding Off:*

54″ × 2.54 (cm/inch) = 137.16 cm = 137 cm

We will round off small so as not to exceed maximum. To convert to meters:

1,3 7. cm

The decimal point is moved two places to the left, making the measurement 1.37.

C. *Reviewing Proportion:* Look at Figure 2.57. Notice the minimum dimension between the underside of the girder and the earth (grade) and the distance between the underside of the floor joist and grade. A 6″ space exists, which will accommodate a girder without raising the entire structure. Thus, a 4×6 was selected. A 4×4 is allowed in many situations, but remember, we are building to increase the strength within the allowable space.

A 2×6 was used here because it is often the smallest size allowed by many municipalities and was selected to keep a low building profile.

Converting the 2×6 floor joist at 16″ o.c.:

The 2×6 is in reality 1.5×5.5 inches.

The 2×6 member is a 1 to 3 ratio, whereas in reality 1.5×5.5 is closer to a 1 to 3.66 ratio.

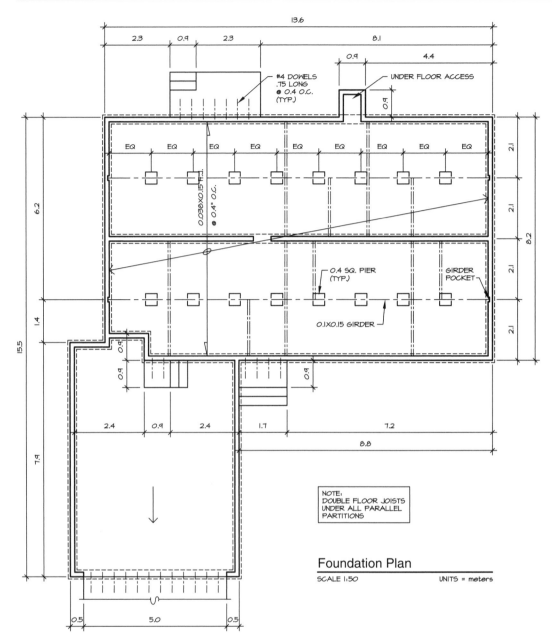

Figure 2.55 Metric foundation plan.

The larger this ratio (see Figure 2.58), the stronger the member, as you are using the member in the direction of the strength based on the direction of the grain.

Metric Conversion:
1.5 × 2.54 = 3.81 cm
5.5 × 2.54 = 13.97 cm

D. *Selecting a Comparable Metric Member:* The 1.5 × 5.5 member converted becomes a 3.81 cm × 13.97 cm unit. When selecting a comparable size from the chart, note that the chart displays sizes in millimeters (mm). The closest is 38 mm × either 100 mm or 150 mm. The 38 mm × 150 mm value is used to round off to the strength.

E. *Checking the Metric Proportion:* A 38 mm × 150 mm member has a proportion of 1:3.95. Compare this with the 1:3.66 in the English system member. The metric proportion is much better.

F. *Computing Cross-Sectional Area:* With the 38 mm × 150 mm member, you have (38 × 150) 5,700 sq mm. The 1.5 (38.1 mm) × 5.5 (139.7 mm) member has a cross-sectional area of 38.1 mm × 139.7 mm = 5,322.57 sq mm. Thus, the 38 mm × 150 mm member has a greater cross-sectional area and a better proportion, giving the structure a stronger foundation.

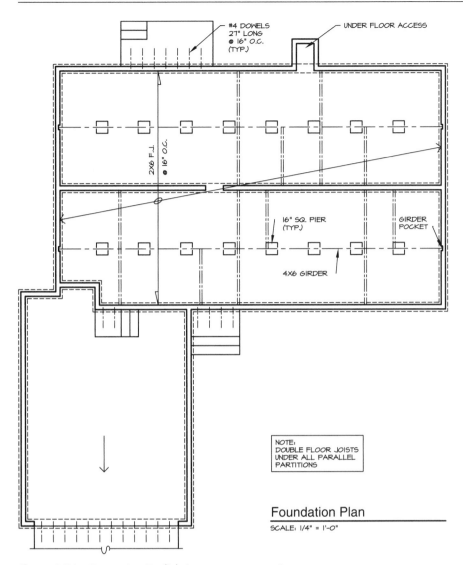

#4 DOWELS
27" LONG
@ 16" O.C.
(TYP.)

UNDER FLOOR ACCESS

2X6 F.J.
@ 16" O.C.

16" SQ. PIER
(TYP.)

GIRDER
POCKET

4X6 GIRDER

NOTE:
DOUBLE FLOOR JOISTS
UNDER ALL PARALLEL
PARTITIONS

Foundation Plan
SCALE: 1/4" = 1'-0"

Figure 2.56 Converting English increments to metric.

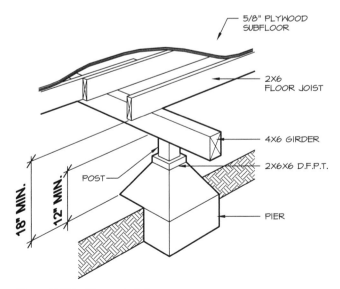

5/8" PLYWOOD
SUBFLOOR

2X6
FLOOR JOIST

4X6 GIRDER

2X6X6 D.F.P.T.

POST

PIER

18" MIN.

12" MIN.

Figure 2.57 Pier and girder.

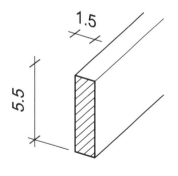

1.5

5.5

A) CROSS-SECTIONAL AREA:
5.5 X 1.5 = 8.25 SQ. INCHES

B) RATIO:
APPROX. 1:3

Figure 2.58 Ratio and cross-sectional area of a 2 × 6.

G. *Scale:* If this foundation plan was drawn on a 24″ × 36″ sheet of paper at a scale of ¼″ = 1′-0″, and now must be drawn on a sheet of paper sized in metrics, its nearest size would be 594 mm × 841 mm. A 24″ × 36″ sheet would be 609.6 mm × 914.4 mm in size.

Scaling Factor

The scaling factor in a metric drawing is very easy to compute because the scale is expressed in proportion relative to the meter. For example, at 1:50, one-fiftieth of a meter is used to express one meter in the drawing; thus, there are 50 meter increments in one meter. Therefore, the scaling factor is 50.

■ HAND DRAWING

Sketching

Sketching is the process of developing eye-hand coordination that aids in the design process. The designer can accurately maintain the proportions that are so essential in design.

Initially, all elements are sketched, from the design of a structure to a specific architectural detail. This is a way of conveying to the CAD drafter the ideas you are trying to deliver to the contractors in the field. Details, in particular, must be resolved before the plans, elevations, and building sections are drafted, as they will dictate the shape and configuration of structural components. The decor around a window, the form of a guardrail, and the connection of a column to a roof are but a few instances exemplifying the control that can be exercised in the freehand detailing process.

Any new idea for assembly should be sketched (freehand) and studied before it is hard-lined manually or drafted on the computer. These detail sketches (**design sketches**) are then sent to the drafter to draw formally. This ability to sketch and communicate puts the employee at a management/supervision level, not at the design level. When we refer to freehand detail, scale is still used, especially at critical intersections.

Drafting

Manual drafting also develops many positive attributes and skills that are needed to sustain employees in the future. These come in the form of:

A. *Patience.* Drafting manually produces a high degree of understanding of one's own limits and timing.
B. *Appreciation for CAD.* Drafting manually allows the CAD drafter to appreciate the increased productivity CAD affords.

C. *Flexibility.* CAD drafters possessing manual drafting skills are more flexible in their ability to create drawings. Suppose, for example, after plotting a plan, that one notices a couple of small errors on a drawing. The errors can be quickly corrected manually to meet a deadline or an appointment.
D. *Presentational drawings.* Many CAD drafters are not proficient in the use of standard drafting equipment. Thus, they are not effective in formatting and producing presentation boards and cutting mats.
E. *Model construction.* Construction of actual mock-up design models, massing models, or presentation models are frequently constructed manually for a client's review.

Summary

The following are advantages of the manually drafted drawing process:

1. Eye-hand coordination is developed.
2. Viewers get a look at the drawing as it will appear to the construction workers in the field.
3. Drawing is done at the scale that will be printed.
4. Hard copies allow you to look at all the drawings in a set one at a time, even during development.
5. Line quality can be varied, depending on need and the intent of the drawing.
6. Hand drawing allows the drafter to think through the drafting process and assess his or her own skills in relation to the task.
7. Hand drafting enhances other skills needed in the office, such as model making, creation of presentation drawings, and even the processes of design or translating design.

■ KINDS OF DRAFTING EQUIPMENT

Basic Equipment

The drafting tools needed by a beginning draftsperson and the basic uses of those tools are shown in Figure 2.59 and are as follows:

A. **Circle template.** A prepunched sheet of plastic punched in various sizes, for use as a pattern for circles without using a compass.
B. **Compass.** A V-shaped device for drafting arcs and circles.
C. **Divider.** A device resembling a compass, used mainly for transferring measurements from one location to another.
D. **Drafting dots.** Circular-shaped tape.
E. **Drafting pencil and lead holders.** Housing for drafting leads.

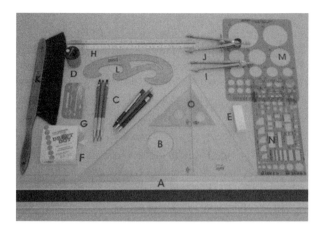

Figure 2.59 Basic drafting equipment.

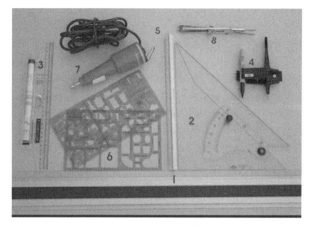

Figure 2.60 Additional drafting equipment.

F. Drafting tape. Tape used to hold paper while drafting.

G. Dusting brush. A brush used to keep drafting surfaces clean and free of debris.

H. Eraser. A rubber or synthetic material used to erase errors and correct drawings.

I. Erasing shield. A metal or plastic card with prepunched slots and holes used to protect some portions of a drawing while erasing others.

J. French curve. A pattern used to draft irregular arcs.

K. Lead pointer. A device used to sharpen the lead in a lead holder.

L. Parallel bar. A straightedge used to draft horizontal lines and base for the use of triangles. Runs on a wire cable at the sides of the bar.

M. Plan template. Prepunched patterns for shapes commonly found in architectural plans.

N. Scale. A measuring device calibrated in a variety of units for ease of translating large objects into a small proportional drawing.

O. Triangle. A three-sided guide used in conjunction with a parallel bar to draft vertical lines and angular lines. The 30°/60° and 45° triangles are basic equipment.

P. Triangle, small. A three-sided guide used to draft vertical lines when lettering.

Additional Drawing and Designing Equipment

In addition to the tools previously listed, a number of others aid in and simplify the drafting process. They are shown in Figure 2.60.

1. Parallel bar. Straightedge.

2. Adjustable triangle. A triangle used to draft odd angles such as those found in the pitch (slope) of a roof.

3. Rolling ruler. Draws horizontal, angular, and vertical lines, has a protractor function, and can be used as a compass.

4. Clip compass. Can be used to hold cutting knives, pencils, inking devices, paintbrushes, felt pens, and the like. Has a 9″ diameter capacity.

5. Metric rule. Scale for international work.

6. Specialty templates. Include furniture, trees, electrical and mechanical equipment, geometric shapes, and standard symbols. Enables the drafter to show, for example, plumbing fixtures in elevation.

7. Electric eraser. Particularly useful when one is working with erasable sepias or ink. Models available include hard-wired, battery-operated, and portable (with power charger).

8. Proportional dividers. Used to enlarge or reduce a drawing to any proportion. Many have golden mean proportions.

Figure 2.61 shows the correct way of using a straightedge. The lead holder is being rotated as a horizontal line is drawn.

Figure 2.61 Parallel straightedge. (Courtesy of Kratos/Keuffel & Esser.)

This list is by no means complete. Your selection of tools will be dictated by office standards and the requirements of particular projects.

Using Triangles

Triangles are generally used in conjunction with a straightedge such as a parallel bar, a T-square, or even another triangle (see Figure 2.62). A combination of triangles can produce 15° and 75° lines in addition to a perpendicular 90° angle, a 45° line, and 30° and 60° lines.

Using Erasing Shields and Erasers to Draw Dotted Lines

Dotted lines, which are usually called **hidden lines** in drafting, can be drawn rapidly by using an erasing shield and an eraser. An electric eraser is more effective than a regular eraser.

First, draw the line as if it were a solid line, using the correct pressure to produce the desired darkness. Second, lay the erasing shield over the line so that the row of uniformly drilled holes on the shield aligns with the solid line. Next, erase through the small holes. The results will be a uniform and rapidly produced hidden (dotted) line.

This technique is particularly effective for foundation plans, which use many hidden lines. There are, however, some questions inherent in drawing hidden lines. If

one hidden line overlaps another, is one deeper (as on a foundation plan), or are they both at the same depth? If a corner has two hidden lines that do not meet, does this mean one is lower than the other? Any mechanical drafting book will explain.

Using the Scale

The most convenient scale to purchase is a triangular scale, because it gives the greatest variety in a single instrument. There are usually eleven scales on a triangle scale, one of which is an ordinary 12″ ruler.

Reading the Scale.   Although we call this instrument a *scale,* there is one portion that is a ruler. If you look at a triangular scale (see Figure 2.63A), you will see a side marked 16 on the edge. It measures 12 inches using $\frac{1}{16}$″ increments. If you can read this, you can read the rest of the information printed on the tool.

Let us say you were assigned to do a drawing at $\frac{1}{8}$″ = 1′-0″. This means that 12 inches is now equal to $\frac{1}{8}$ inch. So let us look at Figure 2.63B. $\frac{1}{8}$ of an inch has been printed as a 12″ ruler as shown by "X." The area next to this 12″ ruler ("X") has large numbers on it starting with "0" and small numbers in between. We must stay with the small numbers. Note that from "0" to the 12 has been marked as "Y." If you wanted 12′-6″, you would first measure the "Y" and then add the 6″ or half of the "X" area.

The large numbers previously mentioned belong to the $\frac{1}{4}$″ scale, shown in Figure 2.63C. In this instance, the "Y" area measures 6′-0″ and additional inches can be added from the 12″ scale marked "X."

The most difficult scale to comprehend is the 3″ scale. It is not listed as a fraction, as this might confuse you in the beginning (see Figure 2.63D). The "X" on this figure shows the length corresponding to 12 inches; just like a 12″ ruler. A 3″ scale is also called $\frac{1}{4}$″ (quarter) scale, not to be mistaken for a $\frac{1}{4}$″ scale. Other scales are:

$\frac{3}{32}$″ on one end and $\frac{3}{16}$″ on the other
1$\frac{1}{2}$″ on one end and 3″ on the other
$\frac{3}{4}$″ on one end and $\frac{3}{8}$″ on the other

Confusion is often caused by the numbers between the two scales. Look carefully at these numbers and notice two sets. One set is closer to the groove that runs the length of the scale and the other is closer to the outside edge. The numbers near the edge will be the feet increments for the smaller scale, and the other numbers will be the feet increments for the larger scale.

It is easy to make an error by reading the wrong number, because the "32" on the $\frac{1}{8}$″ scale is so close to the "32" on the $\frac{1}{4}$″ scale. Similar pitfalls occur in other pairs of scales on the triangle scale.

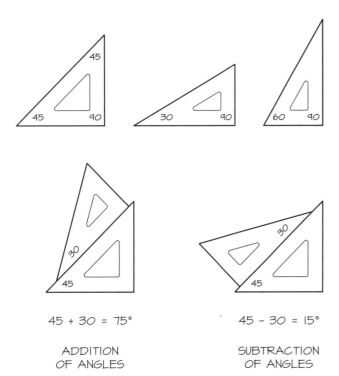

45 + 30 = 75°

ADDITION
OF ANGLES

45 − 30 = 15°

SUBTRACTION
OF ANGLES

Figure 2.62 Triangles and combinations of triangles.

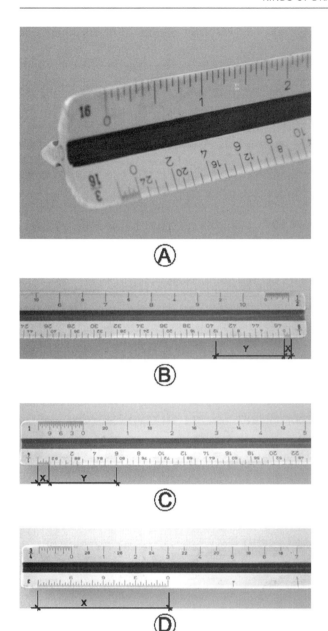

Figure 2.63 Reading a scale.

Most engineering scales use the same principles as architectural scales, except that measurements are divided into tenths, twentieths, and so on, rather than halves, quarters, and eighths. The section on metrics explains these metric scales further.

Using Drafting Tape

A simple but effective method of taping original drawings is to keep the edges of the tape parallel with the edges of the **vellum** (a translucent, high-quality tracing paper), as shown in Figure 2.64. This prevents the straightedge from catching the corner of the tape and rolling it off.

Vellum taped at an angle creates unnecessary frustration for the beginning draftsperson. Drafting supply stores sell tape in a round shape (dot), which is even better.

Rolling Original Drawings

Most beginners begin rolling drawings in the wrong direction. In their attempt to protect the drawings, they often roll the print or the original so that the printed side is on the *inside,* as shown in Figure 2.65B. However, the correct way is to roll the sheet so that the artwork is on the *outside,* as shown in Figure 2.65A.

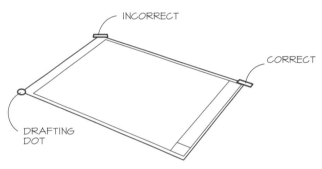

Figure 2.64 Correct placement of drafting tape.

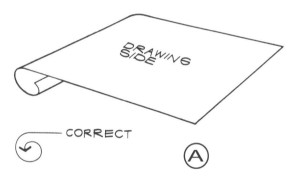

Figure 2.65A Correct way to roll a drawing.

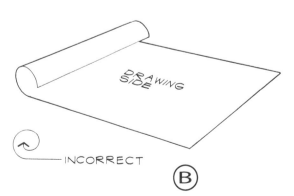

Figure 2.65B Incorrect way to roll a drawing.

When a set of prints is unrolled and read, the drawings should roll toward the table and should not interfere with easy reading by curling up. If originals are rolled correctly, the vellum curls toward the drafting table, preventing it from being torn when drafting equipment slides across it or when it is being reproduced.

■ SELECTING AND USING DRAFTING PENCILS

Types of Leads

Seventeen grades of leads are available, but only a few of these are appropriate for drafting. Harder leads are given an "**H**" designation, whereas softer leads are given a designation of "**B**." Between the "H" and "B" range are "**HB**" and "**F**" leads. The softest "B" lead is 6B (number 6); the hardest "H" lead is 9H (number 9). See Figure 2.66.

Selection Factors.   Only the central range of leads is used for drafting. 2H, 3H, and 4H are good for drafting, while H is good for a medium and dark object lines.

However, many other factors also determine the choice of pencil. Temperature and humidity may dictate that certain leads be used. Manufacturers' designations of the particular grades vary. Also, the natural pressure that the drafter places on the pencil varies from individual to individual. The reproduction method to be used also determines the choice of lead grade.

For reproduction, a crisp line is better than a dark one because a dark, broad line may end up as a blur on the final image. The old diazo prints are still being used today but are rapidly being replaced by copiers. Diazo prints (blue or black lines on a white background) have to block out light, so a dense line is more important when using this reproduction system.

Pencils versus Lead Holders

Wood pencils are fine, but serious drafting requires mechanical lead holders. See Figure 2.67. Wood pencils require sharpening of both the wood and the lead, which is time-consuming. More important, a lead holder allows you the full use of the lead, whereas a wood pencil does not.

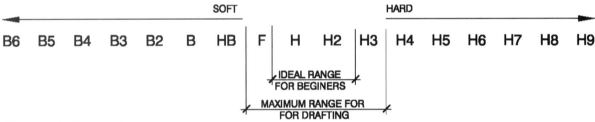

← SOFT								HARD →						
B6	B5	B4	B3	B2	B	HB	F	H	H2	H3	H4	H5	H6	H7	H8	H9

IDEAL RANGE
FOR BEGINERS

MAXIMUM RANGE FOR
FOR DRAFTING

Figure 2.66   Lead hardnesses.

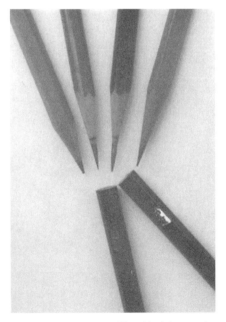
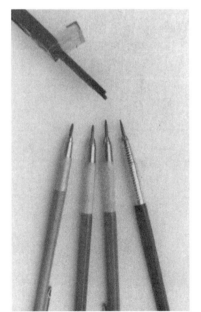

Figure 2.67   Types of lead holders and pencils.

Lead Pointers

A *lead pointer*, a tool used to sharpen drafting leads, is a must. Sandpaper can be used for both wood pencils and lead holders, but it is not nearly as convenient, consistent, or rapid as a lead pointer. A good practice after using a lead pointer is as follows: Take the sharpened lead and hold the pointer perpendicular to a hard surface such as a triangle; crush the tip of the lead slightly; then hone the tip by drawing a series of circular lines on a piece of scratch paper. This stops the lead from breaking on the first stroke. Roll the pencil as you draw to keep a consistent tip on the lead. Draw either clockwise or counterclockwise, depending on whichever produces the best line and is the most comfortable for you. Note the position of your fingers and thumb at the beginning and end of the line.

■ COMPUTER DRAFTING

Computer-Aided Drafting

Computer-aided drafting (CAD) has significantly affected the field of architecture. This section does not instruct you on how to use the computer or the various CAD programs (there are books solely devoted to CAD that do), but rather teaches you how CAD programs can best be used to become an effective tool in an architectural office.

What the Drafter Will Learn

CAD does *not* refer to what the computer allows you to do; rather, it refers to the process of taking the conventions, symbols, and the drawing dimensions and incorporating them into the computer to be adjusted for the task at hand. Literally, we are talking about design that uses the computer as just another tool, albeit a very powerful and convenient one. In this section, we discuss:

- **A.** Office setup and expectations.
- **B.** CAD standards used in the industry, such as line weights, color, and layering.
- **C.** Effective use of 2-D and 3-D spaces. These discussions will help the beginner to become a more effective user of paper space (two-dimensional layout space) and model space (three-dimensional modeling space).
- **D.** Scaling drawings and lettering.
- **E.** Three-dimensional drafting.
- **F.** Effective cartooning.
- **G.** Using vectors in the drawing process.
- **H.** The near future of computers in our industry.

The computer, in the architectural industry, is becoming increasingly important. Just as with other tools, the CAD drafter must learn to use the computer through specific instruction. After the drafter has mastered the techniques, the computer can aid significantly in the creative process. However, in this process, the drafter is controlling the tool, rather than the computer controlling or constraining the drafter. Similarly, the CAD drafter concentrates on translating the intent of the designer into a workable set of construction documents, with the computer as one of his or her creative tools.

Each computer drafter should be well trained so that he or she can prepare a set of construction documents from scratch. Training will allow you, the CAD operator, to integrate your understanding of the system with your knowledge of architectural drawings and standards and become immediately effective in production.

■ OFFICE STANDARDS

Offices have a set of standards that employees must follow. This is essential in the industry, not only because many drafters may be working on the same project, but also to ensure uniformity of the language that the drafters speak. Adhering to standards helps coordinate drawings for a firm's associates both inside and outside the office.

Standards establish sheet size, scales used, standard line and symbol conventions, placement and positions of drawings, and sheet modules, to mention a few items. These standards are often kept on the drafter's desk and are referred to as the **drafting room manual**, the **office procedure manual**, or something similar. Computers are no different. They too have their standards, and although standards may differ slightly from job to job or office to office, they should be rigidly followed. Standards do change, and making or suggesting a revision adds to both their usage and their ability to become viable office solutions.

Although standards are established by individual offices and are often based on existing drafting room manuals, the introduction of computers to the arsenal of production tools has created a need for national and international standards. Associations such as the American Institute of Architects, National Institute of Building Sciences, Construction Specifications Institute, and even the military, to mention just a few, have in fact produced national CAD standards.

When using standards, a drafter should not be so dependent on existing standard templates that he or she is unable to develop new ones if the job calls for them. Flexibility and creativity are important. You may find two types of computer drafters in an office. One drafter can develop new office standards as the need requires. This type of drafter is knowledgeable and flexible and knows how to set up line types, lettering size, sheet size, and scales. A second type is the "running scared" CAD employee, who copies office standards from various offices and uses a large number of CDs or flash drives with predrafted, predetermined templates of sheet sizes, lettering, sizing, and so on. Office managers will evaluate individual performance and conformance to standards, and if you do not keep up with the state of the technology or fail to recognize the needs of the office, your job may be jeopardized.

To help drafters avoid this dilemma, the following pages describe the needs of the architectural office and why certain standards are enforced, how to develop them, and how to understand them.

In this section, we discuss the following topics with regard to standards and CAD use:

1. A profound change in perception
2. Importance of standards in the electronic world
3. Vector versus raster
4. X-referencing (XREF)
5. Oddly scaled drawings and computer manipulation of existing drawings
6. Paper
7. Paper space/virtual space (model space)
8. Scaling factor
9. Layering
10. Updating old drawings
11. Pen setting/line weights/color
12. Lettering size
13. Procedure for the preparation of construction documents
14. Disadvantages
15. Advantages
16. The future of CAD

A Profound Change

The most profound change caused by the advent of computer-aided and computer-assisted drafting is the manner in which we perceive and execute drawings. The first of these changes in perception is the way in which we view structures. With the use of CAD, structures should be drawn at full scale. This is made possible because we are working in virtual space (model space), which is unlimited.

When designing and drawing in full scale on the computer, you can look around the space you are occupying and draw relationships based on real-world sizes. The monitor becomes a window through which you are viewing this full-size structure. The printer/plotter becomes a photograph of this image displayed on the monitor screen (see Figure 2.68).

Standardization in the Electronic World

Standardization in the electronic world is very important because our whole industry is based on communicating ideas. We can do this only if each of the participants—architects, drafters, associates (mechanical, structural, electrical engineers), and so forth—speak the same language.

If a set of drawings has been done in layers, as is often the case, the titles of these layers become critical for identification. To aid in identification, a CAD drafter must use the standards (standard titles) to which the office subscribes and plot them out onto a chart similar to that found in Figure 2.69.

Generally speaking, drawings are categorized by subject—for example, architectural, mechanical, structural, and the like. In manual drawings, "A" is for architectural,

Figure 2.68 Drawing and monitor become one and the same relative to perception.

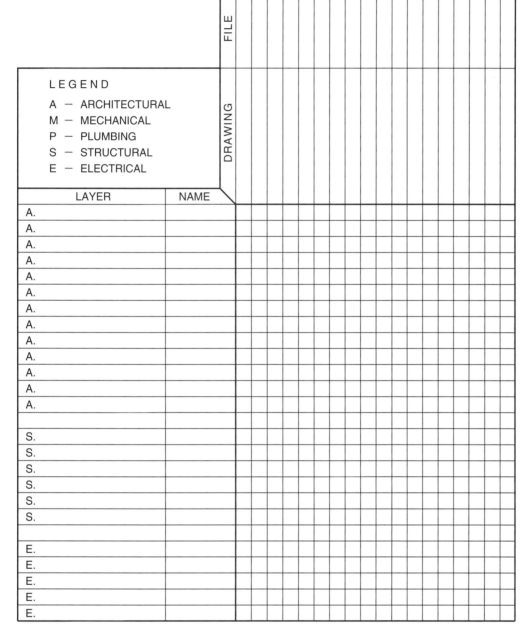

Figure 2.69 Sample layout for layers.

"S" is for structural, and so on. Look at Figure 2.70 for such a breakdown. Notice the thirteen "A" drawings listed in the left column. The walls of the floor plan are drawn on one layer and given the name A-WALL. All of the appliances (such as plumbing) are drawn on another layer called A-FLOR, windows and doors on A-GLAZ and A-DOOR, dimensions on A-ANNO-DIMS, and so on. To produce a drawing for construction, we must print A-WALL, A-FLOR, A GLAZ/DOOR, and A-ANNO, along with a host of other layers, all of which contain reference bubbles and titles. To print a furniture plan for the client,

you would most certainly need layers A-WALL, A-FURN, and A-ANNO.

Let us say you sent the engineer the floor plan described earlier: A-WALL, A-FLOR, A-DOOR, A-GLAZ, A-ANNO-DIMS, reference bubbles, notes, titles, and so forth. The engineer has to know how to load the layers needed for an S drawing. If the structural engineer is producing a roof framing plan or a ceiling joist plan, he or she will initially need not only the wall layer, but also the dimension layer. The dimension layer can be eliminated on the final printing. In this way, the wall (A-WALL) layer

LEGEND

A — ARCHITECTURAL
M — MECHANICAL
P — PLUMBING
S — STRUCTURAL
E — ELECTRICAL

LAYER	NAME	SITE PLAN (A-1.0)	FLOOR PLAN (A-2.0)	CEILING PLAN (A-2.1)	FURNITURE PLAN (A-2.2)	FINISH PLAN (A-2.3)	ELEVATIONS (A-3.0)	SECTIONS (A-4.0)	SCHEDULES (A-5.0)	INT. ELEVATIONS (A-6.0)	FOUNDATION (S-1.0)	FLOOR FRAMING (S-2.0)	ROOF FRAMING (S-3.0)	WALL SECTION (S-4.0)	POWER PLAN (E-1.0)	LIGHTING PLAN (E-2.0)	REFLECTED C.P. (E-3.0)
FILE		2000_A-1.0	2000_A-2.0				2000_A-3.0	2000_A-4.0	2000_A-5.0	2000_A-6.0	2000_S-1.0	2000_S-2.0	2000_S-3.0	2000_S-4.0	2000_E-1.0	2000_E-2.0	2000_E-3.0
A. SITE	A-SITE	●															
A. WALL	A-WALL		●	○	○	○						○	○		○	○	○
A. FIXTURES	A-FLOR		●	○	○												
A. DOORS	A-DOOR		●	○	○											○	
A. WINDOWS	A-GLAZ		●	○	○											○	
A. DIMENSIONS	A-ANNO-DIMS		●			○					○	○					
A. CEILING PLAN	A-CEIL			●													●
A. FURNITURE	A-FURN				●												
A. NOTES	A-ANNO					●											
A. BORDER & TITLE	A-TBLK	●	●	●	●	●	●	●	●		●	●	●	●	●	●	●
A. EXTERIOR ELEVATION	A-ELEV-EXTR						●							○			
A. INTERIOR ELEVATION	A-ELEV-INTR									●							
A. BUILDING SECTION	A-SECT							●									
S. NOTES	S-ANNO										●						
S. DIMENSIONS	S-DIMS										●						
S. FOUNDATION WALLS	S-WALL										●						
S. FOOTING CONVENTIONS	S-FNDN										●						
S. FRAMING MEM. FLOOR	S-FRAM-FLOR											●					
S. FRAMING MEM. ROOF	S-FRAM-ROOF												●				
E. NOTES	E-ANNO														●		
E. EQUIPMENT	E-EQUP														●		
E. WALL FIXTURES	E-FIXT-WALL															●	
E. CEILING FIXTURES	E-FIXT-CEIL																●
E. SUSPENDED CEILING	E-CEIL																●

Figure 2.70 Example of layers and their titles.

is used as a base for a multitude of other drawings. A quick look at Figure 2.70 reveals that the A-WALL layer is used for the floor plan, ceiling plan, furniture plan, and finish plan, as well as the floor framing plan, roof framing plan, and, on the simplified chart, the power plan, lighting plan, and the reflected ceiling plan. This is called cross-referencing, or X-referencing.

Vector versus Raster

It is imperative that all CAD drafters know the difference between vector drawings and raster drawings, because of the ways in which each file format can be used. Both raster and vector images can be manipulated. **Raster** images are made up of pixels; a photo manipulation program must be used with a raster image. You can remove items from the image, and elongate, stretch, or compress the image. You can even change the position of the image relative to the paper and format for presentation. However, you cannot easily change the geometry.

Vector drawings are done both two-dimensionally and three-dimensionally. Vector drawings are actually lines, planes, and geometric shapes drawn in virtual space. Height, width, and depth are described as X, Y, and Z directions. This means you can rotate a three-dimensional form and look at it from any of the six principal directions—front, back, left, right, top, and bottom (or underside)—and an unlimited number of views in between.

For importing a digital drawing from a vendor, you should request a vector drawing. Figure 2.71 shows a single-hung window with a transom made of vinyl and imported as a vector file. Such drawings represent the basic manufacturer's configuration, which can be placed with the header, exterior finish, interior finish, and waterproofing methods to produce a construction detail for a specific application.

Figure 2.72 shows a recommended installation detail. The computer drafter can take this detail and adapt it to a specific application while adding pertinent design features. When requesting both basic shapes and installation details, ask for the file format your office typically uses. Usually, that will be DXF or DWG. The majority of CAD programs can easily manipulate these file types.

DWG versus DXF

If a drawing is to be sent or received electronically, it must be formatted. Although there are other formatting methods, DXF and DWG are most typically used.

The **DWG** format, which is the most desirable, is the easiest for the AutoCAD drafter to use, change, or correct because it has all the ingredients needed to produce the end result.

The **DXF** (short for *drawing exchange format*) strips down the total drawing sequence in a way that makes it easier to translate. Because it is a stripped-down form, you cannot perform certain tasks; although the final visual image is complete, pertinent information is missing and thus it cannot be easily manipulated. It saves the final geometry, but many of the steps used to produce the final geometry are missing. DXF is easier to exchange with other programs. Not all programs can use DWG formats easily. If you wish to send a drawing

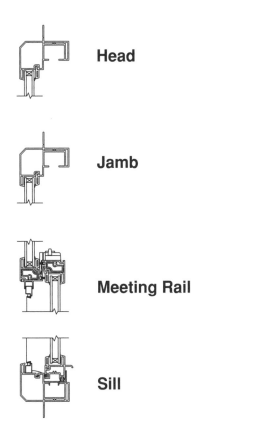

**NEW CASTLE
SINGLE HUNG WINDOW**

Figure 2.71 Vinyl window configurations. (Courtesy of Certainteed Windows. Reprinted by permission from the *Professional Practice of Architectural Detailing,* 3rd edition. Copyright 1999 by John Wiley & Sons, Inc.).

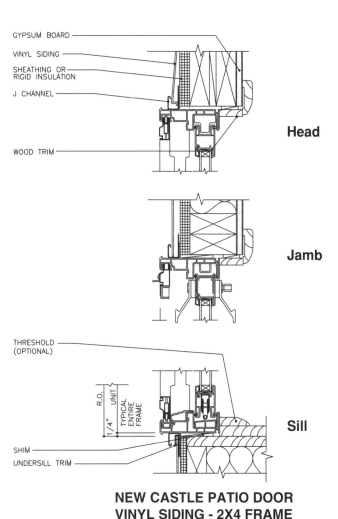

**NEW CASTLE PATIO DOOR
VINYL SIDING - 2X4 FRAME**

Figure 2.72 Manufacturers' installation details in DWG format.

electronically or place a drawing on a web site strictly for viewing, then explore a DWF format.

Various AutoCAD programs cannot open **DWF**-formatted drawings, because this format provides a level of protection useful for maintaining a more secure transmission. Your standards, symbols, layers, sheet setups, and so forth, will not be entirely usable by the person to whom you transmit the file in DWF format.

X-Referencing (XREF)

Cross-referencing, in the architectural industry, refers to the process of referencing one drawing to another by

means of reference bubbles (see Figure 2.73). In the computer industry, the term *X-referencing* (**XREF**) sounds like *cross-referencing,* but it is not the same. XREF means "externally referenced" drawings. XREF is used to combine drawings and keep the entire set of construction documents updated with the most recent version of a drawing. A secondary datum is now being used to produce drawings. The example shown in Figure 2.73 is an electrical plan. The floor plan (master) becomes the externally referenced drawing and is not directly a part of the electrical plan layers.

Computer-generated drawings, with their intricate network of finely tuned layers, titles, and patterns, are

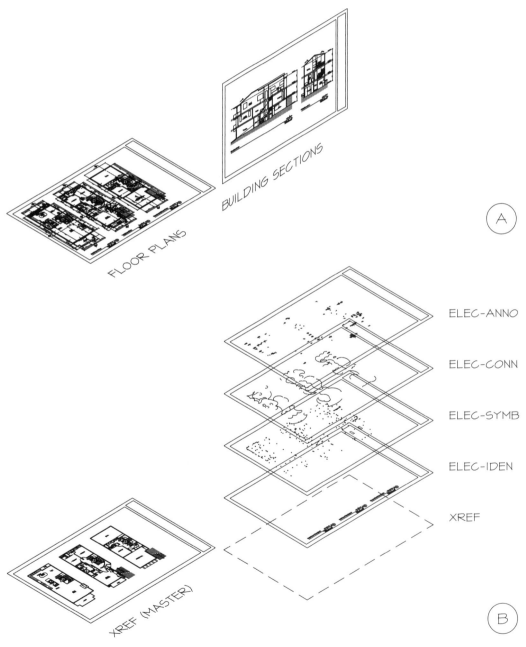

Figure 2.73   XREF.

produced almost as if they were a family. Base drawings, such as exterior and interior walls showing some of the basic fixtures and stair locations, are often referred to as *masters* or *parent drawings*. Their offshoots, such as framing plans, electrical plans, building sections, and so on, are commonly referred to as *children* or *submasters*. The plot sheets serve the parents and children by presenting specific drawings and information (*maids* or *servants*). A composite of these drawings may include title blocks, notes, and other features always found on every sheet (e.g., title block) or those features found only on specific sheets. Because CAD drawings can be done using multiple files, the process of delegating certain information to certain drawings is called *XREFing* and allows certain drawings to be used in multiple ways.

Figure 2.74 shows a sampling of an XREF standard for a hypothetical office. Figure 2.75 provides examples of a master, submaster, and servant. This cross-referencing has the same meaning in manual drawings as it does in CAD drawings, whereas XREF refers to a special process unique to computer-generated drawings.

Oddly Scaled Drawings

A peculiar group of computer-generated drawings that are beginning to find their way into the construction industry are drawings without a specific or known scale. These are drawings that may have been drawn to scale initially, but were resized to fit the paper on which they were plotted. Even worse are drawings and notes that have been reduced so that you need a magnifying glass to read them.

To avoid such a catastrophe, all CAD drafters should be able to cartoon a drawing and adhere to office standards with regard to sizing and heights of lettering.

The reduction process has found its way into the CAD system with a command called "Print to Fit," which prints the drawing on a sheet of paper regardless of scale. If the CAD drafter anticipates how much the drawing will be reduced, office standards for lettering height can be maintained.

If a floor plan would fit a 24 × 36 piece of paper at ¼″ = 1′-0″ and the office standard is to maintain tall lettering and ¼″ tall titles, the drafter must produce lettering at 6″ in height (at ¼″ scale) and titles 12″ tall.

Computer Scanning and Manipulation of Existing Drawings.

Most computers are equipped with scanners and printers. Older drawings (hard copy), diazo prints, vellum originals, and photographs can be scanned into the computer. These drawings can then be altered and changed easily to produce a new master drawing. Once material is "in" the computer, layers (overlays) can be employed to update drawings and produce restoration

drawings. Because of the flexibility and speed with which computers operate, they can technically create almost everything that can be done via reprodrafting, composite drafting, paste-up drafting, scissors drafting, photo-drafting, and more.

Paper

Paper comes in various sizes. The standard and nonstandard sizes are listed in Figure 2.76. Nonstandard-sized paper is listed with asterisks.

Thus, if a final drawing is to be printed/plotted on an 8½″ × 11″ sheet of paper, its template in the computer should be called "A" paper, an 11″ × 17″ sheet of paper would be called "B" paper, and so on.

When drafting manually, the drafter has the entire sheet of paper to work with. Such is not the case with computer-generated drawings. The CAD drafter must be aware of the limits of the printer or plotter. For example, an 8½″ × 11″ paper may have a printable area of only 8″ × 10½″. This proportion holds true with all paper. When you add border lines and title blocks to the drawing sheet, the actual drawing area of the sheet will be reduced to a given standard used in the office. Figure 2.77 shows a diagram of the printable area and the drawing area of an 8½″ × 11″ sheet of paper.

Knowing that the printable area for an 8½″ × 11″ sheet of paper can be 8″ × 10½″, ideally we would set the margins at ¼″ and use a 1″ or ¾″ strip for a title block. Some offices do not even print the borders, but only the title block. If the drawing will be bound, the binding edge is increased to ¾″, leaving a drawing area of 7½″ × 9¾″ (see Figures 2.77B and 2.77C, respectively).

Because most computer drawings are done in layers (layering is covered later in this chapter), one layer may contain the limits within which the drafter must stay. These borders may or may not be printed in the final drawing (see Figures 2.77A and 2.77C, respectively).

Paper larger than 8½″ × 11″ is subdivided into drawing modules. In Figure 2.78, a 24″ × 36″ sheet of paper is shown with a 1½″ left binding border and a ½″ border for the top, bottom, and right side. It will use a 1½″ title block. The remaining drawing area is divided into five horizontal and five vertical spaces, each of which is 4⅝″ × 6½″. This now becomes the office standard for all drawings. Notes will be typed so as not to exceed 6½″ in width (or 13″ if two modules are used) and a vertical height of 4⅝″, 9¼″, 13¾″, 18″, or 22⅝″.

Architectural details are drawn to this module of 4⅝″ × 6½″. This space may be further divided into drawing areas and keynote areas to further exploit paper usage.

Plans, elevations, building sections, and site plans should be drawn within this established matrix so as to allow the remaining space to be used by details, notes,

Preliminary Documentation of Office XREF Standard

Schematic Design / Design Development (MASTER)			
Naming: YearMonthProjectNumber-MAST.dwg (YYMM##-MAST.dwg) 000101-MAST.dwg			
	MAST	Master Design Drawing	Walls, Doors, Windows, Stairs, Fireplaces, Room Labels,
			Plumbing Fixtures, Closets (What you need for the Client)

Design Development / Construction Documents (Sub-Masters)			
Naming: YearMonthProjectNumber-FLOR.dwg (YYMM##-FLOR.dwg) 000101-FLOR.dwg			
XREF	**Listed in order of importance**		**Description**
MAST	**NBHD**	Neighborhood Compatibility	If needed
MAST	**FLOR**	Floor Plans	Poche, Hatching, Notes, Dimensions
MAST	**ROOF**	Roof Plan	
MAST	**ELEV**	Elevations	
MAST	**SECT**	Building Sections	
MAST	**SITE**	Site Plan	Modify TOPO to start Could also include a separate Grading Plan
MAST	**FRAM**	Framing / Foundation	All Structural Drawings
MAST	**ELEC**	Electrical Plans	
MAST	**OTHR**	Other Architecture	If in project program
	TBLK	Titleblock	XREF'd to ALL plotsheets
	TOPO	Survey / Topography	Produced by surveyor

PLOTSHEETS or Layouts w/ modelspaces.			
It is possible to have all sub-masters drawn on their respective plotsheet modelspaces.			
XREF	**Sheet**	**Sheet Title**	**Description**
	T-1.0	Title Sheet	
	T-1.1	General Notes	
	CF-1R	Title 24 / Energy Calcs	
SITE	**A-1.0**	Site Plan	
TOPO	**A-1.1**	Survey / Topography	
NBHD	**A-1.2**	Neighborhood Compatibility	If required for submittal
SITE	**A-1.3**	Grading Plan	If not included in Site Plan
FLOR	**A-2.0**	Floor Plans	
	A-2.1		
ELEV	**A-3.0**	Exterior Elevations	
	A-3.1		
SECT	**A-4.0**	Building Sections	
	A-4.1		
MAST	**A-5.0**	Roof Plan	
INTR	**A-6.0**	Interior Elevations	
	A-6.1		
OTHR	**A-7.0**	Other Architecture	
	A-7.1		
	A-8.0	Schedules	
	A-8.1		
	A-D.1	Architectural Details	
	A-D.2		
FRAM	**S-1.0**	Foundation Plan	
FRAM	**S-1.0B**	Basement Framing Plan	If needed for space reasons
FRAM	**S-1.1**	First Floor Framing	
FRAM	**S-1.2**	Second Floor Framing	
	S-1.3		
FRAM	**S-2.0**	Roof Framing	
	S-2.1		
	S-D.1	Structural Details	
	S-D.2		
ELEC	**E-1.0**	Electrical Plans	
	E-1.1		

Figure 2.74 A sample XREF standard.

MASTER
(PARENT)

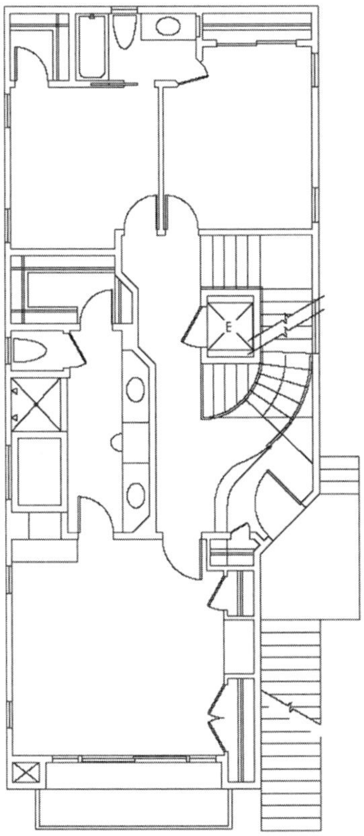

SUBMASTER
(CHILD)

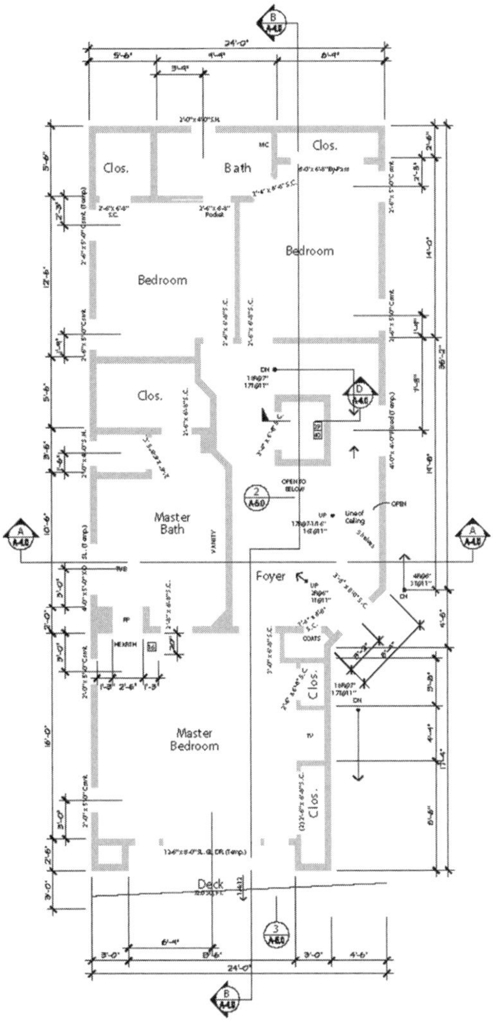

SLAVE
(SERVANT)

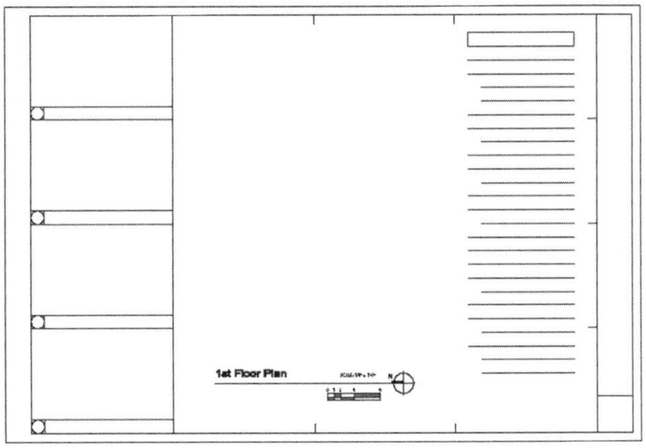

Figure 2.75 A floor plan developed through XREF. (Courtesy of Norman Lebeau, owner.)

Typical Paper(s)
"A" Paper (16)
a. 11" x 8.5"
b. 12" x 9"
c. 10.5" x 7.5" **
"B" Paper (8)
a. 17" x 11"
b. 18" x 12"
c. 15" x 10.5" **
"C" Paper (4)
a. 22" x 17"
b. 24" x 18"
c. 21" x 15" **
"D" Paper (2)
a. 34" x 22"
b. 36" x 24"
c. 30" x 21" **
"E" Paper (1)
a. 44" x 34"
b. 48" x 36"
c. 42" x 30" **
(#) = sheets in an   "E" size sheet
** = nonstandard

Figure 2.76 Typical standard and nonstandard paper sizes.

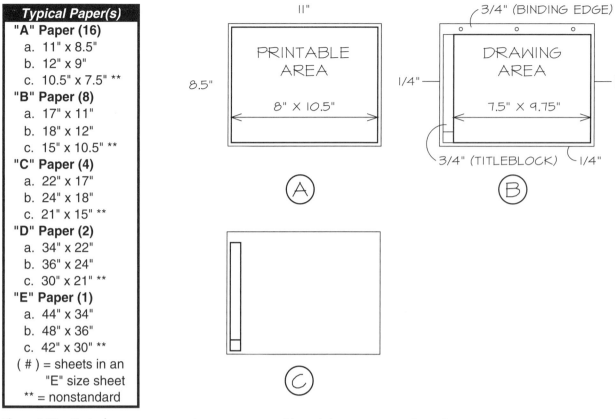

Figure 2.77 Printable and drawing area 8.5″ × 11″.

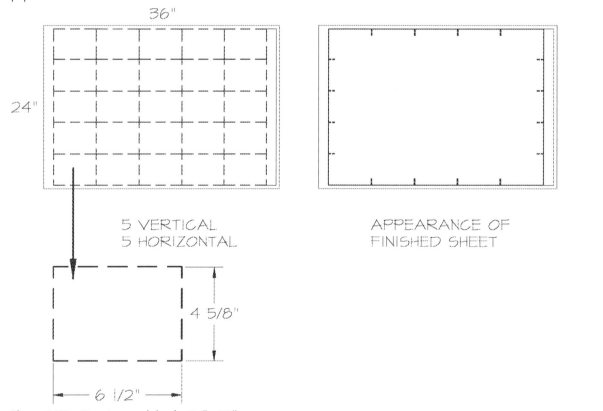

Figure 2.78 Drawing modules for 24″ × 36″.

charts, and schedules. Figure 2.79 shows a site plan, general notes, details, vicinity map, and an index formatted to a 24″ × 36″ sheet of paper with a matrix of five vertical and five horizontal modules.

Figure 2.80 shows this formatting process using a 24″ × 36″ sheet divided into a 5 × 5 module and a 4 × 5 module, and a 30″ × 42″ sheet divided into a 5 × 5 module and a 6 × 6 module. Once the formatting process decision is made in the office, the drafter must comply with these limits when drawing, writing notes, and even detailing. If many drafters are working on one set of working drawings and all subscribe to a single format pattern, not only will the entire set look well organized to the client, but the integral pieces will fit together like a giant puzzle. Clear, precise drawings reduce office liability and increase the visual impact of office documents.

As described earlier, a structure is drawn at full scale on the computer and viewed through a window that is actually the monitor. By filling this entire screen area with a standard-size sheet of paper, you have a formatted screen ready to import drawings. The interior of this drawing sheet is now your new window, which is called a **viewport**. Each module can also be a viewport. Figure 2.81 shows a monitor displaying a 24″ × 36″ sheet of paper. Thus, a viewport becomes a window on the paper through which you can see a full-size building. The computer allows you to zoom up close or fill the viewport with a graphic image such as a floor plan. In this way, you can fill to the extents of the viewport, but you will not be displaying to any given scale.

The best solution to this nonscaled drawing is to fill the viewport with the largest image possible, but to a known scale. This scale may be an architectural scale such as ⅛″ = 1′-0″ or ¼″ = 1′-0″.

2-D (Paper) versus 3-D (Virtual or Model) Space

The difference between two-dimensional (2-D) and three-dimensional (3-D) space can be compared to the difference between manual drafting and computer-aided drafting. In paper (2-D) space, you fill the monitor with a theoretical piece of paper. This theoretical piece of paper is already unrealistic, because it is an image of the actual piece of paper reduced to fit the screen. In manual drafting, the paper is actual size.

In model space or virtual space (3-D), you are drawing full size. When you are "modeling" a drawing, you measure the size of the building exactly. You do not work at a reduced scale.

When printing or plotting a drawing, you must reduce this full-size drawing or model to a scale that will fit on the actual paper size. For this reason, we encourage you

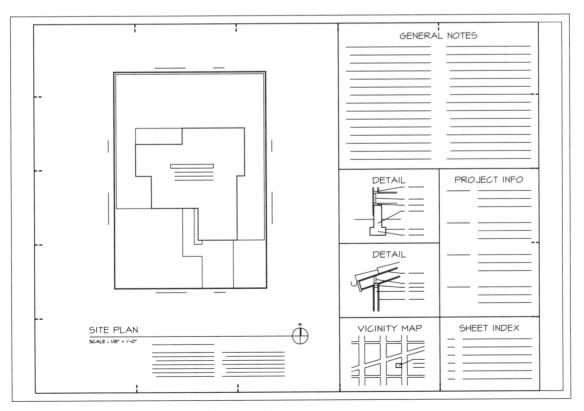

Figure 2.79 Drawing modules for 24″ × 36″ (registered).

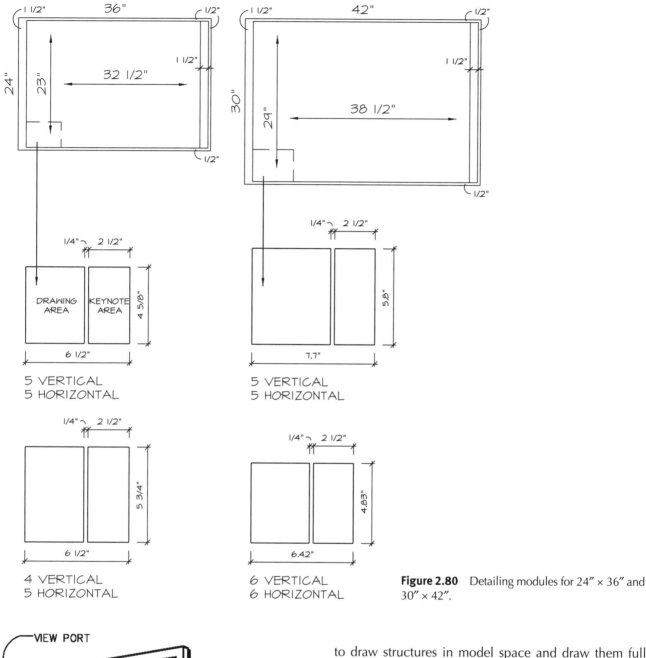

5 VERTICAL
5 HORIZONTAL

5 VERTICAL
5 HORIZONTAL

4 VERTICAL
5 HORIZONTAL

6 VERTICAL
6 HORIZONTAL

Figure 2.80   Detailing modules for 24″ × 36″ and 30″ × 42″.

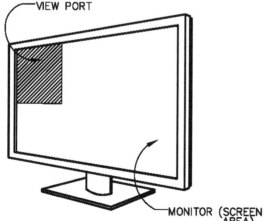

Figure 2.81   Monitor—paper space and viewport.

to draw structures in model space and draw them full scale. Model space, also called **virtual space**, is the closest thing to the real thing.

Figure 2.82 shows various sizes of paper and their drawing areas based on scale. Sizes of paper range from a standard 8½″ × 11″ to a 36″ × 48″. These are listed across the top of Figure 2.82, and the various scales (architectural and engineering) are shown to the left. For example, if you were preparing a floor plan for a building 90′ deep and 135′ wide at a ¼″ = 1′-0″ scale (shaded area on chart) and wanted to find a paper sheet size, note that at the intersection of a 24″ × 36″ column and ¼″ = 1″ row, a 96″ × 144″ figure appears. This means that at a ¼″ scale, and using a 24″ × 36″ piece of paper, a 96′ × 144′ space is available. If a 70′ × 90′ building were

	AP		BP		CP		DP		EP		FP	
(width) X"	11	8	17	14	24	21	36	33	48	45	42	39
(height) Y"	8.5	7.5	11	10	18	17	24	23	36	35	30	29
Scale	TRUE	ADJ	TRUE	ADJ	TRUE	ADJ	TRUE	ADJ	TRUE	ADJ	TRUE	ADJ
3"=1'	3'8x2'10	2'8x2'6	5'8x3'8	4'8x3'4	8'x6'	7'x5'8	12'x8'	11'x7'8	16'x12'	15'x11'8	14'x10'	13'x9'8
1 1/2"=1'	7'4x5'8	5'4x5'	11'4x7'4	9'4x6'8	16'x12'	14'x11'4	24'x16'	22'x15'4	32'x24'	30'x23'4	28'x20'	26'x19'4
1"=1'	11'x8'6	8'x7'6	17'x11'	14'x10'	24'x18'	21'x17'	36'x24'	33'x23'	48'x36'	45'x35'	42'x30'	39'x29'
3/4"=1'	14'8x11'4	10'8x10'	22'8x14'8	18'8x13'4	32'x24'	28'x22'8	48'x32'	44'x30'8	64'x48'	60'x46'8	56'x40'	52'x38'8
1/2"=1'	22'x17'	16'x15'	34'x22'	28'x20'	48'x36'	42'x34'	72'x48'	66'x46'	96'x72'	90'x70'	84'x60'	78'x58'
1/4"=1'	44'x34'	32'x30'	68'x44'	56'x40'	96'x72'	84'x68'	144'x96'	132'x92'	192'x144'	180'x140'	168'x120'	156'x116'
1/8"=1'	88'x68'	64'x60'	136'x88'	112'x80'	192'x144'	168'x136'	288'x192'	264'x184'	384'x288'	360'x280'	336'x240'	312'x232'
1/16"=1'	176'x136'	128'x120'	272'x176'	224'x160'	384'x288'	336'x272'	576'x384'	528'x368'	768'x576'	720'x560'	672'x480'	624'x464'
1/32"=1'	352'x272'	256'x240'	544'x352'	448'x320'	768'x576'	672'x544'	1152'x768'	1056'x736'	1536'x1152'	1440'x1120'	1344'x960'	1248'x928'
3/32"=1'	117'6x90'6	85'6x80'	181'6x117'6	149'6x107'	299'x192'	224'x181'6	384'6x256'	352'6x245'6	512'6x384'6	480'6x373'6	448'6x326'	416'6x309'6

Architectural

	AP		BP		CP		DP		EP		FP	
(width) X"	11	8	17	14	24	21	36	33	48	45	42	39
(height) Y"	8.5	7.5	11	10	18	17	24	23	36	35	30	29
Scale	TRUE	ADJ	TRUE	ADJ	TRUE	ADJ	TRUE	ADJ	TRUE	ADJ	TRUE	ADJ
1/10"=1'	110'x85'	80'x75'	170'x110'	140'x100'	240'x180'	210'x170'	360'x240'	330'x230'	480'x360'	450'x350'	420'x300'	390'x290'
1/20"=1'	220'x170'	160'x150'	340'x220'	280'x200'	480'x360'	420'x340'	720'x480'	660'x460'	960'x720'	900'x700'	840'x600'	780'x580'
1/25"=1'	275'x212'6	200'x187'6	425'x275'	350'x250'	600'x450'	525'x425'	900'x600'	825'x575'	1200'x900'	1125'x875'	1050'x750'	975'x725'
1/30"=1'	330'x255'	240'x225'	510'x330'	420'x300'	720'x540'	630'x510'	1080'x720'	990'x690'	1440'x1080'	1350'x1050'	1260'x900'	1170'x870'
1/40"=1'	440'x340'	320'x300'	680'x440'	560'x400'	960'x720'	840'x680'	1440'x960'	1320'x920'	1920'x1440'	1800'x1400'	1680'x1200'	1560'x1160'
1/50"=1'	550'x425'	400'x375'	850'x550'	700'x500'	1200'x900'	1050'x850'	1800'x1200'	1650'x1150'	2400'x1800'	2250'x1750'	2100'x1500'	1950'x1450'
1/60"=1'	660'x510'	480'x450'	1020'x660'	840'x600'	1440'x1080'	1260'x1020'	2160'x1440'	1980'x1380'	2880'x2160'	2700'x2100'	2520'x1800'	2340'x1740'
1/75"=1'	825'x637'6	600'x562'6	1275'x825'	1050'x750'	1800'x1350'	1575'x1275'	2700'x1800'	2475'x1725'	3600'x2700'	3375'x2625'	3150'x2250'	2925'x2175'
1/100"=1'	1100'x850'	800'x750'	1700'x1100'	1400'x1000'	2400'x1800'	2100'x1700'	3600'x2400'	3300'x2300'	4800'x3600'	4500'x3500'	4200'x3000'	3900'x2900'

Engineering

Adjusted Margins	
Top	0.5"
Bottom	0.5"
Left	1.5"
Right	0.5"
Title Rt.	1"
Title Bot.	0"

Figure 2.82 Paper space maximum.

to be drawn, it would occupy approximately 18″ × 24″ of the 24″ × 36″ sheet. The rest could be used for details, notes, or schedules.

Scaling Factor

Some computer programs are programmed to deal with scale. With these programs, the drafter can size or scale a drawing simply by typing in the scale desired or selecting a scale from a menu. For example, if you wish to print or draw a floor plan at ¼″ = 1'-0″ scale, you simply select this scale and the computer does the rest of the work.

Other programs call for a scaling factor to be used. The CAD drafter must be comfortable with either system. Scaling factor is computed in reference to a foot (12 inches). For example, if a drawing is to be scaled at ¼″ = 1'-0″, you divide 12″ by ¼ inch. Forty-eight (48) becomes the scaling factor for ¼″ = 1'-0″.

Figure 2.83 lists scaling factors for a variety of the most typically used architectural and engineering scales.

Scale	Factor
1'=1'	1
3"=1'	4
1 1/2"=1'	8
1"=1'	12
3/4"=1'	16
1/2"=1'	24
1/4"=1'	48
1/8"=1'	96
1/16"=1'	192
1/32"=1'	384
1"=10'	120
1"=20'	240
1"=25'	300
1"=30'	360
1"=40'	480
1"=50'	600
1"=60'	720
1"=75'	900
1"=100'	1200
1"=200'	2400

Figure 2.83 Scaling factors.

Figure 2.84 shows a 9″ × 12″ and a 24″ × 36″ piece of paper. Using a scaling factor (48) for a ¼″ scale, the numbers in the parentheses indicate how many feet (at ¼″ scale) are available on the 24″ × 36″ sheet of paper. Now go back to Figure 2.82 and see the figures repeated for a number of different-sized sheets of paper and a variety of scales. Next, the drafter must know the same information for the drawing area. See Figure 2.85 and compute.

Figure 2.86 shows the drawing area for a variety of scales and sheet sizes. The drawing area is now called the *viewport*.

Layering

Layering is what makes computer drafting so superior to manual drafting. Layering is the process of creating a series of overlays on which you display different functions

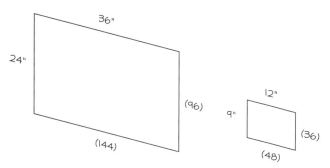

Figure 2.84 Scaling factor (¼″) for 24″ × 36″ and 9″ × 12″.

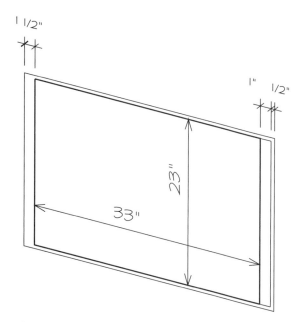

Figure 2.85 Printable area for 24″ × 36″ sheet.

and different types of lines and conventions. The alignment of computer-generated layers is perfect. Selection of the proper layers is done in seconds. Layers may be turned on and off, frozen in place, plotted or not plotted. They can also be grouped and XREFed from other drawings.

Let us now look at a typical set of layers for a construction document. The first layer is often considered the base, unless you are using XREF drawings as a base. This first layer contains the matrix that will act as a datum for the entire drawing. For example, a steel building such as the Madison Building (see Chapter 17) is based on an axial reference system. A matrix locates and positions the steel columns. The matrix will be drawn on the base layer, with the steel columns possibly on the subsequent layer. This base (the datum) can be used for other drawings, so different views subscribe to the same system. Therefore, it becomes even more important that the drafter of tomorrow become familiar with three-dimensional datum drawings (described earlier) so that elevations, building sections, framing plans, and foundation plans can use the same base (datum) layer. In this way, we can cross-reference drawings from the very beginning (XREF drawings).

Each layer can be done in a different color. The use of various colors helps the drafter stay focused on the specific layer on which a particular task is to be accomplished. Colors also help in identifying drawings. Color also has an impact on the quality of lines, as explained in the next section.

If there is an inherent geometry present in the drawing but not used in the finished drawing, the construction lines can be drawn on a layer but never printed, A-NOH plotting layer. Take the case of drawing a winding stair, as shown in Figure 2.87. The construction lines are on one layer, and the drawing of the stair is on another. One need only outline the required portions of the geometry to produce a base drawing, and then repeat the forms to produce the finished drawing.

Setting Up Layers. Look again at the sample of layers and their specific titles in Figure 2.70. Although this is a simplified plan, it does follow many of the examples found in the National CAD Standards pamphlet. Notice the legend and the letter designations for architectural, mechanical, structural, and so on. Learn to identify the standards so that you can tell the difference between correctly and incorrectly drawn documents.

Correct and uniform titles are important, because as you are laying out the structural members of a building, these members must be cross-referenced with the electrical conduit on the electrical drawing, or the heating or

			AP		BP		CP		DP		EP		FP	
	(width) X"		11	8	17	14	24	21	36	33	48	45	42	39
	(height) Y"		8.5	7.5	11	10	18	17	24	23	36	35	30	29
Factor	Feet in 1"	Scale	TRUE	ADJ	TRUE	ADJ	TRUE	ADJ	TRUE	ADJ	TRUE	ADJ	TRUE	ADJ
4	1"=0'-4"	3"=1'	3'8"x2'10	2'8"x2'6	5'8x3'8	4'8x3'4	8'x6'	7'x5'8	12'x8'	11'x7'8	16'x12'	15'x11'8	14'x10'	13'x9'8
8	1"=0'-8"	1 1/2"=1'	7'4x5'8	5'4x5	11'4x7'4	9'4x6'8	16'x12'	14'x11'4	24'x16'	22'x15'4	32'x24'	30'x23'4	28'x20'	26'x19'4
12	1"=1'-0"	1"=1'	11'x8'6	8'x7'6	17'x11'	14'x10'	24'x18'	21'x17'	36'x24'	33'x23'	48'x36'	45'x35'	42'x30'	39'x29'
16	1"=1'-4"	3/4"=1'	14'8x11'4	10'8x10'	22'8x14'8	18'8x13'4	32'x24'	28'x22'8	48'x32'	44'x30'8	64'x48'	60'x46'8	56'x40'	52'x38'8
24	1"=2'-0"	1/2"=1'	22'x17'	16'x15'	34'x22'	28'x20'	48'x36'	42'x34'	72'x48'	66'x46'	96'x72'	90'x70'	84'x60'	78'x58'
48	1"=4'-0"	1/4"=1'	44'x34'	32'x30'	68'x44'	56'x40'	96'x72'	84'x68'	144'x96'	132'x92'	192'x144'	180'x140'	168'x120'	156'x116'
96	1"=8'-0"	1/8"=1'	88'x68'	64'x60'	136'x88'	112'x80'	192'x144'	168'x136'	288'x192'	264'x184'	384'x288'	360'x280'	336'x240'	312'x232'
192	1"=16'-0"	1/16"=1'	176'x136'	128'x120'	272'x176'	224'x160'	384'x288'	336'x272'	576'x384'	528'x368'	768'x576'	720'x560'	672'x480'	624'x464'
384	1"=32'-0"	1/32"=1'	352'x272'	256'x240'	544'x352'	448'x320'	768'x576'	672'x544'	1152'x768'	1056'x736'	1536'x1152'	1440'x1120'	1344'x960'	1248'x928'

Architectural

			AP		BP		CP		DP		EP		FP	
	(width) X"		11	8	17	14	24	21	36	33	48	45	42	39
	(height) Y"		8.5	7.5	11	10	18	17	24	23	36	35	30	29
Factor	Feet in 1"	Scale	TRUE	ADJ	TRUE	ADJ	TRUE	ADJ	TRUE	ADJ	TRUE	ADJ	TRUE	ADJ
120	1"=10'	1/10"=1'	110'x85'	80'x75'	170'x110'	140'x100'	240'x180'	210'x170'	360'x240'	330'x230'	480'x360'	450'x350'	420'x300'	390'x290'
240	1"=20'	1/20"=1'	220'x170'	160'x150'	340'x220'	280'x200'	480'x360'	420'x340'	720'x480'	660'x460'	960'x720'	900'x700'	840'x600'	780'x580'
300	1"=25'	1/25"=1'	275'x212'6	200'x187'6	425'x275'	350'x250'	600'x450'	525'x425'	900'x600'	825'x575'	1200'x900'	1125'x875'	1050'x750'	975'x725'
360	1"=30'	1/30"=1'	330'x255'	240'x225'	510'x330'	420'x300'	720'x540'	630'x510'	1080'x720'	990'x690'	1440'x1080'	1350'x1050'	1260'x900'	1170'x870'
480	1"=40'	1/40"=1'	440'x340'	320'x300'	680'x440'	560'x400'	960'x720'	840'x680'	1440'x960'	1320'x920'	1920'x1440'	1800'x1400'	1680'x1200'	1560'x1160'
600	1"=50'	1/50"=1'	550'x425'	400'x375'	850'x550'	700'x500'	1200'x900'	1050'x850'	1800'x1200'	1650'x1150'	2400'x1800'	2250'x1750'	2100'x1500'	1950'x1450'
720	1"=60'	1/60"=1'	660'x510'	480'x450'	1020'x660'	840'x600'	1440'x1080'	1260'x1020'	2160'x1440'	1980'x1380'	2880'x2160'	2700'x2100'	2520'x1800'	2340'x1740'
900	1"=75'	1/75"=1'	825'x637'6	600'x562'6	1275'x825'	1050'x750'	1800'x1350'	1575'x1275'	2700'x1800'	2475'x1725'	3600'x2700'	3375'x2625'	3150'x2250'	2925'x2175'
1200	1"=100'	1/100"=1'	1100'x850'	800'x750'	1700'x1100'	1400'x1000'	2400'x1800'	2100'x1700'	3600'x2400'	3300'x2300'	4800'x3600'	4500'x3500'	4200'x3000'	3900'x2900'

Engineering

Figure 2.86 Paper sizes at specific scales (½" top, bottom, and right border, 1½" left border, 1" right title-block space).

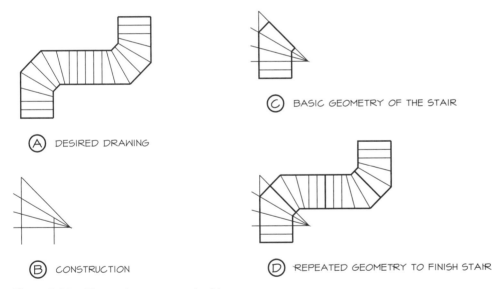

(A) DESIRED DRAWING

(B) CONSTRUCTION

(C) BASIC GEOMETRY OF THE STAIR

(D) REPEATED GEOMETRY TO FINISH STAIR

Figure 2.87 Diagnosing geometry (stair).

air-conditioning ducts found on the mechanical set, that may occupy the same space.

The strategy employed might be staged similarly to that in Figure 2.88. Note the number of layers produced on the left side, the composite drawing for construction in the center, and the drawing used for client consumption on the right side. Note the inclusion of the furniture layer for client consumption and the voiding of the dimensioning layer on the same set.

In the multifile strategy illustrated in Figure 2.89, an example of a three-file system is shown. File No. 1 is the architectural file, which we just looked at in Figure 2.88. File No. 2 is a structural set, and File No. 3 is a lighting plan. Note how various layers are selected to produce still another file. In this example, File No. 4 becomes a lateral plan, and File No. 5 becomes the reflected ceiling plan. As indicated earlier, this process is called "XREFing."

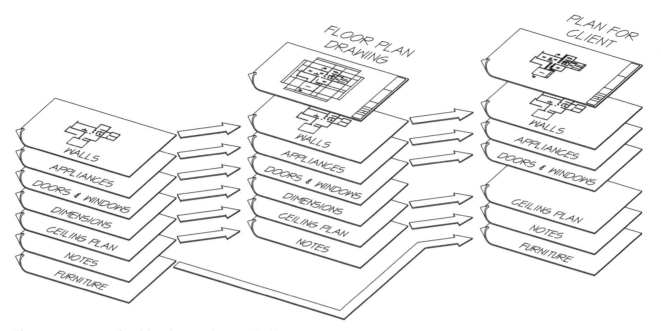

Figure 2.88 Example of the planning for a single file.

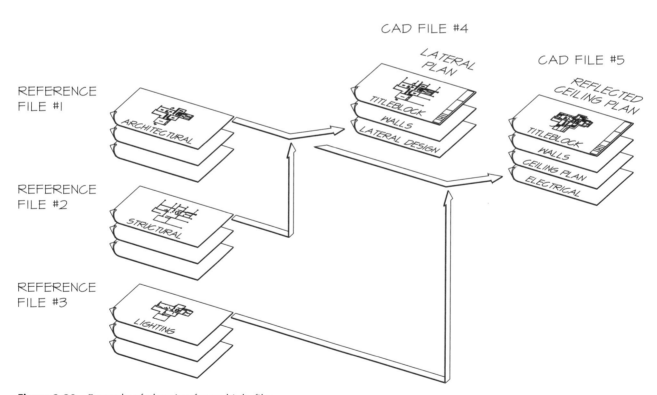

Figure 2.89 Example of planning for multiple files.

Updating Old Drawings in CAD

To update an existing drawing, simply import an old CAD drawing. Retitle the drawing, erase the portions that do not apply, make the corrections on a new layer, and complete the drawing. In this fashion, you will preserve the original drawing in the office's archive. Remember that merely saving the drawing on a flash drive, CD, or DVD will preserve it for about five to seven years. Put the saved drawing on an archivable CD or exterior hard drive to save space in your computer.

Pen Setting and Line Weights

Line weights can be produced by establishing and assigning certain colors as desired pen settings. Figure 2.90 shows common AutoCAD pen settings. The number assigned to the pen can be found on the extreme left side of the chart. Directly adjacent to the pen number is the name of the pen. The names are names of colors. As you can see by the width of the pens, magenta is the strongest and should be used for object lines. The thinnest line is red.

The office may have already established these standards, which may be based on a national standard. You need to know the source and why the office standards were established in this fashion. Knowing why allows you to know the office's game plan.

Pen settings and line weights should be saved on the computer or disk immediately when establishing the layers so that you can employ them as needed.

Pen Settings

color	name	width
1	red	0.008
2	yellow	0.012
3	green	0.008
4	cyan	0.010
5	blue	0.012
6	magenta	0.030
7	white (high ink)	0.020
8	dark grey	0.015
9	light grey	0.015
15	dark red	0.012
30	orange	0.008
174	dark blue	0.010
250	dark grey	0.015
251	med. dark grey	0.015
252	med. grey	0.015
253	med. light grey	0.015
254	light grey	0.015
255	white (low ink)	0.015

Figure 2.90 Pen settings, line weights, and colors.

Figure 2.91 is a summary chart of the items discussed in this section. Sample standard titles are listed to the left, then the colors used, followed by the line types and descriptions of their uses.

Lettering Size

One advantage of a computer is its ability to change scale rapidly. The disadvantage appears, for example, in drawing a floor plan at ¼″ = 1′-0″ scale with ⅛″ tall lettering, then reducing it to a ⅛″ = 1′-0″ scale without any regard to the final height of the lettering. The lettering in this example will be ¹⁄₁₆″ tall and very difficult to read, not to mention that it will not follow the office standard and will look peculiar in a set of drawings.

Graphic scales are often used in lieu of expressing the scale in a proportion (see Figure 2.92A).

Because we are drawing in model space (virtual space), we are able to draw the structure at full scale. However, every drafter must realize the scale to which the drawing will be reduced and printed. For example, a floor plan can be drawn at full scale but may be reduced to ¼″ = 1′-0″ scale when printed on a 24″ × 36″ sheet of paper. Knowing the final display scale is important, because when notes and dimensions are placed on the final print, they must be readable. If the office standard is to have lettering that is ⅛″ tall, with titles ¼″ tall, this lettering height must be translated into a measurement that is full size because we are drawing in full size. At ¼″ = 1′-0″, all lettering (⅛″ in height) must be scaled at 6″ tall and the titles (¼″ tall) at 1′-0″, because the lettering height is measured in scale. For your convenience, two charts, an engineering scale and an architectural scale, are included to help translate various lettering heights to specific heights (see Figure 2.93).

The scale in which you will print/plot your drawing is read across the top of each chart. The desired height of the final text is read down the left column. The intersection of these columns will tell you the height of the lettering. See the shaded area for the ⅛″ tall lettering at ¼″ = 1′-0″ scale for the previous example.

The decimal conversion chart in Figure 2.94 includes the height of lettering in decimals. As every schoolchild knows, ½″ is equal to 0.5″, but equivalents for fractions such as ³⁄₁₆ and ³⁄₃₂ are hard to remember; they are 0.1875 and 0.09375, respectively.

Standards are established for general noting, room titles, and the title of the drawing. For example, it is a prevalent practice to use upper- and lowercase lettering for the title of a drawing, such as "Floor Plan." The font may be Helvetica. Room titles may be in all caps, using the same Helvetica font. Notes and general text should be done in all caps, but in an architectural font. An architectural font can simulate a hand-lettered drawing,

NAME	COLOR	LINETYPE	DESCRIPTION
0	WHITE	Continuous	For making Blocks & Unknown
ANNO	CYAN	Continuous	Text (annotation)
ANNO-DIMS	RED	Continuous	Dimensions
ANNO-IDEN	YELLOW	Continuous	Identification (rooms)
ANNO-KEYN	CYAN	Continuous	Keynotes
ANNO-LEGN	CYAN	Continuous	Legends and Schedules
ANNO-NOTE	CYAN	Continuous	General Notes
ANNO-PATT	RED	Continuous	Hatches (all)
ANNO-PCHE	8 (lt) or 9 (dk)	Continuous	Poche (all)
ANNO-REDL	RED	Continuous	Redlines (corrections to be made)
ANNO-SYMB	YELLOW	Continuous	Symbols (scale, north, section)
ANNO-TTLB	CYAN	Continuous	Title block
ANNO-VIEW	RED	Continuous	Viewports
DOOR	CYAN	Continuous	Doors (plan & elevation)
ELEC	YELLOW	Continuous	Electrical Symbols
ELEC-CONN	CYAN	CENTER2	Electrical Connections
ELEV	CYAN	Continuous	Elevation (colors can vary)
ELEV-BYND	BLUE	Continuous	Objects Beyond
ELEV-OTLN	WHITE	Continuous	Building Outline / Profile
FLOR	CYAN	Continuous	Floor plan (secondary information)
FLOR-DECK	YELLOW	Continuous	Deck
FLOR-HIDD	RED	HIDDEN	Hidden
FLOR-HRAL	RED	Continuous	Handrails & Balcony Railings
FLOR-STRS	CYAN	Continuous	Stairs
FNDN	YELLOW	HIDDEN	Foundation (footings & pads)
FNDN-SHRW	MAGENTA	Continuous	Shearwall
FNDN-SLAB	WHITE	Continuous	Slab
FRAM	YELLOW	Continuous	Framing (posts, headers, rafters)
FRAM-BEAM	WHITE	CENTER	Beams (wood, steel, prefab)
FRAM-JOIS	CYAN	CENTER2	Ceiling Joists
FRAM-SHRW	MAGENTA	Continuous	Shearwall
GLAZ	CYAN	Continuous	Windows (plan & elevation)
ROOF	WHITE	Continuous	Roof Outline (ridges, hips, valleys)
ROOF-BLDG	RED	DASHED	Building Outline
ROOF-OTHR	CYAN	Continuous	Roof (vent, chimney, skylight, etc)
SECT	CYAN	Continuous	Section (colors can vary)
SECT-BYND	BLUE	Continuous	Objects Beyond
SECT-OTLN	WHITE	Continuous	Objects at Section Cut / Profile
SITE	CYAN	Continuous	Site
SITE-BLDG	WHITE	Continuous	Building Outline
SITE-EXST	RED	Continuous	Existing Information
SITE-PLNT	GREEN	Continuous	Plants / Landscape
SITE-PROP	MAGENTA	PHANTOM	Property Line
SITE-RTWL	YELLOW	Continuous	Retaining Wall
TOPO	GREEN	DASHED	Topography (from surveyor)
TOPO-OTHR	BLUE	DASHED2	Topography (faded)
WALL	WHITE	Continuous	Wall (full height)
WALL-HALF	YELLOW	Continuous	Wall (partial height)
XREF	WHITE	Continuous	Cross-Referenced Files (XREFs)
XREF-GHST-OTHER	BLUE	Continuous	Ghost - faded (fixtures, labels, etc)
XREF-GHST-WALL	RED	Continuous	Ghost - light (walls, stairs, etc)

Figure 2.91 Sample preliminary documentation of office layering standard.

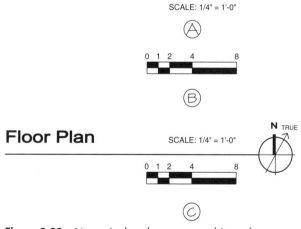

Figure 2.92 Numerical scale versus graphic scale.

thus giving the drawing a distinguishing characteristic that separates it from engineering drawings. There are two additional reasons for using an architectural font. Architectural fonts, as compared with other textbook-type fonts, are described by a simpler geometry. Because the shape definition uses less geometry, it prints faster.

The other reason to use an architectural font is that, because it simulates hand lettering, simple corrections can be done by hand when the computer is down or when speed is of the essence. Of course, the corrections must eventually be done on the computer, because manual corrections will not be reflected in the digital image saved on the computer or peripheral storage device.

Architectural

Scale: Feet in 1": Scale Factor:	3"=1' 1"=0'-4" 4	1 1/2"=1' 1"=0'-8" 8	1"=1' 1"=1'-0" 12	3/4"=1' 1"=1'-4" 16	1/2"=1' 1"=2'-0" 24	1/4"=1' 1"=4'-0" 48	1/8"=1' 1"=8'-0" 96	1/16"=1' 1"=16'-0" 192	1/32"=1' 1"=32'-0" 384
1" Text	4"	8"	12"	16"	24"	48"	96"	192"	384"
3/4" Text	3"	6"	9"	12"	18"	36"	72"	144"	288"
1/2" Text	2"	4"	6"	8"	12"	24"	48"	96"	192"
3/8" Text	1.5"	3"	4.5"	6"	9"	18"	36"	72"	144"
1/4" Text	1"	2"	3"	4"	6"	12"	24"	48"	96"
3/16" Text	0.75"	1.5"	2.25"	3"	4.5"	9"	18"	36"	72"
1/8" Text	0.5"	1"	1.5"	2"	3"	6"	12"	24"	48"
3/32" Text	0.375"	0.75"	1.125"	1.5"	2.25"	4.5"	9"	18"	36"
1/16" Text	0.25"	0.5"	0.75"	1"	1.5"	3"	6"	12"	24"

Engineering

Scale: Feet in 1": Factor:	1/10"=1' 1"=10' 120	1/20"=1' 1"=20' 240	1/25"=1' 1"=25' 300	1/30"=1' 1"=30' 360	1/40"=1' 1"=40' 480	1/50"=1' 1"=50' 600	1/60"=1' 1"=60' 720	1/75"=1' 1"=75' 900	1/100"=1' 1"=100' 1200
1" Text	120"	240"	300"	360"	480"	600"	720"	900"	1200"
3/4" Text	90"	180"	225"	270"	360"	450"	540"	675"	900"
1/2" Text	60"	120"	150"	180"	240"	300"	360"	450"	600"
3/8" Text	45"	90"	112.5"	135"	180"	225"	270"	337.5"	450"
1/4" Text	30"	60"	75"	90"	120"	150"	180"	225"	300"
3/16" Text	22.5"	45"	56.25"	67.5"	90"	112.5"	135"	168.75"	225"
1/8" Text	15"	30"	37.5"	45"	60"	75"	90"	112.5"	150"
3/32" Text	11.25"	22.5"	28.125"	33.75"	45"	56.25"	67.5"	84.375"	112.5"
1/16" Text	7.5"	15"	18.75"	22.5"	30"	37.5"	45"	56.25"	75"

Figure 2.93 Text size for architectural/engineering drawings.

Standard Text Sizes

Standard Text		Optional Text	
1"	1	3/4"	0.75
1/2"	0.5	3/8"	0.375
1/4"	0.25	3/16"	0.1875
1/8"	0.125	3/32"	0.09375
1/16"	0.0625	3/64"	0.046875
1/32"	0.03125		

Figure 2.94 Conversion chart for simple fraction to decimal.

■ A GAME WITHIN A GAME

The idea that there is a game within a game is often found in athletics. Similarly, architecture frequently has games within games. There may be a secondary game involved in the financing of a project, or the exploration of new materials and their application to a project, or a game strategy involved in combining materials in a job. Even the production of construction drawings may hold an inner game, such as the study involved to identify the best way to prepare a set of drawings. This may include a game of document standardization and computer productivity and how best to implement both.

Procedure for Computer Drawings

1. Learn to identify the icons on the screen to determine whether you are in model space or paper space. There will be a "title" (a box) that you can click on to toggle between model space and paper space. You can verify paper/model space by checking the **user coordinate system** (UCS) icon (usually found on the bottom left corner of the screen) (see Figure 2.95).

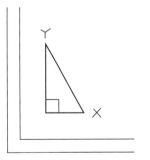
PAPER SPACE (2D)

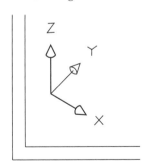
MODEL SPACE (3D)

Figure 2.95 UCS icons.

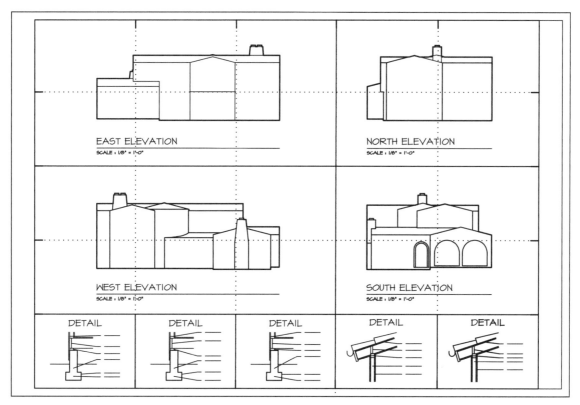

Figure 2.96 Sample cartoon/page layout.

2. If your drawing (paper) is set up for ¼″ scale but the building is larger than the paper will allow, go to "Limits" and change the drawing to a different scale. The office manager may have already done this on the cartoon (also called **page format** or **page layout**) (see Figure 2.96).

3. Cartooning, as discussed in Chapter 6, should be done for the entire set of working drawings before you start any drawings. In this way, a team of CAD drafters working on a single project will know where each drawing will be positioned before they start a particular drawing.

4. The drawing can be drawn anywhere on the sheet, because it will most likely be repositioned on the paper at a later time.

5. Establish your line weights and pen settings. This information may already be available in the office, but you need to know what and how these standards were established.

6. Set up the layers for a particular set of drawings. See the discussion "Layering" earlier in this chapter.

7. Familiarize yourself with the finished drawing (the plot) using the scale you are working with. For example, if the drawing will be plotted at ⅛″ = 1′-0″ scale, and you need to draw a ½″ diagram reference bubble, you will draw it at 4′-0″ in size. Another example using the same ⅛″ = 1′-0″ scale: ⅛″ tall lettering will be drawn at 1′-0″ tall.

8. Consider the following points before you begin drawing:

   a. Confirm the office standard to which you subscribe.

   b. Confirm that all the software you need is operational and registered.

   c. Understand the time constraints and the expectations of your supervisor or administrator.

   d. Review all the preliminary design sketches so you can enhance the design without changing its intent.

   e. Understand the structure and how the design works into this structural pattern.

   f. Study the designer's approach to the environmental forces to correctly orient windows for the maximum amount of light, orientation to the prevailing view and the part of the view to be showcased, and so on.

   g. Review the reference resources for construction materials such as the block modules used for masonry, the stud line, dimensioning procedures for lightweight wood structures, and so on.

   h. Review all of the related drawings (structural, mechanical, electrical, etc.).

Procedure for Preparing the Computer for Computer-Aided Drafting

1. Computer to architectural
2. Setting
   a. Limits
   b. Grids/snap
3. Display
   a. Zoom all
4. Layer
   a. Layer standards: line, color, lettering
5. Review paper/model space
6. Saving
7. Printing

■ POWER OF THE CAD DRAFTER

The power of the CAD drafter at all levels lies not only in understanding the process of how buildings are built, which this book is mainly about, but also in the ability to produce the documents necessary to make this process a reality. To that end, all CAD drafters must:

1. Be divided into different levels of proficiency. Table 2.1 defines the four basic levels of CAD drafting found in an architectural office, and their requirements. Level 1 is the equivalent of a junior drafter. Level 2 may be equated to the journeyman drafter, and Level 3 is considered a senior drafter. Level 4 is reserved for management.
2. Be comfortable working with any version of CAD, not just the latest version. Software programs change so often that it is very difficult to standardize the profession to work in any computer application.

   As you move from office to office, you may be confronted with a large range of programs. We all know that as soon as a 2012 version of any program hits the market, the 2013 version is not far behind.
3. Be aware of the program their associates are using, because it does little good to send them drawings that they cannot manipulate or use.
4. Be comfortable with drawing in full scale (model space) and plotting in paper space.
5. Be able to send and receive drawings via the computer as easily as making a telephone call; send drawing files that can be opened to receive additional information from their associates; or send closed files for viewing only, to protect the office.
6. Be able to draw in 3-D and rotate the 3-D drawing into orthogonals and produce 2-D drawings from them.
7. Be able to work on two different versions of a program without any loss of productivity.
8. Be able to manage their files and know how to compress their files.

This is a list of minimum requirements for an effective CAD drafter. The next level of CAD drafter is a person who can organize and initiate new programs in the office system using existing office standards. The third level of CAD drafter is a person who can troubleshoot the computer and do minimal repair. The final level of computer specialist is the person who can rewrite existing software programs to make them more effective tools for the office.

Setting Up a Computer Drawing

From scratch:

1. Set limits to architectural drawings.
2. Set grid, snap, and units based on the scale of the project.
3. Set up layers using the office standard titles, line type, and colors.
4. Work in the paper modules (see Figure 2.78). Make sure everything fits, including:
   a. Dimension lines
   b. Reference symbols
   c. Titles
5. Work in model space (not in paper space).

At a minimum, a drafter should know:

How to set up the computer:

1. Units
2. Grid
3. Snap
4. Limits
5. Layers
6. Line types
7. Styles
8. How to establish a base layer
9. How to check for XREFs

Tracking a Drawing via the Computer

A 3-D massing model of the structure is the first step in tracking a drawing via the computer. Three-dimensional images are often not 3-D drawings. For example, if the designer sketched or rendered a 3-D image and scanned it into the computer, the model will not be in 3-D in the truest sense of the word. Look at Figure 2.97A. We will refer to this 3-D model as the *preliminary sketch*. Because the preliminary model is drawn in 3-D and in full scale, it may be well to incorporate a person standing in front of the structure for scale. This helps the drafter to realize scale. As the model evolves, based on the client's wishes, budgets, and other design-changing factors, a refined 3-D model is created (see Figure 2.97B). Next, we rotate the object into an orthographic view, a plan view, and a minimum of four elevations. See Figure 2.98.

Table 2.1 CAD Drafting in an Architectural Office

Level 1	Junior Drafter	Level 3	Senior Drafter

Level 1 — Junior Drafter

1. Ability to hardline a designer's ideas
2. Mastery of simple commands such as:
   a. LINE, PLINE, DLINE, MLINE
   b. MOVE, COPY, SCALE
   c. TRIM, EXTEND, STRETCH
   d. INSERT BLOCKS
   e. HATCHING
   f. DTEXT, MTEXT
3. Basic 3-D modeling
4. Use of object snaps
5. Ortho and polar restrictions
6. Keyboard entry (absolute and relative modes)
7. Basic Plan Check revisions (notes, minor geometry changes)
8. File management
9. Layering
10. Dimensions
11. Basic plotting

Level 3 — Senior Drafter

1. Attributes (grouping of entities that contain text)
2. Finding architectural/structural errors based on experience
3. Manage individuals and projects (ability to "hand off" work)
4. Advanced 3-D modeling/visualization (thorough understanding of model-centric design)
5. Thorough understanding of architectural/structural detailing
6. Complete Plan Check revisions (research and change entire working drawings)
7. Suggest/modify page setups and templates
8. Basic program customization
9. Basic programming
10. Advanced rendering
11. Intermediate plotting

Level 2 — Journeyman Drafter

1. XREF
2. Paper space/model space
3. Can follow a design change throughout a set of working drawings
4. Make appropriate design suggestions
5. Text styles and justifications
6. Intermediate 3-D modeling (including model-based/model-centric design)
7. Editing of attributes
8. Filtering
9. Use of object tracking
10. Advanced Plan Check revisions (new geometry/multiple sheets)
11. Program preferences
12. Basic rendering

Level 4 — CAD Manager

1. Network/hardware/software installation, upgrades, and troubleshooting
2. Image editing and photo manipulation
3. Template construction
4. Title block construction
5. Custom blocks/symbols
6. Custom hatches and shapes
7. Ability to make purchase suggestions/decisions
8. Ability to make, implement, and suggest changes to office standards
9. Internet and web site development
10. Graphic design skills
11. Advanced program customization
12. Advanced programming
13. Advanced plotting
14. Advanced collaboration and workgroup tools (LAN/WAN/Internet)

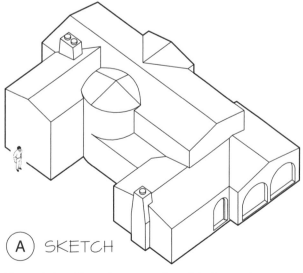

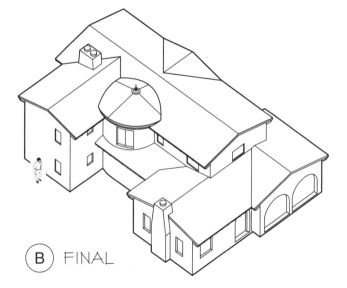

Figure 2.97 Three-dimensional model of a Residence.

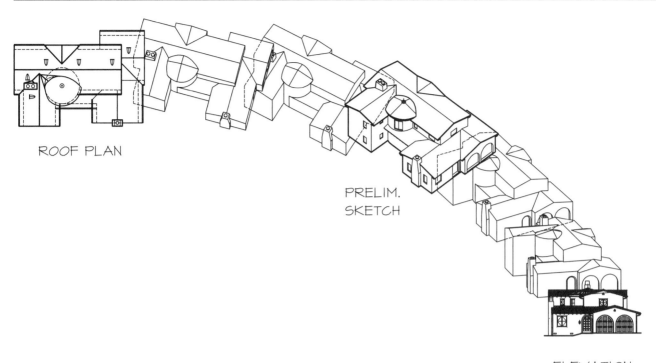

ROOF PLAN

PRELIM.
SKETCH

ELEVATION

Figure 2.98 Rotation of massing model into ortho view.

The structure must now be sliced horizontally to produce a floor plan and/or a reflected ceiling plan, and into a number of vertical slices to produce what are called *building sections*. See Figures 2.99A and 2.99B, respectively, for these types of slices and their respective solutions. By slicing and rotating, we can produce a roof plan, a floor plan, a number of sections, and at least four elevations, as shown in Figure 2.100.

Other drawings can now be generated from this basic set. The floor plan can become the master (XREF) drawing for the roof-framing plan when used in conjunction with the roof plan; the ceiling joist plan can become the basis for the foundation plan and the base for your associates' drawings, such as an electrical plan, structural plan, and/or mechanical plan. See Figure 2.101.

The walls, floors, ceiling, and roof are all initially drawn as solids. Another strategy is to take these planes and further articulate them. Draw the individual rafters, ceiling joists, studs, the concrete slab, and the foundation below it. This can be done on the section before it is rotated into ortho, as shown in Figure 2.102.

The eave can be isolated as shown on Figure 2.103, and then detailed as shown on Figure 2.104.

There is a definite advantage to articulating the structure right on the massing model. The drafter can actually see the construction that is to take place and identify potential problems, which may look as if they are resolved on details but reveal themselves only when the whole building is produced. The greater the understanding of

the building process, the more effective and valuable the employee is to the office.

If the preliminary sketch was further developed or refined to produce presentational drawings, in the form of presentational plans, elevations, renderings, and area sketches, the CAD drafter need only use a stage prior to the rendering to produce the base for elevations, plans, and so on (see Figure 2.105).

Figure 2.105 also shows the reader the stages in producing a 3-D model drawing (refer back to Figure 2.97). Whether the designer develops the 3-D model or it is developed by a CAD drafter, the present method is to:

A. Lay out the main masses of the structure as a 2-D drawing.

B. Lay out this drawing in a 3-D image. Obviously, because there are no heights yet, we will be working with the *x* and *y* axes only.

C. Extrude the heights from this 3-D form.

D. Add the roof shape to the 3-D rectilinear form.

E. Add to this some of the features of the site, such as driveways, walks, and fences.

F. Further articulate the form by adding windows, doors, fireplaces, skylights, etc.

A *wire* (short for wire frame) of the massing model is extremely helpful later to locate the interior forms and help the designer understand the intersections of these geometric forms. This version of the model will aid not only

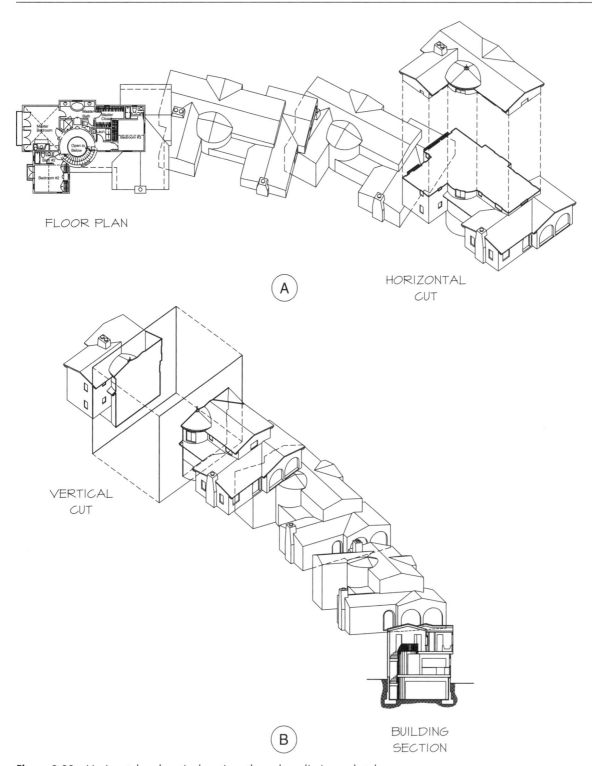

FLOOR PLAN

HORIZONTAL
CUT

(A)

VERTICAL
CUT

BUILDING
SECTION

(B)

Figure 2.99 Horizontal and vertical sections through preliminary sketch.

in the section drawing but in the details as well. The advantage of the computer is best seen here because we can instantly go from wire frame to (hidden) massing model.

Still another use of a 3-D model is for rotation. To see other views of the building, it is important to rotate into ortho to produce plans and elevations.

■ DISADVANTAGES OF A COMPUTER

One of the greatest concerns in the industry is the piracy of drawings. Drawings sent electronically can be copied and duplicated. There is always a possibility that people who are changing jobs may download entire libraries of

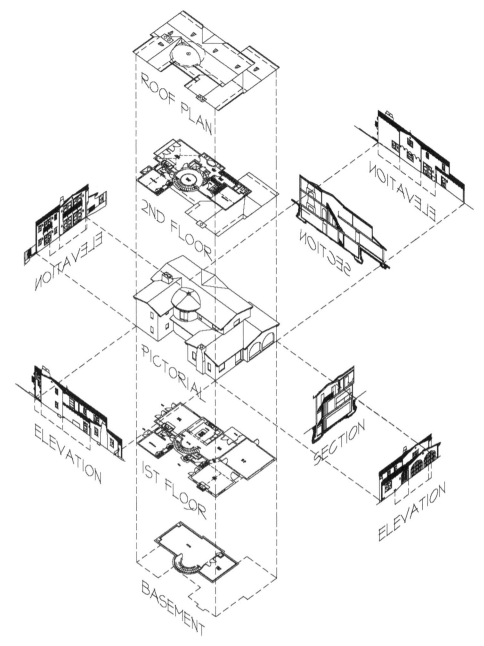

Figure 2.100   Evolution of construction documents.

information and take that information with them to their new firms. Drawings can also be changed or altered. For this reason, many municipalities require a hard copy (printed on paper) with wet ink signatures.

The computer is forever changing. The life cycle of a computer is said to be three years. Small offices, which are the majority in the architectural industry, cannot financially afford to change computers that frequently.

The percentage of downtime, which is the period when a computer or network is not operational for one reason or another, is still high and creates a problem for small offices with few computers. The development of better and faster computers is helping to reduce the amount of downtime, but it is for this reason that offices need a CAD manager.

■ ADVANTAGES OF A COMPUTER

The first advantage with a computer is that you are drawing full size. Fifty-foot-long buildings are drawn fifty feet in length. This is possible because we are drawing in model (virtual) space, which is unlimited. Drafters can now think and measure full-size buildings in actual dimensions, rather than in a reduced scale.

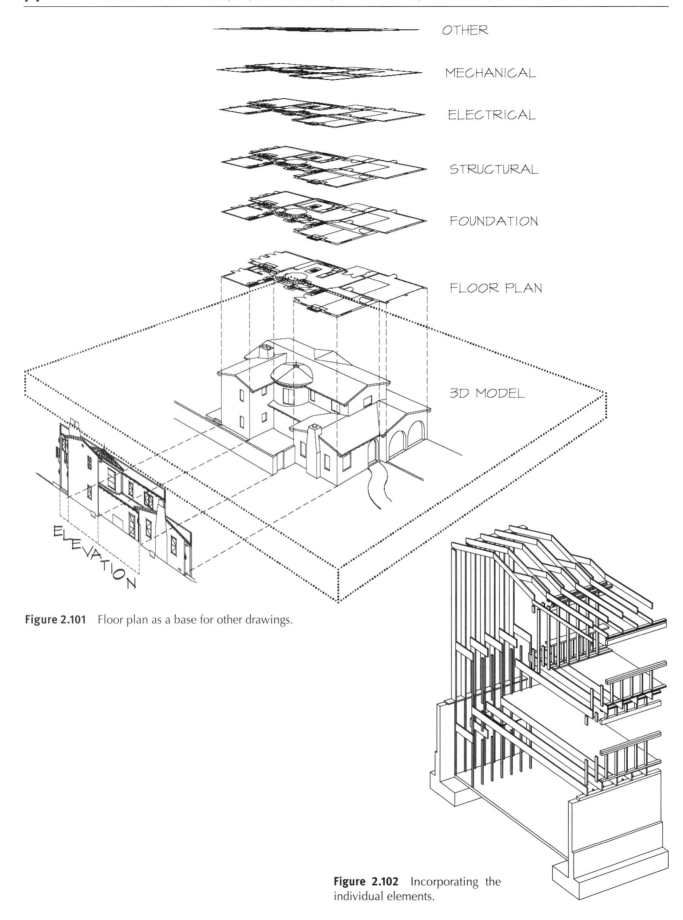

OTHER

MECHANICAL

ELECTRICAL

STRUCTURAL

FOUNDATION

FLOOR PLAN

3D MODEL

ELEVATION

Figure 2.101 Floor plan as a base for other drawings.

Figure 2.102 Incorporating the individual elements.

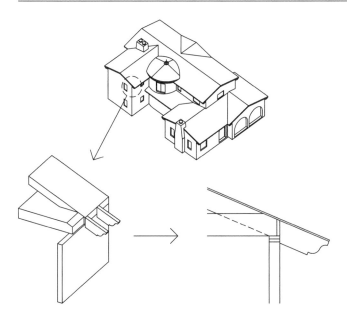

Figure 2.103 Isolating areas for detailing.

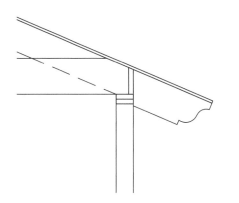

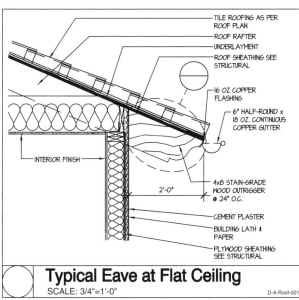

TILE ROOFING AS PER
ROOF PLAN

ROOF RAFTER

UNDERLAYMENT

ROOF SHEATHING SEE
STRUCTURAL

16 OZ COPPER
FLASHING

6" HALF-ROUND x
18 OZ. CONTINUOUS
COPPER GUTTER

INTERIOR FINISH

2'-0"

4x8 STAIN-GRADE
WOOD OUTRIGGER
@ 24" O.C.

CEMENT PLASTER

BUILDING LATH &
PAPER

PLYWOOD SHEATHING
SEE STRUCTURAL

Typical Eave at Flat Ceiling
SCALE: 3/4"=1'-0"
D-A-Roof-001

Figure 2.104 Isolating an area and detailing.

Another advantage is the computer's ability to enlarge or reduce a drawing instantly. A single drawing can be reproduced in a variety of different scales. The computer has the capability to enlarge and reduce much like a paper copier.

A drawing can be displayed on the monitor as a single drawing, or the screen can be split and the original drawing can be displayed adjacent to an enlargement (see Figure 2.106). Two monitors can also be used simultaneously: one displaying the original drawing and the second monitor zooming in to show an enlargement of a given area (see Figure 2.107).

The computer was made for repetitive and redundant tasks. The accuracy and speed with which a computer carries out these tasks is far superior to the abilities of even the best manual drafter.

Computers can be networked so that if many drafters are working on one project, they can communicate with each other. As one drafter changes an element of a drawing—say, a window size—the change will be reflected on the drawing of the computers that are networked (this feature is particularly valuable when XREFed drawings are changed).

The computer programs of today can perform many tasks simultaneously. As a drafter is outlining a floor plan, for example, the computer is also computing the perimeter and the square footage of this polygon.

Because the computer can draw in 3-D, any potential problems, whether in construction, installation, or other areas, can be identified before they occur.

■ FUTURE OF CAD

Advances in the computer industry increased dramatically after the year 2000, making it impossible to accurately forecast the evolution of the computer for the next decade. There may be more computers than people, if you count those in appliances, cell phones, and so forth.

This ever-morphing industry does, however, provide some clues to the future. One need only look at cutting-edge, state-of-the-art computers and plan for offices to incorporate these advances into their operations. There are, for example, eight major movements taking place in the architectural industry:

A. Wireless
B. Skill/tool assessment as a base of compensation
C. The disappearance of the central workspace
D. Model-based or model-centric design as 3-D models, only now being adopted as a base for working drawings
E. Full-size virtual buildings that clients may "walk" through

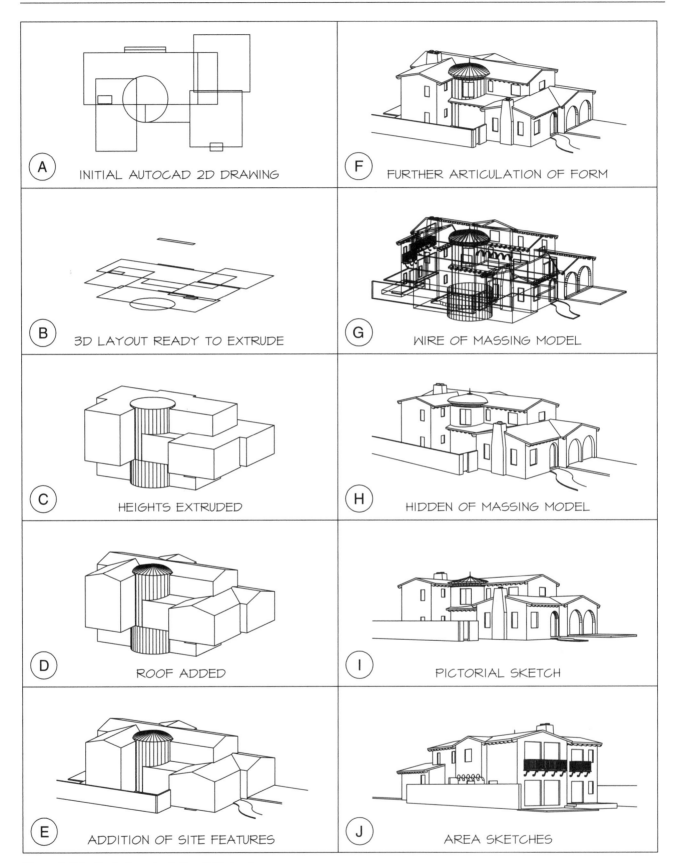

A INITIAL AUTOCAD 2D DRAWING

B 3D LAYOUT READY TO EXTRUDE

C HEIGHTS EXTRUDED

D ROOF ADDED

E ADDITION OF SITE FEATURES

F FURTHER ARTICULATION OF FORM

G WIRE OF MASSING MODEL

H HIDDEN OF MASSING MODEL

I PICTORIAL SKETCH

J AREA SKETCHES

Figure 2.105 Evolution of a 2-D to 3-D sketch.

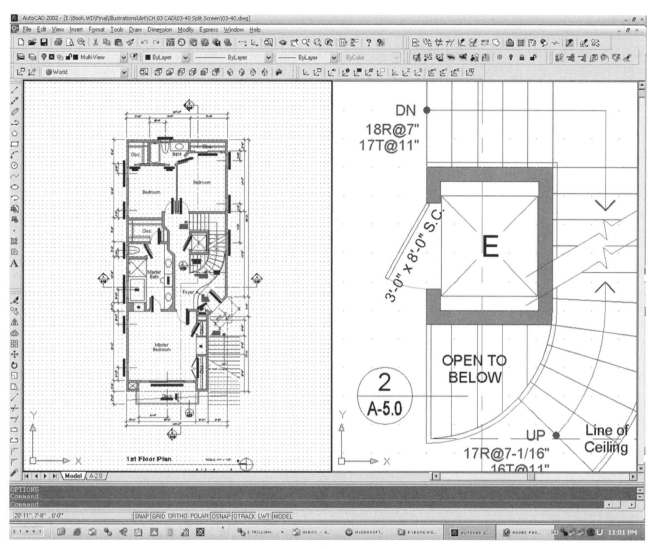

Figure 2.106 Split screen. (Courtesy of Norman LeBeau, owner.)

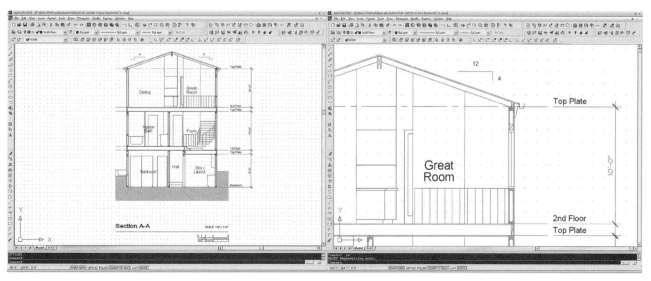

Figure 2.107 Dual screen.

F. Software—pay as you use
G. New delivery methods
H. A future foundation for Revit (see Chapter 3 for more on Revit)

The advent of wireless components has not only begun to affect the configuration of the office, but has also given more freedom to the CAD drafter. Currently, the only limitation is directional; that is, you need to be sure that the infrared beams are directed toward the equipment you wish to control. Wireless printers and copiers are now beginning to appear on the market. As jobs are completed, the CAD stations will be reconfigured to meet the needs of the next project and future projects. The production room will be forever morphing to meet current demands.

Some CAD drafters may choose to work at home and come into the office only for staff meetings. More conventional offices may see this new, minimally staffed office as a radical change from the past, with the office acting only as a docking station for the CAD drafter. Technology is making it increasingly easy for the industry to send and receive drawings.

Some offices may not have CAD drafters at all. CAD drafters may become contractors or subcontractors and bid on various jobs, some of which they might find on web sites. This can provide greater freedom for drafters, allowing them to spend their daylight hours with their families and perform the contracted work during the evenings or early morning hours.

■ CONCLUSION

Throughout this chapter, we have tried to refrain from discussing how to use a computer or the commands used for a specific function. Rather, we have deliberately shown the process by which a set of drawings is produced. Certainly, techniques have changed, moving from manual drafting to computer-generated drafting or use of CAD programs, but the process of building construction has not changed. The changes in the process of building have not resulted from use of the computer or the method of drawing, but from changes in building technology.

The impact of BIM has yet to be fully realized. When this happens—within the next few years, it is hoped—a monumental change will take place in our profession. Earlier exposure of our associates to the national (even global) interest in green architecture, the implementation of LEED in buildings, should introduce architecture to a new era.

3

BIM, REVIT, AND HUMAN CONCERNS

■ INTRODUCTION

In this chapter, we introduce building information modeling (BIM), along with Revit, the computer-program vehicle that makes BIM possible. The human concerns that are an integral part of BIM help us see a larger picture of the world.

The preceding pictures are of a building in San Francisco's Golden State Park, called the California Academy of Sciences. Designed by Renzo Piano, this 2-acre facility took 10 years to plan, 3 years to build, and cost $488 million. It is both a museum and much more than a museum. The complex includes two large "houses": One is a planetarium; the other is a 90'-diameter, four-story rain forest and coral reef where you can see live fish from above and below, and birds in a natural-like habitat. Misters are used to keep the humidity similar to that found along Amazon riverbanks. There are also an African hall and a research museum. Taken altogether, the Academy sends a message about how we should care for our world and the creatures in it.

Most spectacular is the building that houses the museum. The roof is made of insulated earth (top right photo), allowing indigenous birds and plants to live there and making the roof a 400-year-rated roof. Around the perimeter of the natural roof is a trellis with photovoltaic panels mounted on it to capture the natural and free energy from the sun (top left photo). The bottom left photograph shows the entrance; the bottom right photograph shows the roof displaced by the dome. More than 90% of the Academy's original building (concrete and sand) was reused. Its walls are sealed in denim (from recycled old jeans). The structure's basement was designed to receive natural sunlight and in the center there is a piazza—an open space with motorized shades to control the heat and glare. Seeing this building in person makes one truly appreciate a structure that uses just about all of the green technology available today.

Governmental agencies are now beginning to require architectural firms to use CAD programs such as Revit. Although programs other than Revit are available, large firms appear to favor Revit. Many school districts, hospitals, and large commercial projects are also requiring successful contract bidders to use BIM as the instrument for building design and construction. Thus, it behooves architects and designers to be familiar and comfortable with both BIM and Revit.

■ HUMAN CONSIDERATIONS

Though architects must deal with the forces that affect a structure, such as wind, rain, and seismic activity (covered in Chapter 4), they must always stay focused on the main reason the building was designed: people. It is important to understand the critical anthropometric data describing adult men and women, children, and elderly and disabled persons (*anthropometrics* is the science dealing with the measurements of the body in different groups of people). Architects can provide their clients with the best working environment by producing architecture that makes a daily task comfortable. Whether serving food at a counter, working at a computer, or selling tickets for the local philharmonic, it is important that the worker be comfortable. One should also provide comfortable settings for dining, relaxing, and, yes, even studying. Providing the best angle for viewing in a museum or a theater, or for watching a favorite television program, can contribute significantly to human comfort.

To create comfortable environments, we must first understand the limits of the human body. It is vital to study the measurements for such things as clearances under counters and desks, the maximum height a person can reach when getting an item from an upper shelf, and how far an elderly person can reach down to plug in an electrical appliance. Those who maintain public facilities must complete this type of study for many different types of users, including children and persons with special needs such as accommodation of a wheelchair. Dimensions must be considered not only in regard to the limits of individual human bodies—whether standing, sitting, lying down, climbing stairs, squatting, or even kneeling—but also in regard to such diverse conditions as clearances for shopping carts at a market, cars in parking spaces, and so on.

A sampling of these dimensions can be found in Figures 3.1, 3.2, and 3.3. For a more comprehensive discussion of such dimensions, see the general planning and design data section of *Architectural Graphic Standards,* published by John Wiley & Sons in conjunction with the American Institute of Architects.

Note that special studies are continually being performed for specific building types, such as hospitals, research centers, the service bays of automobile mechanic shops, and so on. It would be helpful to explore the Internet to study how people adjust in their leisure environments as well as in their work environments, and learn about *ergonomics,* the science of how people adapt to their environments.

■ AMERICANS WITH DISABILITIES ACT (ADA)

Public building accessibility is a result of legislation for the protection of persons with disabilities. The Americans with Disabilities Act or ADA is a civil rights law, not a building code. This law is divided into four major titles that prohibit discrimination against those who are disabled: Title I, Employment; Title II, Public Services and

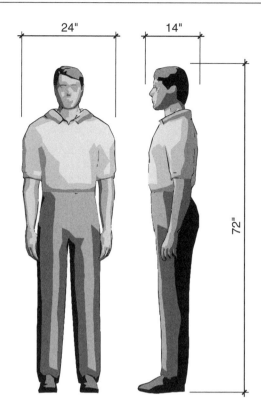

Male : Avg. Width, Depth, & Height

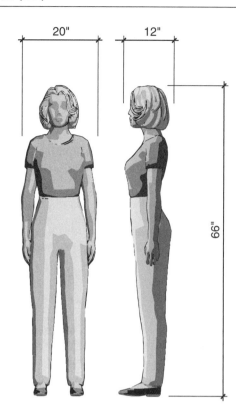

Female : Avg. Width, Depth, & Height

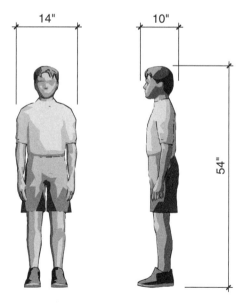

Child : Avg. Width, Depth, & Height

Figure 3.1 Understanding the human figure: average dimensions.

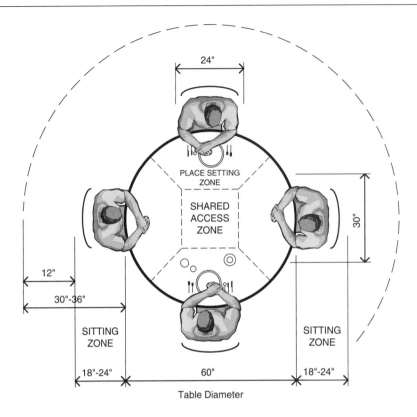

60"-Diameter Circular Table for Four / Optimum Seating

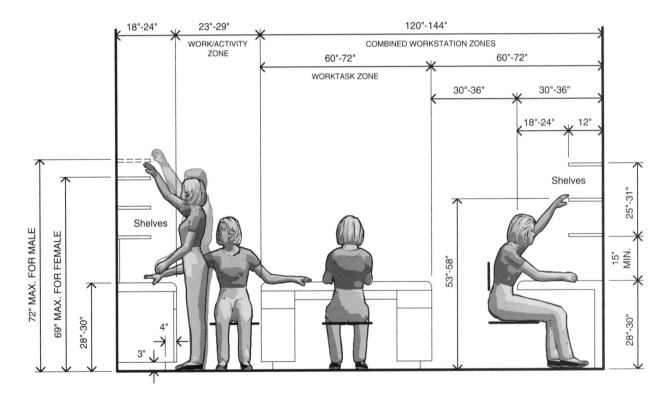

Desk and Workstation Considerations with Shelves

Figure 3.2   Reach.

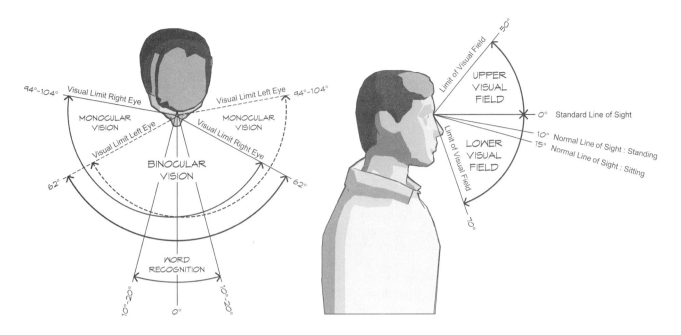

Visual Field in Horizontal Plane   Visual Field in Vertical Plane

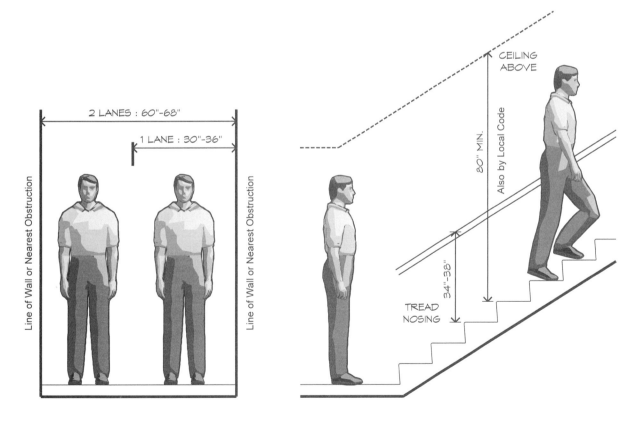

Circulation / Corridors and Passages   General Stair Dimensions

Figure 3.3   Space relative to sight and movement.

Transportation; Title III, Public Accommodations; and Title IV, Telecommunications. Given that the focus of this book is on building design and construction detailing, this chapter discusses Title III, Public Accommodations, and provides graphic illustrations of methods required to be used in public buildings and facilities to accommodate the needs of persons who are disabled.

The dimensions with maximums and minimums are shown only to allow readers a glimpse into the type of concerns we have as a profession. For example, Figure 3.4 shows a wheelchair going up a ramp in a curb. A designer, drafter, office manager, or architect will have to seek out the national standard and always follow that up with a check of state and local municipality regulations. Local or state regulations may be more stringent than federal guidelines and requirements.

To offer greater accessibility to and better accommodations in public buildings for those with disabilities, various representatives of organizations for disabled persons have worked with federal agency officials to establish recommended standards. Requirements implementing these standards have been compiled in a list of elements that will be of concern to you as you prepare drawings and details to satisfy the various required/recommended design criteria:

1. Path of travel—exterior accessibility route to the facility
2. Accessible parking
3. Curb
4. Entrances
5. Interior access route
6. Ramps
7. Stairs
8. Elevators
9. Platform lifts
10. Doors/thresholds/handles
11. Drinking fountains
12. Toilet rooms and bathrooms
13. Water closets
14. Urinals
15. Lavatories and mirrors
16. Sinks
17. Bathtubs
18. Shower stalls
19. Grab bars
20. Tub/shower seats
21. Assembly areas
22. Storage
23. Alarms
24. Signage
25. Public telephones
26. Seating and tables
27. Automatic teller machines
28. Dressing and fitting rooms
29. Register counters
30. Floor materials/finishes
31. Electrical fixture heights

There are also requirements and recommendations for special applications in the following types of buildings:

A. Restaurants and cafeterias
B. Medical care facilities
C. Business and mercantile facilities
D. Libraries
E. Transient lodging facilities

Parking Stalls and Curb Ramps

For specific buildings, the required number of parking spaces for those with disabilities is determined by the total number of spaces provided for that facility. This determination is based on ratios of the cars to be accommodated. An example of ratios for disabled parking may be 4 disabled spaces per 80 total parking spaces. See Figure 3.5. Note that there are provisions for a marked access aisle, a curb ramp, a disabled/handicapped parking sign, and a parking-surface disabled symbol. Figure 3.6 depicts separately the freestanding disabled sign and the parking-surface disabled symbol. In most municipalities, a large fine is imposed on nondisabled persons who use these parking spaces.

Ramps.   Another way of providing exterior accessibility to a facility is through the use of ramps. Figure 3.4 showed a curb ramp detail—one example of providing an accessible exterior route of travel to a specific facility. Ramps have proven to be a desirable method of enhancing accessibility when there are grade changes in

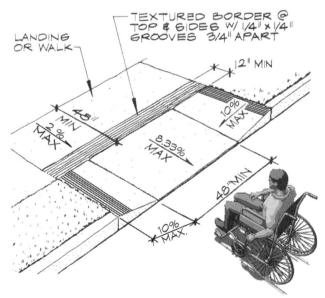

Figure 3.4 Curb ramp.

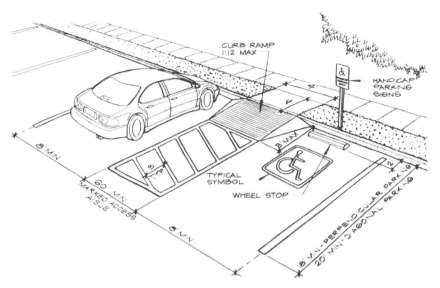

Figure 3.5   Parking spaces.

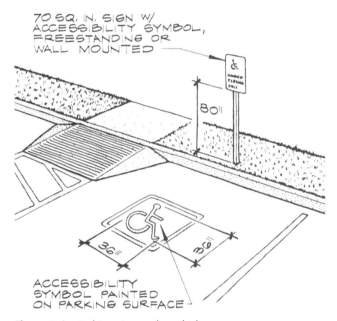

Figure 3.6   Parking sign and symbol.

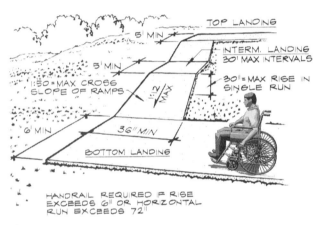

Figure 3.7   Ramp.

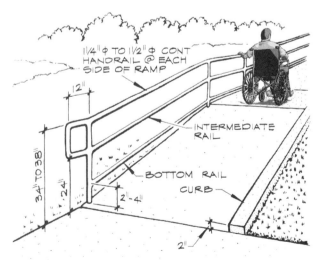

Figure 3.8   Ramp handrail.

the path of travel to a building. Figure 3.7 illustrates an example of an acceptable ramp with various changes in levels. Handrails are required on both sides of a ramp if the rise exceeds 6 inches or the horizontal projection exceeds 72 inches. If handrails are required, they will have to be drawn and detailed in accordance with the applicable requirements. Figure 3.8 depicts handrail requirements for the ramp shown in Figure 3.7.

Wheelchair Space Requirements

In cases where there are no specific rules for a particular planning situation, it is prudent for the architect or designer to be aware of the space needed for maneuverability by someone using a wheelchair. Figures 3.9 through 3.13 give some examples of floor space areas and reaching dimensions that are desirable for those who function from a wheelchair.

Locations for Controls and Shelving. As shown in Figures 3.9 through 3.13, there are dimensional limitations in various directions for a person using a wheelchair. Therefore, controls such as thermostats, window controls,

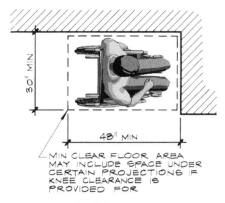

MIN CLEAR FLOOR AREA MAY INCLUDE SPACE UNDER CERTAIN PROJECTIONS IF KNEE CLEARANCE IS PROVIDED FOR

Figure 3.9   Wheelchair space requirements.

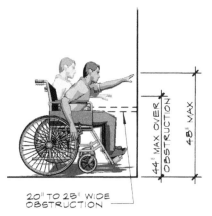

20" TO 25" WIDE OBSTRUCTION

Figure 3.10   Wheelchair space requirements.

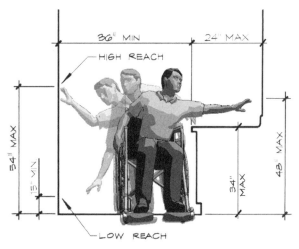

Figure 3.11   Wheelchair space requirements.

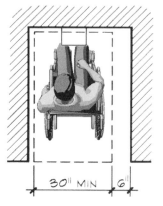

Figure 3.12   Wheelchair space requirements.

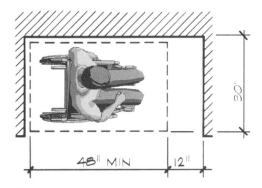

Figure 3.13   Wheelchair space requirements.

electric switches, pull cords, convenience outlets, and the like will have to be located within these reach limitations. Figure 3.14 illustrates such controls. Another concern in regard to reach limitations is accessibility to the bookshelves found in educational and library facilities. Figure 3.15 illustrates maximum shelf heights and passage dimensions for various types of aisles.

Doors and Doorways. The maneuvering capabilities of a person in a wheelchair are important considerations when dealing with accessibility of doors and doorways. These capabilities determine the minimum required floor-plan dimensions. An example of a floor-plan configuration involving a door and doorway access is depicted in Figure 3.16. Note that the door clearance does not include the door thickness or any hardware. Door-swing direction in access corridors will be dictated by required minimum clearances for maneuvering a wheelchair to access doors. If building code requirements specify that certain doors have to swing into corridors, then corridor dimensions may have to be adjusted to satisfy wheelchair clearances. Figure 3.17 illustrates two examples of door-swing directions that affect the dimensional width of a corridor.

Access doors and the various hardware assemblies required for their functioning must also meet certain

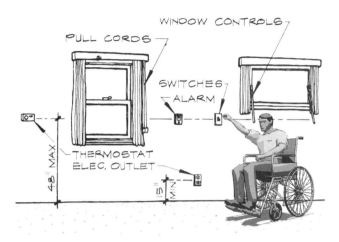

Figure 3.14 Control heights.

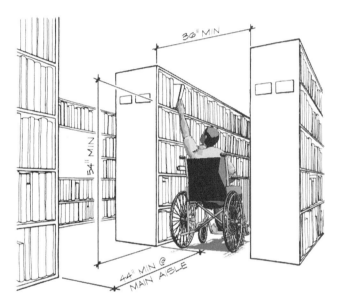

Figure 3.15 Shelf heights.

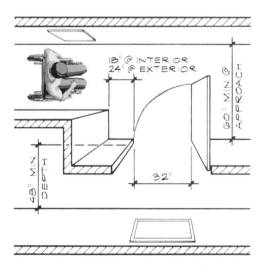

Figure 3.16 Doorway maneuvering clearances.

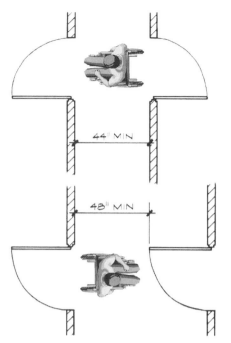

Figure 3.17 Doorway maneuvering clearances.

requirements. For example, regulations confine the selection of door handle hardware to a lever-type U-shaped handle with a minimum and maximum dimensional location above the floor. Similarly, the slopes and heights of door thresholds must satisfy accessibility requirements. An illustration of hardware for door handles and an example of an acceptable threshold are shown in Figure 3.18.

Drinking Fountains. When planning drinking fountain locations, the architect will have to be aware of minimum required dimensions for recessed or projected installations. Figure 3.19 provides a view of these two types of installation, illustrating dimensional clearances as well as the maximum height to the spout and clearance for knee space.

Plumbing Facility Requirements. An important facet of the building design process is the provision of accessible plumbing facilities that accommodate persons with disabilities. These facilities, which include such fixtures as water closets, lavatories, and urinals, are planned to ensure accessibility for those who have disabilities. A floor plan must be designed to provide at least the minimum required space clearances and accessibility to specific plumbing fixtures. Figure 3.20 illustrates an overall pictorial view of a proposed restroom facility that incorporates minimum access clearances for the various plumbing fixtures. Note the required grab bar sizes and locations relative to the water closet. The installation of the various plumbing fixtures is regulated with reference

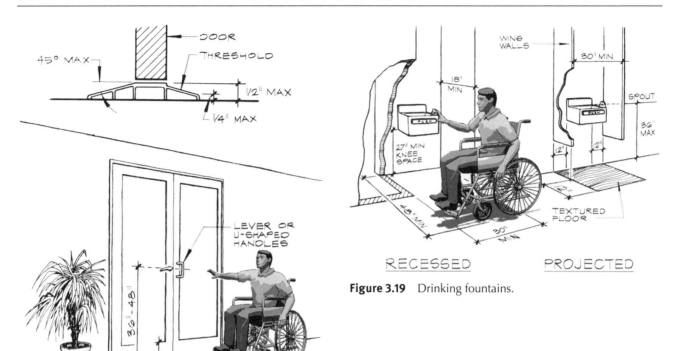

Figure 3.18   Threshold and door hardware.

Figure 3.19   Drinking fountains.

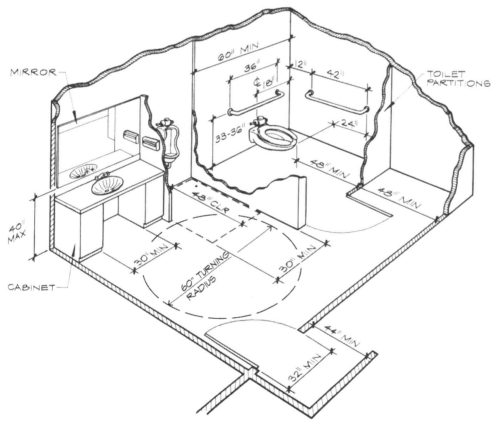

Figure 3.20   Restroom facilities.

to their dimensional height above the floor, side wall clearances, and knee and toe spaces for the use of lavatories. See Figure 3.21.

Note that hot-water and drain pipes are required to be insulated to protect against contact. Lavatory clearances are most important, because the knee will project under the lavatory fixture and will therefore require additional clearance. For a clearer illustration of the required clearances beneath the lavatory, see Figure 3.22. In planning for accessibility to toilet compartments, the location of the door to the compartment will dictate the required fixture layout. See Figure 3.23.

These illustrations are examples of the elements within a public building that the architect must plan for in order to accommodate persons with disabilities.

We have included a few samples of construction documents (partial plans and elevations) showing how ADA information must be displayed and what types of notes might accompany the drawings. If these drawings confuse you, try reading Chapter 8 on floor plans, and Chapter 11 on exterior and interior elevations, before looking at

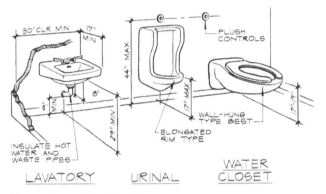

Figure 3.21   Plumbing fixtures.

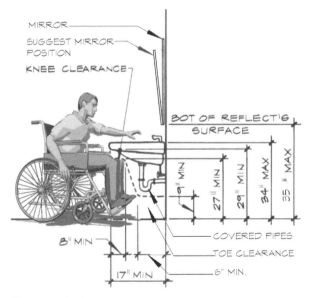

Figure 3.22   Lavatory access.

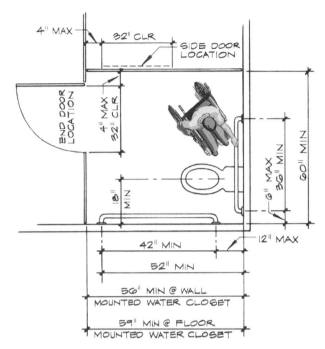

Figure 3.23   Toilet compartment plan.

these sample plans, elevations, and notes again. They are found in Figures 3.24, 3.25, 3.26, and 3.27.

Typically, notes such as the ones seen in Figure 3.26 would be found adjacent to the images found in Figures 3.24 and 3.25. It is also possible that the notes could be included in the specification section of the architectural documents. See Figure 3.26.

■ BUILDING INFORMATION MODELING (BIM)

As described in Chapter 1, BIM is a new way to approach construction documents, particularly working drawings. BIM addresses every characteristic of a building, from material quantities to energy performance, from lighting to site disturbances (to mention just a few). BIM can be an integral part of sustainable design because it allows the architect/designer to explore, investigate, and implement designs that have the least impact on the environment.

In architecture, as in life in general, there is nothing as constant as change. Fortunately, BIM manages change for you. It also keeps you honest, as it does not allow you to avoid a situation by temporarily inserting a "placeholder" unit in your design. Elements' "properties"—a term used by Revit—are based on real-life properties and characteristics. BIM is data driven. It allows you to take a design and enhance its data, but it does so in a holistic manner. This means you cannot be fickle: The change you make on any plan or elevation will be reflected in all drawings. For example, if you put a window on the first floor of a three-story building, Revit will change the

LAVATORY

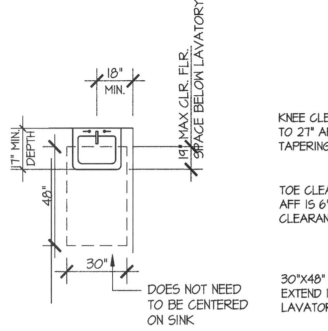

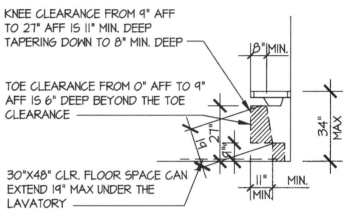

KNEE CLEARANCE FROM 9" AFF
TO 27" AFF IS 11" MIN. DEEP
TAPERING DOWN TO 8" MIN. DEEP

TOE CLEARANCE FROM 0" AFF TO 9"
AFF IS 6" DEEP BEYOND THE TOE
CLEARANCE

30"X48" CLR. FLOOR SPACE CAN
EXTEND 19" MAX UNDER THE
LAVATORY

DOES NOT NEED
TO BE CENTERED
ON SINK

Figure 3.24 Lavatory drawings and specifications.

AMBULATORY STALL

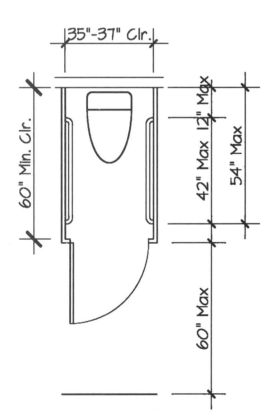

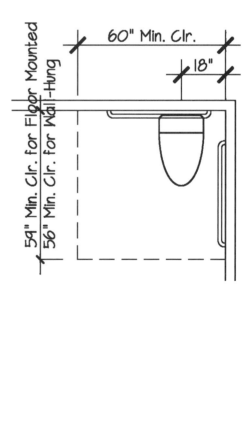

Figure 3.25 Construction documents for a water closet (ambulatory).

Notes:

Lavatory:
- All drain and hot-water pipes under the lavatory must be insulated or covered with a boot or shield to prevent contact.
- All sharp and abrasive surfaces under the lavatory must be covered to prevent contact.
- Doors should not swing into the required clear space.

Faucets:
- Faucets must be operable with one hand and should not require tight grasping, pinching, or twisting of the wrist; lever-operated, push-type, and electronically controlled faucets need to be ADA compliant.
- Force necessary to operate faucet controls is 5 pounds maximum.
- Self-closing valves are to remain open 10 seconds maximum.

Water Closet:
- Toilet (single or multiple accommodation):
  - Toilet is located 18″ from the side wall to its centerline.
  - Flush valve is located on wide side of toilet.
  - Flush valve requires 5 pounds maximum force to operate and is operable with one hand and does not require tight grasping, pinching, or twisting of the wrist.
  - The top of the seat is 17″ to 19″ AFF.
  - The seat does not automatically spring to an open position.
  - The toilet paper dispenser allows for a continuous paper flow and does not control delivery.
  - The toilet paper dispenser is located between 7″ and 9″ from the front of the toilet to the center of the dispenser and 15″ to 18″ AFF.
- Single accommodation toilet:
  - Provide a turning space of 60″ diameter in the restroom, with a clearance height of 27″ minimum.
  - Above the finish floor (AFF), the turning space can overlap clear spaces of other fixtures, and doors can swing into the turning space.
  - Or provide a "T"-shaped turning space of 60″ × 60″ with two 12″ × 24″ notches; the turning space can overlap clear spaces of other fixtures and can use the 27″ clear height for knee and toe clearance on one side only.
  - Doors cannot swing into the required clear space of any fixture.
  - Operable parts of hardware are located 34″ to 45″ AFF.
  - Doors within 10″ AFF should have smooth kick plates the full width and 10″ high.
  - Provide one minimum accessible lavatory.
  - If separate restrooms are provided for each sex, then an accessible restroom should be provided for each sex.
  - If a unisex restroom is provided, it should be accessible.

Figure 3.26   Minimum requirements for toilet and lavatory.

window alignment on the other floors to accommodate it. The program is "parametric" modular; that is, it creates and maintains relationships among elements. Therefore, you must always work in three dimensions. You must see the impact the floor plan has on other drawings. A two-inch change in the columns between floors on a ten-story building will have a monumental impact on the surface of the elevations. Again, to use BIM successfully, you must work with a 3-D model.

Green Architecture

If we are to implement "green" architecture, we must design and build structures with reduced energy use and costs. Residential and commercial buildings account for 40% of our total energy use, 70% of our electricity use, and 12% of our water use. Also, 30% of our greenhouse gas emissions come from structures.

Sustainable design uses environmentally sensitive design to reduce this negative impact on the environment. In the United States, a voluntary system called LEED (Leadership in Energy and Environmental Design) was established as a national standard for design. As many as 69 points (maximum) can be earned for a site design, for good indoor environment quality, and for efficient use of energy, materials, and water. Why are LEED's points critical? Because adherence to LEED criteria may make a project eligible for governmental funding: The higher the points, the higher the possible funding.

A good example of LEED is the Aria Resort and Casino complex, which includes a hotel and spa, the Mandarin Oriental Las Vegas, Veers Towers, and the Crystal retail and entertainment district. The main entry to the City Center (with LEED gold certified buildings) is by way of the Daniel Liebeskinds' Crystal retail center featured on the cover of this book. The Aria, designed by high-profile

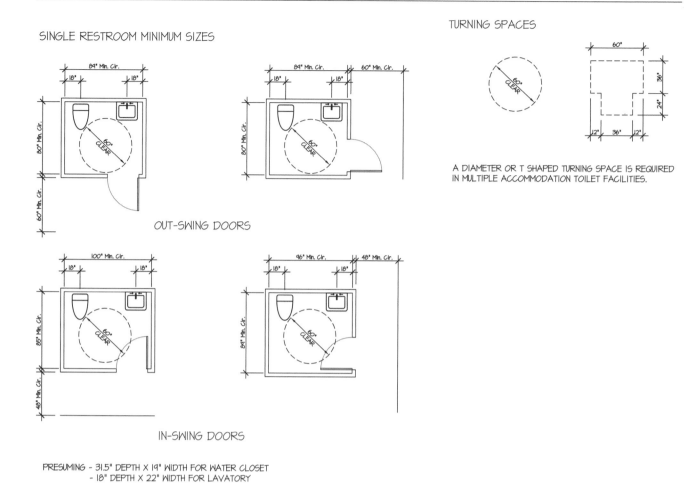

Figure 3.27   Minimum requirements for fixtures, door, and clearance.

architects including Daniel Liebeskind, Pelli Clarke Pelli, and Kohn Pedersen Fox, is one of the first Las Vegas hotels to achieve LEED gold certification, and is the world's largest hotel with LEED gold status.

Revit

BIM is the concept underlying our new way of thinking; Revit is the vehicle that makes the BIM process possible. Although a number of other firms, such as Bentley, ArchiCAD, and VectorWorks, also produce BIM software, throughout this book we describe the BIM process using Revit, the premier program in this area. However, the other programs function in much the same way.

Revit can be used at the onset of design, or the architect or designer can choose (as in the past) to wait until the schematic design stage, when the form has begun to take shape. As a designer/architect begins to develop the initial concept, he or she usually comes to a point in the life of the design when concept starts to take shape and "speaks" to the designer/architect. This is the perfect point at which to develop BIM via Revit. When finished, the project will just say "Here I am."

As you study Revit, remember that you must think in 3-D, even though eventually the drawings you produce for construction will be 2-D. This 3-D visualization of documents is new, especially to beginners; in the past, drafters drew and thought two-dimensionally. In CAD, you set up a series of geometric forms; CAD does not care what it represents. In contrast, in Revit you create elements.

The term *Revit* comes from "Revise Instantly," which the program accomplishes as changes are made. Move one door, and Revit will reflect the change in all other drawings. This is because Revit creates relationships within objects and between objects. If you were to call out (tag) a wall to be made of wood studs with stucco on the exterior and drywall on the inside, all walls would be affected (although you could change one particular wall from drywall to wood paneling). Another feature of Revit is that it allows the user to define the rules with which he or she is working. Remember, there are no layers in Revit. On its plan, Revit uses object categories. In other words, Revit has commands that control the visibility of elements per view. There are three main levels of details to be shown and medium levels of details plus subcategories. The three types of elements are:

1. The host element, called the "Model Element." These can best be described by floors, walls, roofs, ceilings, stairs, or ramps.
2. How to view the Model Element, with the "View Elements" feature.
3. The explanation or annotation (noting) process is called the "Annotation Element." With this feature, you can see the formation of grids for columns, levels, planes, and references.

A subcategory of the Model Element (host element) is the *component element*. It contains everything other than built-in plan items, such as doors, windows, and furniture. Specialty elements for these items, which are not a part of the structure but describe its parameters, are called *annotation elements*. Here you will find such things as dimensions, text notary, loaded tags, and symbols.

Sun and Revit. Revit's power can be appreciated from an example dealing with the sun. If you have ever tried, during the design process, to check the sun and plot its movement over the course of a day, you know that previous methods were a time-consuming process. Until recently, you had to input the latitude, date, time of day, site location, and other such data each time you wanted to perform these calculations in AutoCAD.

Revit has tremendously simplified this task. You do begin in the same way, in that you input the site location, but Revit supplies the latitude and date and displays a pictorial. See Figure 3.28. Note that the path of the sun on that particular day is shown and the shade and shadow from the structure are immediately plotted. If you put the icon onto the sun and move the cursor along its path, you can see the shade areas and the shadow patterns change. Figure 3.29 shows this image on three very important days: June 21 (summer solstice), December 21 (winter solstice), and March 21 (mean position of the sun). This capability is also a great aid for the landscape architect, as it allows you to define areas in total shade, partial shade, and total sun for selecting plants. Among the hundreds of potential uses, this feature also helps a designer position solar roof units for the most effective use of energy.

Design Development

After having designed the structure (preliminary design), the project is given to the CAD drafter to develop the construction documents. When using hand drafting or AutoCAD with BIM via Revit, the process changes: Extensive refinement is needed to translate and develop the preliminary design. The bulk of preliminary design

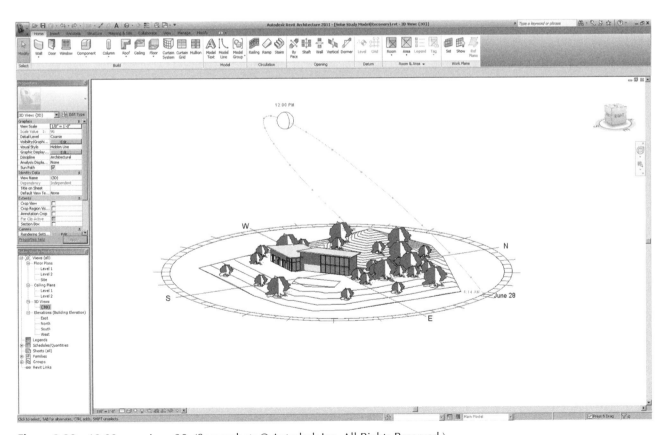

Figure 3.28   12:00 noon June 28. (Screenshots © Autodesk Inc. All Rights Reserved.)

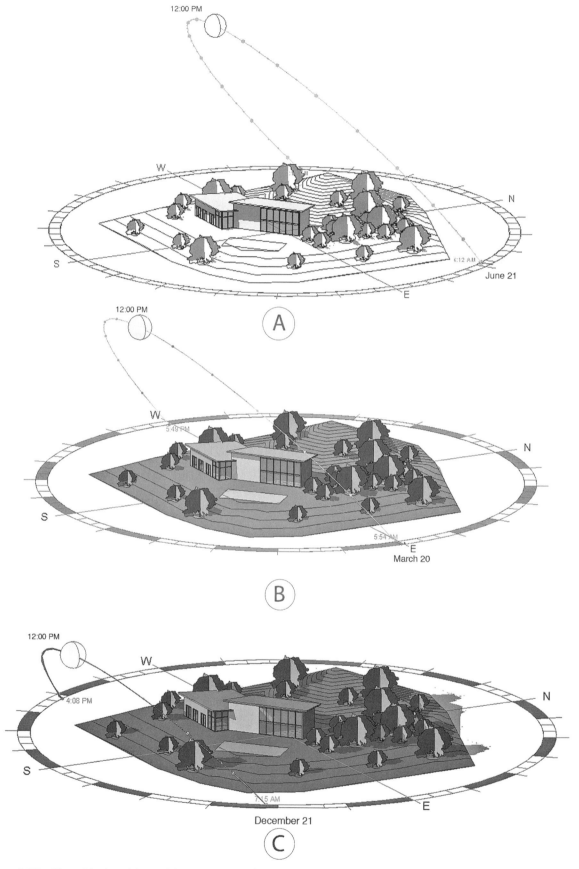

Figure 3.29 Three ideal positions of the sun. (Screenshots © Autodesk Inc. All Rights Reserved.)

questions are resolved by the designer in conjunction with all of the associates (e.g., the structural engineer, the mechanical engineer, the lighting engineer, etc.). Thus, the design phase, which used to be a short period of time (approximately ±10% of the total design time), and the construction document phase, which used to be very time-consuming, now become very brief. The design development period becomes longer, because at this stage many problems can be discovered and resolved that might have been hidden or unresolved during the working drawing stage. The computer program (Revit) reveals these problems because they are visually apparent early in the design stage via 3-D imaging.

In this book, we use a theater and the Madison all-steel building as exemplars. The work drawings will be dealt with as part of the treatment of construction documents in Chapters 16 and 17, respectively. The theater design is used in the figures of this chapter to describe the schematic design process using Revit.

Knowledge Base for Using Revit

Because BIM, implemented by way of Revit, is so front-loaded, the design development phase must be done by a person who is very knowledgeable about architecture. Be it the project architect, the designer, or the architectural technician, the person using Revit must know what the building constraints are before he or she begins work. As a Revit drafter, you must know about the:

Site Plan: Have a working knowledge of how your associates will perform their tasks. Know how the metes and bounds are developed by the civil engineer; have a good grasp of cut and fill and the limits of grading. You must be able to trace water through the site, as well as knowing the prevailing wind or snow loads, bearing pressure of the soil, and the level of bedrock at the site. How the workers understand the drawings and the limits of their ability are determined by the dimensions you provide.

Floor Plan: Truly understand the function of the floor plan. Know the best way to dimension the floor plan, be it built of wood, masonry, steel, or composites. Understand the techniques of the dimension reference system vs. stud-line dimensioning vs. block module using masonry. If the electrical plan is to be done on the floor plan, you must know whether it will be drawn with conventional wiring or by computer and how to represent it in a drawing under another. You must know how shear walls and grade beams are represented, as well as how to represent mesh, dowels, framing anchors, and—most of all—dimensioning.

Schedules: Know the different types of schedules and the office standard for charting them. Understand how the schedule is referenced to the plans, elevations, and building sections. You must know when and how to use a regular schedule as opposed to pictorial schedules. Know how and when to use plumbing schedules, appliance schedules, shear wall schedules, and pier and spread footing schedules.

Interior Elevation: Know how to dimension and what to dimension. Understand how to represent plumbing fixtures, cabinets, and how to profile for clarity. You must also be fully aware of how to represent commercial and residential plumbing fixtures, correctly draw stairs and fireplaces, and the clearances they require.

Exterior Elevation: Know what to dimension and what not to dimension to avoid repetition. Understand the orientation (NSEW) and the order in which to attack the problem, first establishing the datum. Be able to add oddly shaped buildings. Understand how addition, alteration, and tenant improvement differ from new building. A must is the knowledge of a pivot point and a key plan and how they are used. Know how to represent the structure behind the skin, such as bracing, shear walls, and pilasters, and how to represent different materials per AIA standards, while watching out for moisture penetration and condensation and—above all—meeting the requirements of local (and other) building codes.

Roof Plan: Understand plans and their geometry so that water or snow can be accommodated. This makes ridges, valleys, and hips quite important. Know how to designate the material(s) of which the roof is made; that is, know how to show the sheathing (if any), waterproofing, and the final topping.

Foundation: Be able to correctly imagine how the footing might translate in plan view, how hidden lines will show when concrete stops and changes level, and how to show one level of concrete. Figure 3.30 shows an axonometric model of our exemplar theater. On the left top is the menu called "Properties"; directly below it is a menu called "Property Browser," and across the top are various tabs used to refine the form. To start, you must set the limits of the project; the height, width, and depth of each form; the dimension reference system; and need for the datum on the project. See Figure 3.31.

This list is a representative sampling of the minimum knowledge a Revit drafter must possess in order merely to survive, let alone to do a good and efficient job. This is a good instance of "you can't draw what you don't know." Thus, the more you know about architecture, the better and faster you can produce a problem-free set of construction documents. Once the requisite data are all front-loaded in the project file, it becomes easy to produce the working drawings.

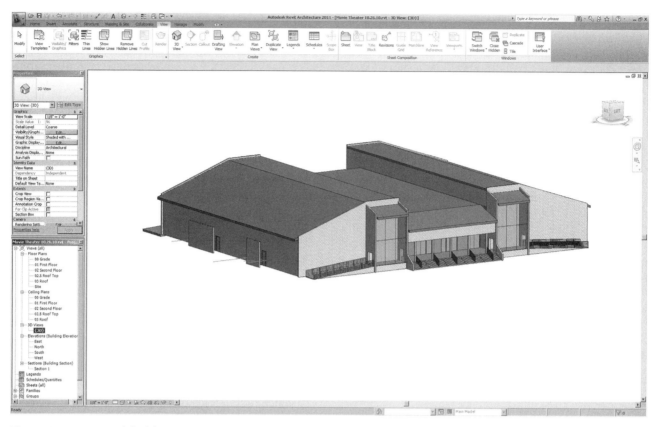

Figure 3.30   3-D model of theater. (Screenshots © Autodesk Inc. All Rights Reserved.)

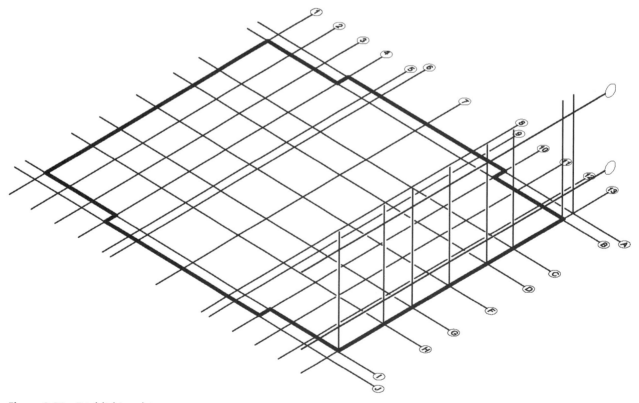

Figure 3.31   Establishing datums.

Share this BIM with your associates. In turn, the engineering and mechanical contractors will invest their time to draw their portions of the work accurately. This will, for example, avoid the problem of a structural beam using the same space as the ductwork.

See Figure 3.32 for establishing datum in 2-D. Both can be done by using the project browser. The walls are the first to be established. Our preference is to have the drafter work with a 3-D object, but some beginning Revit drafters who trained initially on AutoCAD prefer to work with a 2-D object.

Onto these 2-D and 3-D models we will begin to lay out the walls. See Figures 3.33 and 3.34 (both in 3-D). For modeling in 3-D, see Figures 3.35 and 3.36.

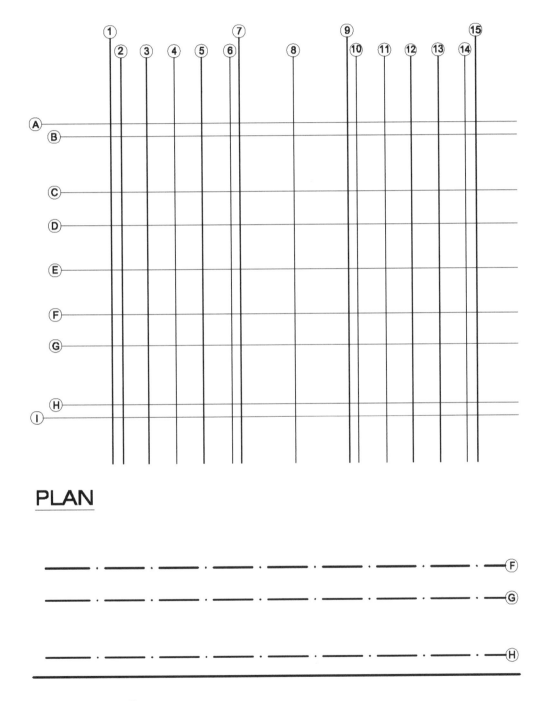

PLAN

ELEVATION

Figure 3.32 Datum in two dimensions.

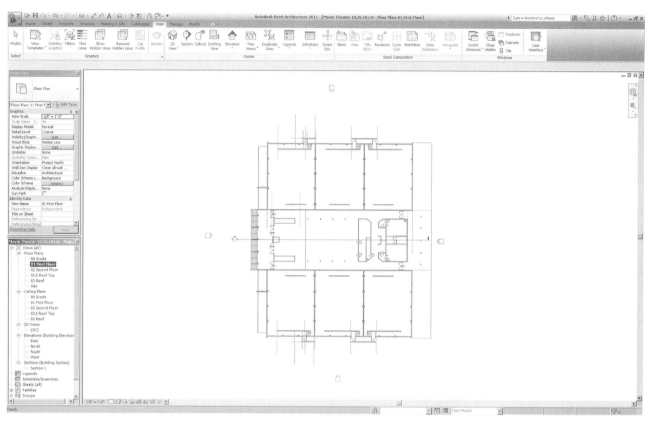

Figure 3.33   Establishing limit for walls. (Screenshots © Autodesk Inc. All Rights Reserved.)

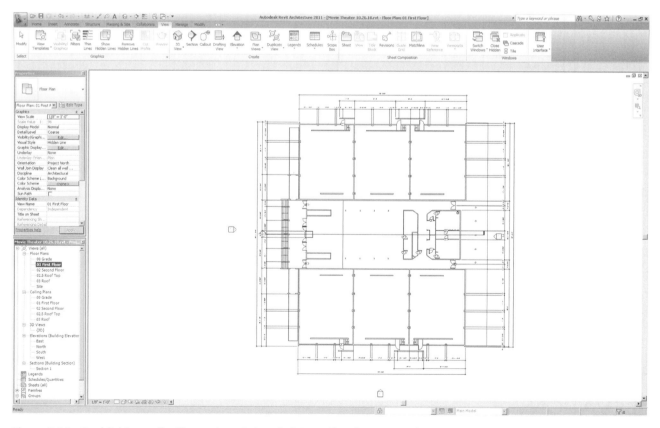

Figure 3.34   Establishing walls. (Screenshots © Autodesk Inc. All Rights Reserved.)

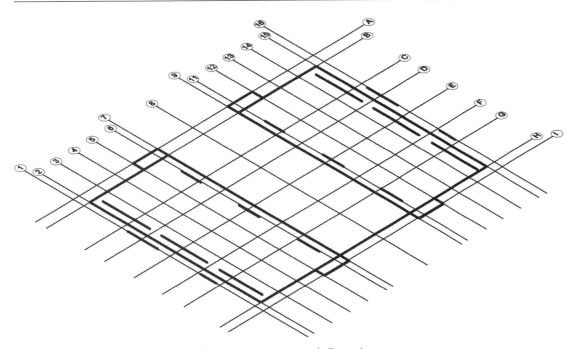

Figure 3.35 Using axial reference plane in conjunction with floor plan.

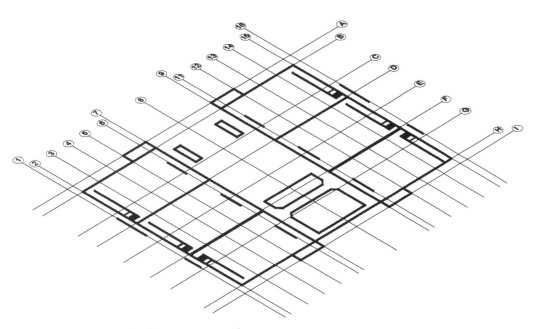

Figure 3.36 Additional information inserted.

Load-bearing walls go in first, pilasters next, then stairs, doors, and plumbing fixtures.

Because the roofs of this structure are hipped and attached to parapet walls (walls that extend above the roof), you may find it easier to work in 2-D, as shown on Figure 3.37; however, Figure 3.38 shows a 3-D model. Any portion of the roof can be removed, as seen in Figure 3.39. Using Revit, you are working in a parametric model, which means that any changes you make on a 2-D elevation or 3-D pictorial translate to all drawings in the parametric modeler. For example, if you work in polyline, when you choose the shape of a wall, Revit will show the change on the 3-D model, change the image to an elevation via the project modeler, and show all the changes you made on the 3-D model.

As the steel columns intersect the roof, as will the pilaster and the block wall, you, as the Revit drafter, can be very precise in locating points that require detailing. Sometime during an early stage, you should check the

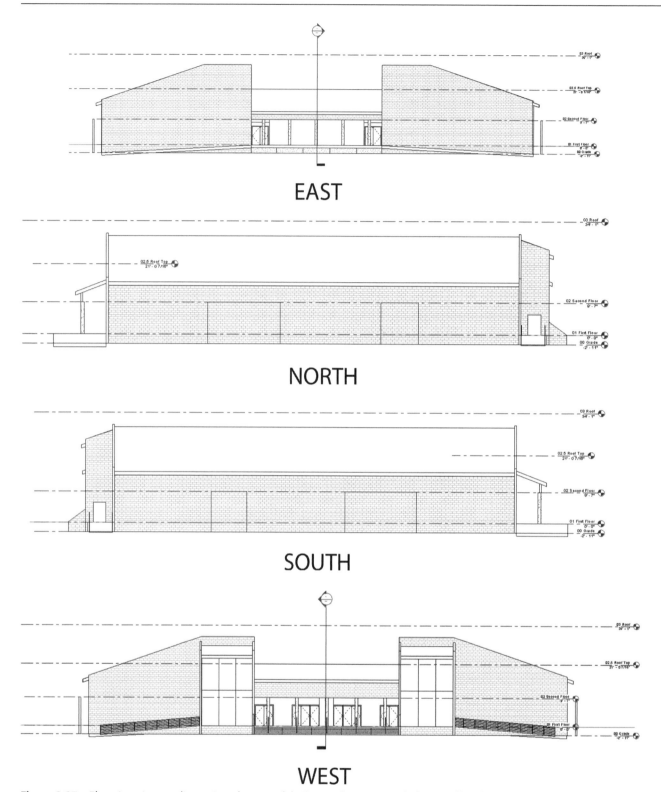

EAST

NORTH

SOUTH

WEST

Figure 3.37 Elevations in two dimensions from model. (Screenshots © Autodesk Inc. All Rights Reserved.)

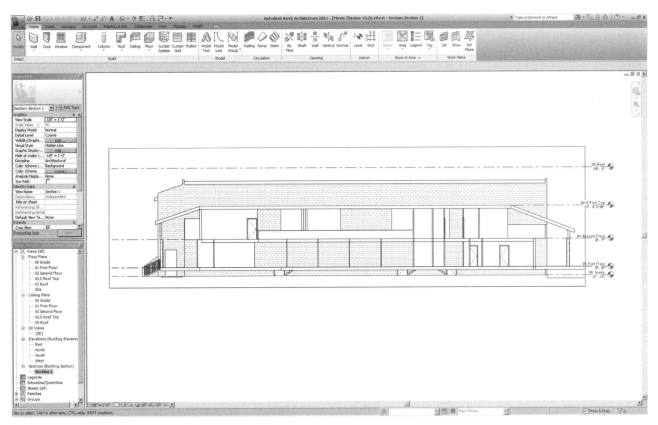

Figure 3.38 3-D image with roof on the structure. (Screenshots © Autodesk Inc. All Rights Reserved.)

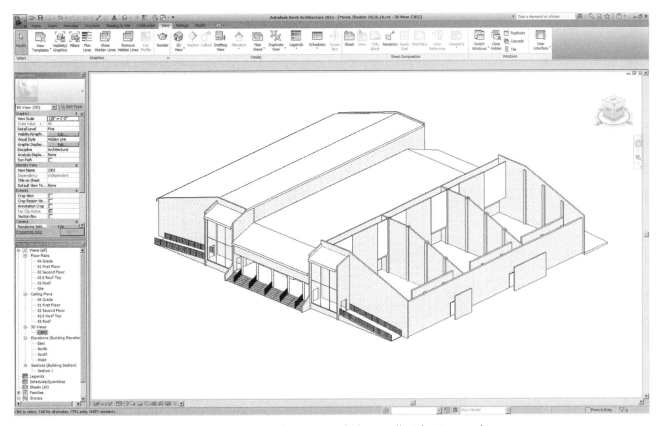

Figure 3.39 3-D model with roof removed. (Screenshots © Autodesk Inc. All Rights Reserved.)

properties menu and designate the proper materials to be used.

For example, if you started using generic 8″ wall during the design stage, you must change that specification to block as soon as possible. It does not make any sense to bring a generic 8″-wide wall to the underside of the roof if the wall material is not correct. See Figure 3.40. The three drawings that are initially used are the plan, the elevation, and the building sections. These will set the dimensional standards for the entire project.

Foundation Plan.   If a foundation plan is to be drawn, you must establish the underside of the floor plan, establish a new datum, and then draw the foundation. The foundation plan can be drawn orthographically, with the floor plan above the foundation plan and its parameters projected on the drawing over the floor plan, in what is called *ghosted mode*. When complete, this drawing will show up on the project browser.

Building Sections.   A building section clarifies the project, as well as revealing the need for details, because it shows the joining of planes. Review Figure 3.38 for the section cut symbols to be used. A partial section is accomplished by moving the cutting plane line to where you want the cut to stop.

Roof Plan.   The roof plan is drawn on top of the floor plan when you are working in 2-D. In 3-D, you must work with the model to refine the shape of the roof.

To better understand this roof planning process, look at the sketch of its central portion in Figure 3.40. The line at the very center is the ridge. This ridge produces a gable-type roof at the central portions. The surrounding portions are higher and so the slope of this gable roof must be drained at its edges. Roof drains, commonly called *scuppers*, were added at strategic points.

As you can see by comparing the sketch with the plan, portions of the low point of the gable roof remained flat to accept air-conditioning equipment. Other portions

sloped down from the vertical plane like a shed roof. Sheet metal saddles, called *crickets*, were positioned to control the flow of water on the roof and to direct water toward the roof drains. The small circles near the roof drains represent the overflow drains provided in case the regular scuppers clog.

On two sides of the structure, we added reference bubbles to correspond with those on the plans and sections. Skylights were not shown because they were deleted earlier at the request of the client.

Roof Framing Plan.   Although the roof framing plan is usually done by the structural engineer, it may be done in-house or sent to an outside source. If outsourced, the structural engineer must be sent an accurate set of plans from which he or she can take off the information necessary to structurally complete the sizes of the framing members. This is a stage where an accurate 3-D parametric (BIM) becomes very useful. The engineer's solution can be done as a total project, or the information can be drawn freehand and later transferred into the BIM model, from which a roof framing plan (working drawing hard copy) can be obtained.

Annotation Categories

This Revit category includes all annotations, symbols, text, and 2-D data that describe how a structure is to be built. This tool does not work or look the same as the tool in AutoCAD. This difference lies primarily in the fact that you can view your parametric modular work in 3-D as well as in 2-D. In fact, you should learn always to think in 3-D even when you are working in 2-D. Students who fail to develop this habit often revert to a 2-D mindset when they are working on plans, elevations, sections, and so on. However, with Revit you can immediately see the impact of your work on the 3-D model, naturally and visually, although you may be working in the 2-D format. This capability helps you develop the absolute mindset of always working in 3-D. As students work on a one-monitor system, they can toggle back and forth from the 2-D model they are drawing, correcting, and annotating to view the model in three dimensions.

Many architectural offices, especially larger ones, lament the fact that our college graduates do not think in 3-D while going through 2-D drawings, and thus are often unaware of or ignore the consequences of their efforts. For example, during detailing, changing the height of the columns by an inch floor to floor will result in the height of a ten-story building changing by ten inches. The change will result in the curtain wall (exterior wall surfaces that hang on the wall surfaces) being 10 inches too large or too small. This is only one example of the myriad problems caused by not thinking of the impact of any change on the whole structure.

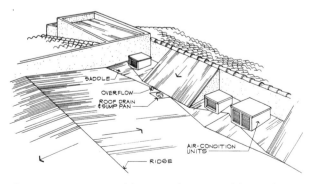

Figure 3.40   Corner of the central portion of the roof.

Order of Revit Operations

The order of Revit operations is outlined in simplified form in Chapters 16 and 17, dealing, respectively, with the steel-and-masonry theater and the all-steel Madison building.

Revit and Energy Considerations

Revit can be used with software tools that analyze energy use. With these capabilities, we are able to quantify the green effect of our structures much earlier in the design stage. Those involved with the project (the design team and the client) will be able to "walk through" the virtual structure so as to actually visualize and see the results and effects of greener design.

For example, we can study lighting via tools that allow use of airport information about the weather at any given latitude and longitude on Earth. In this way, we can see the effects of daylighting. *Daylighting* refers to using natural lighting (sun) to illuminate the structure, thus reducing the use of electrical energy to light (and heat) the building. Thus, high-performance, sustainable design can be realized by using the multifaceted approach made possible with ease via Revit. This is critical in current design, because structures (both residential and commercial, of which there are approximately 81 million in the United States) account for about 40% of all energy consumption in this country. It is our buildings that create the energy shortage! We used to blame automobiles and other vehicles, yet they alone account for only 7% of our energy use.

Federal agencies, state governments, and local governments are all helping to finance green building, whether by grants, tax credits, or other schemes. There are also regulatory incentives from state and local government entities. Architectural firms are eager to employ individuals who are LEED certified, as that status enhances the chances of success when bidding on government-funded projects such as schools.

Revit is linked with Autodesk Green Buildings Studio (GBS), a tool used for building energy analysis. GBS creates a thermal model of the building and even applies local building code presumptions. This can (and should) be done throughout the design stages. Early use enables better orientation of the structure on the site. Daylight can be checked during the design stages. Also, GBS creates an input which in turn enables engineering analysis systems to be used in conjunction with Revit for detailed analyses. This automated input of geometric coordinates saves hundreds of hours of labor. Revit's hidden strength is its ability, when used correctly, to provide information effortlessly, accurately, and quickly.

You can even do estimates of LEED credits for use of recycled material in your draft specifications, as well as reducing waste and improving staff efficiency. Because Revit knows what materials are to be used, it will automatically know what to draw; all it needs is for the drafter to input the size of the room.

Architecture and Trust

Since the time of hand-drawn construction documents, architects have been very protective of their work product. Protection meant keeping the originals and only releasing the prints (usually printed in blue and not capable of being copied). They protected their designs as well as the processes used in the construction documents, such as details to realize their drawings. Copyrights were (and still are) available for architectural renderings and plans, but were used by only a few firms because the application process was quite lengthy and time-consuming. Consequently, the government made copyrights a high priority in its scheduling.

When computers were introduced, the problem of theft and pirating became acute. Over the years, such portable storage devices as flash drives made it very easy for drafters to copy construction documents or parts of them, such as a detail that was time-consuming to produce. When the draftspersons moved to another office or firm, they carried with them a library of conventions and shortcuts that made them quite valuable to the new employer.

Details especially are unique to each job. Nevertheless, poor drafters were using a lot of details on every job without knowing the consequences given the new job characteristics, such as soil conditions, transfer of load (shear transfer), and so on. More experienced drafters would repurpose and reuse their details as datums, tweaking the detail to accommodate weather conditions, moisture conditions, and load-bearing details. Unfortunately for them, details can never be a standard for an exterior bearing wall, because of the infinite variety of soil and other conditions.

Computers also made transmission of construction documents easy, because one could quickly send them to, say, the structural engineer via electronic mail. Hard copies were not needed because the electronic files could be sent immediately. Of course, electronic transmission exacerbated the problem of plagiarism, as files could be easily copied, especially after the introduction of wireless units. Protection was installed in the form of blocks, but for every block a computer hacker found a way in.

Architects were also outsourcing drawing tasks to other countries where labor was cheaper. The work got done seemingly instantly, as the projects were being sent to countries with approximately 12 hours' time difference. This meant the offshore crews were working while domestic ones were sleeping, so drawings were being produced 24 hours per day. One serious drawback to this system was its negative effect on change orders: Havoc was produced when changes in the floor plan were not properly communicated and therefore were not made in the other drawings, such as the elevations, sections, and framing plans (to mention just a few).

The advent of BIM and Revit solved many of these problems, but also created additional ones for our profession. The use of BIM requires us again to build trust as we travel full circle. From jealously protecting and guarding our drawings, details, and innovative ideas, we have had to come to trust our associates—whether in-house or outside the office—with our entire BIM/Revit product. This trust brings us back to the beginnings of our profession and the way its members used to work: sharing, delegating, collaborating, and trusting as a new way of building a new community within the architectural profession. As a medical surgeon must trust his or her operating-room colleagues (such as the anesthesiologist and surgical nurses), so must an architect build a common, thoughtful bridge between contractors, their subcontractors, and the structural, civil, and electrical and mechanical engineers.

Any large contractor will claim that this is not now being done by architectural firms. Therefore, contractors are building their own models based on the 2-D drawings they are given, needlessly recreating a model form that already exists. In addition to demonstrating mistrust, this duplication of work adds cost to the project. The concept of BIM/Revit depends to a great extent on not duplicating files, but rather having access to the original working file.

To best understand the problem, look at Figure 3.41. In this model, the architect becomes the coordinator and resolver of conflicts. This is very difficult to do with a 2-D drawing. Even a trained eye may miss a duct that conflicts with a structural member or a plumbing or

electrical line drawing that conflicts with a beam in the framing plan. Often mechanical engineers will lay out their equipment while overlooking or ignoring the fact that the other engineers and trades need to use the same space. Such conflicts can be avoided by the use of Revit because it shows the structure holistically in 3-D. If all of the engineers would input their information into a single source, any conflict that arises would be shown immediately. In this way, Revit catches human errors in our construction documents that the senior drafter, the job captain, or any of the staff in an office might miss. See Figure 3.42 for a picture of this coordination of associates.

Because Revit is still so new to most drafters, they often fall back to using AutoCAD, because they are comfortable there. Even when Revit, a powerful parametric modeling tool, is used, we see drafters drawing in 2-D rather than 3-D. This is okay for the moment, but eventually we hope that the entire profession will use 2-D drawing only when it is absolutely necessary, and even then continue thinking in 3-D.

As for BIM, it creates a fine line between design, development, and construction documents. When design development is finished, the construction documents (working drawings) will also be all but finished.

Setting Up Revit

The key word here is *setup*. When you use Revit, you cannot work directly from the raw Revit program. You must first set up templates.

One programs the conventions and symbols the way they used to be done in the old drafting room of an office. Therefore, it is really important that the Revit user be very knowledgeable about how buildings are built and what the workers in the field understand. See Figure 3.43.

The best way for an office to begin to use Revit is to take its best project—the project that gave the firm the most trouble—and draw it anew in Revit. This allows the firm to use this template for additional projects. Use

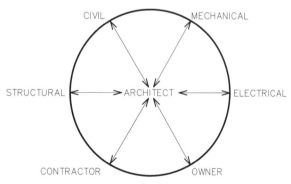

Figure 3.41 Disseminating project information to owner and professional associates.

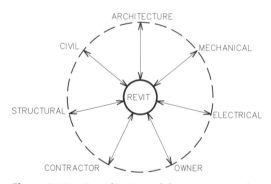

Figure 3.42 Coordination of drawings to catch conflicts.

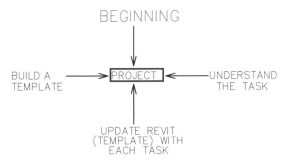

Figure 3.43 Starting with a template.

National Standard or AIA standards to set up a template base. If a better way is found, Revit can instantly change the drawings to incorporate any changes.

If this is your first attempt at using Revit in a small office, you must first define the conventions you will be using and build your template accordingly. If you are involved with military buildings, you must follow their standards (called *military specifications*).

For example, Revit uses a convention to cut a section in a drawing, as shown in Figure 3.44A. In the industry, this might work, but it is not technically correct. Figure 3.44B shows the correct symbol for a full section: a cutting plane line that has a broken dark line with two short dashes. The ends are made up of a pair of circles bound by darkened triangles. This section is a full section, cut through the entirety, as opposed to a partial section, which has the triangular form around a circle on one side only. The full section title has an "X" on both sides, and thus the title of that section is Section X-X. This also helps to alert the contractor and crew to look at both sides to see if it is a partial section or a full section. The arrowheads also show the direction one is looking when viewing the section. Figure 3.44C illustrates another detail in which the darkened beak shows the direction the detail is being viewed. The outside of the building on a detail is always to the left.

As you can see, the working drawing is a means of communication between the architect (or one of the architect's subordinates) and the workers in the field. It is all about communication. In our industry, we have some people speaking English while other workers speak another. To enhance the accuracy of communication and the quality of work, use standard conventions that act as a common language and create a common ground.

A Thought

In the next few years, the use of BIM will probably increase, but mostly in large architectural offices. Some large offices may have hundreds of employees, but our profession consists predominantly of small offices, with one to eight employees.

The smaller offices will not transition to BIM right away, partly because of the implementation cost and partly because of the cost of training staff. After all, when the transition from hand drawing to AutoCAD transpired, it took about ten years to be fully completed.

There are many reasons for the slow adoption of even very promising new methods. The situation somewhat parallels the process of changing from use of the English system to use of the metric system. The older drafters were not eager to learn a new skill, and even the younger professionals were not as familiar with or trained in computer use as they are today. Forty years ago, the original computer games were quite simplistic, and video games did not catch on until more sophisticated games were produced later on. Computers were not as sophisticated as they are now, and telephones were still land lines. Over the past 40 years, things have drastically changed: Today's students grew up with text messaging, the Internet, Facebook, and so on. For them, the transition to AutoCAD is easy, as young pupils are intimately familiar with computers and how they work. Quite a few are bona fide computer geeks who can manipulate

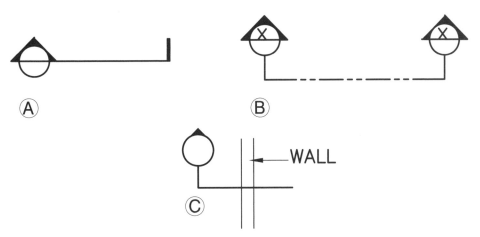

Figure 3.44 Standard conventions in corrected drawings.

software and hardware to make the computer do anything they want it to do.

The learning curve for the transition from AutoCAD to BIM, via programs such as Revit, is even steeper. BIM requires much more than a translation or acquisition of skills: It demands greater and deeper knowledge of architecture and construction. To complete a 3-dimensional drawing, one must change what has been learned in 2-D to a finite 3-D drawing. The front-loaded drawing programs of today require the designer to solve architectural problems, such as conflicts in the positioning of air-conditioning ducts, plumbing, and structural components, up front, well before the construction documents stage and early in the BIM process. This is a disadvantage to the present CAD drafters, who often depend on their skill with AutoCAD rather than their architectural skills to solve their problems. This is why the offices using BIM/Revit must set up a template that the drafter can follow. Too much computer skill and too little architectural knowledge can be deadly to an architectural project.

Summary

The BIM concept has revolutionized the design process and changed how production drawings are produced. At the same time, it has enhanced the use of sustainable/green architecture, thus allowing designers to earn as much as 20 LEED points in the process.

Changes have blurred the distinction between the functions of the designer and the drafter. In fact, many firms have eliminated the terms *draftsman* and *draftsperson* and instead train for their particular uses of Revit.

The main drawback to BIM lies in the need for reeducation of our staff. As educators, we need to look at the needs of architectural offices and find a common denominator for producing a Revit-based curriculum.

The entire thinking process has changed. Our drafters need to be able to understand how buildings are built and work in 3-D first, before they attempt to use Revit. The majority of buildings are designed by looking at the proposed structure from the engineering and green standpoints first, so the task is front-loaded. Among other things, this changes billing procedures, and requires that the designer be constantly looking at the structure. To be useful in the BIM process, a drafter must be able to produce details in their final form, cut sections, and be more focused on drafting and drawing conventions.

We must educate our drafters to be substance drafters rather than surface drafters, not just to know how Revit works, but to understand how Revit can produce structures that are fully thought through. BIM is the new concept, and Revit is the new tool, of our profession.

chapter

4

SUSTAINABLE/GREEN ARCHITECTURE

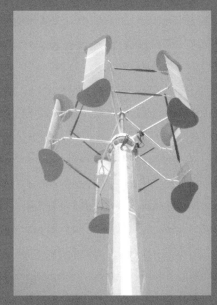

Courtesy of WikiArquitectura.

■ ENVIRONMENTAL AND HUMAN CONSIDERATIONS

As the title of this chapter suggests, **sustainable** and **green** architecture has to do with environmental concerns and what architects, engineers, and students of architecture can do about confronting the crisis of energy, conservation, waste, and so on. If everyone in any facet of the architectural profession takes on the responsibility of addressing these issues, an improved outcome can be expedited.

One cannot place a building on a site without considering the impact the structure will have on the immediate environment. In fact, there are many environmental concerns facing the architectural technician, ranging from seismic to snow, from the effects of the sun to rainfall, and from the control of termites to frost-line depth in certain regions. The results of a national survey conducted by the authors on environmental concerns are printed in the Appendix A survey of regional differences and can be found on the web site for this text at www.wiley.com/go/wakita. An abbreviated list of the most common concerns includes:

1. Climate
2. Soil/geology
3. Seismic activity
4. Fire
5. Energy
6. Foundation design
7. Flooding
8. Distribution of loads/roof loads/vertical loading
9. Structural design
10. Frost depths
11. Drainage
12. Insulation
13. Americans with Disabilities Act (ADA)
14. Water table
15. Exterior finishes

This chapter specifically addresses sun (light, heat, and ultraviolet radiation), sound, deterioration of materials, termites, and underground gases (see Figure 4.1).

■ SUSTAINABLE ARCHITECTURE

The phrase "sustainable architecture" has different meanings for different individuals. For some, it may be as simple as incorporating a solar unit to heat the water for a structure. To others, it may mean harnessing all the forces nature has to offer to sustain a structure. A third—and more comprehensive—approach is to calculate the

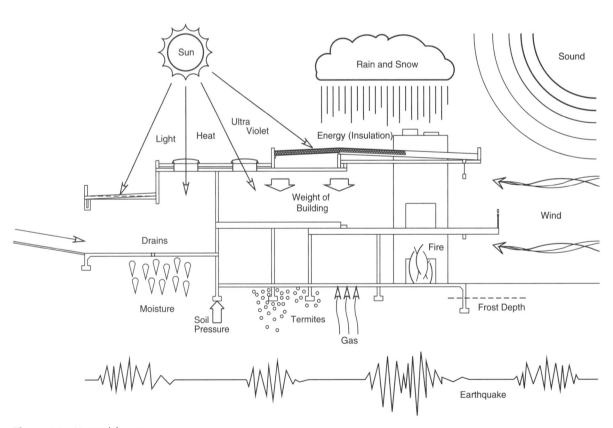

Figure 4.1   Natural forces.

load that a designed structure produces on its immediate surroundings and to provide a solution that successfully reduces this load via natural forces, such as the sun, wind, heat gain and heat loss, and seismic (among others).

In any event, this may be a moot point, because a responsible architect, through his or her formal training, will in the design process call upon all the applicable and naturally available technology to produce the safest and most efficient structure possible. This chapter was written to highlight a few of the concerns that may confront architects and the solutions they may employ to address these concerns. Review Figure 4.1.

LATERAL INFLUENCES

Structures are affected by either high wind conditions or seismic activity/impacts (earthquakes), or both. In many cases, one will be the obviously larger factor, but in either situation, the structure will be required to resist the impact forces. Figure 4.2 illustrates a simple rectangular building and the wind pressure on its sides. The total wind pressure is calculated at the roof and floor diaphragms. This factor is expressed as a force acting on these diaphragms, as indicated by F-1, F-2, and F-3. The diaphragms are considered rigid planes and will distribute the forces into vertical bracing units.

The following are three examples of vertical bracing methods that an architect or structural engineer may implement to resist the lateral forces impinging on the building shown in Figure 4.2.

Figure 4.3 depicts a portion of the west wall in Figure 4.2, where the lateral force F-4 is distributed into the engineered plywood or oriented strand board (OSB) shear walls. The thickness of the plywood panels, the shear connectors, the panel edge nailing, the strapping, and the field nailing are all determined by the force they are intended to resist. The seismic loads, derived from earthquake forces, are generated by the dead weight of the building construction materials. Wind loads are determined by use of historic wind-speed data specific to the building site. The force factors distributed throughout the structure are resolved for seismic impacts in a manner similar to the way forces created by wind conditions are resolved.

Figure 4.4 depicts a steel frame at the opening at the north side of the first-floor level. Windows and garage doors limit the opportunity to use long, rigid wall areas, such as plywood or OSB shear panels, so in that application steel is a desirable solution. The steel columns are cantilevered from a reinforced concrete grade beam. This method may be considered a self-stabilizing frame when used in pairs, or may be called a *flagpole design*

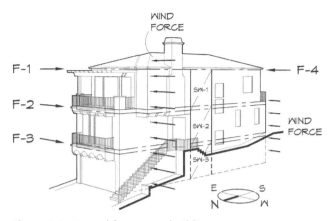

Figure 4.2 Lateral forces on a building.

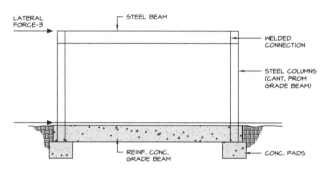

Figure 4.3 Example of steel frame with cantilevered columns.

when used as a singe column. This frame would resist the lateral force F-3.

Another method for resisting the lateral force F-3 is the use of steel columns and a steel beam with welded moment connections at the steel columns and beam connection. This method may be termed a **moment frame** (also referred to as a **rigid frame**). Such a resistive system is named for the moment connection joints within the steel-braced frame. This would be utilized in place of the system shown in Figure 4.4 when the column width or depth is limited. This method is illustrated in Figure 4.5.

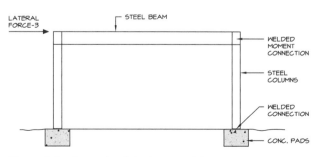

Figure 4.4 Example of steel moment frame.

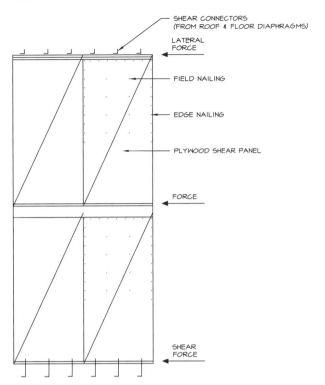

Figure 4.5 Plywood shear panels.

■ ENERGY CONSERVATION

The architect, mechanical engineer, and electrical engineer will constantly be designing and providing methods to conserve energy. These methods will primarily deal with the use of insulation allocated to the roof, wall, and floor assemblies for a specific structure. The assemblies will handle both cold and heat, as well as mechanical and electrical systems, and any innovations that will assist in conserving energy.

Figure 4.6 illustrates a three-story residence in which the entire envelope will be calculated, detailed, and constructed with energy-conserving elements designed to address both warm and cold weather conditions. The first elements are the roof, ceiling, walls, and floors. These will be insulated with a material with an "R" value that will resist heat loss and heat gain. The *R value* is the value assigned to a specific insulating material or a combination of materials that have been tested for their resistive capabilities. One method of combating heat and cold is shown in an example of a roof and exterior wall assembly with insulation at the ceiling and wall locations (see Figure 4.7).

In areas where extreme cold weather conditions prevail in the winter, it is recommended that rigid insulation board be installed at the foundation, around the footing elements, and perhaps under floor slabs. This insulation will prevent excess cold from reaching the floor slab and,

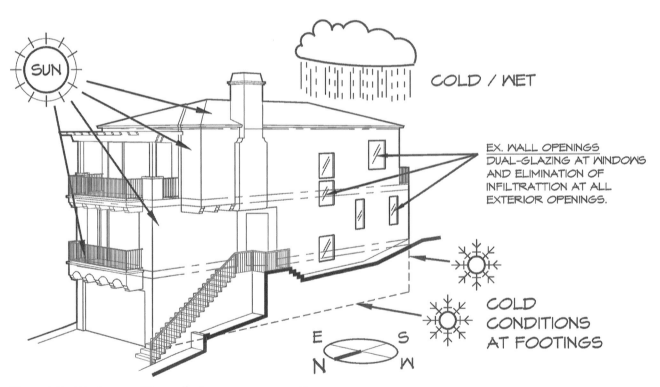

Figure 4.6 Weather conditions affecting energy conservation.

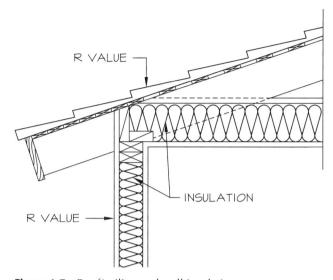

Figure 4.7 Roof/ceiling and wall insulation.

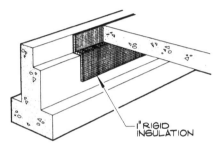

Figure 4.8 Footing insulation. (Reprinted by permission from *Professional Practice of Architectural Detailing*, 3rd Ed., copyright 1999 by John Wiley & Sons, Inc.)

ultimately, the inside of the building. Figure 4.8 shows an example of a footing detail where 1″ rigid insulation board is incorporated at the footing and concrete slab connection. This detail would lower the need for heating and thus reduce the expenditure of energy.

For exterior wall openings, such as windows and doors, where extreme cold and hot weather conditions prevail, it is recommended—and in many municipalities required—that the windows have dual or triple glazing and be installed to prevent air infiltration. Doors should also be weather-stripped and installed to prevent air infiltration.

For many building projects, there may be methods and innovations for heating and cooling systems whereby energy conservation may be attained. One example of supplemental heating is the use of a trombe wall. A trombe wall is a large, massive wall that is typically oriented to absorb the most sunlight during the day; it then radiates the heat back into the living space in the evening when the heat is required to maintain a comfortable temperature. See Figure 4.9.

As mentioned previously, the entire envelope in Figure 4.6 will be calculated and designed with energy

savings in mind. *Envelope* is a term referring to the entire enclosure of the interior living space of a building. This enclosure may utilize insulation materials to prevent heat loss during the winter and heat gain during the summer. An example of a building section for a one-story residence that creates an insulated envelope is illustrated in Figure 4.10.

Figure 4.9 Trombe wall.

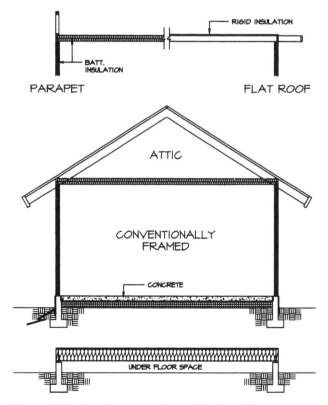

Figure 4.10 Creating an envelope. (Reprinted by permission from *Professional Practice of Architectural Detailing*, 3rd Ed., copyright 1999 by John Wiley & Sons, Inc.).

For the purpose of augmenting lighting conditions in interior spaces, devices such as manufactured skylights and a unit called a "Solatube" are recommended. The Solatube, a reflective tube, is attached to the roof, and a lens is directed to an interior space in the structure. The lens refracts the captured light and disperses it into a specific area. This device can reduce the demand for additional lighting energy.

These and other resources are available for conserving energy in building projects.

■ SOUND

Various types of unpleasant (negative) sounds can enter a structure and cause discomfort to the occupants. Aircraft, vehicles, and trains are some of the sources of sound that create a need to construct buildings that address the problems of sound infiltration. Figure 4.11 depicts some of the major contributors of negative sounds that will be confronted in the detailing and construction of a three-story building. The negative sounds coming from above a building, like those created by various aircraft, will necessitate full sound insulation in the roof and ceiling members and the use of sound-rated windows. For a detail of an insulated wall and ceiling assembly, see Figure 4.7. Sound infiltration through the exterior walls can be controlled through required sound insulation techniques. Insulation of an exterior wall is achieved either with full insulation placed inside the wall or with sheets applied to the outside of the wall. An example of insulated sheets applied to the outside of exterior walls is shown in Figure 4.12.

In projects where concrete masonry units (CMU) are used for the exterior walls, the open cells in the CMU may be filled with a metal baffle or a fibrous filler to de-

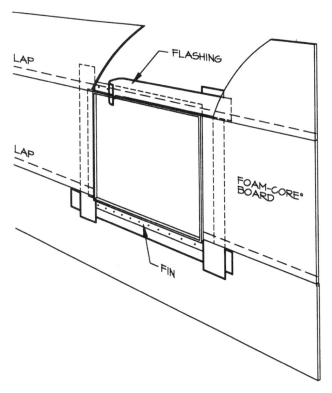

Figure 4.12 Fome-Core® board as a wrap. (Courtesy of International Paper. Reprinted by permission from *Professional Practice of Architectural Detailing,* 3rd Ed., copyright 1999 by John Wiley & Sons, Inc.)

ter or eliminate the infiltration of noise. A standard CMU with two types of insulation is depicted in Figure 4.13.

An effective method of deterring noise transmission through a floor assembly is to use lightweight concrete, carpet, and pad and batt insulation between the floor joists. The finished ceiling below may contain two layers of ⅝"-thick gypsum board attached to resilient channels,

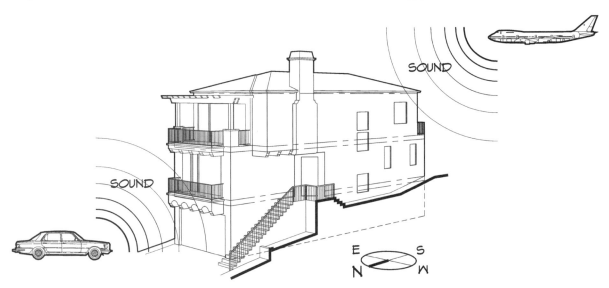

Figure 4.11 Sound-producing forces.

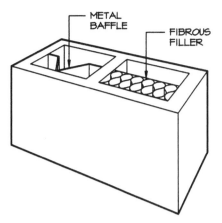

Figure 4.13 Sound insulation in concrete masonry units. (Reprinted by permission from *Professional Practice of Architectural Detailing,* 3rd Ed., copyright 1999 by John Wiley & Sons, Inc.)

which are in turn attached to the wood joists. The resilient channels will provide a vibration isolation separation between the wood joist, which transmits sound, and the living space below. See Figure 4.14.

There are a few wood construction assemblies recommended for deterring sound transmission between the common walls of apartment units or other types of living

units. One method is to provide a double-studded wall with a 1″ air space separating the individual stud walls, along with two layers of gypsum board on both sides of the party wall. Batt insulation is installed between the wood studs. See Figure 4.14.

Another method of interior wall insulation is to construct a wood wall with staggered studs and then continuously weave the sound insulation between the studs. The attachment of gypsum boards to the studs is accomplished with resilient clips. This construction method is shown pictorially in Figure 4.15. This type of assembly is less costly and slightly less effective than that shown in Figure 4.14.

An alternative method for deterring sound transmission through a floor assembly is to have a separate ceiling independent from the floor joist above. This will necessitate separate ceiling joist members with a higher wall plate line to support the floor joist above. The space between the floor joist and the ceiling joist is an ideal arrangement for preventing sound transmission as well as allowing space for plumbing lines, heating ducts, and other equipment requirements. Resilient channels are recommended for the attachment of the gypsum board to the ceiling joist. This detailed assembly is illustrated in Figure 4.16. A drawing depicting this assembly is shown in Figure 4.17.

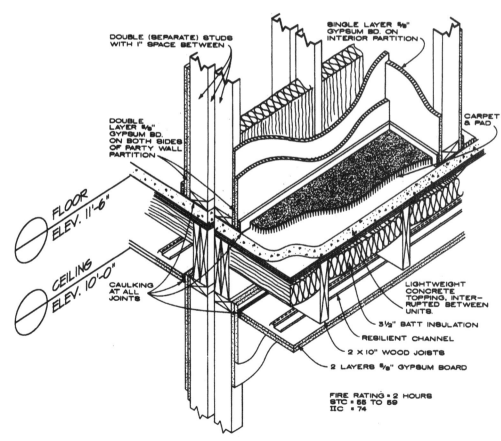

Figure 4.14 Soundproofing between floors. (Reprinted by permission from *Professional Practice of Architectural Detailing,* 3rd Ed., copyright 1999 by John Wiley & Sons, Inc.)

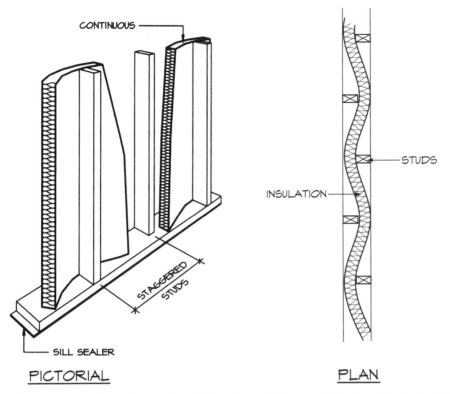

PICTORIAL   PLAN

Figure 4.15 Interior wall sound insulation. (Reprinted by permission from *Professional Practice of Architectural Detailing*, 3rd Ed., copyright 1999 by John Wiley & Sons, Inc.)

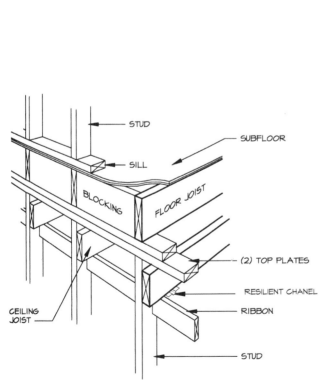

Figure 4.16 Detail of floor-ceiling separation. (Reprinted by permission from *Professional Practice of Architectural Detailing*, 3rd Ed., copyright 1999 by John Wiley & Sons, Inc.)

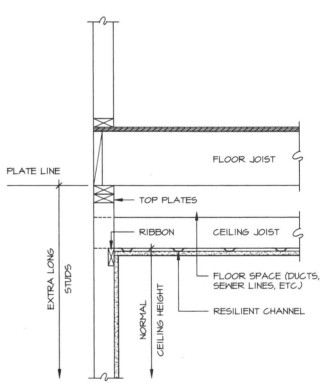

Figure 4.17 Separation of floor joist and ceiling joist. (Reprinted by permission from *Professional Practice of Architectural Detailing*, 3rd Ed., copyright 1999 by John Wiley & Sons, Inc.)

■ SNOW

In geographic areas with snow and prevailing cold climates, the various sections of a structure must be detailed to address these climatic conditions.

As shown in Figure 4.18, the roof structure initially will be designed based on the live load of the snow. This live load figure is usually established by the existing building code in the local municipality. The load may be reduced for each degree of a roof pitch that is more than 20° where snow loads are in excess of 20 pounds per square foot. Special eave requirements are set by the governing building codes. These requirements include a hot or cold underlayment of roofing material on all roofs from the edge of the eave for a distance of up to five feet toward the roof edge.

It should be noted that in areas that are subject to seismic activity, the building official of the municipality will ask that the snow live load also be calculated into the architect's or engineer's lateral design.

It is a good practice, as well as a requirement of the building code, to protect all building exits from sliding ice and snow at the eaves. The use of heat strips and metal flashing at the exit areas in the eave assembly is an acceptable method of deterring ice dams and snow accumulation. Most roof structures with a roof pitch exceeding 70° are considered free of snow loads.

Insulation is required for roof, ceiling, wall, and floor locations. Rigid insulation board is installed at the exterior of the foundation to keep the utility spaces from freezing. See Figure 4.19.

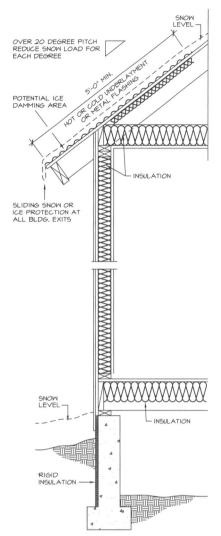

Figure 4.19 Roof/ceiling and wall insulation.

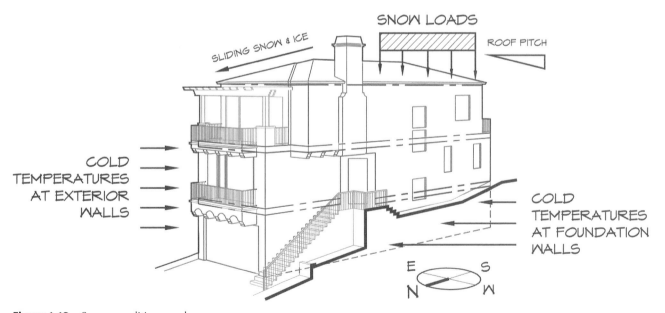

Figure 4.18 Snow conditions and concerns.

■ FIRE AND SMOKE

Fire and smoke are major concerns in the design of all types of structures. Building fires may be ignited by both external and internal causes, ranging from brush or forest fires to various internal causes, including electrical, vehicular, or heating fires.

Fire

Various methods and procedures are used to prevent the destruction of a building by fire. One method is to protect the various materials used in construction of the building. Underwriters Laboratory (UL) conditions, various materials or a combination of materials are tested and given fire rating designations. These fire ratings are expressed as the number of minutes and hours it takes a material to catch fire. For example, a wall may be fire rated as a two-hour firewall, or a specific door may have a rating of sixty minutes. Structural columns can be assembled to provide a four-hour fire rating, whereas a glass panel may be manufactured with a twenty-minute fire rating. Laboratory testing has produced results in a time/temperature chart illustrating temperature in degrees and time in hours.

Figure 4.20 is a chart showing temperatures measured in degrees Fahrenheit (°F) and Celsius (°C) as they relate to a particular length of time measured in hours. An example, using this chart, is a one-hour fire rating for a material or combination of materials that would withstand a fire with a temperature of 1,500°F or 860°C.

Although all parts of a structure are vulnerable to fire, the safety of the occupants and the integrity of the structure can be enhanced by providing construction details that incorporate fire-rated materials to deter a fire or to minimize the spread of a fire. Buildings in high-risk brush fire areas can use exterior materials that will withstand high temperatures. This will give the building's occupants a longer time to evacuate the building in the event of a fire. For example, a cement tile roofing material

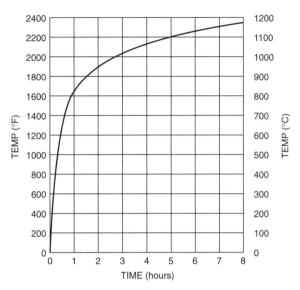

Figure 4.20 Time/temperature curve. (Reprinted by permission from *Professional Practice of Architectural Detailing*, 3rd Ed., copyright 1999 by John Wiley & Sons, Inc.)

can be used for brush fire protection in a single-family residence. The construction detail of the eave and soffit assembly for such a single-family residence is depicted in Figure 4.21 with a reference detail bubble "B" of the construction. Using a nonflammable roof material, the soffit detail is enclosed with a 1"-thick cement plaster finish that will deter a fire from spreading into the attic spaces. This detail is illustrated in detail and pictorial form in Figure 4.22. Note that fireblocking is installed below the soffit area to deter any fire that may occur in the exterior wall. To complete a fire-protective envelope of the exterior materials, this residence has a wood-sided exterior wall finish. There is a layer of one-hour-rated fire-resistant hardboard and fire taping at all the joints of the hardboard. This is installed prior to installation of the

NORTH ELEVATION

Figure 4.21 Exterior elevation—external fire control.

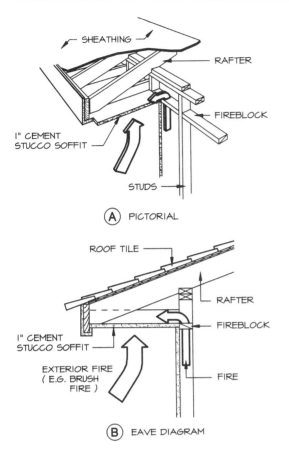

Figure 4.22 Roof tiles, cement stucco soffits, and fireblocking. (Reprinted by permission from *Professional Practice of Architectural Detailing,* 3rd Ed., copyright 1999 by John Wiley & Sons, Inc.)

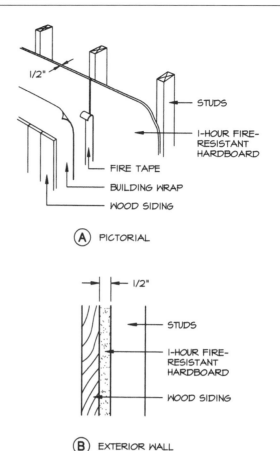

Figure 4.23 Fire-resistant stud walls. (Reprinted by permission from *Professional Practice of Architectural Detailing,* 3rd Ed., copyright 1999 by John Wiley & Sons, Inc.)

wood siding. A detail and a pictorial drawing are shown in Figure 4.23.

Smoke infiltration is a grave concern because most "fire" deaths are actually caused by the smoke rather than the flames or heat. Detailing the openings in walls, such as those for doors and windows, will reduce the potential of smoke infiltration. One means of reducing the infiltration of smoke through doors is to mill the head and jamb sections and the doorstop from one piece of wood. This feature is required by most building codes and fire protection agencies. A detail of a jamb and head section for a door assembly incorporating a one-piece section is illustrated in detail and pictorial form in Figure 4.24.

Another concern in regard to fire is a building's stairs and exits. During the planning of a building, the architect must provide clearly defined pathways to fire exits. Fire exits and their layouts are determined by the governing fire protection agency and the requirements of applicable building codes. Distances between stair exits and the number of exits are also established by the governing

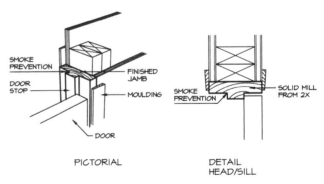

Figure 4.24 Solid-finish jamb and doorstop. (Reprinted by permission from *Professional Practice of Architectural Detailing,* 3rd Ed., copyright 1999 by John Wiley & Sons, Inc.)

agencies. In multilevel buildings, a correct stairwell design will allow people to move quickly down the stairs to an outdoor access without any interferences or obstructions in the exiting path.

A typical requirement for distance between stairwells is that it must exceed half the distance of the diagonal

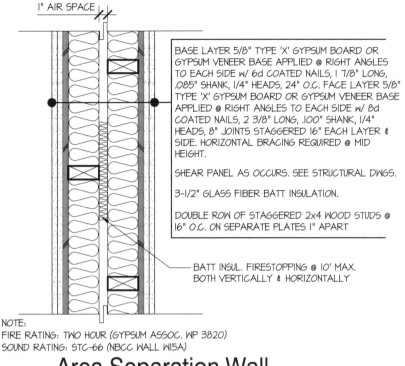

1" AIR SPACE

BASE LAYER 5/8" TYPE 'X' GYPSUM BOARD OR GYPSUM VENEER BASE APPLIED @ RIGHT ANGLES TO EACH SIDE w/ 6d COATED NAILS, 1 7/8" LONG, .085" SHANK, 1/4" HEADS, 24" O.C. FACE LAYER 5/8" TYPE 'X' GYPSUM BOARD OR GYPSUM VENEER BASE APPLIED @ RIGHT ANGLES TO EACH SIDE w/ 8d COATED NAILS, 2 3/8" LONG, .100" SHANK, 1/4" HEADS, 8" JOINTS STAGGERED 16" EACH LAYER & SIDE. HORIZONTAL BRACING REQUIRED @ MID HEIGHT.

SHEAR PANEL AS OCCURS. SEE STRUCTURAL DWGS.

3-1/2" GLASS FIBER BATT INSULATION.

DOUBLE ROW OF STAGGERED 2x4 WOOD STUDS @ 16" O.C. ON SEPARATE PLATES 1" APART

BATT INSUL. FIRESTOPPING @ 10' MAX. BOTH VERTICALLY & HORIZONTALLY

NOTE:
FIRE RATING: TWO HOUR (GYPSUM ASSOC. WP 3820)
SOUND RATING: STC-66 (NBCC WALL W15A)

Area Separation Wall
SCALE: 1 1/2"=1'-0"

Figure 4.25 Two-hour area separation wall detail.

measure of the building. The local building code establishes requirements for the construction of the stairway walls. The stair tower is typically a fire-rated assembly. An example of a wood-constructed two-hour fire wall assembly detail is illustrated in Figure 4.25; in this example, a two-hour wall construction encloses the stairwell.

All fire-rated doors must swing in the direction of the exit access. Note, too, in this example, the required two-hour wall construction that encloses the stairwell. The local building code establishes requirements for the construction of the stairway walls. An example of a pictorial view of a wood-constructed, two-hour, fire wall assembly detail is illustrated in Figure 4.26.

Smoke

The exhausting of smoke is a major concern in fires that occur in buildings. It has been determined that smoke kills more people in building fires than heat itself, flames, or structural failure. Therefore, smoke control, whether through deterring smoke infiltration, as previously discussed, or by exhausting smoke from within the structure, is important. A common method for exhausting smoke from a building that is on fire is to use

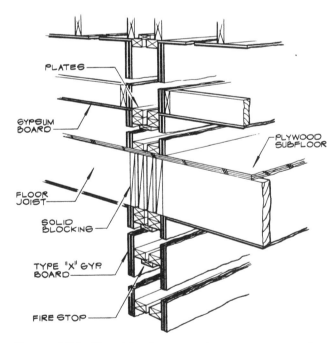

PLATES

GYPSUM BOARD

PLYWOOD SUBFLOOR

FLOOR JOIST

SOLID BLOCKING

TYPE "X" GYP BOARD

FIRE STOP

Figure 4.26 Pictorial view, two-hour area separation wall. (Reprinted by permission from *Professional Practice of Architectural Detailing,* 3rd Ed., copyright 1999 by John Wiley & Sons, Inc.)

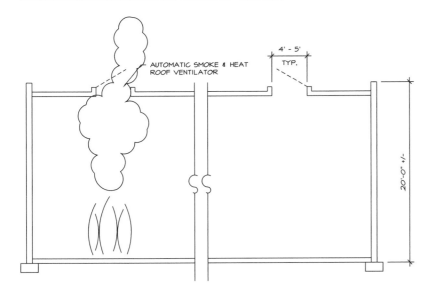

Figure 4.27 Smoke and heat roof ventilators.

automatic roof hatch ventilators. These automatic ventilators, which are usually found in smaller buildings, open individually by means of a device that is activated by either smoke or heat. An example of a roof hatch ventilator that may be installed on a one-story industrial building is illustrated in Figure 4.27. The sizes and locations of these ventilators are determined by the governing fire protection agency and the building code.

Concerning fire and smoke as they relate to the design of a structure, the architect should be aware of the following:

1. How occupants exit from a building in fire and smoke conditions
2. Fire ratings of materials and code requirements
3. Methods of preventing smoke infiltration and the spread of fire
4. Vulnerable areas within a structure
5. Methods of reducing the spread of fire
6. How to protect the integrity of the structural members from fire
7. Methods of exhausting smoke to the outside (the major concern)

■ TEMPERATURE

Outside temperatures affect the design of building structures. In areas with high temperatures, buildings are insulated and provided with various types of mechanical systems to control the temperature within the structure's habitable areas. Temperature also has a large effect on the structural integrity of a building. For example, buildings that are constructed with a concrete frame and a concrete floor system are detailed at various connections

to allow for expansion and contraction of the various concrete elements affected by temperature fluctuations. Figure 4.28 shows a concrete column and a concrete floor beam connection that provides expansion joint clearances, as well as an electrometric pad for ease of movement. Such a pad need not be anchored; it is shock absorbent and returns to its original shape and dimension (the soles of basketball shoes are made of this same material). Electrometric pads are best used for putting temporary gymnasium wood floor over concrete floor.

Another floor condition that may require an expansion joint appears when there is a large expanse of floor area, as shown in Figure 4.29. These expansion joints are

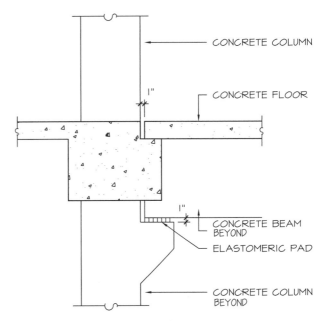

Figure 4.28 Expansion joint detail.

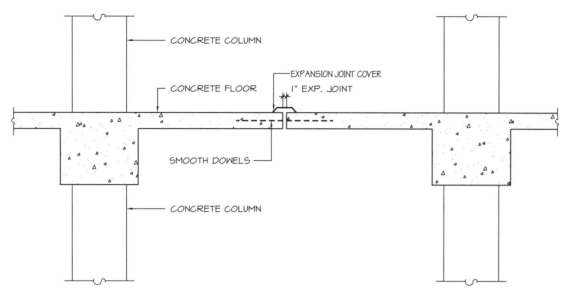

Figure 4.29　Floor expansion joint.

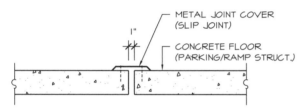

Figure 4.30　Expansion joint cover.

placed in locations that are visually unobtrusive and will not require expensive covering methods. Concrete parking structures with vast areas of concrete floor require that various locations have expansion joints. The expansion joints are normally covered with an aluminum metal strip to allow easy passage of automobile traffic. These joints are referred to as *slip joints*. See Figure 4.30.

■ DETERIORATION

Many steps are taken in detailing the methods used to reduce or eliminate deterioration of the various building materials in a structure. As we have seen, the use of metal flashing for foundation details, roof conditions, and other features provides wood with some protection from deterioration. However, other conditions can also subject wood to deterioration.

For example, future deterioration is a great concern where there are wood posts on concrete porches. Water from rain or hose streams and sprays is a great catalyst for deterioration at the base of a wood post. One method for detailing this connection to prevent deterioration at the base of the post is to elevate the post base above the concrete patio. See Figure 4.31. As shown, a galvanized

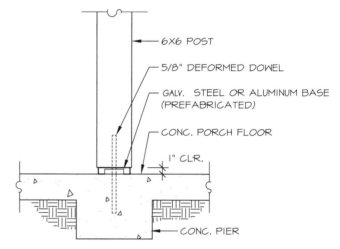

Figure 4.31　Elevated porch post.

metal or aluminum prefabricated base is positioned under the post to provide a 1" clearance above the concrete patio. Openings in the metal base unit will provide for water drainage.

Methods of anchoring exterior wood posts that may be used for fences, balustrades, and wood trellises vary as to how they may be detailed. Figure 4.32 depicts an example of detailing the anchorage of a wooden fence post. This is recommended because the wood post is elevated above the soil and is protected from both soil and water by the concrete pier. Anchorage of the wood post to the concrete pier is achieved by using a manufactured or prefabricated galvanized steel "U" strap and machine bolts. The sloping top perimeter of the concrete pier prevents water from collecting at the base of the post and metal strap.

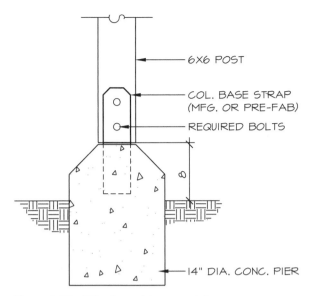

Figure 4.32 Wood post/pier assemblies.

■ DRAINAGE/RAINFALL

The accumulation of rainwater may lead to erosion or flooding problems. Because all regions of the country have specific and particular climatic conditions relative to the amounts of rainfall, the architect will need to anticipate and solve any problems of water drainage that may affect a building's structural areas and site conditions. As a general rule, water must drain away from the building to appropriate drainage devices or catch basins.

Roof Drainage

Roof designs and drainage devices are designed and detailed to dissipate and control rainwater. For example, a very low-pitched roof design will create a slower flow of water runoff, which may reduce the possibility of flooding around a building's foundation. Devices such as code-acceptable manufactured roof drain units or conventional gutters and downspouts should be placed in key locations on the roof to accommodate and control any amount of rainwater. An example of a roof drain is shown in Figure 4.33. Note that an overflow drain is incorporated as a safety measure in case there is blockage in the roof drain. Blockage may be a result of tree leaves, debris, and the like. The solutions for exterior deck drainage are similar to those recommended for a roof drainage system.

Roof drainage that is conducted to the roof eaves or overhangs is detailed in various ways. A recommended method of detailing an eave for dispersing water from the roof areas is to provide a gutter and downspouts. This method will control and direct the water to areas

that will disperse the water away from the building, thus deterring erosion at the perimeter of the building. The concentration of water caused by the downspouts can be quickly dissipated with use of a splash block. Another method of dispersing the water flow concentrated at the eave, in lieu of metal downspouts, is to attach a steel or aluminum chain from the roof gutter to a concrete splash block. The shape of the chain will act to slow the water

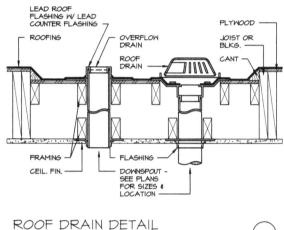

ROOF DRAIN DETAIL

Figure 4.33 Roof drain section. (Reprinted by permission from *Professional Practice of Architectural Detailing,* 3rd Ed., copyright 1999 by John Wiley & Sons, Inc.)

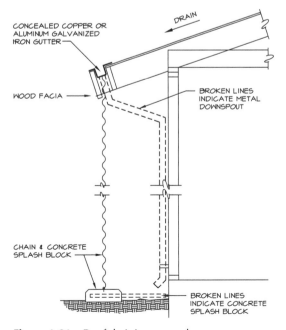

Figure 4.34 Roof draining examples.

flow and further limit the possibility of erosion. These detailed conditions are depicted in Figure 4.34.

Figure 4.35 illustrates another method of dispersing water drainage, which utilizes a gravel-filled pit encased in a concrete or vitreous container. This method may be restricted in areas where the soil conditions are not conducive to dispersing water this way. For instance, this may not be a good idea for hillside property where slides may result. The enclosed gravel areas are referred to as *drywells*.

In areas where soil conditions may dictate how water drainage is dispersed, other methods for roof drainage will be required. If you design drainage for wetland areas, check with your local building department. Figure 4.36, a gray-water option, illustrates a detail in which the downspouts or leaders are connected directly to a vitreous clay pipe that conducts the water to other drainage devices. The sizes of the downspouts or leaders and drainage pipes are determined by the tributary areas of the roof that conduct water to any one of the downspout locations.

When a drainage condition is directing the flow of water to a certain area of a building, such as a garage door, it is recommended that a trough drain, drainage pipes, and an aluminum or cast iron grate cover be used. This construction assembly will minimize the chance of water entering the garage area. See Figure 4.37. Note in the detail that cast iron, vitreous clay, or polyvinyl chloride (PVC) pipe is located at the ends of the trough to conduct the water away from the building.

A frequent problem at a sloping site is how to control the rainwater and reduce the erosion caused by a concentrated rainwater flow. A recommended method is installation of a concrete swale or drainage pipes on the downslope to collect the rainwater and conduct the flow into recommended drainage disbursement or erosion devices. Depending on the slope of the downhill area, numerous swales and drainage pipes may be required.

If the water flow is to be distributed on an existing site, it is recommended that a method of dissipating the flow of water be designed to deter or minimize erosion of the soil. One way to dissipate the concentration of water flow and control soil erosion is to construct a drainage device referred to as a *riprap*. This device is placed in a location where it can collect the water from swales and/or pipes. It is constructed with a concrete base and inlaid with broken concrete or protruding rocks, which are spaced apart to slow down and dissipate the water flow. See Figure 4.38.

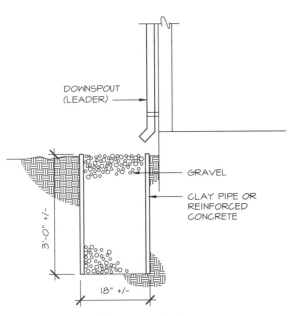

Figure 4.35 Roof downspout drainage.

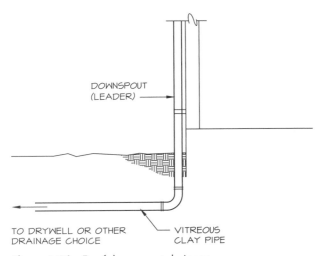

Figure 4.36 Roof downspout drainage.

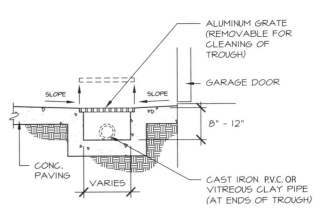

Figure 4.37 Trough drain detail.

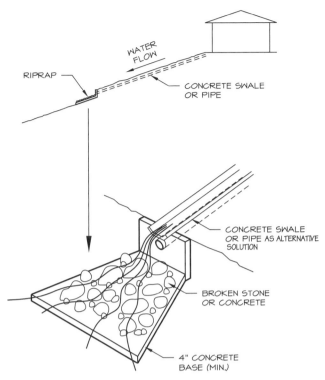

Figure 4.38 Riprap detail.

UNDERGROUND GAS CONTROL

Industrial and manufacturing buildings that are constructed on sites where there is evidence of underground gas, such as methane, will require a method of dissipating the underground gas. A recommended method is to install collector pipes below the concrete floor and vent these pipes to an outside area. Figure 4.39 illustrates the partial foundation plan for an industrial building. It shows the recommended locations of 4″ "0" perforated pipes and reference detail symbols for the required pipe and venting installations. Note, in detail A, that a 24″ × 24″ gravel-filled trench encases the 4″ "0" perforated pipe as a means of collecting the gas. Detail B illustrates a method of venting the gas to the outside air through use of a 2½″ "0" vent in the exterior wall, terminating at a minimum distance of two feet above the roof.

WATER TABLE

The term **water table** has two meanings. The first refers to the elevation (height) at which groundwater is atmospheric. The second refers to an aboveground projection that sheds water away from a structure. A sample detail of a water table at a foundation wall is shown in Figure 4.40.

First, let us establish some basic working facts about water, the movement of water, and water tables:

A. Water will pass easily through clean gravel and sand and seek its own level.
B. Perforated pipe in gravel provides an efficient means of travel for water. A good use for these pipes is under slabs and around basements.
C. Water travels very slowly through silts and very little through clay. Thus, it is important to use gravel to encourage water to flow away from a structure.
D. There are two basic ways of keeping water from penetrating a substructure when the substructure is below the water table. The first is through waterproofing with a barrier and draining the water by way of a **sump pit** (a tank for holding water that is under grade until it is pumped out) and a pump. Note that waterproofing is not 100% effective.
E. Municipalities require that when work is being done in an excavated area below the water table, the area must remain dry during construction. This can be accomplished with a pump or a series of pumps that change the water table configuration, as shown in Figure 4.41. An example of an area where this might occur is shown in Figure 4.42. Compacted fill is located in such a manner that the water table is just below the top of the fill. The foundation of a structure with such a fill will be built as shown in Figure 4.43.

FROST LINE/FROST DEPTH

In many parts of the world, temperatures fall below freezing. Thus, a new level of measurement is introduced in reference to existing grade. This measurement, called the **frost line** or **frost depth**, is a significant datum for building (see Figure 4.44). These lines and numbers on the map represent levels below the grade under which water no longer freezes. This is important, because at these levels the moisture will not become a solid, expand, and cause damage to a foundation system. The figures given on this map are in inches and are for general use only. Frost lines should always be checked, because they are established by local code. The national code requires that a footing be placed a minimum of 1′-0″ below the frost line (see Figure 4.45). The ground will not freeze below the frost line, making this a stable foundation.

To make us truly international or universal, rather than local or national, we must investigate cold climates in other parts of the world. There are climates such as these in the Arctic Circle, where we must deal with permafrost. We see this in one of the U.S. states, Alaska. The existence of permafrost means that the annual mean

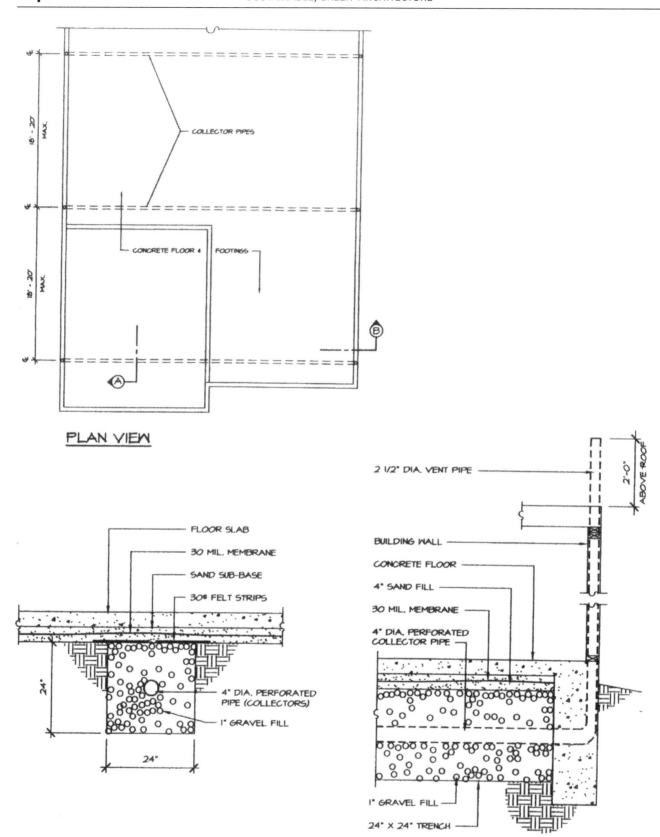

Figure 4.39 Partial building foundation plan.

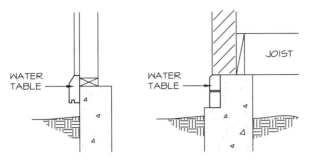

Figure 4.40 Water table at foundation plan.

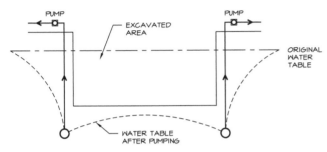

Figure 4.41 Diagram of dewatering.

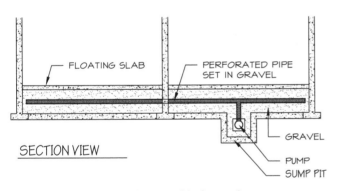

SECTION VIEW

Figure 4.42 Removal of water table from substructure.

temperature is 32°F. These areas are also subject to very high winds, extremely cold temperatures, snow drifts, continuous dark days, and very low sun angles (vertical angle), in addition to permafrost.

How do we deal with this? We raise the floor level or build a gravel bed upon which the building sits. See Figure 4.46. Figure 4.46A shows how a building on permafrost is configured, and Figure 4.46B shows a building built where there is sporadic permafrost.

■ TERMITES AND TERMITE TREATMENT

The durability and longevity of wood are improved by preservative treatment techniques. The treatment of wood is usually recommended for two reasons: (1) the location of a member subjects it to an unsafe amount of moisture content, especially where the climate or site conditions promote decay; and (2) termite infestation.

Termites are a major problem in some of our states. California, Hawaii, and the southeastern states are some of the most heavily infested areas. Although not everyone practices in an infested area, architects should be familiar with the methods used to deal with termite infestation. Figure 4.47 shows the distribution of termite infestation in the United States. The chart is calibrated in modest, moderate, and heavy infestation areas, and reveals that the areas most heavily affected are in our southern states.

When a structure is supported by wood members embedded in the ground, the members should be of an approved **pressure-treated (P.T.) wood.** P.T. wood is impregnated with toxic chemicals at elevated pressures and temperatures. One of the following classes of preservatives is commonly used: (1) oil-borne preservatives, (2) water-borne preservatives, or (3) water-repellent preservatives. Code standards for preservatives and treatments should be in accordance with those of the American Wood Preservers Association. Water-borne or

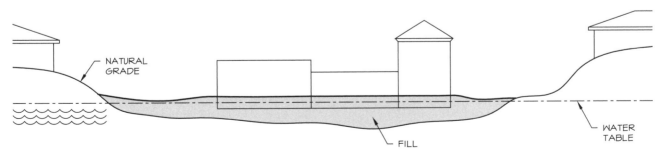

Figure 4.43 Fill at water table.

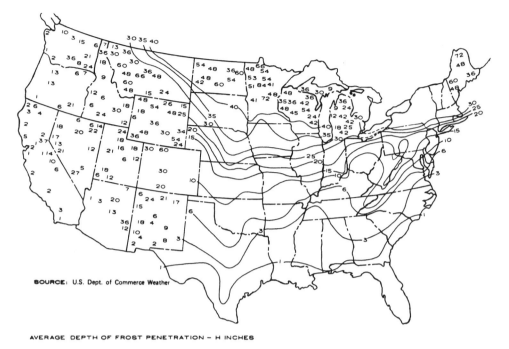

SOURCE: U.S. Dept. of Commerce Weather

AVERAGE DEPTH OF FROST PENETRATION – H INCHES

Figure 4.44 Frost depths. (Reprinted by permission from *Architectural Graphic Standards,* 9th Ed., copyright © 1994 by John Wiley & Sons, Inc.)

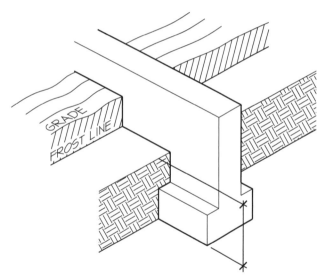

GRADE
FROST LINE

Figure 4.45 Frost line as a datum for footing depth.

water-repellent preservatives should be specified when members are to be painted or when finish materials are to be nailed to the members.

Wood members, such as sills, ledgers, and sleepers, that come in contact with concrete or masonry that itself is in direct contact with earth should be of an approved treated wood and approved by the local building department.

The effectiveness of treated wood depends on several factors: (1) the type of chemical used, (2) the amount of treatment penetration, (3) the amount of treatment retention, and (4) uniform distribution of the preservative.

In the course of detailing, the architect should be cognizant of the application of treated wood. Examples of details incorporating a treated wood mudsill, ledger, and sleeper are illustrated in Figure 4.48.

It should be emphasized that damage from moisture decay and termites develops slowly. Therefore, inspections should be done to ensure that proper clearances are being maintained and that termite barriers have been implemented and installed correctly. See Figure 4.49.

■ ENERGY SOURCES

Wind

If you seek to use wind for energy and cannot use a propeller-type wing unit, there is now an alternative. The U.S. military uses a hybrid form of what is called a **vertical axis wind turbine** (VAWT), which converts wind energy into electrical power. This omnidirectional, low-speed generator can be used practically anywhere that has good wind exposure. Presently, the unit size is 30″ in diameter and 8′ high, weighs 60 pounds, and rotates from a speed of 0 to a 600-rpm peak. It remains visible to birds as the speed increases. See Figure 4.50.

Because of its relatively small size, and the fact that it can be effective in almost any vertical position, this application lends itself to designs that are curvilinear and kinetic in nature.

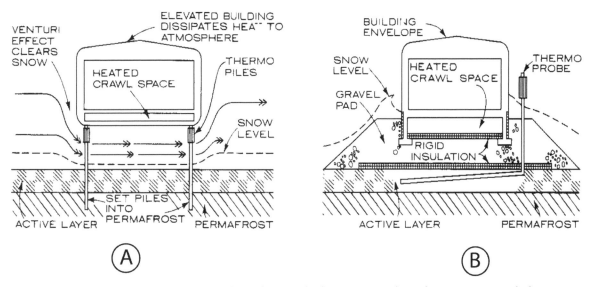

Figure 4.46 Building on permafrost. (Architectural Graphic Standards CD-ROM, John Wiley & Sons Inc. Hoboken, NJ. Copyright 2000.)

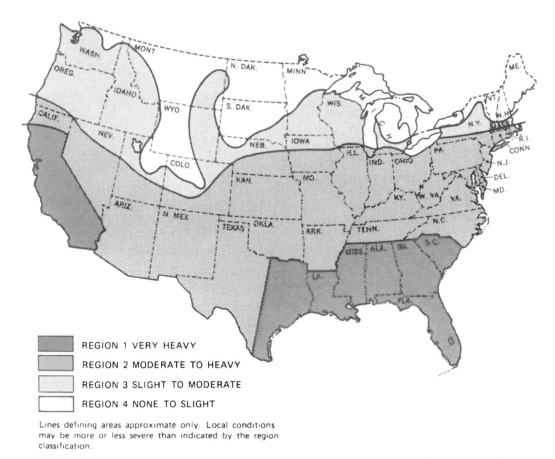

REGION 1 VERY HEAVY

REGION 2 MODERATE TO HEAVY

REGION 3 SLIGHT TO MODERATE

REGION 4 NONE TO SLIGHT

Lines defining areas approximate only. Local conditions may be more or less severe than indicated by the region classification.

Figure 4.47 Regions of termite infestation. (Reprinted by permission from *Architectural Graphic Standards,* 9th Ed., copyright © 1994 by John Wiley & Sons, Inc.)

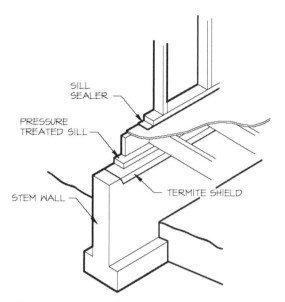

Figure 4.48　Mudsill area.

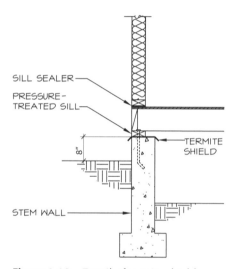

Figure 4.49　Detail of termite shield.

Geothermal

If you are one of the lucky inhabitants of an area that nature has provided with **geothermal** energy (a name that comes from the term *geothermic,* having to do with the heat of the Earth's interior), you should look into the feasibility of tapping into this natural resource. Geothermal energy is accessible in many areas around the world; Figure 4.51 shows the locations of the best of these areas. If you are in one of these geothermal zones, you must first investigate the cost, how you can amortize the cost of installation, and the impact the equipment will have on the aesthetics of the structure. Remember that cost rebates may be available through the federal or state government or from a public utility.

In California, a production well is drilled in excess of a mile to reach the hydrothermal reservoirs where 80%

Figure 4.50　Wind-power air turbine. (Wepower LLC ©.)

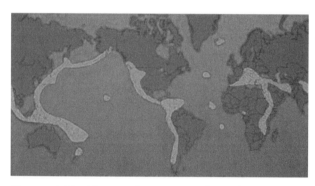

Figure 4.51　Hottest known geothermal areas. (U.S. Department of Energy, Geothermal Education Office. Earth Policy Institute.)

of the state's geothermal energy lies. Steam from these reservoirs, which can reach temperatures of 360°F, is used to turn turbines; the electricity produced thereby is distributed via power lines. The cooled water returns to the reservoir by way of an injection well. Returned water is reheated and may be used over again. The whole process is shown diagrammatically in Figure 4.52.

Areas that have hot springs, such as Idaho, often simply use those springs to heat buildings in the winter. It

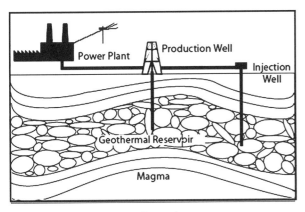

Figure 4.52 Tapping geothermal areas.

might also be practical to go down into the earth some 80 to 100 feet and use the natural temperature of the earth to cool or warm a building.

Solar

One of the best uses of solar energy applications, from both functional and aesthetic standpoints, is the giant metal flower located in Buenos Aires, in the United Nations Plaza. Designed by Eduardo Catalano, the "Floralis Generica" sits in a reflecting pool in a park full of plants and flowers. (The designer chose the name *Generica* to indicate that the installation is a symbol of all flowers.) Its petals, each of which measures 13 meters long by 7 meters wide and incorporates solar panels, close in the evening and remain closed from sunset to sunrise. During the day, it moves in 20-minute intervals to mimic a flower—a perfect marriage between technology and nature. See it on the chapter opener.

Three of the most natural, free, and significant solar energy sources are heat, light, and ultraviolet rays. We can use two out of three of these sources. The third (ultraviolet rays) causes cancer in humans, but is needed by plant life for **photosynthesis,** a process of making food that also creates the oxygen that we breathe.

Knowledge of the Sun. In its simplest form, the sun can be a negative in architecture. If, for example, we let direct sun into a structure in order to get light and heat, we also create a health hazard: prolonged exposure to the sun's ultraviolet rays is known to cause both basal cell carcinomas (skin cancer) and melanoma (a more serious form of cancer).

Position of the Sun. If you can control the temperature extremes and glare that the sun creates in the structure, you will have captured and made the best use of the sun's solar energy. To attain this control, you must determine the longest day and the shortest day at the building site. June 21 and December 21, known as the summer and

winter solstices, respectively, are what we as architectural designers must seek out prior to executing a design. The summer and winter solstices can best be determined by finding the sun's angles to the Earth and locating its latitude. *Latitude* refers to (artificial) horizontal markings we have placed on the Earth; *longitude* refers to the vertical markings we use as a datum. (It is easy to remember which is which when you pronounce these words: Note the shape of your mouth as you say *latitude* or *longitude*. Your lips will get wider when *latitude* is spoken, and the "long" of *longitude* will be pronounced with more vertically formed lips.)

Latitude. Clearly, many of you already know how to find the latitude of a given city. For beginners, we suggest that you access the U.S. Department of Commerce, National Oceanic and Atmospheric Administration (NOAA) web site on your computer. It will direct you to NOAA's new solar calculation. It even gives you specific directions on how to use the solar calculation (remember that you want latitude). For example, if you type in "Berlin, Germany," 52°19′48″ will appear. If you are a student, find out if the architecture department has a device used to measure the vertical and horizontal angles of the sun at a given time based on the latitude of the location. Charts of such information are available; see Figure 4.53 for a listing of states and their latitude range.

Suppose that you were interested in Las Vegas (36° – 10′) and Berlin (52° – 19′ ±). Charts may be available for 52° + and 36° +, such as the one for Berlin found in Figure 4.54, or you may find this information via computer. AutoCAD is preloaded with latitude ranges for almost every city and country in the world. If you input the date, day, latitude, and time of the day, the program will give you the vertical angle and the horizontal movement of the sun. If you want to see the shadow patterns from a building, you must insert the day, date, latitude, and the specific hour before AutoCAD can give you the results. However, the process is cumbersome at best. If you want to follow the shadow pattern for a specific date, it is much quicker and easier to use Revit, which can do this for you. See Chapter 3 for such a display. If you do not have Revit, you could still plot the data in Figures 4.54 and 4.55, though it is a time-consuming process.

In the recent past, one would take the information such as that found in Figures 4.54 and 4.55 and plot the data points to produce a diagram like that in Figure 4.56. View A is a top view, like a CT scan, for 52° latitude and 36° latitude, approximately the latitude of Berlin and Las Vegas. Another method would be to find a series of charts for this desired latitude, similar to those in Figures 4.56B and 4.56C, and laboriously plot the shades and shadows. This would assist the architect in designing the window/glass door locations, patios, landscape, and overhang of the roof, to mention just a few applications.

Alabama	30–35°	Montana	45–49°
Arizona	31–37°	Nebraska	40–43°
Arkansas	33–36°30′	Nevada	35–42°
California	32° 30–42°	New Hampshire	43–45°
Colorado	37–41°	New Jersey	39–41°
Connecticut	41–42°	New Mexico	31–37°
Delaware	38 30′–42°	New York	41–45°
District of Columbia	39°	North Carolina	34–37°
Florida	25–31°	North Dakota	46–49°
Georgia	31–35°	Ohio	39–42°
Idaho	42–49°	Oklahoma	34–37°
Illinois	37°–42°30′	Oregon	42–46°
Indiana	38–42°	Pennsylvania	40–42°
Iowa	41–43°	Rhode Island	41–42°
Kansas	37–39°	South Carolina	32–35°
Kentucky	37–39°	South Dakota	43–46°
Louisiana	29–33°	Tennessee	35–37°
Maine	43–47°	Texas	26–36°
Maryland	38–40°	Utah	37–42°
Massachusetts	42–43°	Vermont	43–45°
Michigan	42–47°	Virginia	36° 30′–39°
Minnesota	43° 30′–49°	Washington	46–49°
Mississippi	30–35°	West Virginia	37–41°
Missouri	36–41°	Wisconsin	42° 30′–47°
		Wyoming	41–45°

Figure 4.53   Range of latitude by state.

Winter Dec 21

	Vertical Angle	Horizontal Angle
Sunrise	0°	S 42°
10:00 am	9°	S 30°
12:00 (Noon)	12°	S
2:00 pm	10°	S 31° W
Sunset	0°	S 42° W

Summer June 21

	Vertical Angle	Horizontal Angle
Sunrise	0°	E 49° S
8:00 am	30°	E 21 1/2° S
10:00 am	54-1/2°	E 35° S
12:00 (Noon)	64-1/2°	S
2:00 pm	56°	S 57° W
4:00 pm	37°	W 1° N
Sunset	0°	E 48° N

Figure 4.54   Berlin (52° − 19±′).

Winter Dec 21

	Vertical Angle	Horizontal Angle
Sunrise	0°	E 34° S
10:00 am	21°	E 60° S
12:00 (Noon)	27°	S
2:00 pm	21-1/2°	S 36° W
4:00 pm	6°	S 60° W
Sunset	0°	S 67-1/2° W

Summer June 21

	Vertical Angle	Horizontal Angle
Sunrise		E 3° S
8:00 am	36°	W 11° N
10:00 am	56°	E 21° S
12:00 (Noon)	80°	S
2:00 pm	62°	W 6° E
4:00 pm	37°	W 11° E
Sunset	0°	W 37-1/2° N

Figure 4.55   Las Vegas (36° −10±′).

What to Expect. If you know how to effectively determine the interaction of the sun and a building, but do so only as an afterthought, you have done a disservice to the client. It is better to consider and verify the factors of heat gain and light penetration before the structure is designed. Validation after the fact is fine, but it is too late to change the design at that point. You must know the effects of the sun on your proposed structure at any time and date, and use that knowledge to inform and enhance your design.

Plotting in 3-D. Check your site and establish the bearing (N, S, E, W). Then plot the movement of the sun on June 21 and December 21 (see Figure 4.57).

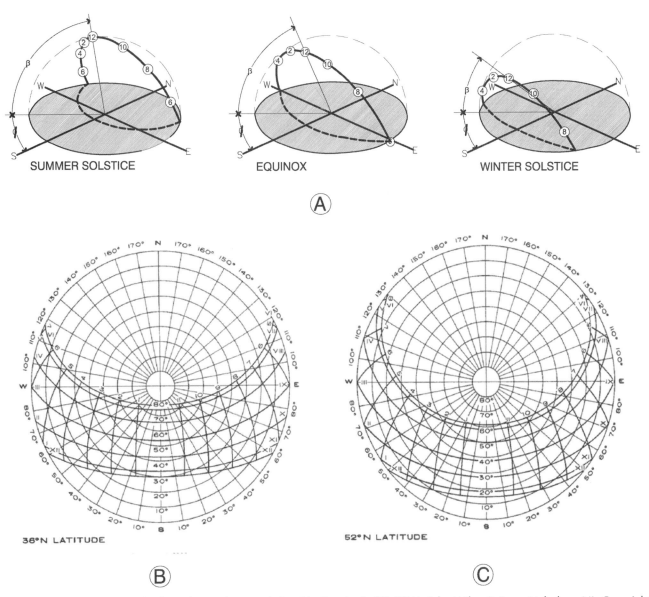

Figure 4.56 Sun position by latitude. (Architectural Graphic Standards CD-ROM, John Wiley & Sons, Hoboken, NJ. Copyright 2000.)

This will give you an idea of how the sun moves across the sky in the winter and the summer. Next, show the step, drawing your sets onto the grid. Now you are ready to design your structure—or maybe not! You will also want to explore the prevailing wind in conjunction with the sun, correlate the annual rainfall, noise, and so on. BIM suggests that you check all the elements in select materials by rotating a 3-D model of the structure on the site, to determine the effects of rain, wind, and other elements on the structure. As educators, we suggest that you study and learn about one design element at a time, even though you will eventually have to consider all of them when you execute a design.

Summary

It is not sustainable to build by exporting significant grade from the site to a landfill or another location; in fact, we feel that trucking tons of soil offsite is just about the least sustainable thing an architect can do. Use the excess earth to improve the flow of water more efficiently, landscape with it to separate private space from public space, or create a berm (ledge or shoulder along the edge of the site) to control street noise.

In this chapter, we have only briefly discussed the leading available energy sources. Many factors must be considered for a green design, including cost, environmental

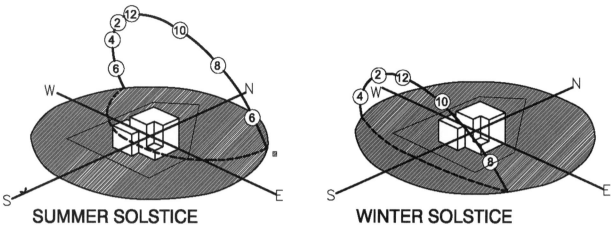

SUMMER SOLSTICE   **WINTER SOLSTICE**

Figure 4.57   Checking massing forms with summer and winter solstices.

impact, and the project's individual contribution to preserving the available energy sources. Maximize the positive global impact of your structure!

For the construction documents, especially the working drawings that are our primary responsibility, you must carefully consider the following:

1. Will the use of a particular design element affect the structure overall? For example, the decision to change from asphalt shingles to a tile roof will also increase the weight of the roof, as well as the cost of the roofing product and the larger roof members required. You must balance the change in the roof framing and size against the greater energy savings yielded by a tile roof.

2. Will this project include alternative energy sources such as the wind turbine discussed earlier? If so, will the manufacturer install the wind turbines, or will this task fall to the contractor? If installation becomes the contractor's job, what type of drawings will the contractor need, working drawings or shop drawings? **Shop drawings** are done by the manufacturer rather than the architectural firm. Any drawings provided by the manufacturer must be compatible with the structure and the existing working drawings, and preserve the uniqueness and structural integrity of the application; do not settle for just a generic solution to a "typical" installation. Many products are required to be installed by the vendor of the product, to maintain and safeguard the warranty.

3. The product must meet local codes and be built in a manner suitable for its intended use. However, the product used must also be compatible with the larger project or structure being executed; it must not look alien or incongruous.

4. Do not use a product just because "everyone" is using it. Do your own investigation to validate its use in your particular project. Determine whether

the product is truly green; do not simply accept the manufacturer's claims or statements in this regard.

■ FUTURE OF ENERGY SOURCES

Even though proven alternative energy sources, such as biofuels, wind, solar, water, and geothermal, currently exist, their technical adoption has not yet delivered enough of a financial advantage for the U.S. population to fully embrace them. It can take twenty to thirty years to amortize the installation cost, and because people often move from residence to residence more frequently than that, they tend not to invest in energy-saving devices and fixtures in their homes. The same is true in the business arena, where many businesses are only tenants and unwilling to improve the landlord's property out of their own pockets. The state and federal governments have thus been forced to subsidize alternative-energy investments with grants, tax rebates, and other incentives so as to break this mindset.

Solid oxide fuel cells (SOFC) have garnered interest since an SOFC system was used in space travel starting in the 1960s, but they have not yet been incorporated into our daily lives because of the cost and low efficiency. We need a clean, efficient, reliable, and affordable SOFC, which until recently had not been available. K. R. Sriohar, a rocket scientist, took one of the inventions he had created for space travel (specifically, a Mars landing), reversed the process, and created a wireless energy-producing cell called the Bloom Energy Cell. Bloom Energy claims that its clean, reliable, and affordable energy source will pay for itself in three years and leave a lower carbon footprint while doing so. The Bloom cell is appropriately termed "plug and play": It is made to fit into any infrastructure and requires no end-user maintenance (Bloom Energy handles all management and maintenance of its systems).

After the company was founded in 2001, it spent a year finding funding and the next three years in research and development. In 2006–2007, it performed field trials, product testing, and validation. 2008 saw the first commercial shipment.

Customers include Bank of America, the Coca-Cola Company, eBay, Cox Enterprises, Staples, and Google. Since its inception, Bloom devices have produced more than 11 million kilowatt hours for its customers; more importantly, users have reduced their carbon footprints by more than 14 million pounds. It has been said that this represents the equivalent of powering 1,000 average U.S. homes (2,000 European homes) and planting a million trees.

Each Bloom Energy Server is comprised of hundreds of fuel cells. These fuel cells, which are about the size of a CD container, are assembled from simple components such as sand and metal. (Look at the bottom of the diagram in Figure 4.58.) One fuel cell can produce enough electricity to power a 25-watt bulb. A stack of these would power a European (7 kw) home, while a twin stack would power a U.S. (2 kw) home. One large Bloom Energy Server (100 kw) could power 100 U.S. homes or a supermarket.

This capability, in conjunction with state subsidies and federal rebates to offset acquisition and installation costs, is expected to make Bloom Energy systems available for the entire country within ten years. Because it is wireless, it can also be used where there is no other electricity capacity, especially in Third-World countries.

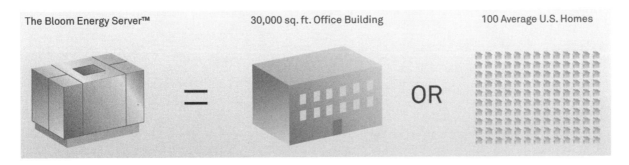

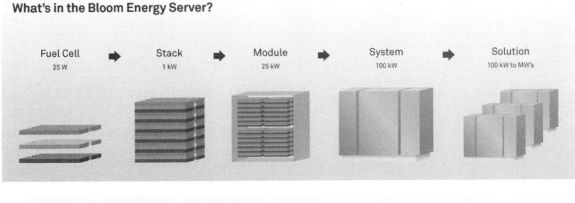

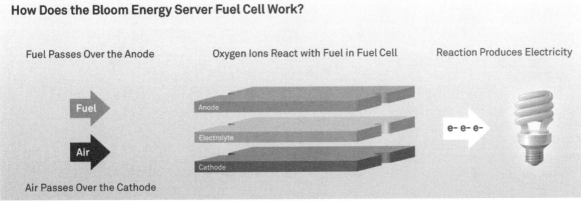

Figure 4.58 Bloom Energy Server. (Courtesy of Bloom Energy.)

chapter

5

CONSTRUCTION MATERIALS
AND METHODS

BUILDING MATERIALS

Materials and Systems

Building construction incorporates various building systems, materials, and construction principles. These systems, materials, and principles are generally selected for the following reasons:

1. The type and use of the proposed structure
2. Governing building code requirements
3. Design and planning solutions
4. Structural concepts
5. Economical considerations
6. Environmental influences
7. Energy requirements

The primary materials utilized in construction systems are the following:

1. Wood—sawn lumber and manufactured lumber, often called *engineered lumber*
2. Concrete
3. Structural steel and light steel framing
4. Masonry
5. Composite systems with a combination of materials
6. Recycled/reclaimed

The use of one or more of the aforementioned materials for a proposed building may be predicated on reasons such as building code requirements or the building occupancy; architectural design; energy and climatic conditions; and the influence of natural forces, including high winds, seismic, infestation, and moisture. The primary components of construction systems include the foundation and floor systems, and the wall and roof systems.

WOOD FLOOR SYSTEMS

Sawn Lumber Floor Joist System

The most conventional wood floor systems use sawn lumber floor joists as the supporting structural members. For a single-story residence, these members may be 2 × 6 or 2 × 8 joists. Although lumber members are named 2 × 6 or 2 × 8, they typically measure 1½″ × 3½″ and 1½″ × 5½″, respectively. This is due to the milling process of the lumber manufacturer. Notice the inch mark when calling out the actual size of the member. This actual size is often called the *net size* and is a common result for sawn lumber. The dimensions of lumber selected will depend on the live and dead load and the span of the joists. Plywood of varying thickness is used as a subfloor for supporting the finish floor material. The spacing

of the floor joists is usually 16″ on center. The structural members are supported by the exterior perimeter concrete foundation walls, and the intermediate supports in the interior include the concrete foundation walls and/or wood girders and concrete piers. See Figure 5.1.

The advantages of utilizing a sawn lumber floor joist system are:

1. Greater span length relative to the size of the joist
2. Requires fewer internal supporting walls and girders
3. Capable of providing floor joist cantilevers
4. Permits insulation material to be placed between the joist members
5. Allows rewiring, making plumbing modifications, or renovating under floor areas
6. Accommodates sloping lots
7. Levels irregular floor elevations or sloping floors

Sawn lumber floor joist systems are not appropriate:

1. In regions highly susceptible to termite infestation and dry rot
2. For buildings that require a minimum amount of noise transmission
3. In buildings desiring a lower silhouette
4. Where a crawl space must be ventilated relative to grade
5. If rats, other wild animals, or other pests may access the crawl space
6. When sustainability is a concern

Construction Principles

1. Ensure that the wood members are not in direct contact with the concrete.
2. Provide recommended under-floor clearances from the soil.
3. Select floor joist sizes that will minimize deflection or floor movement.
4. Provide proper metal flashing to protect wood members from possible moisture.
5. Provide recommended under-floor ventilation.
6. Ensure that the floor is rat-proofed.

Detail ①, as designated on the foundation plan in Figure 5.1, is an isometric drawing of an exterior concrete foundation wall utilizing a wood floor joist and a plywood subfloor. Note the exterior foundation vent for the under-floor ventilation. See Figure 5.2.

Internal Load-Bearing Foundation. Internal load-bearing foundation assemblies are designed to support heavy loads from the floor system, load-bearing walls, and ceiling and roof loads. Such a foundation assembly may be designed as a concrete wall and footing similar to that in Figure 5.2, or with the use of wood girders and concrete piers. The size of the wood girders and

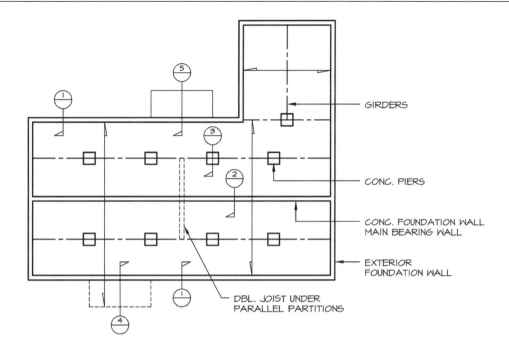

GIRDERS

CONC. PIERS

CONC. FOUNDATION WALL
MAIN BEARING WALL

EXTERIOR
FOUNDATION WALL

DBL. JOIST UNDER
PARALLEL PARTITIONS

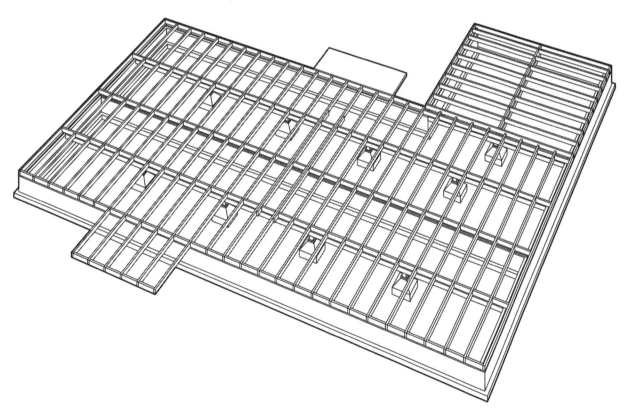

Figure 5.1 Foundation plan: Wood floor joist system.

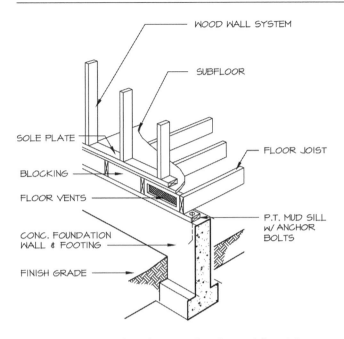

Figure 5.2 Exterior foundation wall with wood floor joist.

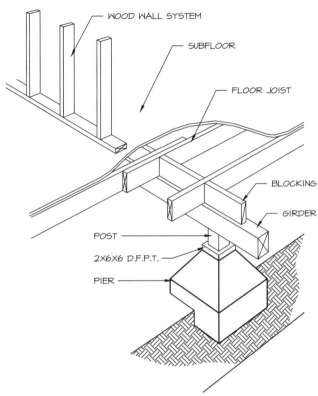

Figure 5.3 Internal pier and girder assembly.

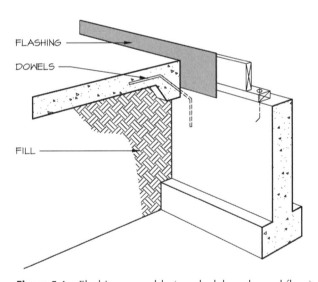

Figure 5.4 Flashing assembly (porch slab and wood floor).

the spacing of the concrete piers are predicated on the amount of structural loading they are required to support. Whenever possible, it is recommended that the wood girders be located directly beneath the load-bearing wall. It is good practice not to extend floor joists to their maximum span, because this approach may cause deflection or movement in the floor system. It is also good practice to add additional rows of girders and piers to provide a stiffer floor system. Figure 5.3 shows an internal pier and wood girder assembly. Note the required solid blocking between the floor joist and its placement directly above the girder, and under the wall partition.

Moisture Protection. As mentioned in the list of construction principles for a wood floor system, it is paramount to protect wood members against moisture. Moisture can cause dry rot, swelling, and buckling of wood members. One method of deterring moisture is to provide an adequate sheet-metal flashing system in areas subject to water seepage.

Detail 5 in Figure 5.1 illustrates a recommended sheet-metal flashing assembly positioned between a concrete porch and a wood floor system. See Figure 5.4.

Wood Plank Floor System

Another wood floor system frequently used is called tongue-and-groove **planking**. This system uses 2 × 6 or 2 × 8 wide wood members. These members, with high stress capabilities, are used to span over wood girders and

concrete foundation walls. This system requires additional rows of girders and piers because the span for the 2″ planking is generally limited to spans from 4′ to 5′.

Figure 5.5 illustrates a wood floor system for a one-story residence utilizing girders as the support for 2″ tongue-and-groove planking. It is recommended that plywood be applied directly over the 2″ planking members for the

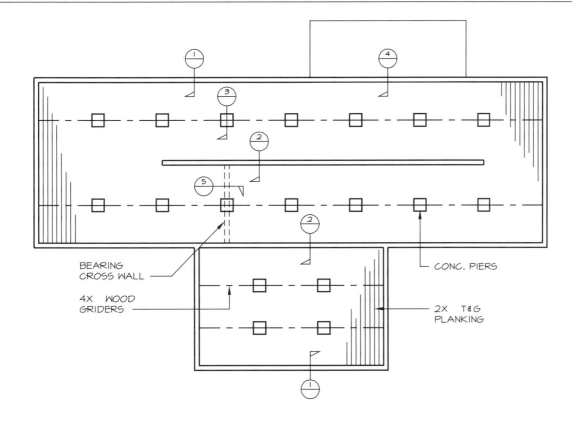

BEARING
CROSS WALL

4X WOOD
GRIDERS

CONC. PIERS

2X T&G
PLANKING

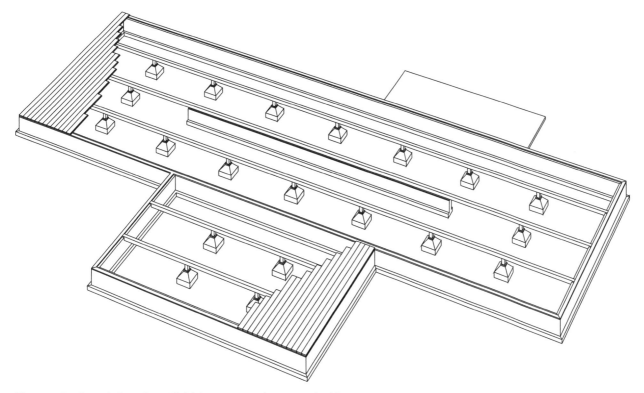

Figure 5.5 Foundation plan: 2″-thick tongue-and-groove planking.

purpose of providing a subbase for the finish floor materials, as well as developing a tie between the various members. Whenever possible, it is recommended that concrete foundation walls and/or girders be positioned directly under paralleling walls. When bearing walls are parallel with the planking members, it will be necessary to provide a 4 × wood girder in the floor system for support. The depth of the girder is governed by the load factor from the wall above and other load-carrying members. Note that the bearing cross-wall member in Figure 5.5 will be installed for support of the load-bearing wall. An isometric drawing depicting the exterior foundation wall for the tongue-and-groove floor system is shown in Figure 5.6.

The advantages of using a tongue-and-groove floor system are that:

1. It provides a stiffer floor with the recommended spacing of girders.
2. It provides a lower building height silhouette, because the added height of the floor joists is eliminated.
3. It has a lower noise factor than a wood floor system.
4. It provides a more rigid subfloor for finish floor materials such as ceramic or concrete tiles.
5. Tongue-and-groove planking is available in greater thickness, which can be used when longer spans are required.

The disadvantages of using a tongue-and-groove floor system are that:

1. Shorter spans will require additional foundation walls, girders, and piers.
2. The system is not conducive to the use of floor cantilevers.
3. The system is susceptible to termite infestation and dry rot (in regions where these problems are endemic).
4. The system does not allow the development of floor beams. Conventional floor joist systems may combine a number of floor joists for the purpose of creating a structural beam.
5. The system does not provide space for blanket insulation.
6. Sustainability is a concern.

Engineered Lumber Wood Floor System

The use of engineered lumber floor joists has proven to be very successful in wood floor systems. Engineered lumber or wood is manufactured by adhering wood strands, veneers, fibers, or particles together to manufacture a new product that can be made to meet certain criteria of strength or shape. Engineered floor joists have been approved by all major building codes.

To see the structural capabilities of this floor joist system, compare the span lengths in the foundation plan illustrated in Figure 5.1 (sawn lumber floor joists) with those of the engineered lumber floor joists shown in Figure 5.7. Two rows of girders and piers have been eliminated from the foundation plan in Figure 5.7 because of the greater strength and load-bearing capacity of the engineered lumber. Other engineered lumber wood members that may be used in a wood floor system are girders and floor beams. These members are developed and fabricated with the use of laminated veneer lumber. The laminated members provide a high allowable bearing stress that is accepted by all major building codes, and are consistent in size and performance. They also reduce the problems of splitting, warping, and checking. The size of these members may range from 1½″ to 7″ in thickness and standard depths may range from 7¼″ to 24″.

An example of the aforementioned engineered lumber joist, illustrating its shape and fabrication components, is shown as an isometric drawing in Figure 5.8. Sizes and structural capabilities will vary among manufacturers of engineered lumber.

Figure 5.9 is a three-dimensional drawing segment of the foundation plan in Figure 5.7, showing the concrete footing, engineered lumber floor joist, engineered plywood subfloor, and wood stud walls.

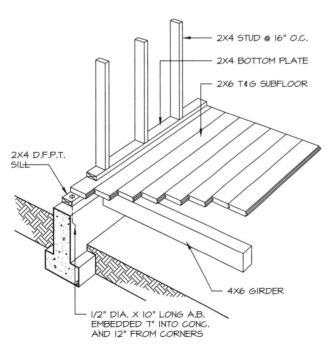

Figure 5.6 Exterior foundation wall with 2″-thick tongue-and-groove planking.

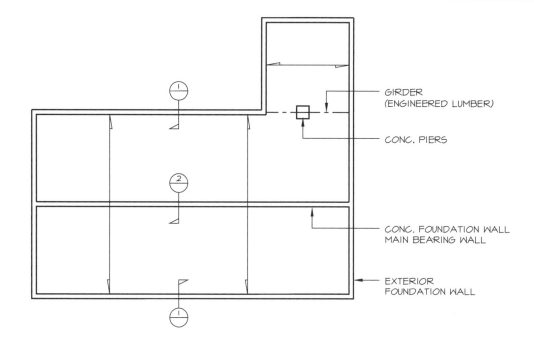

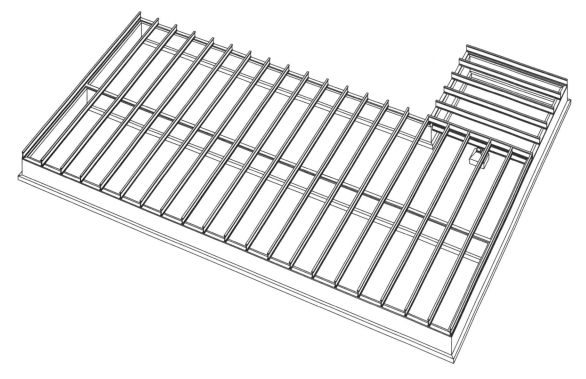

Figure 5.7 Engineered lumber floor joist.

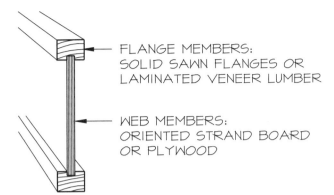

Figure 5.8 Engineered lumber floor shape.

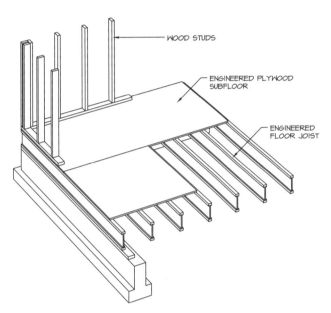

Figure 5.9 Engineered lumber floor system.

The advantages of an engineered lumber wood floor joist system are:

1. Floor joist sizes are uniform.
2. Light weight allows for easier handling on the job.
3. Splitting, checking, warping, and crowning are eliminated.
4. System has greater structural capabilities.
5. Better construction quality of material (no knots).

The disadvantages of an engineered lumber wood floor joist system are:

1. There are limitations on cutting the members in the framing process.
2. There are restrictions on the location in the web sections where holes may be cut.

3. Proper care must be taken to protect these joists prior to installation.
4. The system creates a higher building silhouette because of the increased depth of the joist.
5. One cannot taper the floor joists.

■ WOOD WALL SYSTEMS

Framing Systems

The two most conventional types of wood stud wall framing systems used in construction are the balloon framing system and the Western or platform framing system. The main differences between these two systems are at the intersection of the second-floor framing assembly and the wall.

Balloon Framing

In the construction of two-story structures, the balloon framing system uses continuous wall studs from the first floor level up to the roof assembly. The second-floor supporting members are then framed to the continuous studs. Stud sizes are 2 × 4 or 2 × 6 at 16″ center to center. 2 × blocking is fitted to fill all openings to provide firestops and prevent drafts from one space to another.

Wood or metal members are attached securely at a 45° angle to the top and bottom of the studs and provide horizontal bracing for the walls. In areas subjected to strong lateral forces, sheathing is used for horizontal bracing. Balloon framing is not utilized in all parts of the country; refer to the local codes for allowable use. See Figure 5.10. The use of plywood or **oriented strand board** (OSB) panels may be determined by the governing building code or the structural engineering requirements. This system has a minimum amount of vertical shrinkage and vertical movement and may be used with brick veneer or cement plaster exterior finishes.

Western or Platform Framing

Western or platform framing uses a different procedure. The lower floor walls are assembled first, and then the supporting floor members and subfloor for the upper floor are framed. The upper subfloor and floor joists provide a platform for assembling the upper-floor walls, ceiling joists, and roof framing. The walls are framed with 2 × 4 or 2 × 6 studs at 16″ center to center. Required blocking is 2″ thick and is fitted to provide stiffness to the joist.

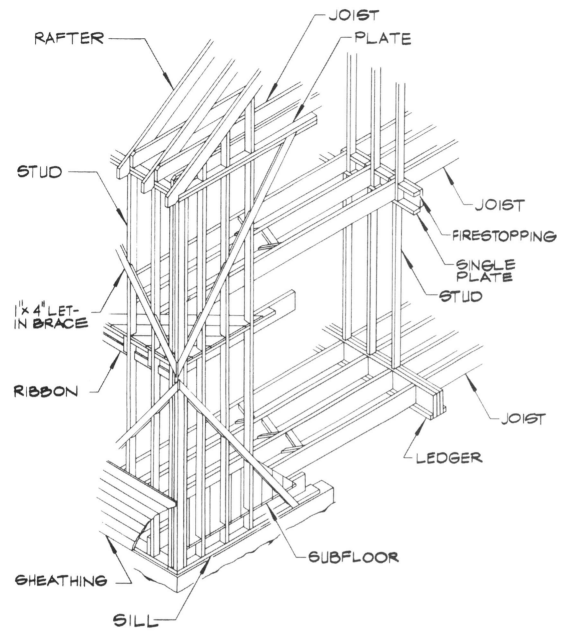

Figure 5.10 Balloon-frame construction. (*Architectural Graphic Standards*, 11th Ed. © by John Wiley & Sons, Inc.)

Solid sheathing, diagonal braces, plywood, or OSB panels may provide lateral bracing. Building code requirements, regional differences, and structural engineering calculations may determine the type of lateral bracing. See Figure 5.11.

Post and Beam Framing

A third method for framing wood structures is the post and beam system. Less common than platform and balloon framing, this method uses a post and beam spacing that allows the builder to use 2 × roof or floor planking. See Figure 5.12. For the best use of this system, a specific module of plank-and-beam spacing must be established. Supplementary bracing is placed on the exterior walls, with options similar to those used in conventional framing systems. You must provide a positive connection between the post and the beam and secure the post to the floor. Different types of metal framing connectors may be used to

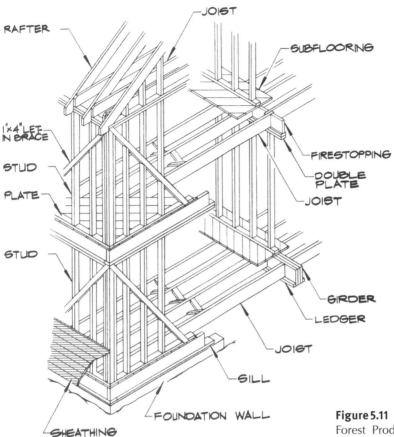

Figure 5.11 Western or platform framing. (Courtesy of National Forest Products Association. Reprinted by permission from *The Professional Practice of Architectural Working Drawings,* 3d Ed., © 2003 by John Wiley & Sons, Inc.)

satisfy these connection requirements. If metal framing connectors are undesirable for aesthetic reasons, then steel dowels may be utilized at the post-to-beam connection and the post-to-floor connection. See Figures 5.13 and 5.14. Because fewer pieces are used in this system, special attention to post-to-beam connections and connections to other members should be given in detailing these conditions. With proper detailing, such connections will securely fasten components of the building together and act as a unit to resist any external forces.

Engineered Lumber Wall Systems

Engineered lumber sheathing panels are used in wood stud wall construction to strengthen and stabilize exterior and interior walls. Engineered sheathing panels used for exterior walls should be protected with building paper, wood siding, or other types of exterior cladding to protect the panels from damage caused by water or other moisture conditions. These panels are fabricated in sizes ranging from 4′ × 8′ to 4′ × 9′ and 4′ × 10′. Panel thickness can range from $^3/_8$″ to $1^1/_8$″, and panels are manufactured using plywood or OSB. See Figure 5.15.

■ WOOD ROOF SYSTEMS

Roof Materials

The principles underlying wood roof systems, and the construction methods used in developing these systems, may depend on the finish roof material and the requirements of its application. The following are examples of finish roof materials used over roof framing systems:

1. Wood shingles or shakes (can be fire treated)
2. Asphalt shingles
3. Clay or concrete tiles
4. Built-up composition, gravel surface, and torch down

PLANK-AND-BEAM
FRAMING

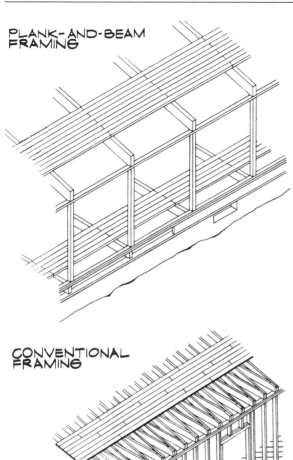

CONVENTIONAL
FRAMING

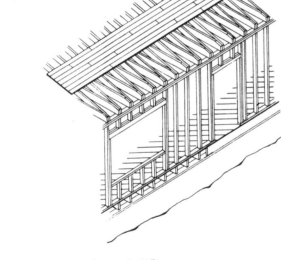

COMPARISON OF PLANK-
AND-BEAM SYSTEM
WITH CONVENTIONAL
FRAMING

Figure 5.12 Pictorial comparison of plank-and-beam framing with conventional framing. (Courtesy of National Forest Products Association. Reprinted by permission from *The Professional Practice of Architectural Working Drawings*, 3d Ed., © 2003 by John Wiley & Sons, Inc.)

5. Aluminum, copper, stainless steel, or galvanized metal
6. Standing seam or corrugated metal
7. Green roof

Wood Roof System Utilizing Sawn Lumber

Sawn lumber members of various dimensions have been used for the construction of wood-framed roofs. Utilizing these members can provide more on-the-job flexibility for roof systems because members can be cut and fitted to the varying conditions that may occur during the roof framing stage. Members required for blocking, bracing members, studs, plates, and others are used to fit the jobsite conditions. An example of sawn lumber roof framing is shown in Figure 5.16. The use of sawn lumber members affords the architect greater latitude in designing the external projections of a roof system, including eave and rake designs. Examples of eave designs are shown in Figures 5.17 and 5.18.

Planking

The term *planking* is used to refer to members that have a minimum depth of 2″ and various widths. The edges of these members are normally tongue and groove. Using such edges enables a continuous joining of members so that a concentrated load is distributed onto the adjacent members. See Figure 5.19.

Plank-and-Beam and Heavy Timber Roof Systems

The plank-and-beam roof system uses heavy wood beam members greater than 2″ in thickness to support roof planking and the finish roofing material. The main supporting wood beam members normally have a modular spacing, such as 6′ to 8′ on center. The spacing of these members is determined by the weight of the finish roofing materials. In general, the architect selects this system for use where he or she wishes to expose the roof structural system for reasons of aesthetics or code requirements. For roof members that must satisfy heavy timber construction requirements, the roof planking must have a thickness of not less than 2″ and must provide a tongue-and-groove or splined connection. The main supporting members must not be less than 4″ in width and not less than 6″ in depth. All supporting wood columns must be at least 8″ in any dimension. See Figure 5.20.

Wood Truss Roof System

Wood roof trusses are available in many sizes, shapes, and lengths. Wood roof trusses are generally fabricated by a manufacturer and delivered to the building site. Trusses are selected according to the manufacturer's stipulated engineered design criteria for the various weights of materials that the trusses must support. One method

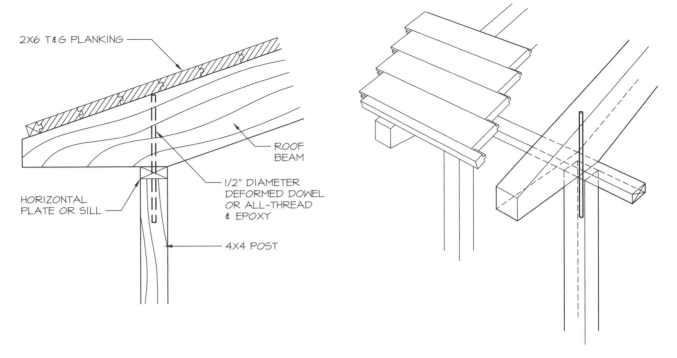

2X6 T&G PLANKING

ROOF BEAM

1/2" DIAMETER DEFORMED DOWEL OR ALL-THREAD & EPOXY

HORIZONTAL PLATE OR SILL

4X4 POST

Figure 5.13 Post-to-beam connection.

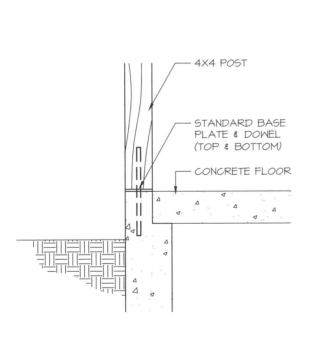
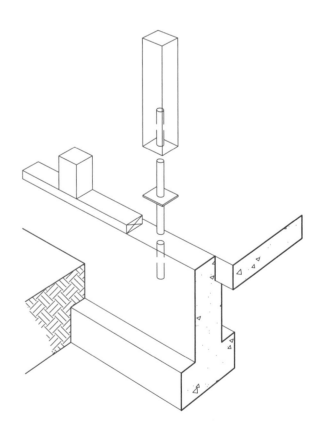

4X4 POST

STANDARD BASE PLATE & DOWEL (TOP & BOTTOM)

CONCRETE FLOOR

Figure 5.14 Post-to-foundation connection.

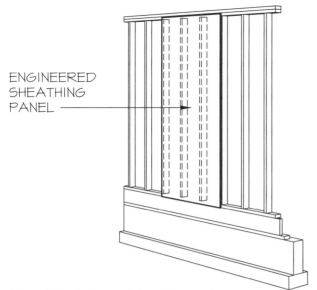

Figure 5.15 Engineered sheathing panel.

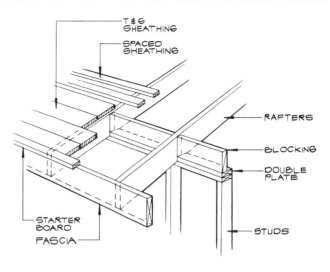

Figure 5.18 Pictorial view, eave detail. (Reprinted by permission from *The Professional Practice of Architectural Working Drawings,* 3d Ed., © 2003 by John Wiley & Sons, Inc.)

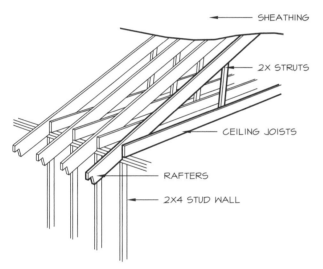

Figure 5.16 Sawn lumber roof system.

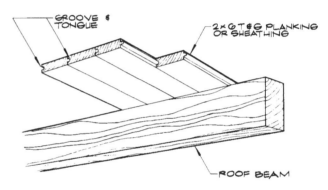

Figure 5.19 Pictorial view of roof planking. (Reprinted by permission from *The Professional Practice of Architectural Working Drawings,* 3d Ed., © 2003 by John Wiley & Sons, Inc.)

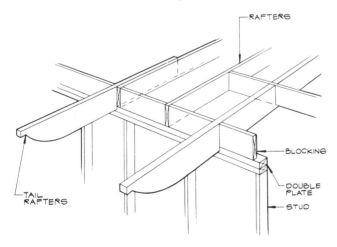

Figure 5.17 Pictorial view, eave detail. (Reprinted by permission from *The Professional Practice of Architectural Working Drawings,* 3d Ed., © 2003 by John Wiley & Sons, Inc.)

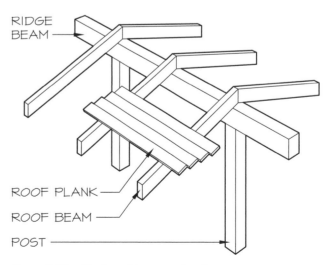

Figure 5.20 Plank-and-beam roof system.

of utilizing a wood truss roof system is to place the trusses on a dimensional module spacing that allows the intermediate roof supporting members to span the trusses. See Figure 5.21. An alternative method is to utilize truss members at a 16″ or 24″ center-to-center spacing.

Panelized Wood Roof System

A panelized wood roof system is a construction method whereby plywood or OSB roof sheathing panels and intermediate supporting members are prefabricated in a manufacturing plant. Generally, the size of these panels is 4′ × 8′ because this is the standard dimension for plywood sheets. The thickness of the plywood sheathing is governed by the structural engineer's specifications. The supporting intermediate members of the plywood are generally 2 × 4 placed at 24″ center to center. Once the panels are fabricated, they are lifted and placed within the 4′ × 8′ module dimensions of the roof's main supporting members. The panels are attached to the main and intermediate supporting members with the metal framing connectors. The main supporting members may be glue-laminated (glu-lam) beams, and intermediate members have a minimum thickness of 4″. This roof framing system is generally used in the construction of industrial and manufacturing buildings. See Figure 5.22.

Engineered Lumber Roof System

The use of engineered lumber members for roof rafters provides a straighter and stiffer frame, which is also more consistent in size and shape, for a wood roof system.

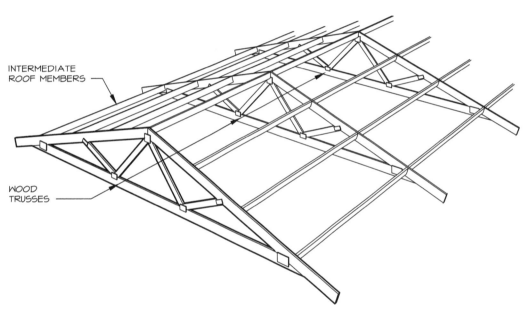

Figure 5.21   Wood truss roof system.

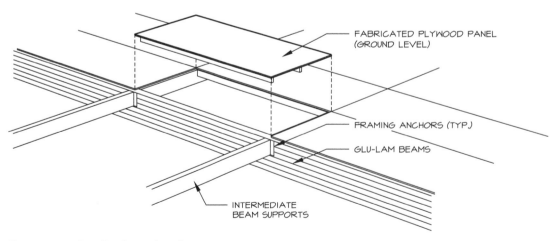

Figure 5.22   Panelized wood roof system.

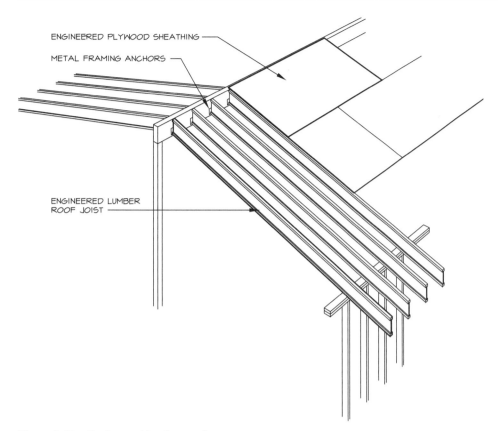

ENGINEERED PLYWOOD SHEATHING

METAL FRAMING ANCHORS

ENGINEERED LUMBER
ROOF JOIST

Figure 5.23 Engineered lumber roof system.

See Figure 5.8. The structural capabilities of these members allow for the use of different types of roofing materials, and can handle snow-loading conditions. When engineered lumber is used, roof pitches may vary from a low pitch to a steep roof condition. The depth of these members may range from 5½" to 16", depending on the particular engineered lumber fabricator or manufacturer. See Figure 5.23.

■ CONCRETE

Concrete Floor System on Grade

When concrete has been selected for a floor system on grade, factors influencing this selection may be the result of the following factors:

1. Acceptable soil conditions
2. Soundproofing requirements
3. Infestation conditions
4. Desire for a low building silhouette
5. Floor material finish
6. Basement condition

There are two main types of concrete floors and foundation systems. One type is the *monolithic system*, also referred to as the *one-pour system*, in which the concrete

floor and foundation are poured in one operation. The other system is referred to as the *two-pour system*. In this system, the foundation walls and footings are poured first, followed by the concrete floor, which is poured separately. Although termed two-pour, it could actually take several pours (three or more), depending on the size of the foundation system.

The construction methods for these two systems differ. In the one-pour system, the trenches become the forms for the foundation, as shown in Figure 5.24. For the two-pour system, formwork is required for the foundation wall. See Figure 5.25. A monolithic footing requires more concrete but less labor, as opposed to a two-pour footing which also requires form lumber.

Concrete Floor Steel Reinforcing

Just as a foundation must be strengthened with steel reinforcing, a concrete floor must be reinforced to prevent cracking. There are two primary methods of reinforcing concrete floor systems on a grade. One method is to use welded wire mesh, which is usually made of number 10 gauge wires spaced 6" apart in each direction. Another method of reinforcing a concrete floor is to use deformed steel reinforcing bars with the spacing in each direction as recommended by a soils engineer. For example, the designation of the size of reinforcing bars and spacing

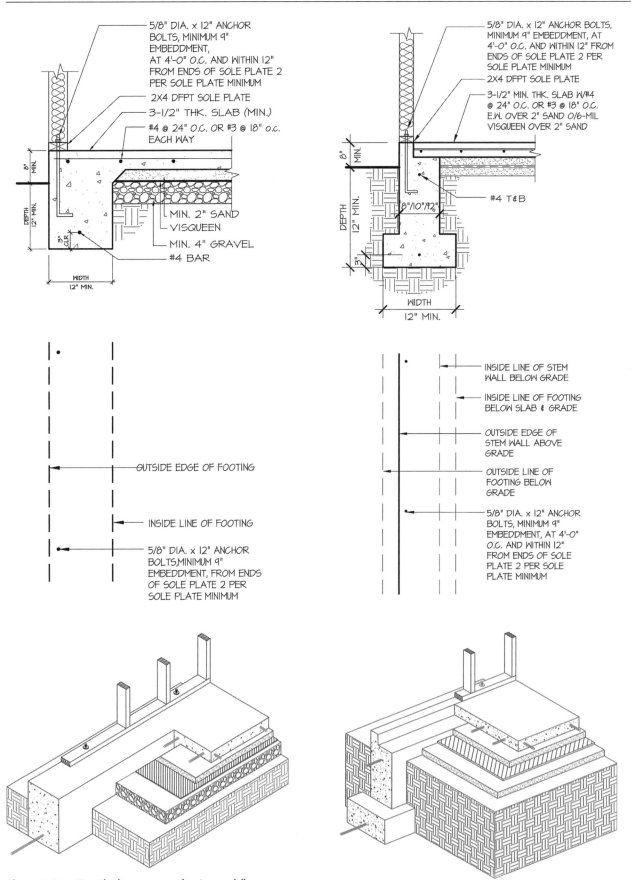

5/8" DIA. x 12" ANCHOR BOLTS, MINIMUM 9" EMBEDDMENT, AT 4'-0" O.C. AND WITHIN 12" FROM ENDS OF SOLE PLATE 2 PER SOLE PLATE MINIMUM

2X4 DFPT SOLE PLATE

3-1/2" THK. SLAB (MIN.)

#4 @ 24" O.C. OR #3 @ 18" o.c. EACH WAY

8" MIN.

DEPTH 12" MIN.

3" CLR.

MIN. 2" SAND
VISQUEEN
MIN. 4" GRAVEL
#4 BAR

WIDTH
12" MIN.

OUTSIDE EDGE OF FOOTING

INSIDE LINE OF FOOTING

5/8" DIA. x 12" ANCHOR BOLTS, MINIMUM 9" EMBEDDMENT, FROM ENDS OF SOLE PLATE 2 PER SOLE PLATE MINIMUM

5/8" DIA. x 12" ANCHOR BOLTS, MINIMUM 9" EMBEDDMENT, AT 4'-0" O.C. AND WITHIN 12" FROM ENDS OF SOLE PLATE 2 PER SOLE PLATE MINIMUM

2X4 DFPT SOLE PLATE

3-1/2" MIN. THK. SLAB W/#4 @ 24" O.C. OR #3 @ 18" O.C. E.W. OVER 2" SAND O/6-MIL VISQUEEN OVER 2" SAND

8" MIN.

DEPTH 12" MIN.

#4 T&B

8"/10"/12"

3"

WIDTH
12" MIN.

INSIDE LINE OF STEM WALL BELOW GRADE

INSIDE LINE OF FOOTING BELOW SLAB & GRADE

OUTSIDE EDGE OF STEM WALL ABOVE GRADE

OUTSIDE LINE OF FOOTING BELOW GRADE

5/8" DIA. x 12" ANCHOR BOLTS, MINIMUM 9" EMBEDDMENT, AT 4'-0" O.C. AND WITHIN 12" FROM ENDS OF SOLE PLATE 2 PER SOLE PLATE MINIMUM

Figure 5.24 Detail of a one-pour footing and floor.

Figure 5.25 Detail of a two-pour footing and concrete floor.

could be number 4 bars at 18″ to 24″ center to center in each direction. The use of deformed steel bars is preferred for most soil conditions. See Figure 5.26.

When confronted with having to hold two different pours of concrete together, such as a concrete porch slab and a main concrete floor, it is recommended that deformed steel dowels be used as the holding connection. These dowels may be number 3 bars at 18″ to 24″ center to center. See Figure 5.27.

Concrete Floor Systems above Grade

There are various types of construction methods for concrete floor systems that are used in above-grade and multilevel concrete floor construction. These concrete floors are erected with the use of various forming and steel reinforcing methods, with assemblies created on the jobsite in preparation for the concrete placement.

One of these methods is referred to as a *two-way flat slab*. The formwork is completely flat. The concrete slab is reinforced in such a way that the varying stresses are accommodated within the uniform thickness of the slab. The concrete slab thickness may vary from 6″ to 12″ in depth. The depth, as well as the steel reinforcing, is determined by the consulting structural engineer. See Figure 5.28.

Another concrete floor system used in many buildings is a two-way solid slab system. In this system, a solid flat slab is supported by a grid of concrete beams running in both directions over supporting concrete columns. In general, a flat slab concrete floor system is very economical because of the simplicity of the formwork. Steel reinforcing bars will be incorporated in projects with recommendations from the structural engineer. These systems impose limitations on the length of spans for the flat slab. See Figure 5.29.

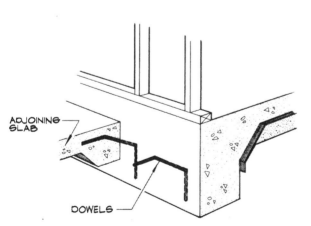

Figure 5.26 Concrete floor reinforcing. (Reprinted by permission from *The Professional Practice of Architectural Working Drawings,* 3d Ed., © 2003 by John Wiley & Sons, Inc.)

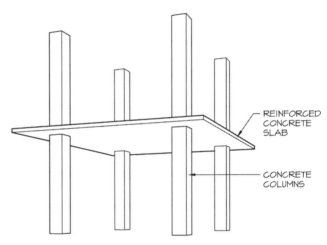

Figure 5.28 Flat slab floor system.

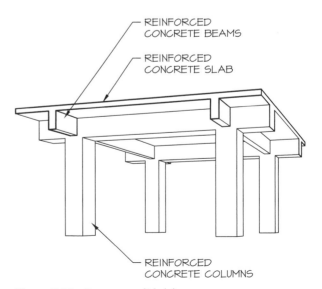

Figure 5.27 Use of steel dowels to tie porch slab to concrete floor. (Reprinted by permission from *The Professional Practice of Architectural Working Drawings,* 3d Ed., © 2003 by John Wiley & Sons, Inc.)

Figure 5.29 Two-way solid slab system.

Precast Prestressed Concrete Systems

The use of precast prestressed concrete structural components for floor systems in buildings has many advantages over the use of concrete poured in place at the jobsite. Precast prestressed concrete components such as slabs, beams, girders, columns, and wall panels are manufactured at a precasting plant and delivered to the building site for erection. Precasting plants offer excellent quality control of materials and workmanship and minimize waste in concrete and steel.

An example of a precast prestressed slab floor system utilizing a precast double-tee-shaped floor slab with support beam is illustrated in Figure 5.30. The thickness of the slab and the amount of steel reinforcing are dictated by the length of the span and the weight that will be loaded onto the floor. The solutions are dictated by the structural engineer's findings. Note in Figure 5.30 that the precast double tees are supported on steel-reinforced concrete walls.

Figure 5.31 shows a solid flat slab reinforced unit that will be lifted into place and supported by concrete beams and concrete columns. This type of precast slab is used for short span conditions.

Figure 5.32 illustrates a precast prestressed hollow-core slab panel. The hollow cores further reduce the

Figure 5.31   Precast prestressed solid flat slab.

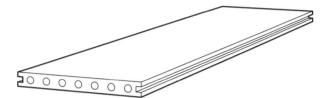

Figure 5.32   Precast prestressed hollow-core slab.

dead weight of the concrete panel. These hollow-core slab panels are best suited for intermediate spans and can be supported by concrete beams and concrete columns.

Figure 5.33 depicts a precast prestressed concrete single tee. This type of precast unit and the double-tee unit are desirable for longer spans. The single tees are used less frequently than the double tees, because the single tee requires a temporary support to relieve tipping. The

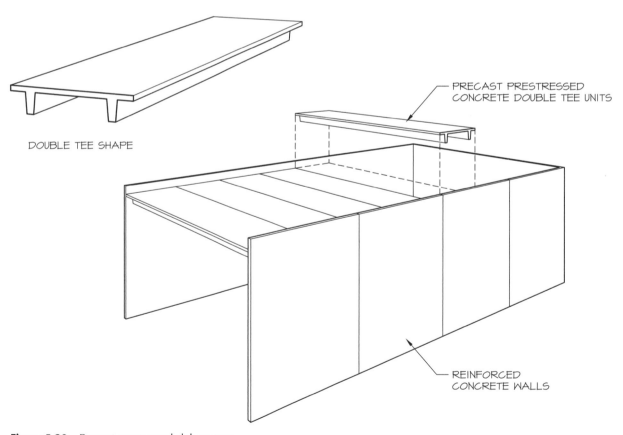

DOUBLE TEE SHAPE

PRECAST PRESTRESSED
CONCRETE DOUBLE TEE UNITS

REINFORCED
CONCRETE WALLS

Figure 5.30   Precast prestressed slab system.

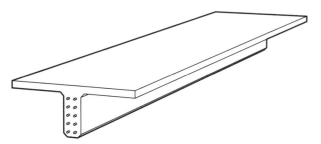

Figure 5.33 Precast prestressed concrete single tee.

examples shown are the most commonly used precast prestressed concrete elements for floor systems; they are also used for concrete roof systems.

Concrete Wall Systems

A commonly used concrete wall system that is poured in place is called a *concrete retaining wall.* As with most poured-in-place concrete, wood forms are constructed on both sides of the wall and tied together to resist the weight and force of the poured concrete. Steel reinforcing bars are required and are attached to the wood forms before the concrete is poured. See Figure 5.34.

Concrete walls are also utilized in basements for below-ground conditions, and can be manufactured as described earlier with wood forms. Metal forms are used in a manner similar to the wood forms, but are best for a more repetitive dimensional system. If the measurements are uniform, the use of modular metal forms is a more efficient system of forming. These forms can be rented and are intended for frequent use. In either case, any basement wall must be waterproofed.

Concrete Tilt-Up Wall System

Tilt-up wall panels are used to support roof and floor loads and serve as shear walls to resist movement due to earthquakes and high wind conditions. See Figure 5.35.

Tilt-up wall construction is a precast construction method in which the wall panels are cast on the jobsite. In most cases, the concrete floor of the building serves as the casting platform for the wall panels. The panels may be of high-strength concrete and relatively thin. Tilt-up construction is especially suitable for commercial and industrial structures.

Generally, fabrication of a tilt-up wall is accomplished with the use of wood forms, reinforcing steel, and a bond-breaker liquid suitable to release the precast panel from the casting platform. After the concrete meets the

A

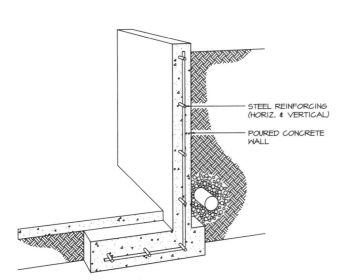

Figure 5.34 Poured-in-place concrete retaining wall.

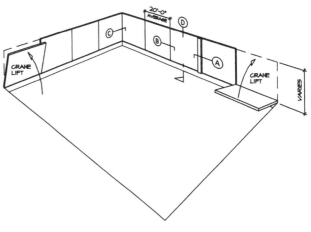

B

Figure 5.35 Tilt-up wall diagram. (Reprinted by permission from *Professional Practice of Architectural Detailing,* 3d Ed., © 2003 by John Wiley & Sons, Inc.)

curing specifications, the panels are lifted into place by a mobile truck crane. See Figures 5.36 and 5.37.

A detailed wall section for a two-story concrete tilt-up wall is illustrated in Figure 5.38. Note that a concrete pour strip is used to connect the wall and the casting slab after the tilt-up wall panel is erected.

Precast Concrete Wall System

A highly successful construction method for concrete walls is the use of precast concrete bearing and non-bearing walls. These walls are manufactured at a casting plant and delivered to the building site for erection. The walls may be cast with various openings in

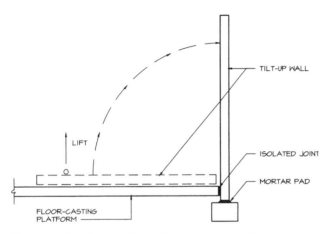

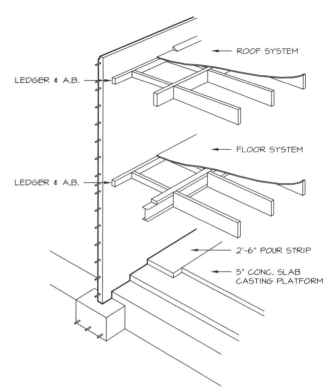

Figure 5.38 Concrete tilt-up wall.

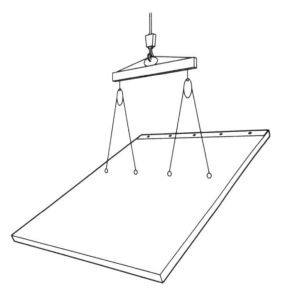

Figure 5.36 Tilt-up wall installation. (Reprinted by permission from *Professional Practice of Architectural Detailing,* 3d Ed., © 2003 by John Wiley & Sons, Inc.)

Figure 5.37 Tilt-up wall section. (Reprinted by permission from *Professional Practice of Architectural Detailing,* 3d Ed., © 2003 by John Wiley & Sons, Inc.)

them, such as for doors and windows. The wall sizes and shapes vary, based on the designs of the architect and the structural engineer. Figure 5.39 depicts a precast concrete wall arrangement with the use of a precast concrete hollow-core floor system. Note that when wall openings are required, they may be incorporated into the internal and external planning. The connections for precast concrete elements, such as for walls, are dictated by the consulting structural engineer's detail. A wall-to-floor connection (section A) is shown in Figure 5.40. This detail does not show the steel reinforcing and grouting required to connect the walls to the floor system to maintain the structural integrity of the building. There are various methods of meeting these structural requirements.

Precast Concrete Roof System

The precast concrete elements used for a structural roof system are similar to those used for precast concrete floor systems. This system is depicted in Figure 5.41, where precast hollow-core planks are supported and incorporated with the use of precast concrete bearing walls. Note that the haunch used to support the hollow-core planks is part of the precast wall unit. Roofing insulation and the finished roofing application are applied directly over the hollow-core planking.

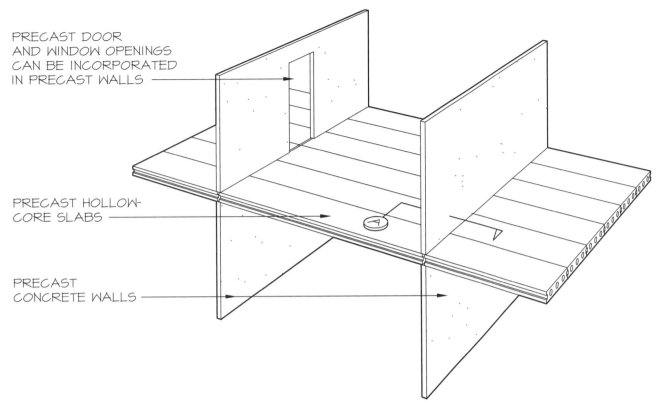

PRECAST DOOR
AND WINDOW OPENINGS
CAN BE INCORPORATED
IN PRECAST WALLS

PRECAST HOLLOW-
CORE SLABS

PRECAST
CONCRETE WALLS

Figure 5.39 Precast concrete bearing walls.

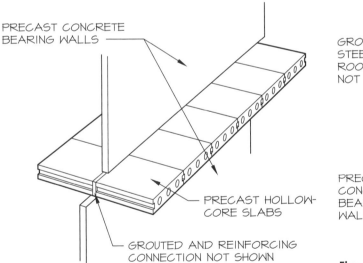

PRECAST CONCRETE
BEARING WALLS

PRECAST HOLLOW-
CORE SLABS

GROUTED AND REINFORCING
CONNECTION NOT SHOWN

Figure 5.40 Precast walls and hollow-core slab.

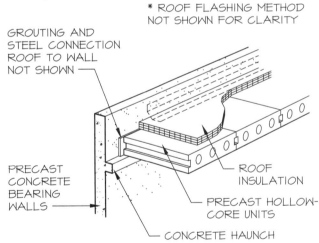

* ROOF FLASHING METHOD
NOT SHOWN FOR CLARITY

GROUTING AND
STEEL CONNECTION
ROOF TO WALL
NOT SHOWN

PRECAST
CONCRETE
BEARING
WALLS

ROOF
INSULATION

PRECAST HOLLOW-
CORE UNITS

CONCRETE HAUNCH

Figure 5.41 Precast concrete roof system.

■ STEEL FLOOR SYSTEM

Steel Floors

One type of steel floor system is a combination of steel decking and concrete. This type of system is referred to as a *composite* construction method. The corrugated steel decking sheets provide reinforcing for the concrete, a form into which the concrete is poured, and a walking surface for the contractors. Corrugated steel decking is available in various shapes, depths, and gauges. One method of attaching steel decking to the steel supporting beams is with the use of steel studs welded to the top flange of the steel beams; this is done before the concrete is poured. Bonding the concrete and steel decking to the steel studs provides the structural capability to withstand horizontal shear forces. Such a composite steel and concrete floor system provides a lighter and stiffer building, as well as an assemblage of noncombustible materials. See Figure 5.42.

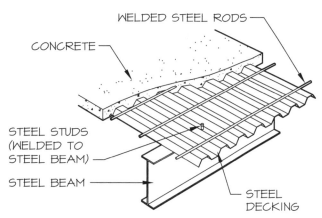

Figure 5.42 Composite steel decking floor system.

■ STEEL STUD WALL FRAMING SYSTEM

Steel Studs

The use of lightweight, cold-formed steel stud members provides a wall framing system for load-bearing and non-load-bearing walls. These walls provide a noncombustible support for fire-related construction and are well suited for preassembly. Moreover, shrinkage is not a concern with steel stud walls. The material of the studs varies from 14- to 20-gauge galvanized steel, with sizes ranging from 1½″ to 10″ in depth. These walls are constructed with a channel track at the bottom and top of each wall and steel studs attached to the channels. Horizontal bridging is achieved with the use of a steel channel positioned through the steel stud punch-outs and secured by welding. See Figure 5.43. Wood sheathing may be attached to steel framing members with self-tapping screws. See Figure 5.44.

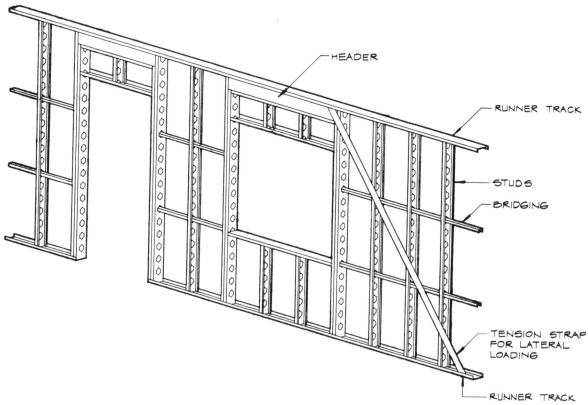

Figure 5.43 Isometric of steel stud wall.

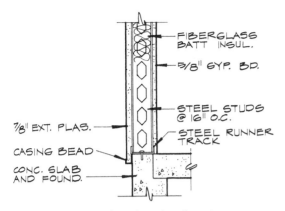

Figure 5.44 Partial steel stud wall section.

■ STEEL DECKING ROOF SYSTEM

Steel Decking

Corrugated steel decking used in steel roof systems is available in various shapes, with steel gauges ranging from 18 to 24 gauge and depths from 1½" to 3". Steel decking roof systems are mainly found in the construction of commercial, industrial, and institutional-type buildings. Figure 5.45 illustrates a roof-to-wall assembly incorporating a 20-gauge galvanized steel decking, which in this case has a fire protection coating to satisfy a building code requirement. For insulation purposes, a 2½"-thick rigid insulation board is installed directly above the steel decking, followed by installation of the built-up roof system.

■ LIGHT STEEL ROOF FRAMING SYSTEM

Steel Framing

Light steel framing members are used in the construction of roof framing systems. These members are available in web depths of 3⅝" to 13½". These light steel members are manufactured from 18- to 24-gauge steel. The attachment of plywood or OSB sheathing and other wood members may be accomplished with the use of self-tapping screws. See Figure 5.46.

■ MASONRY WALL SYSTEM

Masonry

Masonry is widely used for exterior structural walls. The main masonry units are bricks and concrete blocks, which are available in many sizes, shapes, textures, and colors. A primary advantage is that the masonry acts as the formwork for concrete.

Masonry is fire resistant and provides excellent fire ratings, ranging from two to four hours or more. The hour rating is based on the time it takes a fire-testing flame temperature to penetrate a specific wall assembly. Masonry also acts as an excellent sound barrier. When solid brick units are used for an exterior structural wall, the primary assembly is determined by regional geophysical conditions, such as seismic and high winds. For example, steel reinforcing bars and solid grout may be needed to resist lateral forces. Figure 5.47 shows a steel-reinforced brick masonry wall. The size and placement

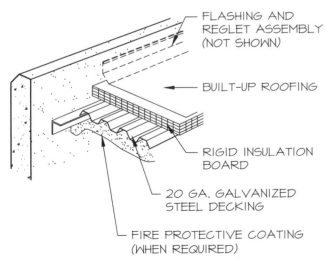

Figure 5.45 Steel roof decking system.

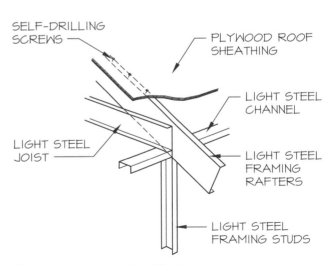

Figure 5.46 Light steel roof framing system.

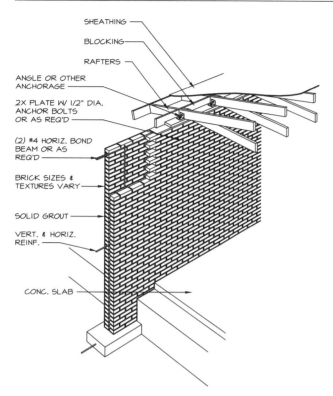

Figure 5.47 Section of reinforced grouted brick masonry wall.

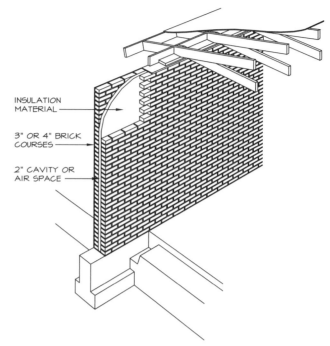

Figure 5.48 Brick cavity wall section.

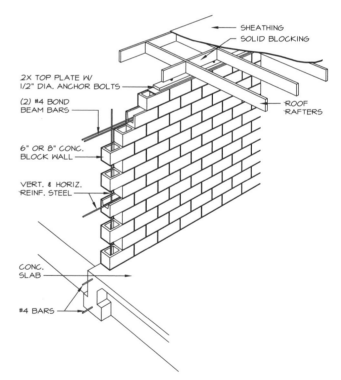

Figure 5.49 Reinforced concrete block wall section.

of the horizontal and vertical reinforcing steel are determined by the structural engineer and the governing building code. In regions without high wind conditions or seismic activity, reinforcing steel and grout are not needed. The unreinforced masonry wall or brick cavity wall is excellent for insulating exterior walls. Two 3″ or 4″ walls of brick are separated by a 2″ air space or cavity. This cavity provides a suitable space for insulating materials, and the two masonry walls are bonded together with metal ties set in the mortar joints. See Figure 5.48.

Concrete masonry units (CMU) for structural walls are generally 6″, 8″, 12″, or 16″ thick, depending on the height of the wall. The hollow sections of these units are called *cells*. Vertical cells may be left empty or filled solid with grout and reinforcing steel; when required, horizontal cells can also include concrete and steel to add strength. As in brick wall construction, the use of unreinforced or reinforced walls will depend on the structural engineer's calculations and the building code requirements. In regions where reinforcing steel and grout are not required, the open cells may be filled with a suitable insulating material. When you utilize a concrete block wall, the dimensions of the blocks affect the height and width of the building; it is best to utilize the modular unit of the block. See Figure 5.49. Window and door openings must satisfy the dimensions of the modular units as well.

Masonry Veneer Wall

Masonry veneer includes the use of brick, CMU, or stone as a non-load-bearing component of the building. The maximum thickness of masonry veneer is regulated

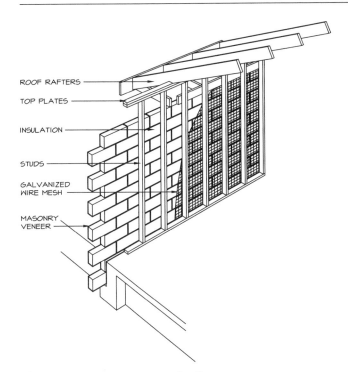

ROOF RAFTERS

TOP PLATES

INSULATION

STUDS

GALVANIZED
WIRE MESH

MASONRY
VENEER

Figure 5.50 Masonry veneer detail.

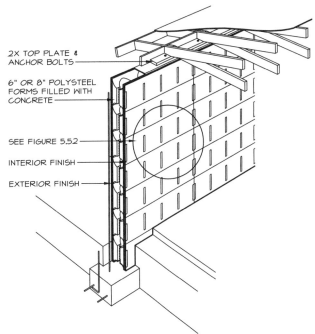

2X TOP PLATE &
ANCHOR BOLTS

6" OR 8" POLYSTEEL
FORMS FILLED WITH
CONCRETE

SEE FIGURE 5.52

INTERIOR FINISH

EXTERIOR FINISH

Figure 5.51 Polysteel forms and concrete wall. (Courtesy American Polysteel, Inc.)

by most building codes and is generally recognized as 5″ or less. *Masonry veneer* may be defined strictly as a masonry finish that is nonstructural and generally used for its architectural appearance. In regions with seismic disturbances, a positive bond between the veneer and a stud wall is required. See Figure 5.50.

■ COMPOSITE SYSTEMS AND COMBINATIONS OF MATERIALS

Systems and Materials

Some construction methods incorporate systems that are assembled with various materials. These are called *composite systems* and may include a combination of materials such as steel and concrete; aluminum and insulation panels; polystyrene, galvanized steel, and concrete; and plastic and wood. These are just a few of the material combinations utilized in building construction. Another example of a composite system is the use of polystyrene and galvanized steel forms for construction of poured concrete walls. See Figure 5.51. This system provides a form for the poured concrete and also possesses excellent insulation qualities, as the polystyrene forms are retained in the structural wall. They are designed to serve as an anchor for the finish materials that will be applied to the exterior and interior faces of the wall. The exterior and interior finishes may be anchored to galvanized steel furring strips that are an integral part

of the form unit. Figure 5.52 depicts a single polysteel form unit.

For structures that are designed to have exterior wall insulation, the architect may select a composite exterior wall system that utilizes a substrate material insulation board and a moisture-proof exterior finish. The thickness of an acceptable substrate may be at least ½″, and an expanded polystyrene insulation board may be from 1″ to 2″ in thickness. The selected thickness may be determined by the required or desired R factor. (The

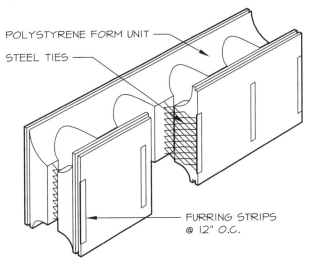

POLYSTYRENE FORM UNIT

STEEL TIES

FURRING STRIPS
@ 12″ O.C.

Figure 5.52 Polysteel form unit. (Courtesy American Polysteel, Inc.)

R factor designates the assigned insulation capability.) It is recommended that the supporting exterior wall members for this system be galvanized steel studs at 16″ center to center or 24″ center to center. This composite system can be attached to the steel studs and the approved substrate with an approved adhesive or a mechanical attachment. The mechanical attachment incorporates a metal screw and washer. See Figure 5.53.

Figure 5.54 illustrates an exterior wall assembly utilizing the aforementioned wall panel. Note that the polystyrene selected is 2″ thick. The parapet detail in Figure 5.55 incorporates the various requirements for using this system.

Wood and plastic are found in a product developed for exterior decking and handrails in construction. This composite product requires virtually no maintenance and is manufactured from a sturdy wood composite. The decking material will not splinter, split, or crack; is resistant to termites, dry rot, and decay; and is available in a wood-like finish. The individual members are straight and true, having smooth or wood-grain finish. The members can be attached using the same method as for sawn lumber; however, predrilling and the use of screws are recommended. This decking material is available in two types. One is a solid 4 × 6 unit that can be supported with structural members spaced at 16″ center to center.

The other type is a 2 × 6 unit that is hollowed to provide a lighter weight for ease of handling. The hollowed member may span over the joists spaced at a maximum of 24″ center to center.

These two products do not require painting, staining, or sealing. Because all members are of exactly the same

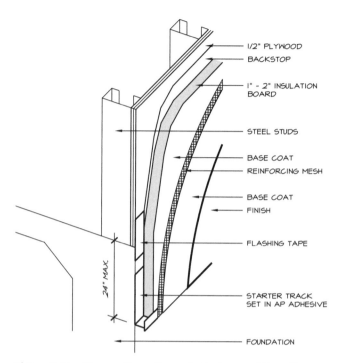

Figure 5.54 Composite wall panel attachment. (Compliments of Dryuit Systems, Inc.)

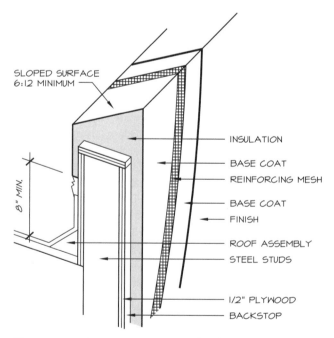

Figure 5.55 Composite parapet detail. (Compliments of Dryuit Systems, Inc.)

Figure 5.53 Composite wall panel. (Compliments of Dryuit Systems, Inc.)

size and shape, the installation process is made easier. See Figure 5.56.

The composite handrail system incorporates 2 × 6 handrails, 2 × 4 side rails, and 2 × 2 balusters. The use of screws with countersunk-type heads is recommended for connection of the various members. All screws must be predrilled. The composite handrail system is depicted in Figure 5.57. This handrail assembly shows the various member sizes that are available for construction of an exterior handrail system. See Figure 5.58.

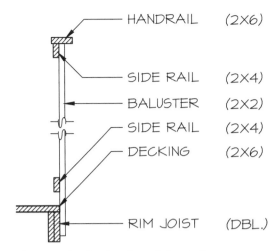

Figure 5.58 Section through handrail.

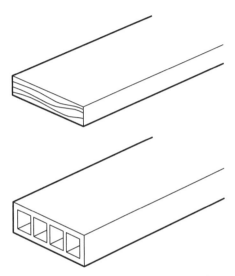

Figure 5.56 Composite decking members.

■ **MATERIAL SELECTIONS**

Material Selection

In the practice of architecture, an architectural firm will be confronted with the issue of selecting a material or materials for a specific project. This selection process is dictated by such factors as the governing building codes, fire department requirements, the architect's design philosophy, environmental influences, and economic considerations. For most structures, the main materials used are wood, concrete, structural steel, masonry, light steel framing, and composite materials. For many structures, a combination of materials may be utilized.

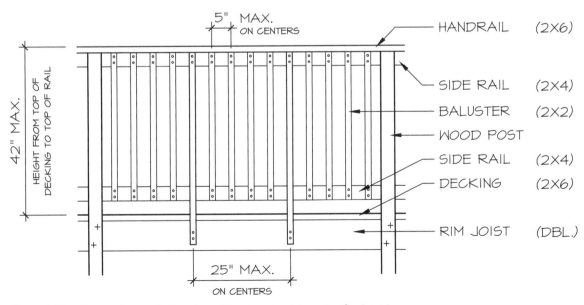

Figure 5.57 Composite handrail system. (Courtesy Louisiana Pacific Corp.)

■ WOOD AS A MATERIAL

Wood Materials

The layout of a floor plan using a wood stud framing system is very flexible in comparison to that of a floor plan using another material. This is because openings in the exterior and interior walls are not restricted by a modular unit or other material constraints. Wood also performs well in environmental conditions such as seismic events or hurricanes.

When a conventional wood stud framing system has been selected for the floor, walls, and roof systems, the floor plan drawings must be graphically correct. For example, a wood stud wall system is presented with the use of two parallel lines, which may be drawn to scale, incorporating the wood stud size in combination with the exterior and interior finishes. An example of a floor plan for a small dwelling, using two parallel lines to represent a conventional 2 × 4 wood stud wall in plan view, is illustrated in Figure 5.59. The exterior walls are dimensioned from the face of the wood stud as abbreviated with the letters "f.o.s.," indicating "face of stud." This method of dimensioning will correspond to the face of the concrete foundation footing, thus providing a good dimensional check for both the floor plan and the foundation plan. For layout purposes, the width of the two parallel lines will be the stud width of 3½″ plus the thickness of the exterior and interior wall finishes. The interior walls are dimensioned to the centerline of the walls, as indicated in Figure 5.59. Note that the 4 × 4 post is dimensioned to the centerline in both directions.

Figure 5.60 represents a view of the corner framing condition for this small dwelling. This is shown to illustrate the actual dimension line as it relates to the stud face dimension. The corner layout is intended to maximize strength and accommodate the connection of the finish materials to the studs. In this example, gypsum board can be screwed to two of the interior corner studs, while the cement plaster can be nailed to the exterior corner stud.

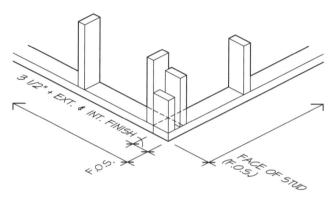

Figure 5.60   Corner framing layout.

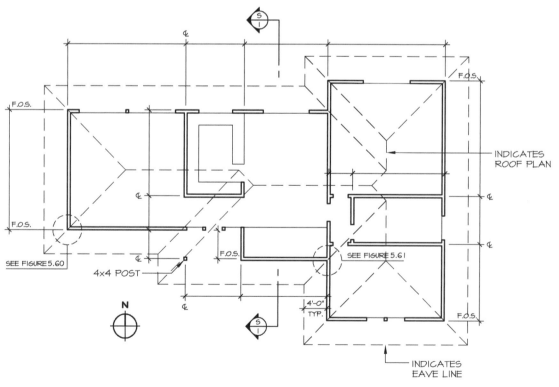

Figure 5.59   Floor plan with 2 × 4 stud framing.

In laying out the interior walls of the floor plan, the two parallel lines are drawn to scale, incorporating the width of the wood stud plus the thickness of the interior wall finishes. See Figure 5.61.

Exterior Elevations

The design and layout for the exterior elevations are developed in conjunction with the floor-plan exterior wall openings, exterior wall material, roofing material, and roof pitch. The architect for this small dwelling has chosen to use a hip roof design, utilizing cement tiles as a finish roof material. The roof plan is illustrated in Figure 5.59. Based on the foregoing considerations, the design and layout for the exterior elevations may then proceed. Figure 5.62 illustrates the design and layout of the South elevation. A plate height of 9′ is measured from

the top of the concrete floor to the top of the 2 × 4 stud plate; the roof plan has determined the 4′ overhang, the roof pitch, and the horizontal soffit at the eaves, which terminate just above the exterior window and exterior door trims. From the South and West elevations, a view is developed on the computer to allow further study and presentation. See Figure 5.63.

Building Section

It is recommended that you study a preliminary building section before developing the exterior elevations. As discussed in the development of the exterior elevations, the architect determined a roof pitch, an eave overhang, and a soffit so as to terminate the finish soffit material directly above the exterior window and door trims. This design requirement also established a 9′ plate height dimension from the top of the concrete floor to the top plate. Generally, the plate heights for light residential wood structures are from 8′-0¾″ to 10′-0″. A wood stud framing system provides flexibility in the design and construction process. Figure 5.64 illustrates a building section that is cut through the floor plan at the building section symbol location on the floor plan in Figure 5.59. As indicated by the building section symbol, the section cut is looking in the westerly direction.

Note that the horizontal soffit at the roof eave terminates just above the normal window and door height of 6′-8″. The size and grade of the wood supporting members in the roof system will be determined later in the working drawings by the architect or the structural engineer.

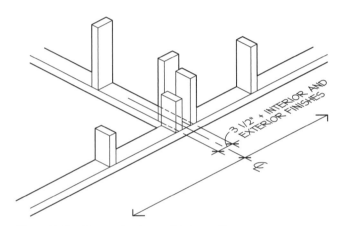

Figure 5.61 Perpendicular wall intersection.

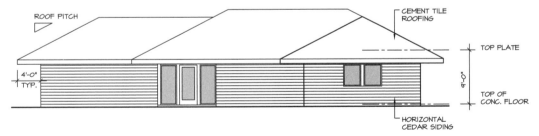

Figure 5.62 South elevation.

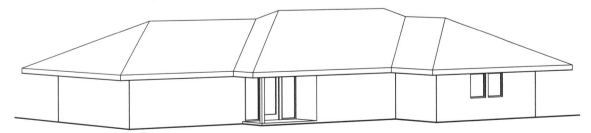

Figure 5.63 South/West exterior view.

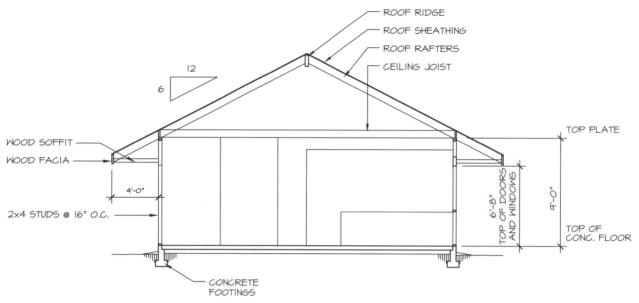

Figure 5.64   Building section.

Wood Post and Beam

Another project to be built with wood may use a different format with a conventional wood stud construction system. For example, a wood modular system may be selected for the structure. This system will incorporate the use of posts and beams spaced at a preferred dimensional distance. The modular distance will depend on the type and size of the floor and roof members that will span between the modular beam systems. These members may use solid tongue-and-groove planking, sawn lumber joists, or engineered lumber joists. Modular post and beam systems may be used in light construction projects, such as a residence, or in the heavy timber construction of a public building. See Figure 5.65.

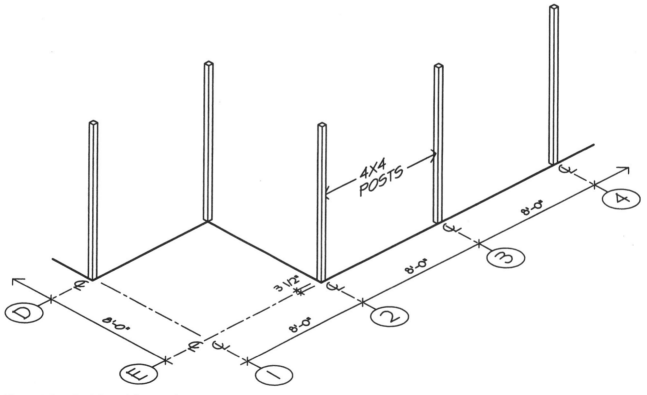

Figure 5.65   Partial modular post layout.

Floor Plan. The initial approach for development of a floor plan to be used in the working drawings for a project utilizing a wood post and beam system is to create a matrix system. This may also be referred to as a *dimensional reference system* (covered in Chapter 2) for the supporting post in each direction. The matrix for the wood post and beam system now provides the basic structural skeleton for the building's structure.

In most cases, this system is used to organize the wood structural members and the simplicity of the structural design. The dimensioning of this wood system is different from that of the conventional wood stud system. See Figure 5.66.

The post and beam construction method that utilizes a matrix system allows the location of any of the supporting columns and its corresponding concrete pier foundation supports. An example of locating a specific column is illustrated in Figure 5.66, where column B-3 has been defined for referencing. Any one of these specific columns can be utilized for the purpose of referencing dimension lines to the interior wall locations.

Exterior Elevations. Development of the exterior elevations for a modular wood post and beam system would depict the wood columns according to the matrix layout, while also establishing the desired wall and bottom-of-beam heights. In addition, the dimensioning of roof overhangs may be referenced from a specific matrix designation. See Figure 5.67. A partial drawing of Figure 5.67 is shown in Figure 5.68.

Building Section. The next major item to consider and analyze is the building sections for the post and beam wood framing method. As previously mentioned, the roof and floor system may consist of tongue-and-groove planking, sawn lumber joist, or engineered lumber members. For this project, the architect decided to use tongue-and-groove planking spanning over the exposed beams, which are to be spaced 8' center to center. Nailed directly over the tongue-and-groove planking will be one layer of 3/8" exterior-grade plywood. To meet energy conservation standards, one layer of insulation board, such as urethane, will be applied over the plywood and

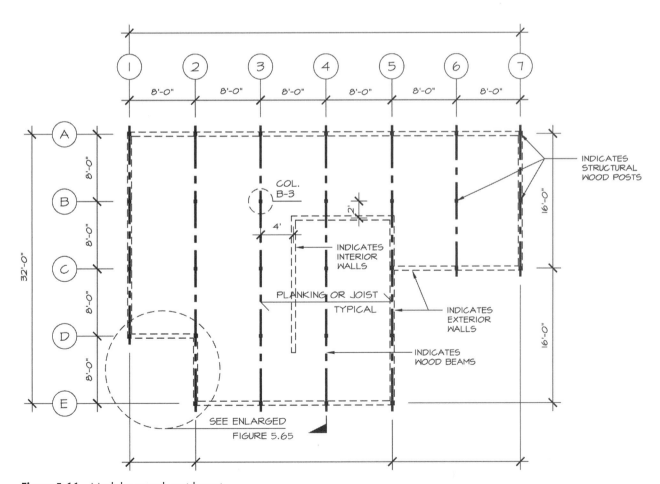

Figure 5.66 Modular wood post layout.

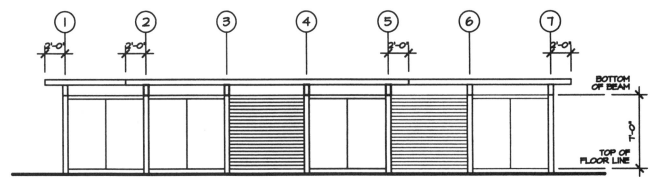

Figure 5.67   Exterior elevation of a post and beam system.

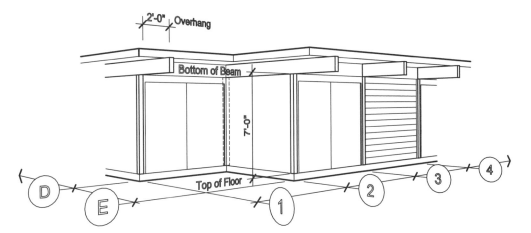

Figure 5.68   Partial drawing of Figure 5.67.

will be the substrate for the application of a built-up roofing system. See Figure 5.69. This building section is viewed along the matrix axis line ④. Figure 5.70 depicts pictorially a view along matrix line ④.

■ CONCRETE AS A MATERIAL

Concrete Material

Once concrete has been selected as the structural material for a building project, it is necessary to decide whether the concrete will be poured in place or whether precast concrete will be used. If precast concrete units have been selected for construction of the exterior and interior walls and the roof system, it is of paramount importance to consult with the project's structural engineer. From the approved preliminary building design, the structural engineer will determine the thickness of the interior and exterior walls. The thickness of a wall will depend on whether it is a load-bearing or non-load-bearing wall and whether it will have to resist wind, snow, or lateral loads. These determinations will allow the architect to lay out the exact wall thickness on the floor

plan. See Figure 5.71. This initial drawing of the floor plan establishes the wall thickness for the load-bearing and non-load-bearing precast concrete walls. The walls shown on matrix lines A, B, and D are non-load-bearing walls and have been determined to be 5″ thick. The wall thickness for the load-bearing walls along matrix lines 1 through 9 are to be 7″ thick. The load-bearing walls have been engineered to support 6″ precast concrete cored slab panels, which will span 21′. The use of a matrix system provides clarity for identifying the various precast concrete panel locations. See Figure 5.71.

The next step in developing the floor plan layout is to provide the building dimensions and the various wall thickness dimensions. Also noted at this time are the directional arrows for the spans of precast hollow-core panels that will support the roof. Indicated on the span directional arrows are the thickness of the concrete cored slab panels, which is 6″, and the abbreviation HC, which means hollow core. A directional arrow is drawn between the matrix symbols ① and ⑨ to further illustrate the bays that the hollow-core precast panels are spanning. On this arrow are noted four bays at 21′ with an overall length of 84′. At this stage, the basic floor plan layout shows the primary structural members.

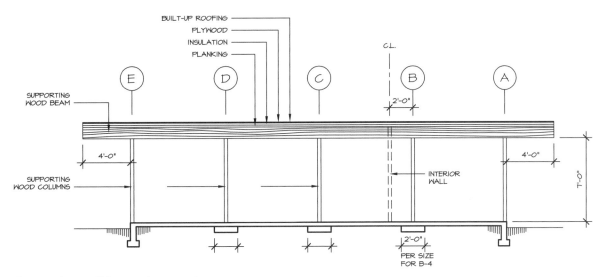

Figure 5.69 Building section on axis 4.

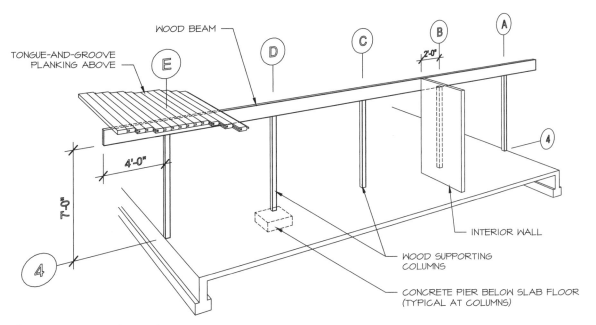

Figure 5.70 Pictorial view along matrix 4.

Exterior Elevations

Because this is a light manufacturing building, it was decided to provide 14'-high ceilings. The ceiling heights thus dictate the wall heights. Figure 5.72 depicts the North elevation, and Figure 5.73 illustrates the West elevation. As shown, these exterior elevations illustrate the dimensioning of such items as the top of the parapet, the ceiling level height above the concrete floor, and the height of the steel overhead doors. These dimensions provide the necessary information for the sizes of the precast concrete wall panels, which will be manufactured and delivered to the building site. Also indicated on the North elevation are the precast sections that are to be finished in a textured scored concrete. See Figure 5.74.

Building Sections

In conjunction with the necessary drawings for the building sections, it will be important to develop the precast panel drawings illustrating the wall dimensions and wall thickness for each specific panel. These panels should be identified with an elevation drawing and a panel identification number. See Figure 5.75. The precast panel to be placed between matrix numbers ① and ② from Figure 5.72 is defined as panel P-1. Panel identification may be shown on the floor plan, or a key plan may be provided.

The number of building sections to be illustrated on a set of working drawings will be the number needed to clearly explain and show the various conditions that exist for a specific building. Figure 5.76 depicts a building

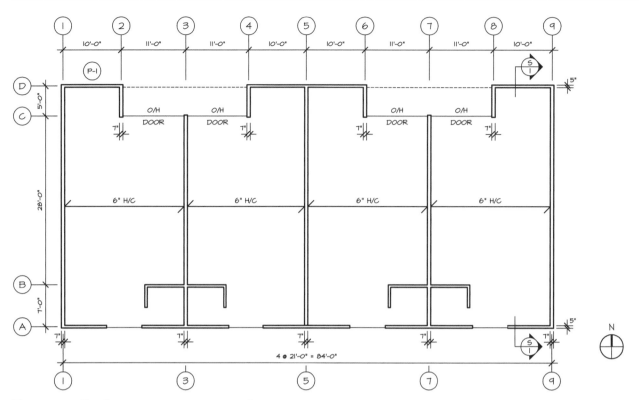

Figure 5.71 Plan layout—precast concrete walls.

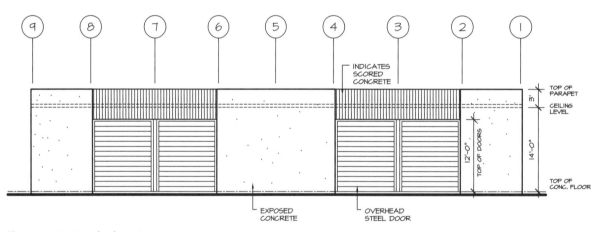

Figure 5.72 North elevation.

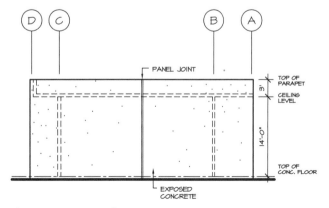

Figure 5.73 West elevation.

section cut in the north-south direction as referenced on the floor plan. The figure illustrates the dimensional heights for the ceiling and parapet and identifies the direction of the precast concrete cored roof panels. At the east and west outside walls, a corbel or haunch, which is formed in the precast wall panel, will be necessary to support the precast cored panels at the end wall conditions. See Figure 5.77. Similar requirements and drawings will be necessary for a project using a poured-in-place concrete construction method. These requirements will pertain to wall height dimensions, wall thickness, steel reinforcing, and any type of architectural feature.

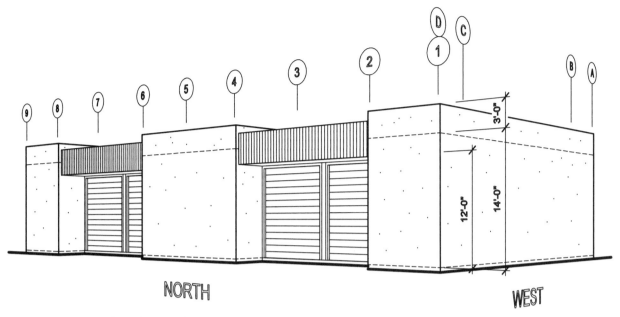

Figure 5.74 View of North/West elevations.

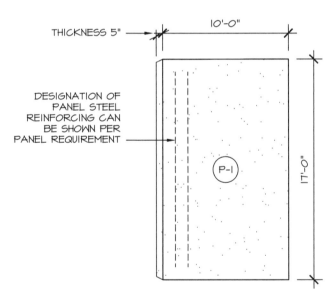

Figure 5.75 Precast concrete panel.

■ STEEL AS A MATERIAL

Steel

When selecting steel as a construction material for a building project, it is necessary to decide whether the steel components are to be structural steel members or light steel framing members. The use of structural steel members, such as "W" shapes, "S" shapes, tubes, or channels, will probably dictate the use of a matrix identification system. For a light steel framing system, the approach will be similar to that used for a wood stud framing system.

If an architectural firm has been commissioned to design and prepare working drawings for an office building incorporating structural steel members, then the game plan is to establish a matrix identification system. A matrix system will identify the column and beam locations as well as spread concrete footings and concrete piers. Before formulating a floor plan layout with the steel column locations, it is necessary to consult with the project's structural engineer for his or her recommended span lengths between the supporting steel columns. With the structural engineer's preliminary recommendations, the architects may proceed with the preliminary studies, incorporating the client's requirements and all the other design considerations necessary in designing a building.

Floor Plan

When creating a floor plan for a building using structural steel members, it is desirable to incorporate continuity and simplicity in the column and beam spacing. This allows for standardization of column and beam sizing while maintaining simplicity in the steel fabrication process. Figure 5.78 depicts a ground-level floor plan that uses a matrix system to identify the column and beam locations. To enclose the steel columns in the finished north or south walls, it will be necessary to have a wall 8" or more thick. The columns along the matrix lines A and D are a minimum of 8" in thickness. Their call-out

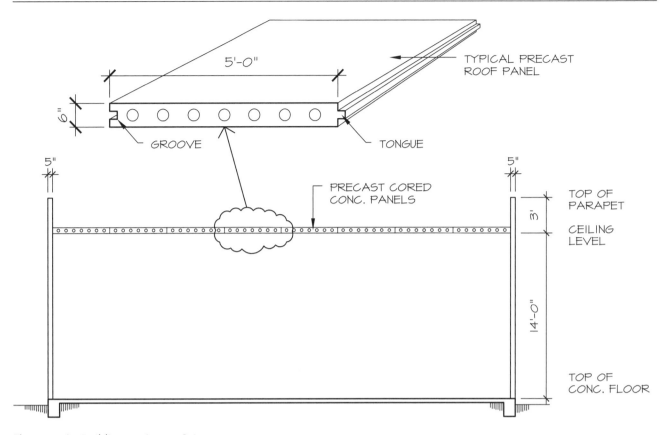

Figure 5.76 Building section on S-1.

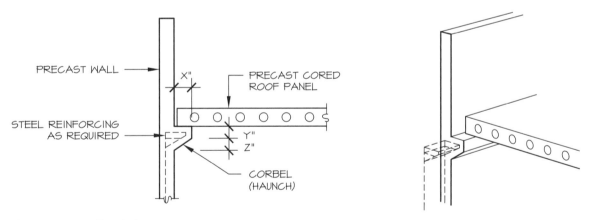

Figure 5.77 Wall corbel.

size is W8 × 15. W describes the wide flange shape; 8 is the depth measured in inches; 15 represents the weight in pounds per linear foot. The east and west walls will be dictated by the flange width of the steel columns along matrix lines ① and ④. These flanges are 4″ wide.

The interior wall partition layout may be dimensioned from the various matrix line identifications. An example is shown on the ground-floor plan where the office partition walls are dimensioned from the column identified at matrix lines ② and C.

Second-Level Floor Plan

In the second-level floor plan, columns and beams will align directly over the ground-floor steel members. However, the column and beam sizes will be different because they are not supporting as much weight as the ground-floor members. The steel columns on the second-floor level will be W6 × 12 members. The finished wall thickness, on the north and south walls, will thus have to be a minimum of 6″ to enclose the columns

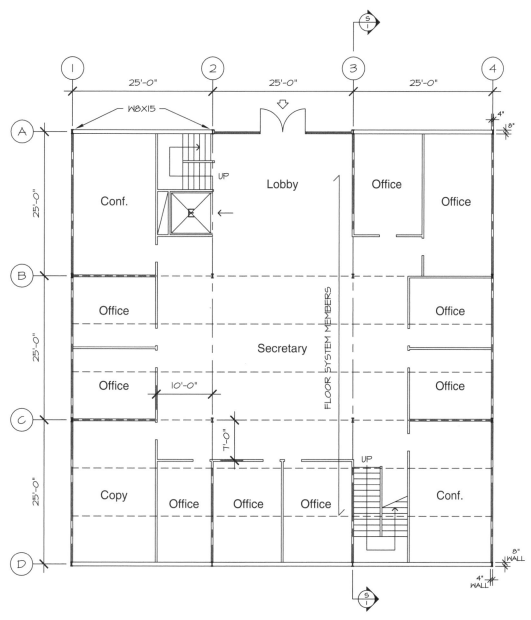

Figure 5.78 Ground-level floor plan.

along matrix lines A and D. See Figure 5.79. The finished wall thickness along matrix lines ① and ④ will have to be a minimum of 4″ because the flange width of the W6×12 steel column is 4″. When dimensioning the wall thickness for the enclosure of steel columns, it is recommended that the properties of the steel members be verified by referring to the *Manual of Steel Construction*.

Exterior Elevations

The process in developing preliminary exterior elevations is to coordinate the basic requirements established by the structural and mechanical engineers. For example, the structural engineer may establish the unsupported heights for selected steel columns, and the mechanical engineer may provide a recommended dimensional clearance for the mechanical ducts. The plenum area is the allocated space between the top of the finished ceiling and the bottom of the floor and roof system members. This space is used for heating and cooling ducts and various plumbing lines. These dimensional requirements are needed for the layout of the preliminary exterior elevations relative to their building heights. See Figure 5.80.

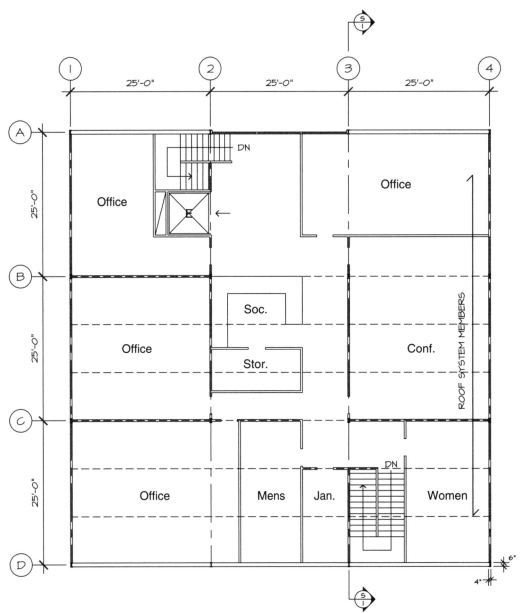

Figure 5.79 Second-level floor plan.

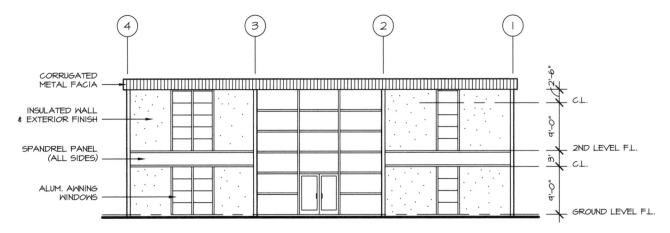

Figure 5.80 North elevation.

Building Sections

The initial layout dimensionally illustrates the recommended floor-to-finished-ceiling height, while also showing the recommended dimensional space for the plenum area. Preliminary engineering calculations provide the approximate steel column and beam sizes necessary for development of the building sections.

Figure 5.81 is taken along matrix line ③, which is in the north-south direction looking eastward. Refer to the ground-level floor plan in Figure 5.78 for the building section designation symbol.

Here the architect decided to use a composite floor and roof system utilizing corrugated steel decking and concrete fill as indicated on the building section. As shown in Figure 5.81, dimensions are provided for the heights of the concrete floor to the bottom of the second floor and the top of the second floor to the bottom of the roof beams. This may also be achieved with the use of vertical elevations relative to the ground-floor concrete slab elevation. A pictorial view of the building section is given in Figure 5.82. A photograph taken at the jobsite illustrates a typical corner first-floor steel column and beam. See Figure 5.83.

Another jobsite photograph (Figure 5.84) illustrates a beam and columns found along matrix line A at the first-floor level.

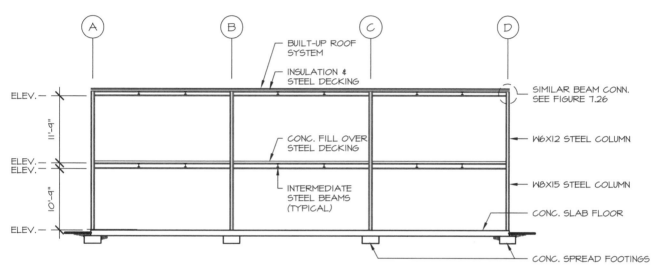

Figure 5.81 Building section.

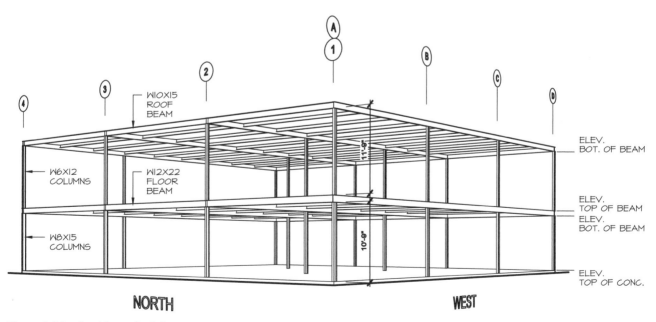

Figure 5.82 Steel frame building system.

Figure 5.83 Photograph of a similar column and beam connection. (Courtesy of Rich Development.)

Figure 5.84 Photograph of ground-floor steel columns and beam.

■ MASONRY AS A MATERIAL

Masonry

Masonry has proven to be a versatile and durable construction material. Various types of masonry products are available for the construction of buildings. In general, reinforced grouted brick masonry units and reinforced CMU are widely used in the construction of residential, commercial, and industrial structures.

Wall thickness and modular layout will depend on whether reinforced grouted brick masonry or concrete masonry units are selected. Brick masonry units are manufactured in a great range of sizes, starting with the standard brick size of 2½" × 3⅜" × 8¼" and ranging to a brick block size of 7⅝" × 5½" × 15½". CMU are often referred to as *concrete block units*. Though sizes vary, a typical modular concrete block unit is rectangular with dimensions of 8" wide, 8" high, and 16" long.

Floor Plan

The initial approach to a floor plan layout is for the architect to select the type of masonry material that will be used in the building project. Suppose an architectural firm has selected CMU for the exterior walls of a small industrial building, utilizing an 8" × 8" × 16" modular system. This selection will now dictate the initial floor plan layout. Because the architect is dealing with a precast modular unit, he or she will delineate the exterior walls to 8" wide while recognizing the length of the modular unit as it relates to dimensioning and wall openings. When possible, it is more practical and efficient to lay out the walls and vertical wall heights with the standard concrete block modular sizes. This will eliminate the need to saw-cut the concrete units, which will lessen the construction costs and save construction time.

An example of a light industrial building floor-plan layout using 8 × 8 × 16 CMU is illustrated in Figure 5.85. This floor plan has used standard size CMU in order to eliminate the process of saw-cutting any of the modular units. The dimensioning of the door and window openings adheres to the length of the modular units, also referred to as *stretchers*. An acceptable method of delineating CMU in plan view is shown in the enlarged portion of Figure 5.85. A view showing a part of the floor plan is depicted in Figure 5.86.

Exterior Elevations

It is paramount to develop and design the exterior wall heights to accommodate the height of the concrete blocks when CMU has been selected for a project. In this case, the CMU are 8" in height, and therefore a multiple of these units will dictate the height to the top of the concrete block wall. Figures 5.87 and 5.88 illustrate a wall height of 16', which translates to 24 courses of 8"-high concrete block units. The window and door heights are also at the height of a multiple of concrete block units. In this case, the tops of the doors and windows will be at a height of 10', which is established with the use of 15 8"-high concrete masonry units. A pictorial view of the North and West elevations is given in Figure 5.89.

Building Sections

The study of the preliminary building sections usually coincides with the development of the exterior elevations, in order to determine the wall heights and the wall material. The study also includes the type of roof system and its material composition. In the example of

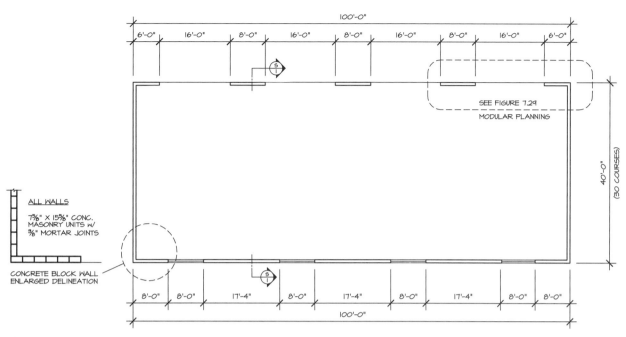

Figure 5.85   Concrete masonry modular units floor plan.

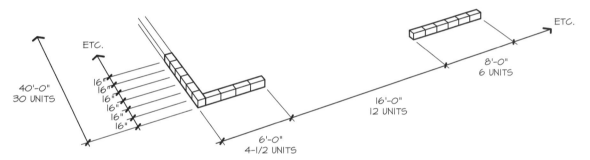

Figure 5.86   Blocks using a modular floor-plan layout.

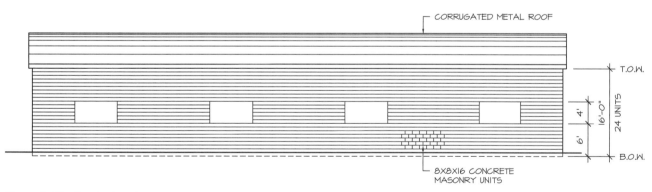

Figure 5.87   South elevation.

the light industrial building, a building section S-1 has been taken in the north-south direction, as indicated in Figure 5.85. This building section delineates the top and bottom of the concrete masonry wall, in which case the height of the masonry wall is established by the desired number and height of the modular CMU. See Figure 5.90. As previously indicated, the wall height has been established by the height and number of concrete block units while addressing the requirements for this type of building. See Figure 5.90.

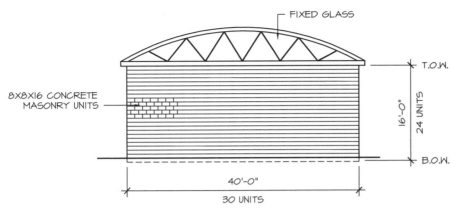

Figure 5.88 East elevation.

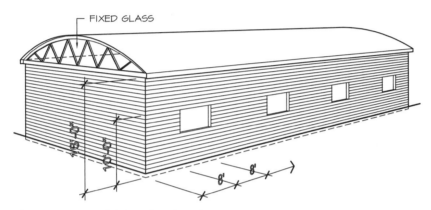

Figure 5.89 North/West elevation view.

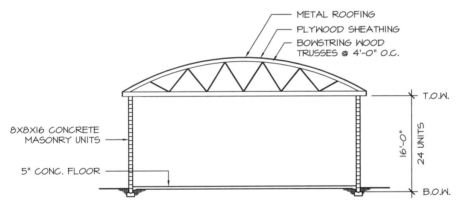

Figure 5.90 Building section S-1.

INITIAL PREPARATION PHASE FOR CONSTRUCTION DOCUMENTS

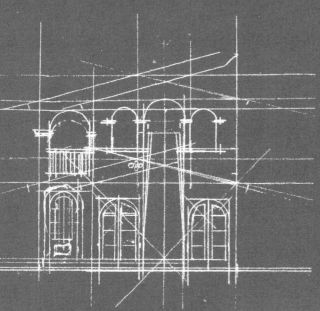

■ WORKING GUIDELINES FOR PREPARING CONSTRUCTION DOCUMENTS

Construction Documents

Guidelines are too important to reduce to a series of steps and formulas to memorize. In fact, working guidelines for drafting are actually attitudes and ideals that are fundamental to good communication. Communication produces understanding; without it, the project will not progress smoothly.

You may think that much of this material is obvious, common knowledge, or common sense. Yet, if these guidelines are known but *not acted upon,* mass confusion and anguish result. They have been arrived at through research in supervision, communication, human relationships, and field experiences, particularly with prospective employers. Remember, in an architectural firm you are not an individual; rather, you are an important part of a team. As a team member, you must know how the others on the team function.

The Rules for Drafting Construction Documents
1. Plan every step of your drawing.
2. Establish some manner in which you can check your work.
3. Understand the decisions you will be asked to make.
4. Know and understand the standards under which you will function.
5. Draft from the other person's point of view.
6. Cooperate, communicate, and work with others.
7. Find out your primary and secondary responsibilities. Don't assume.
8. Think for yourself.
9. Concentrate on improving at least one aspect of your skills with each task.
10. Be sure to follow established office standards. This is critical.

The Rules for Drafting Construction Documents, Expanded
1. *Plan every step of your drawing.* Each drawing has a distinct procedure and an order. Use your mind's eye to completely draw the object first. Make mental and/or written notes about the sequence and anticipated problems. Every sheet of a set of architectural plans subscribes to a basic system. The system may be based on the materials used, methods of erection, limits of the present technology, or even the limits of the builder, to mention just a few. Whatever the controlling and limiting factors are, be aware of them, understand them, digest them intellectually, and put them into effect. Know your options when you have an unusual problem.

2. *Establish some manner in which you can check your work.* Every office has some method of checking drawings. The method may be a check sheet developed by the principal draftsperson or others. Whatever the system, establish a method to check yourself before you submit a drawing to a senior in the firm. This does two things. First, it builds trust between you and your supervisor. If you are conscientious enough to double-check your work, the rapport built between you and your supervisor will be enhanced. In addition, it builds the supervisor's confidence that you have done your best to perform your duty. Always double-check your corrections, too; if done poorly, changes can exacerbate errors.

   This checking method differs with each person and each drawing. Each checking method is based on the construction system used. If you understand the system, you will usually understand how to check it.

   Accuracy transcends all checking systems—accuracy of representation as well as of arithmetic, grammar, and spelling. Nothing causes as many problems in the field as contradictory information, arithmetical tools that are not equal to their parts, or dimensions that do not reflect an established module.

3. *Understand the decisions you will be asked to make.* Know what decisions you will be allowed to make, and know when to ask a superior.

   If you ask a superior for help every time you are confronted with a decision, you are taking up that person's valuable time, reducing the superior's effectiveness, and demonstrating that you are not really ready for the job. Nevertheless, a production draftsperson (a person drafting construction documents) cannot simply change a design decision; the draftsperson may not be aware of all the factors that led to that decision. It might seem obvious to the draftsperson that a particular change would produce a better effect, but the original may have been based on a code requirement, a client's request, cost of production, or any one of hundreds of reasons of which the draftsperson may not be aware.

   Make sure that your duties, responsibilities, and, above all, the decisions you are allowed to make are clearly defined by your superior.

4. *Know and understand the standards under which you will function.* You will encounter a multitude of standards. Just as there are various standards for office attire, ethics, and behavior, so there are drawing standards.

   Each sheet you draw will have a setup standard. Certain offices use certain sheet sizes. Title blocks, border lines, and sheet space allocation are usually set up in advance. In fact, some offices produce what is called a *manual* of "office standards." The standard may call for something as simple as a font style, or as professional as a standard based on building erection procedures. Whether it is a building code, a state-regulated requirement, or a personal whim of an employer, you must incorporate this standard into your documents.

5. *Draft from the other person's point of view.* Your work involves many individuals who will interpret your drawings: people like the subcontractor in the field, the person who assigns you your duties, the client, and the contractor. All of these people influence your approach. For example, when you draft for the subcontractor in the field, your work becomes a medium of communication between the client's needs and the individuals who construct and execute the structure to meet those needs. Before drafting a detail, plan, or section, you must sufficiently understand the trades involved so that you do not ask a person or machine to perform an unreasonable task.

As for drafting from your employer's point of view, first and foremost understand what your task is. It is better to spend a few minutes with your supervisor at the beginning of a drawing, outlining your duties and the firm's objectives and needs, than to spend countless hours on a drawing only to find that much of the time you have spent is wasted.

By the time a drawing task reaches you, the client and the designer have already made a number of design and construction decisions. No matter what the reasons are for these decisions, the office and the client have an understanding, which you must respected and do everything you can to support. If you know of a better solution or method, verify its appropriateness with a superior before you employ it.

6. *Cooperate, communicate, and work with others.* One of the main criticisms from employers is that employees do not know how to work as members of a team. Whereas education requires you to perform as an individual, each person in an office is a member of a team and has certain responsibilities, duties, and functions on which others rely. There may be many people working on a single project, and you must understand your part and participate with others toward achieving a common goal.

Be clear about the way you communicate your ideas. Write memos and notes, write formal letters to other companies, and document correspondence. Keep in mind that you are a representative of your firm and that proper presentation, grammar, spelling, and punctuation reflect the abilities of the firm.

Communication helps you know what the other people in the firm are doing and it helps you to develop an appreciation of the attitudes, goals, and aims of the others with whom you will be working.

Know what is going on in the office and allow others to easily track your progress.

7. *Find out your primary and secondary responsibilities. Don't assume.* Nothing gets an office or an employee in as much trouble as making assumptions. Phrases such as "I thought John was going to do it" not only break down the communication process in an office, but can create discord that disturbs office harmony and breaks down office morale.

Know your responsibilities and how and whom to ask for guidance in case of a change in your responsibilities.

A classic example of this was an office that had two divisions: an architectural division and a structural engineering division. Each prepared a set of drawings and each division assumed that the other would develop a set of details. On the architectural drawings there were notations that read, "See structural drawings for details." The structural group made the detail reference to the architectural set. The details were never drawn, and when the total set was assembled and the lack of details was discovered, the omission caused a great delay and much embarrassment to the firm.

Whenever more than one person works on a project, you need to understand not only your primary responsibilities, but your not-so-obvious secondary responsibilities as well.

8. *Think for yourself.* There is a natural tendency for a draftsperson to feel that all decisions should be made by a superior. However, your supervisor will tell you that certain decisions have been delegated to you.

If you ask for help each time a problem arises or you reach a decision point, your supervisor will not be able to do his or her job effectively. Your immediate supervisor or head draftsperson is earning two to five times as much as you are because of additional responsibilities and experience. Therefore, each time you ask a question and stop production, the cost is that of your salary plus that of your supervisor.

Research the solution before you approach your seniors. Look through reference and manufacturers' literature, construction manuals, similar projects, reference books, and so on. Make a list of problems and questions and work around them until your superior is free and available to deal with them. Arrange your time to suit your supervisor's convenience. THINK and be able to propose solutions or suggestions yourself.

Above all, do not stop production and wait around for a superior to become available; do not follow them around. Employers react very negatively to this.

9. *Concentrate on improving one aspect of your skills with each task.* Constantly improve your speed, your setup, your accuracy. As athletes continuously work to perfect some part of their ability, so should you. Work on your weakest aspect first, even though the tendency is to avoid or shy away from it. For example, if sections are your problem, view and study various sections from the office, texts, or publications. Make yourself familiar with a variety of sections. A draftsperson who can draft, detail, communicate, and research is a valuable commodity in an office and will always be employed, because an office cannot afford to lose such a versatile person.

An employer wants an employee who is punctual, dependable, and accurate; has a high degree of integrity; and is able to work with a minimum amount of supervision.

10. *Be sure to follow established office standards. This is critical.* Office standards are an integral part of the evolution of construction documents. It is not sufficient merely to follow the standards; it is also necessary to understand why they are used. Certain standards are used because associates such as structural, mechanical, electrical, and plumbing engineers use the same documents as those used in the architectural office. Layer titles, basic symbols, and conventions, while simple to implement, must be the same from a Los Angeles office to a New York office.

■ MAKING THE TRANSITION FROM SCHEMATIC DRAWINGS TO CONSTRUCTION DOCUMENTS

Making the transition from approved schematic drawings, to design development drawings, to construction documents is important because it completes the process of making decisions about the physical characteristics of the building. When utilizing BIM or Revit within these three phases, this system does not vary. Once this transition is made, the production of construction documents can proceed.

Accomplishing this transition—the design development phase—requires that the following basic requirements be satisfied and thoroughly investigated:

1. Building code and other requirements, such as those set by the zoning department, fire department, health department, planning department, engineering department, environmental department, and architectural committees
2. Primary materials analysis and selection
3. Selection of the primary structural system and materials

4. Requirements of consultants, such as mechanical, electrical, plumbing, and structural engineers
5. Regional and environmental considerations
6. Energy conservation considerations and requirements
7. Budget alignment
8. Project programming

■ BUILDING CODE REQUIREMENTS

Building codes exist to establish the minimum requirements for life safety. Components of a code cover areas such as exiting, fire resistivity, occupancy, and disability access. Although some things are specified in great detail, such as the maximum rise of a stair and the minimum depth of a tread, some aspects are more general, such as a requirement of two exits for a specific occupancy group. An understanding of these codes aids the architect in the decisionmaking process.

It is extremely important that you research building code requirements, as they are updated occasionally and new requirements are implemented. In multiple housing projects as well as in residential projects, building codes establish minimum physical requirements for various rooms. Figure 6.1 shows the minimum floor areas and dimensions required for the bedroom and kitchen.

Remember that the building department sets minimum standards. An architect sets standards (often above minimum) to satisfy or enhance health and safety. For

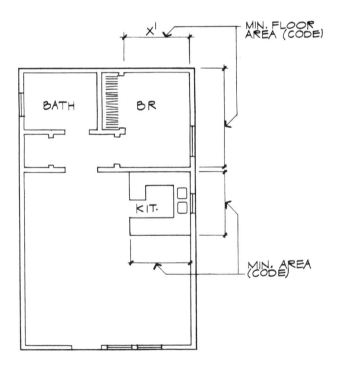

Figure 6.1 Required minimum dimensions.

example, the maximum slope for a disability ramp is 1:12. An architect may choose to use 1:14 as the slope of the ramp to be more accommodating to the individual using a wheelchair.

■ PRIMARY MATERIALS ANALYSIS

Material Analysis

In any building project, among the most important building materials to be selected are those for foundations and floors, exterior and interior walls, and ceiling and roof structures. Several factors influence this selection, and many of these require considerable investigation and research:

1. Architectural design
2. Building codes
3. Economics
4. Structural concept
5. Region
6. Ecology
7. Energy conservation

The importance of selection is illustrated in Figure 6.2. Concrete masonry units have been selected as the material for the exterior walls of a structure. Using this material affects the exterior and interior dimensions, because concrete blocks have fixed dimensions. Establishing the exterior and interior dimensions *before* the production of construction documents is most important, because

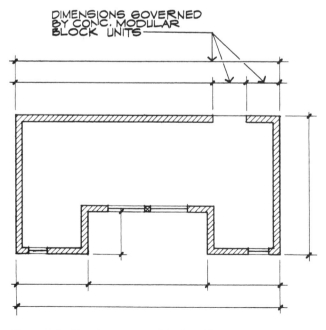

Figure 6.2 Exterior concrete block walls.

other phases, such as structural engineering, are based on these dimensions.

Modular and Nonmodular Units

The term *module* refers to a predetermined dimension from which structures are designed. *Block module* is usually used in conjunction with masonry units, such as bricks, concrete blocks, or structural clay tiles.

Masonry units can be broadly classified as either modular or nonmodular. The mortar joint between two units is usually either ⅜″, ⁷/₁₆″, or ½″ thick. Modular sizes are designed to ensure that final measurements, including mortar joints, are in whole numbers. Nonmodular units result in fractional measurements.

For example, an 8 × 8 × 16 modular concrete block unit measures 7⅝″ × 7⅝″ × 15⅝″, so that a ⅜″ mortar joint produces a final 8 × 8 × 16 measurement to work with. Half sizes are also available, so that when the units are stacked on top of each other, lapping each other by one-half the length of the block, the end of the structure comes out even. See Figure 6.3.

Certain lengths are commonly available. First, all even numbers of feet are available (2′-0″, 8′-0″, 2′-0″, etc.). Second, all odd-numbered feet have four inches added to them (for example, the length closest to 3 feet is 3′-4″; the length closest to 9 feet is 9′-4″; etc.). Third, all even-numbered feet are also available in 8″ increments, such as 4′-8″, 8′-8″, and 32′-8″.

Height is calculated in the same way. Note that 4″ blocks do not completely follow the rules mentioned earlier. A careful examination of the chart will reveal a single rule: All modular dimensions will be 4″, 8″, or 0″ (for example, 3′-4″, 6′-8″, or 10′-0″).

For a nonmodular system, the same size concrete block is used but with a different mortar joint. Odd fractions thus begin to appear. Only heights are shown. The mortar joints—both ⁷/₁₆″ and ½″—affect window and door sizes and heights.

Brick also comes in modular and nonmodular sizes. Examples of sizes for a modular unit are 5⅝″ × 2¼″

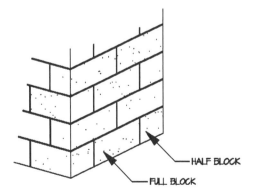

Figure 6.3 Use of half block.

× 7⅝″ for a ⅜″ joint and 3½″ × 2⅜″ × 7½″ for a ½″ joint. 2½″ × 3⅞″ × 8¼″ is a nonmodular size.

Here are some of the things you should consider when deciding whether to use the block module system:

1. Heights of the structure
2. Ceiling heights
3. Size of foundation if walls are masonry units
4. Size of floor plan if foundation wall is made of masonry units
5. Window and door width openings
6. Window and door heights
7. Details of window and doors (e.g., use of brick)

If you have a choice of modular or nonmodular materials, use modular. The dimensions are easier to figure out, and, as contractors report, the structure is faster, easier, and cheaper to build.

Why, then, would you choose nonmodular? You may be forced into nonmodular sizes. For example, building function might dictate overall size, as in an assembly plant. The client may require that a building occupy the full width or depth of a piece of property to maximize site use. An auditorium size is often dictated by seating arrangement or acoustics. A fire department regulation may determine certain size corridors for schools. These are only a few of the reasons for using a nonmodular system. If all these kinds of restraints can be satisfied by using modular units, use modular units. An alternative example is working in another country where standard modular units are not measured in inches.

The cost of cutting masonry units is rapidly decreasing, thus giving greater selection for almost any size structure, although cutting reduces the visual unity of the building and should be used with discretion.

The importance of selecting primary building materials is further shown in Figure 6.4. The roofing material selected here actually governs the roof pitch. This in turn establishes the physical height of the building and also dictates the size of the supporting members relative to the weight of the finished roof material.

■ SELECTING THE PRIMARY STRUCTURAL SYSTEM

The selection of a structural system and its members is influenced by meeting building code requirements; satisfying design elements; and using the most logical system based on sound engineering principles, economic considerations, simplicity, and environmental factors. For most projects, the architect consults with the structural engineer about systems or methods that will meet these various considerations. A structural concept is required before construction documents can be produced (see Figures 6.5 and 6.6). After a structural concept is established, the decisionmaking process is based on supporting that concept.

■ REQUIREMENTS OF CONSULTANTS

Early involvement of structural, electrical, mechanical, and civil engineering consultants is highly recommended. This is especially critical early in the design stage when using Revit. Their early involvement generally results in fewer adjustments having to be made to the finalized preliminary drawings to meet their design requirements. For example, the mechanical engineer's design may require a given area on the roof to provide space for various sizes of roof-mounted mechanical equipment. See Figure 6.7. For projects that require mechanical ducts to be located in floor and ceiling areas, necessary space and clearances for ducts must be provided. Figure 6.8 shows a floor and ceiling section with provisions for mechanical duct space.

The electrical engineer should also be consulted about any modifications to the building that may be required to provide space for electrical equipment. In most cases, the architect or project manager provides for an electrical equipment room or cabinet in the plans. However, with the increasing sophistication and size of equipment, additional space may be required. This increase in the electrical room dimensions may require a floor-plan adjustment, which can even result in a major or minor plan modification. Figure 6.9 illustrates a floor-plan modification to satisfy space requirements for electrical equipment. Elements such as transformers or backup generators may be required to be placed on the site, so the required clearances must also be accounted for.

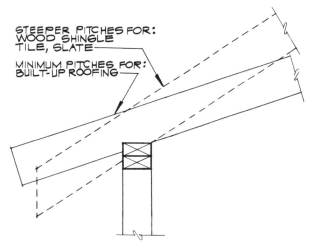

Figure 6.4 Roof material and roof pitches.

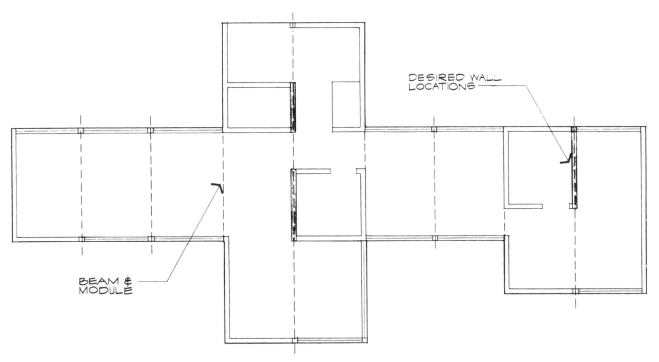

Figure 6.5 Wood post and beam structural system.

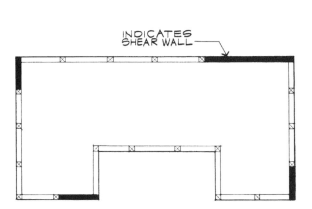

Figure 6.6 Plan view of shear wall locations.

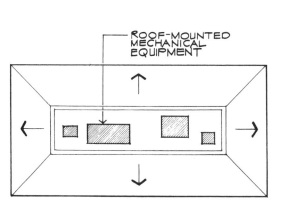

Figure 6.7 Roof plan with mechanical equipment area.

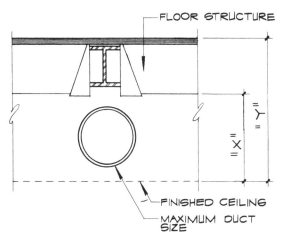

Figure 6.8 Mechanical duct space equipment.

■ REGIONAL CONSIDERATIONS

Regional differences in construction techniques are controlled or influenced primarily by climatic conditions, soil conditions, and natural events and forces such as high winds and seismic activity.

In brief, regional differences influence:

1. Soils or geological requirements
2. Environmental impacts
3. Structural assembly
4. Climatic impacts
5. Material availability

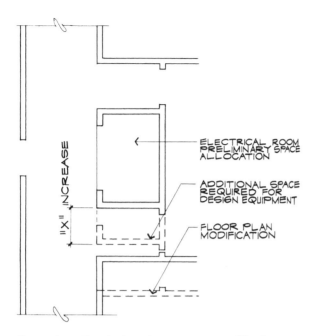

Figure 6.9 Electrical equipment room modification.

Figure 6.10 illustrates a type of foundation used in regions with cold climatic conditions: an exterior foundation wall and footing with a concrete floor. The depth of the foundation is established from the frost line, and insulation is required under the concrete floor.

Where temperatures are mild and warm, the foundation design and construction techniques are primarily governed by soils investigations and local building codes. Figure 6.11 illustrates an exterior foundation detail where the depth of the footing is established to a recommended depth below the natural grade.

Another example of regional influence is change in exterior wall design. Figure 6.12 shows a section of an exterior wall with wood frame construction. This open-frame construction is suitable for mild climates. A wood frame exterior wall recommended for eastern regions is shown in Figure 6.13. Here, solid sheathing is used, and this in turn requires the wood studs to be set in from the face of the foundation wall. This one regional difference can affect many procedures and detailing throughout the construction documents, such as wall dimensioning, window details, and door details.

Not every material is available in every region. For example, if a specific species of lumber is available only on the East Coast, it may not be environmentally or economically feasible to ship that lumber across the

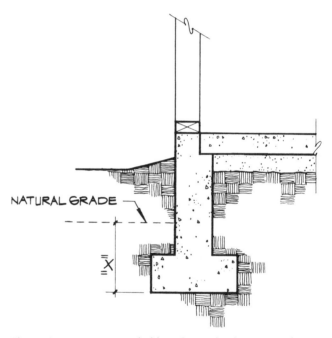

Figure 6.11 Recommended foundation depth in warm climate.

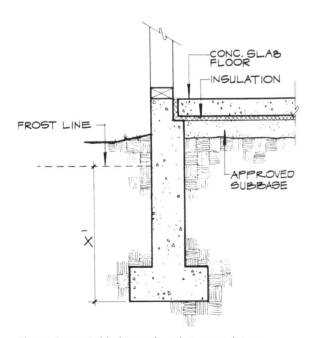

Figure 6.10 Cold-climate foundation conditions.

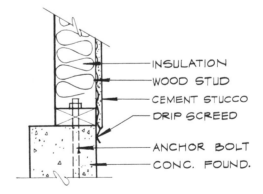

Figure 6.12 Exterior wall: Open-frame construction.

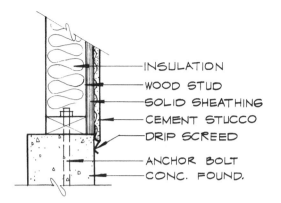

Figure 6.13 Exterior wall: Sheathed frame construction.

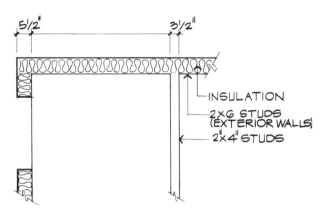

Figure 6.14 Floor-plan wall thickness.

country; hence, these regional considerations would mandate selection of a different timber.

■ ENERGY CONSERVATION

To determine what you must do to satisfy local and federal energy conservation requirements, you must complete preliminary research. These requirements can affect exterior wall material and thickness, amount and type of glazing, areas of infiltration (leakage of air), amount of artificial lighting to be used, thickness and type of insulation, mechanical engineering design, and so forth. For example, a wood building requires exterior walls to be 2 × 6 studs instead of 2 × 4 to allow for the thickness of the building insulation. This particular requirement dictates procedures in the construction document process, such as floor-plan wall thickness and dimensioning, window

and exterior door details, and other related exterior wall details. Figure 6.14 shows a segment of a floor plan that indicates the thickness of walls and the locations of required insulation.

An excellent example of an award-winning mechanical system that produces energy savings is an ice bank. The use of storage tanks in the design of a mechanical system can increase operating efficiency and considerably reduce both the electrical costs and the amount of energy used. An example of this storage-tank approach is the use of ice storage tanks to produce cooling for a large office building. Ice usually forms around the piping that carries the refrigerant located in a tank. The ice is produced during off-peak hours, such as during the night, when energy costs are at their lowest. This then provides the necessary coolant during the following day's peak-use hours. See Figure 6.15.

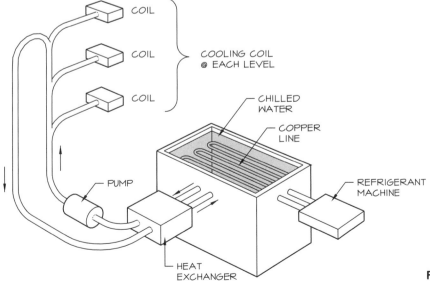

Figure 6.15 Ice bank system.

■ INTERRELATIONSHIP OF DRAWINGS

When you develop construction documents, you must have consistent relationships between the drawings for continuity and clarity. These relationships vary in their degree of importance.

For example, the relationship between the foundation plan and the floor plan is most important, because continuity of dimensioning and location of structural components for both are required. See Figure 6.16. The dimensioning of the floor plan and the foundation plan are identical, and this provides continuity for dimensional accuracy.

The relationship between drawings for the electrical plan and the mechanical plan is also critical. The positioning of electrical fixtures must not conflict with the location of mechanical components, such as air supply grilles or fire sprinkler heads.

Cross-reference drawings with important relationships such as these and constantly review them during preparation of the construction documents. The utilization of programs such as Revit is designed to identify conflicts and aid in determining where revisions are required.

This cross-referencing and review is not as critical with drawings that are not so closely related, such as the electrical plan and the civil engineering plans, or the interior elevations and the foundation plan. Nevertheless, it can still be important.

■ PROJECT MANAGEMENT

For many construction projects, a construction firm uses a time schedule process to coordinate all the trades, materials, and services necessary to finish the project by the scheduled completion date. Architects also use a time schedule for programming the phases of a project.

The primary phases of a project are programming, site analysis, schematic design, preliminary budget, client review, agency review (when required), design development, revised budget, client review, agency review (such as building and planning departments), construction documents, bidding and negotiating, final construction bids, and building and planning department approvals and permits.

■ OFFICE PROCEDURE AND PLANNING STRATEGY

Standards and Procedures

Most offices have a set procedure for planning the transition from schematic drawings to the development and execution of construction documents. In a small office, it may be a simple matter of the principal giving verbal directives to employees until a specific system is understood. In a large office, the system may be an intricate network of preplanned procedures.

There are two items in any office with which the beginner will be confronted. These are described herein as **standards**, standard graphic and written patterns to which the office subscribes, and **procedures**, the methods that are instituted during this transition and by which the standards are implemented.

Standards

Many offices have a booklet called **Office Standards** or the **Drafting Room Manual**. These are critical to both the employee and the employer. In large architectural firms, employees are asked to study and learn these standards. See Figure 6.17. It contains such items as the following:

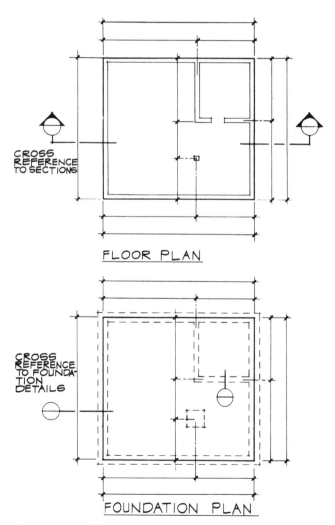

Figure 6.16 Relationship of foundation plan and floor plan.

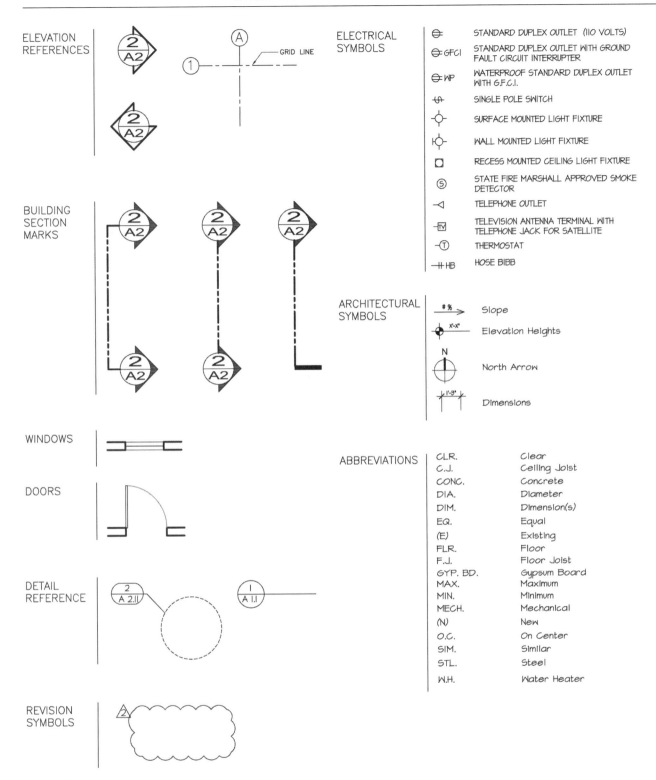

Figure 6.17 Sample of standard conventions.

1. A "Uniform List of Abbreviations" for working drawings
2. Material designations in plan, section, and elevation
3. Graphic symbols
4. Methods of representing doors and windows in both plan and elevation
5. Mechanical, electrical, and plumbing symbols
6. Graphic representations of appliances and fixtures
7. Sheet layout and drawing modules
8. Line weights and layers
9. BIM & Revit

Procedures

Think of the process, as described here, as parallel to a basketball or football game. It is important to understand the role of the owner of the team, the manager, the offense and defense coaches, and the team members, including the team captain. In this comparison, the owner might be viewed as the principal, the manager as the person in charge of the specific job, the offense and defense coaches as professional associates such as the electrical engineer and structural engineer, and, finally, the players as the drafters. The more seasoned the player (drafter), the more responsibility he or she takes on. These players often become the spirit, the determination, and the core around whom new players rally.

To take the analogy a step further, the spectators are the clients who have certain expectations; the umpires and referees can be compared with the building inspectors who check for violation of the rules of the game.

Procedures do, however, have added impacts: on the duration of the project, the cost/investment, and the lifespan of the project being executed. Moreover, our profession also addresses the health and safety, as well as the creative needs, of generations of clients.

■ TRACKING A SET OF WORKING DRAWINGS

Working Drawings

One should be able to locate, at a moment's notice, the precise progress of a set of construction documents. This is particularly critical for the office manager or job captain, who must track the progress of a set of drawings for budgetary reasons. He or she must know whether an entire set will meet the deadline, as well as the progress of a single drawing. In this way, the manager can check the productivity of employees, give an extra push to those falling behind, compliment those working ahead of schedule, and even recommend some for raises.

It is important to understand the total sequence followed by drafters so that individual participants can track their progress in relation to their colleagues to ensure that all drawings produced by the team will progress equally. For an overview of where areas of participation fit into the whole scheme of things in an office, see Figure 6.18. The initial design phase is done either by hand or by computer.

Datum Base

All construction documents should be datum based. If the documents are to be executed with CAD, the first layer should be a datum layer.

The datum is usually based on the material to be used in the construction and the system best suited for that selected material. For example, if steel is selected as the material for constructing a structure, then a matrix system such as the dimensional reference system would be chosen, as it is best suited for constructing with steel.

For ceilings and floors, neutral zones are used to control the space in between; these are referred to as the *control zones* or *control dimensions*. Thus, the entire dimensioning process is dictated by this matrix datum, even to the drafting of details, which also should be datum based. See Figure 6.19.

By Hand

During the design phase, models, renderings, presentational floor and roof plans, elevations, and sections are developed. These are altered or changed after being viewed by the client. Subsequent to this stage, the drafter must realize that design changes cannot be made without the approval of the designer (in conjunction with the client).

The drafter then builds up each drawing through the developmental stages, following basic office standards. The specific stages for the plans, elevations, building sections, and details are covered later in this chapter.

By Computer

If the design phase includes a computer 3-D model, the drafter's task is simple. The 3-D model is rotated into an ortho position to obtain plan, elevation, and building sections. The floor plan, which is a horizontal section, is then used as a datum base for other drawings, such as the framing plan, mechanical plan, electrical plan, or plan of any other consultant (e.g., mechanical, electrical, plumbing, or structural engineer) you might enlist to aid you in the completion of this set of working drawings. This datum base drawing should be imported as a XREF drawing. An XREF is a method of creating an external reference to a drawing that is located in another sheet and used a reference in a current sheet. Thus, every time a drawing is accessed, the most recent version of that drawing—say, the floor plan—is loaded. The various stages now become layers and any combination of layers can be sent to the associates. In fact, these layers in progress can be placed on a web site and downloaded with a specific code given only to the associates.

Designing Working Drawings Both Manually and on a Computer

Design images that have been drawn manually should be translated to digital images. This can be done by

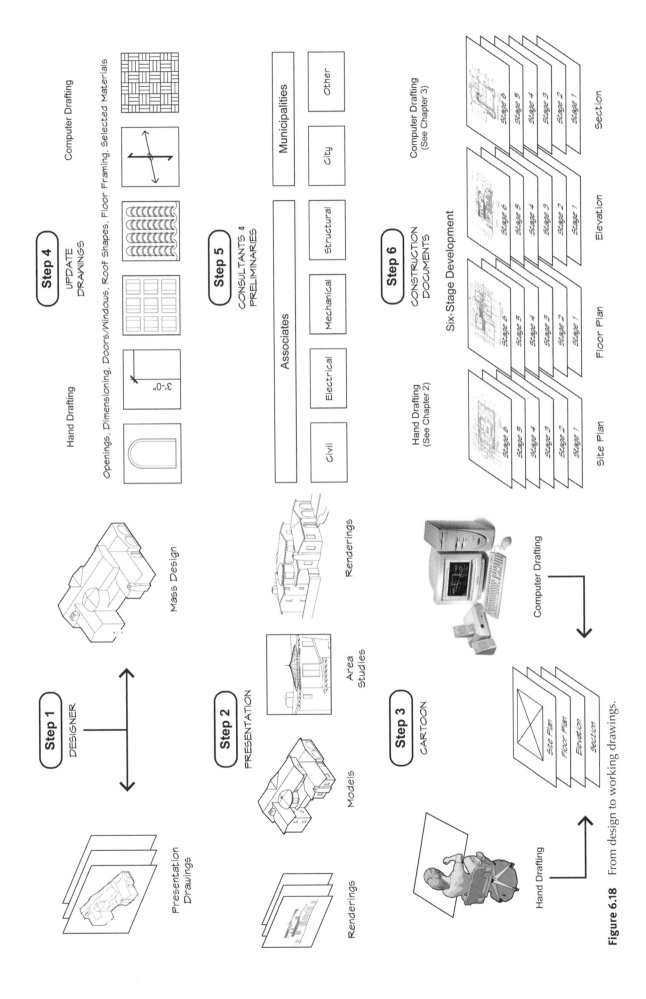

Figure 6.18 From design to working drawings.

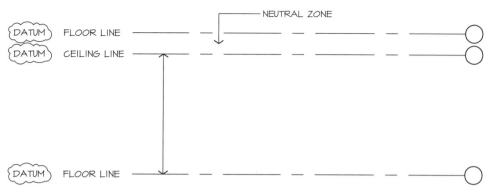

Figure 6.19 Vertical datum layout.

scanning in the presentational plans, elevations, and building sections. Although this scanned-in drawing cannot be manipulated, it can be used as a tracer or corrected by erasing any undesirable information. In programs such as Revit, the trace of specific walls will be identified by a specific construction assembly. For example, a 2 × 4 stud wall with cement plaster and gypsum board on the interior could denote the exterior walls of a residence.

■ FORMAT/CARTOON

Formatting

During the planning phase of developing working drawings, someone in the office may be responsible for the layout of the individual document sheets. The planning phase is most affectionately called the *cartooning* of a set of working drawings. *Mock-up, page format,* and *sheet layout* are other terms, used interchangeably, for the same thing.

Although the cartooning of a set of drawings can be done at full size, a more expedient method is to draw it at a reduced sheet size, 8½″ × 11″ being the most convenient. This can be performed manually or by CAD. In

either case, determining the scale at which a floor plan will be drafted is the biggest problem. See Figure 6.20. As CAD or BIM programs become more sophisticated, the sheet templates are becoming established, but they do allow for customization.

Hand Drafting a Cartoon

When hand drafting (manually drafting) a cartoon, everything is based on proportion. See Figure 6.21.

Computer Cartoon

Computer cartoons are much easier to produce than hand-drafted cartoons. The paper is drawn at full scale in model space, and the drawings are imported into the theoretically full-size sheet in the desired scale to fit. If the plans, elevations, and sections are drawn full scale, the scaling factor is used to create an image in the proper scale. See Figure 6.22.

If drawings are not available, as is usually the case with interior elevations, rectangles can be drawn at the desired scale to occupy the space allocated for a cartoon. See Figure 6.23.

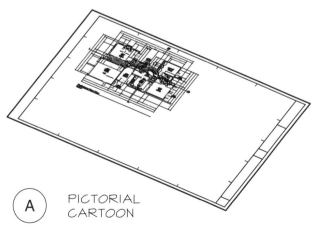

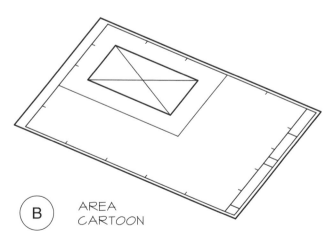

Figure 6.20 Pictorial and area cartoon.

Figure 6.21 Cartoon of the exterior elevation sheet with measurements for positioning the elevations.

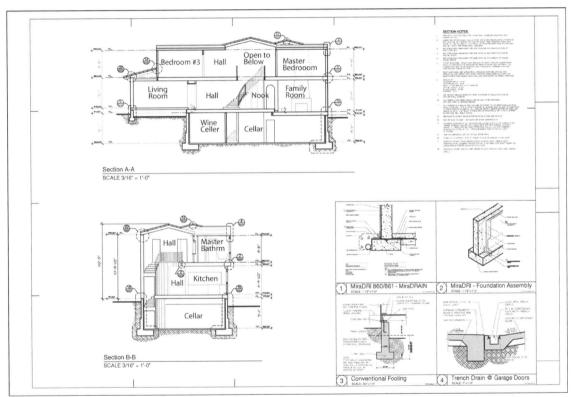

Figure 6.22 Cartoon of building section and details.

Hand-Drafted Preliminary to Computer Cartoon

When the preliminary floor plans, elevations, and sections are drawn by hand, the images can be scanned into the computer and positioned on the sheet at any desired scale. With a computer, you have the capability to enlarge or reduce drawings merely by inputting a scale factor or a proportion ratio.

■ PROJECT BOOK

Project Materials and Specifications

All information about a specific project—the materials selected, the structural system chosen, the exterior finishes and interior finishes, plus all correspondence relating to the project—is documented, collected, and

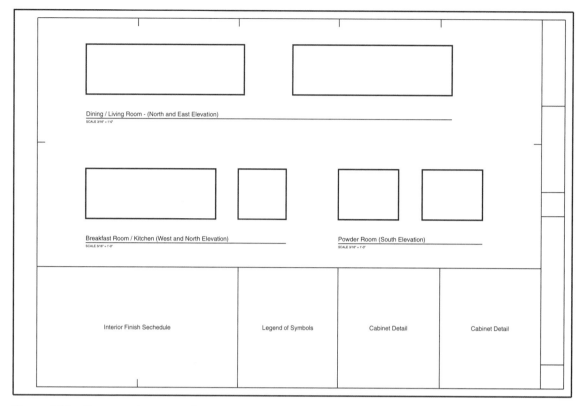

Figure 6.23 Cartoon using rectangles to reserve space.

placed in a *project book*. This can be a simple three-ring binder or a series of binders. Lists of structural considerations, exterior finishes, and interior finishes are shown in Figures 6.24, 6.25, and 6.26, respectively.

Exterior Finishes

In the development of the exterior elevation, the drafter must be able to identify the various materials to be used on the exterior surface, as well as the type of fenestration (windows and doors). As with structural considerations, a chart is again the instrument used to convey the information to the drafter. See Figure 6.25.

Interior Finishes

To allow an accurate drawing of the floor plan, interior elevation, and finish schedule, interior finishes are selected by the client, in conjunction with the architect. The drafter can find this information in the project book on a chart similar to the one shown in Figure 6.26. Although this list is called "Interior Finishes," it can include appliances and other amenities such as fireplaces, a security system, a safe, and so on.

■ NUMBERS—LEGAL, JOB, TASK

Legal Description

Every project has some type of legal description. A simple description might look like this:

Lot #_____ Block #_____
Tract #___, as recorded in book ___, page ___, of the _____ County recorder's office.

STRUCTURAL

1. FOUNDATION	2. TYPICAL WALL FRAMING	3. TYPICAL FLOOR FRAMING	4. TYPICAL ROOF FRAMING
a. Conventional slab-on-grade	a. 2 x ___ wood studs	a. 2 x ___ wood floor joists	a. Conventional (wood rafters & beams)
b. Post-tensioned slab	b. Lap with corner boards	b. 2 x ___ wood floor joists per structural consultant	b. TJI
c. Wood floor	c. Other	c. TJI	c. Trusses
d. Other		d. 1-1/2" lightweight concrete over	d. Trusses and conventional framing
		e. Other	
		Note: Specify any minimum sizes	Note: Specify any minimum sizes

Figure 6.24 Listing of structural considerations.

EXTERIOR FINISHES

A. WALLS

1. STUCCO	2. CEDAR SIDING	3. MASONITE SIDING	4. MASONRY VENEER
a. Sand texture	a. Lap with mitered corners	(specify other manufacturers)	a. Thin set brick (mfg.)
b. Other	b. Lap with corner boards		b. Full brick (mfg.)
		a. Lap with metal corners	c. Stone
		b. Lap with corner boards	d. Stucco stone
		c. V-groove with corner boards	e. Other
		d. Other	

B. TRIMS, BARGES, AND FASCIA

1. SIZE	2. TEXTURE
a. X ___ Trim at windows and doors	a. S4S
___ Whole house	b. Resawn
___ Front elevation only	c. Rough sawn
b. X ___ Barge and fascia with ___ X ___ Trim over	d. Other

C. ROOFING

1. MATERIAL	2. GUTTERS	3. DIVERTERS AT DOORS	
a. Wood shakes	a. At whole house	Composition shingle	
b. Wood shingle	b. At doors only	Wood shake and shingle	Only
c. Concrete "s" tile (mfg.)		Flat concrete tile	
d. Clay "s" tile (mfg.)			
e. Clay 2-piece mission tile (mfg.)	*Note:* Gutters will be assumed		
f. Flat concrete tile (mfg.)	at all tight eave		
g. Composiiton shingle (mfg.)	conditions.		
h. Built-up			
i. Built-up with gravel surface			
j. Other (mfg.)			

D. DECKS AND BALCONIES / E. STAIRS

D. DECKS AND BALCONIES	E. STAIRS	
1. TYPE	1. THREADS	2. STRINGERS
a. 2 X spaced decking	a. Open wood treads	a. Steel stringers
b. Dex-o-Tex waterproof membrane decking	b. Precast concrete threads	b. Wood stringers
c. Other	c. Conc.-filled metal pan treads	
	d. Dex-o-Tex waterprf. membrane	

F. DOORS

1. ENTRY	3. PATIO / DECK
a. 3068 1-3/4" S.C. (mfg.)	a. Aluminum sliding glass door
b. 3080 1-3/4" S.C. (mfg.)	b. Aluminum French doors
c. Other	c. Wood sliding glass door
2. GARAGE	d. Wood French doors
a. Overhead	e. Other
b. Wood roll-up (mfg.)	
c. Metal roll-up (mfg.)	

G. WINDOWS

1.	Aluminum	Wood	2. MUNTINS
a. Sliding			a. All Windows
b. Single-hung			b. Front elevation and related rooms
c. Double-hung			3. Dual Glazed
d. Awning			4. Single and dual glazing per Title 24
e. Casement			5. Other

H. SKYLIGHTS

1. GLASS (mfg.)	2. ACRYLIC (mfg.)		3. GLAZING
Color	Color	Shape	a. Single
a. Bronze	a. Bronze	a. Flat	b. Double
b. Gray	b. Gray	b. Dome	c. Per Title 24 report
c. Clear	c. Clear	c. Pyramid	d. Other
d. White	d. White	d. Other	
e. Other	e. Other		

Figure 6.25 Listing of exterior finishes.

INTERIOR FINISHES

A. WALLS

1. Drywall - Texture	
2. Plaster - Texture	
3. Other	
4. Bullnose Corners	

B. FLOORS

	Carpet	Sheet Vinyl	Ceramic Tile	Other
Entry				
Living				
Dining				
Family				
Den				
Kiitchen				
Nook				
Hall				
Master Bedroom				
Second Bedroom				
Master Dressing Room				
Second Bathroom				
Powder				
Service				

C. CEILING

1. Drywall - Texture	
2. Plaster - Texture	
3. All dropped beams shall be drywall wrapped	
4. All dropped beams shall be exposed	
5. Other	

D. CABINET TOP AND SPLASH

	Ceramic Tile	Corian	Cult. Marb	Cult. Onyx	Plastic Lam.	Wood	Other	Splash Hght.
Kitchen								
Service								
Wet Bar								
Powder								
Linen								
Master Bathroom								
Second Bathroom								

E. INTERIOR DOORS

1. Passage		2. Wardrobe	
Master Bedroom		a. 6'-8" high siding	
a. 3068		b. 8'-0" high siding	
b. 2868		c. 6-'8" high bifold	
c. Other		d. 8'-0" high bifold	
Secondary Bedrooms		e. Other	
a. 2868			
b. 2668			
c. Other			
3. Mirrored			
a. Master Bedroom			
b. Secondary Bedroom			
c. Other			

F. BATHROOM FIXTURES

	Master Bath	Second Bath
1. Tubs and Tub/Showers		
a. 3'-6"x5'-0" cast iron oval tub		
b. 3'-6"x5'-0" porc/stl. oval tub		
c. 3'-6"x5'-0" fiberglass oval tub		
d. 3'-6"x5'-0" 1-piece fiberglass oval tub and surr.		
e. 2'-8"x5'-0" cast iron tub		
f. 2'-8"x5'-0" porc./stl. Tub		
g. 2'-8"x5'-0" 1-piece fiberglass oval tub and surr.		
h. Other		
Note : Specify surrounding material		
2. Showers		
a. Fiberglass pan and surround		
b. Hot mopped ceramic tile pan with ceramic tile surrounding material		
c. Precast pan with surround		
Specify: Type Pan		
Type Surround		
d. Shatterproof enclosure		
e. Curtain rod		
3. Mirrors		
a. 3'-0" high		
b. 3'-6" high		
c. 3'-8" high		
d. 4'-0" high		
e. Full height to ceiling		
4. Medicine Cabinets		

G. KITCHEN APPLIANCES

1. Sink
a. Double
b. Double with garbage disposal
c. Triple
d. Triple with garbage disposal
2. Built-In Oven
a. Double - gas
b. Double - electric
c. Single with microwave
3. Built-in Cooktop
a. Gas
b. Electric
c. Downdraft - gas
d. Downdraft - electric
e. Hood, light and fan above
f. Microwave above
4. Slide-in Range/Oven (30")
a. Gas
b. Electric
c. Downdraft - gas
d. Downdraft - electric
e. Hood, light and fan above
f. Microwave above

Figure 6.26 Listing of interior finishes.

G. KITCHEN APPLIANCES (continued)

- 5. Hi/Low Slide-in Range/Oven (30")
  - a. Gas
  - b. Electric
  - c. Oven below and above
  - d. Oven below, microwave above
- 6. Dishwasher
  - a. Included
- 7. Trash Compactor
  - a. Included
  - *Size*
- 8. Refrigerator
  - a. 3'-3" wide space
  - b. 3'-0" wide space
  - c. Other
  - d. Stub-out for ice maker
  - e. Recessed stub-out for ice maker

H. LAUNDRY

- 1. Dryer
  - a. Gas
  - b. Electric 220V
  - c. Both

I. MECHANICAL

- 1. F.A.U.
  - a. Gas
  - b. Electric
  - c. Zoned - Specify number of units _____
- 1. Air Conditioner
  - a. Included
  - b. Optional

J. PLUMBING

- 1. Water Heater - Gas
  - a. Recirculating
  - b. Water softener - included
  - c. Water softener - loop only
- 2. Exterior Hose Bibb
  - a. Total Required _____
  - b. Locations: _____

L. FIREPLACES

- 1. Prefab Metal
  - a. Manufacturer
  - b. Size
  - c. Gas stub-out
- 2. Precast Concrete
  - a. Manufacturer
  - b. Size
  - c. Gas stub-out
- 3. Masonry Sizes
  - b. Size
  - c. Gas stub-out

K. ELECTRICAL

	Surface Mounted	Rec. Can Light	Square Flush Light	Lum. Clg. (Fluor.)	Lum. Soffit (Fluor.)	Lum. Soffit (Incand.)	Wall Mounted	Pendant	Other
1. Location									
Entry									
Living									
Dining									
Family									
Den									
Kitchen									
Nook									
Stair									
Hall									
Master Bedroom									
Second Bedroom									
Master Dress									
Second Dress									
Master Bath									
Second Bath									
Powder									
Service									

- 2. Outlet for Garage Door Opener
- 3. Exterior W.P. Outlets
  - a. Total Required: _____
  - b. Location: _____
- 4. Phone Outlets - Locations
  - a. _____
  - b. _____
- 5. TV Outlets - Locations
  - a. _____
  - b. _____
- 6. Intercom System
  - a. Wired
  - b. Option
- 7. Security System
  - a. Wired
  - b. Option

M. Miscellaneous Amenities

- 1. Safe
  - a. Wall - location _____
  - b. Floor - location _____
- 2. Wet Bar - Plans
  - Under-counter
  - Ice maker _____
  - Refrigerator, _____
- 3. Other (specify)
  - a.
  - b.

Figure 6.26 *(continued).*

This description must appear on the set of working drawings. It may be on the title sheet or, more appropriately, on the site plan or survey sheet.

The legal description is used when researching your client's site: zoning requirements and limitations, setback requirements, height limits, or any other information you might need for a specific design feature of the project.

Job Number

Every office has its own way of identifying a specific project. Generally, each project is assigned a job number, which might incorporate the year of the project, the month a job was started, or even the order in which the project was contracted. For example, job number 1103 might reflect the third project received in an office in the year 2011. By using this system, an office can rapidly identify the precise year in which a job was contracted and never duplicate a number.

Task Number

All offices use time sheets, or log data into a time spreadsheet; the data include keeping track of the drafter's performance. A drafter might log the time spent on a project by date, the job number, a written description of the task performed, and amount of time, such as:

07–30–11 Job #1103—Tylin Residence—Plans—SD 2.25 hrs.

In a large office, each task is also numbered. Figure 6.27 displays a chart describing the work to be performed as "work packages"; the task number at the left is assigned to the specific package and a column at the right indicates the total man-hours planned for the particular work package. The task numbers jump by ten, allowing the flexibility, on a complex project, to have sub-work packages. For example, 140 Site Visit might use 141 as a task number for measuring an existing structure to be altered.

Figure 6.28 is an example of the total man-hours for a residence. Note the task numbers and the computer display of the corresponding work-package names.

ADDITIONAL SERVICE CHECK LIST
SINGLE-FAMILY SUMMARY OF PLANNED MAN-HOURS

PROJECT NAME: _____

PROJECT NO: _____

PROJECT MANAGER: _____

START DATE: _____

	WORK PACKAGE NAMES	PLANNED MAN-HOURS
110	BUILDING DEPARTMENT PLAN CHECK	
120	BUILDING DEPARTMENT SUBMITTAL	
130	IN-HOUSE PLAN CHECK	
140	SITE VISIT	
150	PRODUCTION ASSISTANT/PRINTING	
160	CONSTRUCTION DOCUMENTS (DIR. & ASSOC. DIR.)	
170	FOUNDATION LAY-OUT (ARCHITECTURAL)	
180	FLOOR PLAN	
190	ARCHITECTURAL BACKGROUND	
200	EXTERIOR ELEVATIONS	
210	BUILDING SECTIONS	
220	DETAILS	
230	INTERIOR ELEVATIONS	
240	ROOF PLAN	
250	STAIR PLANS	
260	NOT USED	
270	NOT USED	
280	FOUNDATION PLAN (STRUCTURAL INFORMATION)	
290	FRAMING PLAN (STRUCTURAL)	
300	TITLE SHEET	
310	SITE PLAN	
320	SCHEDULES	
330	PLAN CHANGE (SINGLE FAMILY)	
340	PROJECT MANAGEMENT (PROJECT MGR./ARCHITECT)	
350	PROJECT MEETINGS (TEAM MEMBERS)	
360	CAD COORDINATION (DIR. OF CAD SERVICES)	
370	CAN BE USED FOR ADDITIONAL WORK	
380	CAN BE USED FOR ADDITIONAL WORK	
390	CAN BE USED FOR ADDITIONAL WORK	
	TOTAL PLANNED MAN-HOURS	

APPROVED BY: _____

Figure 6.27 Task numbers and summary of planned man-hours.

	Summary of Planned Man-Hours	
	Project name: the professional practice or architectural drawings case study—Mr. and Mrs. _____ Residence	
Task No.	**Work Package Names**	**Planned Man-Hours**
310	Site Plan, Roof Plan, and Energy Notes	10
170	Foundation Plan and Details	20
180	Floor Plan and Electrical Plan	20
220/320	Door Window Details and Schedules	32
200	Exterior Elevations and Details	20
210	Building Sections	10
290	Roof Framing and Details	20
230	Interior Elevations	16
130	Project Coordination and Plan Check	18
	Total Hours	166
	166 hours $ _____ Hr. =	$ _____

Figure 6.28 Planned man-hours for a project.

Each week, as the drafters turn in their time sheets, the project manager must ascertain the progress on a particular job or check to see if the project has been budgeted correctly. Figure 6.29 provides an example of such a spot check.

Document Numbering System

Although this book is mainly concerned with architectural working drawings, it also includes other drawings among those that constitute a complete set of construction documents. To keep all of the drawings in their proper spaces, they are numbered differently. For example, the set of architectural drawings can easily be identified by the letter A: Sheets A-1, A-2, A-3, and so on. In contrast, S can be used for structural drawings (S-1, S-2, S-3), E for electrical, L for landscape, and M for mechanical, to mention but a few categories.

	Summary of Man-Hours Through 12-15-93		
310	Site Plan	2 hrs.	40 min.
310	Vicinity Map		20 min.
310	Roof Plan	1 hr.	15 min.
170	Foundation Plan	3 hrs.	15 min.
320	Foundation Details	3 hrs.	55 min.
180	Floor Plan	4 hrs.	5 min.
200	Exterior Elevations	3 hrs.	55 min.
210	Sections (Garage)		15 min.
290	Roof Framing Plan		40 min.
130	Projection Coordination	2 hrs.	5 min.
		Total 22 hrs.	25 min.

Figure 6.29 Progress for a specific time period.

A title sheet includes a legend of all the sheet titles, and page numbers are indicated so that recipients of a set of drawings will know if a page is missing.

■ DRAWING SEQUENCE

Drawing Development

Now to the actual performance—the development of the drawings themselves. As indicated previously, most offices have a game plan. Although such plans may vary slightly from one office to another, Figure 6.30 displays what we feel is a rather typical sequence. The terms **layout** or **block out** in this list mean to roughly draw out so that changes and corrections can easily be implemented. Key or special notes (**keynotes**) refer to the fact that noting is vitally important and actually supersedes the graphic documentation or representations illustrated on the plans.

Preliminary Approach with Computer Model

Following the initial design stages of whatever process is chosen, a massing study is used as a bridge between the design and construction documents (see Figure 6.31). The massing study is initially formed as a three-dimensional model on the computer, making the journey much easier. Review the steps described in Chapter 2 to better understand the process we will now embark upon.

Initially, the 3-D massing model is refined and adjusted to the client's needs (see Figure 6.32). The next step is to convert the refined 3-D model into a series of ortho views. The top view becomes the roof plan, and

Working Drawing Procedures

PROJECT

1. Lay Out Unit Floor Plans—¼″
   ____Block out walls.
   ____Doors and windows.
   ____Cabinets, appliances, and fixtures.
   ____Dimension overalls.
   ____Calculate square footages.
2. Lay Out Roof Plan—⅛″
   ____Indicate exterior line of building.
   ____Indicate roof lines and pitch.
3. Lay Out Building Sections—¼″
   ____Indicate type of framing.
   ____Dimension floor and plate heights.
4. Lay Out Exterior Elevations—¼″
   ____Indicate doors and windows.
   ____Indicate exterior materials.
   ____Dimension floor and plate heights.
5. Lay Out Addenda Plans—¼″
   ____Partial floor plans.
   ____Exterior elevations (per step #4).
   ____Roof plan (per step #2).
6. Project Manager to Select Keynotes
   ____Floor plans.
   ____Exterior elevations.
   ____Interior elevations.
   ____Sections.
7. Project Manager to Select Details
   ____Doors and windows.
   ____Exterior elevations.
   ____Interior elevations.
8. Project Manager to Lay Out Framing and Mechanical Study
   ____Overlays.
9. Plot
   ____Floor plans.
   ____Addenda plans/exterior elevations/roof plans.
   ____Sections.
   ____Submit package to structural, T-24 engineers, and applicable consultants.
   ____In-house back check of package (designer and project architect).
   50% Complete
10. Floor Plans—¼″
   ____Lay out electrical plan.
   ____Finish interior/exterior dimensions.
   ____Note plans.
   ____Reference details.

11. Lay Out Interior Elevations and Fireplaces—¼″
   ____Indicate ceiling heights.
   ____Dimension cabinet heights.
   ____Dimension appliances.
   ____Note interiors.
   ____Dimension fireplaces.
   ____Note fireplaces.
12. Architectural Detail Sheets
   ____Finish all details.
   Consultant design information due for in-house plan check and application to drawings.
13. Addenda
   13.1 Partial Floor Plans
   ____Electrical.
   ____Dimension.
   ____Note—plans.
   ____Reference details.
   13.2 Roof Plans—¼″
   ____Reference details.
   ____Reference notes.
   13.3 Exterior Elevations
   ____Reference details.
   ____Reference notes.
   ____Exterior materials finish schedule.
14. Sections
   ____Reference notes.
   ____Coordinate consultant design.
15. Title Sheet
   ____Code tabulation.
   ____Consultant information.
   ____Vicinity map.
   ____Sheet index.
16. Final Coordination
   ____Building department submittal information.
   ____Final plotting for building department.
   ____Submit for plan check.
   90% Complete
17. Formal In-House Plan Check
   ____Plan check.
18. Building Department Plan Check
   ____Incorporate correction into plans.
   ____Coordinate client/cyp in-house plan checks and incorporate into plans.
   ____Final plot for building department submittal.
19. Signatures
   ____ Upon building department approval (permit), route plan set for consultant approval and signatures.
   100% Complete
   Ready for plotting and submittal

Figure 6.30   Working drawing procedure game plan.

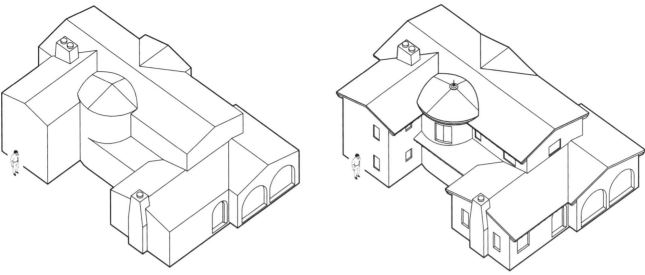

Figure 6.31 Preliminary massing model of the Clay residence.

Figure 6.32 Refined 3-D model of the Clay residence.

the front, rear, and side views become the elevation (see Figure 6.33). This is the process of taking a building (drawn in 3-D) and slicing it. The horizontal slice produces a floor plan when the inside is detailed. The vertical slice becomes a building section when rotated into an ortho position (see Figure 6.36). A summary of the various views available via rotation can be seen in Figures 6.34 and 6.35.

Stages and Layers of Production Drawings

The pictorial and preliminary floor plan shown in Figure 6.37 can be scanned and used as a construction layer for computer drawings. If the 3-D model is digital, we can then rotate the object into the required views as described earlier.

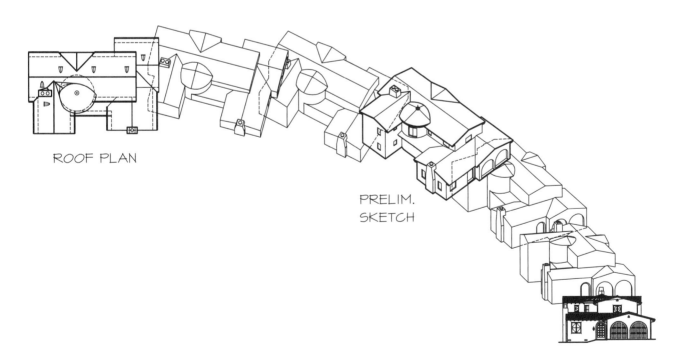

ROOF PLAN

PRELIM. SKETCH

ELEVATION

Figure 6.33 Rotation of massing model into ortho view.

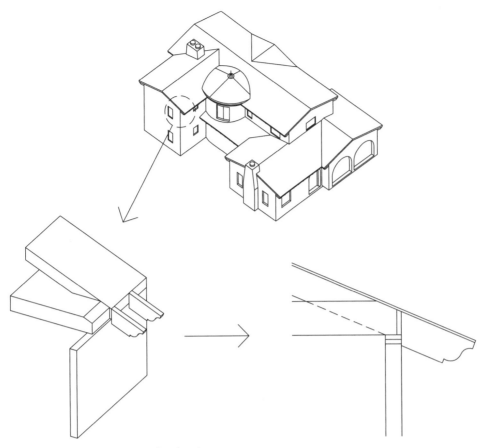

Figure 6.34   Isolating areas for detailing.

Producing the initial stage of working drawings by rotation sets the stage for the following five to six stages of layers to be produced by the CAD drafter. More complex projects may call for more stages, but we think that five is the absolute minimum number of stages for any set of construction drawings.

Stages

STAGE I   (Figure 6.38). The floor plan becomes the basic pattern for all other drawings in the set. If a computer is used, grids and snaps are set to produce the pre-established modules, such as a block module when masonry is used or a matrix for steel.

STAGE II   (Figure 6.39). The interior and exterior walls with their limits are drawn in this stage. Columns and openings should also be included at this stage. The designer called for rounded corners. Figure 6.40 shows a pictorial and a detail of how this is accomplished. This stage may become the datum stage for the foundation plan.

STAGE III   (Figure 6.41). Stair positioning is critical at this stage. Plumbing fixtures also become a critical part of the drawing. For an office, partitions are frequently drawn at this stage, as are non-load-bearing walls and the positions for openings and doors not previously positioned by rotation of the 3-D model.

STAGE IV   (Figure 6.42). Dimensioning, including values, is accomplished here. You must dimension to face or center of stud for wood, follow a block module for masonry, and position the columns correctly using the axial reference plane method for steel.

STAGE V   (Figure 6.43). The drawing is cross-referenced with other drawings, plans, sections, and details.

STAGE VI   (Figure 6.44). All text and titles should be placed on one layer. Refer to the standard for type-face, size, and positioning.

Stages and layers may appear to be the same to the beginning CAD drafter, but in reality they are different. An example is the floor plan shown in Figure 6.37. This is a drawing done in six or seven stages, but there are as many as fifteen layers. The greater the number of layers, the easier it is to change or alter the drawing. As any office employee will tell you, there is nothing more constant than change. The client may find a better piece of equipment that has to be dimensioned into the drawing, the Department of Building and Safety may require a larger clearance than originally expected, the structural engineer may request a longer wall for a lateral bracing—any number of changes, from various sources, may be made and have to be incorporated into the drawings.

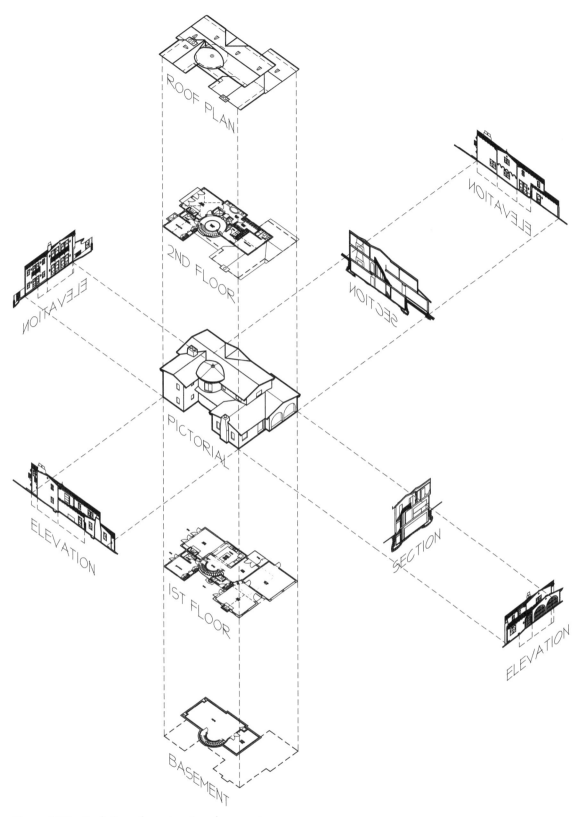

Figure 6.35 Evolution of construction documents.

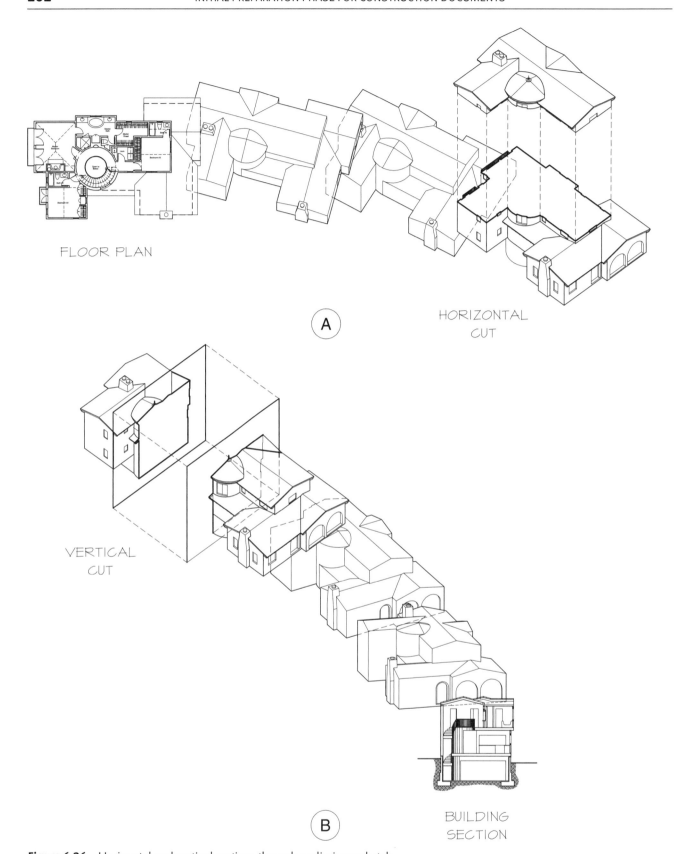

FLOOR PLAN

HORIZONTAL CUT

A

VERTICAL CUT

BUILDING SECTION

B

Figure 6.36 Horizontal and vertical sections through preliminary sketch.

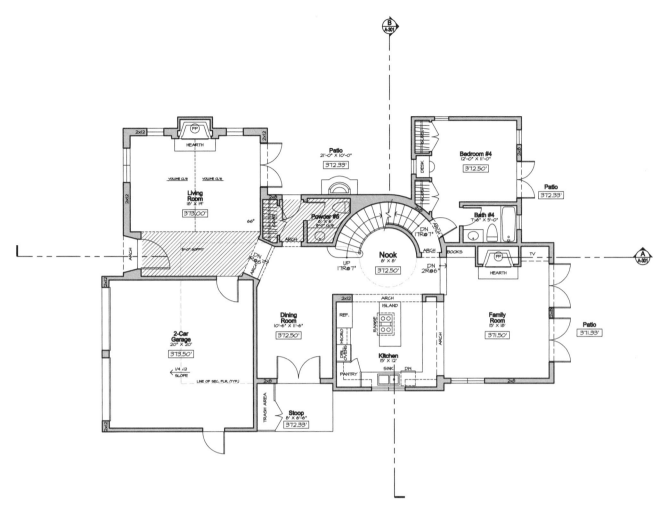

Figure 6.37 Pictorial and preliminary floor-plan layout.

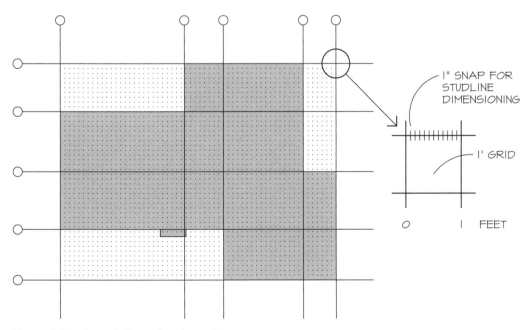

I" SNAP FOR
STUDLINE
DIMENSIONING

I' GRID

O   I   FEET

Figure 6.38 Stage I: Floor-plan datum layer.

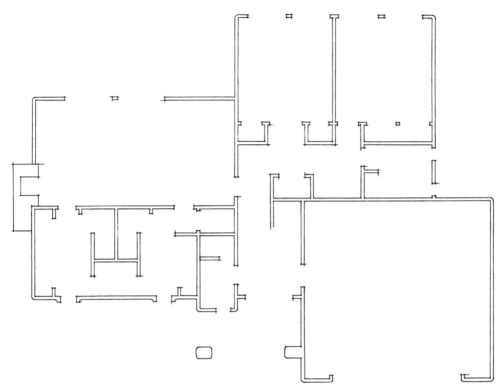

Figure 6.39   Stage II.

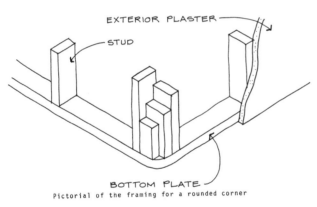

EXTERIOR PLASTER

STUD

BOTTOM PLATE
Pictorial of the framing for a rounded corner

A

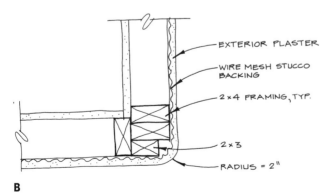

EXTERIOR PLASTER

WIRE MESH STUCCO
BACKING

2×4 FRAMING, TYP.

2×3

RADIUS = 2″

B

Figure 6.40   Framing at rounded corners.

The importance of being able to alter a drawing easily then becomes paramount.

When using BIM or Revit, you can follow this same process of stages. The stages are a guideline of how to create construction drawings. Revit does not follow a strict set of guidelines; it allows the drafter to provide data as the data are received, and does not have to get input in a linear pattern. For instance, if it is determined that the exterior walls will be 2×6 studs and the interior walls are 2×4 studs, the wall type can be created without drawing a single line. This typically occurs in Stage II of CAD drawing. Also, with Revit, Stage V is automatically determined in the parametric referencing system built into the Revit software. To the novice Revit or BIM user, the stages will aid in a more organized method of development.

Some layers may contain similar conventions—for example, text on one layer and dimensions on another. The CAD drafter may work a little on each layer as the drawing process progresses, as described in the stages of evolution. Additional layers may have to be developed as needed. An example of this is the text titled "ANNO" (annotation). The text layer can be divided into a multiple number of layers. One layer may be used for room titles only, a second layer may be used for general construction notes, and all other incidental notes may be on a third. The same can be said about dimensions. Column

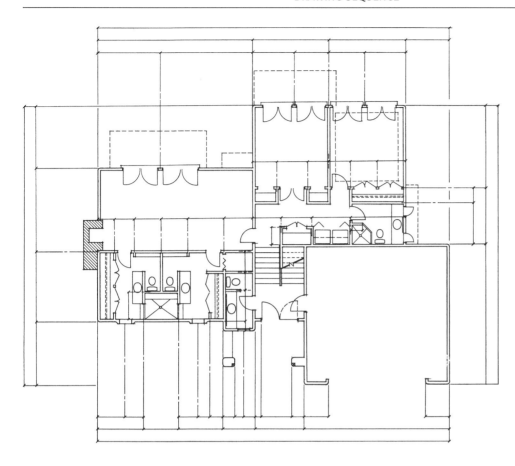

Figure 6.41 Stage III: Stairs and plumbing fixtures.

dimensions may be on one layer, and bearing wall dimensions on a second layer; non-bearing walls and the dimensions for partitions may be on a third. In this manner, the CAD drafter can finish each layer in his or her sequential order. An architectural office may utilize a standard layering practice as proposed in the national standards, or it may develop its own method.

The final plot sheet of the first-floor plan of the Clay residence is shown in Figure 6.45. This sheet has twenty layers, but many of the layers have been combined, resulting in a set of drawings with eleven layers:

1. Plot Sheet. Figure 6.45 includes the title block and the notes on separate sheets.
2. The floor plan is divided into the following layers:
   A. Datum Layer—Figure 6.46. This layer shows the perimeter layout for a block module if the building is made of masonry. Space is plotted at the given module if a module is used (e.g., 50″ module). If steel is used, the module at which the steel columns are set by the structural engineer appears (e.g., 10′-0″ o.c.). When the structure is to be framed in wood, the grid may be set at one-foot increments and the snap at one-inch increments for stud line dimensioning. Whatever the game plan is for the structure in question, the datum layer becomes the pattern by which all other

drawings are established and on which they are based. This perimeter drawing can be used to estimate square footage or to estimate the perimeter of the form.
   B. Figure 6.47. All walls are drawn on this layer. It may be split further into two additional layers, one showing bearing walls only, and non-bearing walls on the other. If a wall is moved, one can see immediately whether it is a load-bearing wall that affects the structure, or a non-bearing wall that does not affect the calculation or engineering of the structure. If the walls were already drawn in 3-D, validate that indeed they were extruded from the massing model. A rotation of the 3-D model can be used for this layer. All openings can be done at this point, but the drafter might choose, again, to put them on another layer.
   C. Figure 6.48. Plumbing fixtures, stairs, cabinets, and fireplaces are drawn on this floor layer. They can also be drawn on separate layers.
   D. Figure 6.49. All hidden lines are drawn on this layer. They may be outlines of cabinets, soffits, or ceiling level changes. Whatever the reason for using hidden lines, they are placed on this level, avoiding the need to change line types within a layer. This too can be divided into wall and floor layers.

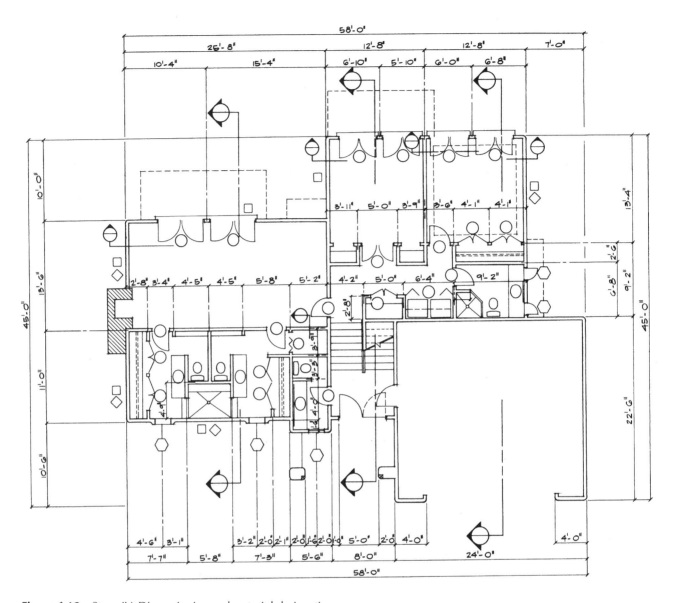

Figure 6.42   Stage IV: Dimensioning and material designation.

E. Figure 6.50. Because openings were positioned on a previous layer, the conventions used to identify doors, windows, and, in some instances, large cabinets are drawn at this point. As can be seen on this layer, the doors that lap are identified. It will also help later in the positioning of light switches to ensure that none are placed behind doors.

F. Figure 6.51. This is the most critical of all of the layers in this set because it establishes the parameters and limitations for all the other drawings, elevations, sections, framing, and so forth. The numerical values must adhere to the module being used. If the structure is a wood stud construction, the dimensions must be set to face of stud (outside walls) or center of stud (inside

walls). They must be positioned so the workers in the field (carpenters in this instance) can immediately find them and use the measurements efficiently and accurately. Dimension everything. Do not leave anything to chance. Do not force the carpenters to compute figures. Be sure the total equals the sum of its parts. See Chapter 8, "Floor Plan," and review the sections on dimensioning practices.

G. Figure 6.52. This is the lettering layer. In most instances, it is split into two layers, one for room titles and another for lettering. The name of the drawing, north arrow, scale, and any other office-standard titling identification can be placed on a third lettering layer.

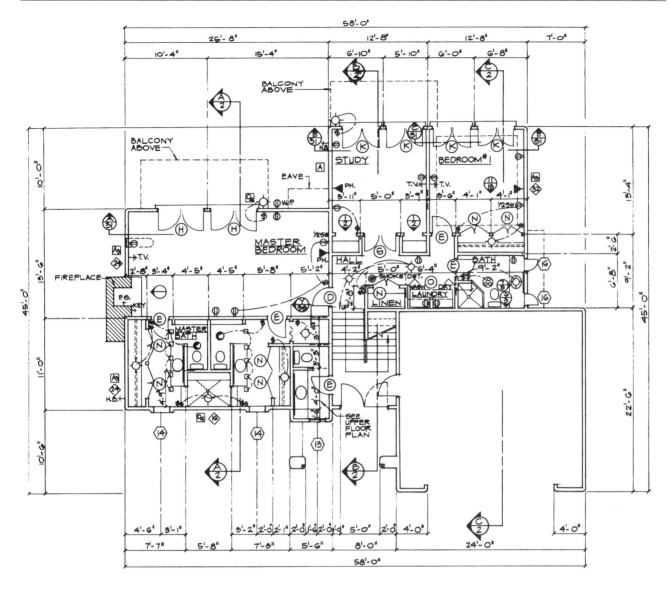

Figure 6.43 Stage V: Referencing.

H. Figure 6.53. Walls can be pouchéd (darkened) on this layer. For the floor plan, all walls are shaded in the same intensity. On a framing plan, the bearing walls can be shaded dark and the non-bearing walls left unpouchéd. Patterns for furred ceilings, floor material, fireplace hearths, and any other patterns can be done on this layer or, again, as in previous layers, split into multiple layers if the patterns are complex.

I. Figure 6.54. This section and symbol layer is a critical communicative layer. It references one area of a drawing to a detail, schedule, or building section. You will notice reference bubbles for a variety of referrals. Each of these can be placed on a separate layer.

J. Patios, barbeques, and other outside forms that do not affect the floor plan, yet set the proper context for the floor plan, can be placed on another layer. The outside forms on this floor plan were so minimal that an example is not shown.

K. Figure 6.55. XREF(ed) and positioned on all sheets is the standard office title block and notes (Figure 6.56).

L. As can be seen in Figure 6.45, a set of notes is positioned on the extreme right side. As with details, these may be predrawn or preformatted notes and should be placed on a layer by themselves.

M. Notice the revisions to the notes and in the revision portion of the title block on Figure 6.45. All revisions should be placed on a separate layer.

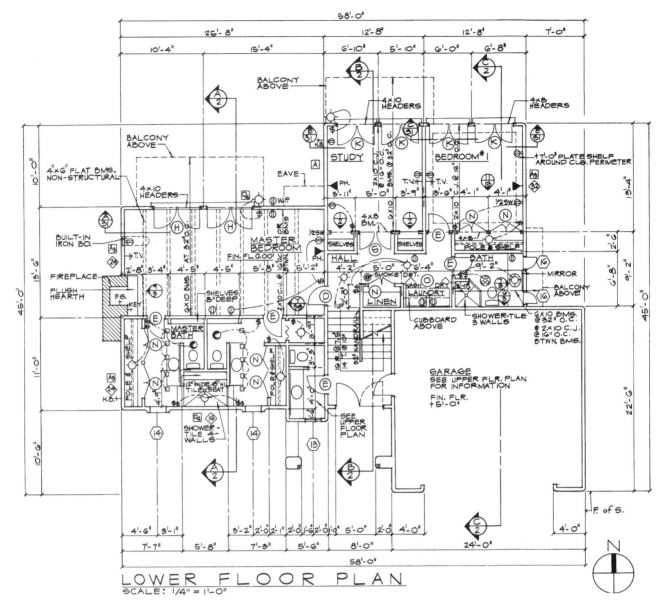

Figure 6.44   Stage VI: Final plot sheet of lower floor plan.

■ DELIVERY METHODS

Delivery or Reproduction

The method of actually printing or plotting a drawing is called the *delivery* or *reproduction* method.

If an engineering copier is used (which reproduces much like a large plain-paper copier), a drafter can paste drawings, notes, and charts onto one large sheet and produce a composite drawing. Even photographs and vendors' literature can be pasted or taped on with page-mending tape. Corrections can be done easily with the use of white correction fluid or a simple cutout.

With CAD, the delivery system takes on a completely new look. Because the entire drawing is electronic, any

electronic device can be used as a delivery method, starting with plotters and printers for a hard copy, and moving to PDFs that can be printed out or sent via email.

At one time, there was a cardinal rule in our industry: "Never give the client the originals!" Today we are essentially giving up our originals by sending electronically based drawings. There are both positives and negatives to sending electronic copies of our documents.

On the positive side,

1. Our consultants get the exact base sheet on which they can compute and draw the framing plans and structural details.

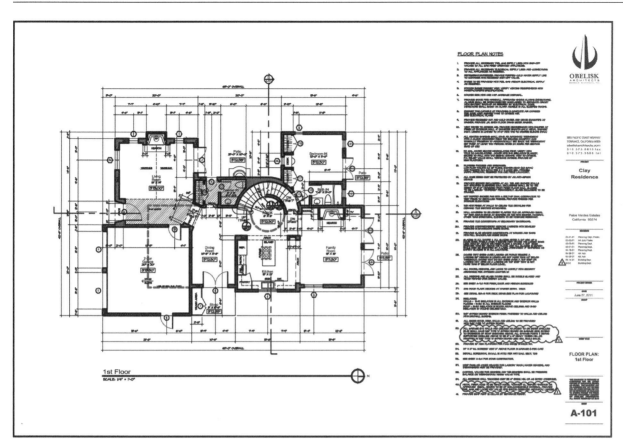

Figure 6.45 Plot sheet: First-floor plan.

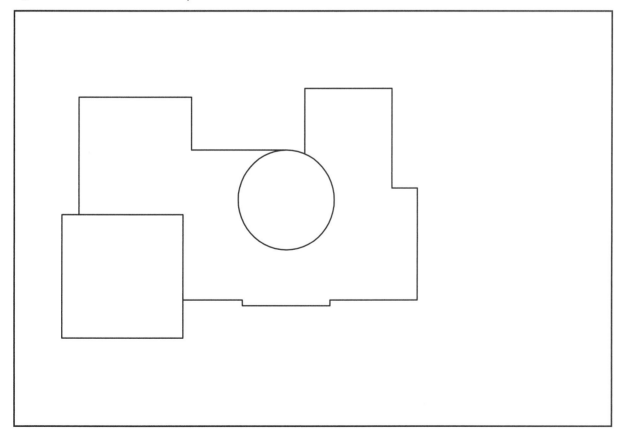

Figure 6.46 Master: Datum layer.

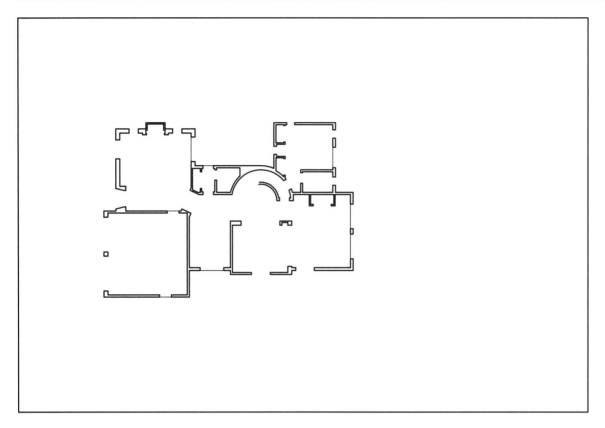

Figure 6.47   Master: Wall layer.

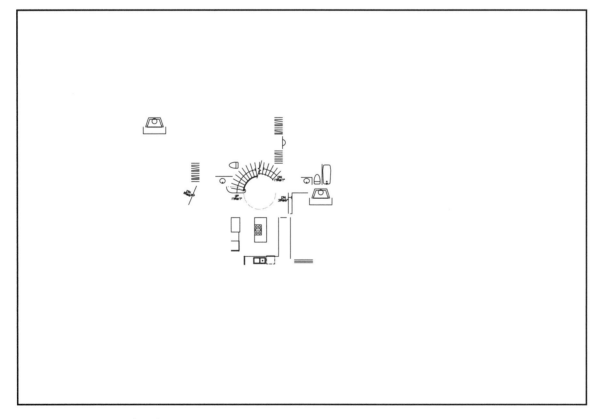

Figure 6.48   Master: Floor layer.

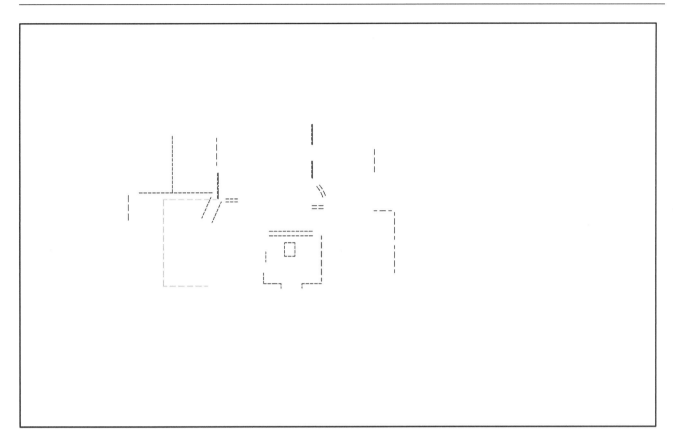

Figure 6.49 Master: Wall and floor hidden layer.

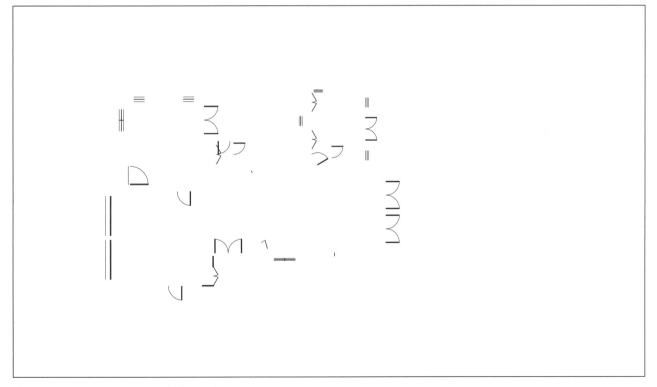

Figure 6.50 Master: Door and glazing layer.

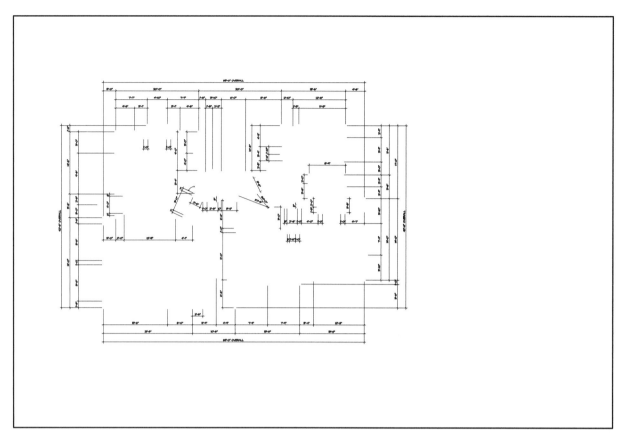

Figure 6.51   Master: Dimensions layer.

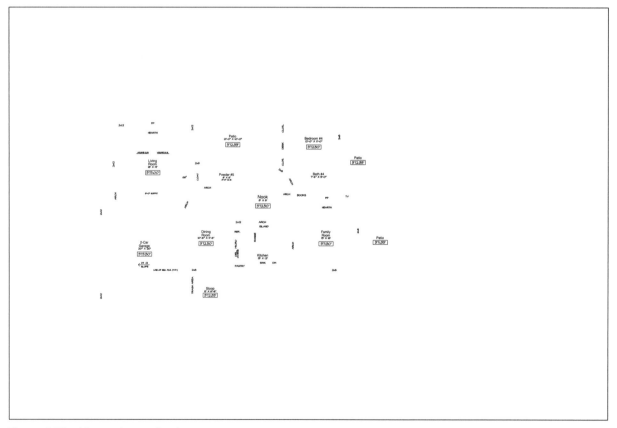

Figure 6.52   Master: Annotation layer.

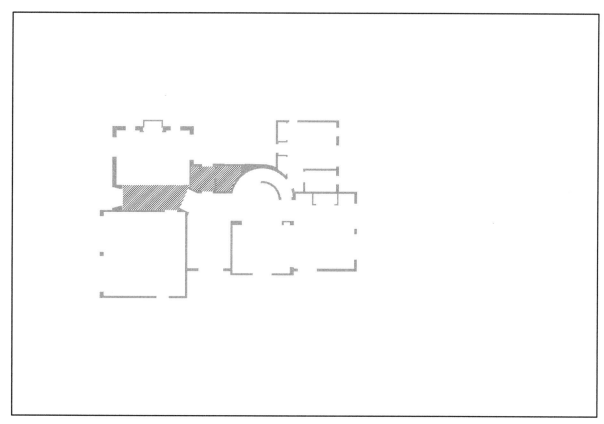

Figure 6.53 Master: Pattern and pouché layer (hatch).

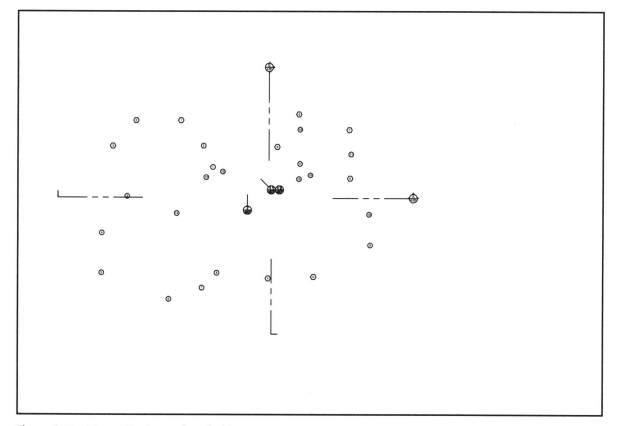

Figure 6.54 Master: Section and symbol layer.

Figure 6.55   XREF: Title block.

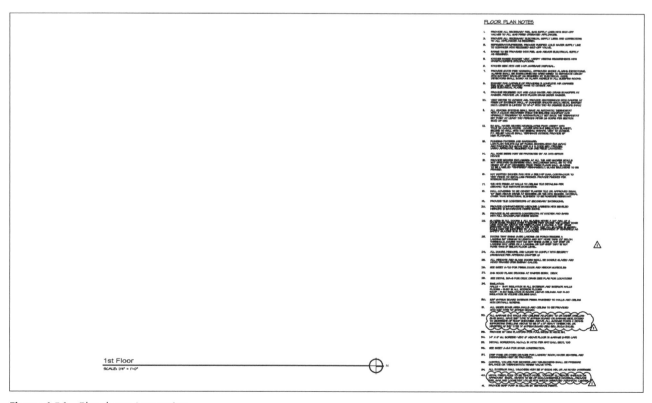

Figure 6.56   Plot sheet: Annotation.

2. For an out-of-stage project, multiple copies can be at another location.

3. Corrections can be made instantly in the field and relayed to the home office.

4. There is no downtime for mail delivery, as was the case with hard copy.

On the negative side,

1. There is a potential for piracy of the drawings.

2. Building departments require wet-copy signatures for permits.

3. Viruses can destroy parts of an image, creating an incorrect set of drawings.

4. Someone can be working on a set of drawings that appears to be the original but is not.

P A R T

Document Evolution

The information contained in Chapters 7 through 13 is meant to be the foundation of, or the basis (datum) for, all construction documents. For example, the material about floor plans applies to any method of drawing. Whether you are using hand (manual) drafting, computer drafting, or the three-dimensionally oriented Revit, the process is essentially the same. This is true no matter what set of drawings you are producing, from final construction document display to be used for the building department, to 2-D image drawings required by the client, contractors, or for bidding (getting estimates).

Chapter 7   **Site and Grading Plan**

Chapter 8   **Floor Plan**

Chapter 9   **Foundation and Roof Plans, Floor and Roof Framing Systems**

Chapter 10   **Building Sections**

Chapter 11   **Exterior and Interior Elevations**

Chapter 12   **Schedules: Door, Window, and Finish**

Chapter 13   **Architectural Details and Vertical Links (Stairs/Elevators)**

7

SITE AND GRADING PLAN

■ SITE ANALYSIS

Site Analysis Defined

The purpose of **site analysis** is to determine the best use of the site, and find a layout that capitalizes on site attributes to optimize fulfillment of the client's needs while respecting the inherent site conditions. A site analysis is a specific study of the project site.

Important components of research in site analysis include, but are not limited to, determining:

- Boundaries
- Topography
- Drainage
- Traffic (vehicular, pedestrian, transportation)
- Setbacks
- Weather (rain, sun, snow, wind)
- Lot shape (orientation)
- Site utilities (electric, gas, telephone, TV, water)
- Zoning (easements, covenants)
- Vicinity
- Neighborhood character (both positive and negative elements)
- Past, present, and future conditions

Community Research

Location within a country, county, state, province, and city are all factors in understanding a site. A large view of the site situated in its larger surroundings will aid in developing the site. In addition to the physical aspects of the site, become familiar with the activities that occur in the neighboring area, both positive and negative. These features range from a monthly festival or an annual parade to graffiti incidence and crime patterns.

Neighborhood Research

Understand the site within the context of the adjacent properties. This may require a two- to three-block study, in a refinement of the larger scale study described earlier. For a larger building, this research might expand to five or six blocks around the site.

Climate Research

Site-specific climate research must include factors such as temperature range, rainfall and snowfall, humidity, prevailing winds, and sun direction, as well as regional concerns such as earthquakes, hurricanes, and tornadoes. All of these factors will affect the approach to site design and layout, although some will be more important than others in any given situation. See Figure 7.1.

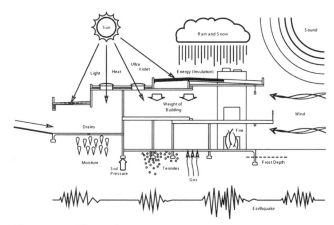

Figure 7.1 Climate impacts.

Site-Specific Research

Each site is identified by a legal description. Some legal descriptions are written according to metes and bounds, but most sites in more developed areas are identified according to plats, subdivision maps, and area maps. Although the format will vary from one municipality to the next, a legal description will typically read something like: Lot **6**, Block **27**, Tract **4289**, as recorded in the Richmond County Map Page 5-69. Once you have this information, you can determine more specific information about the site, such as setbacks, zoning requirements and limitations, development covenants, building area, redevelopment district requirements, and required dedications and easements.

Setbacks are predetermined restrictions that aid in determining the limits on a building footprint. For example, a site may require that the structure not encroach upon a strip of land 20′ in front, 5′ from each side, and 15′ in the rear; these are the required setback dimensions where building is not allowed. A height limitation will determine the maximum allowable height of a structure. In most cases, there are also limits on the maximum allowable area or square footage of a building. Often a **floor area ratio (FAR)** is established, so that the site cannot be completely covered from setback to setback.

Zoning—a municipal system of controlling what activities and structures are permitted on a piece of property—is determined by a governmental agency that has a primary purpose of public protection, implemented by rules harmonizing allowable land uses with owners' desires and the highest and best use of a site. This is what keeps high-rise office buildings and industrial production facilities from being built on a block of two-story residences. **Dedications** are portions of a site identified by the governing agency as a required contribution of land for an express public purpose. Most common is a dedication for a new road or a road expansion, which can vary in scale from a couple of feet to a strip ten or twenty feet wide. Another example is a required greenbelt area.

Often site owners are not compensated for a dedication; it is considered a cost of development. A site may also be subject to *easements*, which are portions of the property that others have the right or permission to use in some way even though the owner retains title to the land; most common are utility right-of-way easements.

Many city and county agencies have established **redevelopment districts** within their jurisdictions. Land use in redevelopment districts must, for various reasons, follow a different set of use and building guidelines to achieve an overarching, specific public goal. In many cases, these guidelines are more stringent than zoning requirements for other areas, but in some cases they may be less restrictive.

Utility Research

In some areas, such as Manhattan, determining the availability of electricity, gas, sewer, water, telephone, and cable television may be as simple as visiting a public works or engineering counter. In other areas, such as Wyoming, finding this information may be much more involved, and one may have limited utility options. In large cities, most utilities are immediately available, and typically are routed underground in the street or under sidewalks. In the Wyoming countryside, each site owner may have to have a well drilled to access fresh water, and bear the cost of bringing in the lines for electrical and telephone service; natural gas, sewer, and cable TV may not even be options. Obviously, these considerations bear heavily on the possible uses of the site and the type of structure that can be placed there. To fully understand the utility limitations and requirements of a site, one must also determine the depth, pipe diameter, pipe material, and pressure available. See Figure 7.2.

Circulation Research

Understanding how people will approach or access a site will affect your design for the site. Are there bus and train stops or metro stations near the site? Do service trucks or fire trucks figure prominently in the traffic pattern study? Perhaps there is an elementary school nearby, or vehicles can make a right turn only? Consider future development as well: Is there an electric trolley stop planned near the site, or a future police or fire station adjacent to the site?

Sensory Research

Document and observe significant views to and from the site, both positive and negative. Understand the impact of building and window placement in relation to

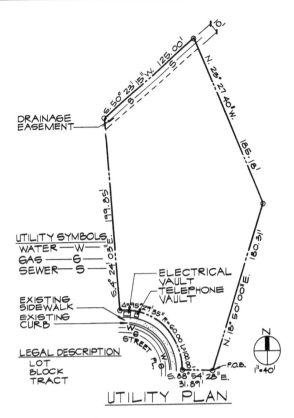

Figure 7.2 Utilities.

those views. Often noise, such as from vehicles, trucks, trains, buses, or airplanes, can affect site conditions. Even smells should be taken into account: It takes only one design of a building downwind from a dairy farm or paper mill for the designer to learn never to overlook the "scentscape" of a site again! See Figure 7.3.

Natural Features

Significant natural features often include the views discussed earlier, but natural elements such as a winter spring or creek, a rock outcropping, or a vertical bluff can strongly influence the layout of a site. See Figure 7.4.

The three natural elements that perhaps will most affect a site plan are the **existing contours**, or the slope of the site; the **soil type** and **bearing capacity** (how the soil supports the structure of the building); and the **geology**, the nature of the earth's structure beneath the soil elements. Geological concerns also include things like archeological/prehistoric sites that might affect the future building foundation or even location. This is discussed further in this chapter, in detail.

In some regions, native and preexisting trees are protected, whether by law or covenant. In many cities in California, for example, the California live oak, walnut, and others are in this category and may not be removed or damaged.

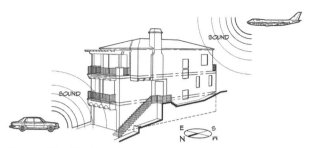

Figure 7.3 Tracking impacts.

Figure 7.4 Natural features.

Man-Made Features

Man-made features that are on a site or adjacent to the site should be documented as well. Elements such as existing structures, buildings, walls, curbs, gutters, sidewalks, power poles, light poles, and fire hydrants are often difficult to move or relocate. Even if they can be moved, it is usually very expensive to do so; alternatives should be explored before deciding to relocate an existing feature.

On occasion, man-made features will limit access to a site. (Perhaps there is a center divide on a street, with no left turn lane or median cut to allow vehicles into your site.) Document and record all of these features, as they will further shape the site plan.

■ SITE ANALYSIS APPLIED

Implementing Site Analysis

Accumulation of research on a specific site will allow the architect to establish a series of important supporting documents, some of which will require the consultation of a civil engineer. Many drawings may be needed to further develop the analysis of the site, including:

- Vicinity plan
- Location plan

- Plat map
- Topographic map
- Site plan/plot plan
- Grading plan
- Drainage plan
- Erosion control plan—storm water system mitigation plan (SWSMP)
- Utility plan
- Circulation plan
- Landscape plan
- Irrigation plan

Not all of these drawings are created for every job, but the more complex jobs may require all of them.

The Vicinity Map

A **vicinity map** provides an overall view of the region around the specific site to better introduce the surrounding neighborhood or district. Often this map will be provided on the cover sheet of a set of working drawings. See Figure 7.5.

The Location Plan

A **location plan** helps the viewer see the proposed project in relation to the specific area where the work is to be accomplished. This is particularly important on large-scale projects such as campuses or warehouse facilities. See Figure 7.6.

The Plat Map

The site plan is developed in stages, each dealing with new technical information and design solutions. The first step in site plan development is the **plat map**. This map, normally furnished by a civil engineer, is a land plan that delineates the property lines with their bearings, dimensions, streets, and existing easements. The information from the plat map forms the basis of all future site development. The property line bearings are described by degrees, minutes, and seconds; the property line dimensions are noted in feet and decimals. These are termed the **metes and bounds**. See Figure 7.7.

Even when the architect is furnished with only a written description of the metes and bounds of the plat map, a plat map can still be derived from this information. Lot lines are laid out by polar **coordinates**; that is, each line is described by its length plus the angle relative to true north or south. This is accomplished by the use of compass direction, degrees, minutes, and seconds. A **lot line** may read N 6° 49′ 29″ W (this describes the lot line as running north six degrees forty-nine minutes, twenty-nine seconds westerly). See Figure 7.8. In some U.S.

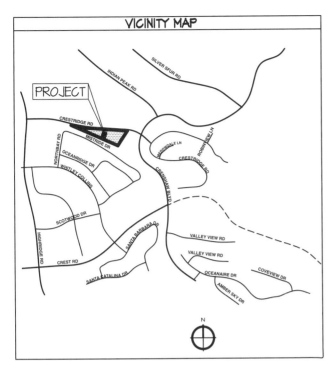

Figure 7.5 Vicinity map.

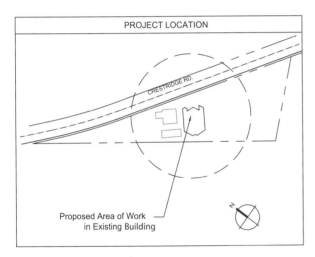

Figure 7.6 Location plan (map).

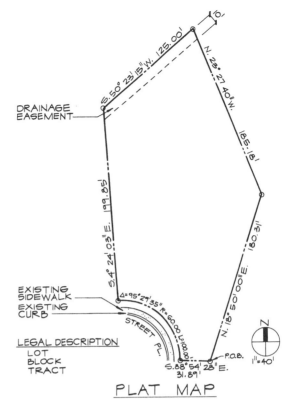

Figure 7.7 Plat map. (Reprinted by permission from *The Professional Practice of Architectural Working Drawings,* 3d Ed., © 2003 by John Wiley & Sons, Inc.)

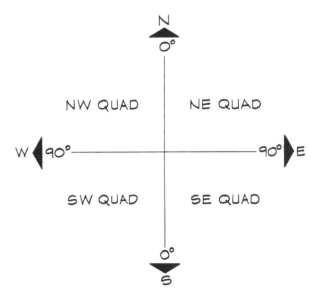

Figure 7.8 Compass quadrants.

counties, a boundary description can be retrieved via the Internet from the county in which the plat is located.

Drawing a Plat Map

Figure 7.9A shows a plat map with the given lot lines, **bearings**, and dimensions. To lay out this map graphically, start at the point labeled **P.O.B. (point of beginning)**. From the P.O.B., you can delineate the lot line in the northeast quadrant with the given dimension. See Figure 7.9B. The next bearing falls in the northwest quadrant, which is illustrated by superimposing a compass at the lot line intersection. See Figure 7.9C. You can delineate the remaining lot lines with their bearings and dimensions in the same way, eventually closing at the P.O.B. See Figures 7.9D, 7.9E, and 7.9F. For a plat map layout, accuracy is critical; thus, it is preferable to accomplish this task on a computer.

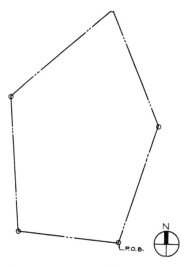

Figure 7.9A   Point of beginning.

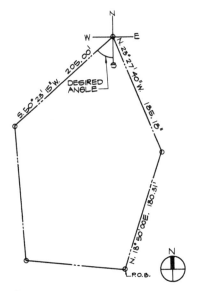

Figure 7.9D   Point of beginning and third angle.

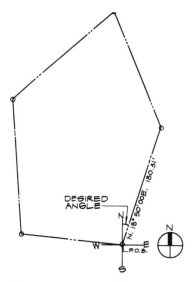

Figure 7.9B   Point of beginning and first angle.

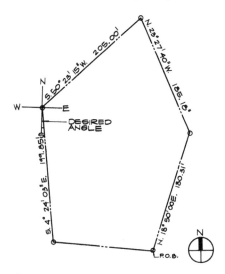

Figure 7.9E   Point of beginning and fourth angle.

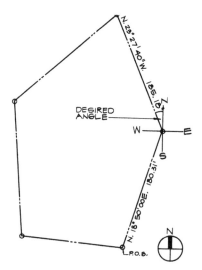

Figure 7.9C   Point of beginning and second angle.

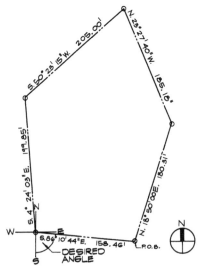

Figure 7.9F   Point of beginning and fifth angle.

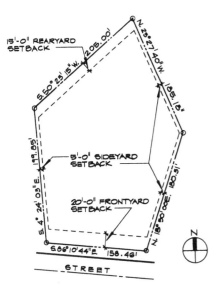

Figure 7.9G Site plan with building setbacks.

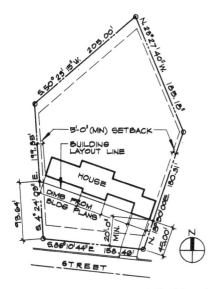

Figure 7.9H Site plan with building location. (Reprinted by permission from *The Professional Practice of Architectural Working Drawings*, 3d Ed., © 2003 by John Wiley & Sons, Inc.)

With the completion of the plat map layout, a specific plot of ground has been established. The boundary of a plat will also influence the development of the property. For the purpose of the architectural construction drawings, this portion of the drawings is called the **site plan** or **plot plan**. This drawing can now be utilized to determine the city-required **setbacks** (distance between the building and the lot line) required for aesthetics or life safety. In Figure 7.9G, the front yard, side yard, and rear yard setbacks are illustrated for the purpose of defining the governing building setback locations.

The next step in site plan development is to provide a dimensional layout for a proposed building. One method, as shown in Figure 7.9H, is to provide a dimension

along the west and east property lines. Starting from the front property line, establish a line parallel with the front of the building, to determine the angle of the front of the house in relation to the front property line. In addition, from this parallel line, dimensional **offsets** of the building can be established. Note also in Figure 7.9H that all required yard setbacks will be maintained without encroachments.

■ THE TOPOGRAPHY MAP

The Function of a Topography Map

For most projects, the architect adjusts the existing contours of the site to satisfy the building design and site improvement requirements. **Finish grading** is the process of adjusting existing contours so that they are in the desired position for the final stage of the site improvement process. The architect needs a topography or topographical map to study any slope conditions that may influence the design process. Usually, a civil engineer prepares this map and shows, in drawing form, the existing **contour lines** and their accompanying numerical elevations. Commonly, these contour lines are illustrated by a type of broken line. The **topography map** is actually a plat map, and its broken lines and numbers indicate the grades, elevations, and contours of the site. See Figure 7.10.

Site Cross-Sections

A topography map can appear complex. However, a **cross-section** or a cutaway view through any portion of the site can make the site conditions clearer; this will also be valuable for the finish grading. See Figure 7.11. The fall of the contours will represent the fall, or change of elevation, from the front or rear of the site.

To make a cross-section, draw a line on the topography map at the desired location. This is called the **section line**. Next, draw a series of horizontal lines, using the same scale as the topography map and spacing equal to the grade elevation changes on the topography map. These lines represent the vertical elevation of the grade. Project each point of grade change to the appropriate elevation line. Now connect the series of grade points to establish an accurate section and profile through that portion of the site. In many cases, multiple cross-sections are required to better understand the existing or proposed grade.

■ THE SOILS AND GEOLOGY MAP

Soils investigations evaluate soil conditions such as type of soil, moisture content, expansion coefficient, and soil bearing pressure. **Geological investigations** evaluate

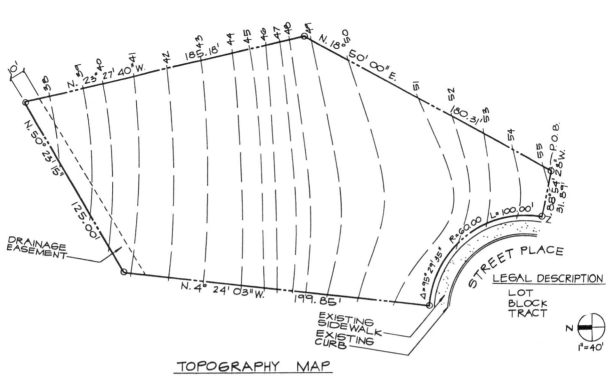

Figure 7.10 Topography map.

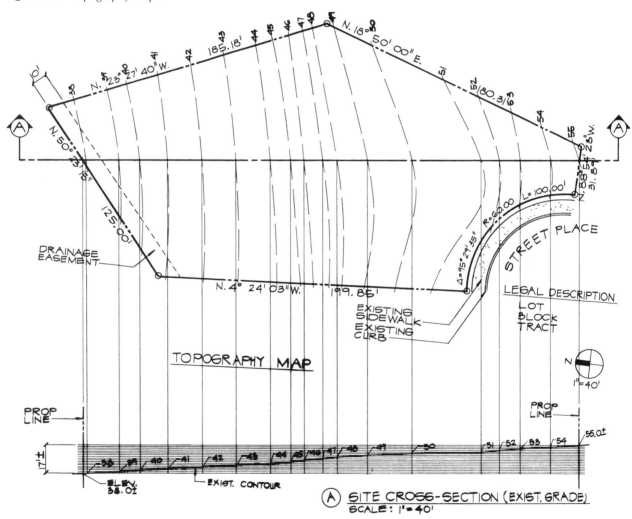

Figure 7.11 Topography map with section lines and cross-section.

existing geological conditions such as fault lines and bedding planes, as well as potential geological hazards.

Field investigations may include test borings at various locations on the site. These drillings are then plotted on a plat map, with an assigned test boring identification and a written or graphic report. This report provides findings from the laboratory analysis of boring samples under various conditions. See Figure 7.12.

When there are concerns about geological instability and soil, the particular problem areas may be plotted on a **soils and geology map** for consideration in the design process. Figure 7.12 shows a plat map with each test boring identified. This map becomes a part of the soils and geological report. Borings are done close to the location of the proposed work established by the architect or the area of structural concern. Figure 7.13 shows a **boring log** in graphic form. Notice the different types of information presented in the sample boring log. Figure 7.14 shows a geological cross-section.

Architects are not significantly involved in preparing drawings for geology and soils information other than locating the proposed work on a site plan and perhaps a site section. However, it is important to have some understanding of their content and representation in order to understand how it may affect design. It will most directly affect the foundation design, system, and size of foundation.

BORING: 79-7   **ELEVATION:** 677'

| DEPTH IN FEET | TEST DATA | | | SAMPLE NUMBER | SOIL DESCRIPTION |
	MC	DD	BC		
5					FIRM, MOIST, SANDY TO GRAVELLY CLAY (CL-CH) — TOPSOIL & SLOPEWASH — NOTE: WATER SEEPS BELOW 22 FEET — STIFF, MOIST, YELLOW GRAVELLY CLAY (CL) — TOPSOIL & SLOPEWASH
10					DENSE, MOIST, LIGHT BROWN CLAYEY SAND (SC) W/ MINOR GRAVEL — FRIARS FORMATION
15					HARD, DAMP, DARK GREEN SILTY TO SANDY CLAY (CL) — FRIARS FORMATION
20				7-2	
25					
30					
35					HARD, DAMP, BROWN SILTY CLAY (CL) — FRIARS FORMATION
40					HARD, DAMP, GREEN SILTY CLAY (CL) — FRIARS FORMATION
45					REFUSAL IN META-VOLCANIC ROCK

Figure 7.13 Example of a boring log. (Reprinted by permission from *The Professional Practice of Architectural Working Drawings*, 3d Ed., © 2003 by John Wiley & Sons, Inc.)

■ THE SITE PLAN

Drawing a Site Plan on the Computer

When drawing a site plan, the easiest way to start is to call your civil engineer and ask for a digital copy of the site topography for the project. This drawing becomes the base drawing on which various layers are drawn, such as setbacks, building location, dimensions, noting, and so on. See Figure 7.15.

If a drawing is available as a hard copy but not digitally, you can scan the drawing into the computer, and then size and scale it. If you are fortunate enough to have Revit to draw site plans, then it's just a matter of following the procedure outlined in Figures 7.9A through 7.9F.

In most CAD programs, this is not the case; the drafter must adjust his or her thinking to accommodate the computer. For example, in the majority of instances, the computer has been programmed to view the east compass bearing as 0°, north as 90°, west as 180°, and south as 270°. If you need to draw a property line N 18° 50' 00" E, you must understand that line will be drawn in the wrong location if you do not adjust the math. For the purpose of giving the computer the proper command, you must subtract 18° 50' from 90° and instruct the computer to draw a line 71° 10'. Let us continue

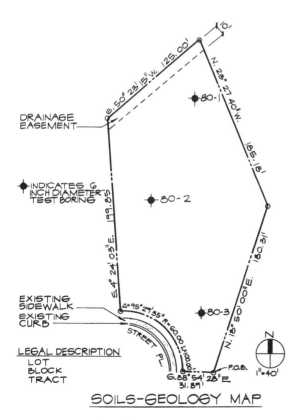

Figure 7.12 Soils-geology map.

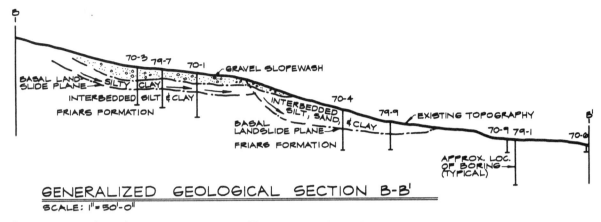

GENERALIZED GEOLOGICAL SECTION B-B'
SCALE: 1" = 50'-0"

Figure 7.14 Geological cross-section. (Reprinted by permission from *The Professional Practice of Architectural Working Drawings*, 3d Ed., © 2003 by John Wiley & Sons, Inc.)

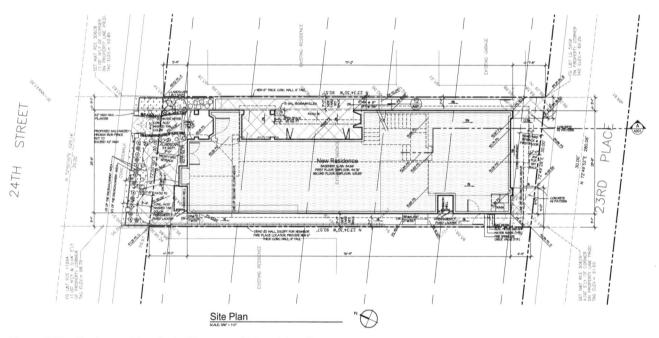

Site Plan

Figure 7.15 Site layout (site plan). (Courtesy of Mr. & Mrs. Givens.)

drawing this lot (developed on Figure 7.9) and construct the second line of 23° 27' 40". Because north is 90°, we must add 27° 40' 40" to 90°, giving us 113° 27" 40', and relay this instruction to the computer. Understand that the computer bearing 0° is the east direction on a compass. It may prove to be simpler to develop the entire site boundary without correcting angles until you have closed back to the P.O.B., and then rotate the drawing 90° to the correct orientation.

A final note: You will find no key for degree unless it has been programmed into the computer. Often you can type in % % d to get the degree symbol. Once the final line is drawn, you must ensure that the polygon is totally closed and you can hatch texture without fear of the texture bleeding outside of the site boundaries.

Revit Site Plan

Revit allows an architect to create a three-dimensional site plan with contours.

The first component to introduce is the topography of the site. This can be accomplished by importing a topography map produced by the civil engineer, or you can develop it by selecting points around the footprint of the ground-floor plan. Once topography is established, modifying a "topo" is a matter of editing the data or shape. You can add trees, shrubs, plantings, and sod by selecting the appropriate materials from the library and placing them where you want them. Moreover, plants sit in the proper elevation on the site when so placed. See Figure 7.16. At any stage, additional elements, such as property lines, setbacks, utilities, and dimensions, can be added to the site plan.

For most building designs, cutting and filling grade areas are required. A shortfall of Revit, albeit one that is easily overcome, is that Revit will not recall the original topography. It is necessary to make a copy of the completed site and name it something different to keep track of the original data. Once this is done, cut and fill can be determined in reference to the original topography. See Figure 7.17.

Architects may choose to create a project with a north orientation, but when modeling in Revit true north must be accounted for so that solar studies can be accurately depicted and proper representation of shades and shadows can be viewed. In addition, the vertical height relative to sea level will be required (default set to 0' at sea level). Without these two critical adjustments, a site plan may be valid but models, shades, and shadow will not. See Figure 7.18.

Revit is a remarkable program that offers extremely accurate data for a project and for a site plan. Elements like cut and fill yardage can easily be broken down and distributed to contractors for accurate bidding and construction scheduling.

Procedural Stages for Site Plan Development

STAGE I The architect requests a digital drawing of the site plan illustrating the property lines, existing grade contours, and any major physical features such as trees, utility poles, or any other feature that may dictate or influence the site plan process. This digital drawing is provided by a civil engineer (see Figure 7.19).

STAGE II Easements that are allocated for utility purposes, such as sewers, are depicted on the drawing with a broken line. This stage of the drawing also shows the

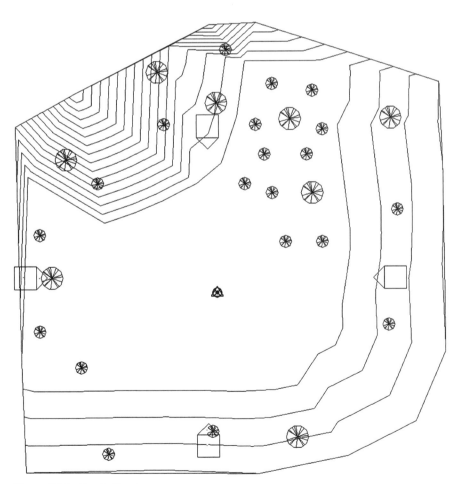

Figure 7.16 Revit site plan.

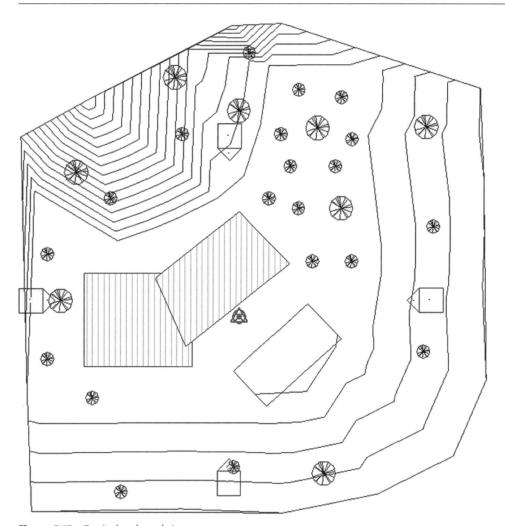

Figure 7.17 Revit developed site.

adjacent streets, street curbs, sidewalks, and pathways (see Figure 7.20). After the final preliminary building designs and their relationship to the influencing factors of the building site are determined, the building is placed on the site plan.

STAGE III   The placement of the building is derived from the final preliminary designs relative to the orientation of the sun, prevailing winds, governing setback requirements, and any existing easements. A solid line depicts the perimeter lines of the building, and a broken line indicates walls beneath. This is done to ensure that the setback dimension lines are to the perimeter wall lines. See Figure 7.21.

STAGE IV   Items such as the driveway, patio slab, garage, and any other significant features are included on the site plan. See Figure 7.22.

STAGE V   Provide the finish contour lines, which are drawn with a solid line and connected to their correlating grade elevations. The numerical elevation grades have been added, representing one-foot

intervals. Dimension lines and their values are now shown from the property lines to the perimeter wall lines of the building for layout purposes. Also shown in this stage are the property line dimensions and their bearings. See Figure 7.23.

When dimensioning a site plan, locating the building is the primary goal. There are no other plans in an architectural set of drawings that will position the building on the site. That is not to say other dimensions are not important: They are, but the locating of patios and other site features is secondary.

STAGE VI   The final stage includes all the required noting. The finish noting on the site plan includes material finish, the walkway material, and any required specifications. In addition, the title and notes are included on the plot sheet. See Figure 7.24.

For clarity, all the various floor elevations should be labeled on the site plan. In addition, a symbol legend should be provided, to define those symbols used on the

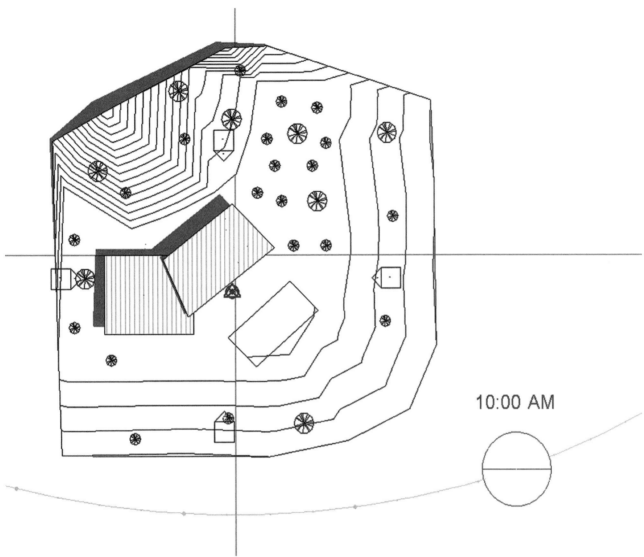

Figure 7.18 Revit shades and shadows.

site plan. Finally, the title of the drawing is shown, along with the north orientation arrow, the street name, and the scale for the site and roof plan drawings.

■ THE GRADING PLAN

Grading

The grading plan shows how the topography of the site will be changed to accommodate the building design. This plan shows the existing grades and proposed grades, which are termed **finished grades**. It also indicates the finished grade elevations and the elevations of building floors, walks, and site walls. Existing grade lines are shown with a broken line, and proposed finished grades with a solid line. Finished grading lines represent the end result or desired layout once the site is graded. See Figure 7.25.

The grading plan drawing illustrates and defines the various alterations of the land contours that are needed to develop the site for a specific structure. It is an important and powerful tool that helps the architect in site development.

Floor Elevations

Once the orientation and location of the building have been established, the process of preparing a grading plan may begin. The first step is to designate tentative floor-level elevations, which will be determined by the structure's location in relation to the existing grades. It should be noted that in the process of designing a grading plan, tentative floor elevations may have to be adjusted to satisfy the location of the finished contours and their elevations. With the establishment of the floor-level elevations, it will then be necessary to reshape the

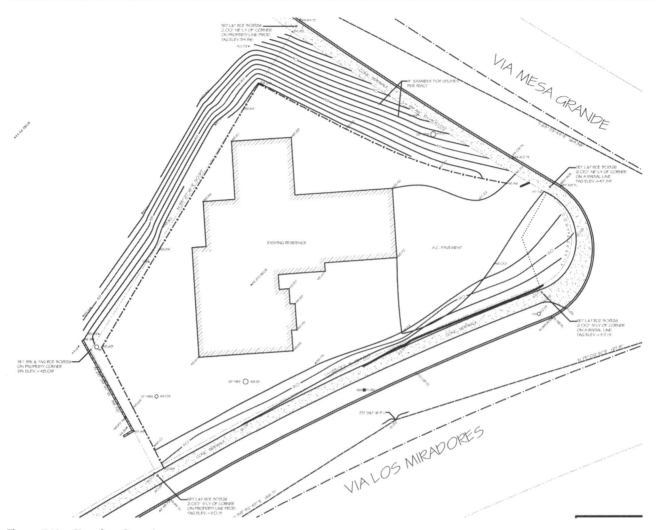

Figure 7.19   Site plan: Stage I.

existing grade lines to satisfy floor clearances and site drainage control. See Figure 7.26.

For the purpose of providing proper drainage around the building, the designer should encourage surface drainage to flow to each side of the building, and follow the natural slope of the site. Finished contour elevations will be shaped to provide a gentle slope around the front and sides of the building. A minimum 2% slope is recommended for proper drainage of soil areas.

The adjacent natural grade can be reshaped to provide a more gradual slope and maintain proper drainage and floor clearances.

Orienting a residence on the site with a minimum amount of finished grading is the most environmentally sensitive response to a site. Once the primary location and floor elevation have been established for the garage, the formation and planning for the residence may

now proceed, with the intention of ensuring compatibility with the existing grade elevations and the contour configurations of the existing grades. The architect may decide to develop a building configuration that will accommodate minimal finished grading conditions and provide a development that is more compatible with the natural terrain.

In designing a more severe slope, as in cases where a building pad must be enlarged, a maximum slope ratio is laid out. **Slope ratios** are laid out with horizontal scaled increments for the tentative slope ratio. For instance, in some counties a ratio of 2:1 is the minimum slope allowed for each site contour. This would allow a site to increase one foot in height for every two feet traveled in the horizontal direction. A slope ratio of 3:1 is a more gradual slope, and in many areas an ideal target for slope stability. Slope ratio is anticipated for the grade cut for the placement of the building. Increments will start

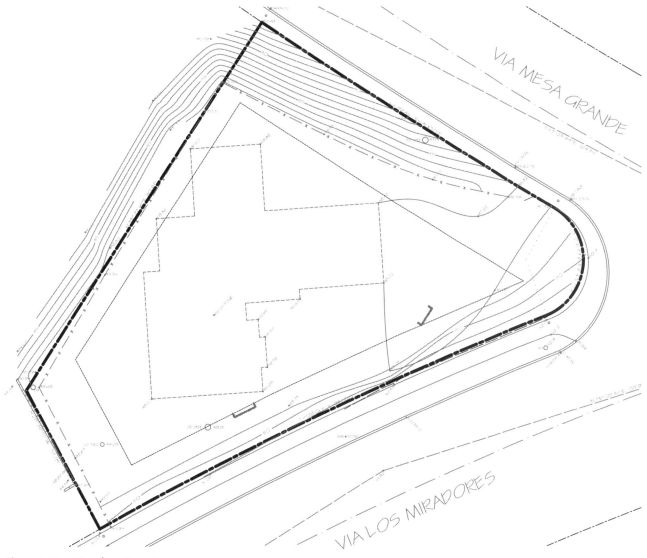

Figure 7.20 Site plan: Stage II.

from the established grades adjacent to the building. Once the various increments have been plotted, these points can be connected. In most cases, all finish grade elevations start at an existing or natural grade elevation and terminate at the respective existing grade elevation. See Figure 7.27.

Cut and Fill Procedures

Contour changes will require either the removal of soil—a **cut** into the existing contours—or the opposite, the addition of soil to the site; the latter is called **fill**. In reshaping contours with cut and fill procedures, one can provide a relatively level area for construction. Depending on the soil's condition and soil preparation, the maximum allowable ratio for cut and fill slopes may

vary from 1½:1, 2:1, or 3:1. A ratio of 3:1 means that for each three-foot distance on the horizontal, there is a minimum one-foot change in vertical elevation. A slope of 3:1 establishes a stable slope that is less likely to slide. In some municipalities, a maximum slope of 3:1 is required for cut and fill. To clarify grading conditions, grading sections should be taken through these areas. See Figure 7.28.

Another approach is to develop a level area on a site for the construction of a residence. The level area, called a **building pad**, will have a minimal slope for drainage of approximately 2%. The creation of a building pad will provide the architect with more flexibility in the design, because he or she will not be constrained by grade elevations, floor transitions, building shapes, or other considerations.

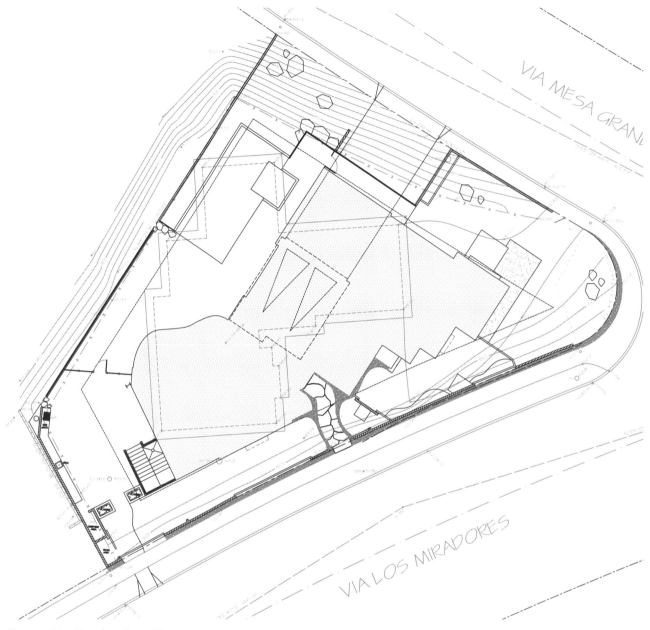

Figure 7.21 Site plan: Stage III.

One approach in developing a building pad is to try to create a balance cut and fill. In this approach, the earth that is cut from the site slope is dispersed and used as the fill material to increase the building pad site. The fill material must then be **compacted** to an acceptable soil-bearing capacity if a structure is to be founded in the fill area. To develop the size, shape, and grading for the building pad, it is recommended that an assumed pad elevation be established. This pad elevation may be determined by what is referred to as a **daylight grade elevation**, defined as that point or elevation where the cut and fill portions of the site grading intersect at a given grade elevation.

■ THE SITE AND GRADING PLAN

Site Plan and Grading Plan

In this section, we discuss and illustrate another example of grading design and the various criteria that dictate design solutions, this time for a two-story residence. The

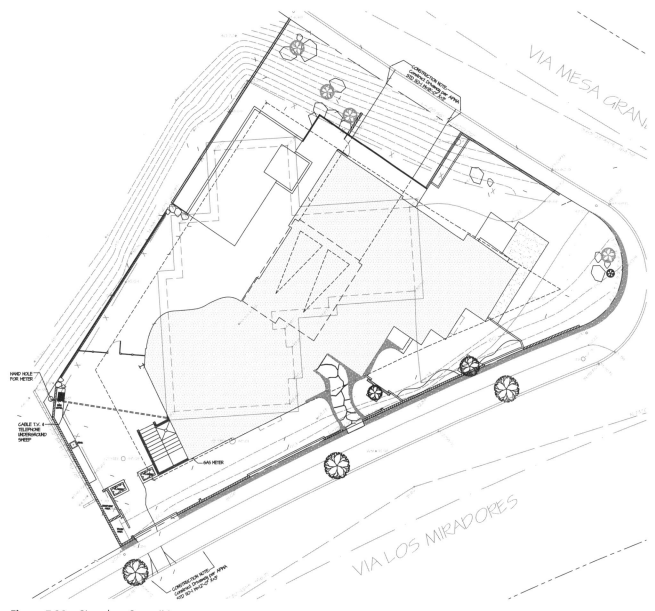

Figure 7.22 Site plan: Stage IV.

topography map for this project is shown in Figure 7.29. Note that the natural or existing grades are indicated with a broken line and a designated number indicating the grade elevation of each contour line.

For this project, the initial concern was the driveway access and slope relative to the garage floor elevation. The desired maximum slope of the driveway does not exceed one foot in ten feet (1:10). This translates into a slope of 10%. Starting at the southerly property line, which is the front property line, the existing contour grade elevation is 375.00'. From this existing grade elevation of 375.00', it is desirable to maintain a maximum driveway slope of 10% within the 15'-0" building

setback area. This design solution then establishes the garage floor elevation at 372.50'. This condition is illustrated in Figure 7.30. Note that a trench drain is located in front of the garage to divert any water accumulation from the sloping driveway. This trench drain will have a grate cover and drain lines to dissipate the water.

Another concern in dealing with sloping driveways is the transition from the street and the driveway apron elevation to the sloping portion of the driveway. This concern is illustrated graphically in the driveway transition section shown in Figure 7.31. Note the hypothetical driveway transition, depicted with a broken line, which

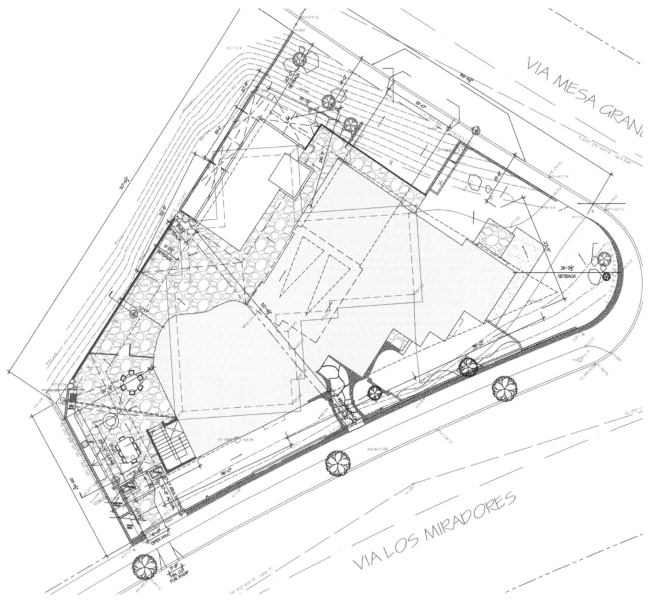

Figure 7.23   Site plan: Stage V.

shows steep slope transitions that may cause under-car damage and/or bumper scraping.

The first step is to develop the grading for a driveway that will provide acceptable slopes for access to the garage, which will in turn determine the garage location and floor elevation. Starting at the street grade elevation, the initial grade transition from the street to the driveway should not be so steep as to scrape the bumper of an automobile. The initial maximal slope ratio is approximately one foot vertically to ten feet horizontally (1:10), or a 10% slope. A slope of 20% or a 1:5 ratio would be the maximum allowable in most jurisdictions.

Although a 20% driveway can be utilized with appropriate transitions of 10% at the beginning and ending of the 20% area, approximately eight to ten feet of 10% grade, then 20%, and then another eight to ten feet of 10% will allow a smoother transition for vehicles. A goal for a contoured lot is to work with the existing topography, but an ideal smooth slope of 12.5% or less is comfortable. In addition to the vertical slope, the length of a driveway maximum cross-slope, measured at the width, would be 10% (ideally, less than 5%). In each region of the country, the local municipality will establish the maximum for this condition.

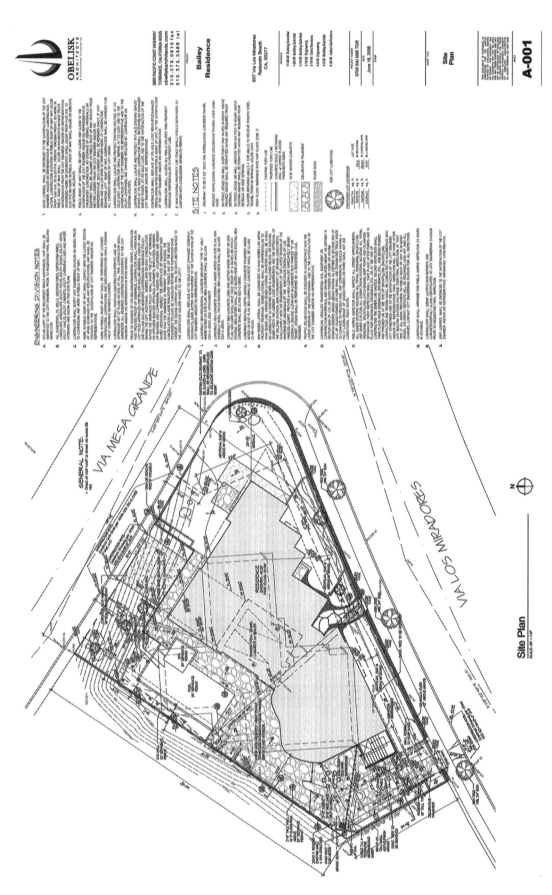

Figure 7.24 Site plan: Stage VI. (Courtesy of the Bailey residence.)

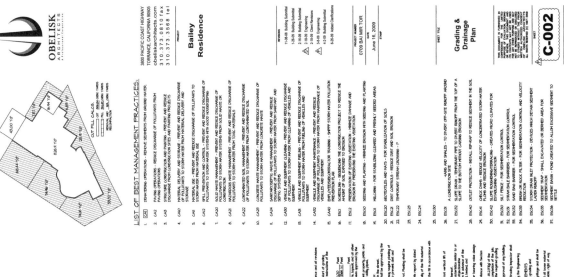
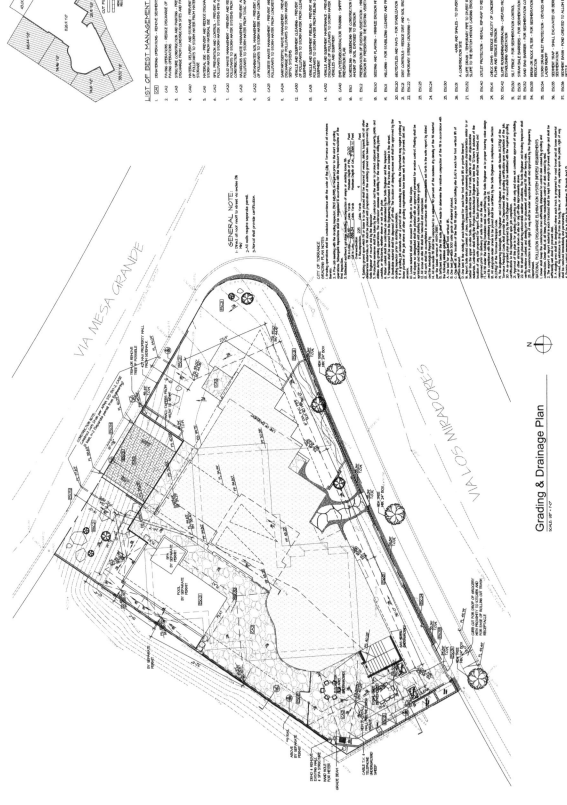

Figure 7.25 Grading plan. (Courtesy of the Bailey residence.)

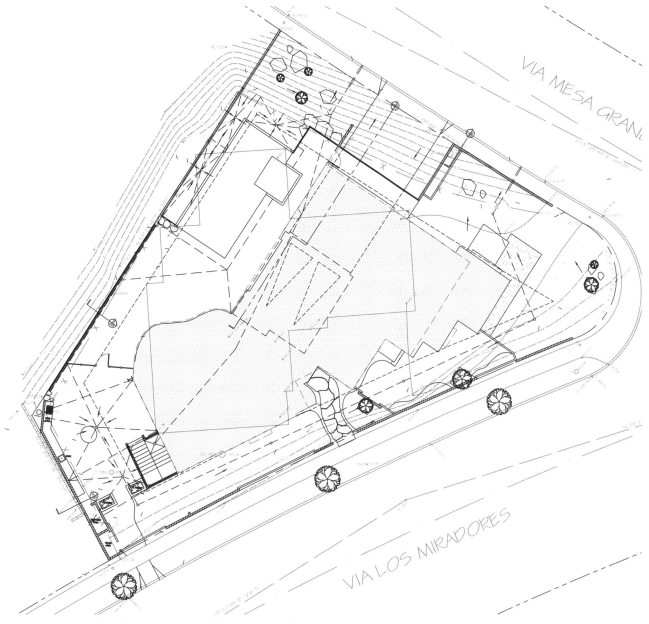

Figure 7.26 Initial grading. (Courtesy of the Bailey residence.)

It is not recommended that one exceed a 20% driveway slope, which is a one-foot transition for each five feet horizontally. A maximum 4% slope is recommended for the side-to-side slope or **cross-slope** of the driveway. As mentioned previously, the garage floor elevation has been established at 372.50'. From the garage floor elevation, a 6" floor transition will determine the first-floor elevation to be 373.00'. The garage floor and first-floor elevations will now become the basis for the finished grading design. See Figure 7.32. The existing grade lines of the site slope gently down from the southerly property line to the northerly property line. This condition, based on the established garage and first-floor elevations, will require an earth cut at the front or southerly area of the site, with the soil removed being relocated to the rear or northerly portion of the site, which becomes a fill area. The solid lines illustrate the finish grade contours, as depicted in Figure 7.32. Note that the finish grade line elevations connect to the existing grade line elevations. Figure 7.32 graphically illustrates a cross-section of the building site cut in a south-to-north direction. The broken line depicts the approximate existing grade, and the

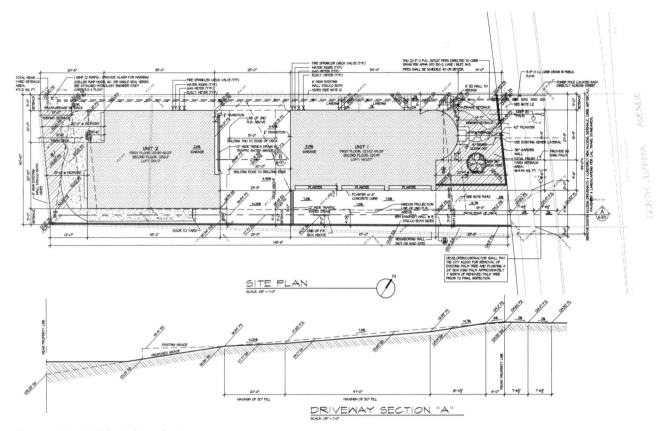

SITE PLAN
SCALE: 1/8" = 1'-0"

DRIVEWAY SECTION "A"
SCALE: 1/8" = 1'-0"

Figure 7.27   Finished slope design.

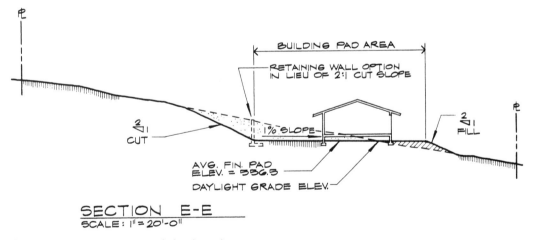

SECTION E-E
SCALE: 1" = 20'-0"

Figure 7.28   Cross-section with finish grades.

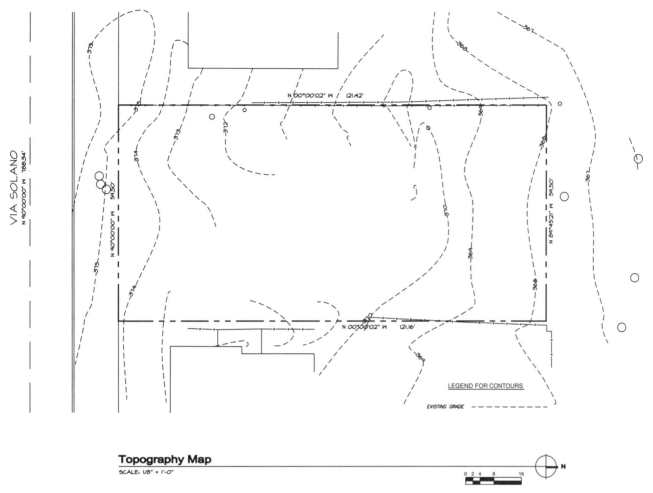

Figure 7.29 Topography map.

solid line and shaded areas show the finished grade line and fill areas. Additional cross-sections in relationship to abutting properties are illustrated in Figure 7.33.

The maximum slope or gradient for cut and fill slope conditions may be determined by the type of soil found on the site and local agency requirements. Various soil types react differently to potential soil erosion. For most cases, the maximum slope or gradient may range from 1, to 1½:1, to 2:1. These ratios translate into 66% and 50% slope conditions, respectively. See Figure 7.34.

Commercial Site Grading

For sloping sites that are going to be developed for commercial and office use, the grading design will have to address automobile and pedestrian access to the building. The transition from the street to the parking area should provide easy access relative to the driveway slope and the slope of the parking area. Grade transitions that require stairs and landings will also require ramps for people with disabilities, which are regulated by the ADA requirements. See Figure 7.35.

■ THE DRAINAGE PLAN

A **drainage plan** establishes the path by which water travels on a site, often in a controlled method via a nonerosive device. Such devices include pipe, area drains, sub-drains, drains, catch basins, drainage swales, diverters/interceptors, and bio-filters. Other controlled methods include shaping of grade, berms, driveways, splash walls, riprap, and velocity reducers. **Area drains** are inlets that allow excess water collected on the surface of an area to be rerouted with pipes below grade. A drain is typically located in a hard paved area where a **sub-drain**, sometimes called a **french drain**, collects excess water below grade (for example, behind a retaining wall). These too are

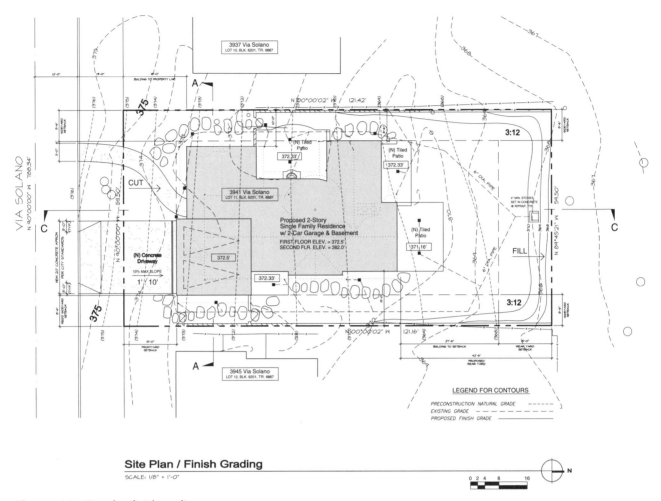

Site Plan / Finish Grading

SCALE: 1/8" = 1'-0"

Figure 7.30 Site plan/finish grading.

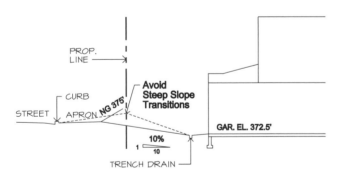

Figure 7.31 Driveway transition section.

connected to a pipe and outlet. On large sloping sites, it is difficult to control water and channel the flow into area drains. In these cases, a **swale**, a "V"-shaped catching device, is used to divert the water flow. These swales will gather the excess water and carry it to a **catch basin**. **Bio-filters** are a new addition to the drainage arsenal. Bio-filters are devices designed to catch harmful chemicals or silt in surface runoff. There are many types of bio-filters; consult regional codes

for proper choice and fabrication. Often shaping the grade with berms or a 2% slope can route runoff in the right direction. Even a driveway can have a low point to guide water; a splash wall or raised curb are also effective methods. When water flow is excessive, implementation of a velocity reducer or a riprap area may be required. This slows the water flow and disperses the water in a fashion that limits erosion potential. See Figure 7.36.

The site may require that floor elevation changes be utilized to enhance the compatibility between the structure and the existing grades. The residence shape may follow the contours of the existing grade elevations and result in a unique shape or configuration. Note that some excavation will occur below the floor levels in order to provide the under-floor clearances required by building codes for wood floors.

After completing an analysis of the existing grades and their contours, in conjunction with the architectural planning of the residence, a grading plan can be prepared.

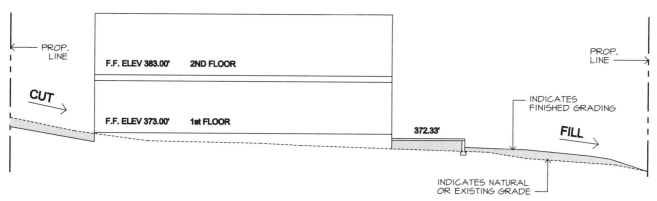

Figure 7.32 Site grading cross-section.

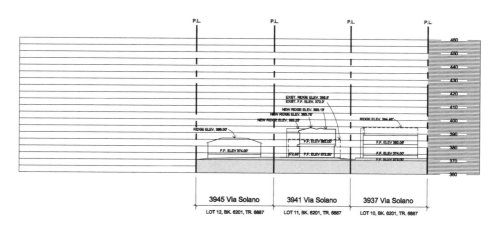

Cross Section "B-B"

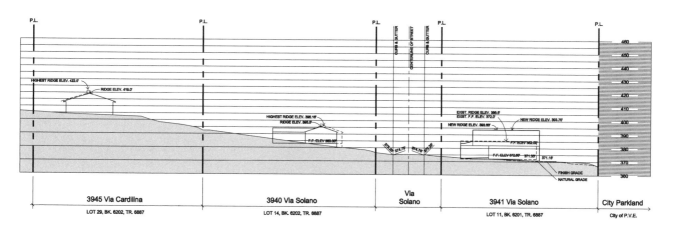

Cross Section "A-A"

Site Sections

SCALE: 1" = 30'-0"

Figure 7.33 Site sections.

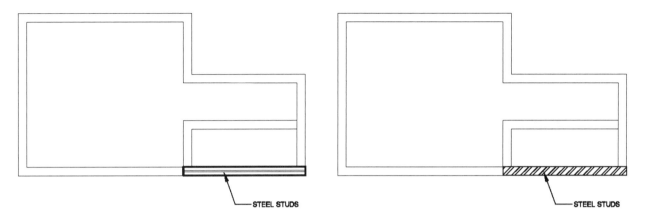

Figure 7.34 Slope ratios.

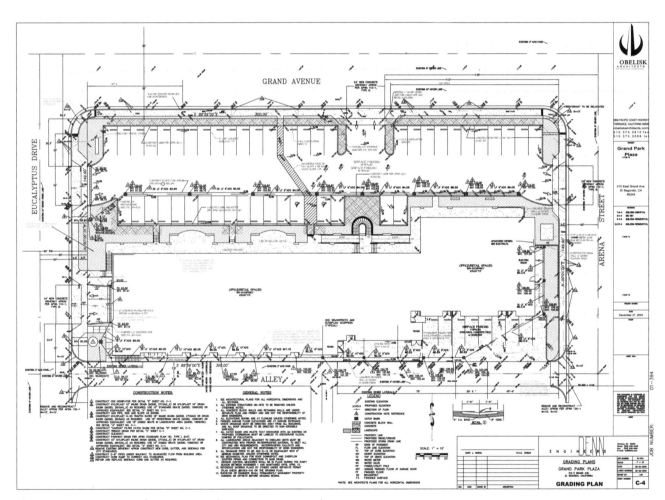

Figure 7.35 Existing grade. (Courtesy of Denn Engineers and Mr. Kizirian.)

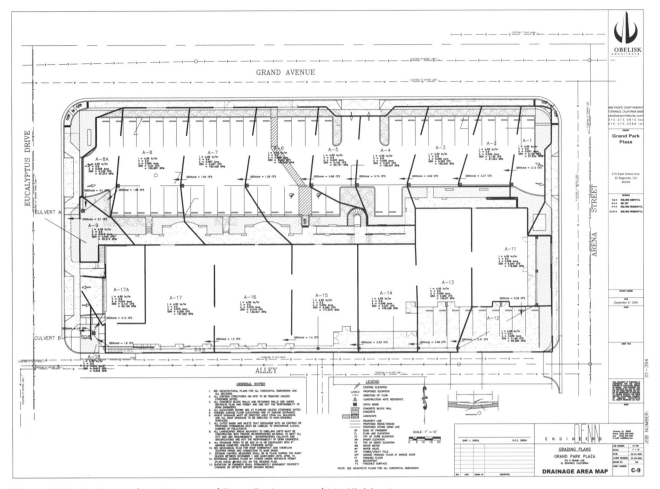

Figure 7.36 Drainage plan. (Courtesy of Denn Engineers and Mr. Kizirian.)

■ THE EROSION AND SEDIMENT CONTROL PLANS

When construction of a building occurs in winter months, the governing agency will require a plan that demonstrates how runoff is to be controlled onsite. This plan is called an *erosion control plan*. Such a plan graphically demonstrates that water will not carry off silt, dirt, or contaminants from a site into storm drains, waterways, or neighboring sites. These can be designed utilizing:

- Sediment control
  - Silt fence
  - Hay-bale barriers
  - Sediment traps
  - Silt curtain
  - Sediment mat
  - Filter logs
- Erosion control
  - Temporary ditch checks

- Mulch
- Erosion control blankets
- Compost
- Erosion stabilization mats

These are a few methods that could be further researched when planning for erosion control. See Figure 7.37.

■ THE UTILITY PLAN

Plotting of existing utilities is necessary to the site improvement process. See Figure 7.2. Such a plan should show the location of all existing utilities, including sewer laterals, water and gas lines, and telephone, TV cable, and electrical service lines. This drawing then provides a basis for locating new utility connections. It may also influence the locations of transformers, generators, electrical rooms, and meter rooms in the structure itself.

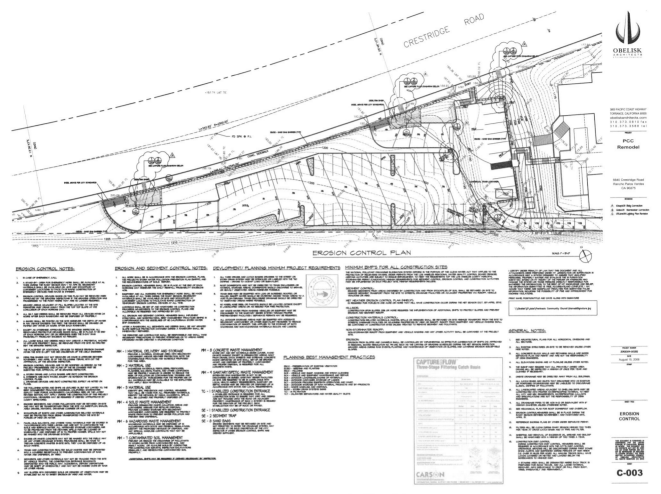

Figure 7.37 Erosion control plan. (Courtesy of Peninsula Community Church.)

■ THE CIRCULATION PLAN

In designing large complexes—more specifically, complexes with heavy vehicular circulation—it may become necessary to create a plan that articulates the flow of vehicular travel. These forms of plans are not complex to develop, but are informative to clients, city officials, and architects who are determining appropriate and efficient circulation design. See Figure 7.38.

■ THE LANDSCAPE, IRRIGATION, AND DRAINAGE PLANS

Landscape Plan and Plant List

The final stage of site development for most projects is landscaping. The landscape drawing shows the location of trees, plants, ground covers, benches, fences, and walks. Accompanying this is a **plant list**, identifying plant species with a symbol or number and indicating the size and number of plants. See Figure 7.39. Often a landscape architect will be hired as a consultant to specify the ideal plant materials and make recommendations for the **hardscape** surrounding the project.

Irrigation Plan

An irrigation plan often accompanies the landscape plan. This drawing is typically separate from the landscape plan, but is directly influenced by the locations of plant material. This plan shows all water lines, points of connection, control valves, and types of watering fixtures required for irrigation. See Figure 7.40.

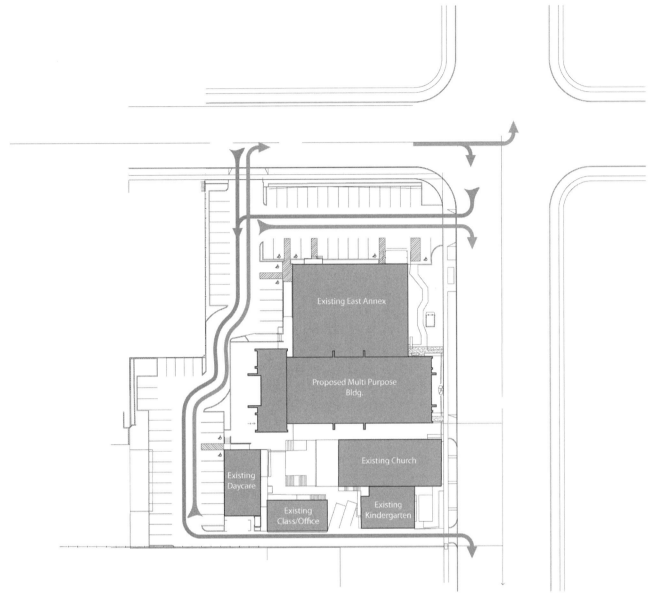

Figure 7.38   Circulation plan.

■ THE SITE IMPROVEMENT PLAN: AN OVERVIEW

The basic requirement for all construction documents is clarity. The site improvement plan is no exception. It can incorporate any or all of the plans just discussed, depending on the complexity of the information that must be communicated and on office practice.

The primary information to be found in the site improvement plan is:

1. Site lot lines with accompanying bearings and dimensions
2. Scale of the drawing
3. North arrows
4. Building location with layout dimensions
5. Paving, walks, walls with their accompanying material call-outs, and layout dimensions

Figure 7.41 shows the primary information found on a site improvement plan. The building layout dimension lines must be noted to their respective property lines, providing two measuring points at each side of the property lines. This, in turn, provides the location of the building on the site. This is helpful when the property lines do not parallel the building. This method may apply to patios, walks, paving, and walls, which are also dimensioned on the site improvement plan.

Site plans for large sites, such as multiple-resident housing projects, must show primary information, such

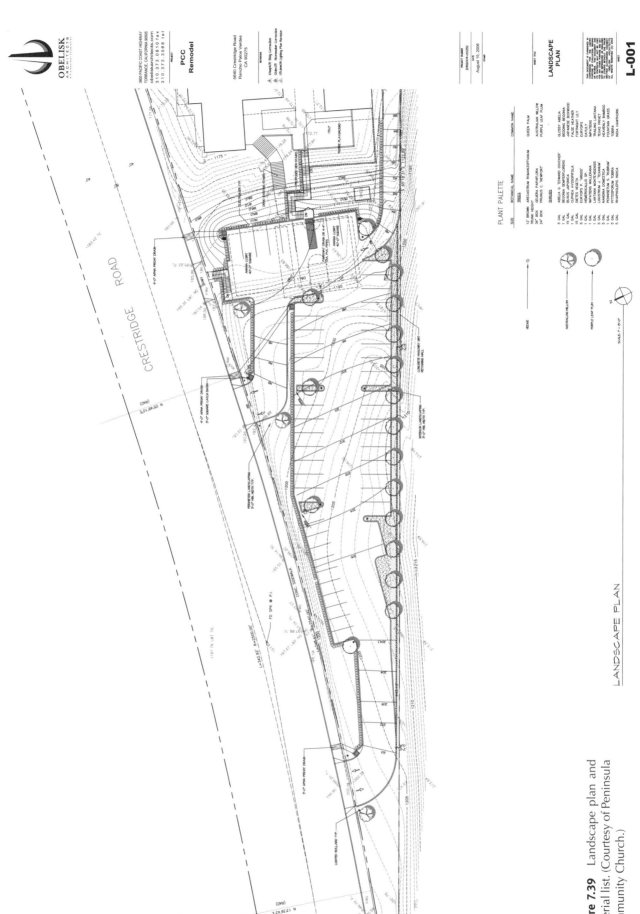

Figure 7.39 Landscape plan and material list. (Courtesy of Peninsula Community Church.)

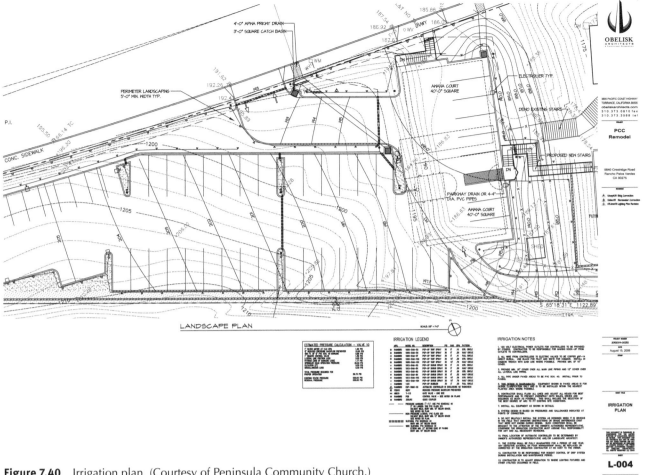

Figure 7.40 Irrigation plan. (Courtesy of Peninsula Community Church.)

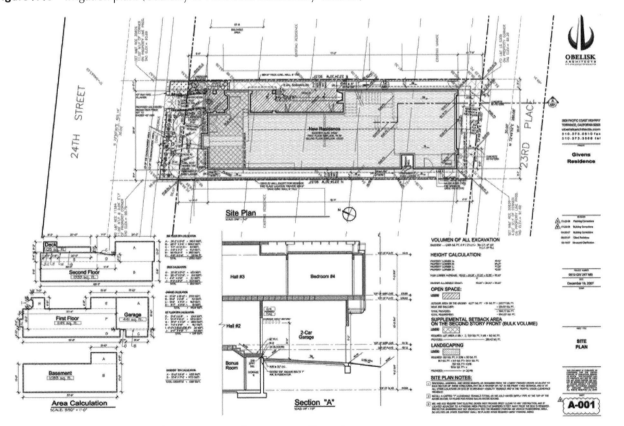

Figure 7.41 Site improvement plan. (Courtesy of Mr. & Mrs. Givens.)

249

1. Vicinity map
2. Property lines
   a. Lengths — each side
   b. Correct angles if not 90°
   c. Direction
3. Adjoining streets, sidewalks, parking, curbs, parkways, parking areas, wheel stops, lanes, and lighting
4. Existing structures and buildings and alleys
5. Structures and buildings to be removed
   a. Trees
   b. Old foundations
   c. Walks
   d. Miscellanea
6. Public utilities locations
   a. Storm drain
   b. Sewer lines
   c. Gas lines
   d. Gas meter
   e. Water lines
   f. Water meter
   g. Power line
   h. Power pole
   i. Electric meter
   j. Telephone pole
   k. Lamp post
   l. Fire plugs
7. Public utilities easements if on property
8. Contours of grade
   a. Existing grade — dotted line
   b. Finish cut or fill — solid line
   c. Legend
   d. Slopes to street
9. Grade elevations
   a. Finish slab or finish floor
   b. Corners of building (finish)
   c. Top of all walls
   d. Amount of slope for drainage

10. Roof plan — new building
    a. Building — hidden line
    b. Roof overhang — solid line
    c. Garage
    d. Slopes (arrows)
    e. Projecting canopies
    f. Slabs and porches
    g. Projecting beams
    h. Material for roof
    i. North arrow
    j. Title and scale
    k. Show ridges and valleys
    l. Roof drains and downspouts
    m. Parapets
    n. Roof jacks for TV, telephone, electric service
    o. Note building outline
    p. Dimension overhangs
    q. Note rain diverters
    r. Skylights
    s. Roof accessways
    t. Floodlight locations
    u. Service pole for electrical
11. New construction
    a. Retaining walls
    b. Driveways and aprons
    c. Sidewalks
    d. Pool locations and size
    e. Splash blocks
    f. Catch basins
    g. Curbs
    h. Patios, walls, expansion joints, dividers, etc.
12. North arrow (usually toward the top of sheet)
13. Dimensions
    a. Property lines
    b. Side yards
    c. Rear yards
    d. Front yards

    e. Easements
    f. Street centerline
    g. Length of fences and walls
    h. Height of fences and walls
    i. Width of sidewalks, driveway, and parking
    j. Utilities
    k. Locations of existing structures
    l. Note floor elevation
    m. Dimension building to property line
    n. Setbacks
14. Notes
    a. Tract no.
    b. Block no.
    c. Lot no.
    d. House no.
    e. Street
    f. City, county, state
    g. Owner's name
    h. Draftman's name (title block)
    i. Materials for porches, terraces, drives, etc.
    j. Finish grades where necessary
    k. Slope of driveway
    l. Scale (1/8", 1"-30', 1"-20', etc.)
15. Landscape lighting, note switches
16. Area drains, drain lines to street
17. Show hose bibbs
18. Note drying yard, clothes line equipment
19. Complete title block
    a. Sheet no.
    b. Scale
    c. Date
    d. Name drawn by
    e. Project address
    f. Approved by
    g. Sheet title
    h. Revision box
    i. Company name and address (school)

Figure 7.42 Sample site plan checklist.

as utility locations, driveway locations, and building locations. Further examples of site development plans appear in later chapters. See Figure 7.42 for a site plan checklist.

■ SIZE AND LOCATION

Size and Location

As you position the structure on the site and subsequently position architectural features adjacent to the building, two considerations come to mind: size and location.

Size includes width, length, and thickness (sometimes even height), plus location dimension. See Figure 7.43; in this illustration, the positioning that must be determined to accommodate a large commercial building and allow for parking we call *location dimension*.

Often the size of a commercial building has a large impact on the location of the building, and in some cases the shape of the building is affected by the need for parking areas.

Driveway and Curb

Often one side of your site will be bounded with a sidewalk, parkway, and a small curb. In most cities, this portion adjacent to a street is maintained by the Department of Public Works or some other such municipal agency. Permits are required to break the curb for a driveway; permits can be obtained from the appropriate agency or agency subdivision (perhaps the city's Road Department Bureau or engineering department). Based on the size of the curb, the agency will configure an angle at which you can cut the curb to form the driveway. See Figure 7.44.

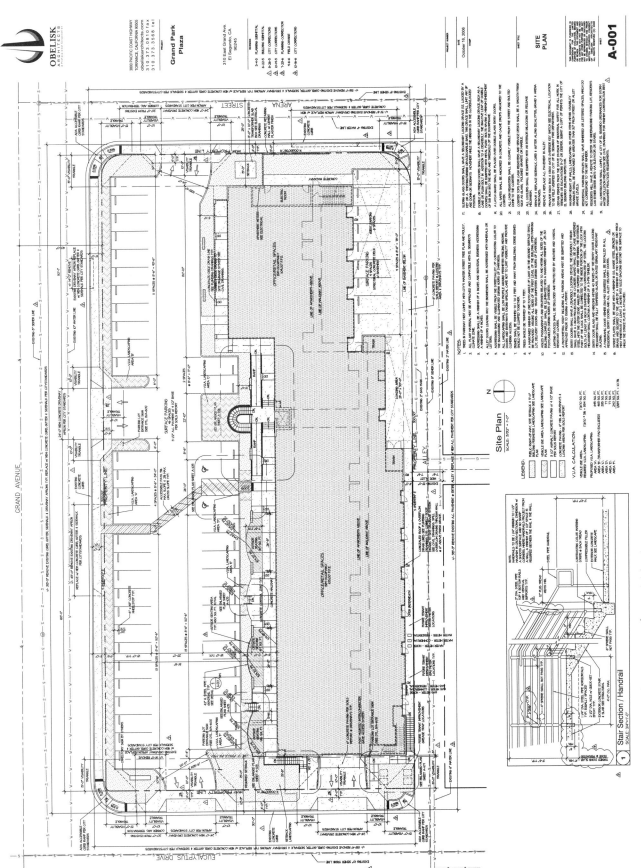

Figure 7.43 Site buildings located. (Courtesy of Mr. Kizirian.)

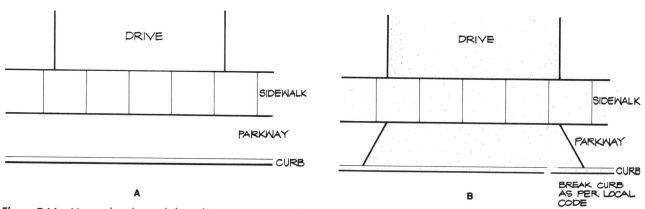

Figure 7.44   How to break a curb for a driveway. (Reprinted by permission from *The Professional Practice of Architectural Working Drawings,* 3d Ed., © 2003 by John Wiley & Sons, Inc.)

FLOOR PLAN

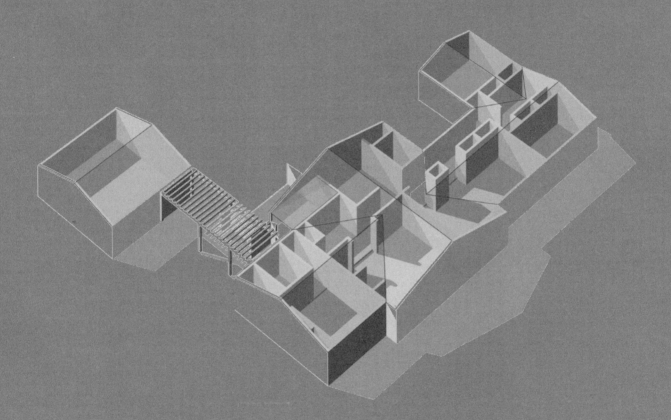

■ TYPES OF FLOOR PLANS

The point of reference for working drawings is the floor plan: a drawing viewed from above with the roof removed. Actually, it is a horizontal cut (section) taken at approximately eye level. See Figure 8.1.

To better understand this, imagine a knife slicing through a structure and removing the upper half (on a single-story structure, the half with the roof). The remaining half is then viewed from the air. This becomes the floor plan. See Figure 8.2.

The floor plan for a split-level residence is more complicated. In the following example, the entry, powder room, and garage are at the mid-level, which is also the level of the street and sidewalk. Use this level as a point of reference.

The stairs at the rear of the entry lead to the upper and lower levels. The lower level contains the master bedroom, master bath, study, bedroom, laundry, and bathroom. See Figure 8.3. The upper level contains the living room with a wet bar, and the dining room, kitchen, breakfast room, and foyer. See Figure 8.4. When these are translated into a floor plan, they appear as in Figures 8.5 and 8.6. The mid-level is duplicated and common to both drawings.

A second approach is to use a **break line** (a line with a jog in it to indicate that a portion has been deleted), showing only a part of the garage on one of the plans.

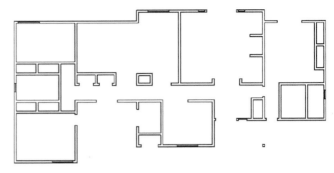

Figure 8.2   Floor plan.

Another approach is to use a straight break line through the garage, and draft it showing only part of the garage on one of the plans.

In a two-story building, a single room on the first floor is sometimes actually two stories high. If this room were a living room, for example, it would be treated as a normal one-story living room on the first-floor plan; however, the area would be repeated on the second-floor plan and labeled as upper living room or just labeled "open."

To simplify the image to be drafted, not every structural member is shown. For example, in a wood-framed structure, if every vertical piece of wood were shown, the task would be impossible. Simplifying this image of the wood structure is done with two parallel lines.

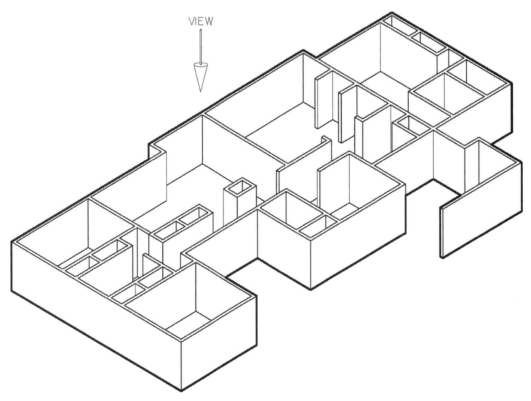

Figure 8.1   Cutaway pictorial floor plan.

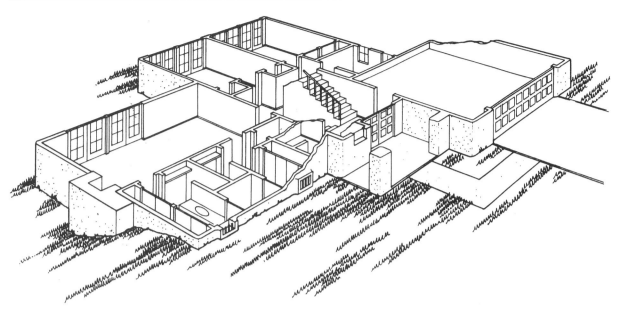

Figure 8.3 Pictorial of lower-level floor plan. (Courtesy of William F. Smith—Builder.)

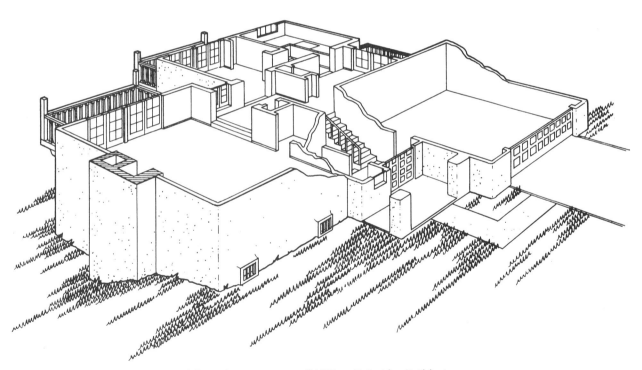

Figure 8.4 Pictorial of upper-level floor plan. (Courtesy of William F. Smith—Builder.)

Sometimes the insulation is shown in symbol form and is not shown through the total wall. See Figure 8.7. The same parallel series of lines can also be used to represent a masonry wall by adding a series of diagonal lines. See Figure 8.8. Steel frame can be represented as shown in Figure 8.9.

Wood Framing

Figure 8.10 shows the appearance of a corner of a wood frame structure. Each side of the wall is built separately. An extra stud is usually placed at the end of the wall; it extends to the edge of the building. It therefore acts as

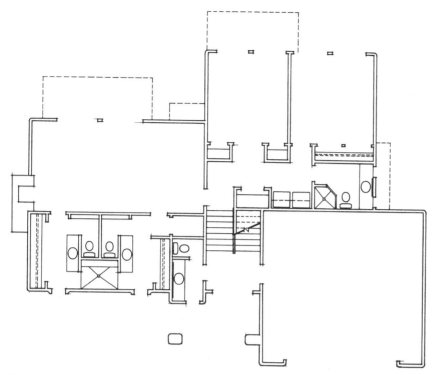

Figure 8.5 Lower-level floor plan. (Courtesy of William F. Smith—Builder.)

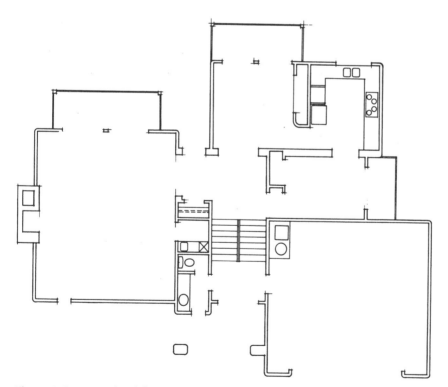

Figure 8.6 Upper-level floor plan. (Courtesy of William F. Smith—Builder.)

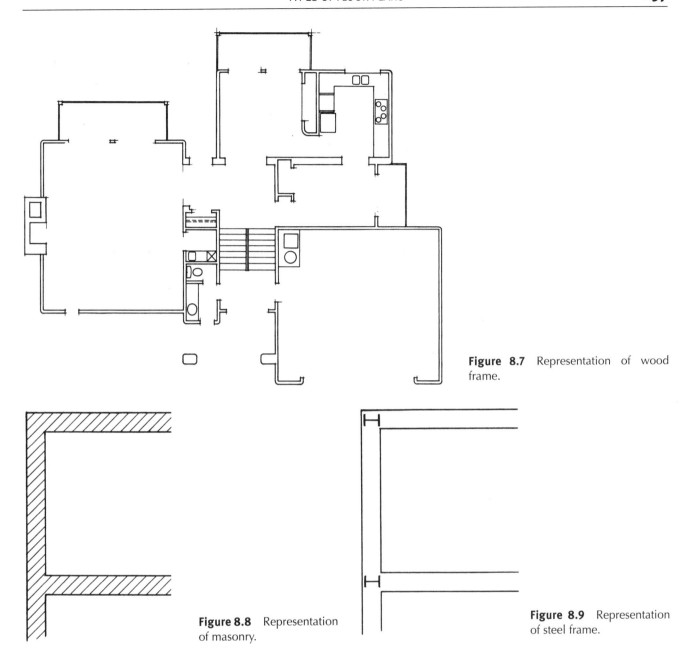

Figure 8.7 Representation of wood frame.

Figure 8.8 Representation of masonry.

Figure 8.9 Representation of steel frame.

a structural support, and gives a larger nailing surface to which wall materials can be anchored.

Figure 8.11 shows the pictorial intersection of an interior wall and an exterior wall, and a plan view of that same intersection.

Walls are not the only important elements in the framing process, of course. You must also consider the locations of doors and windows and the special framing they require. See Figure 8.12.

Interior Dimensioning. Because a wood-framed wall is a built-up system—that is, a wall frame of wood upon which plaster or another wall covering is added—dimension lines must sometimes be drawn to the edge of studs and sometimes to their center.

Figure 8.13 shows how the corner of a wood-framed wall is dimensioned to the stud line. Figure 8.14 shows how an interior wall intersecting an exterior wall is dimensioned. It is dimensioned to the center so that the two studs which the interior wall will join can be located.

The process of drawing each stud in a wall becomes tiresome. So, usually two lines drawn 6″ apart (in scale) are used to represent wood. To make sure that the person reading this set of plans does know that the stud is being dimensioned and not the exterior surface, the extension is often brought inside the 6″-wide wall lines. Another way to make this clear is to take extension lines to the outside surface and write "**F.O.S.**" (**face of stud**) adjacent to the extension lines. See Figure 8.13.

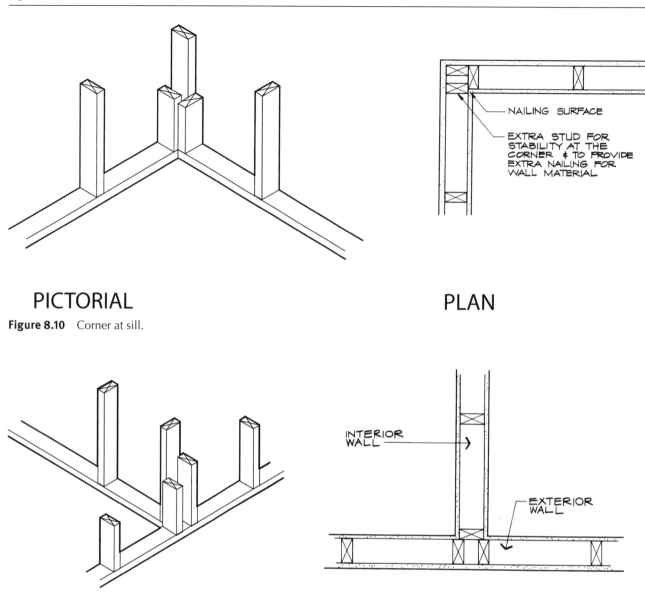

PICTORIAL   PLAN

Figure 8.10 Corner at sill.

PICTORIAL   PLAN

Figure 8.11 Intersection of exterior wall in interior wall.

Dimensioning interior walls requires a centerline or an extension line right into the wall intersection, as shown in Figure 8.14. A centerline is more desirable than a solid line.

Windows and doors are located to the center of the object, as shown in Figure 8.15. When a structural column is next to a window or door, the doors and windows are dimensioned to the structural column. The size of a particular window or door can be obtained from a chart called a *schedule*. This schedule can be found by locating the sheet number on the bottom half of the **reference bubble** adjacent to the window or door. See Figure 8.16. (A *reference bubble* is a circle with a line drawn through it horizontally.)

Exterior Dimensioning. Normally, three to four dimension lines are needed on an exterior dimension of a floor plan. The first dimension line away from the object includes the walls, partitions, centers of windows and doors, and so forth. See Figure 8.17. The second dimension line away from the object (floor plan) includes walls and partitions only. If, in establishing the second dimension line, you duplicate a dimension, eliminate the dimension line closest to the object. The third dimension line away from the object is for overall dimensions. The first dimension line away from the structure should be measured ¾″ to 1½″ from the outside lines of the plan to allow for notes, window and door reference bubbles, equipment that may be placed adjacent to the structure,

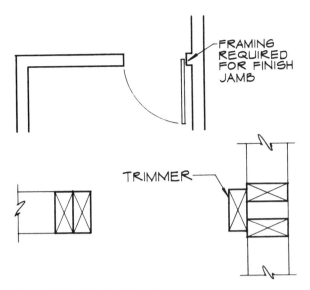

Figure 8.12 Framing for a door.

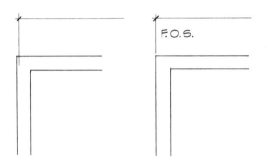

Figure 8.13 Dimensioning corners.

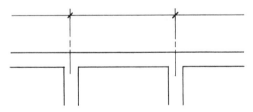

Figure 8.14 Dimensioning interior walls.

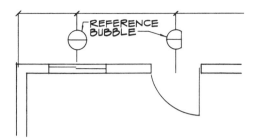

Figure 8.16 Use of reference bubbles on doors and windows.

and so on. The second dimension line away from the structure should be approximately ⅜″ to ½″ away from the first dimension line. The distance between all subsequent dimension lines should be the same as the distance between the first and second dimension lines.

A large jog in a wall is called an *offset*. Because the jog is removed from the plane that is being dimensioned, you must decide whether to use long extension lines or to dimension the offset at the location of the jog.

If the jog were lengthy, it would be better to dimension the jog on its own. See Figure 8.18 for a small jog. This would be dimensioned on the second or the third dimension line, and the fourth dimension line would become the overall.

Objects located independently or outside of the structure, such as posts (columns), are treated differently. First, the order in which the items are to be built must be established. Will the columns be built before or after the adjacent walls? If the walls or the foundation for the walls are to be erected first, then major walls near the columns are identified and the columns are located from them. Never dimension from an inaccessible location! See Figure 8.19.

Masonry

When walls are built of brick or concrete block instead of wood frame, the procedure changes. Everything here is based on the size and proportion of the masonry unit

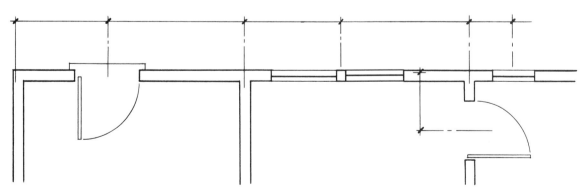

Figure 8.15 Dimensioning doors and windows.

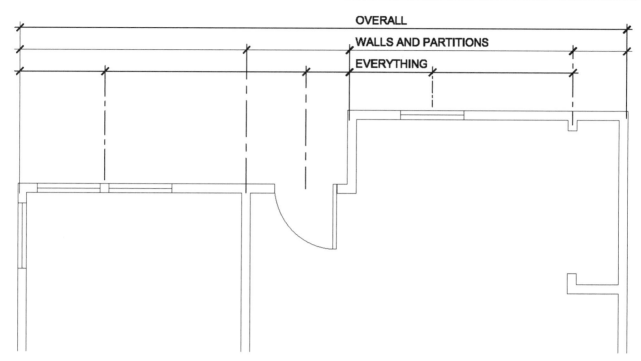

Figure 8.17   First dimension line away from the object.

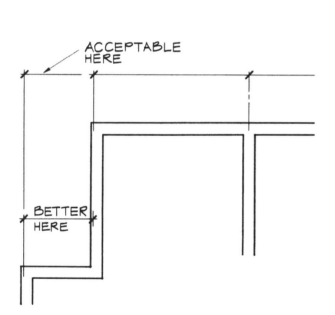

Figure 8.18   Offset dimension locations.

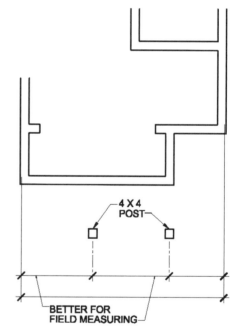

Figure 8.19   Locating columns from the structure.

used. Represent masonry as a series of diagonal lines. See Figure 8.20. Show door and window openings in the same way as you did for wood-framed structures. You may represent concrete block in the same way as brick for small-scale drawings, but be aware that some offices do use different material designations. See Figure 8.21. (These methods of representing concrete blocks were obtained from various sources, including association

literature, AIA standards, and other reference sources.) Extension lines for dimensioning are taken to the edge (end) of the exterior surface in both exterior and interior walls. See Figure 8.22.

Pilasters, which are columns built into the wall by widening the walls, are dimensioned to the center. See Figure 8.23. The size of the pilaster itself can be lettered adjacent to one of the pilasters in the drawing. Another

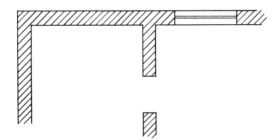

Figure 8.20 Masonry floor plan.

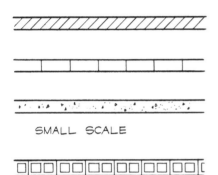

SMALL SCALE

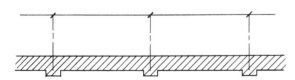

Figure 8.21 Concrete block material designations used on floor plans.

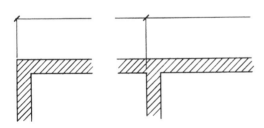

Figure 8.22 Dimensioning masonry walls.

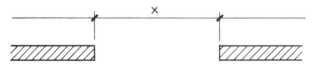

Figure 8.23 Dimensioning pilasters.

method of dealing with the size of these pilasters is to refer the reader of the plan to a detail with a note or reference bubble. All columns consisting of masonry or masonry around steel are also dimensioned to the center.

Windows and Doors. Windows and doors create a unique problem in masonry units. In wood structures, windows and doors are located by dimensioning to the center and allowing the framing carpenter to create the proper opening for the required window or door size. In masonry, the opening is established before installation of the window or door. This is called the **rough opening**; the final opening size is called the **finished opening**.

The rough opening, which is usually the one dimensioned on the plan, should follow the masonry block module. See Figure 8.24. This block module and the specific type of detail used determine the most economical and practical window and door sizes. See Figure 8.25. Therefore, you should provide dimensions for locating windows, doors, interior walls, and anything of a masonry variety to the rough opening. See Figure 8.26. A floor plan of a truck wash constructed of masonry is shown in Figure 8.27.

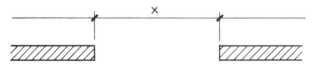

Figure 8.24 Rough opening in masonry wall.

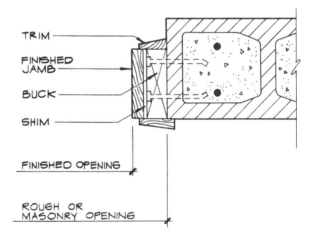

Figure 8.25 Door jamb at masonry opening.

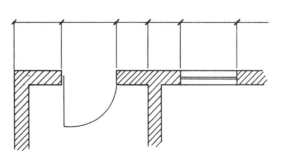

Figure 8.26 Locating doors and windows.

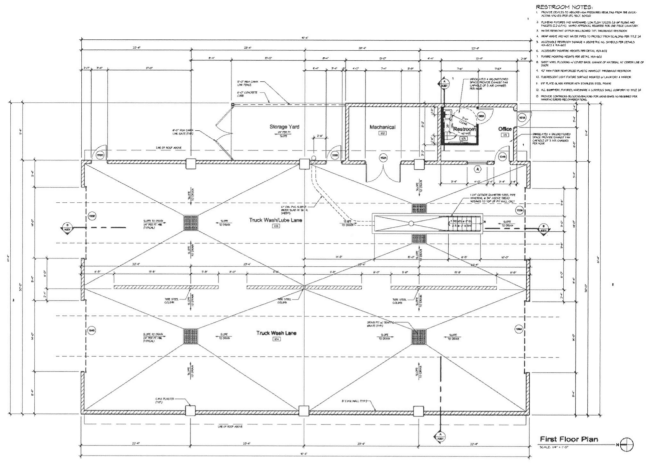

Figure 8.27 Masonry floor plan of a truck wash. (Courtesy of Royal Truck Wash.)

Steel

There are two main types of steel systems: **steel stud** and **steel frame**. Steel studs can be treated like wood stud construction. As with wood stud construction, you need to dimension to the stud face rather than to the wall covering (skin).

There are various shapes of steel studs. See Figure 8.28. Figure 8.29 shows how these shapes appear in the plan view. Drawing each steel stud is time-consuming, so two parallel lines are drawn to indicate the width of the wall. See Figures 8.28A, B, and C. Steel studs can be called out by a note.

If only a portion of a structure is steel stud and the remainder is wood or masonry, you can shade (**pouché**) the area with steel studs or use a steel symbol. See Figure 8.30.

Dimensioning Columns. Steel columns are commonly used to hold up heavy weights. This weight is distributed to the earth by means of a concrete pad. See Figure 8.31. This concrete pad is dimensioned to its center,

as Figure 8.32 shows. When you dimension the steel columns that will show in the floor plan, dimension them to the center. See Figure 8.33. This relates them to the concrete pads. Dimensioning a series of columns follows the same procedure. See Figure 8.34. The

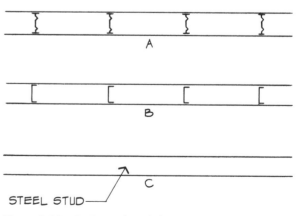

Figure 8.28 Basic steel stud shapes.

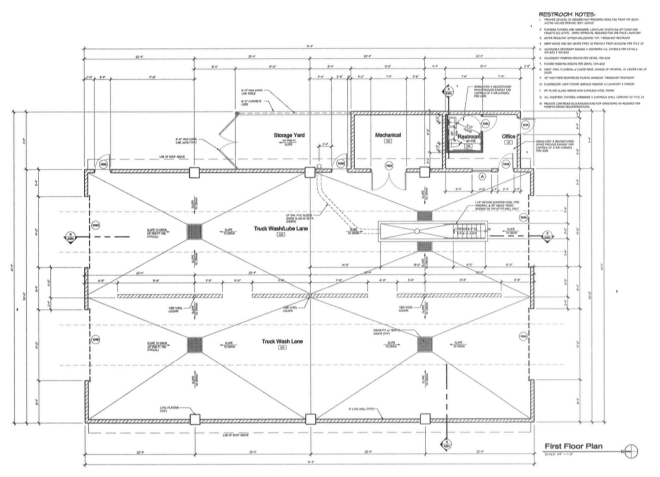

Figure 8.29 Representation of steel studs in a floor plan.

dimensions are taken to the centers of the columns in each direction.

Sometimes, the column must be dimensioned to the face rather than to the center. As Figure 8.33 shows, the extension line is taken to the outside face of the column. Axial reference planes are often used in conjunction with steel columns, as shown in Figure 8.34, and the column may be dimensioned to the face. (The dimensional reference system was discussed in Chapter 2.) A sample of a portion of a floor plan dimensioned with and without a series of axial reference planes is shown in Figures 8.35A and 8.35B. Because of the **grid** pattern often formed by the placement of these columns, a centerline or a plus (+) type symbol is often used to simplify the drawing. See Figure 8.36.

Dimensioning Walls. Walls, especially interior walls that do not fall on the established grid, have to be dimensioned—but only to the nearest dimension grid line. Figure 8.37 is a good example of an interior wall dimensioned to the nearest column falling on a grid.

Combinations of Materials

Because of design or code requirements for fire regulations or structural reasons, materials are often combined: concrete columns with wood walls; steel mainframe with wood walls as secondary members; masonry and wood; steel studs and wood; and steel and masonry, for example. Figure 8.38 shows how using two different systems requires overlapping dimension lines with extension lines. Because dimension lines are more critical than extension lines, extension lines are *always* broken in favor of dimension lines. The wood structure is located to the column on the left side once and thereafter dimensioned independently.

Wood and Masonry. Wood and masonry, as shown in Figure 8.39, are dimensioned as their material dictates: the masonry is dimensioned to the ends of the wall and the rough opening of windows, while the wood portions are dimensioned to the center of interior walls, center of doors, and so forth. The door in the wood portion is dimensioned to the center of the door and to the inside

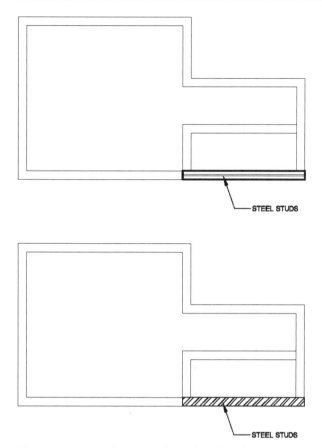

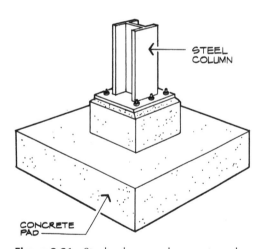

Figure 8.30 Combination of wood and steel.

Figure 8.31 Steel column and concrete pad.

edge of the masonry wall. This assumes that the block wall will be built first.

Masonry and Concrete. Masonry walls and concrete columns, shown in Figure 8.40, are treated in much the same way as wood and concrete columns. In both instances, the building sequence dictates which one becomes the reference point. See Figure 8.41. Here,

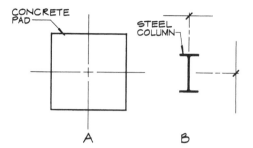

Figure 8.32 Dimensioning concrete pads and steel columns.

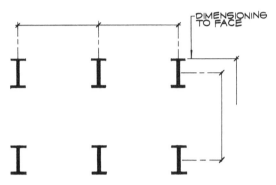

Figure 8.33 Dimensioning a series of columns.

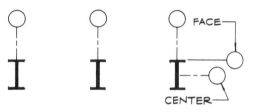

Figure 8.34 Dimensioning a series of columns by way of the axial reference plane.

steel and masonry are used in combination. Using the dimensional reference system, the steel is installed first. The interior masonry wall is then located from the nearest axial reference plane, and dimensioned according to the block module for that kind of masonry. Additional axial reference plane sub-bubbles are provided. Numbers are in decimals. Because one face of the masonry wall is between 1 and 2, $7/10$ of the distance away from axial reference plane 1, the number 1.7 is used in the sub-bubble. Also, because the same wall is also halfway between A and B, A.5 is used as a designation. Another example of the process is found in Figure 8.42. The fabricators will locate the steel first, then the masonry wall. Dimension "X" relates one system to another.

Doors in Plan View

The general method of dimensioning a window or a door was discussed earlier. Here, we examine a variety of

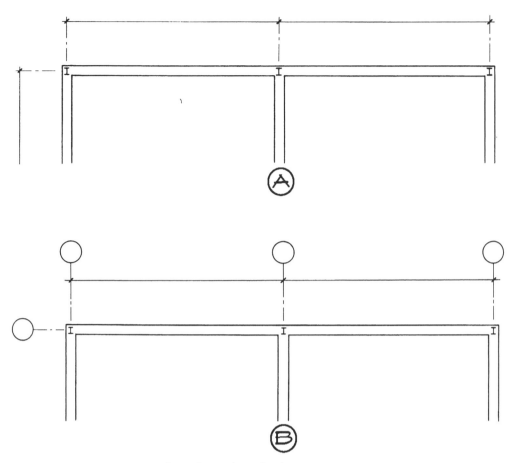

Figure 8.35 Dimensioning a floor plan with steel columns.

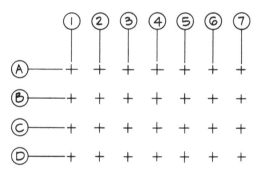

Figure 8.36 Columns forming a grid pattern.

doors and windows and how to draft them. Figure 8.43 shows a sampling of the most typically drafted doors.

Hinged. Doors A and B in Figure 8.43 show the main difference in drafting an **exterior hinged door** versus an **interior hinged door**. A straight line is used to represent the door and a radial line is used to show the direction of swing. Door "I" shows the same kind of door with its thickness represented by a double line. Doors A, B, and I are used in the floor plans to show flush doors, panel doors, and sculptured doors (decorative and carved).

Flush. Flush doors, as the name indicates, are flush on both sides. They can be solid on the interior (solid slab) or hollow on the inside (hollow core).

Panel. Panel doors have panels set into the frame. These are usually made of thin panels of wood or glass. A variety of patterns are available. See *Sweet's Catalog File* under "Doors" for pictures of door patterns. Also see the earlier discussion of elevations for a drafted form of these doors.

Sculptured and Decorative. Sculptured and decorative doors can be carved forms put into the doors in the form of a panel door, or added onto a flush door in the form of what is called a *planted* door. Different types of trim can also be planted onto a slab door.

Double Action. Door C in Figure 8.43 represents a double-action door, a door that swings in both

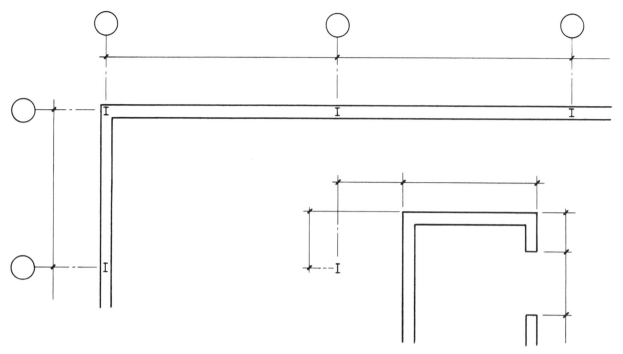

Figure 8.37 Locating interior walls from axial reference bubbles.

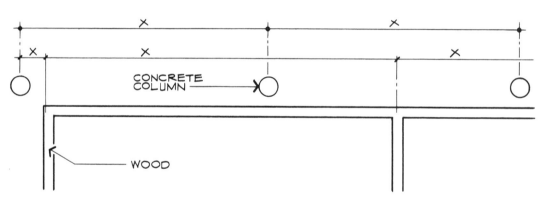

Figure 8.38 Concrete and wood.

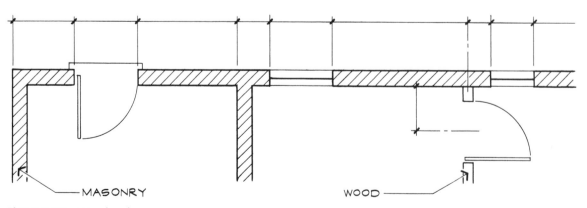

Figure 8.39 Wood and masonry.

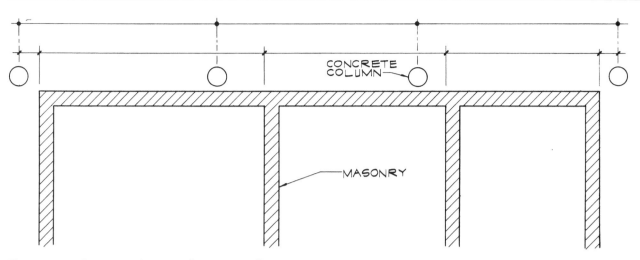

Figure 8.40 Concrete columns and masonry walls.

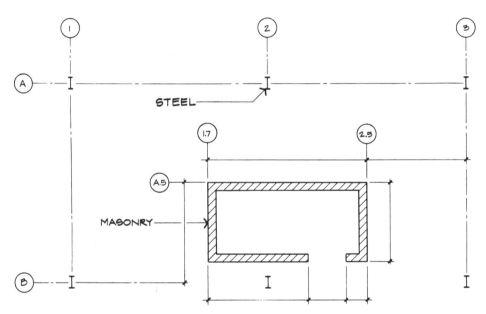

Figure 8.41 Steel and masonry.

directions. Double-action doors can be solid slab, panel, or sculptured.

Sliding. Two types of sliding doors are shown in Figure 8.43. Door D, when used on the exterior, typically is made of glass framed in wood or metal. Pocketed sliding doors are rarely found on the exterior because the pocket is hard to weatherproof, and it is difficult to keep rain, termites, and wind out of the pocket.

Folding. Doors F and G are good doors for storage areas and wardrobe closets.

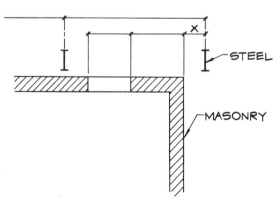

Figure 8.42 Steel and masonry.

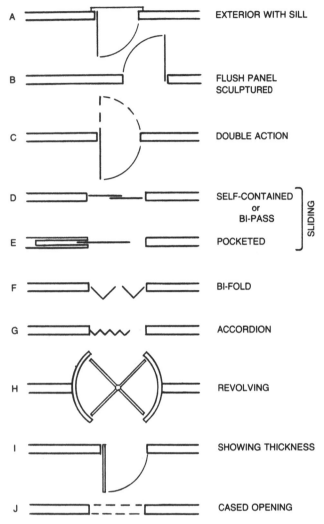

Figure 8.43   Doors in plan view.

Revolving.   Where there is a concern about heat loss or heat gain, a revolving door is a good solution. See door H, which shows a cased opening, that is, an opening with trim around the perimeter with no door on it.

Windows in Plan View

Typical ways of showing windows in the plan view are shown in Figure 8.44. When a plan is drawn at a small scale, each individual window, of whatever type, may simply be drawn as a fixed window (Window A, Figure 8.44), depending for explanation on a pictorial drawing (as shown in Chapter 12). Ideally, casement, hopper, and awning-type windows should be used only on the second floor or above, for the sake of safety. If they are used on the first or ground floor, they should have planters or reflection pools or something else around them to prevent accidents.

Sizes of Doors and Windows

The best way to find specific sizes of windows and doors (especially sliding glass doors) is to check *Sweet's Catalog File*. There you will find interior doors ranging from 1'-6" to 3'-0" and exterior doors ranging from 2'-4" to 3'-6". Sizes of doors and windows also depend on local codes. Local codes require a certain percentage of the square footage to be devoted to windows and doors to provide light and ventilation. These percentages often come in the form of minimum and maximum areas as a measure of energy-efficient structures. Still another criterion for door size is consideration of wheelchairs and the size required for building accessibility (ADA compliance).

■ SYMBOLS

Electrical and Utility Symbols

Just as chemistry uses symbols to represent elements, architectural floor plans use symbols to represent electrical and plumbing equipment. Figure 8.45 shows the ones most typically used. These are symbols only. They do not represent the shape or size of the actual item. For example, the symbol for a ceiling outlet indicates the *location* of an outlet, not the shape or size of the fixture. The description of the specific fixture is given in the specifications document.

Some symbols are more generally used than others in the architectural industry. A floor plan, therefore, usually contains a legend or chart of the symbols being used on that particular floor plan.

Number Symbols

Symbols 1, 2, and 3 in Figure 8.45 show different types of switches. Symbol 2 shows a weatherproof switch, and symbol 3 shows a situation in which there might be a number of switches used to turn on a single light fixture or a series of light fixtures. See Figure 8.46. A centerline type line is used to show which switch connects with which outlet. This is simply a way of giving this information to the electrical contractor. (However, Figure 8.46 is not a wiring diagram.) If one switch controls one or a series of outlets, it is called a two-way switch. A three-way switch comprises two switches controlling one outlet or a series of outlets. Three switches are called a four-way, and so on. Thus, you name switches by the number of switches plus one. For example, the number 3 is placed next to the switch when there are two switches, the number 4 for three switches, and so on. See Figure 8.46 for examples of switches, outlets, and their numbering system.

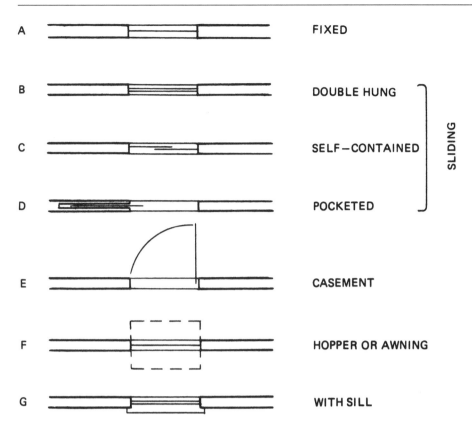

A □──────□ FIXED

B □──────□ DOUBLE HUNG ⎤
SELF—CONTAINED ⎥ SLIDING
C □──────□ POCKETED ⎦

D □──────□

E ══════ CASEMENT

F ══════ HOPPER OR AWNING

G ══════ WITH SILL

Figure 8.44 Windows in plan view.

Symbol 4 in Figure 8.45 represents a duplex convenience outlet with two places to plug in electrical appliances.

Numbers are used to indicate the number of outlets available other than the duplex, the most typical. For example, if a triplex outlet is required, the number 3 is placed beside the outlet symbol. A number in inches, such as 48″, may be used to indicate the height of the outlet from the floor to the center of the outlet. See Figure 8.45, symbols 6, 7, and 9.

Letter Symbols

A letter used instead of a number represents a special type of switch. For example, "K" is used for key-operated, "D" for dimmer, "WP" for weatherproof, and so forth.

As with switches, letter designations are used to describe special duplex convenience outlets, for example, "WP" for waterproof. A duplex convenience outlet is generally referred to by the public as a wall plug.

The call letters "GFI" mean ground fault interrupt. They designate a special outlet used near water (bathrooms, kitchens, etc.) to prevent electric shock. "SP" designates special purpose—perhaps a computer outlet on its own circuit and unaffected by electrical current flowing to any other outlet.

A combination of a switch and a regular outlet is shown in Figure 8.45, symbol 8. This illustration shows a duplex convenience outlet that is half active (hot) at all times. In other words, one outlet is controlled by a switch and the other is a normal outlet. The switch half can be used for a lamp, and the normal outlet for an appliance.

Other Symbols

A square with a circle within it and two lines represents a floor outlet. See symbol 13, Figure 8.45. The various types of light outlets are shown by symbols 14 through 18.

A *flush outlet* is one in which the fixture will be installed flush with the ceiling. The electrician and carpenter must address the problem of framing for the fixture in the members above the ceiling surface. See symbol 21, Figure 8.45.

A selection of miscellaneous equipment is shown in symbols 22 through 36.

Special Explanation

Symbols 24, 25, 26, 28, 31, and 32 in Figure 8.45 require special explanation.

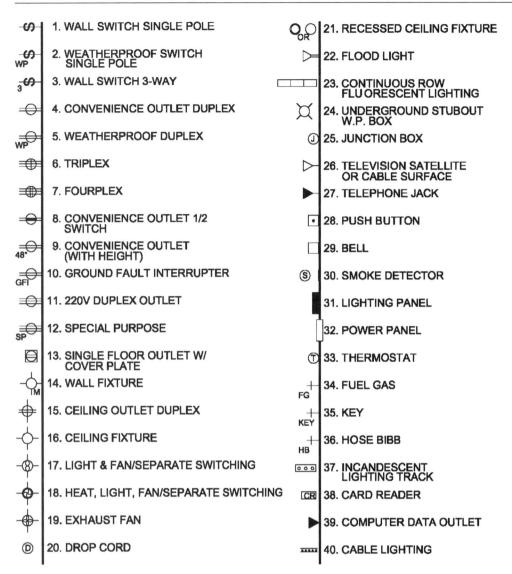

Figure 8.45 Electrical and utility symbols.

Symbol 24—Used for electrical connections (usually on the outside) for such things as outdoor lighting and sprinkler connections.

Symbol 25—A "J" box is an open electrical box that allows the electrician to install fixtures or tie wires together at that location.

Symbol 26—This is not the TV antenna itself, but the point at which you connect a television antenna line from cable or satellite dish.

Symbol 28—Location to push a button to ring a door-bell or chime.

Symbol 31—The connection between the utility company and the structure where the power panel is installed.

Symbol 32—As the structure is zoned for electrical distribution, circuit breaker panels are installed.

This allows you to reset a circuit at a so-called substation without going outside to the main panel or disturbing the rest of the structure.

Symbol 34 represents a gas outlet, and 35 a control for fuel gas. Symbol 34 would be used to indicate a gas jet in a fireplace, and 35 would be used to indicate the control for the gas, probably somewhere near the fireplace. Symbol 36 is a hose bibb, a connection for a water hose.

Symbols 37 through 39 represent present-day symbols. Incandescent track lighting is shown in 37; 38 indicates a card reader for a security door, such as a hotel room door or conference room door, that is opened by a card reader. Symbol 39 represents an outlet through which to receive computer data. Symbol 40 indicates two wires mounted on the ceiling for attachment of the movable and repositionable light often referred to as *cable lighting*.

Electrical and Computers

Although most residences are still wired in the conventional manner, use of the computer to control circuitry is beginning to find its way into the architectural construction world. Similarly, the approach to lighting a small structure is rapidly changing. Today we are being asked to think in terms of the following:

1. What type of general lighting would be appropriate for a given structure?
2. What wall washes, by color and intensity, should be used in a specific area?
3. What specific tasks are to take place in an area, and what kind of lighting would satisfy the requirements of this task?
4. What type of mood do we wish to create, and how will we dim or employ colored lights to produce that specific mood?
5. How should the floor area be lit to facilitate the safe movement of people through a corridor at night or during the day, as in a school environment?
6. How can we efficiently light stairs, both to identify the positions of the steps and to show where they begin?
7. How will specialty lighting be employed, such as fiber optics or neon lighting to identify an entry area or light located to produce a light beacon to the sky at night?

Electrical wiring falls into three basic categories: conventional, retrofit, and centralized controller (computer).

1. Conventional—This system presently exists in the majority of today's structures. Lights are hardwired from switch to outlet, and the system is not very flexible (see Figure 8.46).
2. Retrofit
   a. Radio Frequency—An old conventional toggle-style switch is replaced by what we will refer to as a "smart switch." The smart switch is capable of transmitting and receiving signals to and from other outlets (modules). This system is ideal in building additions and alterations where the cost of rewiring can become prohibitive. Radio-wave signals can be disturbed by steel studs, the chicken wire present in older walls as a base mesh for stucco or plastic, or by distance (approximately 25′ distance limit).
   b. Power Line Carrier (PLC)—Also uses smart switches, but rather than sending a radio-wave signal, it sends an electrical pulse through the existing

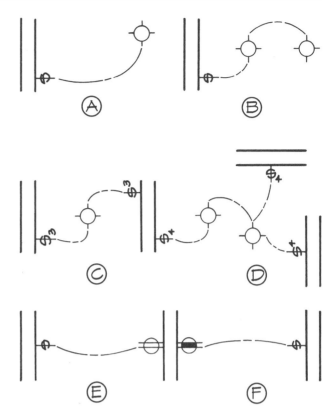

Figure 8.46 Switch to outlet (conventional).

wiring. A single switch can be replaced with a smart switch with multiple controls. This enables one smart-switch location to control multiple outlets, fixtures, appliances, and so forth. HomeTouch by Lite-Touch, Inc. is an example of such a system.

3. Centralized Controller (computer)—Using low-voltage wires, the switches are connected to a central processor. We no longer think in terms of a single light switch controlling a bank of lights, but rather a single control station with as many as nine buttons that can control any or all lights in a structure. These *control stations*, which are wall-mounted keypads, replace the old-fashioned switches and dimmers (see Figure 8.47B). Note that nine switches and dimmers are replaced with one control station the size of a single-gang toggle switch.

Figure 8.47A is a conventional switch similar to that shown in Figure 8.45. With a simple circle added to an existing switch, a drafter can indicate that a smart switch should be installed. Thus, you can easily adjust an existing drawing. Figure 8.47B shows a slight variation of the same smart switch that is drafted from scratch.

The first major change is in the way we think about lighting. Do not think of a room with its lighting controlled by a single switch; instead, plan lighting scenes. Position the lighting to create a visual pathway through a structure. Consider how you would light the exterior

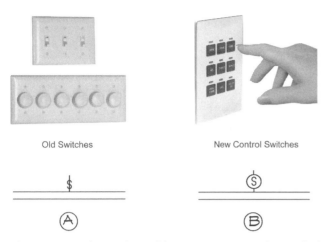

Figure 8.47 Change from old to new smart switches (called *control stations*).

of the structure for visual impact or to deter possible intruders (possibly motion-activated flashing lights). Think in terms of how best to secure your house electrically, by opening or closing windows or draperies. Controls can also be programmed to provide music throughout a structure, to activate a television, or even to dramatically showcase works of art.

The next step to take with your client is to decide from which locations you would like to control these various lighting scenes. Let us now look at the three basic components in this type of control system. As mentioned before, the first are the control stations, wall-mounted keypads suitable for use in both wet and dry areas of a structure. The second is the central control unit (CCU). The CCU is the brain of the system, that is, where the programming resides. It receives signals from the control stations and then processes them. Each control

station is connected to the CCU with low-voltage wire. This is very different from the old system, in which the lights were hooked up to the control station. Once programmed, the CCU will maintain the information even during a power outage or spike—and, yes, the CCU can be programmed for times when the occupants are away on vacation. Lighting can be programmed to give the structure an appearance of being occupied and then returned to its original setting upon the owners' return. The client can be trained to program his or her own system, or the system installer can reprogram the system via the telephone. Thus, a technician need not come to the structure to reprogram the CCU.

Control modules make up the third component. These are self-contained modules that actually do the work. Receiving their instructions from the CCU, they dim lights; drive motorized devices to open skylights, windows, and draperies; raise or lower the screen in a home theater; or merely turn on the garden and pool lights (see Figure 8.48).

Drawing for the Installer

The next task is to convey to the installer the information about the system you have designed, the location of the control stations, and the number of control points you have at one location. The number of control points at a given location can be dealt with using a chart. A *routing schedule* (a chart similar to that shown in Figure 8.49) can easily be developed and become part of the electrical plan. The first column identifies the location of the control station in the structure, and the second column actually tells the manufacturer the actual number of control points needed. Each control station in that location (say #1) is then labeled, such as 1A, 1B, 1C, 1D, and so on.

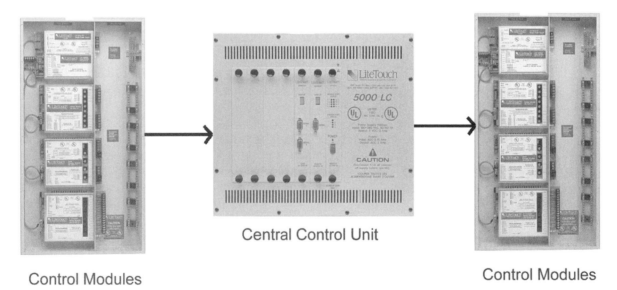

Figure 8.48 Three components of the Lite-Touch system.

Routing Schedule								
Number of Housed	Individual	Connected to System	Number of Outlets	Dimmer % (100% is Full)	Location	Type	Remarks	
1	6	1A	E-1	4	100	LIVING	GENERAL	-
		1B	E-2	6	60	LIVING	SPOT	-
		1C	E-3	2	40	LIVING	MOOD	-
		1D	c	1	100	OUTSIDE	SECURITY	-
		1E	M	2	40	HALL	PATH	-
		1F	L	2	80	DINING	GENERAL	-
2	4	2A	E-1	2	100	DINING	GENERAL	
		2B	F-2	2	80	DINING	GENERAL	
		2C	L	4	80	OFFICE	SPOT	

Figure 8.49 Routing schedule.

Each group of outlets—for example, six outlets in the ceiling in the living room—is then given a call letter. In this chart, the designation E-1 is used for the general light in the living room, E-3 is used for mood lighting, and E-2 may be used as a spotlight for paintings.

Control-station groups can be identified with a single number (see Figure 8.50A). The symbol should be a square. The outlets are connected as in the conventional method, but are not connected to the control stations identified by a C and an S with a line through it. Now look at Figure 8.50B. The outlets are connected to a symbol that should be a square. The symbol should not duplicate those already used for the control stations.

The electrical symbols shown in this chapter are mostly used in residential applications, although most of them are similar in commercial, institutional, and industrial settings. For hospitals, you need a symbol for a nurse call system or signal center system and very specialized auxiliary systems. You may also need to run

a multitude of equipment for surgery at one time, and provide a system that cannot be compromised during surgery. In an office or school building, you may need an electrical door opener or interconnecting telephone service and in-floor ductwork for a computer room.

Appliance and Plumbing Fixture Symbols

Many templates are available for drafting plumbing fixture and kitchen appliances. A good architectural template contains such items as:

- Circles
- Various kitchen appliances
- Door swings
- Various plumbing fixtures
- Electrical symbols
- Typical heights marked along edges

Figure 8.51 shows some of these fixtures and appliances.

■ OTHER FLOOR-PLAN CONSIDERATIONS

It is often necessary to show more than one or two building materials on a floor plan. Let us take a college music building as an example of a structure that has a multitude of walls of different materials, including:

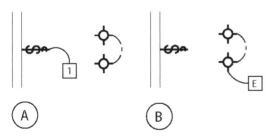

Figure 8.50 Routing symbol for control stations/outlets.

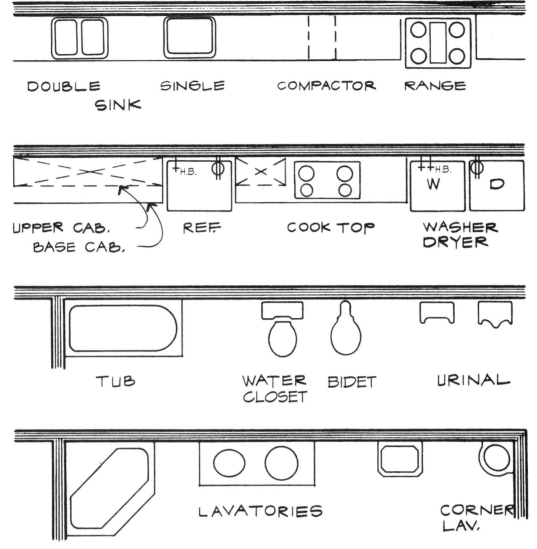

Figure 8.51 Appliance and plumbing fixtures.

1. Masonry
2. Wood studs
3. Two types of soundproof partitions
4. Low walls
5. Low walls with glass above

We need to establish an acceptable symbol for each material and to produce a legend similar to that in Figure 8.52. A sample of a partial floor plan using some of these materials symbols is shown in Figure 8.53.

Combining Building Materials

Because of ecological requirements (such as insulation), structural reasons, aesthetic concerns, and fire regulations, materials often must be combined. For example, insulation may be adjacent to a masonry wall, a brick veneer may be on a wood stud wall, and steel studs may

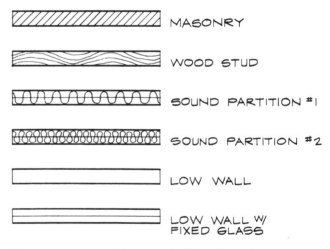

Figure 8.52 Legend for music building floor plan.

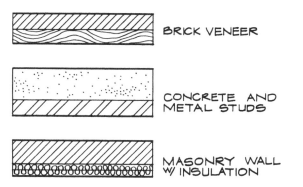

Figure 8.53 Partial floor plan: Music building.

be next to a concrete block wall. Figure 8.54 shows examples of what some of these combined-materials walls will look like on the floor plan.

Repetitive Plans and Symmetrical Items

If a plan or portions of a plan are symmetrical, a centerline can be used and half of the object dimensioned. If a plan is repetitive—for example, an office building or an apartment or condominium—each unit is given a letter designation (Unit A, Unit B, etc.). These are then referenced to each other and only one is dimensioned.

For example, suppose you are drafting a floor plan for an eight-unit apartment structure; these eight units are to be divided into four one-bedroom units and four two-bedroom units, all using the same basic plans. Your approach could be to draft the overall shape of the structure, and then draft the interior walls only on one typical unit and label it completely. The remaining units (three of each) are referenced to the original unit by a note such as "See Unit A for dimensions and notes."

The whole plan is made by putting the fully drafted plans in the proper position to produce the overall shape.

Dimensional Reference Numbers and Letters

The dimensional reference system was discussed earlier (see Chapter 2). Responsibility for placement of the letters and numbers, and often the drafting of the dimensional reference bubbles, rests with the structural engineer. Because the structural engineer is responsible for sizing and locating the columns for proper distribution of the building weight, only the structural engineer can make the proper choices. This information can then be taken and put in the reference bubbles on the foundation plan, building section, framing plans, and so forth.

Pouché Walls

The word *pouché*, mentioned earlier, refers to the process of darkening the space between the lines that represent

wall thickness on a floor plan. A special pouchéd wall can easily be done on the computer with lines or dots. However, each line type must mean something. It might mean an existing wall, or a wall to be, or even a new wall. Figure 8.54 shows an example of pouchéd walls.

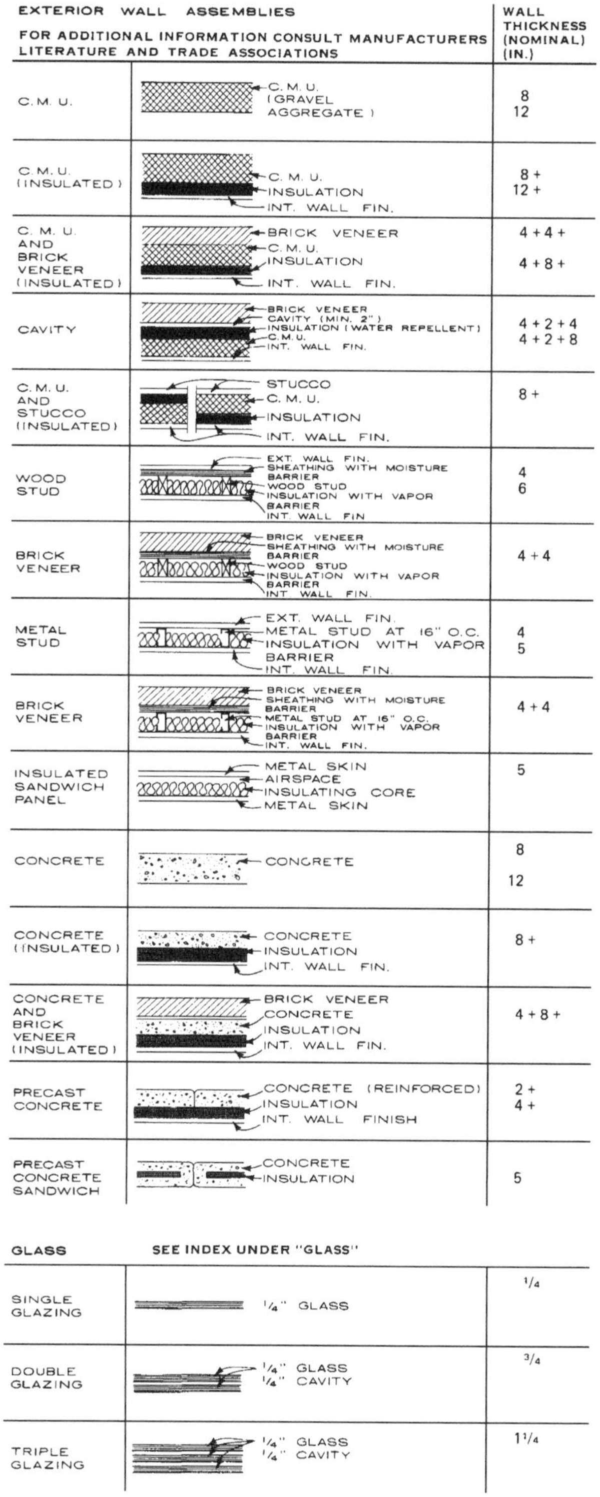

Figure 8.54 Combinations of building materials.

Stairs

An arrow is used on the plan of the stair to show the direction in which the stair rises. See the partial floor plan in Figure 8.55. Notice how the arrowheads show direction and how the number and size of the treads and risers are indicated.

Noting Logic

The basic approach used for noting (notation) logic is to show a complete set of working drawings as if a complete set of specifications were included. *Specifications* are the written documentation of what is drafted; they give information that is not given in the drawings. Brand names, model numbers, installation procedures, and quality of material are just a few of the items included and discussed in a set of specifications. Thus, inclusion of the specifications affects the noting on the floor plan.

Because of the precise descriptions contained in the specifications, only general descriptions are necessary on the floor plan. For example, it is sufficient to call out a "cooktop" as a generic name and let the specifications take care of the rest of the description. "Tub" and "water closet" are sufficient to describe plumbing fixtures.

Because further description would only confuse the drawing, these items should be described in the specifications (*specs*). In other words, specific information should not be duplicated. If it is, changes can present problems. For example, suppose brand "A" is selected for a particular fixture and is called out as brand "A" on

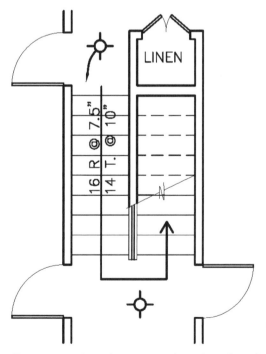

Figure 8.55 Stair directions and number of treads.

the floor plan rather than by its generic term. Later, it is changed to brand "B." Now both the floor plan and specs must be changed; if one is missed, a discrepancy that can cause confusion results.

Electrical Rating

Many architectural firms that superimpose the electrical plan on top of the floor plan note the **electrical rating** necessary for a particular piece of equipment; for example, range 9KW, oven 5KW, dishwasher 1.5KW, and refrigerator 110V. Electrical ratings can also be included in an electrical appliance schedule if one exists. It is important to track electrical ratings so as not to overload a circuit and trip the circuit breaker, or cause snow to appear on the TV screen every time you use, say, a dishwasher.

Room Sizes

Because sizes of rooms are often found on presentation drawings (scaled drawings), some people think that sizes of rooms (9 × 12, 10 × 14) belong on a floor plan. *They do not.* These approximate sizes are fine for client consumption, but are useless in the construction process.

Providing Satisfactory Dimensions

One of the most common criticisms from the field (workers on the job) is that the floor plans do not contain enough dimensions. Because these people cannot scale the drawings (something we would not want them to do anyway), they are dependent on dimensions; be sure they are all included! Remember that notes take precedence over the drawing itself. If a member is called a 2 × 10 but is drawn as a 2 × 8, the note takes precedence.

Sampling of Other Types of Floor Plans

Not all floor plans fit on a sheet, even a 36 × 48 sheet. The Vista del Largo structure is a good example. To maintain readability, the plan was cut in half, and it uses a key plan at a very small scale located on the bottom right corner of the sheet to show how the cut was made and how to reassemble it. Look at Figure 8.56.

A structure such as the Costa home, which falls into the category of a restoration drawing, is seldom seen in the field of architecture relative to the percentage of drawings produced. See Figure 8.57.

Also rarely used is a space plan that shows furniture for a residence; this does, however, give the client a better understanding of the physical constraints and benefits of the structure. See Figure 8.58. However, it is a good plan to superimpose an electrical plan over such a

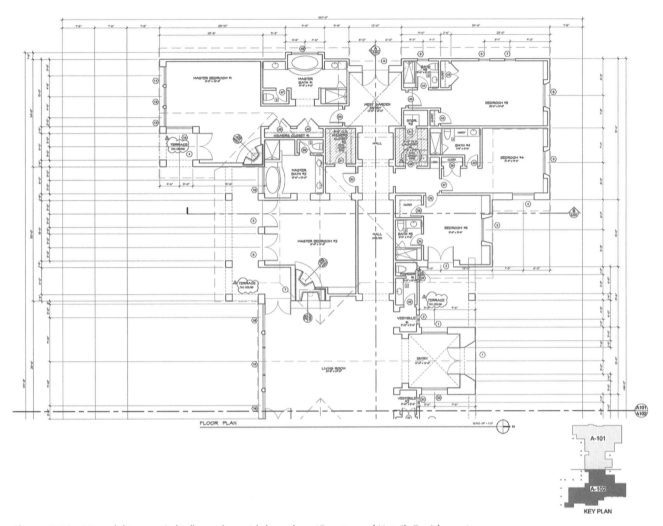

Figure 8.56 Vista del Largo: Split floor plan with key plan. (Courtesy of Katnik Residence.)

space plan for the simple reason that, based on the furniture layout, an electrical plan can be developed from it. For an example, see Figure 8.59.

A good example of a small commercial plan appears in Figure 8.60. In this figure, we are looking at Grand Park Plaza, which is a steel structure of mixed use; it ties in a commercial venture that is also mixed use. In Japan, we find buildings in which the basement is used for parking, the first floor as a supermarket, the following floors for shopping, and the top floors for food courts or a children's playground.

Checklist: Checking Your Own Drawing

There are so many minute details to remember in the development of a particular drawing that most offices have worked out some type of checking system. A **checklist** (or check sheet) is one frequently used device. It lists the most commonly missed items in chart form, making it easy for you to precheck your work before a checker is

asked to review a particular drawing. See Figure 8.61 for a floor-plan checklist.

■ DRAWING A FLOOR PLAN WITH A COMPUTER

The procedure for drawing a floor plan on a computer is somewhat different from that normally used only a few years ago to draw a floor plan manually. However, the information placed on the floor plan, as well as the dimensioning techniques and the formal representations used, remain valid for construction purposes.

The floor plan should be layered out on the grid the designer used. The structure may be built on a four- or five-foot grid, and this grid should be drawn on the datum layer. If there is no set module, the datum grid can be set to one- or two-foot increments (see Figure 8.62). If the structure is built of masonry, there may be a block module to which this grid can be set.

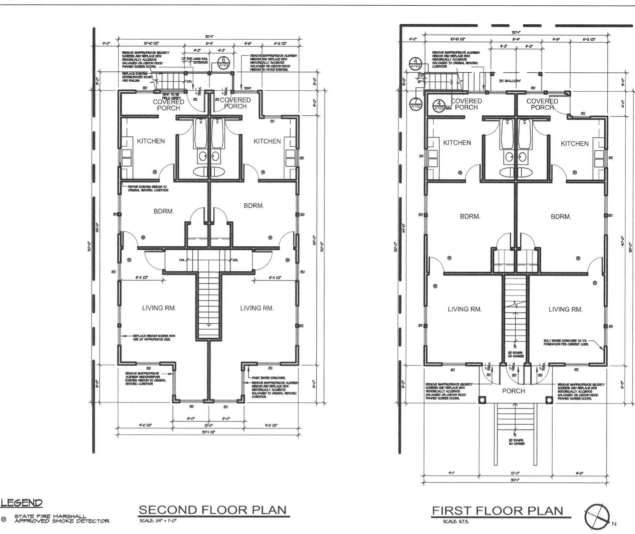

SECOND FLOOR PLAN
SCALE: 1/4" = 1'-0"

FIRST FLOOR PLAN
SCALE: N.T.S.

Figure 8.57 Historical building restoration drawings.

Multiples of 16″ have become a favorite spacing, inasmuch as most building products come in multiples of 16″. Thus, 16, 32, and 48 become easy modules to locate. In working with steel, the columns may be set to a larger grid, such as 12′-6″ spacing. If the grid is this large, set your snaps (spacing where the cursor will momentarily stop) to a smaller spacing. If you are rounding off walls to the nearest 3″, then 3″ will be a good distance to set your snaps. In dimensioning conventional stud construction, the snap should be set at 1″, allowing the drafter to dimension to the face of stud (FOS) (see Figure 8.63).

Let us take a look at the computer drawings, done in six stages, for the first-floor plan of the Adli residence. Remember, you may need more than ten layers to accomplish these six stages.

STAGE I (Figure 8.64). This is the most critical stage because it sets the field of work and the basic outlines for the structure. If we were working with steel, the col-

umns would be set and positioned during this stage. The properties of the outline can be listed, so that plan users can immediately find the square footage of the structure and its perimeter. This outline can be used to position the structure on the site, to verify the required setbacks, or to compare this figure with the allowable buildable area of a particular site.

STAGE II (Figure 8.65). All walls are established at this stage. Exterior walls and interior bearing walls can be put on one wall layer, and all non-bearing walls can be placed on a secondary wall layer. Column locations and all openings are drawn on still another layer. Openings for doors and windows may also be placed on separate layers. Completion of this stage may produce four to six layers. Preliminary energy calculations can be done easily at this stage.

STAGE III (Figure 8.66). At this stage, door and window conventions are drawn, along with any connectors such as for stairs, ramps, escalators, elevators, and

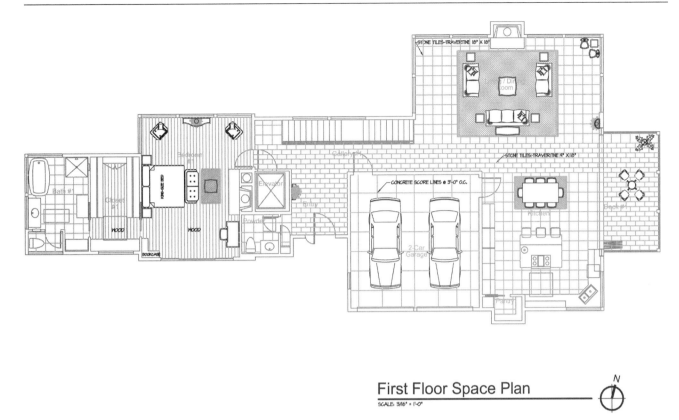

First Floor Space Plan
SCALE: 3/16" = 1'-0"

Figure 8.58   Colinita residence: Furniture plan. (Courtesy of Colinita Residence.)

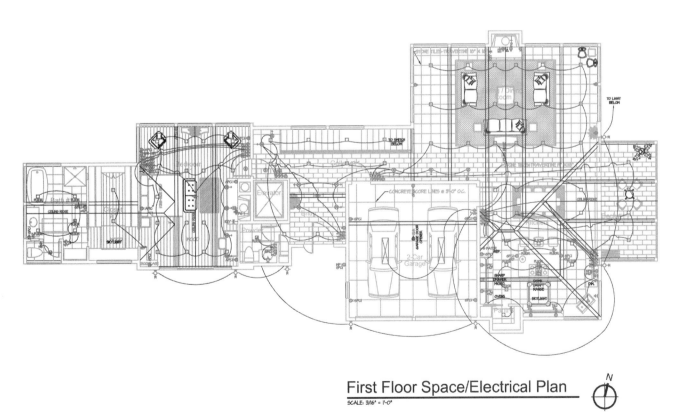

First Floor Space/Electrical Plan
SCALE: 3/16" = 1'-0"

Figure 8.59   Colinita residence: Electrical plan based on furniture plan. (Courtesy of Colinita Residence.)

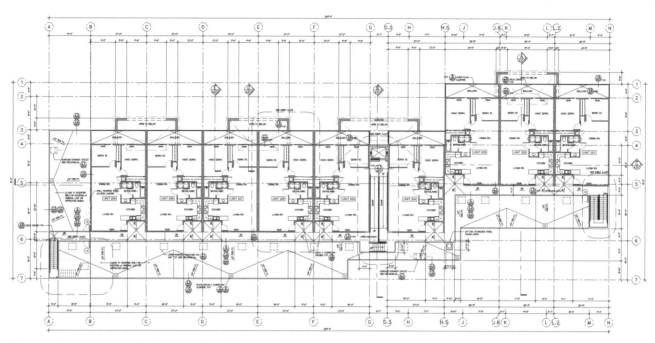

Figure 8.60 Commercial plan: Grand Park Plaza. (Courtesy of Mr. Kizirian.)

lifts. Partitions for office layouts are done now, as well as indications for plumbing fixtures such as sinks and toilets, and built-in cabinets such as kitchen cabinets, shelves and poles in wardrobe closets, built-in bookcases, reference tables, and the like.

STAGE IV   (Figure 8.67). This is the sizing and location stage. All the necessary dimensioning is done now. You must verify block modules and stud-line dimensioning, or adhere to the dimensional reference system if one is being used. Work to numerical values (maximum and minimum) and tolerances to which the workers in the field can build.

STAGE V   (Figure 8.68). This could easily be called the communication stage, because what is produced in this stage must communicate with all the other drawings. Reference symbols are used to connect one drawing with another. Detail references, reference to schedules, and building section reference bubbles are drawn at this stage. This allows the reader to look to other sources for additional information about a portion of the floor plan. Section symbols refer us to the multiple building sections throughout this plan. Detail reference bubbles explain in greater detail the nature of the cabinets and columns and how they are connected with other structural members. Interior elevation reference bubbles show, for example, how a fireplace may be finished, or the appearance of cabinets in an examination room of a medical facility; they can also be used to reference windows and doors to schedules

for size or for details on the physical makeup of a particular window or door.

STAGE VI   (Figure 8.69). All noting and titles are added in this stage, but in many instances the designer may have inserted the room titles when presenting the floor plan to the client. These titles may be relocated at this stage, for clarity, so that they do not interfere with the dimensions, appliances, and so forth. Room titles can be placed on one layer, and other notes, such as those identifying columns or materials, can be placed on another layer. Lettering size may be a determinant for the different layers or the font being used. Main titles should be of existing fonts in the computer program, and all construction notations should be done with an architectural lettering font for ease of correction.

Creating a Floor Plan Using Revit

Beginning with Revit.   Before you start a floor plan using Revit, you must have executed a comprehensive three-dimensional model in Revit, as this becomes the link between one drawing and another. Using a pull-down menu similar to one shown in Figure 8.70 helps you to locate the floor plan.

Producing the Floor Plan.   Anything you can do in AutoCAD, you can do in Revit. However, there are many things Revit can do, if used correctly, that AutoCAD

OTHER FLOOR PLAN CONSIDERATIONS

1. Walls
   a. Accuracy of thickness
   b. Correctness of intersections
   c. Accuracy of location
   d. 8-inch wall
   e. Openings
   f. Pony walls designated
   g. Pouché
2. Doors and windows
   a. Correct use
   b. Location
   c. Correct symbol
   d. Schedule reference
   e. Header size
   f. Sills, if any
   g. Show swing
   h. Direction of slide if needed
3. Steps
   a. Riser and treads called out
   b. Concrete steps
   c. Wood steps
4. Dimensioning
   a. Position of line
   b. All items dimensioned
   c. All dimensions shown
   d. All arrowheads shown
   e. Openings
   f. Structural posts
   g. Slabs and steps
   h. Closet depth
   i. Check addition
   j. Odd angles
5. Lettering
   a. Acceptable height and appearance
   b. Acceptable form
   c. Readable
6. Titles, notes, and call-outs
   a. Spelling, phrasing, and abbreviations
   b. Detail references
   c. Specification references
   d. Window and door references
   e. Appliances
   f. Slabs and steps
   g. Plumbing fixtures
   h. Openings
   i. Room titles
   j. Ceiling joist direction
   k. Floor material
   l. Drawing title and scale
   m. Tile work
      (1) Tub
      (2) Shower
      (3) Counter (kitchen and bath)
   n. Attic opening—scuttle
   o. Cabinet
   p. Wardrobe
      (1) Shelves
      (2) Poles
   q. Built-in cabinets, nooks, tables, etc.
7. Symbols
   a. Electric
   b. Gas
   c. Heating, ventilating, and air conditioning
8. Closets, wardrobes, and cabinets
   a. Correct representation
   b. Doors
   c. Depths, widths, and heights
   d. Medicine cabinets
   e. Detail references
   f. Shelves and poles
   g. Plywood partitions and posts
   h. Overhead cabinets
   i. Broom closets
9. Equipment (appliances)
   a. Washer and dryer
   b. Range
   c. Refrigerator
   d. Freezer
   e. Oven
   f. Garbage disposal
   g. Dishwasher
   h. Hot water
   i. Forced draft vent
10. Equipment (special)
    a. Hi-Fi
    b. TV
    c. Sewing machine
    d. Intercom
    e. Game equipment (built-in)
    f. Other
11. Legend
12. Note exposed beams and columns
13. Special walls
    a. Masonry
    b. Veneers
    c. Partial walls, note height
    d. Furred walls for plumbing vents
14. Note sound and thermal insulation in walls
15. Fireplaces
    a. Dimension depth and width of fire pit
    b. Fuel gas and key
    c. Dimension hearth width
16. Mail slot
17. Stairways
    a. Number of risers
    b. Indicate direction
    c. Note railing
18. Medicine cabinet, mirrors at bath
19. Attic and underfloor access ways
20. Floor slopes and wet areas
21. Hose bibbs
22. Main water shut-off valve
23. Fuel gas outlets
    a. Furnace
    b. Range
    c. Oven
    d. Water heater
    e. Fireplace
24. Water heater: gas fired
    a. 4″ vent through roof
    b. 100 sq. in. combustion air vent to closet
25. Furnace location: gas fired
    a. Exhaust vent through roof
    b. Combustion air to closet
26. Electric meter location
27. Floodlights, wall lights, note heights
28. Convenience outlets, note if 220V, note horsepower if necessary
29. Note electric power outlets
    a. Range 9 KW
    b. Oven 5 KW
    c. Dishwasher 1.5 KW
    d. Refrigerator 110 V
    e. Washer 2 KW
    f. Dryer 5 KW
30. Clock, chime outlets
31. Doorbell
32. Roof downspouts
33. Fire extinguishers, fire hose cabinets
34. Interior bathroom, toilet room fans
35. Bathroom heaters
36. Kitchen range hood fan and light
37. Telephone, television outlets
38. Exit signs
39. Bathtub inspection plate
40. Thermostat location
41. Door, window, and finish schedules
42. Line quality
43. Basic design
44. Border line
45. Title block
46. Title
47. Scale

Figure 8.61 Floor-plan checklist.

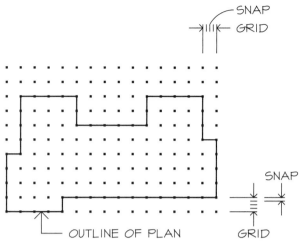

Figure 8.62   Setting grids and snaps to a module.

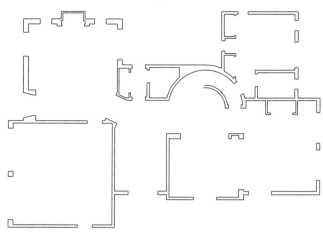

Figure 8.65   Stage II: Exterior/interior wall and openings.

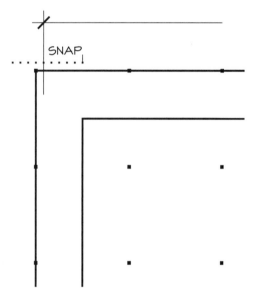

Figure 8.63   Grid versus snap.

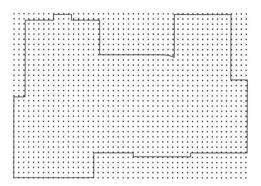

Figure 8.64   Stage I: Setting the datum and building outline.

cannot. Most noteworthy is its ability to catch human error. This is because it standardizes the drawings. In AutoCAD, you draw individual drawings (floor plan, elevations, sections, and so on), whereas in Revit you draw the entire model of the building in 3-D and then develop (for example) the floor plan, dimensioning, and notes; validate wall locations; and so on. You do this two-dimensionally while thinking in three dimensions, so all of the information in this chapter is valuable. The conventions are standard.

Catching human error is not as easy or complete as it might sound. If you put in the wrong dimension, as in Figure 8.71, and your original intent was to make wall "A" parallel with "B" and "C," Revit will not do so. In keeping with the dimensions you entered, the top wall will be dimensioned from face of stud to center of wall, whereas the dimension on the bottom is dimensioned from face of stud to face of stud. On a 2×4 system, this creates a discrepancy of $1\frac{3}{4}$". In trying to position this wall, the computer will slide the one wall over $1\frac{3}{4}$". To repair this, the original wall ("B" and "C") must be drawn parallel in the original building model and dimensioned later. However, unlike AutoCAD, Revit will dimension to a stud line.

If a change is made to a floor plan, such as the location of a door or window, Revit will reflect this change in all other drawings, such as the elevation section, framing plans, and so on. However, if the building was a six-story structure, a change in the first-floor plan window would not carry over to or appear on the second-floor plan or another other floor plans. If you intended for the windows to be aligned vertically, it would be best to make the change on the exterior elevation, whereupon all subsequent floor plans would be changed.

You must build the template of a floor plan based on what is standard in our industry. A template should work as well in New York as in California, as in Alabama as

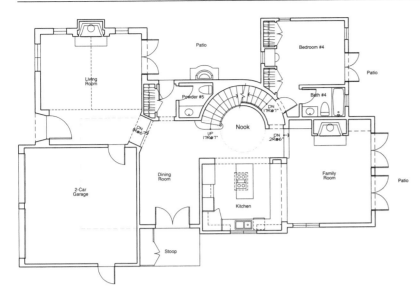

Figure 8.66 Stage III: Plumbing fixtures, stairs, windows/doors, and partitions.

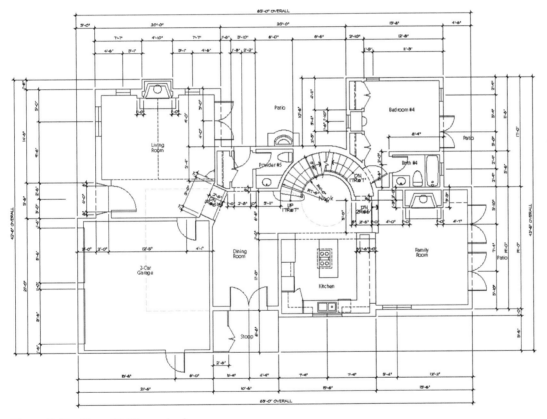

Figure 8.67 Stage IV: Dimensioning.

in England, as in France as in China. You may work on buildings in Texas, but what you draw should be understood all over America or Asia or Europe if you are to become a master of our profession.

Revit Checklist—Floor Plan

1. Visualize the task at hand. Is it modeling or annotation? If you are a drafter or designer, be sure you understand the important parts of this structure that should not be compromised.
2. If there is a module or pattern, set the grid.
3. Refine the grid by setting up a snap.
4. If annotating, set up your monitor so you can see if there is any impact on the model-use viewports, and/or use two monitors.

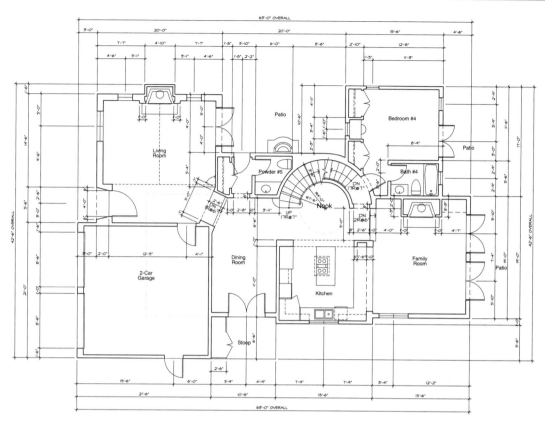

Figure 8.68 Stage V: Noting and references, both detail and section.

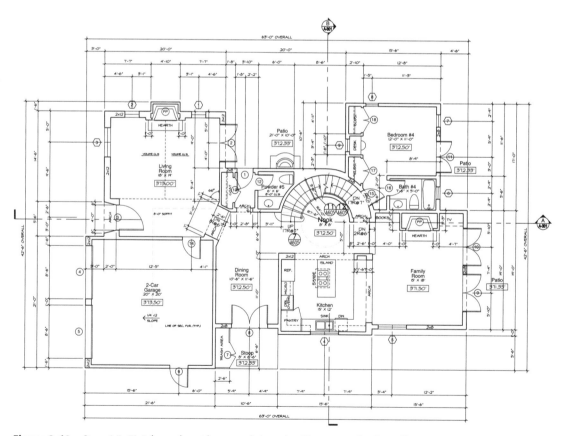

Figure 8.69 Stage VI: Finish work—titles, pouché, scale. (Courtesy of Mike Adli, owner.)

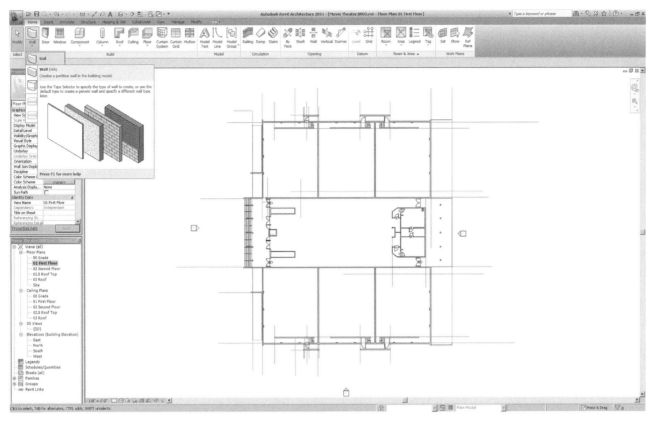

Figure 8.70 Starting a floor plan in Revit. (Screenshots © Autodesk Inc. All Rights Reserved.)

5. Review AIA standards and align drawings with its standards.

6. Be sure to make a drawing template.

7. You cannot create a template as you build your first set of drawings on Revit. Build a template before you begin your first Revit drawings.

8. Be sure the massing model is complete before you begin construction drawings.

9. Check special items that are required by the planning department and/or building department.

Troubleshooting a Floor Plan

1. Always enlarge the drawings to locate walls that are misaligned. Make any necessary corrections before you dimension.

2. Check to see that the floor plan, along with its dimensions, notes, and title, will fit on the drawing sheet. If it does not, a scale change is one option; drawing the two halves of the plan on two separate sheets with a key plan is an alternate choice.

3. Make sure you have the proper material designations to complete a specific job.

4. Ensure that you have enough space to comply with the axial reference. Plan on the correct spacing between the dimension lines and the structure.

5. Check that you have correctly employed line qualities.

6. Ensure that section lines and other conventions were used correctly.

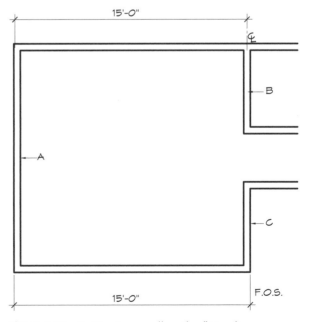

Figure 8.71 Positioning a wall on the floor plan.

9

FOUNDATION AND ROOF PLANS, FLOOR AND ROOF FRAMING SYSTEMS

■ FOUNDATION INTRODUCTION

A foundation plan is a drawing that shows the location of all concrete footings, concrete piers, and structural underpinning members required to support a structure. The main purpose of all the foundation footings is to distribute the weight of the structure over the soil.

■ TYPES OF FOUNDATIONS

Foundation Selection

While there are many types of foundation systems, two primary types of floor systems are used in foundation plans. These floor systems are constructed of concrete or wood or a combination of both. Each floor system requires a foundation to support the floor system and the structure.

Concrete Slab Floor: Foundation Plans

If you have selected concrete as the floor material for a specific project, first investigate the types of **foundation footing details** required to support the structure before drawing the foundation plan. The **footing design** will be influenced by many factors, such as the vertical loads or weight it is to support, regional differences, allowable soil bearing values, established frost-line location, and recommendations from a soils and geological report for reinforcing requirements. Figure 9.1 illustrates a concrete footing and concrete floor with various factors influencing design.

A broken line represents the footing and foundation wall, located under the concrete slab or grade. This broken line is referred to as a **hidden line.** The solid line shows the edge of the concrete floor slab as projected above the grade level. Broken lines are mainly used to show footing sizes, configurations, and their locations below grade level or below a concrete floor; solid lines show those above. See Figure 5.25.

An interior bearing footing might look like Figure 9.2. If it does, draw the plan view of this detail only with

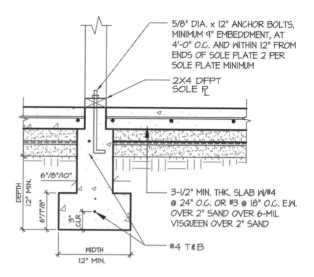

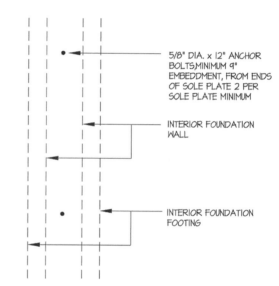

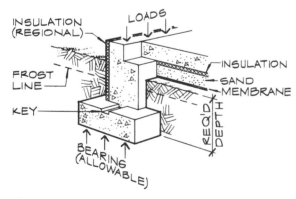

Figure 9.1 Concrete footing and floor with various influencing design factors.

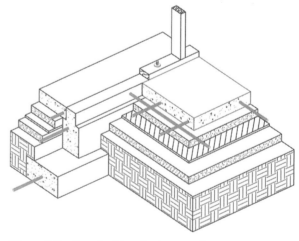

Figure 9.2 Detail of interior bearing footing.

broken lines, because all the configurations are under the concrete slab floor and grade.

Often, concrete curbs above the concrete floor levels are used to keep the garage floor within a few inches above the driveway while keeping the wood eight or more inches from the ground. Curbs are ideal in areas where wood studs must be kept free of floor moisture. See Figure 9.3.

When you are faced with drawing concrete steps and a change of floor level, you may draw a plan view reflecting this section. See Figure 9.4.

To aid in visualization of the foundation of the structure and its various components, a three-dimensional image was produced. Two major segments were enlarged to help readers visualize the interior shapes and connections. One can actually see the exterior bearing footing and the change in level in Figure 9.5.

Drawing the Foundation Plan

Lay your tracing or create a new drawing layer over the floor-plan drawing, then draw the configuration of the floor plan, as well as the internal walls, columns, fireplaces, and so on, that require foundation sections. After this light tracing, you are ready to finalize the drafting.

The final drafting is a graphic culmination, in plan view, of all the foundation walls and footings. Start with all the interior bearing and non-bearing foundation conditions. Represent these with a dotted line according to the particular sections in plan view. Figure 9.6 shows an example of a foundation plan for a residence, incorporating the plan views similar to Figures 9.2, 9.3, 9.4, and 9.5 as previously discussed.

Usually, various notes are required for items to be installed before the concrete is poured. An item like a **post hold-down** or column base (a U-shaped steel strap for bolting to a post and embedded in concrete so as to resist lateral forces; see Figure 9.7) should be shown on the foundation plan, because its installation is important in this particular construction phase. Note the **call-out** for this item on Figure 9.6.

Drawing Fireplaces. A drawing of a masonry fireplace on the foundation plan should have the supporting walls cross-hatched. (To **crosshatch** is to shade with crossed lines, either diagonal or rectangular.) Show the fireplace footing with a broken line. When numerous vertical reinforcing bars are required for the fireplace, it is necessary to show their size and location, because they are embedded in the fireplace.

Strengthening Floors. Requirements for strengthening concrete floors with reinforcing vary by project, so it is

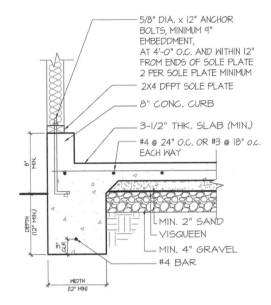

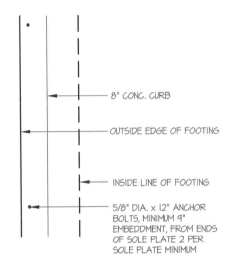

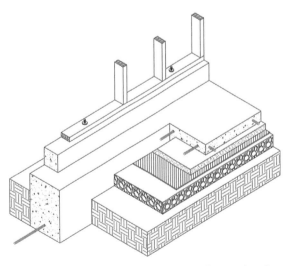

Figure 9.3 Exterior bearing footing with raised curb.

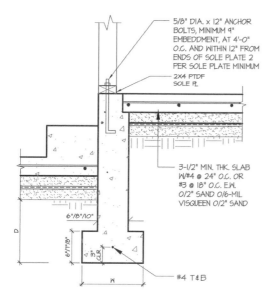

5/8" DIA. x 12" ANCHOR BOLTS, MINIMUM 9" EMBEDDMENT, AT 4'-0" O.C. AND WITHIN 12" FROM ENDS OF SOLE PLATE 2 PER SOLE PLATE MINIMUM

2X4 PTDF SOLE PL.

3-1/2" MIN. THK. SLAB W/#4 @ 24" O.C. OR #3 @ 18" O.C. E.W. O/2" SAND O/6-MIL VISQUEEN O/2" SAND

6"/8"/10"

6"/7"/8"

3" CLR.

#4 T&B

M

D

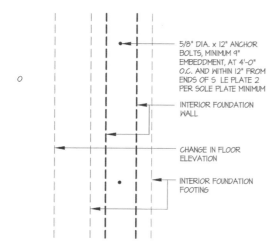

5/8" DIA. x 12" ANCHOR BOLTS, MINIMUM 9" EMBEDDMENT, AT 4'-0" O.C. AND WITHIN 12" FROM ENDS OF S LE PLATE 2 PER SOLE PLATE MINIMUM

INTERIOR FOUNDATION WALL

CHANGE IN FLOOR ELEVATION

INTERIOR FOUNDATION FOOTING

0

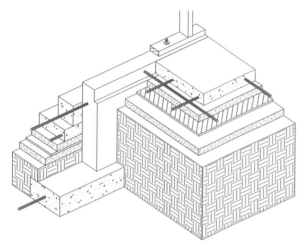

Figure 9.4 Interior bearing footing.

important to show their size and spacing on the foundation plan. The foundation plan in Figure 9.6 calls for a $6 \times 6 \times 10 \times 10$ welded wire reinforcing mesh to strengthen the concrete floor. This call-out tells us that the mesh is in $6'' \times 6''$ squares and made of number 10 gauge wire in both directions. Figure 9.8 shows how the reinforcing mesh and a plastic membrane are placed before the concrete is poured. Deformed reinforcing bars are also installed to strengthen the concrete slab floors. The size and spacing of these bars are determined by factors such as excessive weights expected to be carried by the floor and unfavorable soil conditions.

Sloping Concrete Areas. When concrete areas have to be sloped for drainage, indicate this on the foundation plan. You can do this with a directional arrow, noting the number of inches or 1% slope for the concrete. See Figure 9.6; there a garage slab is sloped to a door.

Your foundation plan dimensioning should use the identical dimension-line locations of the floor plan. For example, centerline dimensions for walls above should match centerline dimensions for foundation walls below. This makes the floor and foundation plans consistent. When you lay out dimension lines, such as perimeter lines, leave space between the exterior wall and first dimension line for foundation section symbols. As Figure 9.6 shows, you must provide dimensions for every foundation condition and configuration. Remember, the people in the field do not use measuring devices; rather, they rely on all the dimensions you have provided on the plan.

In some cases, the foundation dimensioning process may require you to make adjustments for stud wall alignments. For example, if studs and interior finish must be aligned, be sure to dimension for foundation offset correctly to achieve the stud alignment. See Figure 9.9. In this figure, the $3\frac{1}{2}''$ stud, the foundation wall, and the footing of the exterior wall are not aligned with the interior foundation wall and footing.

Provide reference symbols for foundation details for all conditions. Provide as many symbols as you need to remove any guesswork for the contractors in the field. As Figure 9.6 shows, the reference symbol will have enough space within the circle for letters and/or numbers for detail and sheet referencing.

Foundation Details for Concrete Slab Floor

For most cases, foundation details are drawn using an architectural scale of $\frac{3}{4}'' = 1'-0''$, $1'' = 1'-0''$, $1\frac{1}{2}'' = 1'-0''$, or $3'' = 1'-0''$.

Scale selection may be dictated by office procedure or the complexity of a specific project. The more complex a

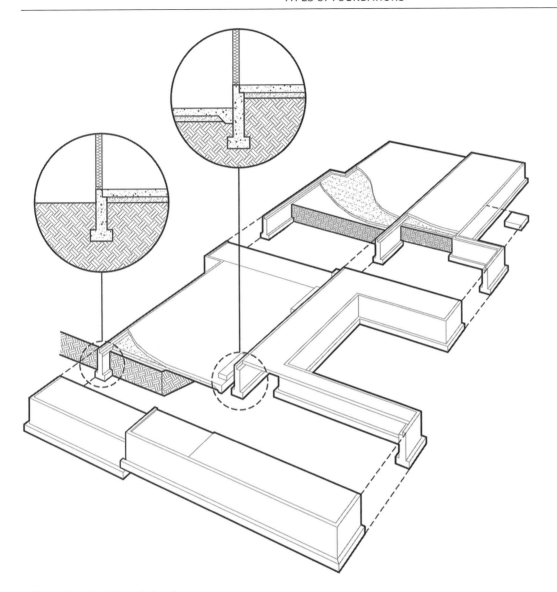

Figure 9.5 3-D foundation image.

detail is, the larger the scale you will require to provide the additional information.

Different geographical regions may necessitate variations in footing depth, size, and reinforcing requirements. Check the specific requirements for your region to determine all of the variables required.

Foundation details for the residence shown in Figure 5.26 are drawn to incorporate a **two-pour system**; that is, the foundation wall and footing are poured first and the concrete floor later. Figure 5.26 shows the exterior bearing footing drawn in final form. In colder regions, the joint between the foundation wall and concrete floor slab is filled with insulation. In severe climates, one could also insulate the underside of the entire slab or even the footings themselves.

The interior bearing footing detail should also be drawn to reflect a two-pour system with call-outs for all the components in the assembly.

Powder-actuated nails, or **shot-ins** as they are often called, can be used to replace the bolt in some municipalities. Because the nails are only a few inches long, a footing may not be required. However, they should be used only on non-bearing walls in the interior of a structure. These can often be found in tenant improvement projects where non-bearing partition walls are used for space layout. Shot-ins are not used for exterior or bearing walls, because under stress the connection will fail.

Wood Floor: Foundation Plans

Prepare a foundation plan for a wood floor the same way you do for a concrete slab floor. First determine the different footing types required to support the structure. Include in the design the footing width, stem wall dimensions, and the depth below grade. Show earth-to-wood clearances, sizes and treatment of wood members,

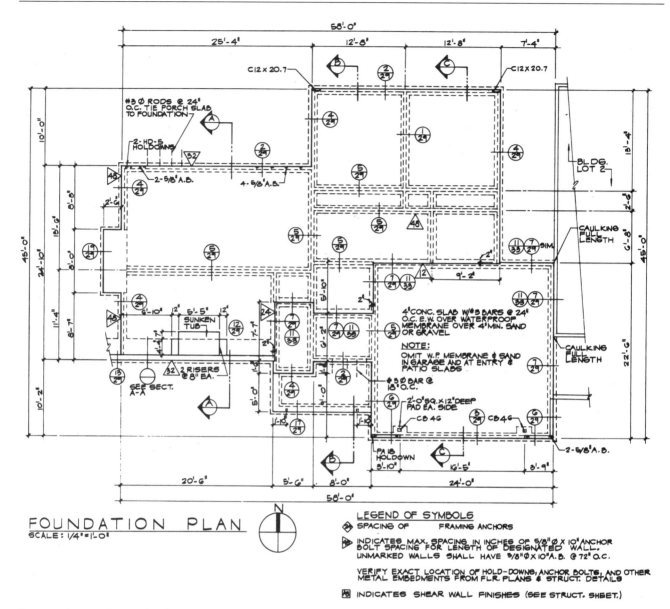

Figure 9.6 Foundation plan for a concrete floor.

floor sheathing, and the exterior wall and its assembly of components above the sheathing or subfloor level. See Figure 9.10. Interior bearing footing requirements can be done the same way, as they are very similar to the exterior footing system. In the plan view, the interior bearing footing will look similar to the exterior bearing footing in Figure 9.10.

When laying out the foundation plan for a wood floor system, provide intermediate supporting elements located between exterior and interior bearing footings. You can do this with a pier and girder system, which can be spaced well within the allowable spans of the floor joists selected. (This layout will be reviewed later in the discussion of the foundation plan.)

The girder-on-pier detail can be sketched in the same way as the previous details. Figure 9.11 describes the concrete pier in plan view. The pier spacing depends on the size of floor girder selected. With a 4 × 6 girder, a 5' to 7' spacing is recommended under normal floor loading conditions. Regional building codes help you to select floor joists and girder sizes relative to allowable spans.

Drawing the Foundation Plan

Begin the foundation plan by drawing the outside line of the exterior walls, the centerline of the interior load-bearing walls (walls supporting ceiling, floor, and

Figure 9.7 Post hold-down at the base of a column.

Figure 9.8 Reinforcing mesh and plastic.

roof), and curb and stud edges that define a transition between the wood floor members and the concrete floor. It is not necessary to locate non-bearing wall conditions for wood floors, because floor girders can be used to support the weight of the wall or double floor joists.

As a review of this procedure, Figure 9.12 shows a foundation with wood floor construction, incorporating the plan views shown in Figures 9.9, 9.10, and 9.11. The floor plan is the same one used for the concrete floor foundation plan. The spacing for floor girders and the concrete piers supporting the girders is based on the selected floor joist size and girder sizes. The floor girders can be drawn with a broken line; the piers, being above grade, should be drawn with a solid line. Dimension the location of all piers and girders. Wherever possible, locate floor girders under walls. Show the direction of the floor joists and their size and spacing directly above the floor girders. The fireplace foundation and reinforcing information can be designated as indicated earlier.

The foundation plan in Figure 9.13 shows a concrete garage floor connected to a house floor system with #3 dowels at 24" on center (or as local code dictates). This call-out should also be designated for other concrete elements, such as porches and patios. If a basement exists,

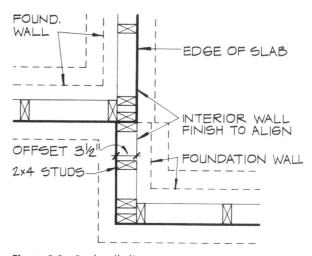

Figure 9.9 Stud wall alignment.

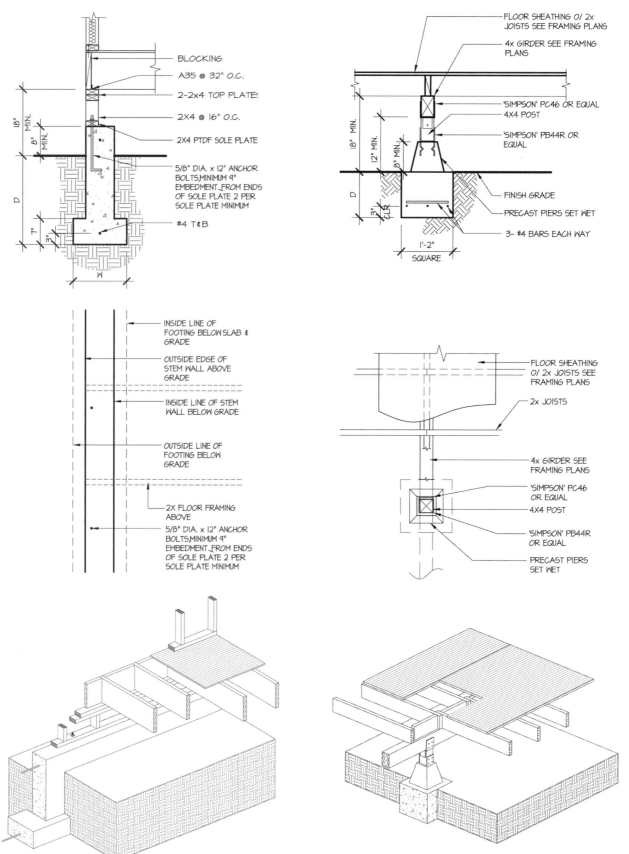

Figure 9.10 Raised wood exterior bearing footing detail.

Figure 9.11 Pier and girder detail.

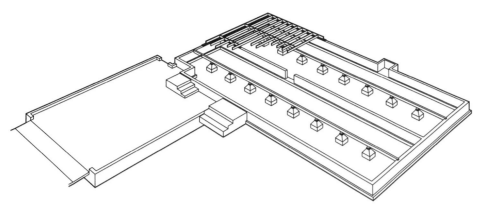

Figure 9.12 Foundation plan for a raised wood floor.

the supporting walls can be built of concrete block. The concrete-block wall will be cross-hatched on the foundation plan to indicate masonry construction. See Figure 9.14. The footing system will be referenced and detailed as seen in Figure 9.15.

Incorporate dimensioning and foundation detail symbols the same way you did for a concrete foundation. In this instance, however, the detail reference symbol shows arrowheads on the circular symbols, as recommended by state and national standards. An important note to be located on the foundation plan drawing is the number of foundation vents required, and their sizes, material, and location. This requirement is established by governing building codes.

The foundation plan is ideally suited for computer drawing. There are two main reasons for this. As every trained manual drafter knows, the repetitious drawing of piers and girders is a thing of the past, as is the drawing of dotted or hidden lines around the perimeter of the stem wall on the foundation. On the computer, you just change the layer and line type, and offset the lines, and you immediately have the outline of a footing or foundation.

Foundation Details for a Wood Floor Foundation

Finished drawings for the foundation details can be drafted with **call-outs** (identification reference system) and dimensions for each specific detail. As with a concrete floor foundation, sizes, depths, and reinforcing requirements vary regionally. Finished details for exterior and interior bearing footings, as well as a typical pier and girder, are shown in Figures 9.9, 9.10, and 9.11. Figure 9.16 illustrates the use of concrete-block stem wall for a foundation supporting a wood floor. Figure 9.17 combines Figure 9.10 with a porch and stair connected to the exterior foundation detail. Here, dowels

have been added to tie the concrete porch to the building, and metal flashing has been used to protect against rot from water seepage.

Figure 9.18 shows a foundation detail through the garage concrete floor and house floor. This important detail shows the placement of dowels and provisions for a nailer in which a finished interior material can be secured at the concrete foundation wall. Remaining foundation sections are drafted in the same way, using investigative sketches for reference.

■ EXAMPLES

Example 1: A Building with Masonry Walls

When projects use concrete or masonry for exterior and interior walls, the walls may continue down the concrete footing. Figure 9.19 shows an exterior masonry wall and concrete footing. If interior walls are also constructed of masonry, the foundation section is similar to Figure 9.19. Drawing the foundation plan using masonry as the foundation wall requires delineation of the foundation walls by cross-hatching those areas representing the masonry.

The building in this example is a theater with exterior and interior masonry walls. The foundation plan, details, and photographs of the construction of the foundation follow.

The foundation plan, shown in Figure 9.20, defines all the masonry wall locations as per Figure 9.19. The footings are drawn with a broken line. For this project, **pilasters** are required to support steel roof beams. A *pilaster* is a masonry or concrete column designed to support heavy axial and/or horizontal loads. The footing width is not called out, but rather refers to the foundation plan for a specific pilaster footing dimension. Many projects use

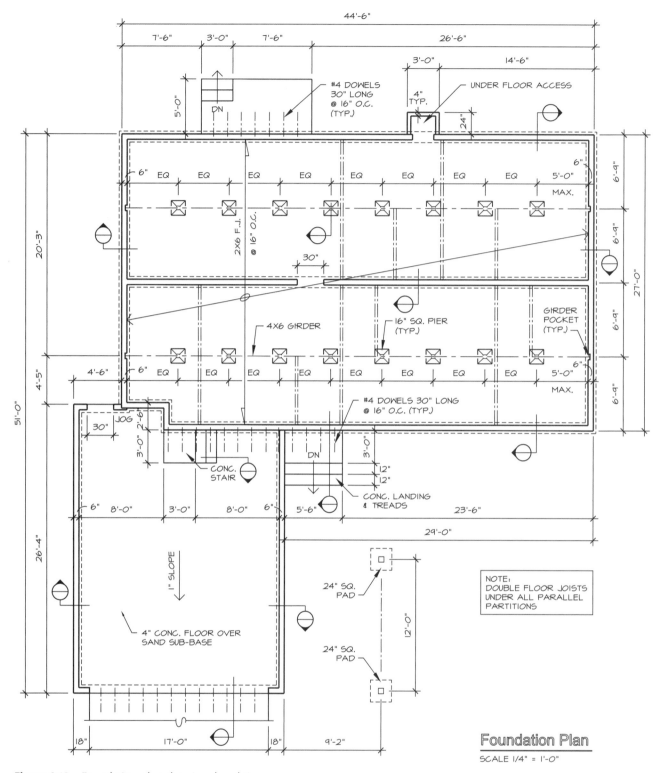

Figure 9.13 Foundation plan showing dowel ties.

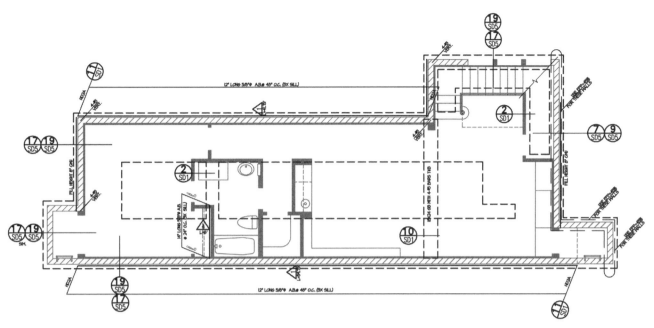

Figure 9.14   Basement foundation plan. (Courtesy of Mr. and Mrs. Givens.)

a schedule, because the total loads acting on the pilaster vary based on location.

An example of a pad schedule is shown in Figure 9.20. Locate the pad schedule directly on the foundation plan sheet for ease of reference. It should show dimensions for all footings, walls, and pad locations, with reference symbols clearly defined for specific conditions. Similar notes are provided for items such as ramp and floor slopes, pilaster sizes, and required steel reinforcing.

From the information on the foundation plan, the various foundation conditions are laid out on the site using chalk lines. In Figure 9.21, the footing for the masonry walls and pilasters is clearly visible on the right side of the structure.

When **chalking** has been completed for the footing locations, trenching for these details is dug and made ready for the pouring of concrete. Once the reinforcing bars and footings are installed, the masonry work can begin. Figure 9.22 shows masonry work in progress. Note the pilasters and chalking for the various concrete pads.

Example 2: A Foundation Using Concrete Pads and Steel Columns

The way foundation plans are drawn varies depending on the method of construction for a specific structure. The example here is of a structure requiring concrete pads to support steel columns, with a continuous footing to support masonry walls.

Steel columns are also required to support heavy axial loads and they, in turn, require a foundation. These foundation members are commonly referred to as concrete piers or **concrete pads**. The size of these pads varies with different loading conditions. Because of the various pad sizes, you may need to use a column pad schedule. This schedule should note the column designation, size, depth, and required steel reinforcing.

This foundation plan, as Figure 9.23 shows, is handled differently from the foundation plan in Example 1. First, establish the column locations as they relate to the **axial reference locations**; then draw and delineate masonry walls. Concrete pads located under a concrete floor are represented with a broken line. See Figure 9.23. Figure 9.24 provides a visual example of this column pad footing detail in section. The column pad sizes may vary due to varying loads, and may be sized using a pad schedule or noted directly on the foundation plan. In this case, sizes are noted on the foundation plan. At the bottom of the foundation plan drawing, provide a **legend** defining the size and shape of the steel column and the base stem that supports it.

Because of all the critical information required in the field, a schedule for column base plates and their required anchorage may be necessary. Put this on the plan. Dimensioning this type of foundation depends on the axial reference locations, which are identical to the floor-plan referencing. Other foundation conditions are dimensioned from these axial reference lines.

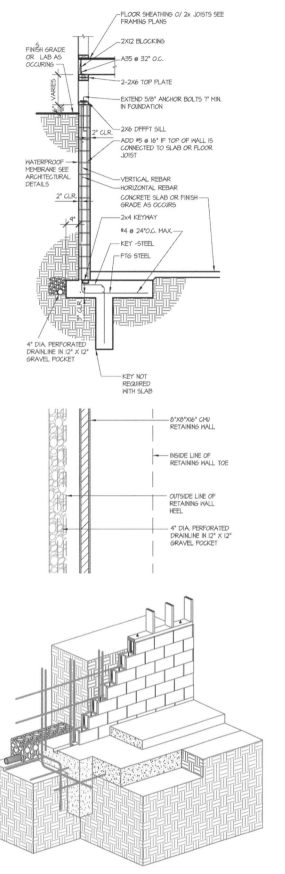

FLOOR SHEATHING O/ 2x JOISTS SEE FRAMING PLANS

FINISH GRADE OR LAB AS OCCURING

2X12 BLOCKING

A35 @ 32" O.C.

2-2X6 TOP PLATE

6" VARIES

EXTEND 5/8" ANCHOR BOLTS 7" MIN. IN FOUNDATION

2" CLR.

2X6 DFFFT SILL

ADD #5 @ 16" IF TOP OF WALL IS CONNECTED TO SLAB OR FLOOR JOIST

WATERPROOF MEMBRANE SEE ARCHITECTURAL DETAILS

VERTICAL REBAR

HORIZONTAL REBAR

2" CLR.

CONCRETE SLAB OR FINISH GRADE AS OCCURS

2x4 KEYWAY

9"

#4 @ 24"O.C. MAX.

KEY -STEEL

FTG STEEL

4" DIA. PERFORATED DRAINLINE IN 12" X 12" GRAVEL POCKET

KEY NOT REQUIRED WITH SLAB

8"X8"X16" CMU RETAINING WALL

INSIDE LINE OF RETAINING WALL TOE

OUTSIDE LINE OF RETAINING WALL HEEL

4" DIA. PERFORATED DRAINLINE IN 12" X 12" GRAVEL POCKET

Figure 9.15   Concrete-block retaining wall at basement.

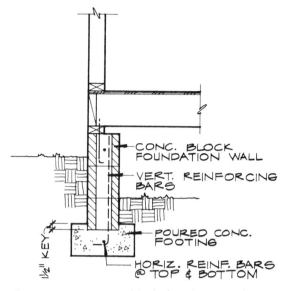

CONC. BLOCK FOUNDATION WALL

VERT. REINFORCING BARS

1½" KEY

POURED CONC. FOOTING

HORIZ. REINF. BARS @ TOP & BOTTOM

Figure 9.16   Concrete-block foundation wall supporting a wood floor.

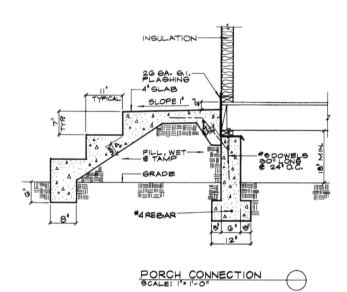

INSULATION

26 GA. G.I. FLASHING

4" SLAB

SLOPE 1"

11" TYPICAL

7" TYP

FILL, WET & TAMP

#5 DOWELS 20" LONG @ 24" O.C.

18" MIN.

GRADE

6"

8"

#4 REBAR

3" 6" 3"

12"

PORCH CONNECTION
SCALE: 1"=1'-0"

Figure 9.17   Drafted detail of a porch connection.

After you complete all the necessary dimensioning, show section reference symbols and notes. Figure 9.23 has a double broken line representing a continuous footing underneath, which connects to all the concrete pads. The main purpose of this footing is to provide continuity for all the components of the foundation.

The concrete pads are the main supports for this structure. Figure 9.25 shows the trenching and some formwork for a concrete pad. Note particularly the placement

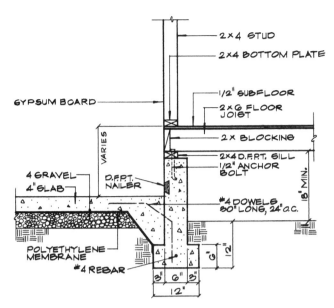

Figure 9.18 Drafted detail of change of level from a wood floor to a concrete slab.

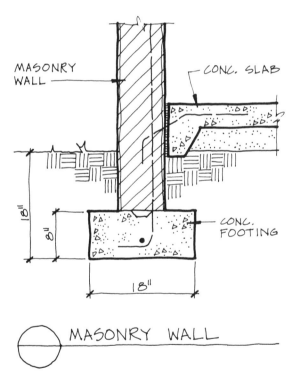

Figure 9.19 Exterior masonry wall and footing.

of the reinforcing steel and the footing, which is used to tie all the pads together. After the concrete is poured and anchor bolts embedded, the steel column with the attached base plate is bolted to the concrete pad. See Figure 9.26.

When columns are used for structural support, **concrete caissons** may be needed in unfavorable soil conditions. A *concrete caisson* is a reinforced column designed specifically for the loads it will support and is located at a depth that has good soil bearing capacity. The concrete caisson shown in Figure 9.27 is used on a sloping site to provide firm support for a wood column, which in turn is part of the structural support for a building. Figure 9.28 shows a jobsite drilling rig making holes for concrete caissons.

Most construction sites that require caissons use them in multiple locations where they are all tied together. The system of caissons is tied at the top with a **grade beam**. This beam acts as a grid of beams that ties all the caissons together and provides the foundation for walls or posts that will sit on top of them. The idea is to provide support for walls where the foundation does not rely on soil bearing capacity up high but down low at the bottom of the caisson, where soil bearing capacities are more ideal. If you visualize a table and its legs, the grade beam is the table top and the legs of the table are the caissons. See Figure 9.29.

Example 3: A Concrete Floor at Ground-Floor Level

The foundation plan in Figure 9.30 is for a small two-story residence with a concrete floor at the ground-floor level. The plan view drawing of the foundation sections is similar to those in Figures 5.25, 9.2, and 9.3.

Everything that is to be installed prior to the pouring of the concrete must be noted on the foundation plan. If items are located on other drawings, the foundation contractor may miss them, causing problems after the pouring. Specific locations call for anchor bolt placement, steel column embedment, post hold-down hardware, and other symbols, all explained in the legend. Dimensions for the location of all foundation walls and footings are shown with reference symbols for the various footing conditions.

Figure 9.31 demonstrates the importance of noting all the required hardware or concrete accessories on the foundation plan. You can well imagine the problems that would arise if these items were not installed before the concrete was poured. Trenching and formwork for the foundation are shown photographically in Figure 9.32. The next step in completing the foundation phase of this residence is the pouring of the concrete and finishing of the concrete floor in preparation for the wood framing. Often, a checklist is also furnished to provide specific information required for a project. See Figure 9.33.

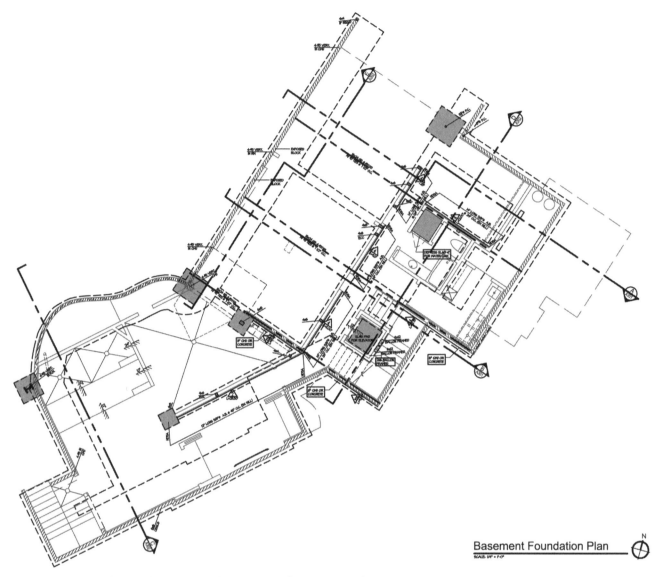

Figure 9.20   Foundation plan layout with masonry walls. (Courtesy of the Bailey Residence.)

■ SUMMARY OF TYPICAL CONVENTIONS FOR FOUNDATION PLAN

Refer to Figure 9.34 as you review the items in the following list.

A. Plan view of an exterior bearing footing for a slab-on-grade.

B. Plan view of a footing with a concrete curb, such as a garage. Also represents bearing footing for a wood floor system.

C. Plan view of an interior bearing footing for a slab-on-grade system.

D. Convention could represent a pier or a concrete pad for a column.

E. A widening of the footing portion of a foundation for a column; actually a combination of B and D.

F. A plan view of a masonry wall and footing.

G. A system showing a pier and girder convention.

H. Centerlines as shown here represent dowels.

I. The diamond shape, triangle, and rectangle are used to identify such things as anchor bolt spacing, shear wall finishes, and spacing of framing anchors.

J. A multiple convention, indicating pad, pedestal, steel column, and base plate sizes. The letter refers you to a schedule in which the plate size, pad size, or even the reinforcing are described.

Figure 9.21 Chalking for foundation layout. (Courtesy of AVCO Community Developers, Inc., and Mann Theatres Corporation of CA.; William Boggs Aerial Photography. Reprinted with permission.)

Figure 9.22 Foundation development. (Courtesy of AVCO Community Developers, Inc., and Mann Theatres Corporation of CA.; William Boggs Aerial Photography. Reprinted with permission.)

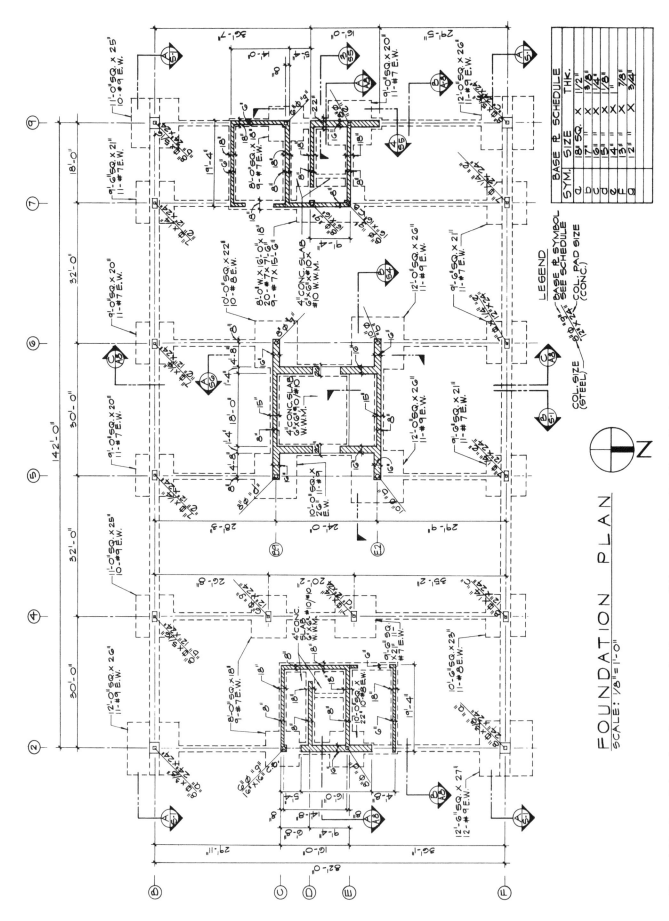

Figure 9.23 Foundation plan: Concrete pads. (Courtesy of Westmount, Inc., Real Estate Development.)

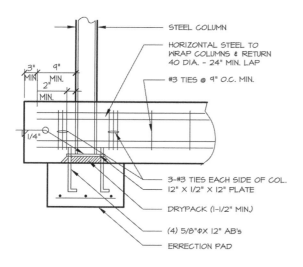

STEEL COLUMN

HORIZONTAL STEEL TO WRAP COLUMNS & RETURN 40 DIA. - 24" MIN. LAP

#3 TIES @ 9" O.C. MIN.

3" MIN.   9"   2" MIN.
MIN.

1/4"

3-#3 TIES EACH SIDE OF COL.
12" X 1/2" X 12" PLATE

DRYPACK (1-1/2" MIN.)

(4) 5/8"ΦX 12" AB's

ERRECTION PAD

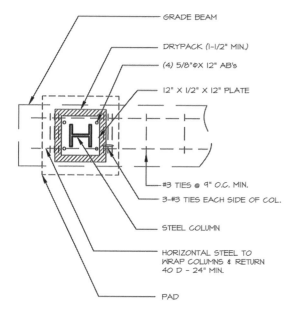

GRADE BEAM

DRYPACK (1-1/2" MIN.)

(4) 5/8"ΦX 12" AB's

12" X 1/2" X 12" PLATE

#3 TIES @ 9" O.C. MIN.

3-#3 TIES EACH SIDE OF COL.

STEEL COLUMN

HORIZONTAL STEEL TO WRAP COLUMNS & RETURN 40 D - 24" MIN.

PAD

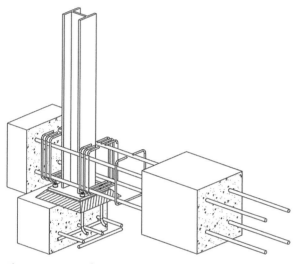

Figure 9.24 Column to footing detail.

Figure 9.25 Forming for concrete pad. (William Boggs Aerial Photography. Reprinted with permission.)

Figure 9.26 Steel column on concrete pad.

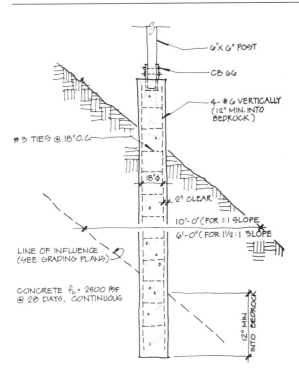

6"X 6" POST

CB 66

4- # 6 VERTICALLY
(12" MIN. INTO
BEDROCK.)

#3 TIES @ 18" O.C.

18"Ø

2" CLEAR

10'-0" (FOR 1:1 SLOPE)
6'-0" (FOR 1½:1 SLOPE)

LINE OF INFLUENCE
(SEE GRADING PLANS)

CONCRETE f'c = 2500 PSF
@ 28 DAYS. CONTINUOUS

12" MIN.
INTO BEDROCK

CONCRETE CAISSON

Figure 9.27 Concrete caisson.

K. The (+) symbols represent anchor bolt locations for shear walls. This symbol should be accompanied with a note similar to the following:
½″ dia. A.B. @ 12″ o.c. (shear wall)

L. The ([) shapes represent hold-downs at shear walls.

M. Shows the location of under-floor vents and/or crawl hole from one chamber of under-floor space to another. As shown, the rectangle should be dimensioned.

N. The four hidden lines shown in this convention represent an interior bearing footing for a slab-on-grade system. If the stem wall and width of the footing vary from location to location, dimensions for them are indicated right at the location on the foundation plan.

O. A masonry retaining wall. As in the previous example, the plan view could be dimensioned if these walls are of varying sizes throughout a structure.

P. A non-bearing footing for a slab-on-grade system.

Q. Matrix used to represent concrete slab reinforcement. The size of the reinforcing is noted; for example, #4 @ 18″ o.c. each way. It is not shown through-

out the foundation plan, but only on a portion of it and noted as typical.

R. An under-floor access, with the rectangle having an X as the actual opening through the foundation wall. This symbol can also be used for a window well in a basement area.

■ EXTERIOR AND INTERIOR WALLS

Figure 9.35 shows a partial floor plan of the living room wall adjacent to the bedroom that begins as an exterior wall and turns into an interior wall. The problem reveals itself when we remove the slab, as seen in Figure 9.36. Note that although the stem wall is not aligned, the plates are. If we align the foundation, the plates (sills) are out of alignment, resulting in a framing problem.

There are a couple of ways of representing this condition. One, as shown in Figure 9.37A, is to actually show the offset by jogging the hidden lines. Another method, as shown in Figure 9.37B, is to show the exterior/interior foundation wall as continuous and identify the jog with a note.

Drafting a Foundation on the Computer

STAGE I (Figure 9.38). The first stage is always the datum or base stage. The floor plan must be used for the base or datum stage. XREF the floor plan.

STAGE II (Figure 9.39). The second stage involves outlining the structure with a single line and positioning the interior bearing walls. Take care in identifying any exterior walls that become interior walls for sill (bottom plate) placement.

STAGE III (Figure 9.40). Locate additional items such as concrete pads and establish the configuration of the footing.

STAGE IV (Figure 9.41). If depressed slabs are needed to accommodate materials such as ceramic tile or brick pavers, concrete steps or stairs, or elevator shafts, they are shown at this or an earlier stage. Solid lines may be changed to dotted lines at this point. It is just a matter of changing layers and changing line type.

STAGE V (Figure 9.42). Dimensioning takes place at this stage. Remember, the dimensions on the floor plan are to face of stud (FOS), and dimensions here should be the same as those on the foundation plan.

STAGE VI (Figure 9.43). All noting takes place at this point, the final stage. Remember that main titles should conform to the standard office font, and all other noting should be done with an architectural lettering font that allows for easy manual correction.

Figure 9.28 Drilling holes for concrete caissons. (William Boggs Aerial Photography. Reprinted with permission.)

■ A STEEL STRUCTURE

The foundation plan for the Madison Steel Building, discussed in Chapter 17 and also used for examples of the tenant improvements in Chapter 18, is presented in this section as an example of a foundation plan for a commercial building.

Stage I

For this all-steel building, all drawings were produced using the dimensional reference system (see Figure 9.44). Thus, the datum or base for the foundation plan is the matrix.

Stage II

The structural engineer has established the size of the various concrete pads and pipe columns and provided us with engineering details (see Figure 9.45). These important pieces of information would be translated into a drawing in the next stage.

Stage III

As you compare the beginning stages of the ground-level plan and the ground-floor plan, you will see differences at the stair area (see Figure 9.46). When the complete set of drawings was submitted for building department plan

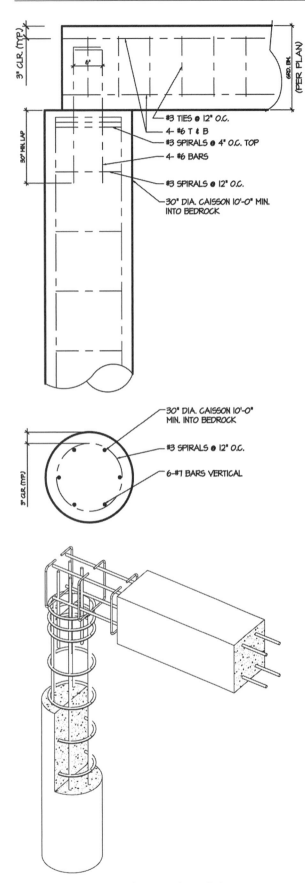

Figure 9.29 Caisson design with grade beam system.

check, changes were made. We next drafted columns (circles) and their respective support pads (squares). We obtained their sizes and shapes from the structural engineer.

Stage IV

Dimension lines were the first addition to the drawing at this stage. We used the reference plane system (see Figure 9.47). All subsequent dimensions were referenced to this basic set on the top and to the left. In the lobby area (central portion of the plan), where the walls do not align with the existing reference bubbles, we added new bubbles. We showed partial and full section designations.

Stage V

Dimensions were added for the concrete-block foundation walls. We also dimensioned the width of all footings (see Figure 9.48). A single detail is used for all of the foundation walls and footings. The material designation for the concrete-block walls and variations in dimensions in the footing and width of the walls were added. Also, the section reference notations were filled in, using the section designation symbols.

Stage VI

At this stage we added all remaining numerical values and filled in the reference bubbles on the matrix in the dimensional reference system (see Figure 9.49). The reference B.9, for example, indicates that there is a column at an intermediate distance between B and C of the axial reference plane. B.9 is approximately $9/10$ of the distance between B and C. If there were another column that was $8/10$ of the way between B and C, it would be designated B.8.

Around the perimeter of the structure are a series of squares drawn with dotted lines. These represent concrete pads that distribute the weight bearing down on the columns. The leader pointing to the hidden line indicates the size and thickness of the concrete pad and reinforcing.

At the center of these hidden lines is another rectangle with a smaller rectangle inside, representing a steel column. The leader pointing to this area explains these. For example, $7 \times 7 \times 1/4$, $12'' \times 24''$, means that the column is a 7"-square column, $1/4''$ thick (wall thickness), mounted onto an "e" base plate. This "e" base plate size can be found in the base plate schedule at the lower right of Figure 9.49. Here, "e" is equal to a 14"-square by 1"-thick plate. This plate rests on another concrete pad, often called a **pedestal**, 12" by 24" thick.

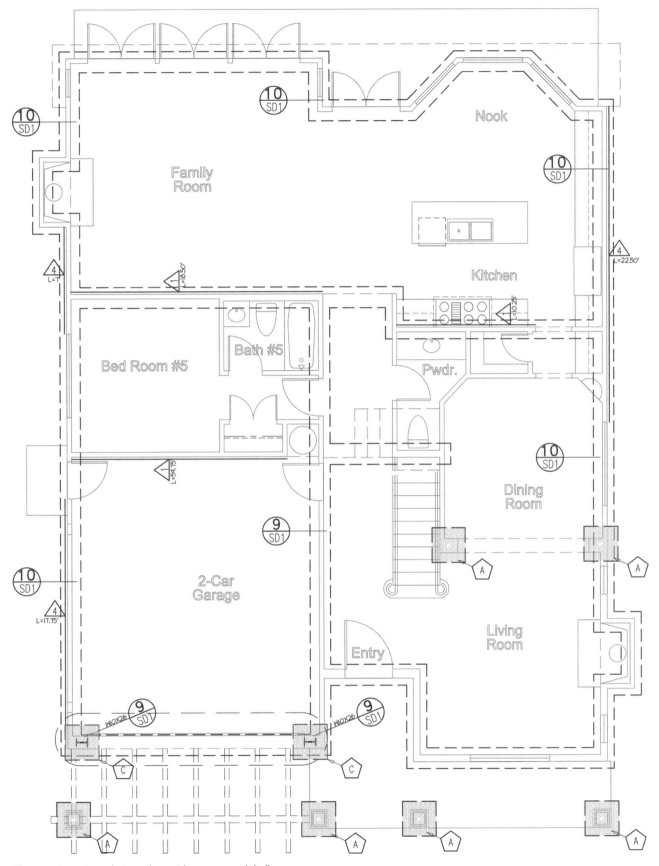

Figure 9.30 Foundation plan with concrete slab floor.

Figure 9.31   Foundation with embedded hardware.

Contained within the masonry walls are some steel columns, with concrete pads that are also noted using the schedule. Next to the schedule is a legend explaining the noting method. The title and North arrow finished this sheet.

■ ROOF PLANS AND FRAMING SYSTEMS

Methods of Representation

There are two main ways to represent floor, ceiling, and roof framing members as part of construction documents: drawing framing members on the floor plan or drawing them separately.

Roof Framing Systems

As you look at the various framing plans, you may see many conventions that require clarification. For this

reason, we have included a chart of typical conventions in Figure 9.50. You may find it helpful to flag this chart as you look at the various framing plans and use it as you would a dictionary, that is, as a reference table that defines the conventions used. The lettered explanations of these conventions correspond to the chart in Figure 9.50.

A. A beam, header, or lintel over an opening, door, or window within a wall. Takes a call-out, such as "BM #2 4 × 10 HDR, DF #1."

B. Used to show the direction of a framing member or a system of framing members, such as floor joists, rafters, or ceiling joists. Lettering occurs right along the line, indicating size, name, and spacing; for example, "2 × 6 ceiling joist at 16" o.c." Note that a half arrowhead is on one side and another half on the opposite side.

C. The line with the half arrowheads is the same as described in definition B. The diagonal line with a full arrowhead on both ends indicates the duration of the system, for example, where a particular system

Figure 9.32   Foundation trenching, forming, reinforcement bar, and anchor bolt locating.

of ceiling joists begins and ends. When sizes of the ceiling joists vary in length or size, this symbol is used to convey to the contractor what size framing member to use and where.

D. A beam, girder, or joist over a post.

E. A beam, girder, or joist under and supporting a post.

F. The employment of a framing anchor or joist hanger at the intersection of two members.

G. A structural post within a wall.

H. Two framing systems on the drawing. For example, one might represent ceiling joists, and the other roof rafters.

I. "W12 × 44" is a call-out for a steel beam or girder. When these members are sequentially repeated, the centerlines are still drawn to represent them, but the description (call-out) is abbreviated with the letters DO, which is short for "ditto."

J. In using conventional wood framing, which is subject to lateral forces such as wind and seismic, a plywood membrane is often placed on all or a portion of the complete wall surface. An adjacent triangle symbol refers readers to a nailing schedule to ensure minimums for nails to secure the plywood to the studs. These are called *shear walls* or *shear panels*.

K. An alternative way to demonstrate shear walls.

L. The rectilinear box that contains the 8'-2" dimension is a convention used to indicate height of an object in plan view. The two dashed lines may represent the top of a beam or the plate line at a wall.

M. The use of three lines, instead of two, represents a double joist at the partition.

N. A post on top of a beam; similar to E, but with a post size notation.

O. An opening in a floor, ceiling, or roof system. The two lines surrounding the opening represent the doubling of the joists, and the dark L-shape indicates the use of framing anchors or hangers. The large X is the area of the opening. This convention is used for skylights and openings in the ceiling or roof for chimneys, a hatch, or attic access.

FOUNDATION PLAN AND DETAIL CHECKLIST

1. North arrow
2. Titles and scale
3. Foundation walls 6″ (solid lines)
   a. Overall dimensions
   b. Offset dimensions (corners)
   c. Interior bearing walls
   d. Special wall thickness
   e. Planter wall thickness
   f. Garage
   g. Retaining wall
4. Footings – 12″ (hidden lines)
   a. Width of footing
   b. Stepped footing as per code
   c. Fireplace footing
   d. Belled footing
   e. Grade beams
   f. Planter footing
   g. Garage
   h. Retaining wall
5. Girder (center to center)
   a. Size
   b. Direction
   c. Spacing (center to center)
6. Piers
   a. Size
   b. Spacing (center to center)
   c. Detail
      (1) 8″ above grade (finish)
      (2) 8″ below grade (natural)
      (3) 2 × 6 × 6 redwood block secure to pier
      (4) 4 × 4 post
      (5) 4 × 4 girder
      (6) 2 × ? floor joist (o.c.)
      (7) Subfloor 1″ diagonal
         (a) T&G
         (b) Plyscord
      (8) Finish floor (usually in finish schedule)
7. Porches
   a. Indicate 2″ lip on foundation (min.)
   b. Indicate steel reinforcing (3/8″ – 24″ o.c.)
   c. Under slab note: Fill, puddle, and tamp
   d. Thickness of slab and steps

8. Subfloor material and size
9. Footing detail references
10. Cross-section reference
11. Column footing location and sizes
12. Concrete floors
   a. Width of footing
   b. Stepped footing as per code
13. Fireplace foundation
14. Patio and terrace location
   a. Material
   b. See porches
15. Depressed slabs or recessed area for ceramic tile etc.
16. Double floor joist under parallel partitions
17. Joist—direction and spacing
18. Areaways (18″ × 24″)
19. Columns (centerline dimension and size)
20. Reinforcing—location and size
   a. Rods
   b. Wire mesh
   c. Chimney
   d. Slabs
   e. Retaining walls
21. Apron for garage
22. Expansion joints (20′ o.c. in driveways)
23. Crawl holes (interior foundation walls)
24. Heat registers in slab
25. Heating ducts
26. Heat plenum if below floor
27. Stairs (basement)
28. Detail references
   a. "Bubbles"
   b. Section direction
29. Trenches
30. Foundation details
   a. Foundation wall thickness (6″ min.)
   b. Footing width and thickness (12″ min.)
   c. Depth below natural grade (12″ min.)
   d. 8″ above finish grade (FHA) (6″-UBC)

e. Redwood sill or as per code (2 × 6)
f. ½″ × 10″ anchor bolts, 6′- 0″ o.c. 1′ from corners, embedded 7″
g. 18″ min clearance bottom, floor joist to grade
h. Floor joist size and spacing
i. Subfloor (see pier detail)
j. Bottom plate 2 × 8
k. Studs—size and spacing
l. Finish floor (finish schedule)
31. All dimensions—coordinate with floor plan dimensions
32. Veneer detail (check as above)
33. Areaway detail (check as above)
34. Garage footing details
35. Planter details
36. House-garage connection detail
37. Special details
38. Retaining walls over 3′-0″ high (special design)
39. Amount of pitch of garage floor (direction)
40. General concrete notes
   a. Water-cement ratio
   b. Steel reinforcing
   c. Special additives
41. Note treated lumber
42. Special materials
   a. Terrazzo
   b. Stone work
   c. Wood edge
43. Elevations of all finish grades
44. Note: Solid block all joists at midspan if span exceeds 8′-0″
45. Specify grade of lumber (construction notes)
46. Pouché all details on back of vellum
47. Indicate North arrow near plan
48. Scale used for plan
49. Scale used for details
50. Complete title block
51. Check dimensions with floor plan
52. Border lines heavy and black

Figure 9.33 Foundation plan checklist.

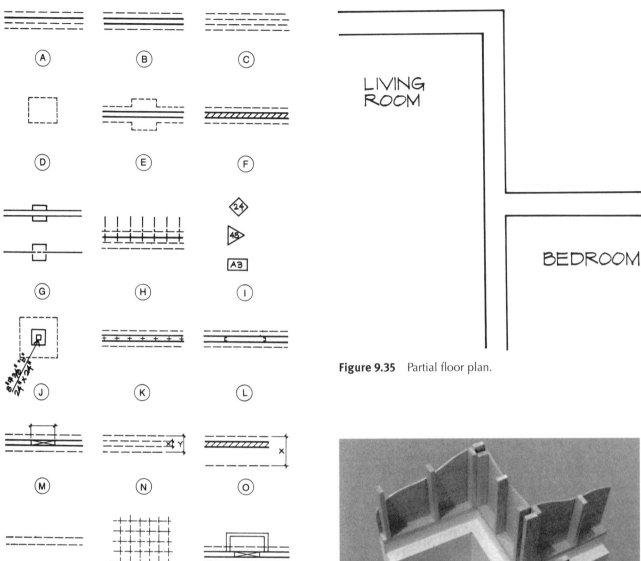

Figure 9.34 Conventions used on foundation plan.

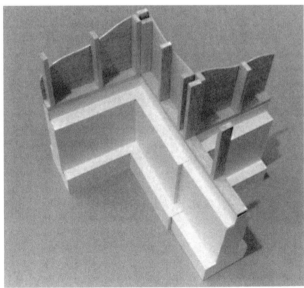

Figure 9.35 Partial floor plan.

Figure 9.36 Offset in the foundation.

Roof Plan

A roof plan is a simple look at the top view of a structure, as if you were aboard a helicopter. Unless you are looking at a flat roof, the view is usually distorted, because a roof plan cannot reveal the entire surface of the roof in its true shape and size if there are slopes involved.

There are a multitude of roof forms. Among the most commonly known are flat parapet, gable, hip, and shed roofs.

Most small structures, especially residential structures, use a flat, gable, or hip roof; the determination of

roof type is influenced by the prevailing rain or snowfall. Throughout this section, we will devote most of our attention to the hip roof. If you can configure a hip roof, a gable or flat roof will be a simple task.

Our approach will be to create a roof system that is geometrically correct and consistent in pitch, while

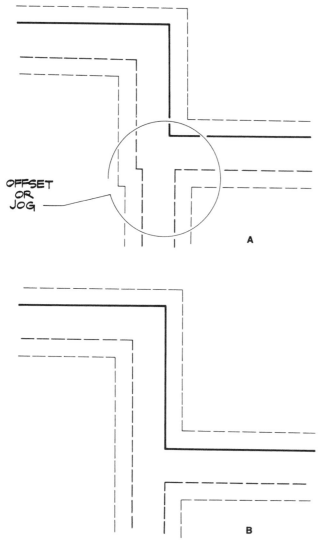

OFFSET OR JOG

A

B

Figure 9.37   Partial foundation plan.

avoiding flat areas that can entrap rain, thus causing leaks through the roof structure. Note the roof structure in Figure 9.51. Between the two roof systems, you will notice a flat (parallel to the ground) line. This space can trap water, causing deterioration of the roof material and, eventually, leaks. A short-term solution is to place a triangular metal form to induce the water to travel outward. Figure 9.52 shows a standard solution for a roof that was configured incorrectly to begin with. See Figure 9.51 for the geometrically correct way to solve the problem in this roof outline.

We describe here the procedure you should follow for even the simplest of roof outlines. With this knowledge, you will be able to create even the most complex outline. Once you know the system, you may even alter the building configuration slightly to avoid problematic roof areas in your plan.

Solution to Problem 1

STEP I.   Identify the perimeter of the roof as shown in the plan view in Figure 9.53. Be sure to dimension the overhang.

STEP II.   Reduce the shape to rectilinear zones. Find the largest rectilinear shape that will fit into the roof configuration. Figure 9.54A shows an outline of a roof, and Figure 9.54B shows the selection of the major area, as designated by the number "1." The major area is not selected according to square footage, but by greatest width. Look at another shape, similar to the preceding outline, in Figure 9.55A. Because the dimension of the base designated by the letter "B" is larger than base A, the major zone is zone 1, as shown in Figure 9.55B.

STEP III.   Locate both the hip rafter and the ridge. See Figure 9.56A. A 45° triangle is used to ensure the

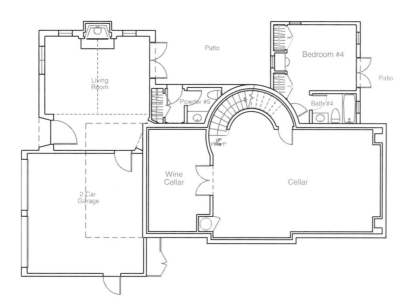

Figure 9.38   Stage I: Establishing datum (using floor plan).

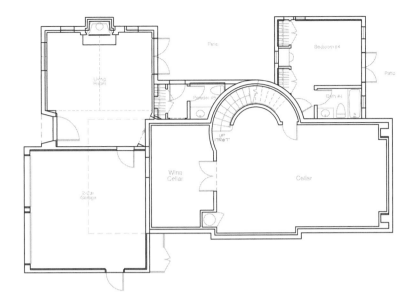

Figure 9.39 Stage II: Outline structure.

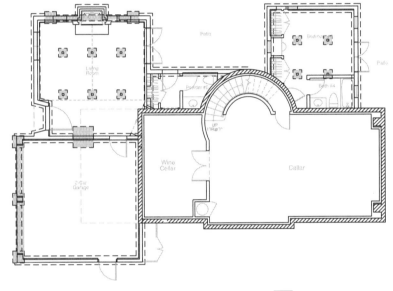

Figure 9.40 Stage III: Positioning bearing walls and posts/pads.

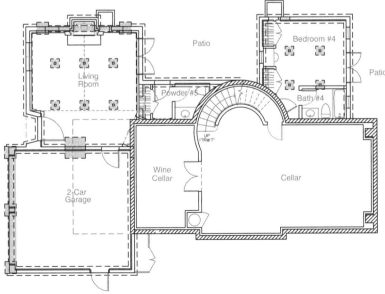

Figure 9.41 Stage IV: Steps, depressed slabs.

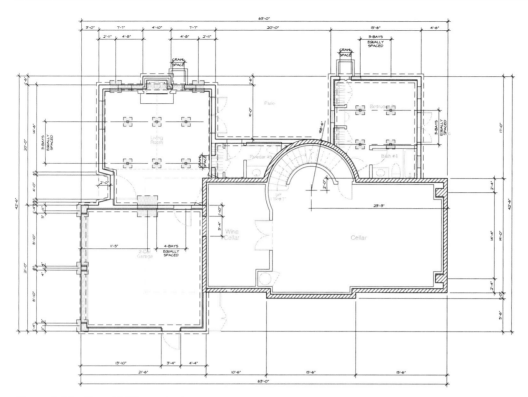

Figure 9.42   Stage V: Dimensioning.

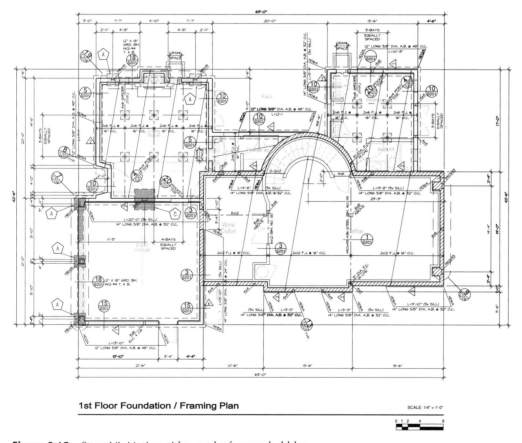

1st Floor Foundation / Framing Plan   SCALE: 1/4" = 1'-0"

Figure 9.43   Stage VI: Noting, titles, and reference bubbles.

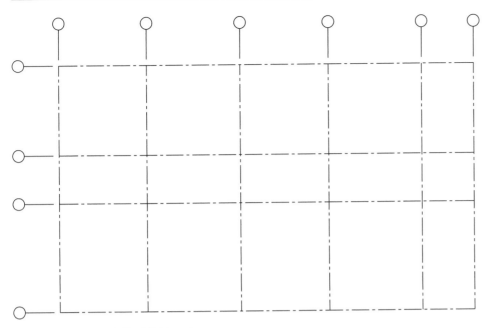

Figure 9.44 Stage I: Establishing datum.

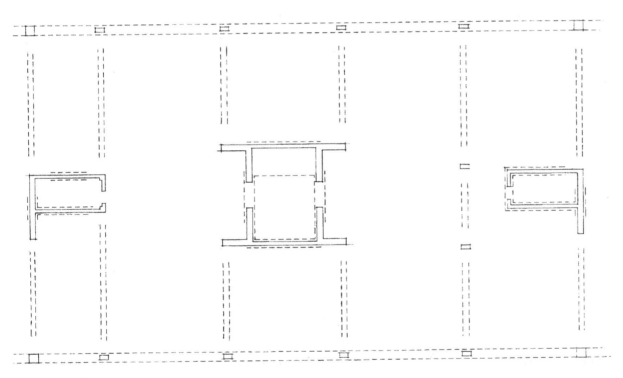

Figure 9.45 Foundation plan: Stage II.

same pitch (angle of roof) on both sides of the roof, as shown in Figure 9.56B. This is possible when the corners are at 90° to each other.

Note, in Figure 9.57, that the outline has been organized into three zones: the main zone (1) in the center, with zones 2 and 3 above and below. These angles have been identified by the letters "A," "B," and "C." For the sake of this solution, any angle such as A, which is 90°, will be called an *inside* corner. The other two corners (nos. 2 and 3) have angles greater than 90° and are referred to as *outside* corners.

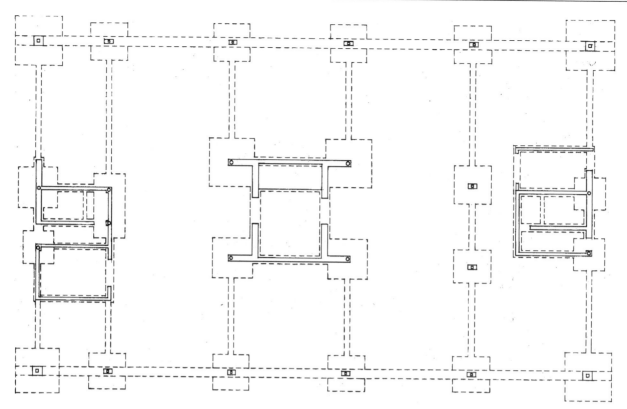

Figure 9.46 Foundation plan: Stage III.

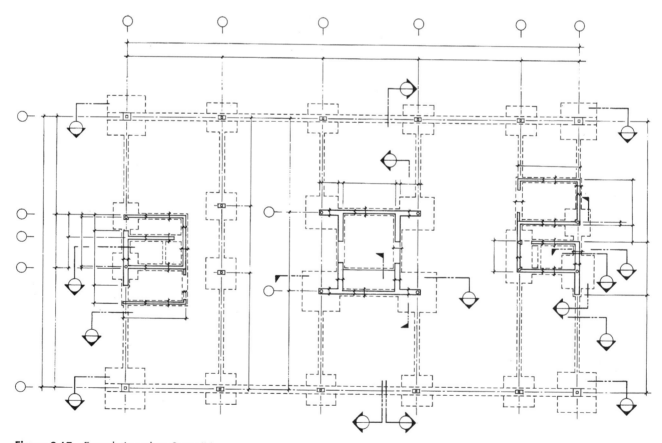

Figure 9.47 Foundation plan: Stage IV.

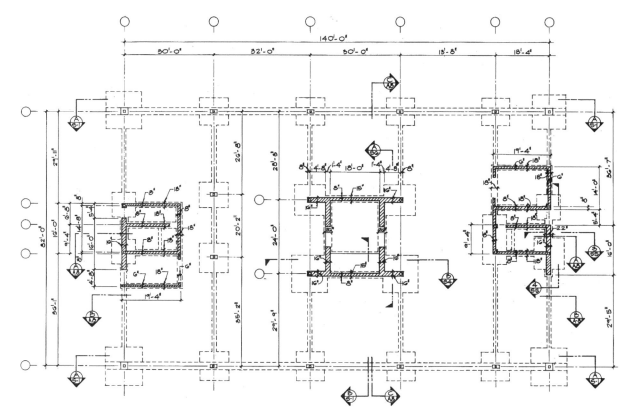

Figure 9.48 Foundation plan: Stage V.

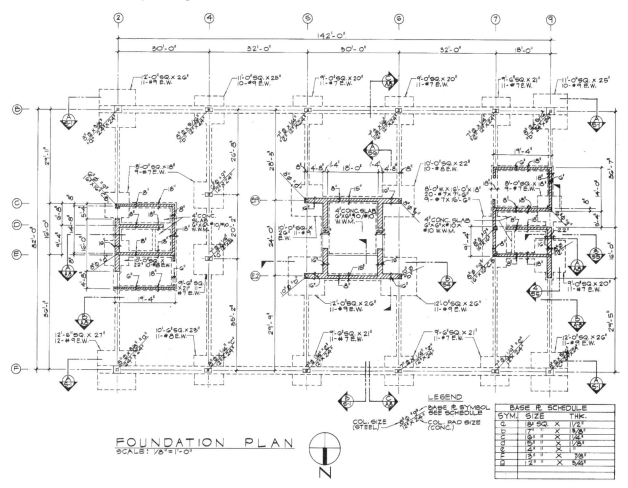

FOUNDATION PLAN
SCALE: 1/8"=1'-0"

LEGEND

BASE PL SYMBOL SEE SCHEDULE

COL. SIZE (STEEL)

COL. PAD SIZE (CONC.)

BASE PL SCHEDULE		
SYM.	SIZE	THK.
a	18" SQ. X	1 1/2"
b	7" X	3/8"
c	6" X	1/4"
d	5" X	1/8"
e	4" X	
f	3" X	7/8"
g	12" X	3/4"

Figure 9.49 Foundation plan: Stage VI.

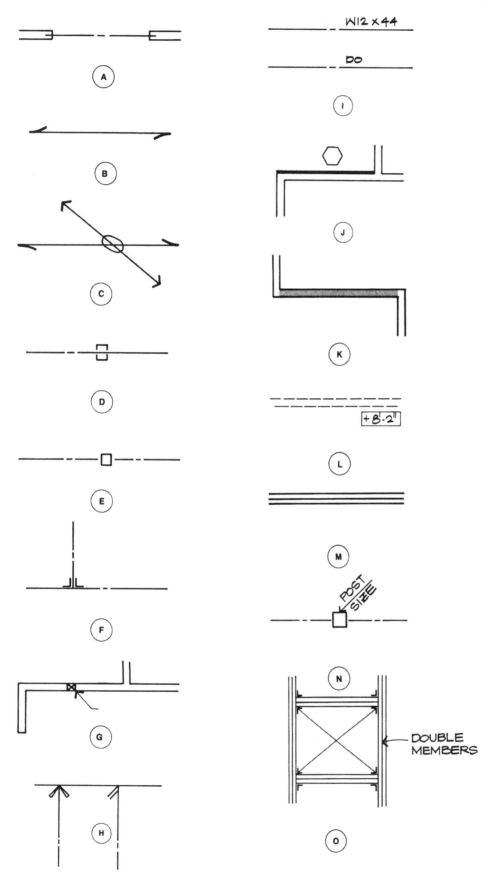

Figure 9.50 Summary of typical framing conventions.

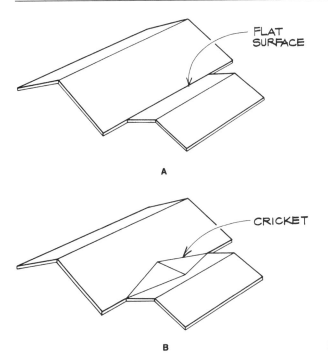

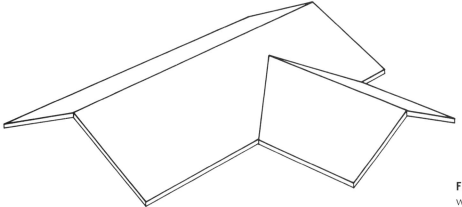

Figure 9.51 Incorrectly configured roof.

Figure 9.52 Ideal solution to avoid water problem.

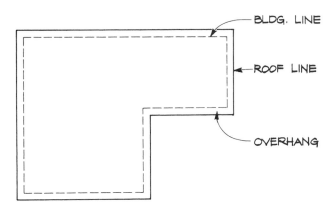

Figure 9.53 Draft the perimeter of the roof to be configured.

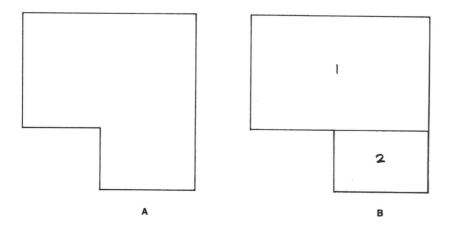

Figure 9.54   Find the major zone.

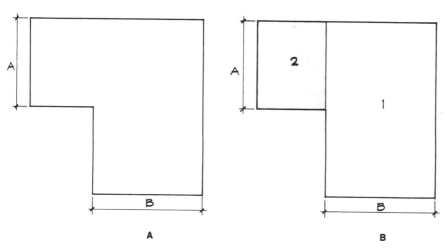

Figure 9.55   Letting the largest width determine the major zone.

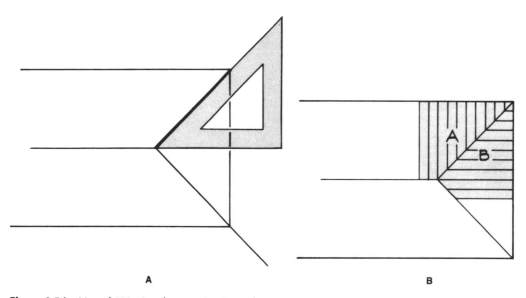

Figure 9.56   Use of 45° triangle to maintain pitch.

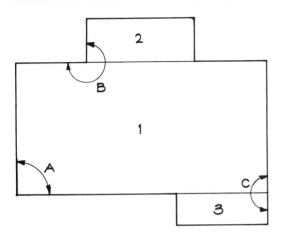

A - INSIDE (ANGLE) CORNER
B - OUTSIDE (ANGLE) CORNER
C - OUTSIDE (ANGLE) CORNER

Figure 9.57 Defining inside and outside corners.

STEP IV. Configure the roof. Let us take this configuration and develop it into a hip roof with the information already learned.

Taking the major zone identified as zone 1 in Figure 9.58A, we strike 45° hip lines from each of the inside corners to form the main structure around which the other two zones will appear.

We now approach zone 2 in Figure 9.58B with an eye out for inside and outside corners. There are two of each. The inside corners at the top are drawn toward the center of the rectangle. The outside corners have their 45° lines going away from the zone 2 rectangle, thus forming the valleys of the roof.

The same approach is used for zone 3 as was used for zone 2. In the process of drawing the outside corners, you will notice that the one on the right overlaps an existing line (see Figure 9.58C). When this happens, the lines cancel each other, creating a continuous plane. See Figure 9.58D, which displays the final roof shape.

As you look at the final roof form, it may appear foolish to have gone through such an elaborate system, because you may have been able to visualize the finished roof from the beginning. Let's reinforce and validate the procedure by attempting roofs of varying complexities.

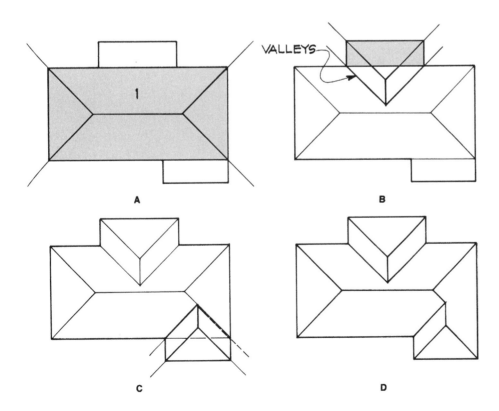

Figure 9.58 Solving hip roof Problem 1.

Solution to Problem 2

Step I.   Figure 9.59A displays an area in the center that appears to be the major zone. By square footage, it might be, but remember, the major zone is the zone with the greatest width.

Step II.   In Figure 9.59B, notice the relocation of the major zone by greatest width. Compare zone 1 with zone 2. The one with the greatest width will produce the highest ridge because it takes longer rafters in the framing of this roof.

Step III.   Figure 9.59C shows all of the zones with roofs outlined. Remember the outside/inside corner rule.

Step IV.   As can be seen in the previous step, many of the lines overlap. In Figure 9.59D, we show them side-by-side for ease of understanding, but in reality they are on top of each other. This means they cancel each other and are erased.

To continue this exploration of problems, we have selected an outline in which the major roof configuration will all but disappear as we develop the roof.

Solution to Problem 3

Step I.   In Figure 9.60A, the main zone is situated vertically through the center of the total form. Check this area, in width, with a horizontal rectangle drawn through the top.

Step II.   Draw the hip and ridge lines as shown in Figure 9.60B. Identify inside and outside corners, and proceed with drawing both the hip and valley lines.

Step III.   As the lines overlap each other, which happens in three locations, these locations are identified with dotted lines (see Figure 9.60C). Notice that three of the four hip lines of the major zone are eliminated in the process.

There are configurations in which the major zones are well hidden. There are also shapes that have overlapping zones. These are by far the most difficult challenges. The following five-step example demonstrates a solution for such cases.

Solution to Problem 4

Step I.   Covering all but the top illustration, see if you can identify the major zone on this outline of the structure in Figure 9.61A.

Step II.   Validate your initial selection with Figure 9.61B. Next, identify the second largest zone, which has been "X"ed out. Notice the overlap of zones 1 and 2.

Step III.   Solve zones 3 and 4 next. Two lines will overlap, causing their removal, as shown in Figure 9.61C.

Step IV.   Zone 2 has inside corners only, as shown in Figure 9.61D. Solve zone 2 as you did zone 1. The points that overlap have been identified with the letters W and X. These are outside corners, which become valleys. Extend point X toward zone 1, and W toward zone 2. These lines will intersect a hip line, identified by the letters Y and Z, respectively.

Step V.   Y and Z are connected to form a ridge (see Figure 9.61E). This ridge is slightly lower than the ridge of zones 1 and 2. The hip lines below points Y and Z are also eliminated to form the final roof configuration.

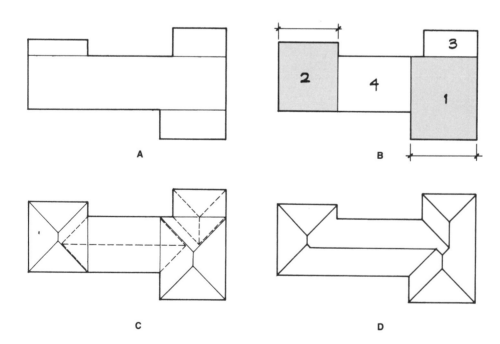

Figure 9.59   Problem 2.

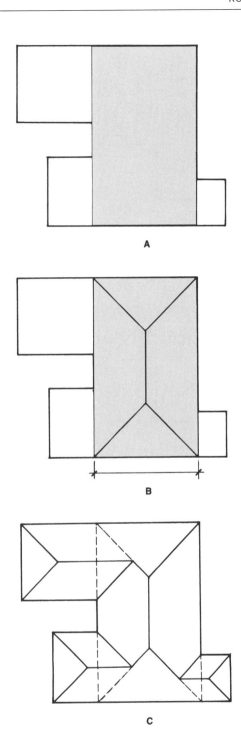

Figure 9.60 Problem 3.

Saving the most challenging for last, we encounter a shape that includes an angle other than 90° around the perimeter. At first glance the task of roofing this outline seems difficult, but if you apply the principles set out in this chapter, the solution is easier than it may first appear.

Solution to Problem 5

STEP I. Extending the center portion toward the left (Figure 9.62A) does not produce the rectangle with the largest width, so change your approach and solve the major zoning as explained in the next step.

STEP II. After you have checked the various possible zones, we hope you have selected zone 1 and zone 2 as shown in Figure 9.62B.

STEP III. With all inside corners in zones 1 and 2, the solution is simple (see Figure 9.62C). Zone 3 should also be easy, with two inside and two outside corners, and thus will be shown as a finished section in the next step.

STEP IV. Zone 4 has four outside corners, two of which overlap zone 1. To find the ridge, use the upper two outside corners and extend the ridge well into zone 1, as shown in Figure 9.62D. The valleys will start at points X and Y.

Because points X and Y are not the normal outside angles (180° or 270°), they must be bisected. It is easier to bisect the outside rather than the inside angle around points X and Y because these angles are less than 180°. This can be accomplished by measuring the angle with a protractor and mathematically dividing the angle, or by using a method, which you may have learned in a basic drafting class or in a geometry class, that requires use of a compass.

The compass is set at any radius and an arc is struck, using X and Y as the center of the arc. See Figure 9.63A. Next, open the compass wider than the original settings and strike two more arcs, starting where the original arc struck the angular lines. See Figure 9.63B. Let's call this new intersection Z. When a line is drawn through Z and X (or Z and Y, depending on which angle you are bisecting), you have bisected the angle.

STEP V. Extend the bisecting lines from X and Y to the inside until they hit the ridge. We have identified these points as M and N in Figure 9.62E.

STEP VI. Next, connect M and N, as shown in Figure 9.62F. This line represents another valley at a different angle and defines the true geometric shape of zones 1 and 4 as they intersect each other. The dotted line, which is the underside of the hip of zone 1, is eliminated in a roof plan but may be shown on a subsequent roof framing plan.

Changing Configuration

After having configured an outline of a roof to its correct geometric shape, you can readily convert it to other than a hip roof. For example, consider the roof shown in Figure 9.64A.

To change this roof to a gable roof, you simply extend the ridges to the edge of the roof, as shown

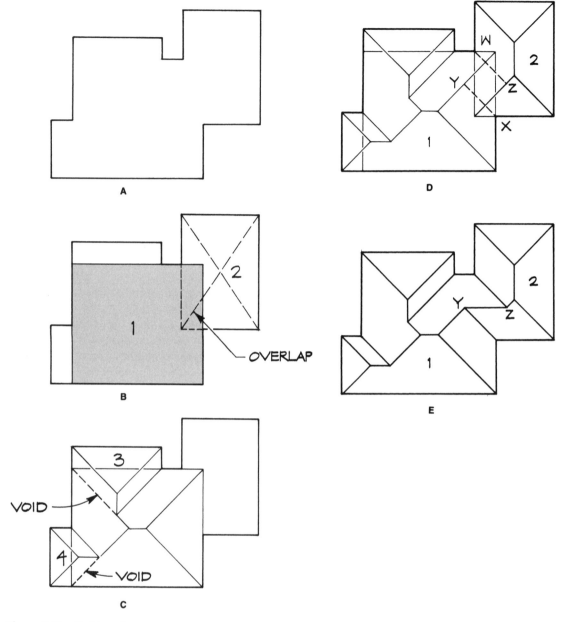

Figure 9.61 Problem 4.

by the arrows. The final gable roof is displayed in Figure 9.64B. Notice the return of the valley lines (marked X).

In the next example, found in Figure 9.65, the arrows provide the slight bit of interpretation needed for the top right corner of the structure.

Skylight Attic Location—Ventilation

A roof plan in conjunction with an exterior elevation gives the designer a perfect opportunity to position and check the appearance of such things as an attic ventilating system that must comply with energy standards.

Standards have been instituted by local, state, and even federal commissions for energy conservation. An effective system may be as simple as a screened opening or a screened opening enhanced with a mechanical device.

Because heat rises, it is best to place ventilating systems as high as possible, at the ends of a roof, for thorough ventilation—also taking into consideration the prevailing winds and any other environmental factors that may dictate their position. Code may also allow a reduction of required venting for a combination of high and low vents that encourages **convection**, which is the drafting of the cool air in place of the hot air and vice versa.

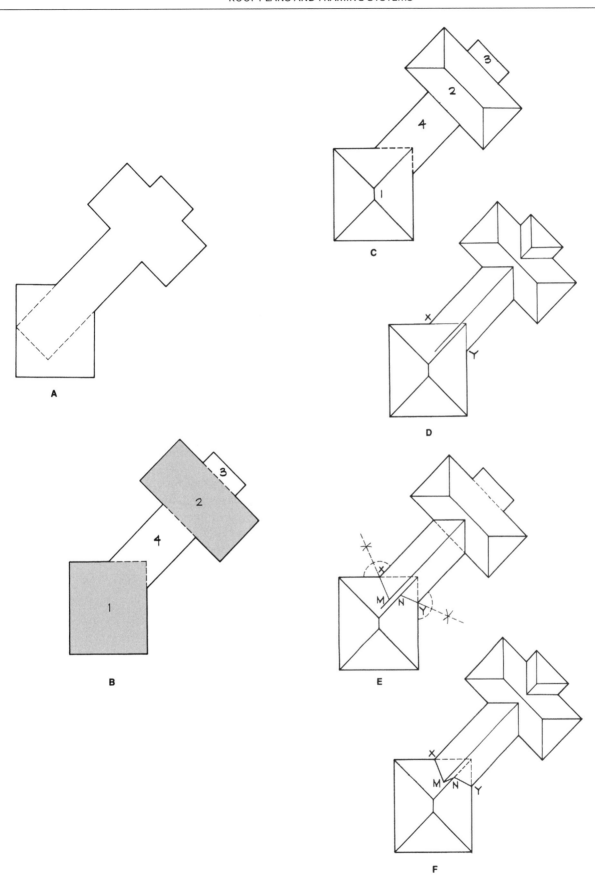

Figure 9.62 Problem 5.

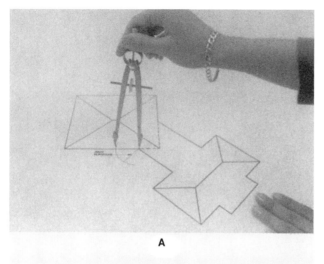

A

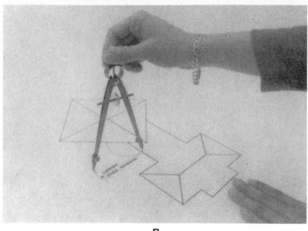

B

Figure 9.63   Bisecting an angle.

Traditionally, ventilation systems were placed on the ends of gable roofs, on the gable portion of a roof, or at the eaves of a hip roof. Today, roof-surface-mounted units and ridge ventilating systems are presently available, as well as numerous mechanical systems for industrial, commercial, and residential structures.

The position of skylights must always be verified on the roof plan. This will ensure that you are not cutting through a strategic area, such as a hip or valley of the roof. For example, the skylight shown at the bottom of Figure 9.66 does not bridge any structural roof member, so it can be placed in the desired location directly above the room below. However, this is not the case with the skylight at the top of this figure, because it crosses a hip member (a pleated plane); therefore, it must be moved to another area, which is shown as a dotted line. The opening below may be in the original position, but with the skylight shifted, the light shaft will be bent. See Figure 9.67.

A Newly Built Major Roof Zone

Rather than restricting yourself to a particular outline, you can alter the configuration with porches, balconies, colonnades, and so on. Simply following the outline of the structure would produce an unusual roof that is difficult to frame. The simple addition of a roof over the entry can protect the entry, create the basis for a better structural form, and even simplify the roof form. See Figure 9.68. A simpler roof allows easier construction and creates a system that is structurally stable; thus, if it answers a functional need (covered entry), it is the best of all solutions. See Figure 9.69.

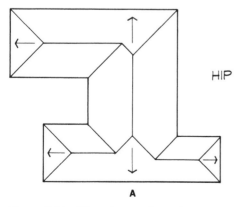

HIP

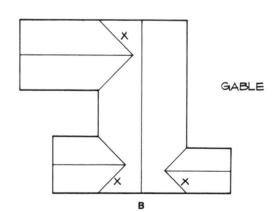

GABLE

A   B

Figure 9.64   Changing configuration.

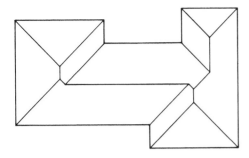

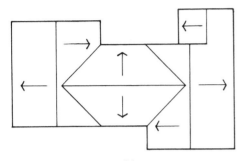

Figure 9.65 Hip to gable conversion.

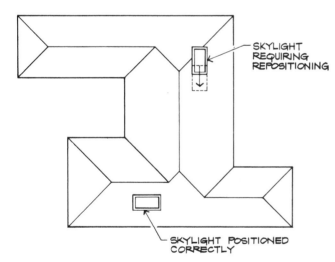

Figure 9.66 Verifying skylight location.

Drawing a Roof Plan on the Computer

STAGE I The roof plan shown in Figure 9.70 requires an accurate drawing of the perimeter of the structure. One of the initial stages of the floor plan becomes the datum and should be XREFed into the system.

STAGE II (Figure 9.71). Add to the outline the various zones to be roofed by isolating the geometry used by the designer and later used by the structural engineer

to properly structure this geometric form with its component parts.

STAGE III (Figure 9.72). The chimney to the fireplace and skylights are positioned, and the roof ridges and valleys are added to the roof structure.

STAGE IV (Figure 9.73). Skylights and chimneys that cut through ridges and valleys are resolved through detailing. Roof slopes and venting of the attic are done at this stage. Heat rises, so it is recommended that the ridge vents be placed as high atop the roof as possible. A portion of the roof may be hatched or delineated to show the roof material covering this structure.

STAGE V (Figure 9.74). The plotting and titling stage may include elevation call-outs of the top of the roof. This is typically required when the municipality has height restrictions.

Drawing a Roof Framing Plan on the Computer

The roof framing plan may be drafted by a structural engineer; an alternate, and usually less expensive, strategy may be to provide the structural engineer with a set of digital drawings on which the engineer may calculate the sizes for all of the necessary structural components (rafters, headers, sheet walls, etc.). These can then be translated in the architectural office as a CAD drawing.

For a better understanding of the system that will be used to build the roof structure, refer to the examples in Chapters 14 and 15.

STAGE I (Figure 9.75). An early stage of the second-floor plan becomes the datum for the evolution of this drawing.

STAGE II (Figure 9.76). The walls that are bearing the weight of the roof are identified.

STAGE III (Figure 9.77). With the bearing and non-bearing walls identified, the drafter will not have any trouble in also placing the direction and duration symbols on the drawing. The drafter can also isolate the most important headers and beams listed by the engineer and isolate critical beams that may be missing from the engineer's sketch. Shear walls are also located, drawn, and referenced to a schedule.

STAGE IV (Figure 9.78). All noting and referencing occurs in this stage.

Drawing Framing Members on the Floor Plan

This first method illustrates and notes ceiling and/or floor framing members directly onto the finished floor plan. It is a good method to use when the framing conditions are simple and do not require many notes. The goal is to reference symbols that will not be confused with the other finished floor-plan information.

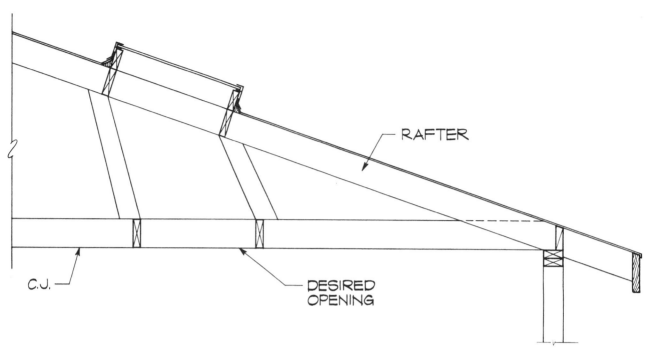

Figure 9.67 Skylight with bent light shaft.

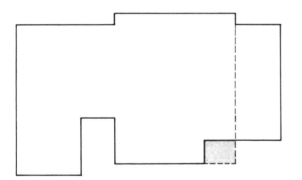

Figure 9.68 Changing the outline.

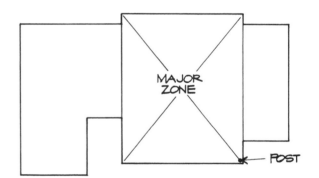

Figure 9.79 shows the lower-floor plan of a two-story residence. This plan contains all the information and symbols needed. Note how the ceiling joist size, spacing, and direction are illustrated in bedroom #1 and the study. Note also the use of broken lines to represent exposed ceiling beams in the master bedroom. As you can see, if a great deal more framing information were required, the drawing would lose its clarity.

The upper-floor plan of this residence designates ceiling joist sizes, spacing, and direction, as well as roof framing information such as rafter sizes, spacing, and direction; ridge beam size; and the size and spacing of exposed rafter beams in the living room.

See Figure 9.80. Headers and beams for framing support over openings are also shown in this figure. If you are using this method to show framing members, you can delineate beams with two broken lines at the approximate scale of the beam or with a heavy broken line.

The structural design of beams and footings is calculated by finding the total loads that are distributed to any specific member. This total load is found by computing the tributary area affecting that member. Figure 9.81 illustrates a cross-section showing the various tributary areas that contribute loads to the ridge beam, floor beam, and foundation footing.

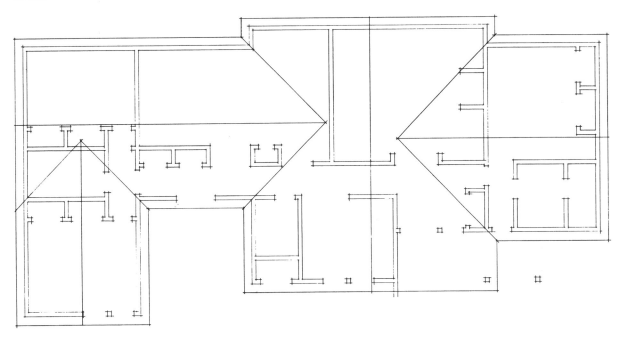

Figure 9.69 Roof to match zoning.

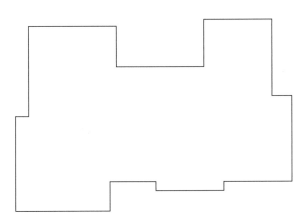

Figure 9.70 Stage I: Datum.

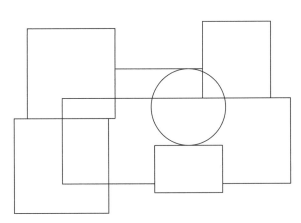

Figure 9.71 Stage II: Isolating geometry.

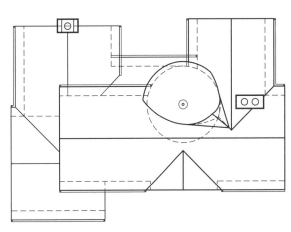

Figure 9.72 Stage III: Defining roof shape.

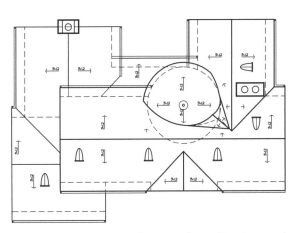

Figure 9.73 Stage IV: Chimney, slope direction, and vents.

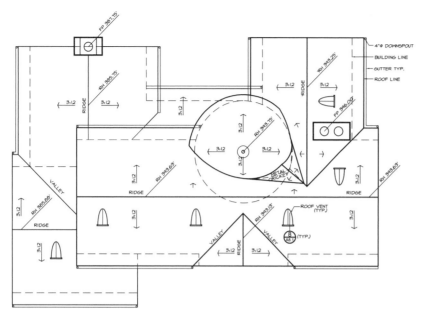

Figure 9.74   Stage V: Noting.

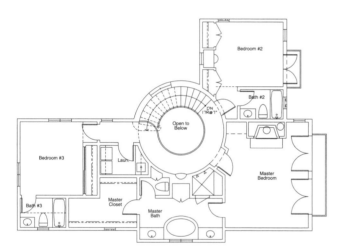

Figure 9.75   Stage I: Floor plan as datum.

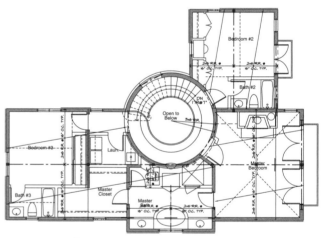

Figure 9.77   Stage III: Direction, duration, shear, and beams.

Figure 9.76   Stage II: Identifying bearing and non-bearing walls.

Drawing Framing Members Separately

The second way to show ceiling, floor, and roof framing members is to provide a separate drawing that may be titled "2nd Floor Framing," "Floor Framing," or "Roof Framing." You might choose this method because the framing is complex or because construction document procedures require it.

The first step is the same as that taken when drawing on the foundation plan. Duplicate or XREF all the walls, windows, and door openings. The line quality of your tracing should be just dark enough to make these lines distinguishable after you have reproduced the drawing. In this way, the final drawing, showing

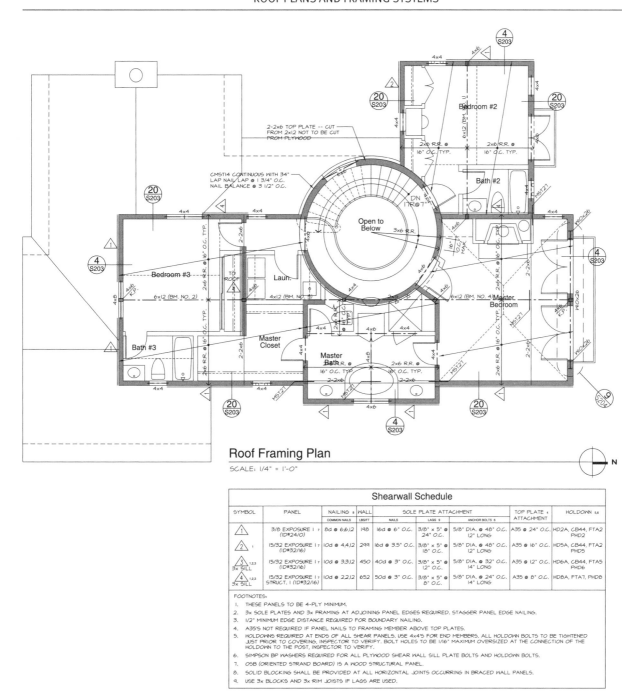

Roof Framing Plan

SCALE: 1/4" = 1'-0"

Shearwall Schedule

SYMBOL	PANEL	NAILING 8		WALL LBS/FT	SOLE PLATE ATTACHMENT			TOP PLATE 4 ATTACHMENT	HOLDOWN 5,6
		COMMON NAILS			NAILS	LAGS 9	ANCHOR BOLTS 9		
△1	3/8 EXPOSURE I 7 (ID#24/0)	8d @ 6,6,12		198	16d @ 6" O.C.	3/8" x 5" @ 24" O.C.	5/8" DIA. @ 48" O.C. 12" LONG	A35 @ 24" O.C.	HD2A, CB44, FTA2 PHD2
△2 1	15/32 EXPOSURE I 7 (ID#32/16)	10d @ 4,4,12		299	16d @ 3.5" O.C.	3/8" x 5" @ 18" O.C.	5/8" DIA. @ 48" O.C. 12" LONG	A35 @ 16" O.C.	HD5A, CB44, FTA2 PHD5
△3 1,2,3 3x SILL	15/32 EXPOSURE I 7 (ID#32/16)	10d @ 3,3,12		450	40d @ 3" O.C.	3/8" x 5" @ 12" O.C.	5/8" DIA. @ 32" O.C. 14" LONG	A35 @ 12" O.C.	HD6A, CB44, FTA5 PHD6
△4 1,2,3 3x SILL	15/32 EXPOSURE I 7 STRUCT. I (ID#32/16)	10d @ 2,2,12		652	50d @ 3" O.C.	3/8" x 5" @ 8" O.C.	5/8" DIA. @ 24" O.C. 14" LONG	A35 @ 8" O.C.	HD8A, FTA7, PHD8

FOOTNOTES:
1. THESE PANELS TO BE 4-PLY MINIMUM.
2. 3x SOLE PLATES AND 3x FRAMING AT ADJOINING PANEL EDGES REQUIRED. STAGGER PANEL EDGE NAILING.
3. 1/2" MINIMUM EDGE DISTANCE REQUIRED FOR BOUNDARY NAILING.
4. A35'S NOT REQUIRED IF PANEL NAILS TO FRAMING MEMBER ABOVE TOP PLATES.
5. HOLDOWNS REQUIRED AT ENDS OF ALL SHEAR PANELS. USE 4x4'S FOR END MEMBERS. ALL HOLDOWN BOLTS TO BE TIGHTENED JUST PRIOR TO COVERING, INSPECTOR TO VERIFY. BOLT HOLES TO BE 1/16" MAXIMUM OVERSIZED AT THE CONNECTION OF THE HOLDOWN TO THE POST, INSPECTOR TO VERIFY.
6. SIMPSON BP WASHERS REQUIRED FOR ALL PLYWOOD SHEAR WALL SILL PLATE BOLTS AND HOLDOWN BOLTS.
7. OSB (ORIENTED STRAND BOARD) IS A WOOD STRUCTURAL PANEL.
8. SOLID BLOCKING SHALL BE PROVIDED AT ALL HORIZONTAL JOINTS OCCURRING IN BRACED WALL PANELS.
9. USE 3x BLOCKS AND 3x RIM JOISTS IF LAGS ARE USED.

Figure 9.78 Stage IV: Noting. (Courtesy of James Orland, CE.)

all the framing members, can be made darker like a finished drawing. This provides the viewer with clear framing members, while the walls are just lightly drawn for reference.

Figure 9.82 shows the floor plan of the first floor of a two-story, wood-framed residence with all the framing members required to support the second floor and ceiling directly above this level. Because the second-floor

framing and ceiling for the first floor are the same, this drawing is titled "2ND FLR. Framing Plan."

First, draft in all the floor beams, columns, and headers for all the various openings. Then incorporate the location and span direction of all the floor joists into the drawing. In Figure 9.82, the floor joist locations and span directions are shown with a single line and arrowhead at each end of the line. This is one way to designate these

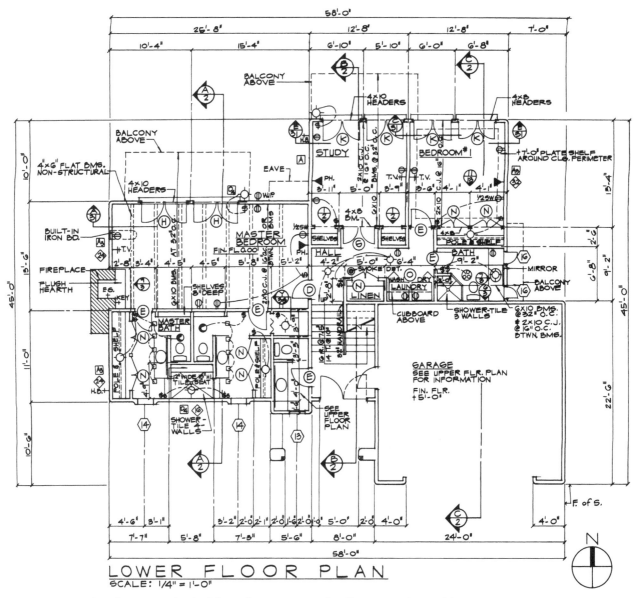

Figure 9.79   Ceiling framing on finished floor plan. (Courtesy of William F. Smith—Builder.)

members. Another method is shown later when the roof framing plan is discussed.

Dimensioning for framing plans mainly applies to beam and column locations. Provide dimensioning for all floor beams and columns located directly under load-bearing members. These members, such as walls and columns, are located on the second floor. Dimensioning for these members is similar to that on a floor plan. When you have finished the drawing, provide the required notes for all the members included in the drawing.

Drawing the ceiling plan for the second-floor level involves only the immediate ceiling framing members. A

ceiling plan will typically be incorporated into the roof framing plan unless it is too complex. In that case, it will show headers over openings and ceiling joist location, span, direction, size, and spacing for a specific ceiling area. This is also where applicable notes and dimensioning are shown.

The final framing plan for this project is the roof framing plan. See Figure 9.83. As mentioned previously, another way to show framing members is to draw in all the members that apply to that particular drawing. This obviously takes more time to draw, but is clearer for the viewer.

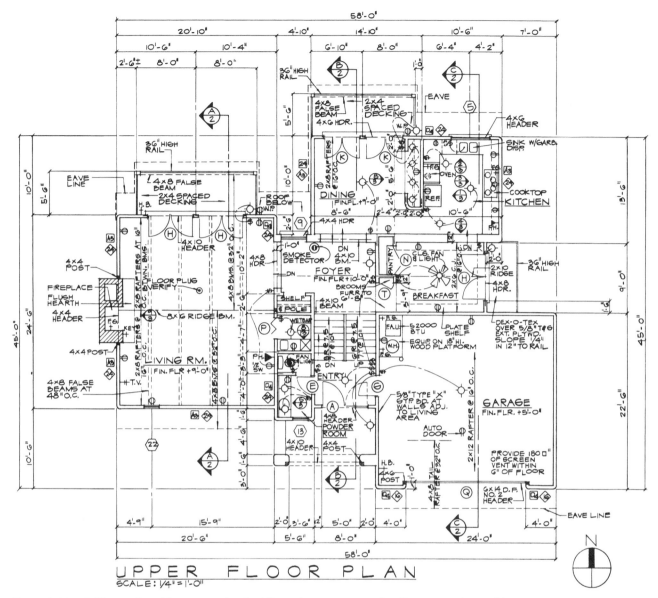

Figure 9.80 Ceiling and roof framing on finished floor plan. (Courtesy of William F. Smith—Builder.)

■ FRAMING WITH DIFFERENT MATERIALS

Framing Plan: Wood Members

When wood structures have members spaced anywhere from 16″ to 48″ on centers, show them with a single line broken at intervals. Figure 9.84 shows the roof framing plan for this residence, which incorporates all the individual rafters, ridges, **hip rafters** (the members that bisect the angle of two intersecting walls), and supporting columns and beams under the rafters. Show the rafters, which are closely spaced, with a single line. Although this method is tedious, it does provide clarity and an actual member count for the contractor to work from. Lightly draft the walls so that the members directly above are clear. Provide dimensioning for members with critical locations, as well as call-outs for the sizes, lumber grade, and spacing of all members.

Framing Plan: Steel Members

When you are using steel members to support ceilings, floors, and roof, show all the members on the framing

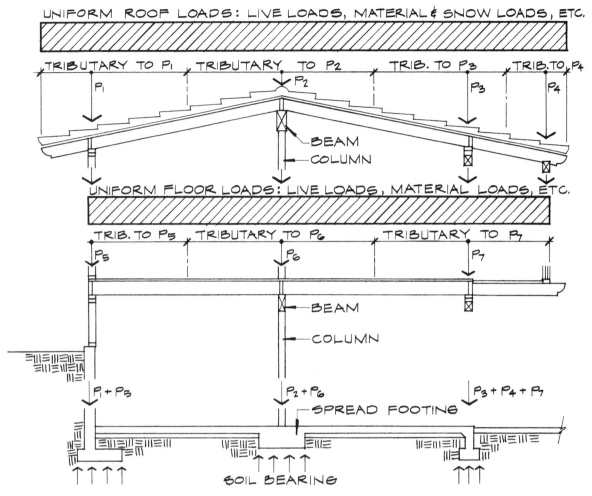

Figure 9.81   Tributary loading section.

plans. The method of drawing the framing plan is similar to the method for drawing wood framing plans.

After you have selected a method, draw the steel members with a heavy single line. See Figure 9.85, which is a roof framing plan for a theater using various-size steel members and steel decking. The interior walls have been drawn with a broken line, which distinguishes the heavy solid beam line and the walls below. As you can see, all the various beam sizes are noted directly on the steel members. Some members have an abbreviated "DO" as their call-out; this tells the viewer that this member is identical to the one noted in the same framing bay.

In some cases, a beam may also be given a roof beam number, noted as "RB-1," "RB-2," and so on. The structural engineer uses this beam reference in the engineering calculations. It can also be incorporated into a roof beam schedule, if one is needed. Any elements that require openings through a roof or floor should be drawn

directly on the plan. On Figure 9.85, an open area for skylights and a roof access hatch are shown with a heavy solid line.

A framing plan can also be useful to show detail reference symbols for connections of various members that cannot otherwise be shown on the building sections. Figure 9.85 shows several detail symbols for various connecting conditions. Show building section reference symbols at their specific locations.

Axial reference lines form the basis for dimensioning steel framing members. These lines provide a reference point for all other dimensioning. Axial reference symbols are shown on all the major beam and wall lines. From these, subsequent dimension lines to other members are provided. These same reference lines are used on the foundation plan.

Beam and column elevation heights are often shown on the framing plan. See the axial reference point H-10 in Figure 9.85. The diagonal line pointing to this particular

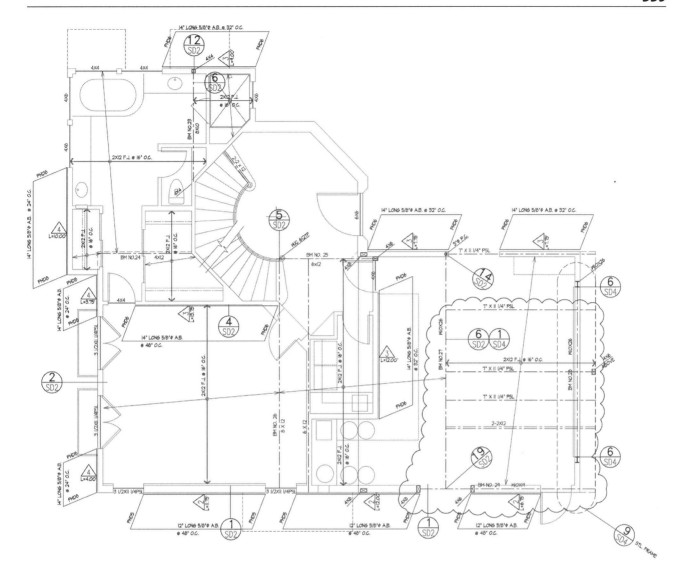

(Bld'g. 2) 2ND FLR. FRAMING PLAN

SCALE: 1/4" = 1'-0"

Figure 9.82   Second-floor framing plan. (Courtesy of James Orland, CE.)

beam has an elevation height of 31'-7½" noted on the top of the diagonal line. This indicates the height to the top of the beam. If the height at the bottom of that beam were required, you would note it underneath the diagonal line. Columns usually only require the elevations to the top of the column.

An aerial photograph showing a stage of the roof framing is shown in Figure 9.86. You can clearly see the main supporting steel members, as per axial reference lines ③, ④, ⑩, ⑪, and ⑫, and some placement of the steel decking on top of these members.

Framing Plan: Wood and Steel Members

Framing plans using both wood and steel members to support ceilings, floors, and roof are drawn in a similar fashion to framing plans using steel alone. Steel members are drawn with a heavy solid line and the wood members with a lighter line broken at intervals. You can also show wood members with a solid line and directional arrow.

Figure 9.87 shows a floor framing plan using steel and wood members to support the floor. This particular

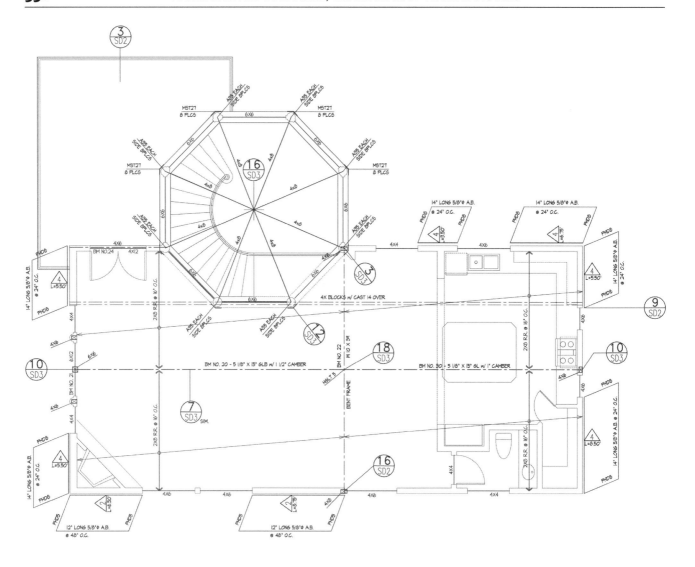

(Bld'g. 2) ROOF FRAMING PLAN

SCALE: 1/4" = 1'-0"

Figure 9.83   Roof framing plan. (Courtesy of James Orland, CE.)

building is supported mainly on round steel columns, with the wall being used only to enclose a lobby and stairwells. For clarity, draw these columns in lines, and be careful to align them with each other. After you have laid out the required columns and walls below, draw in the main steel members with a solid heavy line. The designation of floor trusses spaced at 24″ on centers is shown between these steel members.

Because these members are closely spaced, a solid line is used with directional arrows at the end and the size and spacing of trusses are noted directly above the solid line. The bottom of the line shows a notation,

"FJ-3." This is the abbreviation for floor joist number 3, which is referenced in the structural engineer's calculations and may be used in a floor joist schedule. When you are asked to draw a similar framing plan, be sure to show the joist for all bay conditions. As we saw earlier, "DO" is shown between axial reference lines ⑦ and ⑧. When you use this abbreviation, be sure it is clear. Detail reference symbols are shown for the connections of various members. Sizes and shapes for all the steel columns have been designated, as has the elevation height to the top of each column. Building section reference symbols and locations are shown. Whenever

schedule for the plywood subfloor or the location of the fire draft stops within the floor framing.

To understand this structure better, look at the series of framing photographs. Figure 9.88 is a close-up view of a main steel floor beam and column with joist hangers located at the top of the beam in preparation for attachment of the floor truss members.

In Figure 9.89, floor joist trusses have now been attached to the hangers and nailed in place. Reference symbols for connection details should be located throughout the framing plan drawings. Figures 9.90 and 9.91 give examples of what these details may look like during the actual construction phase.

Framing Plan Checklist
1. Titles and scales.
2. Indicate bearing and non-bearing walls.
    a. Coordinate with foundation plan.
    b. Show all openings in walls.
3. Show all beams, headers, girders, purlins, etc.
4. Show all columns; note sizes and materials.
5. Note roof access way to attic—if occurs.
6. Note ceiling joist sizes, direction, spacing.
7. Draw all rafters; note sizes and spacing.
    a. Show skylight penetrations.
    b. Show chimney penetrations.
8. Draw overhangs.
    a. Indicate framing for holding overhangs up.
    b. Dimension width of footings.
9. Note shear walls and length of wall.
10. Note roof sheathing type, thickness, and nailing.
11. Indicate all ridges and valleys. Note sizes.
12. Note all differences in roof and floor levels.
13. Provide all shear schedules.
14. Provide material specifications.
15. Provide nailing schedule.
16. Note structural observation requirements.

■ FLOOR FRAMING

Conventions

The basic conventions for floor framing are generally the same as those used in roof or ceiling framing plans.

The floor plan should be used, with XREF. In this manner, not only do you keep the size of the file small, but any corrections or changes in the floor plan will be reflected in the framing plan.

This section discusses a second-floor framing plan that will be drawn onto the first-floor plan. Two systems will be shown, the first with conventional framing and the second with engineered lumber. In discussing engineered lumber, we will show how to use the computer framing program developed by Boise Cascade called "BC Framer."

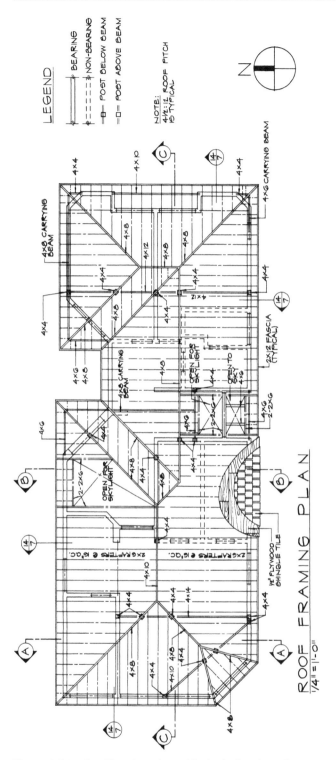

Figure 9.84 Roof framing plan with single line for rafters.

possible, take these sections directly through an axial reference plan.

Dimensioning for this type of project relies totally on axial reference planes as they relate to the column locations. Usually, you should locate notes satisfying various requirements on this same drawing. For example, these notes might designate the thickness, type, and nailing

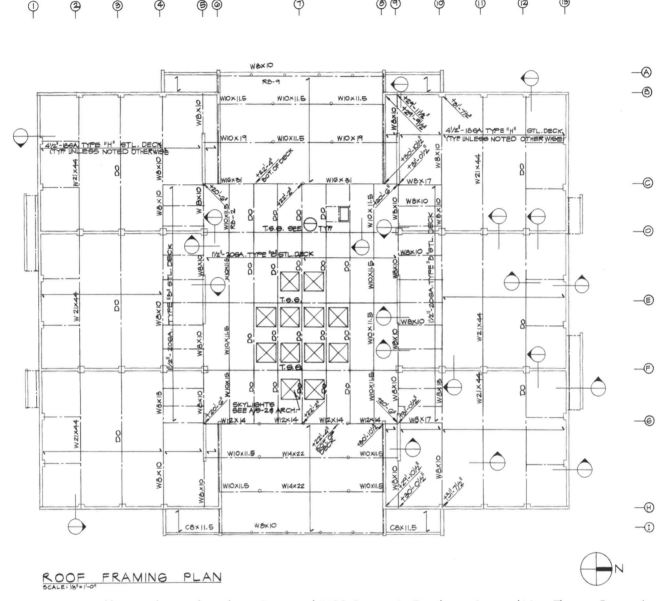

ROOF FRAMING PLAN
SCALE: 1/8" = 1'-0"

Figure 9.85   Roof framing plan: Steel members. (Courtesy of AVCO Community Developers, Inc., and Mann Theatres Corporation of California.)

Conventional Floor Framing Plan

STAGE I (Figure 9.92). Use an early stage of the floor plan that shows all the walls and openings in the structure. Fireplaces, elevators, and stairs should be included and externally referenced in the drawing set so that the framing around them can be included.

STAGE II (Figure 9.93). The various areas to be framed include openings and are identified as zones. An example of the framing that will be employed for openings is shown in Figure 9.94. If not already done, identify any bearing walls with hatching (texturing).

STAGE III (Figure 9.95). Shear walls are drawn at this stage and referenced to a schedule that is shown directly below the framing drawing. Headers, beams, and openings are defined, using a centerline. Critical columns and posts should also be identified.

STAGE IV (Figure 9.96). This stage shows the direction of the floor joist and its duration. A half arrowhead is used to indicate direction, and a full arrowhead indicates the duration. They are connected with a dot.

STAGE V (Figure 9.97). In this stage, information as to size and space is filled in along the direction lines. Headers, beams, and columns are identified, along with the hardware and the connectors used. Referencing and titling complete the drawing.

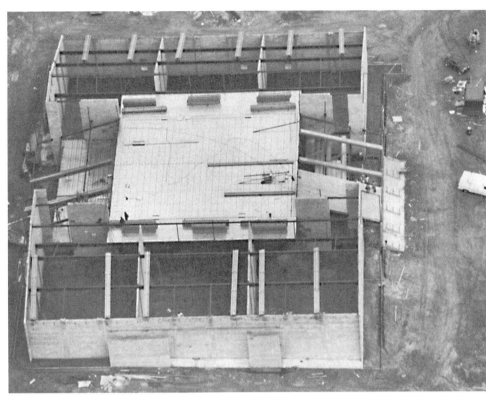

Figure 9.86 Roof framing. (Courtesy of AVCO Community Developers Inc. and Mann Theatres Corporation of California; William Boggs Aerial Photography. Reprinted with permission.)

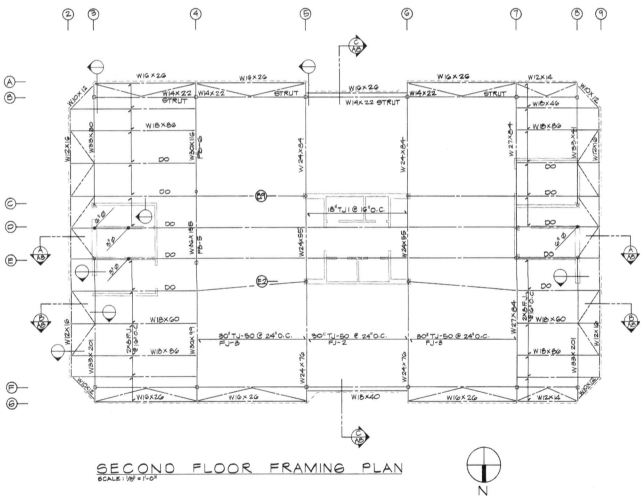

SECOND FLOOR FRAMING PLAN

SCALE: 1/8" = 1'-0"

N

Figure 9.87 Framing plan: Second floor. (Courtesy of Westmount, Inc., Real Estate Development.)

Figure 9.88 Main steel floor beam and column with joist hangers. (Courtesy of Westmount, Inc., Real Estate Development; William Boggs Aerial Photography. Reprinted with permission.)

Figure 9.89 Floor joist trusses attached to hangers and nailed in place. (Courtesy of Westmount, Inc., Real Estate Development; William Boggs Aerial Photography. Reprinted with permission.)

Figure 9.90 Beam and column connection. (Courtesy of Westmount, Inc., Real Estate Development.)

Figure 9.91 Floor beam to main beam assembly. (Courtesy of Westmount, Inc., Real Estate Development.)

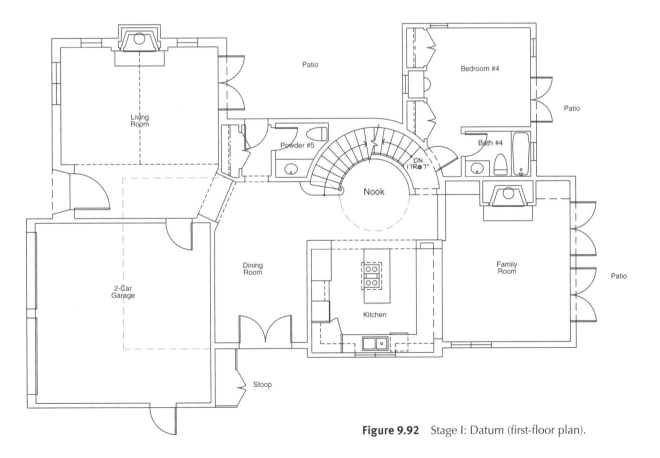

Figure 9.92 Stage I: Datum (first-floor plan).

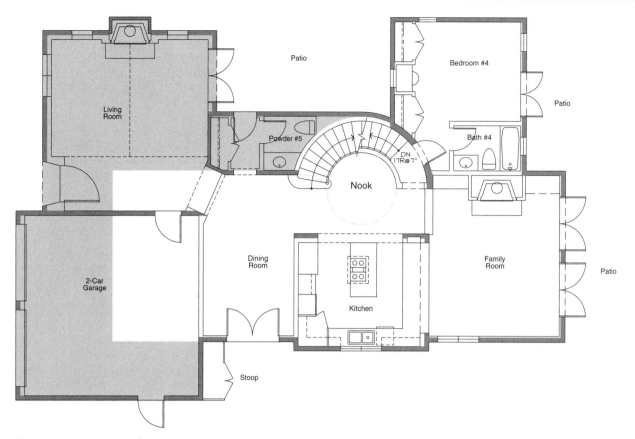

Figure 9.93 Stage II: Selecting zones.

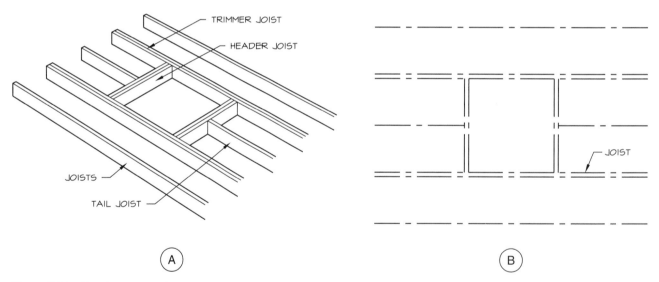

Figure 9.94 Framing an opening.

Floor Framing above Masonry or Concrete

The graphic display of the floor framing on a masonry or concrete wall looks similar to the previously discussed roof framing plan, in that it also uses the same symbols and conventions. An example of a first-floor framing plan over a basement with walls made of con-

crete masonry units (CMU) is shown in Figures 9.98 and 9.99.

Floor Framing Plan with Engineered Lumber

Rather than using the conventional method of framing described throughout this chapter, here we introduce the

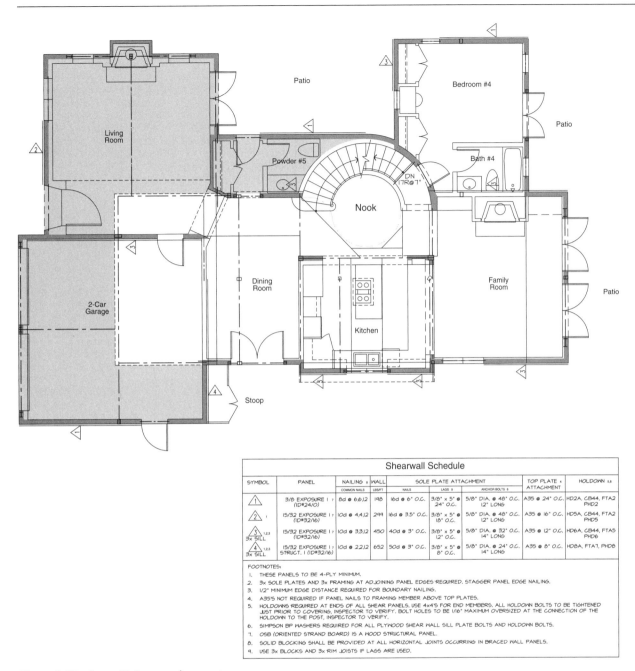

Figure 9.95 Stage III: Structural support.

second floor framing system using engineered lumber. These drawings will become part of the structural set under normal circumstances, and not part of the architectural set of construction documents.

Normally, the first-floor plan is sent to the manufacturer of the engineered lumber. For an example, we will use a plan drawn by Boise Cascade that utilizes the 9½″-high Boise Cascade 400 series. This will be noted as 9–1/2 BCI-400.

The drawing is done by Boise Cascade drafters on a system similar to that of a standard AutoCAD program.

The BC Framer, as it is called, reconciles the space allocated for the thickness of the floor determined by the designer, which is given to the manufacturer along with the floor plan. The manufacturer then takes the information provided by the office and translates it into the framing plan, as shown in Figure 9.100A. A pictorial of the assembly is shown in Figure 9.100B. Samples of the series of pictorial details are shown in Figure 9.100C, and a list of required materials and hardware appears in Figure 9.100D. A separate cost estimate is provided to the office, along with any engineering calculations

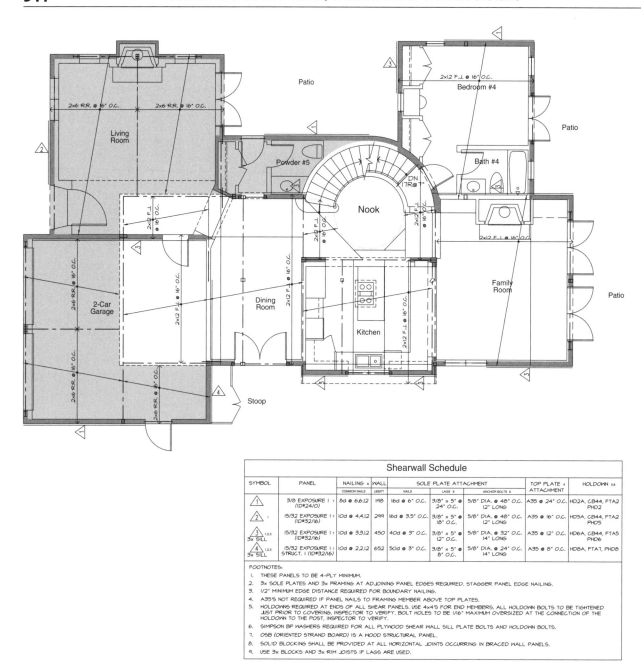

Shearwall Schedule									
SYMBOL	PANEL	NAILING 8	WALL	SOLE PLATE ATTACHMENT			TOP PLATE 4 ATTACHMENT	HOLDOWN 5,6	
		COMMON NAILS	LBS/FT	NAILS	LAGS 9	ANCHOR BOLTS 8			
△1	3/8 EXPOSURE 1 7 (ID#24/0)	8d @ 6,6,12	198	16d @ 6" O.C.	3/8" x 5" @ 24" O.C.	5/8" DIA. @ 48" O.C. 12" LONG	A35 @ 24" O.C.	HD2A, CB44, FTA2 PHD2	
△2 1	15/32 EXPOSURE 1 7 (ID#32/16)	10d @ 4,4,12	299	16d @ 3.5" O.C.	3/8" x 5" @ 18" O.C.	5/8" DIA. @ 48" O.C. 12" LONG	A35 @ 16" O.C.	HD5A, CB44, FTA2 PHD5	
△3 1,2,3 3x SILL	15/32 EXPOSURE 1 7 (ID#32/16)	10d @ 3,3,12	450	40d @ 3" O.C.	3/8" x 5" @ 12" O.C.	5/8" DIA. @ 32" O.C. 14" LONG	A35 @ 12" O.C.	HD6A, CB44, FTA5 PHD6	
△4 1,2,3 3x SILL	15/32 EXPOSURE 1 7 STRUCT. I (ID#32/16)	10d @ 2,2,12	652	50d @ 3" O.C.	3/8" x 5" @ 8" O.C.	5/8" DIA. @ 24" O.C. 14" LONG	A35 @ 8" O.C.	HD8A, FTA7, PHD8	

FOOTNOTES:

1. THESE PANELS TO BE 4-PLY MINIMUM.
2. 3x SOLE PLATES AND 3x FRAMING AT ADJOINING PANEL EDGES REQUIRED. STAGGER PANEL EDGE NAILING.
3. 1/2" MINIMUM EDGE DISTANCE REQUIRED FOR BOUNDARY NAILING.
4. A35'S NOT REQUIRED IF PANEL NAILS TO FRAMING MEMBER ABOVE TOP PLATES.
5. HOLDOWNS REQUIRED AT ENDS OF ALL SHEAR PANELS. USE 4x4'S FOR END MEMBERS. ALL HOLDOWN BOLTS TO BE TIGHTENED JUST PRIOR TO COVERING, INSPECTOR TO VERIFY. BOLT HOLES TO BE 1/16" MAXIMUM OVERSIZED AT THE CONNECTION OF THE HOLDOWN TO THE POST, INSPECTOR TO VERIFY.
6. SIMPSON BP WASHERS REQUIRED FOR ALL PLYWOOD SHEAR WALL SILL PLATE BOLTS AND HOLDOWN BOLTS.
7. OSB (ORIENTED STRAND BOARD) IS A WOOD STRUCTURAL PANEL.
8. SOLID BLOCKING SHALL BE PROVIDED AT ALL HORIZONTAL JOINTS OCCURRING IN BRACED WALL PANELS.
9. USE 3x BLOCKS AND 3x RIM JOISTS IF LAGS ARE USED.

Figure 9.96 Stage IV: Direction of joist and duration.

required by the governing department of building and safety.

The service is total and makes the preparation of framing plans a delight for the architectural office. However, the senior drafters must be able not only to read the framing plans, but also to ensure their proper integration with the rest of the drawings. The drafters must also initially consider the space that must be provided for any overlooked items: duct space for heating and air-conditioning units; space for venting appliances such as ranges and water heaters; space for electronic appliances and access for electrical lines from the fixtures to the computers and for the drainpipes that run from the roof through the floors and walls. All of these matters should be resolved before you submit the plans for framing drawings. Such thoroughness will also provide the workers in the field with a clear picture of potential problems that can be averted. This is further accomplished with comprehensive details, partial sections, and full sections.

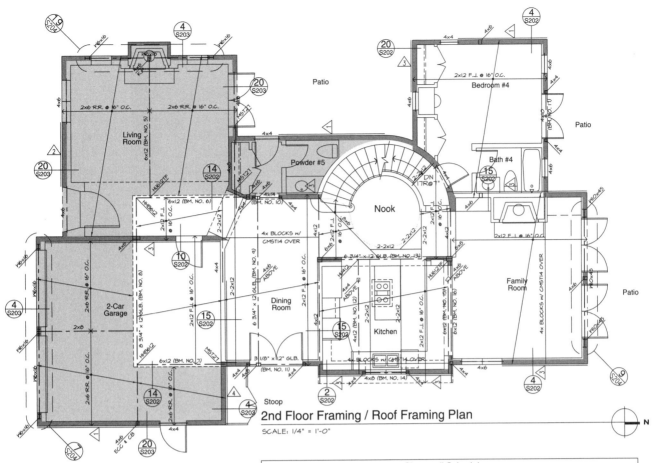

2nd Floor Framing / Roof Framing Plan

SCALE: 1/4" = 1'-0"

N

Figure 9.97 Stage V: Complete floor framing plan. (Courtesy of James Orland, CE.)

Shearwall Schedule

SYMBOL	PANEL	NAILING 8		WALL	SOLE PLATE ATTACHMENT			TOP PLATE 4 ATTACHMENT	HOLDOWN 5,8
		COMMON NAILS	LBS/FT	NAILS	LAGS 9	ANCHOR BOLTS 6		
△1	3/8 EXPOSURE 1 (ID#24/0)	8d @ 6,6,12	198	16d @ 6" O.C.	3/8" x 5" @ 24" O.C.	5/8" DIA. @ 48" O.C. 12" LONG	A35 @ 24" O.C.	HD2A, CB44, FTA2 PHD2
△2 1	15/32 EXPOSURE 1 (ID#32/16)	10d @ 4,4,12	299	16d @ 3.5" O.C.	3/8" x 5" @ 18" O.C.	5/8" DIA. @ 48" O.C. 12" LONG	A35 @ 16" O.C.	HD5A, CB44, FTA2 PHD5
△3 1,2,3 3x SILL	15/32 EXPOSURE 1 (ID#32/16)	10d @ 3,3,12	450	40d @ 3" O.C.	3/8" x 5" @ 12" O.C.	5/8" DIA. @ 32" O.C. 14" LONG	A35 @ 12" O.C.	HD6A, CB44, FTA5 PHD6
△4 1,2,3 3x SILL	15/32 EXPOSURE 1 STRUCT. 1 (ID#32/16)	10d @ 2,2,12	652	50d @ 3" O.C.	3/8" x 5" @ 8" O.C.	5/8" DIA. @ 24" O.C. 14" LONG	A35 @ 8" O.C.	HD8A, FTA7, PHD8

FOOTNOTES:
1. THESE PANELS TO BE 4-PLY MINIMUM.
2. 3x SOLE PLATES AND 3x FRAMING AT ADJOINING PANEL EDGES REQUIRED. STAGGER PANEL EDGE NAILING.
3. 1/2" MINIMUM EDGE DISTANCE REQUIRED FOR BOUNDARY NAILING.
4. A35'S NOT REQUIRED IF PANEL NAILS TO FRAMING MEMBER ABOVE TOP PLATES.
5. HOLDOWNS REQUIRED AT ENDS OF ALL SHEAR PANELS. USE 4x4'S FOR END MEMBERS. ALL HOLDOWN BOLTS TO BE TIGHTENED JUST PRIOR TO COVERING, INSPECTOR TO VERIFY. BOLT HOLES TO BE 1/16" MAXIMUM OVERSIZED AT THE CONNECTION OF THE HOLDOWN TO THE POST, INSPECTOR TO VERIFY.
6. SIMPSON BP WASHERS REQUIRED FOR ALL PLYWOOD SHEAR WALL SILL PLATE BOLTS AND HOLDOWN BOLTS.
7. OSB (ORIENTED STRAND BOARD) IS A WOOD STRUCTURAL PANEL.
8. SOLID BLOCKING SHALL BE PROVIDED AT ALL HORIZONTAL JOINTS OCCURRING IN BRACED WALL PANELS.
9. USE 3x BLOCKS AND 3x RIM JOISTS IF LAGS ARE USED.

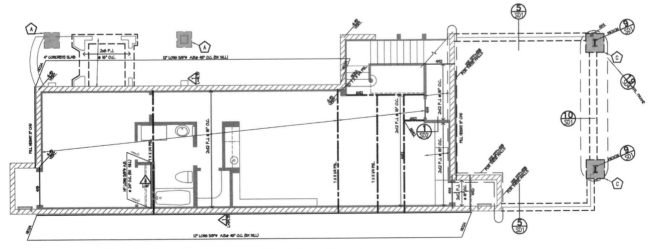

Figure 9.98 First-floor framing plan. (Courtesy of Mr. & Mrs. Givens.)

Figure 9.99   First-floor framing.

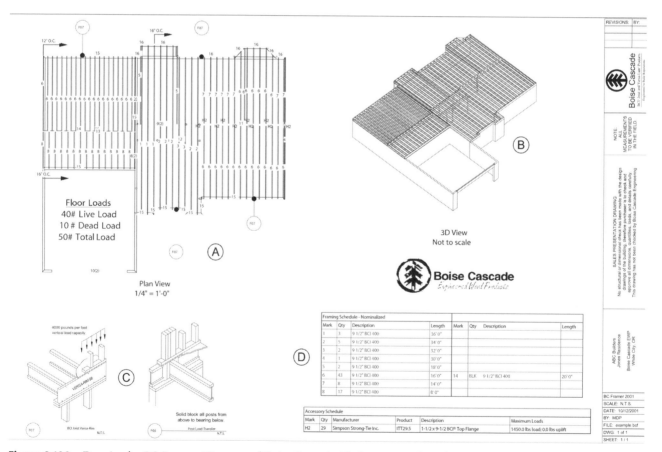

Figure 9.100   Drawing by BC Framer. (Courtesy of Boise Cascade, Timber & Wood Products Division.)

10

BUILDING SECTIONS

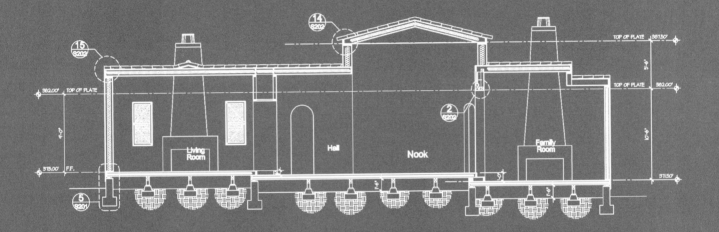

■ BUILDING SECTIONS DEFINED

A **building section** cuts a vertical slice through a structure or a part of a structure. For the computer, it is a cut along the *z–x* axis or the *z–y* axis. It is also an integral part of the dimensional reference system described earlier in this book. Figure 10.1 shows a vertical slice cut through a wood-framed, two-story residence. To further examine the various roof, floor, and wall conditions found at the location of that particular slice, we can enlarge the elements and then call it a **detail**, as seen in Figure 10.2.

■ DRAWING A BUILDING SECTION

To draw a building section, make a cross-section giving relevant architectural and structural information. When given the task of drawing a building section, you first need to gather basic information, including:

1. Type of foundation
2. Floor system
3. Exterior and interior wall construction
4. Beam and column sizes and their material
5. Plate or wall heights
6. Floor elevations
7. Floor members, size, and spacing
8. Floor sheathing, material, and size
9. Ceiling members, size, and spacing
10. Roof pitch
11. Roof sheathing, material, and size
12. Insulation requirements
13. Finished roof material
14. Ceiling heights

Although it may not be possible to gather all of this data early in the design stage, it is possible to construct the parts that are known and add data as the information comes in. When you have gathered this information, select a suitable architectural scale. Usually, the scale ranges from $\frac{1}{8}'' = 1'\text{-}0''$ to $\frac{1}{4}'' = 1'\text{-}0''$. The scale depends on the size and complexity of the project and should be chosen to maintain clarity. Most commercial jobs use $\frac{1}{8}''$, and most residential jobs use $\frac{1}{4}''$.

As you draw the building section, visualize the erection sequence for the structure and the construction techniques for the material(s) being used. See Figure 10.3.

The first step is to show the concrete floor and foundation members at that particular location. Although foundation details should be drawn accurately, they need not be dimensioned or elaborated upon; all the necessary information will be called out in the larger-scale drawings of the individual foundation details.

Next, establish a **plate height**. (A *plate* is a horizontal timber that joins the tops of studs.) Here the plate height is noted, measuring from the top of the concrete floor to the top of the two plates (2–2 × 6 continuous) of the wood stud wall. This height also establishes the height to the bottom of the floor joist for the second-floor level. Once the floor joists are drawn in at the proper scale, repeat the same procedure to establish the wall height that will support the ceiling and roof framing members.

As indicated, the roof pitch for this particular project is a ratio of 3 to 12; the roof rises 3 inches for each 12 inches of horizontal measurement (the roof rises 3 feet, for every 12 feet). You can draw this slope or angle with an architectural scale, or you can convert the ratio to an angle degree. Draw the roof at the other side of the building in the same way, with the intersection of the two roof planes establishing the ridge location. Mission clay tile was chosen for the finished roof material for this project.

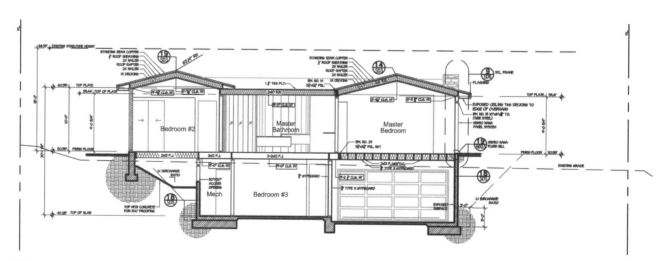

Figure 10.1 Vertical slice through a building. (Courtesy of the Bailey Residence.)

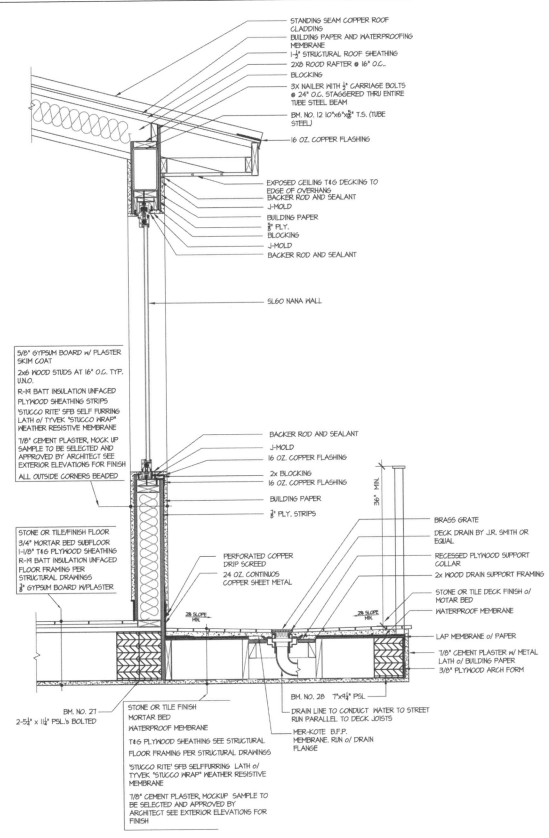

STANDING SEAM COPPER ROOF CLADDING
BUILDING PAPER AND WATERPROOFING MEMBRANE
1-1/2" STRUCTURAL ROOF SHEATHING
2X8 ROOD RAFTER @ 16" O.C..
BLOCKING
3X NAILER WITH 1/2" CARRIAGE BOLTS @ 24" O.C. STAGGERED THRU ENTIRE TUBE STEEL BEAM
BM. NO. 12 10"x6"x3/8" T.S. (TUBE STEEL)
16 OZ. COPPER FLASHING

EXPOSED CEILING T&G DECKING TO EDGE OF OVERHANG
BACKER ROD AND SEALANT
J-MOLD
BUILDING PAPER
3/8" PLY.
BLOCKING
J-MOLD
BACKER ROD AND SEALANT

SL60 NANA WALL

5/8" GYPSUM BOARD W/ PLASTER SKIM COAT
2x6 WOOD STUDS AT 16" O.C. TYP. U.N.O.
R-19 BATT INSULATION UNFACED PLYWOOD SHEATHING STRIPS
'STUCCO RITE' SFB SELF FURRING LATH O/ TYVEK "STUCCO WRAP" WEATHER RESISTIVE MEMBRANE
7/8" CEMENT PLASTER, MOCK UP SAMPLE TO BE SELECTED AND APPROVED BY ARCHITECT SEE EXTERIOR ELEVATIONS FOR FINISH
ALL OUTSIDE CORNERS BEADED

BACKER ROD AND SEALANT
J-MOLD
16 OZ. COPPER FLASHING
2x BLOCKING
16 OZ. COPPER FLASHING
BUILDING PAPER
3/8" PLY. STRIPS

36" MIN.

BRASS GRATE
DECK DRAIN BY J.R. SMITH OR EQUAL
RECESSED PLYWOOD SUPPORT COLLAR
2x WOOD DRAIN SUPPORT FRAMING
STONE OR TILE DECK FINISH O/ MOTAR BED
WATERPROOF MEMBRANE
LAP MEMBRANE O/ PAPER
7/8" CEMENT PLASTER W/ METAL LATH O/ BUILDING PAPER
3/8" PLYWOOD ARCH FORM

STONE OR TILE/FINISH FLOOR
3/4" MORTAR BED SUBFLOOR
1-1/8" T&G PLYWOOD SHEATHING
R-19 BATT INSULATION UNFACED FLOOR FRAMING PER STRUCTURAL DRAWINGS
3/8" GYPSUM BOARD W/PLASTER

PERFORATED COPPER DRIP SCREED
24 OZ. CONTINUOS COPPER SHEET METAL

2% SLOPE MIN.

2% SLOPE MIN.

BM. NO. 27
2-5 3/4" x 11 1/4" PSL.'s BOLTED

STONE OR TILE FINISH
MORTAR BED
WATERPROOF MEMBRANE
T&G PLYWOOD SHEATHING SEE STRUCTURAL
FLOOR FRAMING PER STRUCTURAL DRAWINGS
'STUCCO RITE' SFB SELFFURRING LATH O/ TYVEK "STUCCO WRAP" WEATHER RESISTIVE MEMBRANE
7/8" CEMENT PLASTER, MOCKUP SAMPLE TO BE SELECTED AND APPROVED BY ARCHITECT SEE EXTERIOR ELEVATIONS FOR FINISH

BM. NO. 28   7"x9 1/4" PSL

DRAIN LINE TO CONDUCT WATER TO STREET RUN PARALLEL TO DECK JOISTS

MER-KOTE B.F.P. MEMBRANE. RUN O/ DRAIN FLANGE

Wall Section thru Master Bedroom
SCALE: 1"=1'-0"

Figure 10.2   Portion of a section. (Courtesy of the Bailey Residence.)

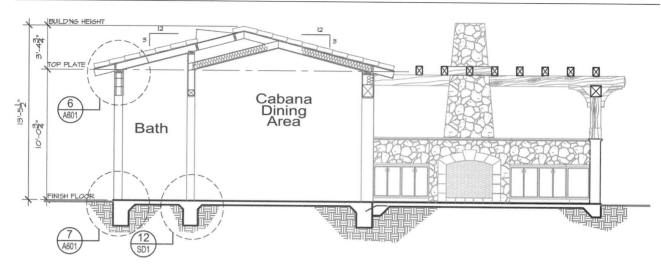

Figure 10.3 Building section. (Courtesy of Mr. & Mrs. Thompson.)

When you have drawn in all the remaining components, such as stairs and floor framing elevation changes, note all the members, roof pitch, material information, and dimensions. See Figure 10.4.

Figure 10.5 shows various reference symbols. These symbols refer to an enlarged drawing of those particular assemblies. To demonstrate the importance of providing enlarged details, Figure 10.5 shows a building section of a wood-framed structure with critical bolted connections. A reference symbol (the number 1 over the number 8, in a reference bubble) is located at the roof framing and wall connection. This connection is made clear with an enlarged detail, showing the exact location and size of bolts needed to satisfy the engineering requirements for that assembly. See Figure 10.6.

Number and Place of Sections

Draw as many building sections as you need to convey the necessary information, with the greatest possible clarity, to the contractors building the structure.

Building sections are used to investigate various conditions that prevail in a structure. These sections can point out flaws in the building's structural integrity, and this information can lead to modifications in the initial design.

The number of building sections required varies according to the structural complexity of the particular building. For a simple rectangular building, you may need only two building sections to clearly provide all the required information. However, for a building with a more complex shape, you may require five or more sections to provide all the structural and architectural information. See Figure 10.7.

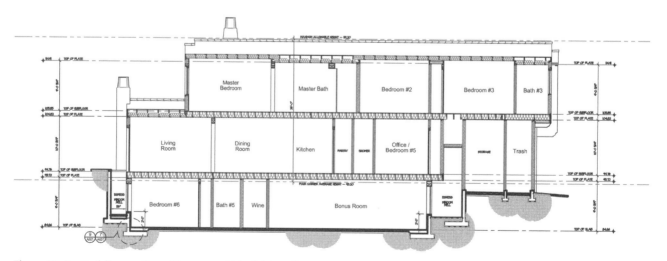

Figure 10.4 Building section. (Courtesy of Mr. & Mrs. Givens.)

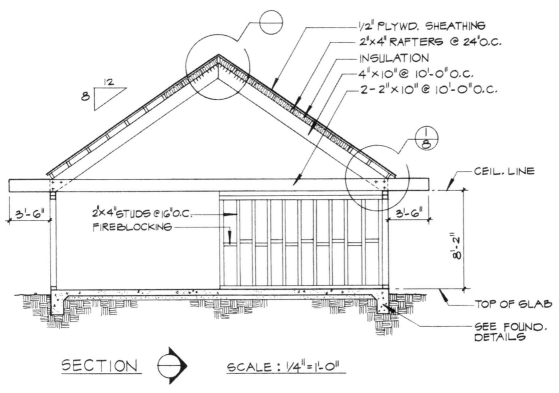

Figure 10.5 Structural section.

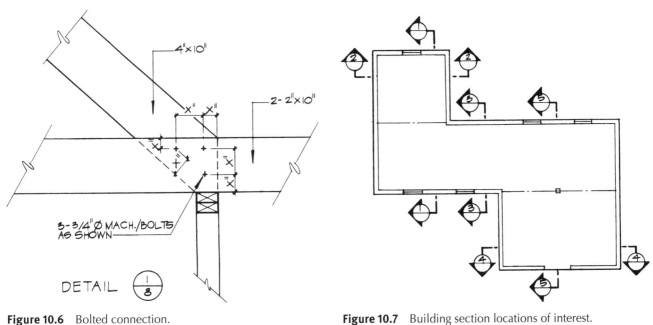

Figure 10.6 Bolted connection.

Figure 10.7 Building section locations of interest.

■ TYPES OF BUILDING SECTIONS

Because the design and complexity of buildings vary, types of sections also vary. The type of section that will best demonstrate the required data is the determining factor in choosing the required types of sections.

Wall Sections

Simple structural conditions may only require wall sections to convey the necessary building information. Structural sections for a small industrial building, for example, might use wall sections.

In most cases, wall sections can be drawn at larger scales, such as ½" = 1'-0". These larger-scale drawings allow you to clearly elaborate building connections and call-outs without having to draw separate enlarged details.

Figures 10.8, 10.9, 10.10, and 10.11, which are for an industrial building, also show how wall sections are incorporated into a set of construction documents. Figure 10.8 shows the floor plan with two main exterior and one interior bearing wall conditions. These wall conditions are referenced to wall sections and are shown in Figures 10.9, 10.10, and 10.11.

To draw a wall section, first select a scale that clearly shows the wall and foundation assembly details, as well as adjacent structural members and components. Then, using wall section 1, Figure 10.9, as an example, draw and dimension the footing for the masonry wall. Because you are drawing at a large scale, you can note all the footing information directly on the wall section, thereby making separate foundation details unnecessary. Next, draw the masonry wall using 8 × 8 × 16 concrete block as the wall material. Because a modular unit is being used for the wall construction, a wall height is established that satisfies the 8" concrete-block increments. Draw the roof-to-wall assembly at the desired height above the concrete floor, with the various framing connections and members needed to satisfy the structural requirements. After you finish the drawing, add notes for all members, steel reinforcing, bolts, and so forth. Other wall sections, as shown in Figures 10.10 and 10.11, are drawn and noted similarly. Note that while Figure 10.11 is similar to Figure 10.9, different roof framing conditions exist.

In short, large-scale wall sections allow the structural components and call-outs to be clearly drawn and usually make larger-scale details, such as framing connections and foundation details, unnecessary.

Full Sections

For projects with complex structural conditions, you should draw an entire section. This gives you a better idea of the structural conditions in that portion of the building, which can then be analyzed, engineered, and clearly detailed.

Figure 10.12 shows a building section through a residence that has complex framing. Here you can clearly understand the need for a full section to see the existing conditions. When doing a full section, you should draw this type of section in a smaller architectural scale, ¼" = 1'-0". Again, when you use a smaller scale for drawing sections, you must provide enlarged details of all relevant connections. The circled and referenced conditions in Figure 10.12, for example, will be detailed at a large scale.

Whether in the areas of schematic design or design development, a design section can be created to aid in the design process. A design section utilizes no structural detail; in fact, it is a drawing that describes volume within a building and graphically holds space for the future structure. See Figures 10.13 and 10.14.

Notice the level of interior detail in Figures 10.15 and 10.16. The option of providing interior detail within the section allows the client to better understand the relationship of the elements inside the room. In this regard, a design section also serves another important purpose: It is one of the few drawings that explain the volume of the rooms. This is also helpful to the consultants, such as mechanical, electrical, and structural engineers. With this kind of section, the mechanical engineers can best determine the space allotted for them to work in, the electrical engineers can determine which types of fixtures will best light the room, and structural engineers can shape the structure to achieve the shape concept designed by the architect.

Partial Sections

Many projects have only isolated areas that are structurally complex. These areas are drawn in the same way as a cross-section, but they stop when the area of concern has been clearly drawn. This results in a partial section of a structural portion.

In addition to the structural aspect of sections, the designed shape of the building is exposed to better demonstrate the 3-D aspect of the space. The section is an aid in realizing the space, for both the builder and the client.

The partial section shown in Figure 10.17 illustrates the structural complexities existing in that portion. Additional detailing is required to make other assemblies clear.

One of these assemblies, for example, may require a partial framing elevation to show a specific roof framing

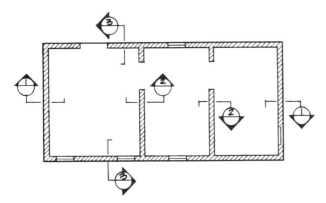

Figure 10.8 Floor plan of an industrial building.

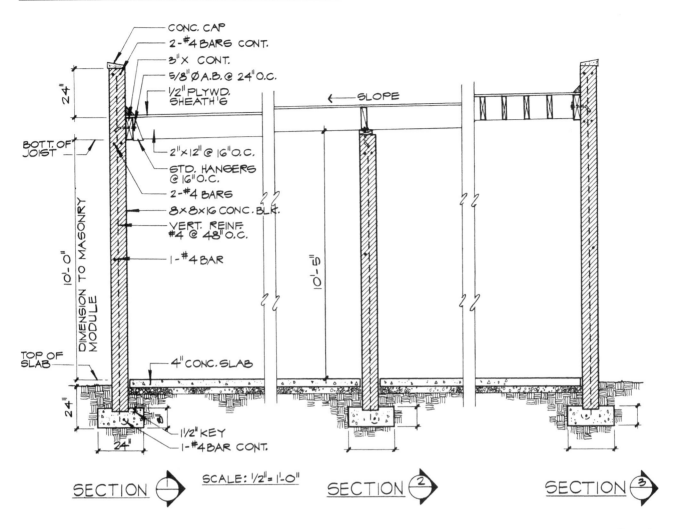

Figure 10.9 Exterior wall section. **Figure 10.10** Interior wall section. **Figure 10.11** Exterior wall section.

condition. This condition may be referenced by the use of two circles—each with direction arrows, reference letters, and numbers—attached to a broken line. Figure 10.18 shows this partial framing elevation, as referenced on Figure 10.17.

Steel Sections

For buildings built mainly with steel members, use elevations to establish column and beam heights. This approach coincides with the procedures and methods for the shop drawings provided by the steel fabricator.

Figure 10.19 shows a structural section through a steel-framed building. In contrast to sections for wood-framed buildings, where vertical dimensions are used to establish plate heights, this type of section may establish column and beam heights using the top of the concrete

slab as a beginning point. Each steel column in this section has an assigned number because the columns are identified by the use of an axial reference matrix on the framing plan, shown in Figure 10.20.

Building Sections Checklist
1. Sections that clearly depict the structural conditions existing in the building
2. Sections referenced on plans and elevations
3. Dimensioning for the following (where applicable):
   a. Floor to top plate
   b. Floor to floor
   c. Floor to ceiling
   d. Floor to top of wall
   e. Floor to top of column or beam
   f. Cantilevers, overhangs, offsets, etc.
   g. Foundation details

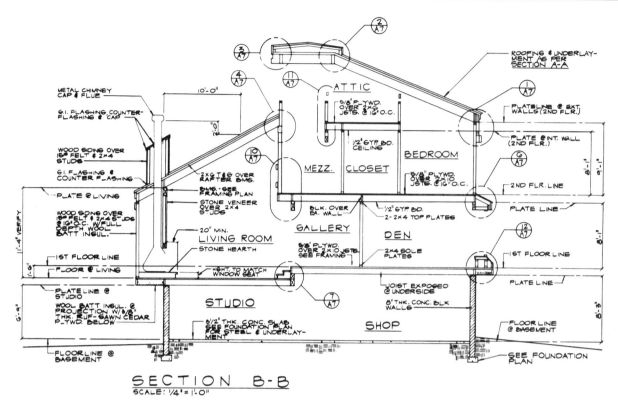

Figure 10.12 Full section. (Courtesy of Steve L. Martin.)

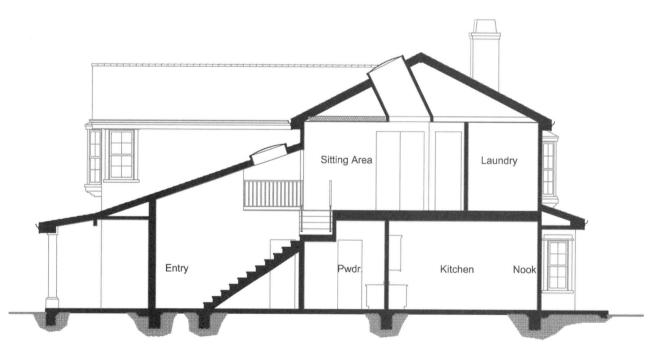

Figure 10.13 Building design section.

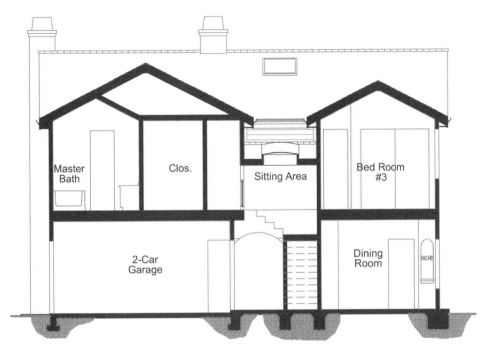

Figure 10.14 Building design section.

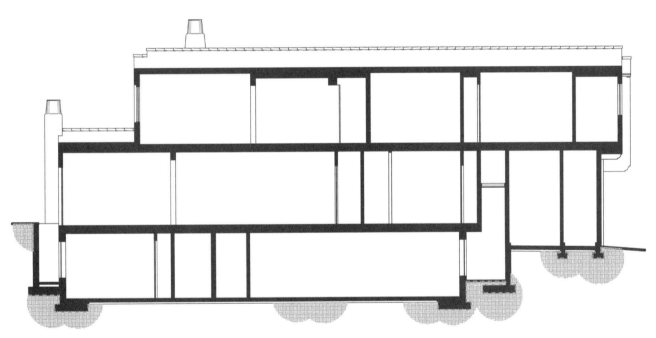

Figure 10.15 Building design section.

4. Elevations for top of floor, top of columns and beams
5. Call-out information for all members, such as:
  a. Size, material, and shape of member
  b. Spacing of members
6. Call-out information for all assemblies, including fire assembly rating (if enlarged details are not provided)
7. Column and beam matrix identification, if incorporated in the structural plan
8. Call-out for subfloor, insulation location and size, and sheathing assembly
9. Roof pitches and indication of all slopes
10. Reference symbols for all details and assemblies that are enlarged for clarity

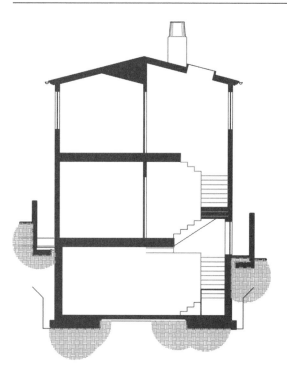

Figure 10.16 Building design section.

11. Designation of material for protection of finish for roof, ceiling, wall, and structural members
12. Structural notes applicable to each particular section, such as:
    a. Nailing schedules
    b. Splice dimensions
    c. Structural notes
13. Structural sections corresponding accurately to foundation, floor, and framing plans
14. Scale and title of drawing section

■ DRAFTING A BUILDING SECTION

After deciding where a section is to be taken so as to reveal the greatest amount of information, a grid pattern is drafted. The horizontal lines of the grid represent the floor line and the plate line (at the top of the two top plates). All of the vertical lines represent the walls of the structure or column locations. See Figure 10.21.

A scale of ¼" = 1'-0" is ideal, but because of the size of the structure or the limits of the sheet, a scale of ⅛" = 1' -0" might be used.

Before you decide on a smaller scale, explore the possibility of removing redundant portions of the building by virtue of break lines. See Figure 10.9. If the building is symmetrical, a partial section, as shown in Figure 10.17, may suffice.

From Floor Plan to Building Section

If the building section is to be drawn at the same scale as the floor plan, the drafter need only transfer measurements by projecting or extending lines down from the floor plan to section. If the building section is drafted at twice the size of the floor plan, you can simply transfer the measurements and double the scale.

With the computer, you do not have a problem with scale, because the floor plan and the building section, along with the entire set of construction documents, are drawn at full scale in model space. Only when you import the drawings into paper space do you need to add a scaling factor.

If the floor plan was drawn in paper space at a scale of ¼" = 1'-0" rather than at full scale in model space, you can quickly change the scaling factor, using the computer, from the ¼" plan to another scale.

Pitch

If a pitch (an angle) is involved and it is constant, an adjustable triangle is handy. Another option is to actually measure the pitch. If you have a template, look for a pitch scale printed on its side. If you are in the market for a plan template, check the various brands carefully, because there are templates that will measure pitch; have markings for typical heights of equipment from the floor; and even plot spacing, such as for 4" and 6" tile, 16" spacing for stud and joist position, and door swings, among other items.

If you understand the process of drafting a building section, you might develop a shortcut method. For example, if you have access to a plain-paper copier that enlarges and reduces, it would be a simple matter to reproduce an eave detail to the proper scale. Then, with the same pitch on a sheet, place it under the building section and trace.

■ DRAFTING A BUILDING SECTION OF A RESIDENCE

The building section is second only to the floor plan in importance, because it reveals how the building is assembled, describes the collective parts of the building, and demonstrates the volume of each specific building area. The building section allows the discovery of essential details. In many instances, for example, the building section reveals potential problems in the intersection of walls, floors, stairs, ceilings, and roof.

In Revit or a three-dimensional model, the building section can be sliced or sectioned or flattened. The various construction members, such as the studs and rafters,

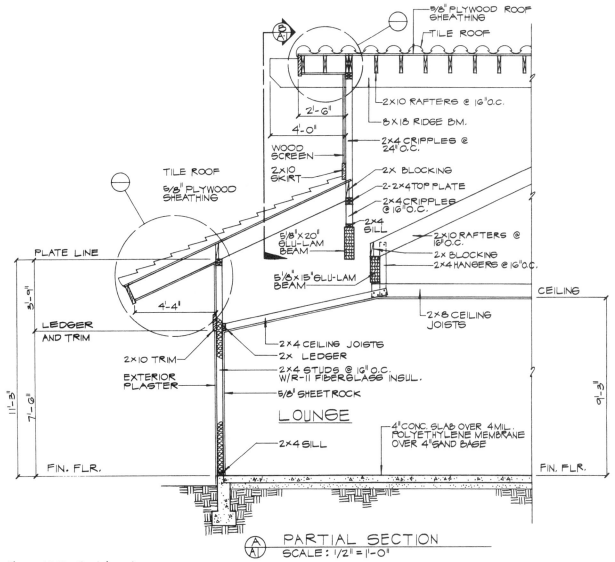

Figure 10.17 Partial section.

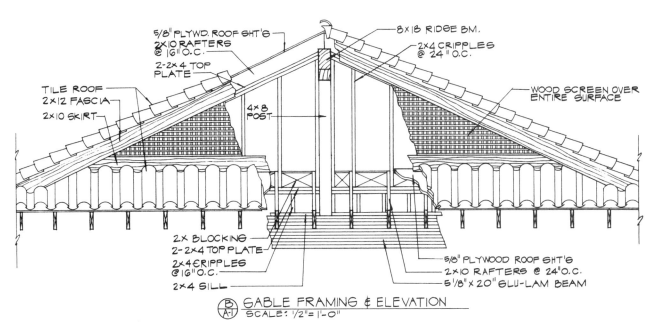

Figure 10.18 Framing elevation.

357

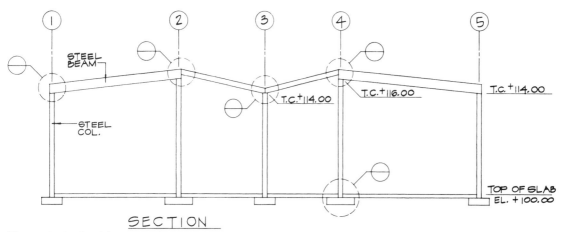

Figure 10.19 Steel frame section.

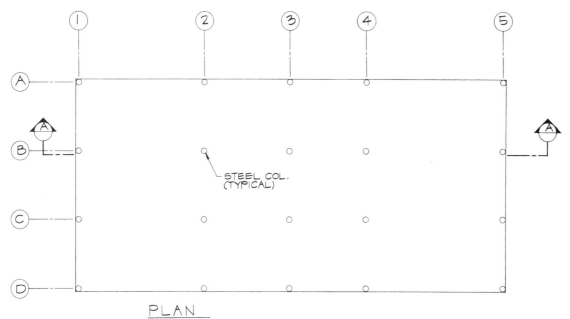

Figure 10.20 Column matrix.

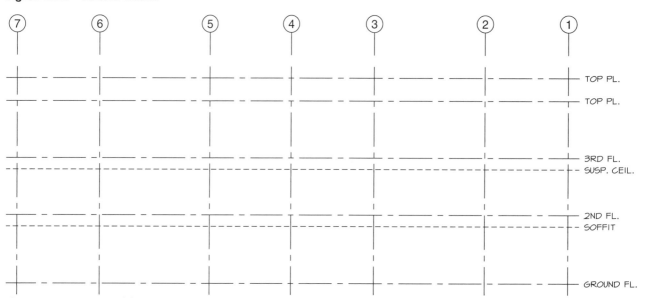

Figure 10.21 Layout of the grid pattern.

can then be rotated in a three-dimensional model to reveal and explain the construction features that are not readily obvious in a two-dimensional drawing.

STAGE I (Figure 10.22). If a flattened 3-D section is available, use this as the datum for future stages. All wall locations, plate heights, and level changes must be verified and corrected at this stage. If a flattened model is not available, the first stage of a 2-D drawing will establish the base or datum. Start by establishing the grade and its relationship with the floor line. Using this floor line as the main baseline, establish and measure the plate lines and floor lines of subsequent floors. In larger buildings, measurement may be in decimals. This is particularly true in steel structures, where the tips of the columns and tops of the floor girders are critical during installation.

STAGE II (Figure 10.23). The outline of the structure is now positioned, including the roof. On 3-D drawings, the walls are already positioned, but in a 2-D drawing the walls must be positioned by aligning the datum lines with a partial floor plan where the cut occurs (see Figure 10.24). In the schematic stage of design, a section may look very similar to the one in Figure 10.23.

STAGE III (Figure 10.25). The thicknesses or widths of the foundation, walls, ceiling, and roof are drawn at this stage. Everything is drawn to net or actual size, not nominal size, to produce an accurate assembly drawing. Previously drafted details showing similar shapes and parts can be imported and used. This stage, which is actually a refinement of the Stage II drawing, constitutes a design development stage of a section.

STAGE IV (Figure 10.26). This is said to be the most enjoyable stage, because the building begins to take on character with the addition of material designations and the array of the end views of ceiling joists, floor joists, and rafters. Concrete takes on its own character adjacent to grade (soil).

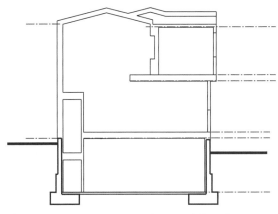

Figure 10.23 Stage II: Outlining of foundation, walls, and roof.

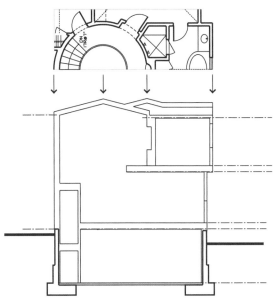

Figure 10.24 Stage II: Aligning datum with floor plan.

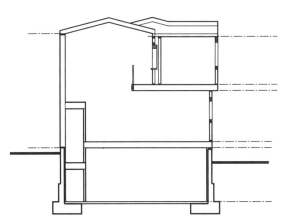

Figure 10.25 Stage III: Sizing members and outlining configuration.

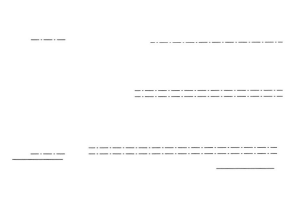

Figure 10.22 Stage I: Establishing datum.

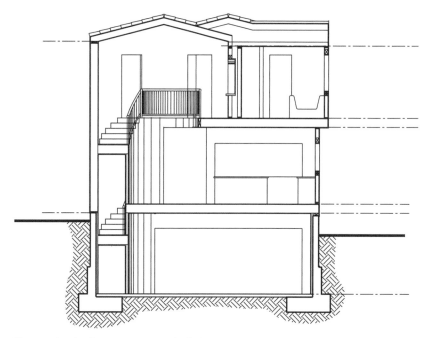

Figure 10.26 Stage IV: Materials designation, array joists.

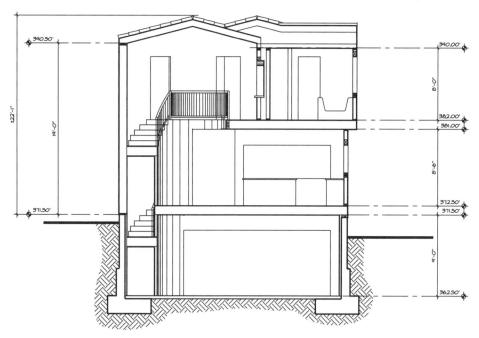

Figure 10.27 Stage V: Dimensioning.

STAGE V (Figure 10.27). Stage V is the most critical to the accuracy of the project. All vertical dimensions are included at this stage. The most critical aspects are the dimensions for the floor to plate and definition of the neutral zones on the project. Horizontal dimensions should not appear in this stage, but rather on the floor plan, with the exception of describing the shape of a soffit or any other feature not seen in the floor plan. Note the call-out of elevation heights such as the top of subfloor 372.50′ (see Figure 10.27).

STAGE VI (Figure 10.28). All notes and referencing are included in this stage. Notes should be generic if the

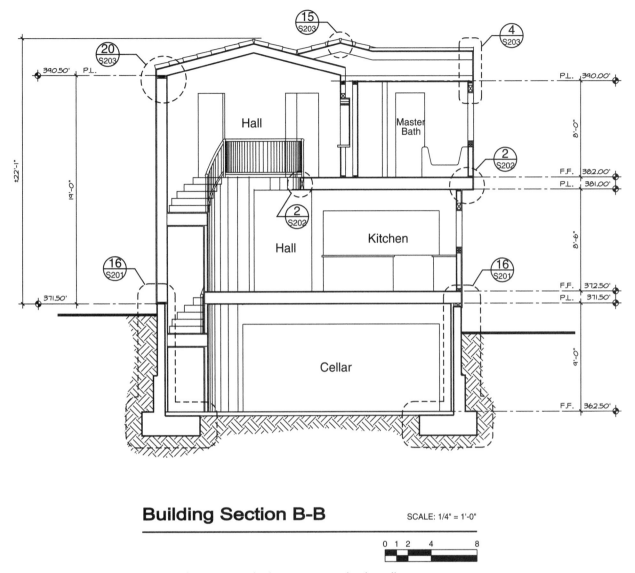

Building Section B-B

SCALE: 1/4" = 1'-0"

0 1 2   4   8

Figure 10.28 Stage VI: Noting, referencing, and titles. (Courtesy of Mike Adli.)

specific materials are described in the specifications. Titles must be given to all of the parts, including the names of rooms through which the section cut occurs. Reference bubbles are positioned and are referred to footing details, eave details, stair details, and so on. Remember, the *title* is a name given to this building section. If it is a full section, as in our example, two letters are used—for example, A-A, B-B, C-C. The first letter indicates the beginning of the section, and the second letter indicates the end of the cut.

The following two examples are completed sections that started as the design sections seen in Figures 10.13 though 10.16. Figures 10.29 and 10.30 are the completed sheets as presented to the client and to the Department of Building and Safety.

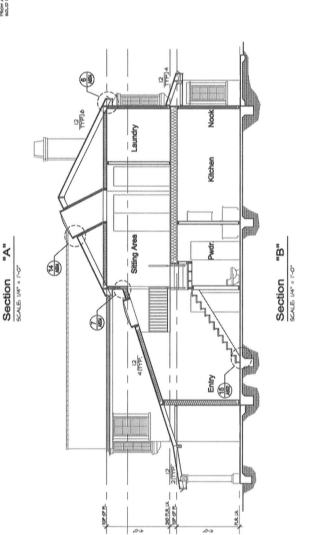

Figure 10.29 Completed sheet of building sections. (Courtesy of John Katnik.)

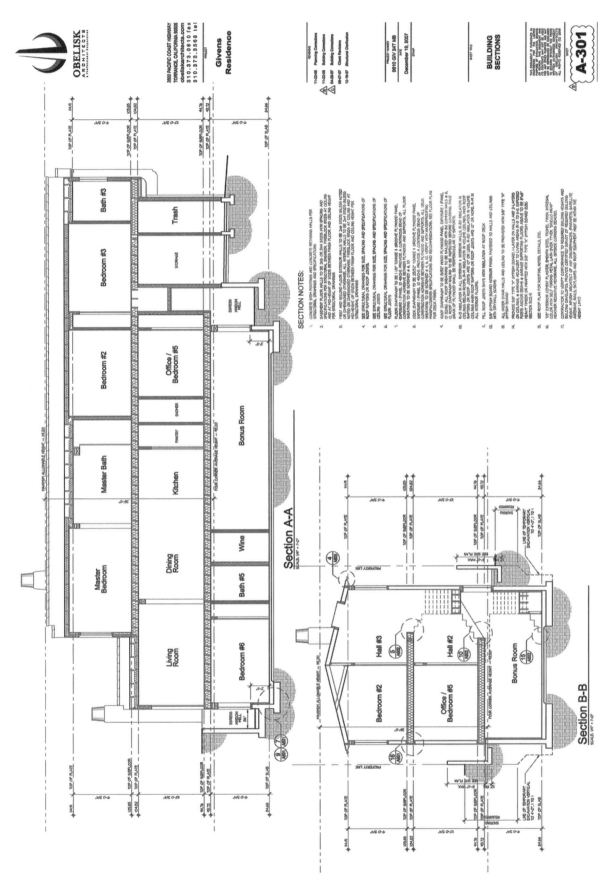

Figure 10.30 Completed sheet of building sections. (Courtesy of Mr. & Mrs. Givens.)

11

EXTERIOR AND INTERIOR ELEVATIONS

■ INTRODUCTION TO EXTERIOR ELEVATIONS

Purpose of Exterior Elevations

The main purpose of exterior elevations is to describe the outer skin, and often the subskin, of the structure and show vertical dimensions that do not appear on any other drawing. Its datum is the floor-to-floor measurements and/or floor-to-plate measurements.

Throughout this chapter, you will find examples of drawings done to meet this purpose. Hand drawing and computer applications will be described, as well as the impact BIM and Revit have had on the drawing of exterior elevations.

Here is a simple list of what you should do—and what drawing users will expect to find—on an exterior elevation of a simple residence:

1. Describe exterior materials found on the structure.
2. Provide a location for horizontal and vertical dimensions not found elsewhere.
3. Show, by using hidden lines, structural members found inside the walls. (Diagonal bracing is a good example of such hidden members.)
4. Show the relationship of elements, such as the height of the chimney in relationship to the roof of the structure.
5. Incorporate reference bubbles for building, window, and door sections.
6. Show any exterior design elements that cannot be shown elsewhere.
7. Show stepped footings, if there are any.
8. Describe building finishes and colors.

Basic Approach

In mechanical or engineering drafting, the elevations are described as the front, side, and rear. In architecture, exterior elevations are called *North, South, East,* and *West.* See Figure 11.1. Figure 11.2 shows how we arrive at the names for exterior elevations.

Orientation

The North, South, East, and West elevations may not be true directions (e.g., not true north or true east). They may have been taken from an "orientation north," or, as it has been called in other regions, **plan North**, which may not be parallel to true north. When the boundaries of a structure are not parallel with true north, an orientation north is established, and used from then on to describe the various elevations. See Figure 11.3.

These terms, then, refer to the direction the structure is facing. In other words, if an elevation is drawn of the

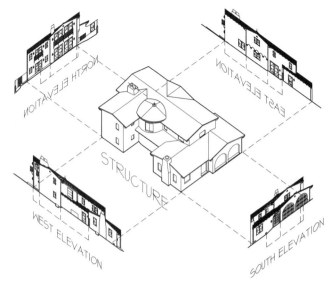

Figure 11.1 Multiview drawing of a structure.

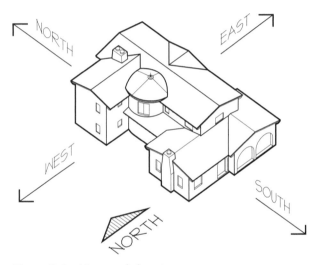

Figure 11.2 Names of elevations.

face of a structure that is facing south, the elevation is called the *South elevation;* the face of the structure that is facing west is called the *West elevation,* and so on. Remember, the title refers to the direction the structure is facing, *not* to the direction in which you are looking at it.

Finally, because of the size of the exterior elevations, they are rarely drawn next to the plan view as in mechanical drafting. See Figure 11.4.

Method 1: Direct Projection

You can draft exterior elevations by directly projecting sizes from the plan views or sections. Figure 11.5 shows

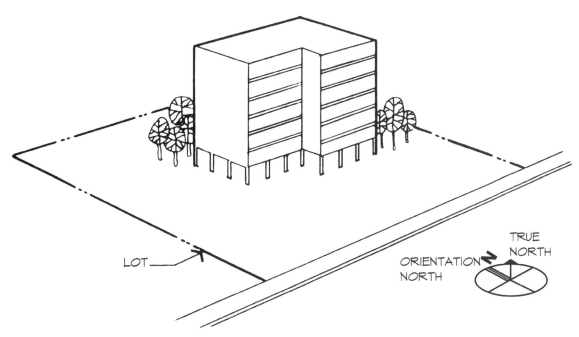

Figure 11.3 Use of orientation north.

Figure 11.4 Elevation arrangement. (Courtesy of Mike Adli.)

how elevations can be directly projected from a plan view (a roof plan, in this case). Figure 11.6 shows how the heights are obtained. Locations of doors, windows, and other details are taken from the floor plan. Figure 11.7 shows a slightly more complex roof being used to form the roof shape on an elevation.

Method 2: Dimensional Layout

You can also draft exterior elevations by taking the dimensions from the plans and sections and drafting the elevation(s) from scratch. First, lightly lay out the critical vertical measurements. In the example shown in

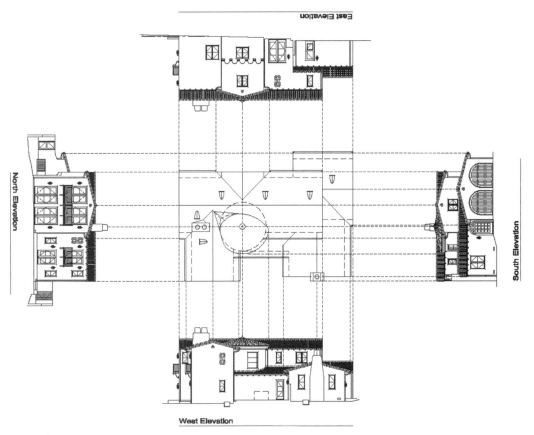

Figure 11.5   Obtaining width and depth dimensions.

Figure 11.6   Heights from wall sections. (Courtesy of Mike Adli.)

Figure 11.8, these measurements are the **subfloor** (top of plywood or concrete) line and the **plate line** (top of the two top plates above the studs). See Figure 11.9A. This measurement is taken directly from the building section.

The second step establishes the location of the walls and offsets in the structure from the floor plan. Draw these lines lightly, because changes in line length may be required later. See Figure 11.9B.

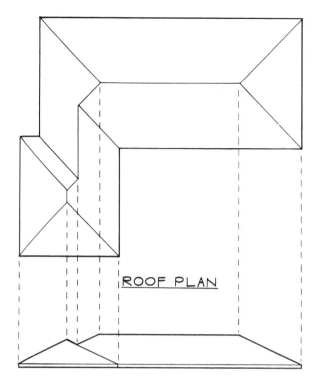

ROOF PLAN

ELEVATION OF ROOF

Figure 11.7 Roof elevation from roof plan.

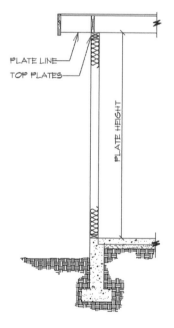

PLATE LINE
TOP PLATES

PLATE HEIGHT

Figure 11.8 Subfloor to plate line.

Third, establish the grade line (earth) in relationship to the floor line. See Figure 11.9C. This dimension is from the building sections or footing sections.

Next, as Figure 11.9D shows, add the roof configuration. To better understand the relationship between the roof and the rest of the structure, draw the **eave** (portion of a roof that extends beyond the wall) in a simple form, as shown in Figure 11.9E. These dimensions are found on the building section. The finished roof shape depends on the roof framing plan or the roof plan for dimensions. See Figure 11.9F.

Finally, windows and doors are located. Sizes are found on the window and door schedule, and locations on the floor plan. Material designations, dimensions, notes, and structural descriptions complete the elevation. See Figure 11.9G.

Figure 11.10 shows a typical example of an exterior elevation. Go back to the beginning of the chapter and compare Figure 11.10 with the simple list of elements.

Choice of Scale

Selection of the scale for elevations is based on the size and complexity of the project and the available drawing space. For small structures, $\frac{1}{4}'' = 1'-0''$ is a common scale. For a larger project, a smaller scale can be used. The exterior elevation is usually drawn at the same scale as the floor plan. For medium and large elevations, you may have to decrease the scale in relationship to the floor plans.

Because we are dealing with small structures, two to four stories in height, we are using the largest scale allowed by the available drawing space not exceeding $\frac{1}{4}'' = 1'-0''$.

Odd-Shaped Plans

Not all plans are rectangular; some have irregular shapes and angles. Figure 11.11 shows several building shapes and the north designation. For these kinds of conditions, all elevations are drawn.

Shape A. Figure 11.12 shows the exterior elevations for a relatively simple L-shaped building and how these elevations were obtained using the projection method.

Shape B. The elevations for Shape B in Figure 11.13 present a unique problem on the East and particularly the South elevation. Because the fence is in the same plane as the south side of the structure, include it in the South elevation. Had the fence been in front of the structure, you could either delete it or include it in order to show its relationship to the structure itself.

The inclusion of the fence may pose additional problems, such as preventing a view of portions of the structure behind. You can overcome this difficulty in one of two ways: Either eliminate the fence altogether (not show it) or use a break line, as shown in Figure 11.13. This allows any item behind it, such as the window, to be exposed, referenced, and dimensioned. Break lines still allow dimensioning and descriptions of the fence.

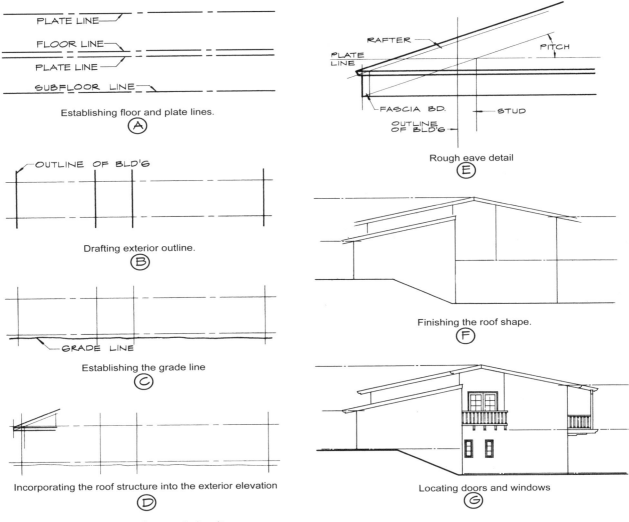

Establishing floor and plate lines.
Ⓐ

Drafting exterior outline.
Ⓑ

Establishing the grade line
Ⓒ

Incorporating the roof structure into the exterior elevation
Ⓓ

Rough eave detail
Ⓔ

Finishing the roof shape.
Ⓕ

Locating doors and windows
Ⓖ

Figure 11.9A   Establishing floor and plate lines.
Figure 11.9B   Drafting exterior outline.
Figure 11.9C   Establishing the grade line.
Figure 11.9D   Incorporating the roof structure into the exterior elevation.
Figure 11.9E   Rough eave detail.
Figure 11.9F   Finishing the roof shape.
Figure 11.9G   Locating doors and windows.

Shape C. The two portions on the right of the South elevation and all of the East elevation are *not* true shapes and sizes, because they are drawn as direct 90° projections from the *left* portion of the plan view. This is sometimes a problem. See Figure 11.14. The West and North elevations will also be distorted. See Figure 11.11.

To solve this problem, we use an **auxiliary view**: a view that is 90° to the line of sight. The elevations are projected 90° to the sight lines and a break line is used to stop that portion which is not true. Notice on Figure 11.15 how the break line splits the South elevation into two parts. Each part is projected independently of the other, and its continuation, which is not a true shape, is voided.

The South elevation in Figure 11.14 appears to have three parts rather than two, as in Figure 11.15. In the latter case, the third part will be left to the East elevation. With a more complex shape, a break line beyond the true surface being projected can be confusing. See Figure 11.16. To avoid confusion, introduce a **pivot point** (P.P.; the point at which the end of one elevation becomes the beginning of another elevation), and show it as a dotted (hidden) line or a centerline-type line (dots and dashes). See Figure 11.17.

Pivot points can cause a problem in selecting a title for a particular elevation. To avoid confusion, introduce a **key plan**. The key plan is usually drawn on the bottom right corner of the drawing sheet. See Figure 11.18.

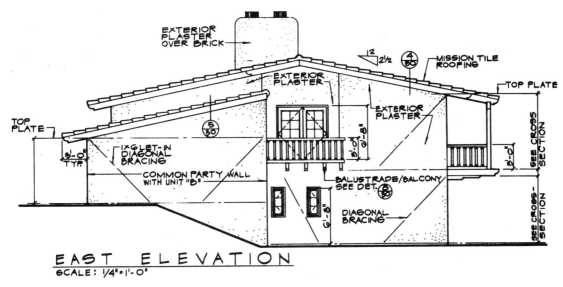

Figure 11.10 Drafted East elevation of a condominium. (Courtesy of William F. Smith—Builder.)

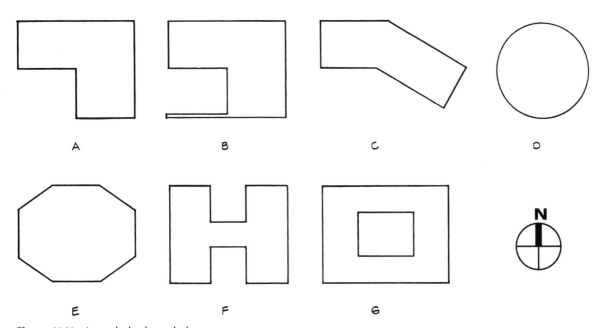

Figure 11.11 Irregularly shaped plans.

Draw and label a reference bubble for every necessary elevation. These reference bubbles will become the titles for the elevations. If the surface contains important information about the structure or surface materials, it deserves a reference bubble. Figure 11.19 shows how these elevations are represented with titles and pivot-point notations.

Shape D. With Shape D from Figure 11.11, nothing is true shape or size, regardless of the direction of the elevation. See Figure 11.20. Figure 11.21 shows a pivot point together with a **fold-out** (called a **development drawing** in mechanical drawing).

Shape E. Shape E in Figure 11.11 can be drawn in one of three ways: first, by drawing it as a direct projection so that one of the three exposed faces will be in true shape and size; second, by using a key plan and drawing each surface individually; and third, by drawing it as a fold-out similar to Figure 11.21. Choose the method that will best explain the elevations. For example, if all other sides are the same, the direct-projection method may be the best. If every wall surface is different, then the key plan or fold-out method would be best.

Shape F. Surfaces that will be hidden in a direct projection, such as some of the surfaces of Shape F

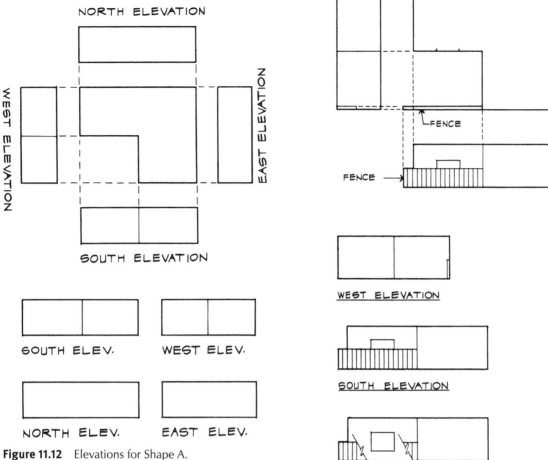

Figure 11.12 Elevations for Shape A.

Figure 11.13 Elevations for Shape B.

in Figure 11.11, can effectively be dealt with in one of two ways. The first uses a key plan and the second uses a combination of an elevation and a section. Both methods are shown in Figure 11.22. The combination of the section and the elevation shows the structure and its relationship to the elevation more clearly.

Shape G. Shape G in Figure 11.11 can be drawn simply as the South elevation, North elevation, East elevation, and West elevation using a direct-projection method. The interior space (atrium) can also be drawn as a direct projection with titles "Atrium North Elevation," "Atrium South Elevation," "Atrium East Elevation," and "Atrium West Elevation." A way to simplify this is shown in Figure 11.23.

■ DRAWING DOORS AND WINDOWS

Draw doors and windows on elevations as close as possible to the actual configuration. Horizontal location dimensions need not be included, because they are

on the floor plan; likewise, door and window sizes are contained in the door and window schedule. However, vertical location dimensions are shown with indications of how the doors and windows open.

Doors

Doors and their surface materials can be delineated in various ways. Illustrations A and B in Figure 11.24 show the basic appearance of a door with and without surface materials—wood grain, in this instance. Illustration C shows the final configuration of a dimensioned door. Note that the 6'-8" dimension is measured from the floor line to the top of the floor. The other line around the door represents the trim. For precise dimensions for the trim, consult the door details. Illustrations D and E of Figure 11.24 show how a door opens or slides. Panel doors are shown in illustration F, and **plant-on doors** (doors with decorative pieces attached) are shown in illustration G.

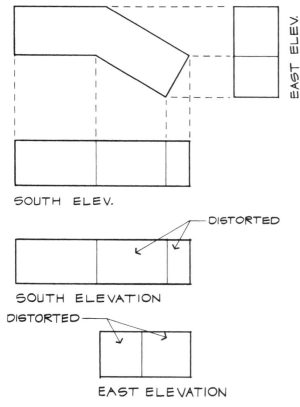

SOUTH ELEV.

SOUTH ELEVATION

DISTORTED

EAST ELEVATION

Figure 11.14   Elevations for Shape C.

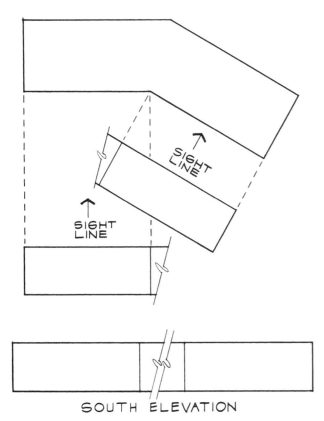

SOUTH ELEVATION

Figure 11.15   Elevations with new sight line. (William Boggs Aerial Photography. Printed with permission.)

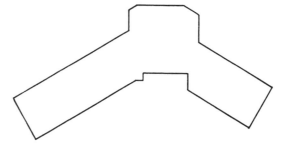

Figure 11.16   Complicated shape.

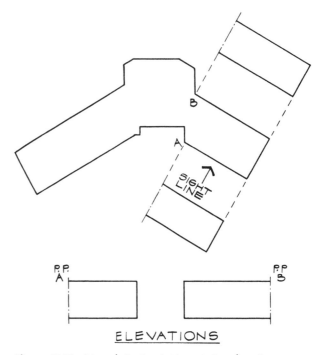

ELEVATIONS

Figure 11.17   Use of pivot point in exterior elevations.

Windows

Windows are drafted much like doors. Their shape, their operation, and the direction in which they open are represented. Double-hung windows and louver windows are obvious exceptions because of their operation. See Figure 11.25.

On double-hung and sliding windows, one portion of the window is shown in its entirety, whereas the moving section shows only three sides of the window. Using the sliding window in Figure 11.25 as an example, the right side of the window shows all four sides because it is on the outside. The left section shows only three sides, because the fourth side is behind the right section.

Fixed Windows.   If the window is **fixed** (nonopening), as shown in Figure 11.26, you must know whether the

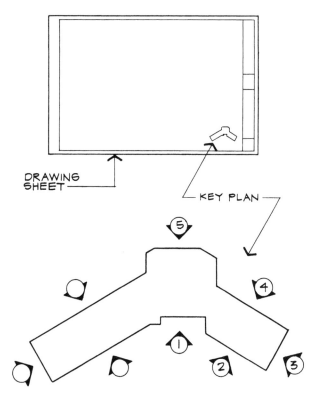

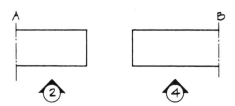

Figure 11.18 Using a key plan.

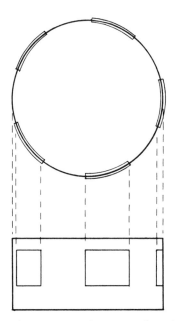

Figure 11.19 Elevations using key plan.

Figure 11.20 Elevations of a cylinder.

window is to be shop made (manufactured ahead of time) or constructed on the job. If the frame can be ordered—in aluminum, for example—treat it like other manufactured windows and include it in the window schedule. If the window is to be job made (made on the site), provide all the necessary information about the window on the window schedule or exterior elevations, as shown in Figure 11.27. However, keep all this information in one place for consistency and uniformity.

Referencing Doors and Windows

Reference doors and windows with bubbles. Bubbles can refer to details or to a schedule for size. See Figure 11.27. If, for some reason, there are no schedules or details for a set of drawings, all information pertaining to the windows or doors will be on the exterior elevations near or on the windows and doors or on the floor plan at the door or window location. See Figure 11.26.

■ MATERIAL DESIGNATIONS

Describing the Materials

The exterior elevations also describe the exterior wall surface material. For a wood structure, describe both the surface covering and any backing material. **Wood siding**, for example, is described with the backing behind it. See Figure 11.28.

In some cases, one word, such as *stucco*, describes the surface adequately unless a special pattern is to be applied. Here, the drafter assumes that the contractor understands that the word **stucco** implies building paper (black waterproof paper), mesh (hexagonal woven wire), and three coats of exterior plaster. Often a more detailed description of the material is found in the specifications. The "stucco" finish, for example, might be described as "20/30 steel trowel sand."

Even if the complete wall is made up of one material, such as concrete block (as opposed to a built-up system as in wood construction), describe the surface. See Figure 11.29.

Drawing the Materials

A facsimile of the material is shown in both Figures 11.28 and 11.29. The material representation does not fill the complete area but is shown in detail around the perimeter only, which saves production time. Figure 11.30 shows more of the area covered with the surface material, but in a slightly more abstract manner. Another method is to draft the surface accurately and erase areas for notes.

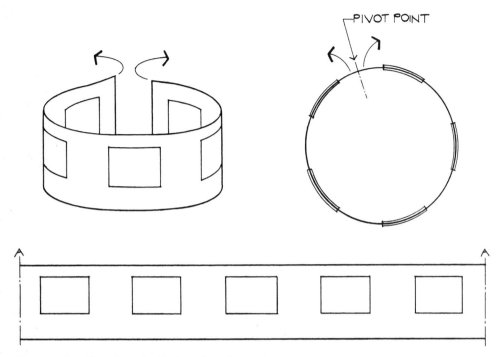

Figure 11.21 Elevation of cylinder using pivot point.

Figure 11.31 shows other materials as they might appear in an exterior elevation. These are only suggestions. Scale and office practice dictate the final technique. See Figure 11.32.

Eliminating Unnecessary Information

Because exterior elevations are vital in the construction document process, unnecessary information should be eliminated. Shades and shadows, cars, bushes and trees, people and flowers add to the look of the drawings but serve no purpose here. These components are utilized for presentation elevations, client documents, city preliminary revisions, or landscape plans. If AutoCAD or Revit are used, layers can be voided to accomplish this.

■ NOTES

Order of Notes

Notes on elevations follow the same rules as notes on other drawings. The size of the object is first, then the name of the material, and then any additional information about spacing, quantity, finish, or methods of installation. For example,

1 × 8 redwood siding, rough sawn over 15# (15 lb) building felt

or

Cement plaster over concrete block, smooth finish

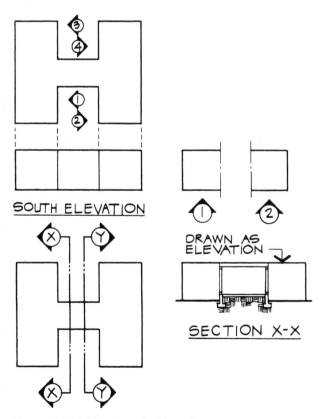

Figure 11.22 Elevations for Shape F.

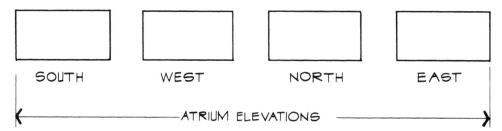

Figure 11.23 Simplified elevation titles.

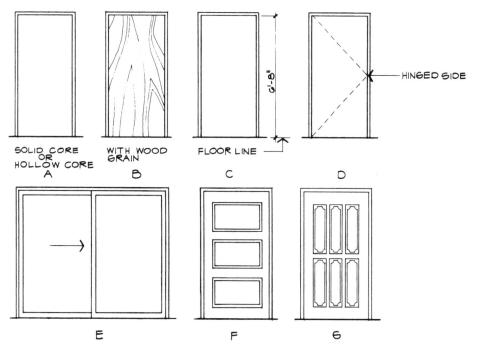

Figure 11.24 Doors in elevation.

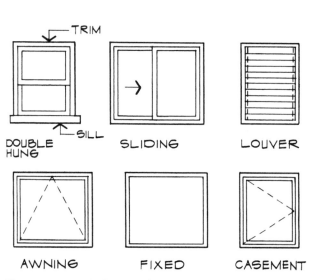

Figure 11.25 Windows in elevation.

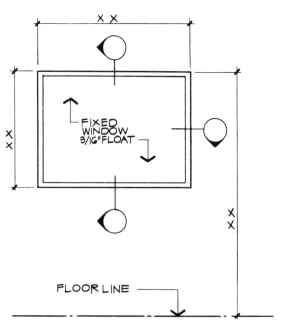

Figure 11.26 A fixed window.

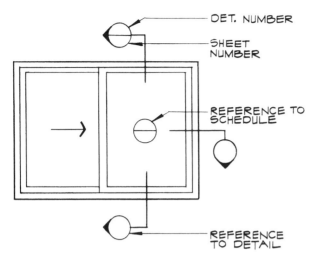

Figure 11.27 Referencing doors and windows.

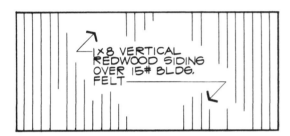

Figure 11.28 Wood siding in elevation.

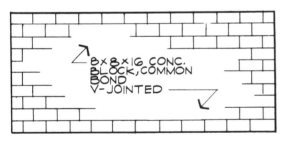

Figure 11.29 Concrete block in elevation.

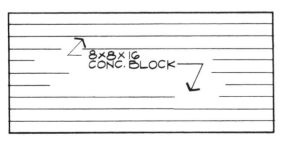

Figure 11.30 Abbreviated concrete-block pattern.

or
Built-up composition gravel roof
or
1 × 6, let-in bracing

In the second example, no specific sizes are needed, so the generic name comes first in the note.

Noting Practices

Noting practices vary from job to job. A set of written specifications is often provided with the construction documents. Wall material on a set of elevations may be described in broad, generic terms, such as "concrete block," when the specific size, finish, stacking procedure, and type of joint are covered in the specifications.

If there are differences between the construction documents and the specifications, the specifications have priority (the specs control). In the construction documents, often the same material note can be found more than once. If an error is made or a change is desired, many notes must be revised. In the specifications, where material notes are mentioned once, only a single change has to be made.

There are exceptions. When there are complicated changes and variations of material and patterns on an elevation, it is difficult to describe them in the specifications. In this case, the information should be located on the exterior elevations. See Figure 11.32.

■ DOTTED LINES

Doors and Windows

Dotted lines are used on doors and windows to show how they operate. See illustration D of Figure 11.24 and the awning and casement windows in Figure 11.25. These dotted lines show which part of the door or window is hinged. See Figure 11.33. Not all offices like to show this on an elevation. One reason is that the direction the door swings is shown on the floor plan and therefore does not have to be indicated on the elevations.

Foundations

At times, you may have to delineate the foundation on the elevations in order to explain the foundation better. Dotted lines are used in various ways relating to the foundation. Dotted lines (centerline-type lines are also used) show the top of a slab, as in Figure 11.34. They are also used to show the elevation of the footings. See Figure 11.35 for elevations of a two-pour footing and a one-pour footing or to delineate a basement.

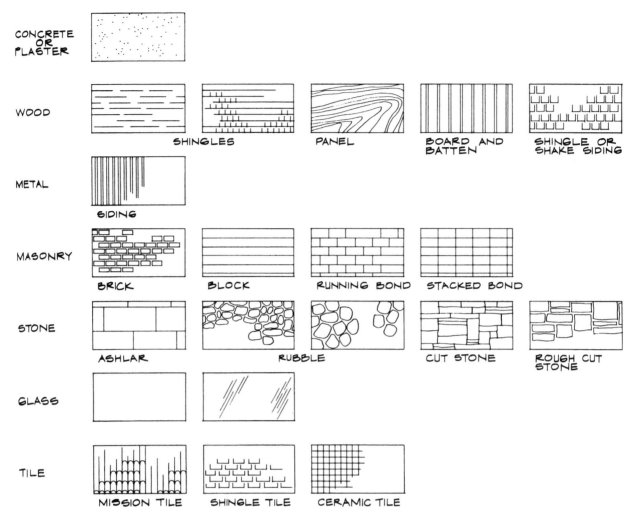

CONCRETE OR PLASTER

WOOD — SHINGLES / PANEL / BOARD AND BATTEN / SHINGLE OR SHAKE SIDING

METAL — SIDING

MASONRY — BRICK / BLOCK / RUNNING BOND / STACKED BOND

STONE — ASHLAR / RUBBLE / CUT STONE / ROUGH CUT STONE

GLASS

TILE — MISSION TILE / SHINGLE TILE / CERAMIC TILE

Figure 11.31 Material designations.

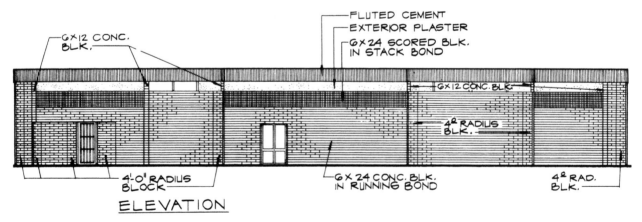

FLUTED CEMENT
EXTERIOR PLASTER
6×24 SCORED BLK. IN STACK BOND

6×12 CONC. BLK.

6×12 CONC. BLK.

4ᴿ RADIUS BLK.

4'-0" RADIUS BLOCK

6×24 CONC. BLK. IN RUNNING BOND

4ᴿ RAD. BLK.

ELEVATION

Figure 11.32 Masonry structure with variations in building patterns.

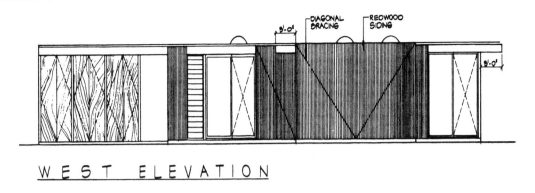

WEST ELEVATION

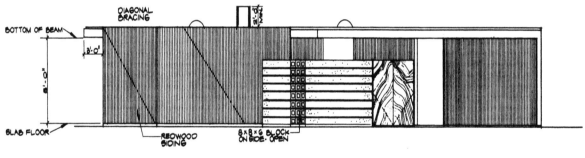

SOUTH ELEVATION

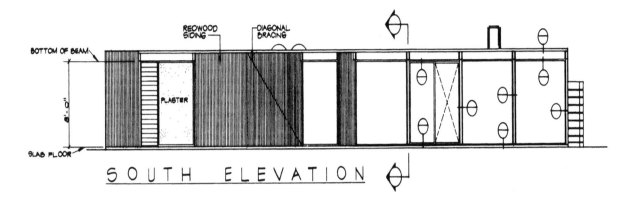

EAST ELEVATION

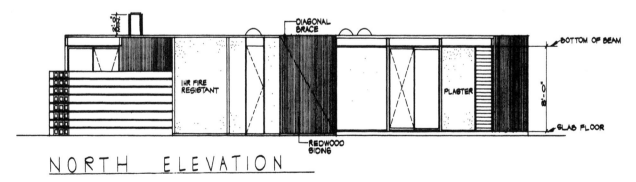

NORTH ELEVATION

Figure 11.33 Elevation in wood.

Dotted lines are also used to describe a **stepped footing**. When the property slopes, the minimum depth of the footing can be maintained by stepping the footing down the slope. See Figure 11.36.

Structural Features

Structural features below the grade can be shown by dotted lines if this helps to explain the structure. See Figure 11.37. Dotted lines can also be used to help show structural elements of the building. In Figure 11.10, centerline-type lines (which can also be used) show **let-in braces** (structural angular braces in a wall). (The plate line is the top of the two horizontal members at the top of the wall, called **top plates**.) In Figure 11.34, dotted lines show the top of the roof, which slopes for drainage; a **pilaster** (a widening of the wall for a beam); and a beam (a laminated beam) or for window wells.

As with doors and windows, the footing on an elevation can be referenced to the foundation plan, details, and cross-sections. The system is the same. Reference bubbles are used. See Figure 11.38.

Whatever the feature, the dotted line is used for clarity and communication. How can you keep the message clear for construction purposes? How can you best communicate this on the drawings?

■ CONTROLLING FACTORS

Each type of construction has unique restrictive features that you need to know about to effectively interpret the transition from design elevations to production of exterior elevations in the construction documents.

Wood Frame Structures

With wood frame structures, elevations are usually dictated by plate line heights. The **plate height** is measured from the floor to the top of the two top plates. See Figure 11.8. Efficient use of material is dictated by this dimension because studs are available in certain lengths and sheathing usually comes in 4′ × 8′ sheets.

Floor, Plate, and Grade Lines. When the floor elevations and plate heights are established, the first thing to draw is the floor line and its relationship to the grade. Next, draw the plate line. If the structure is of post

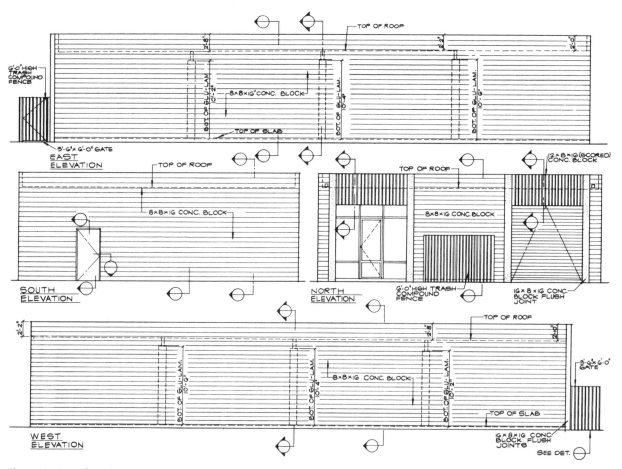

Figure 11.34 Elevation in masonry.

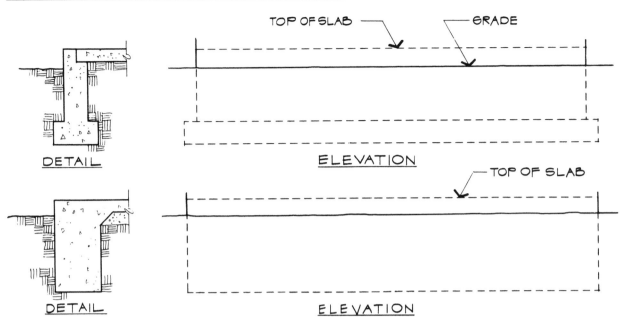

DETAIL   ELEVATION

DETAIL   ELEVATION

Figure 11.35 Showing the foundation on an elevation.

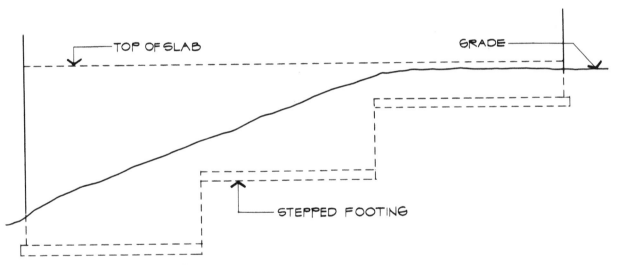

Figure 11.36 Stepped footings in elevation.

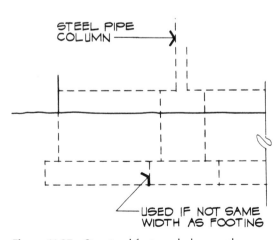

Figure 11.37 Structural features below grade.

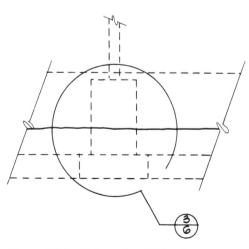

Figure 11.38 Referencing hidden lines.

and beam construction, measure from the floor line to the bottom of the beam. Some offices prefer to put these dimensions on the building sections.

Find the distance between the floor line and the grade line from the grading plan, foundation plan, footing details, and building sections. If the lot is relatively flat, just draw a grade line with the floor line measured above it and the plate line height above the floor as a start. If the site is not flat, carefully plot the grade line from the grading plan, foundation plan, and details or the site plan.

Some site plans, grading plans, and foundation plans indicate the grade height, marked F.G. (finished grade), in relation to the structure at various points around the structure. In Figure 11.39, the grade line is figured by making a grid where the horizontal lines show grade heights and vertical lines are projected down from the structure. Once this grade line is established, the top of the slab—that is, the floor line—is drawn. The plate line is then measured from the floor line. There is no need to measure the distance between the grade and the floor line. See Figure 11.40.

Masonry Structures

Masonry structures, such as those of brick or concrete masonry units (CMU), must be approached differently. The deciding factor here is the size of the concrete block or brick, the pattern, the thickness of the joint, and the placement of the first row in relationship to the floor. Unlike wood, which can be cut in varying heights, masonry units are difficult to cut, so cutting is minimized. As Figure 11.32 shows, dimensions of the masonry areas are kept to a minimum. In a wood frame structure, the lumber can be cut to size on the job. In masonry, the size of the masonry units often dictates such things as the location of windows and doors, the modular height, and so on. Some of the controlling factors in steel construction are: the size of the structural members; the required ceiling heights; and the **plenum** area (the space necessary to accommodate the mechanical equipment and ductwork). See Figure 11.41. Refer to the discussion of noting, earlier in this chapter, for suggested practices and sample illustrations.

Steel Structures

Structures in which the main members are steel and the secondary members are, for example, wood, are treated differently from wood structures or masonry. The configuration is arrived at in the same way and representation of material is the same, but dimensioning is completely different.

Drawing an exterior elevation for a steel structure is a relatively simple task. Usually, the floor elevations on a multistory structure of steel are established by the architect. The building section usually provides the necessary

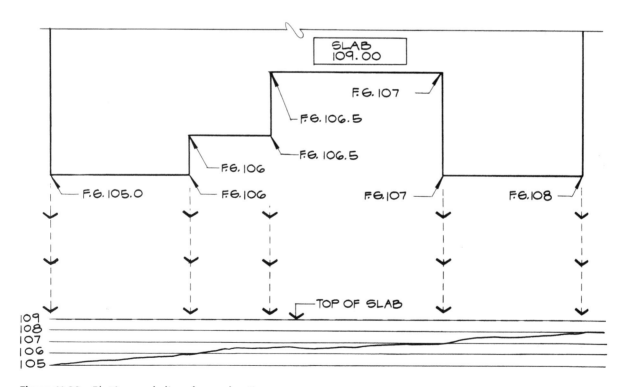

Figure 11.39 Plotting grade lines for an elevation.

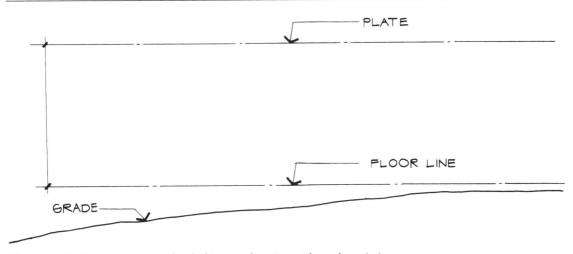

Figure 11.40 Preliminary steps for drafting an elevation with grade variation.

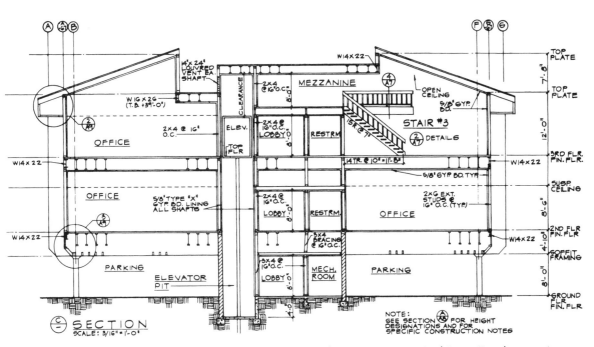

Figure 11.41 Section of a steel and wood structure. (Courtesy of Westmount, Inc., Real Estate Development.)

height requirements. See Figure 11.41. Figure 11.42 is a checklist for exterior elevations.

■ DRAFTING AN EXTERIOR ELEVATION

Drawing an exterior elevation is a straightforward procedure, because most of the structural and shape descriptions have been completed by the time it is drafted: The shape of the roof, the size of the site component parts, the shape and size of the foundation, and all of the vertical heights were determined when drafting the building section. For a small structure, such as those contained in this book, we believe it is the easiest drawing to accomplish.

Guide to Dimensioning

Do not dimension anything on the exterior elevation that has been dimensioned elsewhere, unless you are using Revit. For example, the distance between the floor line and the plate line is dimensioned on the building section and should not be repeated on the exterior elevation. In contrast, windows have been described (width and height) on the schedule, yet their positions in relation to the floor line have not. This makes the exterior elevation an ideal place to dimension these positions, as well as

EXTERIOR ELEVATIONS

1. Natural grade
2. Finish grade
3. Floor elevations
4. Foundation (hidden lines)
   a. Bottom of footing
   b. Top of foundation (stepped footing)
   c. Detail reference
5. Walls
   a. Material
      (1) Wood
      (2) Stucco
      (3) Aluminum
      (4) Other
   b. Solid sheathing
      (1) Plywood
      (2) 1 × 6 diagonal
      (3) Other
   c. Diagonal bracing (hidden lines)
6. Openings
   a. Heights
      (1) Door and window min. 6'-8"
      (2) Post and beam special
   b. Doors
      (1) Type
      (2) Material
      (3) Glass
      (4) Detail reference
      (5) Key to schedule
   c. Windows
      (1) Type
      (2) Material

   (3) Glass — obscure for baths
   (4) Detail reference
   (5) Key to schedule
   d. Molding, casing and sill
   e. Flashing (gauge used)
7. Roof
   a. Materials
      (1) Built-up composition, gravel
      (2) Asphalt shingles
      (3) Wood shingles or shake
      (4) Metal-terne-aluminum
      (5) Clay and ceramic tile
      (6) Concrete
   b. Other
8. Ground slopage
9. Attic and subfloor vents
10. Vertical dimensions
11. Window, door fascia, etc. detail references
12. Roof slope ratio
13. Railings, note height
14. Stairs
15. Note all wall materials
16. Types of fixed glass and thickness
17. Window and door swing indications
18. Window and door heights from floor
19. Gutters and downspouts
20. Overflow scuppers
21. Mail slot
22. Stepped foundation footings — if occur
23. Dimension chimney above roof

Figure 11.42   Exterior elevations checklist.

such architectural features as signage on a commercial building.

Descriptions

Anything that can be described better by drawing should be drawn, and anything that would be better as a written description should be included in the specifications. Noting should use generic terms. It would be sufficient to label the exterior covering (called **skin**) "redwood siding" or "stucco" (exterior plaster), rather than describing the quality of the siding or the number of coats and quality of the stucco.

Concerns

Compare the exterior elevation to the human body. In both instances, the outside cover is called the *skin*. Directly below the skin is the muscle. The muscle might be comparable to the substructure that strengthens a structure, such as metal straps, let-in braces, and shear panels. See Figure 11.43. The purpose of these members is to resist outside forces, such as wind, hurricanes, and earthquakes. The skeleton within a human body is

analogous to the "bone structure" of a building, which is in the form of a network of wood pieces, called *studs*.

The exterior elevation addresses the "skin and muscle," and the building section emphasizes the skeletal form.

Use of Hidden Lines

Hidden lines are used on an exterior elevation to reveal structural members behind the surface. See Figure 11.34. Notice, in this figure, the use of hidden lines to show the slope of the roof, the pilaster, the hinged side of doors and windows; in Figure 11.33, hidden lines are used to show diagonal bracing.

Now look at Figure 11.44. The outline of a gable roof (roof plan) is translated into elevations. Notice that in the front view the small bend in the roof at the top right corner does not show, whereas in the rear view the entire shape is shown and the right-side view shows only a single roof but nothing behind it. Hidden roof lines are not shown.

Pictorial vs. Written Description

It often takes a combination of a drawing and a generic description to describe a material used for covering the outer surface of a structure. For example, a series of horizontal lines is used to describe siding, a row of masonry units, or possibly a texture pattern on exterior plaster.

■ WEATHERPROOFING

Weatherproofing a structure basically means keeping out wind, rain, and ultraviolet rays (UVR) of the sun. UVR reduction is necessary because these rays are harmful to

Figure 11.43 Revealing let-in brace.

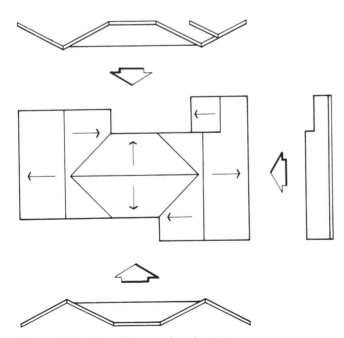

Figure 11.44 Visualizing roof in elevation.

human skin and will fade the color of drapery, furniture, and carpets. In a residence, the solution is rather simple. Large overhangs on roofs can eliminate these harmful rays, as can the newly developed high-performance glass used in windows.

Windows and doors are now made, or can be retrofitted, with weatherstripping. This keeps the structure energy efficient and prevents dust from entering the structure as a result of driving winds.

As you may have learned in a science course, the structure of water is different in its various phases: solid, liquid, and vapor. Therefore, a variety of materials are used to combat the migration of moisture from the outside to the inside of structures.

Generally, a cover is placed over the structure (especially the walls), much like a raincoat on a human. Yet, depending on the material of the raincoat, the wearer's body heat, the temperature of the air, and especially the humidity (moisture in the air), the inside surface of the raincoat will react differently. So it is with buildings. Buildings do perspire. Consider the following scenario: Driven by wind, moisture migrates from the outside to the inside of a structure in the form of vapor. This moisture changes its state through condensation because of temperature change and is unable to leave the inside of the wall. As night approaches, the temperature drops drastically, and the moisture now expands as it becomes a solid (ice). If this moisture happens to be inside the wood or insulation within the wall, it can cause terrible deterioration and damage. Had a vapor barrier been used, moisture might come from the inside of the structure and condense along this membrane as it tried to escape.

Solution to Condensation

A solution to condensation in the attic and under-floor space in a wood floor system can easily be achieved by proper ventilation and recirculation of the air. This is done with small openings through which venting can take place, using the wind as an ally, or the air can be recirculated mechanically, as is often done for bathroom ventilation.

Figure 11.45 is a map of the United States. Notice how it is divided into three major zones. Zone A experiences severe damage to structures as a result of condensation. Zone B experiences moderate damage, whereas the damage in Zone C is slight to almost none. This does not mean that there will never be moderate-to-severe damage in mountainous areas in Zone C; rather, this is a more generalized look at large geographic areas. Therefore, the drafter must be aware that a building in Southern California will *not* be dealt with in the same way as a building in the Dakotas, nor can a building in southern Texas be treated the same as one in Colorado.

Waterproofing

Waterproofing can be achieved in four ways:

1. The use of admixtures that render concrete impermeable.
2. Hydrolytically, by applying a waterproofing coat of asphalt or plastic to a surface.
3. Chemically, by applying a specially formulated paint to a basically porous surface such as concrete. Upon contact with water, this chemical crystallizes, sealing the pores. Such products are used more often for a retro-fix than initial construction.
4. The use of a membrane. Older houses used **bituminous-saturated felts** (also called **building felts**), which have recently been replaced with asphalt-saturated kraft paper.

For a structure in Zone A, you may wish to select a material that will keep the colder side of the wall wind resistant and airtight and require that the material be a vapor retardant. On the warm side of the wall, you might wish to stop the migration of moisture into the wall by using a foil-backed lath product. There are a number of products on the market today that can be specified by the project architect, including a vaporproof membrane, a membrane that can breathe, and a self-sealing membrane for ice and water, as shown in Figure 11.46.

A drafter must know what is being used to properly ensure that he or she uses the correct convention and notation for drawings and details.

Counterflashing

Anytime you break the surface of a waterproof membrane, whether it is plastic or paper, a second sheet (usually of heavier weight) is used. This sheet, called *counterflashing*, is found around openings and at the ends of the membrane, inasmuch as these are the places most likely to leak. In Zone C, for example, where asphalt-saturated (grade D) kraft paper is often used, a heavier-grade band of kraft paper, called *sisal-kraft*, is used. In other instances, a strip of self-sealing vapor membrane may be used around the opening. In either case, it should be done carefully so as to shed water lapping and overlapping so as to let gravity take its natural course and help eliminate moisture.

Referencing

Referencing is the process of referring a specific area to an enlarged detail. Thus, the top half of the reference bubble indicates the name of the detail, and the bottom number indicates the sheet on which the particular detail can be found. On a complete set with details of all conditions, you would see detail reference bubbles around all windows, doors, beam connections, and so on.

Noting

Whenever possible, noting is done outside the elevation within the right margin. You cannot fit all of the

ZONE A—Severe

Zone B—Moderate

Zone C—None to Slight

Figure 11.45   U.S. condensation hazard zones.

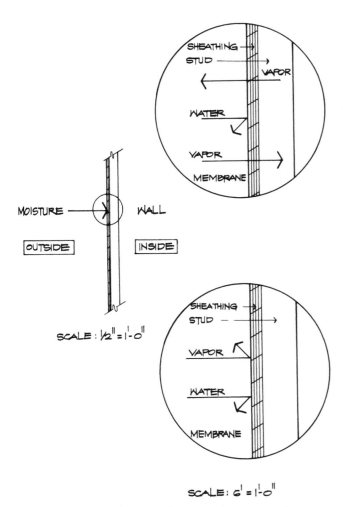

Figure 11.46 Breathing membranes and vapor membranes.

notes in one place without having to use long leaders pointing to the subject. Therefore, certain notes are made inside the elevation to reduce the length of the leaders. A good rule of thumb in regard to leaders is not to allow them to cross more than one object line, never cross a dimension line, and keep the leader length to a minimum.

Many offices use **keynoting**, a procedure of numbering and placing all of the notes on one side (usually the right). You then place a leader in the desired location and, rather than placing the note at the end of the leader, you use a reference bubble that refers to the correct note.

The advantage of keynoting is the standardization of the notes. Keynoting also allows the drafter to make direct references to the specification numbers right on the notes. Numbering systems recommended by the American Institute of Architects are similar to the numbering system used by libraries and can be incorporated here.

DRAWING AN ELEVATION WITH AND WITHOUT A MODEL

With a 3-D model, the drafter needs only to rotate the image into an ortho mode and flatten it to create a base form for the elevation.

If a 3-D model is unavailable, the CAD drafter should use the base layer of the building section for the geometry layer under the base layer (datum layer) for the elevation.

Because we are drawing the structure full-scale, the drawings will transfer directly. If the drawings are prepared in paper space and/or the scale of the building section and elevation are to be drawn differently, the first stage of the building section must be changed in scale to suit the elevation.

STAGE I The next move is to import the floor plan and position the walls as shown in Figure 11.47. The floor plan is temporarily positioned above the datum elevation drawing and rotated for each of the respective North, South, East, and West elevations. This drawing constitutes the base or datum stage of a set of elevations.

STAGE II (Figure 11.48). The total outline of the structure is accomplished in this stage. The geometry of the roof and additional floor lines and plate lines are also incorporated as they change throughout the structure.

STAGE III (Figure 11.49). Doors and windows are positioned. It is best to get digital images from the manufacturer, and then size and position them. If the structure is subject to lateral loads, shear walls may be included at this stage, as would stepped footing or any other structural components.

STAGE IV (Figure 11.50). Line weight should be adjusted at this stage while adding texture. Adding texture may be fun, but restraint is recommended, so as not to disturb any notes or dimensions.

STAGE V (Figure 11.51). This is the dimensioning stage. Remember, the dimension for floor line to plate line should be noted once on the building section and should not be repeated here. Simply refer the floor-to-plate-line dimension to the section. Only those vertical dimensions that do not appear on the building section should appear here. Header height, ridge heights, handrail and guardrail dimensions, and heights of fences and walls adjacent to the structure are examples of actual dimensions that will appear on the exterior elevation.

STAGE VI (Figure 11.52). This is the noting, titling, and referencing stage, as well as final stage of the exterior elevations. Notes should be generic; only the specifications should cite the precise quantity, brand names, model numbers, and so forth.

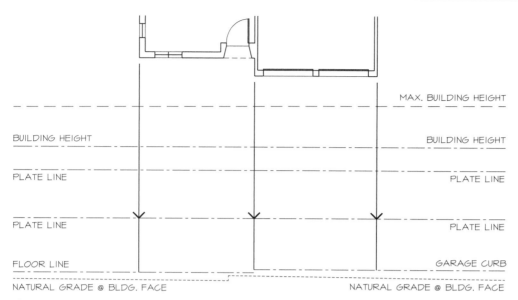

MAX. BUILDING HEIGHT

BUILDING HEIGHT   BUILDING HEIGHT

PLATE LINE   PLATE LINE

PLATE LINE   PLATE LINE

FLOOR LINE   GARAGE CURB

NATURAL GRADE @ BLDG. FACE   NATURAL GRADE @ BLDG. FACE

Figure 11.47   Stage I: Establishing a base (datum).

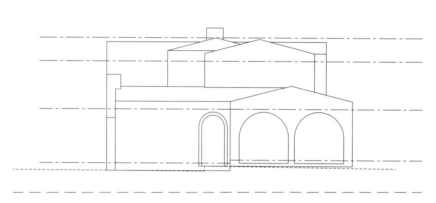

Figure 11.48   Stage II: Outline of structure.

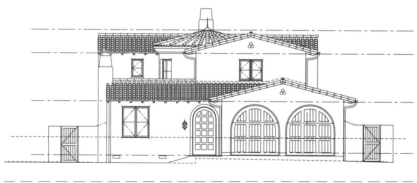

Figure 11.49   Stage III: Positioning doors, windows, and the like.

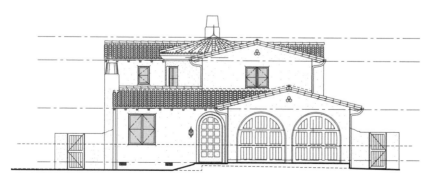

Figure 11.50   Stage IV: Adding texture and adjusting line quality.

■ EXTERIOR ELEVATION USING BIM/REVIT

Using the pull-down menu shown in Figure 11.53A, activate the exterior elevation option. The exterior elevation is already drawn because of the three-dimensional model originally produced in Revit. You need only to annotate the drawing and dimension it. (Figure 11.53B shows the corresponding menu item for interior elevations.)

With Revit, a cardinal principle has changed here: that of putting on the exterior elevation dimensions that exist on the building section. In the past, when changes were made on dimensions (say, height measurements), a sharp drafter would also make that change on both the section and the exterior elevations. Unfortunately, being human, even the sharpest drafter or architect might not

remember to make the change everywhere it appeared; when the dimension occurs in two or more places, it is easy to miss one. This is the basic reason for the principle mandating that there be only one "master" place giving dimensions. Now, though, the principle can be relaxed, because such oversights and omissions will not happen with BIM/Revit; in this system, a change in one drawing will change all related drawings. For example, a change in ceiling height often affects details and interior elevations. Using BIM/Revit, these changes would be made automatically. One exception is that a change in the first floor will not change the plan on the second floor, unless the plans were locked in on the original model.

Your first task is enhancement of the image, to make not only a technical drawing but also a visually readable drawing with a multitude of line qualities. We must divide the dark, medium, and light lines into a scheme of

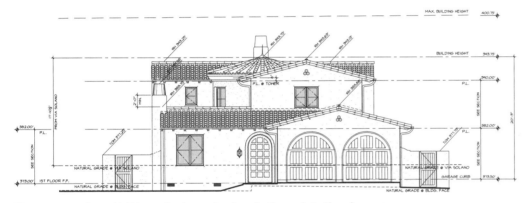

Figure 11.51 Stage V: Dimensioning stairs, handrails, and similar elements.

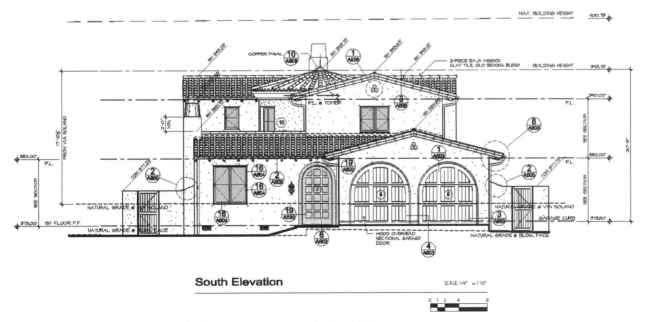

South Elevation

Figure 11.52 Stage VI: Noting and referencing. (Courtesy of Mike Adli.)

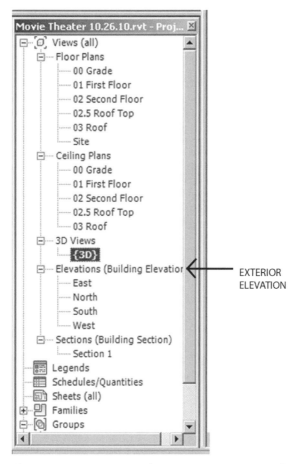

EXTERIOR
ELEVATION

INTERIOR
ELEVATIONS

Figure 11.53A Exterior elevation menu. (Screenshots © Autodesk Inc. All Rights Reserved.)

Figure 11.53B Interior elevation menu. (Screenshots © Autodesk Inc. All Rights Reserved.)

nine line weights: 3 dark, 3 medium, and 3 light. This is critical in an elevation, because there are planes that are dominant by virtue of how close they are to the viewer and wall planes that are slightly farther away from the viewer, and planes that are way in the back.

The second task is to dimension the floor datums. Use either floor-to-floor or floor-to-plate lines, leaving the neutral zone for the framing members and space for mechanical, electrical, and so on.

The third task is to locate and dimension the windows and doors. Always locate these dimensions to the datum (floor to header).

Fourth, insert any dimension required on the elevations for roof height. Drafters often miss the dimension for heights off the floor to the top of a guardrail. You must also show the substructure; diagonal bracing, shear panels, pilasters, slopes on parapet walls, and the like are indicated with hidden (dotted) lines.

Noting should be next. Describe the material(s) to be used on the exterior walls, around windows and doors, moulding as part of the design, signage, and anything else unique to the design.

Finally, insert the detail symbols and conventions. Roofs have a pitch. Show the slope ratio or slope direction. Refer all windows and doors, balcony, roof overhead, and so on to their respective details and/or schedules.

Refer to the checklist at the beginning of this chapter for reminders. Note, though, that this drawing checklist is a general and abbreviated list; students working for an architectural firm should follow the firm's particular checklist or punch list and its unique materials designations.

■ INTERIOR ELEVATIONS

Interior Elevations Purpose

The whole purpose of **interior elevations** is to expose the interior walls so as to locate fixtures, appliances, and cabinets and reveal any additional framing necessary to accommodate fixtures. Interior elevations are necessary when the architect wants to control the visual effects of the interior walls of the structures. Although normally such elevations are not part of the submission, building departments do require an interior elevation showing ADA-compliant elements.

This section gives many examples of interiors, from residential structures as well as commercial and industrial buildings.

For interior elevations, you draw an outline of what you see, based on the measurements of the ceiling height and the width of the walls. Things that are not in the contract are not drawn solid. For example, a refrigerator often is not included in the contract; neither are the washer and dryer. Hence, these should be drawn with a hidden (dotted) line so as to reveal the wall behind, to show the construction of the base molding and/or the outlets needed to power the particular appliance. If there are no cabinet details, the cabinet form coming toward the viewer should be shown in profile instead of voided out, as previously discussed. Do not forget to show the base molding!

Sources of Measurements

Use the floor plan and building sections for accurate measurements of the width and height of an interior elevation wall. When you use these plans, remember that these dimensions are usually to the stud line or centerline of the wall. Interior elevations are drafted to the plaster line.

Interior elevations may not always be drafted at the same scale as the floor plans or sections. Because this requires a scale transition, use caution to avoid errors. In some of the examples in this chapter, the same scale is used and the drawings are directly projected from the plan and section; this is done only to show the theory of where to obtain shapes and configurations.

Information Shown on Interior Elevations

Some architectural offices draft interior elevations for every wall of every room. Although this very careful approach can avoid errors, many wall surfaces are so simple that they do not require a formal drafted interior elevation. These simple walls depend primarily on the interior finish schedule for their proper description.

Use interior elevations when you need to convey an idea, dimension, construction method, or unique feature that is better described by drafting than by a written description in the specification. For example, in a residence, the kitchen, bathrooms, special closets, and wet bars have walls that are usually drafted. On a commercial structure, you may select typical office units, showing bookcases, cabinets, display cases, and so on. In an industrial structure, you may draw the locations of

equipment, conveyor belts, and special heights for bulletin boards or tool racks.

In short, interior elevations are the means of controlling the construction and surface finishes of the interior walls of a structure, and of providing information to contractors. If the contractor does not have the expertise or personnel to do a specific task, specialists (*subcontractors*) will be brought in to assist.

Naming Interior Elevations

In exterior elevations, the titles assigned—North, South, East, and West—are based on the direction the structure faces. In interior elevations, this is reversed: The title is based on the direction in which the viewer is looking. For example, if you are standing in a theater lobby facing north, the interior wall you are looking at has the title "North Lobby Elevation" (see Figure 11.54). To avoid confusion when you are naming an interior elevation, use reference bubbles like those shown in Figure 11.55.

The reference symbol shown on the left is the same as the one used in the foundation plans and framing plans to refer to details. Remember that the reference bubble is a circle with a darkened point on one side, which points to the elevation being viewed and drawn.

The reference symbol shown on the right in Figure 11.55 shows a circle with a triangle inside it. The point of the triangle tells the viewer which elevation is being viewed, and the placement of the triangle automatically divides the circle in half. The top half is filled in with a letter or number, which becomes the name of that interior elevation. The lower half contains the sheet number on which the interior elevation can be found (see also Figures 11.56 and 11.57).

Figure 11.56 shows a floor plan and a symbol used to show multiple elevations. Letter "A" is for the North elevation, "C" is for the South elevation, "B" for the West elevation, and "D" for the East elevation. Figure 11.57 shows two types of **title references** (manner in which the interior elevations are titled for ease of cross-references with the floor plan).

Choosing a Scale

The most desirable scale for an interior elevation is ½" = 1'-0". Most floor plans are drafted at ¼" = 1'-0", so using the half-inch scale makes the translation from floor plan to interior elevation easy: You only need to use a pair of dividers and double every measurement. Interior elevations are seldom drawn larger than this.

If the drawing space does not permit you to use a ½" = 1'-0" scale, or if the scale of the drawing calls for a smaller interior elevation, you may use a ⅜" = 1'-0"

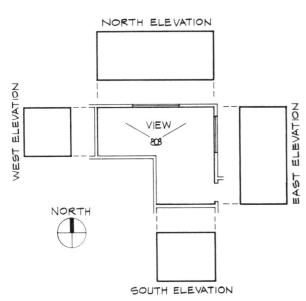

Figure 11.54   Naming interior elevations.

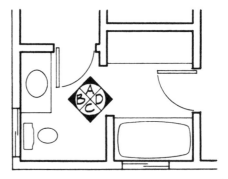

Figure 11.56   Symbol used to show multiple interior elevations.

Figure 11.57   Interior elevation titles.

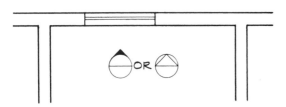

Figure 11.55   Interior elevation reference bubbles.

or ¼″ = 1′-0″ scale. The scale could also depend on the complexity of the wall to be shown.

Using Dotted Lines

Dotted lines are used extensively on interior elevations. As in the drafting of exterior elevations, the dotted line is used to show door-swing direction—for example, for cabinets or for bifold doors on a wardrobe closet. See Figure 11.58. Dotted lines are also used to represent items hidden from view, such as the outline of a kitchen sink, shelves in a cabinet, or the vent above a hood vent, range, or cooktop.

Dotted lines are also used to show the outline of objects to be added later or those **not in the contract** (designated as **N.I.C.**). For example, the outline of a washer and dryer or refrigerator is shown; even though the appliances themselves are N.I.C., space must be allowed for them. The wall behind the appliance is shown, including duplex convenience outlets, and molding or trim at the base of the wall.

Other Drafting Considerations

To draft interior elevations of cabinets, you must know the type, countertop material, heights, general design, and number of cabinet doors.

There are three main types of cabinet doors: **flush**, **flush overlay**, and **lip**. As Figure 11.59 shows, flush overlay doors cover the total face of the cabinet. The front surface of the cabinet, called the **face frame**, does not show. The flush door is shown in Figure 11.60 and the lip door in Figure 11.61. Because the face frame of the cabinet shows when either lip or flush cabinet doors are used, the face frame appears the same in the interior elevation.

Material Designation and Noting

Materials for interior elevations are represented similar to the materials for exterior elevations. Noting is kept simple and generic terms are often used. Specific information, brand names, workmanship notes, procedures, applications, and finishes are placed in the specifications. Later in this chapter you will see examples of generic noting for such items as ceramic tile countertops, an exhaust hood (with a note to "See specs."), and metal partitions.

Outline of Interior Elevations

The outline of an interior elevation represents the outermost measurement of a room. Objects that project

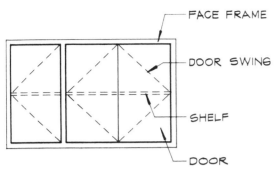

Figure 11.58 Typical elevation of cabinet.

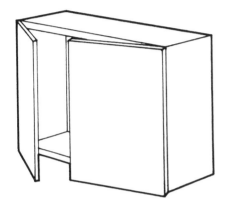

Figure 11.59 Flush overlay doors.

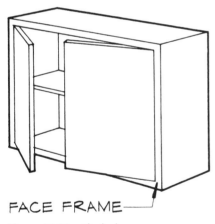

FACE FRAME

Figure 11.60 Flush doors.

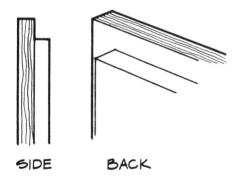

SIDE   BACK

Figure 11.61 Lip door.

toward the viewer, such as cabinets, beams, and air-conditioning ducts, are drawn. Some architectural offices deal with these as if they were in section, but most prefer to treat them as shown in Figures 11.62 and 11.63. Note in Figure 11.63 that the tops of the cabinets have been eliminated in drafting the outline of the cabinet.

Planning for Children and Persons with Disabilities

Always have information available on standards affecting facilities that should be usable by children and persons with disabilities. Here are some of the standards established by several states for disabled persons:

1. Door opening: minimum size 2'-8" clear
2. Restroom grab bars: 33" to 36" above the floor
3. Towel bars: 3'-4" maximum above floor
4. Top of lavatory: 34" maximum above floor
5. Drinking fountains: 3'-0" maximum

Many standards can be obtained by writing to the proper authority, such as the state architect's office. Most standards are presented in the form of a drawing. See Chapter 3 for specifics, and see Figures 11.71 and 11.72 for examples.

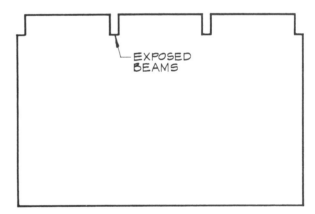

Figure 11.62 Exposed beams.

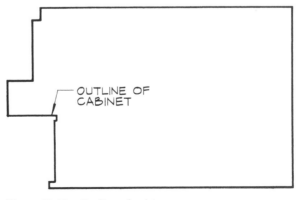

Figure 11.63 Outline of cabinet.

■ DIMENSIONS AND INTERSECTIONS

Dimensions

When you draft a set of interior elevations, do not repeat dimensions that appear elsewhere. For example, you need not indicate the width of rooms on the interior elevation. In fact, avoid repeating dimensions at all costs.

In a similar way, you do not need to dimension the interior elevation of the counter shown in Figure 11.64, because it will occupy the total width of the room. The boundaries, which are the walls, are already dimensioned on the floor plan.

The interior elevations for Figure 11.64 will show a counter, walls, window, and an opening. The portion of the counter that returns toward the opening should be dimensioned either on the floor plan or on the interior elevations, but not on both. See Figure 11.65.

Notice how the base cabinet is dimensioned; in fact, the space between the door and the cabinet could have been dimensioned instead. Deciding whether to dimension the space or the cabinet is based on which is more important. If the space is left for an appliance or some other piece of equipment, then the space should be dimensioned.

The interior elevation is also the place to provide such information as the location of medicine cabinets, the heights of built-in drawers, the locations of mirrors, the required clearance for a hood above a range, and the heights of partitions.

Intersection of Wall and Floor

Interior elevations can also show, in a simple way, the wall and floor intersection. This can be achieved by applying a topset, covering the floor, or using a base or a base and a shoe. This creates a transition between the floor and wall planes. **Topset** is made of flexible material such as rubber and placed on the wall where it touches the floor. With **coving,** the floor material is curved upward against the wall. A **base** is used to cover, or as a guide to control, the

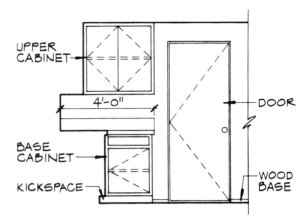

Figure 11.65 Partial interior elevation.

thickness of the plaster on the wall, and a **shoe** covers the intersection between the wall and floor. See Figure 11.66.

■ DRAFTING AN INTERIOR ELEVATION: EXAMPLES

A Kitchen

Figure 11.67 shows a perspective view of a kitchen. The main portion has lip doors on the cabinets, and the extreme left side (not shown in the perspective) has flush overlay doors. Different types of cabinet doors are not usually mixed on a single project; here the intention is simply to show the different methods used to represent them on an interior elevation. Figure 11.68 shows a floor plan of the perspective drawing in Figure 11.67. Note the flush overlay cabinet on the left and the lip or flush cabinets on the right. The upper and base cabinets, slightly to the left of center, project forward.

Figure 11.69 shows the drafted interior elevation of one side of the floor plan of the kitchen. You should take careful note of these points:

1. The difference in the method of representing a flush overlay and a lip door on the cabinets
2. The outlining of the cabinet on the extreme right side of the drawing
3. The use of dotted lines to show door swing, shelves, and the outline of the sink
4. The handling of the forward projection of the upper and base cabinets slightly to the left of center
5. Dimensions and, eventually, the location of notes

A Lobby and Restroom

Figure 11.70 shows a partial floor plan for the lobby and restroom area of an office building. Figure 11.71 shows

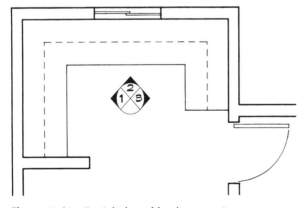

Figure 11.64 Partial plan of food preparation area.

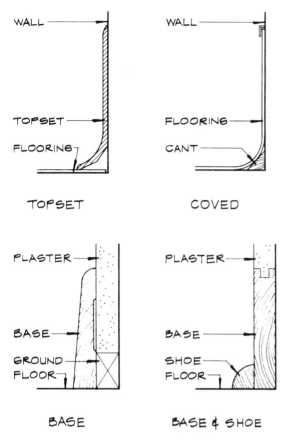

Figure 11.66 Intersection of wall and floor.

the North elevation of the men's toilet. Because this is a public facility, access for persons with disabilities is shown on both the partial floor plan and the interior elevation.

■ COMPUTERS AND INTERIOR ELEVATIONS

The drafting of a set of interior elevations for any structure, be it commercial, industrial, or residential, becomes a relatively painless task when you enlist the aid of a computer. Textures are easily applied to a drawing by using the appropriate commands. If you are drawing full scale in model space, you can transfer heights from the datum layer of the sections and the width and depth of a room from the floor plan.

Cabinet outlines, plumbing fixtures, and many other outlines can be imported from a set of previously developed drawings, or frequently can be found in a collection of shapes. A collection may include configurations and conventions for electrical, cabinetry, plumbing, and other categories, all stored in a library file of symbols and conventions.

The unique shapes of fireplaces, elevators, lifts, handrails, stairs, and so on can be purchased in a generic format, or exact sizes can be obtained from the manufacturers.

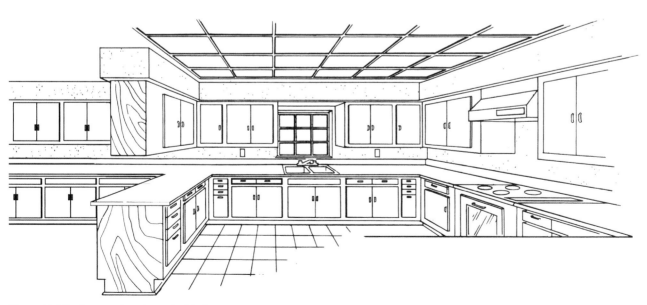

Figure 11.67 Perspective view of a kitchen.

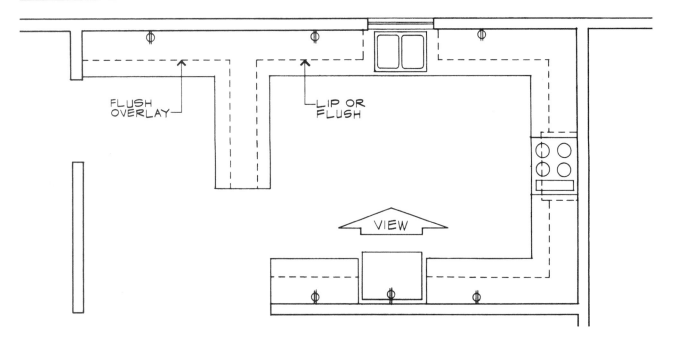

Figure 11.68   Partial floor plan of kitchen.

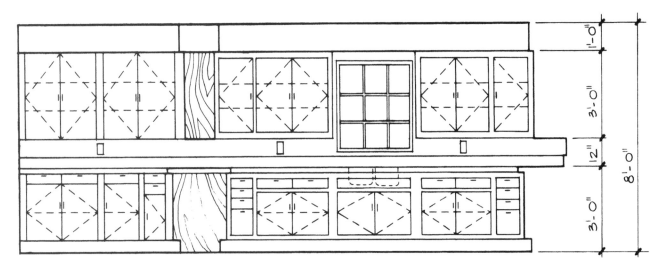

Figure 11.69   Interior elevation of Figure 11.67.

■ EVOLUTION OF A SET OF INTERIOR ELEVATIONS

This section is devoted to the various developmental stages of interior elevations. The Kavanaugh residence was selected to illustrate this. It has an exposed ridge and vaulted ceilings in some of its rooms, including the master suite, dining room, family room, library, kitchen, living room, and guest room. See Figure 11.62 and its accompanying text for a description of how to pictorially draw exposed beams in an interior elevation. The early stages of the floor plan are shown in Figure 11.72.

STAGE I   (Figure 11.73). Stage I, called the **ease** or **datum stage**, sets the parameters. These include the width from wall to wall and the height, and the changes that may occur in the floor or ceiling level. Before beginning this stage, the drafter should consult the project book and become familiar with the sizes and shapes of the various kitchen appliances, plumbing fixtures, cabinets, washer and dryer, and so forth.

STAGE II   (Figure 11.74). Once the maximum size of the room is determined, the real outline of the interior elevation is established by drawing in the soffits, cabinets, fireplaces, and so on. Doors and windows may

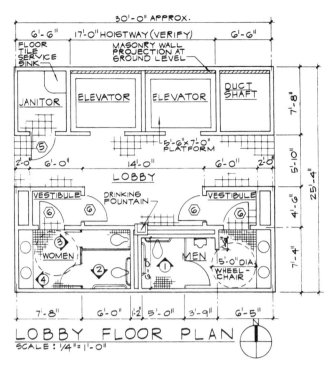

Figure 11.70 Partial floor plan of lobby and restroom. (Courtesy of Westmount, Inc., Real Estate Development.)

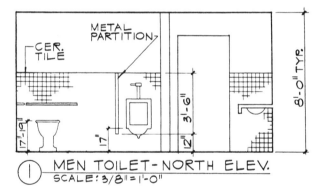

Figure 11.71 Men's toilet: North elevation. (Courtesy of Westmount, Inc., Real Estate Development.)

also be included in this stage. The total outline is now converted to a dark outline.

STAGE III　(Figure 11.75). This is the stage at which various products are added to what is basically an empty room: bathtubs, toilets, built-in bookshelves, fireplaces, and so on.

STAGE IV　(Figure 11.76). Material designations and patterns, such as ceramic tile wainscots, fire extinguishers, bulletin boards, and decorative added forms, are included along with texturing. Some of the shapes for such items as plumbing fixtures can often be obtained from the manufacturer. Swings on cabinet doors and outlines (dotted) of fixtures behind the exposed face,

such as a sink, flues from fireplaces, and shelves, are also added at this stage.

STAGE V　(Figure 11.77). This is the dimensioning stage. Remember, we must locate and size all items. A good example is a mirror. It must first be sized, and its placement or position on a wall must be given to the installer. If the installation is at all complex, a detail should be drawn. If a description is needed, the detailer must know whether the item is described in the specifications. If it is, a generic title is all that is needed at this stage.

Dimensioning also calls for setting limits, such as the clearance of a water closet (toilet) between a wall and a cabinet. Some building codes require a minimum 15″ distance between the center of the water closet and the adjacent wall.

STAGE VI　(Figure 11.78). Notes, references, and titles are included at this stage. Use the following checklist as a guide, or develop your own.

A. Call-outs for all surface materials, other than those included on the finish schedule.

B. A description of all appliances, even those that are not on the surface facing the observer: for example, sinks, garbage disposals, recessed medicine cabinets.

C. A description of items that are not standard. The open shelves in a master bedroom are a classic example.

D. The use of standard conventions to denote shelves, cabinet door swings, drawers, and so forth.

E. Any clearances that must be maintained; those needed for refrigerators and microwave ovens or any client-specific equipment.

■ INTERIOR ELEVATIONS USING BIM/REVIT

Because a three-dimensional model already has been produced when you are using BIM/Revit, the beginning form of the interior elevation already exists in a simplified pattern and is accessed via a pull-down menu (see Figure 11.53B). The drafter's job now is to complete the image, add detail, reference to existing details, do dimensioning when necessary, and note the materials used.

The pull-down menu is used again to obtain the designed outline form of the interior elevation. Before you begin enhancement of the interior elevations, double-check the existing datums, especially for the width and height of each room.

The objects that are closest to the viewer are dark. The objects farther away from the viewer are just a bit lighter, but still dark in relation to such things as doors,

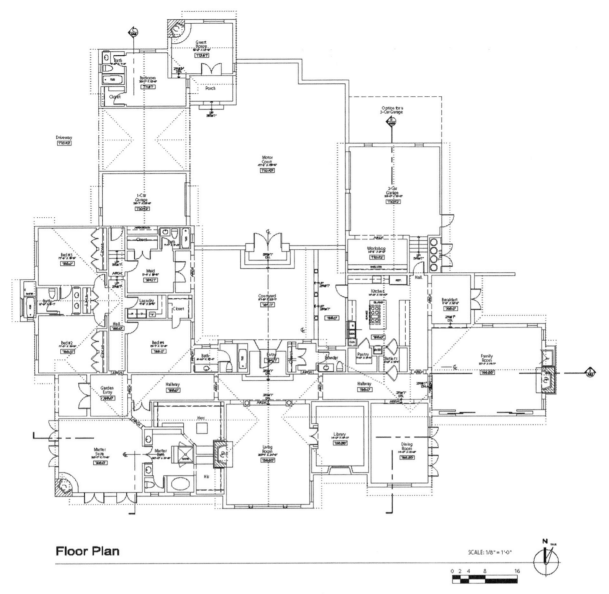

Floor Plan

SCALE: 1/8" = 1'-0"

0 2 4   8   16

Figure 11.72   Kavanaugh plans. (Courtesy of Kavanaugh Development.)

windows, dimensions, and so on. Remember, this is not just a technical drawing with standard line types; it is also a piece of artwork putting the design into visual images so that the craftspersons in the field can easily visualize their task.

The second stage is to put in the appliances and fixtures. In the third stage, you add material designations and patterns. Fourth is dimensioning as needed to help the craftsperson. Finally, you will add noting, referencing, and of course titles and scale.

When you look at some of the ornate structures built in the past, such as those shown in Figures 11.79 and 11.80, you might wonder how the actual construction document looked. Figure 11.79 is the entry to the performance and training center for the famous Lipizzaner stallions. Figure 11.80 is one of the interior spaces of the

world-famous Vienna State Opera (Wiener Staatsoper). Both are located in Vienna, Austria. In fact, elaborate concept sketches were developed by the artists who were commissioned to design these structures, and there was a well-planned coordination between the sculptor and the artist. In some instances, small design models were constructed and sketches were drawn onto the elevations.

In the case of the Hearst castle, San Simeon, the designer Julia Morgan actually drew sketches onto the elevations, which were based on the already-placed sculptures that had been collected by William Randolph Hearst, the great newspaper publisher.

Almost every U.S. resident—and many tourists—know about Disneyland in California. Across from Disneyland, there is still another Disney amusement park, called

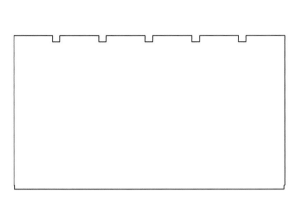

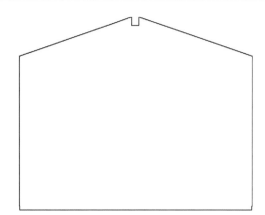

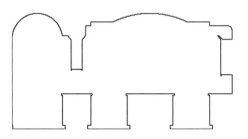

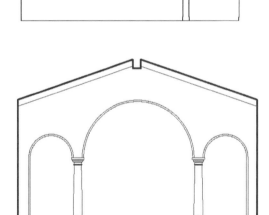

Figure 11.73 Stage I: Datum.

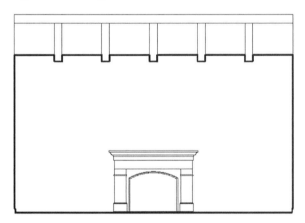

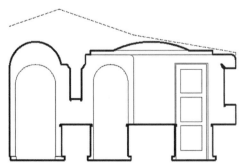

Figure 11.74 Stage II: Real outline and doors and windows.

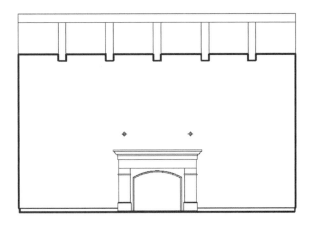
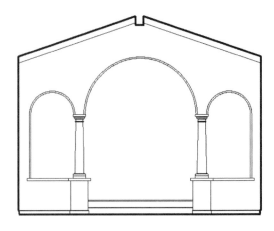

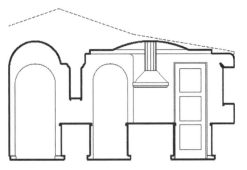
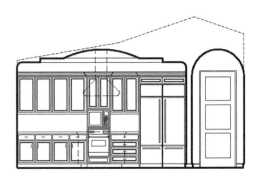

Figure 11.75 Stage III: Products and appliances.

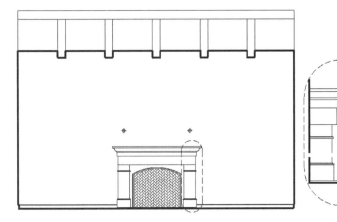
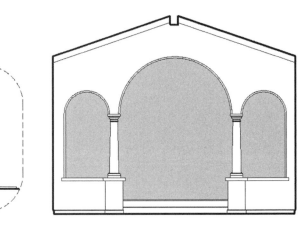

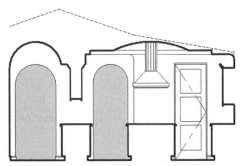
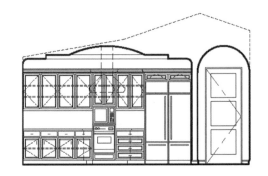

Figure 11.76 Stage IV: Material designation and patterns.

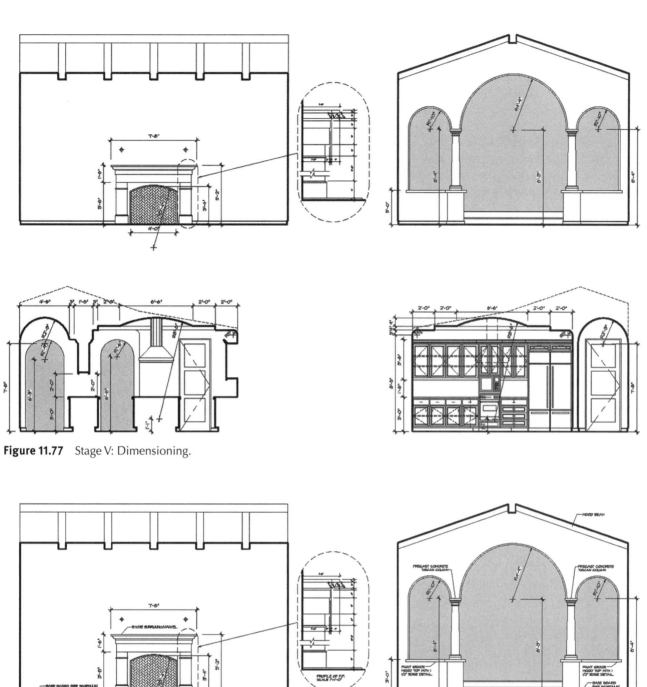

Figure 11.77 Stage V: Dimensioning.

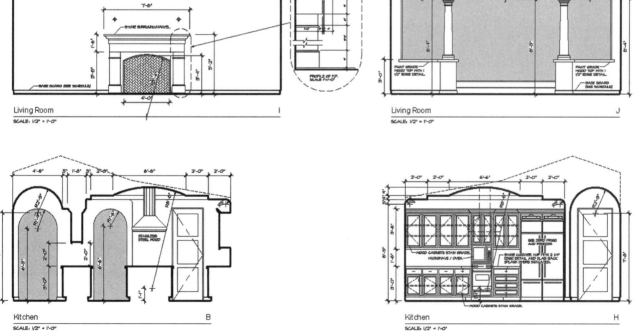

Figure 11.78 Stage VI: Noting, referencing, and titles. (Courtesy of Kavanaugh Development.)

California Adventure. The centerpiece of this park is a man-made 150-foot-high mountain. Atop this mountain sits a large "grizzly bear" rock formation (see Figure 11.81). How does one build such a large mountain, and especially the grizzly bear feature? This is where computers come into play. Miniature models were sculpted and 3-D scanners were used to produce an exact digital image of the model, which was used to plan and draw the rebar structure needed to duplicate the exact shape of the models. Wire mesh and hand-meshed concrete plaster were used to complete the effect.

This technique was also used to complete the second rendition of the MGM lion in front of the MGM Grand Hotel in Las Vegas (shown in Figure 11.82). The lion, as every movie fan knows, is MGM's iconic trademark that opens each of its movies with a roar. Architects and designers alike depend on the computer and 3-D scanners to produce large-scale drawings from a desired model. For example, this enabled the designer to reproduce the lion structure by forming the steel framework to which wire mesh and hand-meshed concrete plaster were applied.

The computer/scanner combination is a great partnership, making it possible to draw complex buildings and structures in three dimensions. Using BIM is a good example of turning 3-D drawings into workable and precise construction documents, via computer-aided design software, such as Revit.

Figure 11.79   Lipizzaner training and performance structure, Vienna, Austria.

Figure 11.81   Disney theme park icon. (© Disney.)

Figure 11.80   Vienna State Opera, Austria.

Figure 11.82   MGM lion, Las Vegas, Nevada. (Courtesy of CityCenter Land, LLC.)

SCHEDULES: DOOR, WINDOW, AND FINISH

■ SCHEDULES DEFINED

A **schedule** is a list or catalog of information that defines the doors, windows, or finishes of a room. The main purpose of incorporating schedules into a set of construction documents is to provide clarity, location, sizes, materials, and information for the designation of doors, windows, room finishes, plumbing and electrical fixtures, and other such items.

■ TABULATED SCHEDULES: DOORS AND WINDOWS

Schedules may be presented in tabulated or pictorial form. Although tabulated schedules in architectural offices vary in form and layout from office to office, the same primary information is provided.

Figures 12.1 and 12.2 are examples of tabulated door and window schedules. The door schedule provides a space for the symbol, the width and height, and the thickness of the door. It also indicates whether the door is to be **solid core** (SC) or **hollow core** (HC). The "type" column may indicate that the door has raised panels, or that it is a slab door or french door, and so forth.

Information

The material space may indicate what kind of wood is to be used for the door, such as birch or beech, and if it is paint-grade or stain-grade quality. Space for remarks is used to provide information, such as the closing device or hardware to be used, or the fire rating required for the door. In some cases, where there is insufficient space for remarks, an asterisk (*) or symbol number may be placed to the left of the schedule or in the designated box and referenced to the bottom of the schedule with the required information. This information must under no circumstances be crowded or left out. For any type of schedule that includes lettering, provide sufficient space in each frame so that your lettering is not cramped or unclear.

DOOR SCHEDULE							
KEY	WIDTH	HEIGHT	THICK.	TYPE	MATERIAL	GLAZING	REMARKS
①	16'-0"	7'-0"	1 3/4"	A	STAIN		ROLL-UP SECTIONAL GARAGE DOOR.
2	3'-6"	7'-0"	1 3/4"	B	PAINT GRD. WOOD		
3	2 – 2'-6"	7'-0"	1 3/4"	C		TEMP.	FRENCH DOORS
4	2 – 2'-6"	7'-0"	1 3/4"	C		TEMP.	FRENCH DOORS
5	2 – 2'-6"	7'-0"	1 3/4"	C		TEMP.	FRENCH DOORS
6	2 – 2'-6"	7'-0"	1 3/4"	C		TEMP.	FRENCH DOORS
7	2'-8"	7'-0"	1 3/4"	D	PAINT GRD. WOOD		
8	2'-8"	7'-0"	1 3/8"	D	PAINT GRD. WOOD		SELF-CLOSING, TIGHT FITTING 20 MINUTE RATED DOOR
9	2'-8"	7'-0"	1 3/8"	D	PAINT GRD. WOOD		
10	2 – 1'-4"	7'-0"	1 3/8"	D	PAINT GRD. WOOD		
11	2'-6"	7'-0"	1 3/8"	D	PAINT GRD. WOOD		
12	2'-6"	7'-0"	1 3/8"	D	PAINT GRD. WOOD		
13	2'-0"	7'-0"	1 3/8"	D	PAINT GRD. WOOD		
14	2'-6"	8'-0"	1 3/8"	D	PAINT GRD. WOOD		
15	2 – 2'-6"	8'-0"	1 3/8"	E	PAINT GRD. WOOD		BY-PASS
16	2'-8"	8'-0"	1 3/8"	D	PAINT GRD. WOOD		
17	2'-8"	8'-0"	1 3/8"	D	PAINT GRD. WOOD		
18	2 – 3'-6"	8'-0"	1 3/8"	E	PAINT GRD. WOOD		BY-PASS
19	2'-6"	8'-0"	1 3/8"	D	PAINT GRD. WOOD		
20	2'-6"	8'-0"	1 3/8"	D	PAINT GRD. WOOD		
21	2'-8"	8'-0"	1 3/8"	D	PAINT GRD. WOOD		
22	2 – 3'-0"	8'-0"	1 3/8"	E	PAINT GRD. WOOD		BY-PASS
23	2'-8"	8'-0"	1 3/8"	D	PAINT GRD. WOOD		
24	2 – 2'-6"	8'-0"	1 3/8"	D	PAINT GRD. WOOD		
25	2'-6"	8'-0"	1 3/8"	D	PAINT GRD. WOOD		
26	2'-6"	8'-0"	1 3/8"	D	PAINT GRD. WOOD		
27	2'-6"	8'-0"	1 3/8"	D	PAINT GRD. WOOD		
28	2'-6"	8'-0"	1 3/8"	D	PAINT GRD. WOOD		

Figure 12.1 Door schedule.

WINDOW SCHEDULE

KEY	WIDTH	HEIGHT	TYPE	MATERIAL	GLAZING	HEAD HGT. FROM F.F.	REMARKS
①	6'-0"	5'-6"	A	VINYL		7'-0"	SINGLE HUNG
2	2'-0"	5'-6"	B	VINYL		7'-0"	SINGLE HUNG
3	2'-0"	5'-0"	B	VINYL		7'-0"	SINGLE HUNG
4	6'-0"	5'-0"	A	VINYL		7'-0"	SINGLE HUNG
5	4'-0"	5'-0"	J	VINYL		7'-0"	SINGLE HUNG
6	4'-6"	5'-0"	J	VINYL		7'-0"	SINGLE HUNG
7	4'-0"	5'-0"	J	VINYL	TEMP.	7'-0"	SINGLE HUNG
8	2'-0"	5'-0"	B	VINYL	TEMP.	7'-0"	SINGLE HUNG
9	2'-0"	5'-0"	B	VINYL	TEMP.	7'-0"	SINGLE HUNG
10	6'-0"	5'-0"	A	VINYL		7'-0"	SINGLE HUNG, EGRESS
11	1'-6"	3'-8"	E	VINYL	TEMP.	8'-0"	SINGLE HUNG
12	1'-9"	5'-6"	B	VINYL		8'-0"	SINGLE HUNG
13	3'-8"	5'-6"	F	VINYL		8'-0"	SINGLE HUNG
14	1'-9"	5'-6"	B	VINYL		8'-0"	SINGLE HUNG
15	2'-6"	5'-0"	G	VINYL		8'-0"	SINGLE HUNG, EGRESS
16	4'-0"	3'-8"	C	VINYL		8'-0"	SINGLE HUNG
17	6'-0"	5'-0"	A	VINYL		8'-0"	SINGLE HUNG, EGRESS
18	2'-0"	3'-8"	E	VINYL	TEMP.	8'-0"	SINGLE HUNG
19	2'-6"	5'-0"	G	VINYL	TEMP.	8'-0"	SINGLE HUNG, EGRESS
20	6'-0"	5'-0"	A	VINYL		8'-0"	SINGLE HUNG, EGRESS
21	3'-0"	5'-0"	D	VINYL		8'-0"	SINGLE HUNG
22	1'-9"	5'-6"	B	VINYL		7'-0"	SINGLE HUNG
23	3'-8"	5'-6"	F	VINYL		7'-0"	SINGLE HUNG
24	1'-9"	5'-6"	B	VINYL		7'-0"	SINGLE HUNG
25	2'-6"	5'-0"	G	VINYL		8'-0"	SINGLE HUNG, EGRESS
26	2'-6"	5'-0"	G	VINYL		8'-0"	SINGLE HUNG, EGRESS
27	5'-0"	3'-8"	H	VINYL	TEMP.	8'-0"	SINGLE HUNG
28	3'-0"	3'-8"	I	VINYL	TEMP.	8'-0"	SINGLE HUNG
29	3'-0"	3'-8"	I	VINYL	TEMP.	8'-0"	SINGLE HUNG
30	3'-6"	3'-6"					SKYLIGHT
31	3'-6"	3'-6"					SKYLIGHT

Figure 12.2   Window schedule.

Symbols

Symbol designations for doors and windows vary in architectural offices and are influenced by each office's procedures. For example, a circle, a hexagon, or a square may be used for all or part of the various schedules; these are the most commonly used. Typically, we do not use triangles, as these symbols are used for revision numbers or for shear walls. Figure 12.3 illustrates symbol shapes and how they may be shown. There are various options, such as using a letter or number, or both, and various shapes. Door and window symbol shapes should be different from each other. To clarify reading the floor plan, the letter "D" at the top of the door symbol and the letter "W" at the top of the window symbol are used. The letter "P" is used for plumbing fixtures, "E" for electrical fixtures, and "A" for appliances. Place the letter in the top part of the symbol. Whatever symbol shape you select, be sure to make the symbol large enough to accommodate the lettering that will go inside the symbol.

When you provide lines for the anticipated number of symbols to be used, allow extra spaces for door and window types that may be added.

■ PICTORIAL SCHEDULES: DOORS AND WINDOWS

Pictorial Representation

In many cases, tabulated schedules cannot clearly define a specific door or window. In this case, you can add to a schedule a call-out with a pictorial drawing of a door or window adjacent to the schedule, as shown in Figure 12.4. Door 1 is difficult to explain, so a pictorial representation makes it clearer.

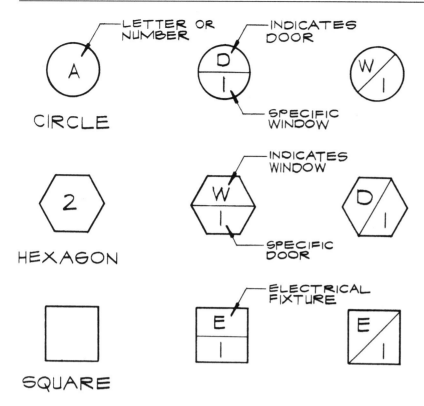

Figure 12.3 Symbol designations.

Pictorial Schedules

A pictorial schedule, as distinct from a pictorial representation, is totally pictorial. Each item is dimensioned and accompanied by data such as material, type, and so forth. Figure 12.5 shows a pictorial schedule of a window. A pictorial schedule provides section references for the **head**, **jamb**, and **sill** sections, so you no longer need to reference the exterior elevations. (The *head* is the top of a window or door, *jamb* refers to the sides of a window or door, and the *sill* is the bottom of the window or door.)

■ CHOOSING A TABULATED OR PICTORIAL SCHEDULE

Tabulated

Your choice of a tabulated schedule may involve the following factors:

1. Specific office procedures
2. Standardization or simplicity of doors and windows selected
3. Large number of items with different dimensions
4. Ease of changing sizes

5. Regular shapes
6. Repetition of call-outs

Pictorial

Choice of a pictorial schedule may involve the following factors:

1. Specific office procedures
2. Unusual and intricate door or window design requirements
3. Very few doors and windows in the project, or very few types used
4. Desired clarity for window section referencing
5. Irregular shapes
6. Mixing types and shapes within a specific assembly

■ INTERIOR FINISH SCHEDULES

Interior finish schedules provide information such as floor and wall material, trim material, and ceiling finish. The layout of an interior finish schedule varies from office to office, because of prevailing office philosophy and specific information the firm receives for various types of projects.

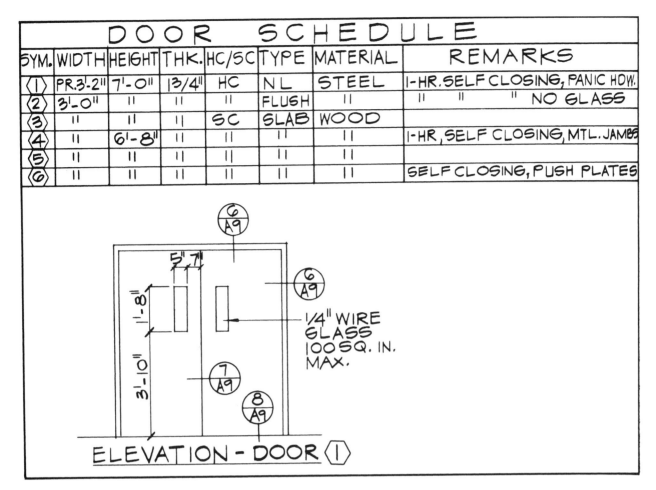

Figure 12.4 Pictorial representation on a tabular schedule.

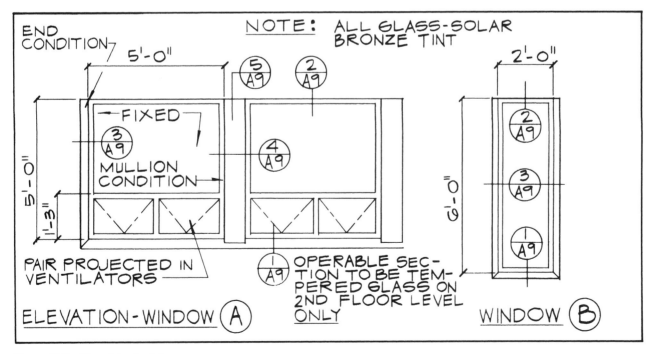

Figure 12.5 Pictorial schedule.

Figures 12.6 and 12.7 show interior finish schedules. The column allocated for room designation may show the room name or an assigned space number or both. This selection may be dictated by the project itself. Another method of defining finishes combines the room finish schedule with a room finish key, which uses numbers and letters to indicate the various materials to be used for floors, walls, and so forth. An example of this type of schedule is shown in Figure 12.8. Using space numbers is more logical for a large office building, for example, than for a very small residence. Once again, when extensive information is required in the remarks section of the schedule, use an asterisk (*) or footnote number for reference at the bottom of the schedule.

■ ADDITIONAL SCHEDULES

The use of other types of schedules depends on office procedure and the type of project. For example, if a project has many types of plumbing and appliance fixtures in various areas, provide additional schedules to clarify and to locate items with their designated symbols.

Figure 12.9 shows a plumbing fixture schedule, and Figure 12.10 shows an appliance schedule. This is an alternative method of identifying the fixtures and appliances that are required for a specific project scope. If these types of schedules are not used in a project, the fixture types, manufacturers, catalog numbers, and other information needed must be included in the project specifications.

For most projects, the specifications will augment information found in the schedules. Examples of information usually found in the specifications include the window manufacturer, the type and manufacturer of the door hardware, and the type and manufacturer of paint for the trim.

■ SCHEDULES AS THEY RELATE TO STRUCTURAL ENTITIES

Shear Wall Finish Schedule

For building projects that may require various structural components, such as shear walls resisting lateral forces or spread concrete footings of various sizes carrying different loads, it is good practice to provide schedules for the various structural entities so as to maintain clear drawings.

Figure 12.11 is an example of a shear wall finish schedule. This schedule and the various finishes reflect the need for this kind of schedule to provide clarity when reviewing the structural drawings. A partial lateral floor plan is shown in Figure 12.12 to illustrate how shear walls are drawn.

Figure 12.6 Interior finish schedule.

INTERIOR FINISH SCHEDULE

ROOM	FLOOR					BASE						WALLS						CEILING						CABINET			PAINT AND STAIN — WALLS				CEILING				TRIM			CABINET			REMARKS
	CARPET	HARDWOOD	MARBLE	CERAMIC TILE	CONCRETE	PAINT GRADE 2 1/4" BASE	STAIN GRADE 4" BASE	MARBLE	STONE	CERAMIC TILE	NONE	5/8" GYP. BD.	5/8" TYPE "X" GYP. BD.	WAINSCOT	STAIN-GRADE WOOD PANELING	FULL-HEIGHT CERAMIC TILE	CEMENT PLASTER	5/8" GYP. BD.	5/8" TYPE "X" GYP. BD.	STAIN GRD. T&G AND BEAMS	STAIN GRD. WOOD BEAM&PLAST.	CEMENT PLASTER	RED BRICK	STAIN GRADE SOLID WOOD	PAINT GRADE	MELAMINE	PAINT	ENAMEL	FAUX FINISH	WALL PAPER	PAINT	ENAMEL	STAIN	NOT APPLICABLE	PAINT	ENAMEL	STAIN	PAINT *	ENAMEL	STAIN *	
B01 MECHANICAL ROOM																																									
B02 CONFERENCE ROOM																																									
B03 CONFERENCE ROOM																																									
B04 HALL																																									
B05 EXISTING LOBBY																																									
B06 EXISTING OFFICE																																									
B07 COPY ROOM																																									
B08 EXISTING OFFICE																																									
B09 EXSITING OFFICE																																									
B10 EXISTING CORRIDOR																																									
B11 EXISTING OFFICE																																									
B12 EXISTING OFFICE																																									
B13 EXISTING RESTROOM																																									
B14 EXISTING CHIOR ROOM																																									
B15 OFFICE																																									
B16 KITCHEN																																									
B17 EXISTING CORRIDOR																																									
B18 MULTI-PURPOSE ROOM																																									
B19 STORAGE																																									
B20 WOMEN'S																																									
B21 MEN'S																																									
B22 HALL																																									
B23 EXISTING JANITOR																																									
B24 STORAGE																																									
B25 EXISTING NURSERY RROM																																									
B26 OFFICE																																									
B27 EXISTING CRIB ROOM																																									
B28 EXISTING RESTROOM																																									
B29 EXISTING MECHANICAL ROOM																																									

Figure 12.7   Interior finish schedule.

Pier/Spread Footing Schedule

Another example of a schedule that is related to a structural entity is a pier and/or spread footing schedule. This type of schedule is recommended when there are numerous spread footings of various sizes. This occurs on many commercial buildings. Figure 12.13 illustrates an example of a pier/spread footing schedule. Note the variances in the steel reinforcing requirements, the sizes of the base plates, the number and sizes of the anchor bolts, and other items. Figure 12.14 depicts how the schedule symbols may be shown on a structural foundation plan.

A copy of a schedule can be made and attached to a set of drawings as required by the scope of work. As a project is altered, a new copy can replace the earlier one to represent the changes. In most cases, a spreadsheet or the computer program will aid in the development of a schedule (see Figure 12.15).

■ CAD-GENERATED AND COMPUTER-DRAFTED SCHEDULES

To illustrate a project utilizing the abilities of a CAD-generated plotting system in developing schedule layouts, three examples are given in the following figures.

Figure 12.16 shows an example of a computer-generated interior finish schedule. This schedule can be revised quickly with a computer while still preserving the basic layout for future projects.

Figure 12.17 depicts a window schedule with drawings of some of the window types that will be

ROOM FINISH SCHEDULE

NO.	ROOM	FINISHES				CEIL. HGT.	ROOM AREA	REMARKS
		FLOOR	BASE	WALLS	CEILING			
101	RECEPTION	B	1	A	2	9'-0"	110▫'	
102	OFFICE	A		B	2	8'-0"	170▫'	
103	OFFICE	A		B	2	"	180▫'	
104	OFFICE	A		B	2	"	185▫'	
105	WOMENS TOIL.	C	1	A	1	7'-6"	30▫'	
106	MENS TOILET	C	1	A	1	7'-6"	25▫'	

ROOM FINISH KEY

FLOORS		BASES		WALLS		CEILINGS	
A	CARPET	1	WOOD	A	5/8" SHEETROCK	1	5/8" SHEETROCK
B	OAK PARQUET			B	1x6 T&G CEDAR	2	SUSP. AC. TILE
C	CERAMIC TILE						

Figure 12.8　Room finish schedule—key type.

incorporated into this project. As discussed previously in this chapter, the pictorial form adds clarity and demonstrates the symbology for window sections. Note in the glazing column that the clouded (shaded) areas refer to tempered glass. This has been done to satisfy a building department requirement and is referenced to a delta one symbol, which stands for a building department requirement. The architect has also added notes to indicate the alignment of the windows and doors. Notes relating to building code requirements are shown below the window types.

The types of doors specified for this project are shown in pictorial form (see Figure 12.18). Types of doors have been depicted pictorially for clarity and referencing. A clouded area for a specific door illustrates a revision and requirement by the governing building department. These types of doors are keyed with a letter on the door schedule. The computer offers the flexibility to alter or revise the schedule layouts for projects that may have different requirements.

■ SCHEDULE TEMPLATES

If a set of construction documents was produced on the computer, chances are that a basic office standard template (pattern) was produced. Every CAD drafter should be able to produce a new basic template as office standards change. The new pattern will change as the technology changes for architectural installation of windows, doors, and so forth.

Schedule templates can be produced on the computer by simply drawing lines and arranging them horizontally and vertically. The text for the main title and the column titles is entered by typing the word "key" in each position, as a placeholder. If the first phrase is positioned and centered carefully, the remaining columns will also be centered. Next, edit the word "key" to reflect the desired column titles and change the size if necessary. The text will automatically center the new titles. Look at Figure 12.19. Because we are producing a generic schedule, put a hyphen (dash) in the unused spaces as a placeholder. The user of this schedule need only replace the

FIXTURE SCHEDULE

SYMB.	EQUIPMENT DEASCRIPTION	MOUNTING LOCATION	MFR / MODEL NO.	FIN NOTES
1	WATER CLOSET FLUSH VALVE	SURFACE / FLOOR	AMERICAN STD 3043.102	WHITE
2	URINAL FLUSH VALVE	SURFACE / WALL	AMERICAN STD 6541.132	WHITE
3	LAVATORY (SEE 8/501) (SELF-RIMMED)	SURFACE / COUNTERTOP	AMERICAN STD 0410.021	WHITE
4	FLUSH VALVE		SLOAN OPTIMA	CHROME
5	FAUCET	CENTER SET	SLOAN OPTIMA	CHROME

ACCESSORY SCHEDULE

SYMB.	EQUIPMENT DESCRIPTION	MOUNTING LOCATION	MFR / MODEL NO.	FIN NOTES
1	PAPER TOWEL DISPENSER	SURFACE / WALL	BRADLEY 237-11	STAINLESS STEEL
2	SOAP DISPENSER	SURFACE / COUNTERTOP	BRADLEY 6326-68	STAINLESS STEEL
3	PAPER TOWEL DISPENSER	SEMI-RECESS WALL	BRADLEY 237-10	STAINLESS STEEL
4	SANITARY NAPKIN/ TAMPON DISPENSER	SURFACE/ WALL	BRADLEY 426-FREE	STAINLESS STEEL
5	1 1/4" DIA. GRAB BAR (SEE DTL. 4/501)	SURFACE / WALL	BRADLEY 812-7	STAINLESS STEEL
6	TOILET SEAT COVER DISPENSER	SURFACE/ WALL	BRADLEY 583	STAINLESS STEEL
7	TOILET TISSUE DISPENSER	SURFACE/ WALL	BRADLEY 5402	STAINLESS STEEL
8	SANITARY NAPKIN DISPOSAL	SURFACE/ WALL	BRADLEY 4722-15	STAINLESS STEEL
19	GEOMETRIC HC SYMBOLS (SEE DETAIL 3/501)	SURFACE/ WALL		PLASTIC
20	ACCESSIBLE RESTROOM SIGN (SEE DETAIL 1/501)	SURFACE/ WALL		PLASTIC

Figure 12.9 Plumbing fixture schedule.

hyphens with the desired information: height, width, material, and so on. All of the information will be automatically centered or placed with the margin to the left, as shown in the "Material" column in Figure 12.20.

Of course, you can take an example from a previous job that has been produced manually and scan it into the computer. Whichever method you use, it is best to put the information on a separate layer. This makes it easy to do changes, revisions, or corrections.

Figure 12.21 is a depiction of a completed series of schedules as presented to the building department for review. Depending on the size of the project, all schedules can be placed on the same sheet for organization's sake.

■ SCHEDULES USING BIM OR REVIT

Computer-Developed Schedule

If a set of construction documents was produced using BIM or Revit, odds are the schedules can be generated automatically. The schedules are tied to the parametric design of the software, which will generate the table for you. This is the ideal situation, as the software's capabilities improve the accuracy of the schedules for both the size and quantity of windows, doors, and finishes. Previously, it was common for a drafter to spend hours reviewing a series of schedules; here the software does

APPLIANCE SCHEDULE

SYM.	ITEM	MANUFACTURER	CATALOG NO.	REMARKS
1	COOKTOP	APPLIANCES INC.	RU38V	WHITE
2	MICROWAVE	"	JKP65G	
3	DISHWASHER	"	GSD2500	WHITE
4	DISPOSER	"	GFC510	

Figure 12.10 Appliance fixture schedule.

Shear Wall Finish Schedule

Sym	Wall Material	Blocked / Unblocked	Nailing Size & Spacing	Stud Size	Anchor Bolts & Number	Remarks
S 1	1/2" GYPSUM WALLBOARD	UNBLOCKED	5d COOLER @ 7" O.C.	2 X 4	(6) 1/2" DIA. X 10"	-
S 2	5/8" GYPSUM WALLBOARD	BLOCKED	6d COOLER @ 7" O.C.	2 X 4	(8) 1/2" DIA. X 10"	-
S 3	3/8" PLYWOOD STRUCT - 1	BLOCKED	8d @ 3"	2 X 4	(5) 5/8" DIA. X 10"	FIELD NAILING : 8d @ 12" O.C.
S 4	1/2" PLYWOOD STRUCT - 1	BLOCKED	10d @ 3"	3 X 4	(8) 5/8" DIA. X 10"	FIELD NAILING : 8d @ 12" O.C.
S 5	- -	-	- -	-	-	-
S 6	- -	-	- -	-	-	-
- -	- -	-	- -	-	-	-
- -	- -	-	- -	-	-	-

Figure 12.11   Shear wall finish schedule example.

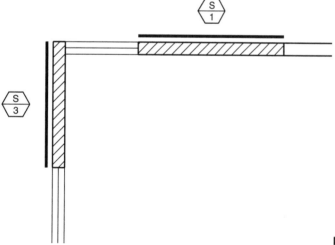

Figure 12.12   Shear wall in plan view.

Pier/Spread Footing Schedule

Sym	Size	Depth	Reinforcing	Base Plate Size	Anchor Bolts & Number	Remarks
P1	1'-6" X 1'-6"	10"	(3) 1/2" DIA. BARS ONE WAY	N.A.	N.A.	KEEP STEEL 3" CLR. OF EARTH
P2	2'-6" X 2'-6"	12"	(4) 1/2" DIA. BARS EACH WAY	6" X 6" x 1/4"	(2) 5/8" DIA.	KEEP STEEL 3" CLR. OF EARTH
P3	3'-6" X 3'-6"	12"	(5) 1/2" DIA. BARS EACH WAY	7" X 7" X 3/8"	(4) 5/8" DIA.	KEEP STEEL 3" CLR. OF EARTH
P4	-	-	-	-	-	-
-	-	-	-	-	-	-
-	-	-	-	-	-	-

Figure 12.13 Pier/spread footing schedule example.

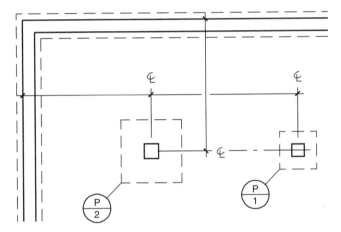

Figure 12.14 Pier/spread footing example.

much of the thinking for you. There are opportunities to customize the schedules and the data on the schedule, but it is truly amazing how far we have come from the traditional methods of scheduling. See Figures 12.22 and 12.23.

Revit Schedule

In traditional drafting, we constructed schedules much like a spreadsheet is built: cell by cell. With Revit those days are gone. The program is designed to create schedules of many components of a building, not just windows, doors, fixtures, and finishes. For example, when you place a new window, the program automatically numerates it in the floor plan and cross-references it to the window schedule. Most of the data you need for the schedule is already built into the software. The schedule will report with absolute accuracy the data you input. That is great news—provided the information is correct. However, if it is determined that a change is desired (say, a window would be better in a larger size), you can simply enlarge it and the program will automatically update the schedule.

You will have to spend some downtime with Revit customizing the schedules to look the way you want them to look.

A view tab is utilized to bring up specific schedules. The lengthy list of options is almost limitless, ranging from building areas, to electric equipment, to facias or even eave gutters. All of these tabs are broken down even further to allow you to select or mark the fields you require for your customized schedule. Additional data can be customized by building level. Though this function may not be required for door or windows, it is ideal for floor area calculations.

Once the schedule is formatted as desired, it is simply a matter of dragging and dropping it onto the desired sheet and location to plot it.

WINDOW SCHEDULE

SYM.	WIDTH	HEIGHT	TYPE	FRAME	SCR.	GLAZ. AREA	VENT. AREA	REMARKS
○								
○								
○								
○								
○								
○								
○								
○								
○								
○								
○								
○								
○								
○								

Figure 12.15 Predrawn schedules.

INTERIOR FINISH SCHEDULE

ROOM	FLOOR: CARPET	HARDWOOD	STONE	CERAMIC TILE	CONCRETE	BASE: PAINT GRADE 8" BASE	PAINT GRADE 5" BASE	STAIN GRADE 8" BASE	STONE	CERAMIC TILE	NONE	WALLS: 5/8" GYP. BD. W/SKIM-COAT	CERAMIC TILE WAINSCOT	WAINSCOT	STAIN-GRD WOOD PANELING	FULL-HEIGHT CERAMIC TILE	STUCCO	CEILINGS: 5/8" TYPE 'X' GYP BD	STAIN GRD. WOOD PANELING	STAIN GRD. T&G AND BEAMS	STAIN GRD WOOD BEAMS/PLAST	STUCCO	CABINETS: RED BRICK	STAIN GRADE ALDER	PAINT GRADE	MELAMINE	PAINT/STAIN WALLS: PAINT	ENAMEL	FAUX FINISH	WALL PAPER	CEILING: PAINT	ENAMEL	STAIN	NOT APPLICABLE	TRIM: PAINT	ENAMEL	STAIN	CABINET: PAINT #	ENAMEL	STAIN #	REMARKS
LIVING RM.	X							X				X						X									X				X				X						
DINING RM.	X							X				X						X									X				X				X						2X6 WOOD PLANK DECKING AT FAM. RM. DECK
FAMILY RM.	X																			X							X							X	X						
KITCHEN			X									X						X						X			X				X				X					X	
NOOK			X									X						X						X			X				X				X						
POWDER				X						X		X						X							X						X				X			X			
LAUNDRY				X						X		X						X							X		X				X				X						
2-CAR GARAGE					X						X	X						X									X				X				X						
STAIRWELL	X							X				X						X									X				X				X						
HALL	X							X				X						X									X				X				X						
MAST. BDRM.	X							X				X						X									X				X				X						
MAST. BATH				X						X		X						X							X		X				X				X			X			
WALK-IN CLOSET	X							X				X						X									X				X				X						
BED RM. #2	X							X				X						X									X				X				X						
BATH #2				X						X		X						X							X		X				X				X			X			
BED RM. #3	X							X				X						X									X				X				X						
BATH #3				X						X		X						X							X		X				X				X			X			
BED RM. #4	X							X				X						X									X				X				X						
BATH #4				X						X		X						X							X		X				X				X			X			
CELLAR					X						X	X						X									X				X				X						
WINE				X					X												X			X							X				X						

Figure 12.16 Interior finish schedule.

WINDOW SCHEDULE

KEY	WIDTH	HEIGHT	TYPE	MATERIAL	GLAZING	HEAD HGT. FROM F.F.	REMARKS
①	2'-4"	5'-0"	D	PAINT GRD. WOOD		8'-0"	CASEMENT
2	2'-4"	5'-0"	D	"		8'-0"	CASEMENT
3	4'-8"	5'-2"	A	"		8'-0"	FRENCH CASEMENT
4	4'-8"	4'-0"	A	STAIN GRD. WOOD	TEMPERED	6'-8"	FRENCH CASEMENT
5	4'-8"	5'-0"	A	PAINT GRD. WOOD		8'-0"	FRENCH CASEMENT
6	2'-0"	4'-0"	D	"	TEMPERED	6'-8"	CASEMENT
7	2'-0"	4'-0"	D	"		6'-8"	CASEMENT
8	2'-0"	4'-0"	D			6'-8"	CASEMENT
9	2'-0"	3'-0"	B	"		8'-0"	CASEMENT
10	6'-0"	4'-0"	C	"		6'-8"	FIXED
11	2'-0"	4'-0"	D	"		6'-8"	CASEMENT
12	4'-0"	4'-0'	A	"		6'-8"	FRENCH CASEMENT, EGRESS (12.25 SQ. FT.)
13	4'-0"	3'-6"	A	"		6'-8"	FRENCH CASEMENT
14	2'-0"	3'-0"	B		TEMPERED	6'-8"	CASEMENT
15	2'-0"	4'-0"	E	"		6'-8"	FIXED, SEE ELEV
16	4'-0"	4'-0"	A	"	TEMPERED	6'-8"	FRENCH CASEMENT
17	2'-0"	4'-0"	D	"		6'-8"	CASEMENT
18	2'-0"	4'-0"	E	"	TEMPERED	6'-8"	INSWING CASEMENT, SEE ELEV
19	2'-0"	4'-0"	D	"	TEMPERED	6'-8"	CASEMENT
20	2'-0"	4'-0"	E	"		6'-8"	INSWING CASEMENT, SEE ELEV
21	2'-0"	3'-0"	B			6'-8"	CASEMENT

WINDOW TYPES

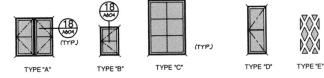

TYPE "A" TYPE "B" TYPE "C" TYPE "D" TYPE "E"

NOTES:

1. ALIGN TOP OF WINDOWS WITH TOP OF DOORS SO THAT TOP EDGES OF DOORS AND WINDOWS ALIGN IN A LEVEL PLANE ABOVE FINISH FLOOR.

2. ALL ESCAPE OR RESCUE WINDOWS SHALL HAVE A MINIMUM NET CLEAR OPENABLE AREA OF 5.7 SQ. FT. THE MINIMUM NET CLEAR OPENABLE HEIGHT DIMENSION SHALL BE 24". THE MINIMUM NET CLEAR OPENABLE WIDTH DIMENSION SHALL BE 20" WHEN WINDOWS ARE PROVIDED AS A MEANS OF ESCAPE OR RESCUE, THEY SHALL HAVE A FINISHED SILL HEIGHT NOT MORE THAN 44" ABOVE FIN. FLR.

3. SKYLIGHTS SHALL HAVE A NON-COMBUSTIBLE FRAME GLAZED WITH DUAL GLAZING OF HEAT STRENGTHENED OR FULLY TEMPERED GLASS OR SHALL BE A 3/4-HOUR FIRE-RESISTIVE ASSEMBLY

4. WINDOWS WITH SILLS LESS THAN 5'-0" ABOVE TUB OR SHOWER FLOOR SHALL BE TEMPERED

Figure 12.17 Window schedule and types of windows.

DOOR SCHEDULE

KEY	WIDTH	HEIGHT	THICK.	TYPE	MATERIAL	GLAZING	REMARKS
①	2'-8"	6'-8"	2 1/4"	C	PAINT GRD. WOOD	TEMP.	FRENCH DOORS (SEE ELEVATIONS)
2	(2)-3'-0"	8'-0"	2 1/4"	E	"	TEMP.	FRENCH DOORS (SEE ELEVATIONS)
3	4'-0"	8'-0"	2 1/4"	A	STAIN GRD. WOOD		
4	8'-6"	8'-3"		D	"		GARAGE OVERHEAD SECTIONAL DOOR (SEE ELEVATIONS)
5	8'-6"	8'-3"		D	"		GARAGE OVERHEAD SECTIONAL DOOR (SEE ELEVATIONS)
6	3'-0"	6'-8"	2 1/4"	K	PAINT GRD. WOOD		
7	(2)-2'-0"	5'-0"		F	"		TRASH AREA, GATE
8	(2)-3'-0"	8'-0"	2 1/4"	E	"	TEMP.	FRENCH DOORS (SEE ELEVATIONS)
9	(2)-3'-0"	8'-0"	2 1/4"	E	"	TEMP.	FRENCH DOORS (SEE ELEVATIONS)
10	(2)-3'-0"	8'-0"	2 1/4"	E	"	TEMP.	FRENCH DOORS (SEE ELEVATIONS)
11	(2)-2'-6"	6'-8"	2 1/4"	E	"	TEMP.	FRENCH DOORS (SEE ELEVATIONS)
12	2'-6"	6'-8"	1 3/4"	J	"		
13	(2)-2'-0"	6'-8"	1 3/4"	G	"		
14	3'-0"	6'-8"	1 3/4"	J	"		20 MIN. RATED, SELF-CLOSING & TIGHT FITTING
15	2'-8"	6'-8"	1 3/4"	J	"		
16	2'-6"	6'-8"	1 3/4"	J	"		
17	(2)-2'-0"	6'-8"	1 3/4"	G	"		
18	(2)-2'-0"	6'-8"	1 3/4"	G	"		
19	2'-6"	6'-8"	1 3/4"	J	"		
20	(2)-2'-6"	6'-8"	1 3/4"	G	"		
21	(2)-3'-0"	8'-0"	1 3/4"	E	"	TEMP.	FRENCH DOORS (SEE ELEVATIONS)
22	(2)-3'-0"	8'-0"	1 3/4"	E	"	TEMP.	FRENCH DOORS (SEE ELEVATIONS)
23	(2)-2'-6"	6'-8"	1 3/4"	E	"	TEMP.	FRENCH DOORS (SEE ELEVATIONS)
24	(2)-2'-0"	6'-8"	1 3/4"	G	"		
25	(2)-2'-0"	6'-8"	1 3/4"	G	"		
26	2'-6"	6'-8"	1 3/4"	J	"		
27	2'-8"	6'-8"	1 3/4"	J	"		
28	2'-8"	8'-0"	1 3/4"	J	"		
29	2'-8"	8'-0"	1 3/4"	J	"		
30	(2)-1'-6"	8'-0"	1 3/4"	G	PAINT GRD. WOOD		
31	2'-8"	8'-0"	1 3/4"	J	PAINT GRD. WOOD		
32	(2)-1'-0"	8'-0"	1 3/4"	G	"		
33	2'-6"	8'-0"	1 3/4"	J	"		
34	2'-8"	6'-8"	1 3/4"	H	"		
35	2'-8"	6'-8"	1 3/4"	J	"		
36	(2)-4'-0"	6'-8"	1 3/4"	B	"		
37	2'-6"	6'-8"	1 3/4"	J	"		

<u>DOOR TYPES</u>

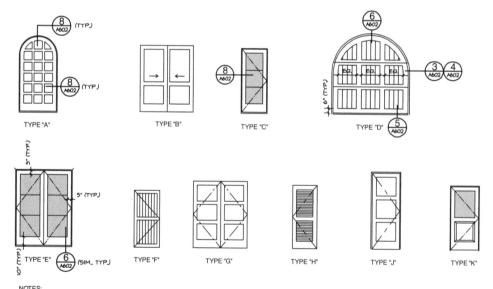

TYPE "A" TYPE "B" TYPE "C" TYPE "D"

TYPE "E" TYPE "F" TYPE "G" TYPE "H" TYPE "J" TYPE "K"

<u>NOTES:</u>
1. ALL DOORS TO BE SOLID CORE.
2. BOTTOM OF INTERIOR DOORS TO BE 3/8" ABOVE FIN. FLR.

Figure 12.18 Door schedule and types of doors.

Window Schedule

Key	Width	Height	Type	Material	Glazing	
⬡⟨-⟩	-	-	-	-	-	
-	-	-	-	-	-	
-	-	-	-	-	-	
-	-	-	-	-	-	
-	-	-	-	-	-	
-	-	-	-	-	-	
-	-	-	-	-	-	
-	-	-	-	-	-	
-	-	-	-	-	-	
-	-	-	-	-	-	

Figure 12.19 Partial template of a schedule with placeholder.

Window Schedule

Key	Width	Height	Type	Material	Glazing	
⟨1⟩	2'-4"	5'-0"	D	PAINT GRADE WOOD	-	
2	2'-4"	5'-0"	D	-	-	
3	4'-8"	5'-2"	A	-	-	
4	4'-8"	4'-0"	A	STAIN GRADE WOOD	TEMPERED	
5	4'-8"	5'-0"	A	PAINT GRADE WOOD	-	
6	2'-0"	4'-0"	D	-	TEMPERED	
7	2'-0"	4'-0"	D	-	-	
8	2'-0"	4'-0"	D	-	-	
9	2'-0"	3'-0"	B	-	-	
10	6'-0"	4'-0"	C	-	-	

Figure 12.20 Replacing the placeholder with live information.

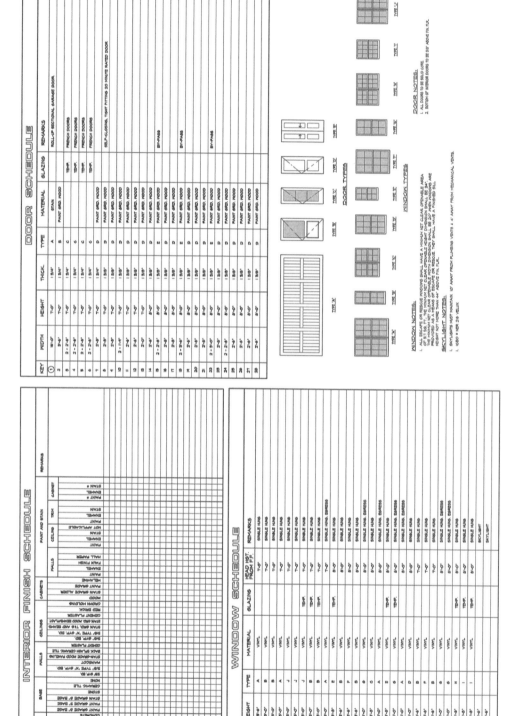

Figure 12.21 Completed door, window, and finish schedules on a plot sheet.

Window Schedule								
Mark	Type	Width	Height	Head Height	Sill Height	Family	Family and Type	Description
1	36" x 48"	3' - 0"	4' - 0"	6' - 0"	2' - 0"	Casement 3x3	Casement 3x3 with Trim: 36"	
2	16" x 72"	1' - 4"	6' - 0"	9' - 0"	3' - 0"	Fixed	Fixed: 16" x 72"	
3	36" x 60"	3' - 0"	5' - 0"	8' - 0"	3' - 0"	Casement 3x3	Casement 3x3 with Trim: 36"	
4	24" x 24"	2' - 0"	2' - 0"	5' - 0"	3' - 0"	Fixed	Fixed: 24" x 24"	
5	36" x 24"	3' - 0"	2' - 0"	5' - 0"	3' - 0"	Fixed	Fixed: 36" x 24"	
6	24" x 48"	2' - 0"	4' - 0"	11' - 0"	7' - 0"	Fixed	Fixed: 24" x 48"	
7	36" x 48"	3' - 0"	4' - 0"	7' - 0"	3' - 0"	Casement 3x3	Casement 3x3 with Trim: 36"	

Figure 12.22 Completed window schedule utilizing Revit.

Door Schedule					
Mark	Width	Height	Head Height	Family and Type	Description
1	6' - 0"	7' - 0"	7' - 0"	Sliding-2 panel: 72" x 84" Metal	
2	6' - 0"	7' - 0"	7' - 0"	Sliding-2 panel: 72" x 84" Metal	
3	6' - 0"	7' - 0"	7' - 0"	Sliding-2 panel: 72" x 84" Metal	
4	6' - 0"	7' - 0"	7' - 0"	Sliding-2 panel: 72" x 84" Metal	
5	6' - 0"	7' - 0"	7' - 0"	Sliding-2 panel: 72" x 84" Metal	
6	6' - 0"	7' - 0"	7' - 0"	Sliding-2 panel: 72" x 84" Metal	
7	2' - 6"	7' - 0"	7' - 0"	Single-Flush: 30" x 84"	
8	2' - 6"	7' - 0"	7' - 0"	Single-Flush: 30" x 84"	
9	2' - 6"	7' - 0"	7' - 0"	Single-Flush: 30" x 84"	
10	2' - 6"	7' - 0"	7' - 0"	Single-Flush: 30" x 84"	

Figure 12.23 Completed door schedule utilizing Revit.

ARCHITECTURAL DETAILS
AND VERTICAL LINKS
(STAIRS/ELEVATORS)

THE PURPOSE OF ARCHITECTURAL DETAILS

Architectural **details** are enlarged drawings of specific architectural assemblies. These details are usually provided by the architect, and structural details are furnished by the structural engineer.

Architectural details are done for many different construction assemblies, including door and window details, fireplace details, stair details, and wall and roof assemblies. The number and kind of details needed for a given project depend entirely on the architect's estimate of what is needed to clarify the construction process. The contractor may request additional architectural details in the construction stage.

FREEHAND DETAIL SKETCHES

Architectural detailers often start with **freehand sketches** and an architectural scale in order to solve different construction assemblies in a structure. Once the details have been formulated in a scaled freehand sketch, they are then ready to be drafted in final form. Many details, such as standard foundation and wall assemblies, are relatively straightforward and do not require freehand sketches. The following sections provide examples of residences to give you an understanding of what is required.

The drawing of details from scratch requires a drafter who understands detailing relative to the detail area available. One should not draft a detail and plot it to fit the space, but rather should begin with the office format sheet and then decide whether **keynotes** (notes written in chart form off to one side of the detail) will be used and what type of noting will be used. The steps required to create a detail and to determine what formatting to use are covered later in this chapter.

USING DETAILS IN CONSTRUCTION DOCUMENTS

Freehand Detail Sketches: Mountain Residence

Architectural details encompass many construction assemblies, such as this mountain residence with unique foundation details. This residence was selected because of its unusual geometric shape, similar to that of a pentagon. Figure 13.1 shows a freehand sketch detail of an exterior bearing footing for this residence. There are some nonstandard conditions in this detail, such as steel anchor clips for connection of the floor joists to the mudsill (for lateral support), steel reinforcing placement in the wall for earth retention, and location of (and installation requirements for) a footing drain. Figures 13.2

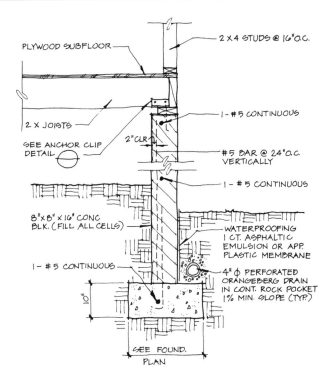

Figure 13.1 Detail of exterior bearing footing.

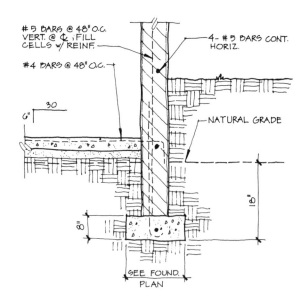

Figure 13.2 Detail of exterior footing.

and 13.3 show two other exterior footing conditions. Figure 13.2 shows a concrete floor condition below grade, and Figure 13.3 shows the wood deck connection to the exterior footing. Finally, Figure 13.4 shows an interior concrete-block wall and its foundation.

Figure 13.5 shows a square concrete pier and reinforcing bars required to support a heavy concentrated load distributed by a 6 × 6 post. Study each of these carefully before proceeding further.

If you are asked to detail a wood beam and masonry wall connection, with the required assembly information, first draw a freehand sketch that includes the necessary information. Figure 13.6 shows such a sketch. The size of the steel plate dictates the masonry wall offset, and the embedment of the anchor bolts is 10".

An important factor in architectural detailing is providing details that are an integral part of the architectural design of the building. For example, if floor cantilevers and wood soffits are an integral part of the design (see Figure 13.7), first design and solve these assemblies in sketch form, before completing the final detail. Creativity and craftsmanship in architectural detailing are as important as any other factors in designing a structure.

In this particular residence, we thought that the top of the **head** section of the windows and doors should have a direct relationship to the eave assembly. Therefore, we detailed the eave assembly with the various wood members forming a wood soffit directly above the head section of the window. See Figure 13.8. We sketched in detail the windowsill and exterior wall assembly projecting down from the head section. Using both Figures 13.7 and 13.8, it was possible to design and detail the **jamb** section for this particular opening, using the established head and sill section as a guide for the detailed assembly.

Details: Beach Residence

Foundation Details. The architectural details for this beach residence project were fairly conventional, but were still worth investigating with freehand drawings. For example, we sketched the foundation details for this two-story residence to take into account the sandy soil conditions. Figure 13.9 shows a detail for the exterior bearing wall. Because this soil did not provide good bearing qualities, we used horizontal reinforcing rods at the top and bottom of the foundation wall. Non-bearing walls still required a minimal footing to support the weight of the wall and a depth of concrete to receive the anchor bolts. Because this residence has a change of floor levels, we provided a detail through the floor transitions. Figure 13.10 shows a detail at a location that has incorporated the **risers** and **tread**. (A *riser* is the vertical dimension of a stair step and the *tread* is

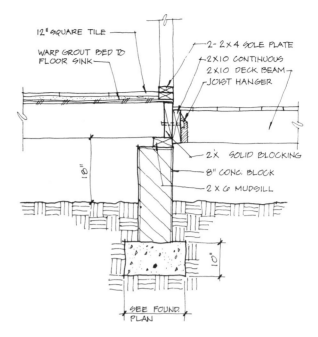

Figure 13.3 Detail of deck at exterior footing.

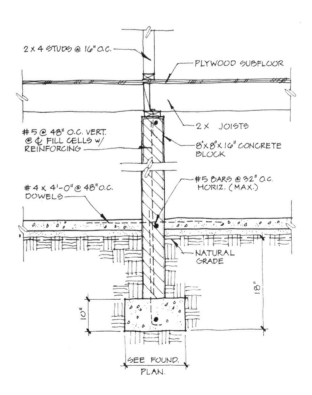

Figure 13.4 Detail of interior concrete-block wall.

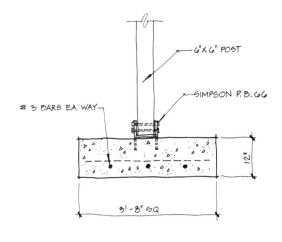

FOOTING @ WOOD POST

Figure 13.5   Detail of footing at wood post.

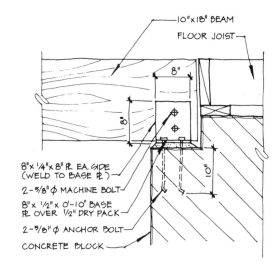

WOOD BEAM CONNECTION

Figure 13.6   Detail of wood beam connection.

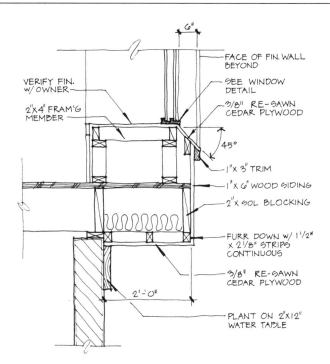

FLOOR FRAMING CANTILEVER

Figure 13.7   Detail of floor framing cantilever.

Details for Framing Assemblies.   Architectural details for framing assemblies were also provided in these construction documents. One example is the eave detail. First, the project designer did a freehand drawing. The freehand drawing was then given to a drafter for final drawing. Figure 13.12 shows the freehand sketch. Figure 13.13 shows a study of a deck and handrail detail located directly above a recessed garage door. The deck assembly at the building wall is also detailed, because proper flashing and drainage are needed to prevent water leaks.

Details: Theater

In some projects, such as the theater discussed in depth in Chapter 16, structural complexities may dictate various construction assemblies. For example, a masonry and steel structure has many architectural details that are governed by structural engineering requirements. The detailer must coordinate these details with the structural engineer. Figure 13.14 shows a detail for a steel beam connection, in which the beam, steel decking, and concrete floor thickness have already been designed by the structural engineer. From these required members, the architectural detail is developed, showing wall materials, ceiling attachment, and under-floor space for

the horizontal dimension.) The risers and tread are dimensioned, as are rebar ties for the connection of the upper concrete floor. (Rebar ties act as dowels to join two concrete elements.)

A large storage area and a mechanical room were located in the basement. A detail was needed to show the assembly for the basement and floor-level changes. See Figure 13.11. The wood stud wall has been offset in front of the upper-level concrete floor to provide a nailing surface for the wall finishes at both levels.

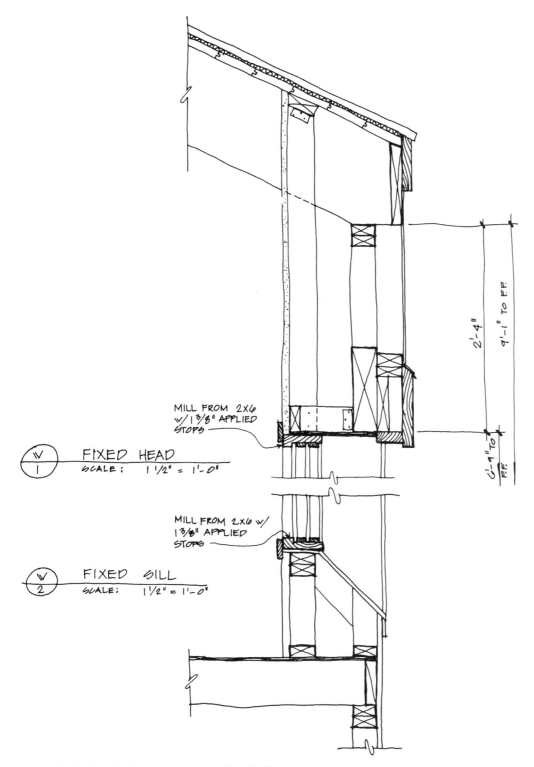

Figure 13.8 Detail of eave and window head sill.

mechanical and electrical runs. When critical information must be explained, or is explained on a separate sheet, the procedure is to add a note on the architectural drawing to "See Structural." This refers the reader to the structural engineer's drawings, which provide such information as type and length of welds for steel connections, and size and weight of steel members. Note the call-out on the steel beam of "W 8 × 10." The "W" refers to the shape of the beam (here a **wide flange**), the "8" refers to the approximate depth of the beam (8 inches), and

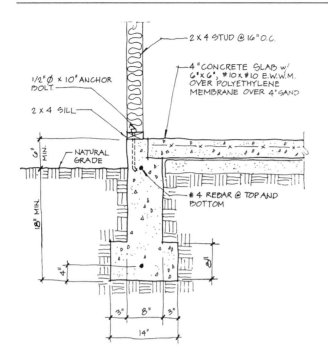

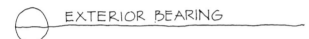

EXTERIOR BEARING

Figure 13.9 Detail of exterior bearing footing.

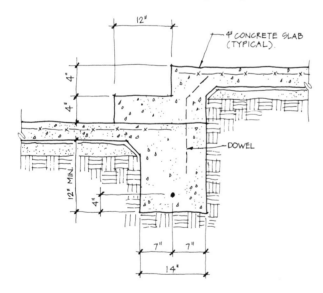

CHANGE OF LEVEL w/STEP

Figure 13.10 Detail of change of level with step.

the "10" refers to the weight of the beam per linear foot (10 lb per linear foot).

A second example is shown in Figure 13.15. The steel stud framing is terminated at the bottom of the steel beam, and extensive galvanized iron flashing has been

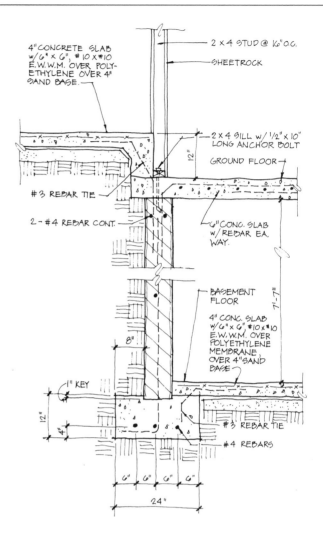

CONC. BLOCK WALL @ BASEMENT

Figure 13.11 Detail of concrete-block wall at basement—slab.

used to cover and protect the intersection of the various members at the ridge.

Some complex architectural details require much study before the finished detail can be drafted. The eave and column detail shown in Figure 13.16 is intricate and shows the entire column assembly from the foundation to the roof, including the eave detail. Notes refer the viewer to other details for more information. Usually, it is unnecessary and unadvisable to repeat all the information from one detail to another, as changes made on one detail must also be made on any other affected details and drawings.

Many projects require a specific architectural detail to show conditions that will satisfy a governing building code requirement. Figure 13.17, for example, shows exactly where a fire protection coating is

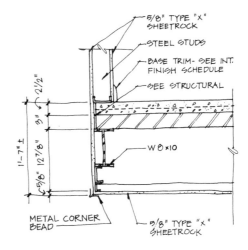

Figure 13.14 Detail of typical connection at a steel beam.

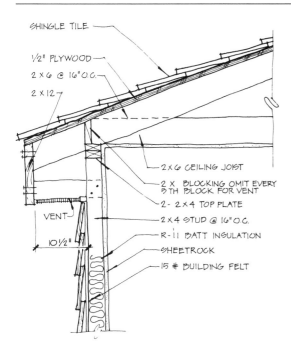

Figure 13.12 Eave detail.

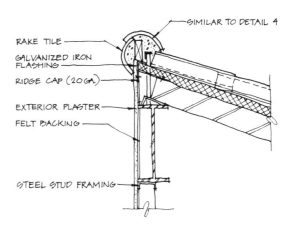

Figure 13.15 Detail of ridge at mechanical well.

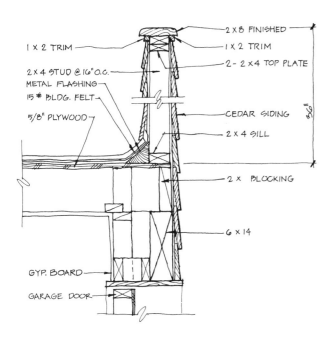

Figure 13.13 Detail of deck railing and header at garage.

required under a steel roof decking that covers the structural steel angle on a masonry wall. This information is combined with a roof parapet detail. Figure 13.18 shows another detail for areas requiring fire protection.

A third example of a condition requiring a detail is of a disability ramp, which must show the required number of handrails, the height of the handrails above the ramp, and the clear space required between the handrail and the wall. This information is combined with the structural requirements for the support of a low wall on the outside of the ramp.

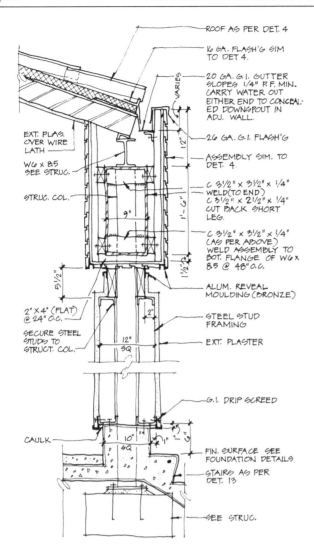

ROOF AS PER DET. 4

16 GA. FLASH'G SIM TO DET 4.

20 GA. G.I. GUTTER SLOPES 1/4" P.F. MIN. CARRY WATER OUT EITHER END TO CONCEAL-ED DOWNSPOUT IN ADJ. WALL.

26 GA. G.I. FLASH'G

ASSEMBLY SIM. TO DET. 4.

C 3 1/2" X 3 1/2" X 1/4" WELD (TO END) C 3 1/2" X 2 1/2" X 1/4" CUT BACK SHORT LEG.

C 3 1/2" X 3 1/2" X 1/4" (AS PER ABOVE) WELD ASSEMBLY TO BOT. FLANGE OF W6 X 85 @ 48" O.C.

ALUM. REVEAL MOULDING (BRONZE)

STEEL STUD FRAMING

EXT. PLASTER

G.I. DRIP SCREED

FIN. SURFACE SEE FOUNDATION DETAILS

STAIRS AS PER DET. 13

SEE STRUC.

EXT. PLAS. OVER WIRE LATH

W6 X 85 SEE STRUC.

STRUC. COL.

2" X 4" (FLAT) @ 24" O.C.

SECURE STEEL STUDS TO STRUCT. COL.

CAULK

EAVE AND COLUMN DETAIL

Figure 13.16 Eave and column detail. (Reprinted by permission from *The Professional Practice of Architectural Working Drawings,* 3d Ed., © 2003 by John Wiley & Sons, Inc.)

■ HARD-LINE (HAND-DRAFTED AND CAD)

Actually, this chapter should begin here, with hard-lining of details, because that is what the final appearance of details should be. We hope we have not led you to believe that most detailing is done freehand—quite the contrary. Detailing is done freehand only at the conceptual level and confirmation stage to check whether, in fact, what was seen in the mind's eye really works. Freehand details are also used as a means of communication from the mind of the designer to the real world of the drafter.

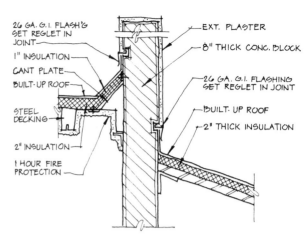

26 GA. G.I. FLASH'G SET REGLET IN JOINT

1" INSULATION

CANT PLATE

BUILT-UP ROOF

STEEL DECKING

2" INSULATION

1 HOUR FIRE PROTECTION

EXT. PLASTER

8" THICK CONC. BLOCK

26 GA. G.I. FLASHING SET REGLET IN JOINT

BUILT-UP ROOF

2" THICK INSULATION

PARAPET DETAIL

Figure 13.17 Parapet detail. (Reprinted by permission from *The Professional Practice of Architectural Working Drawings,* 3d Ed., © 2003 by John Wiley & Sons, Inc.)

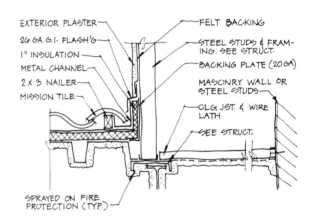

EXTERIOR PLASTER

26 GA G.I. FLASH'G

1" INSULATION

METAL CHANNEL

2 X 3 NAILER

MISSION TILE

FELT BACKING

STEEL STUDS & FRAM-ING. SEE STRUCT.

BACKING PLATE (20 GA)

MASONRY WALL OR STEEL STUDS

CLG. JST. & WIRE LATH

SEE STRUCT.

SPRAYED ON FIRE PROTECTION (TYP.)

BASE FLASHING DETAIL

Figure 13.18 Base flashing detail. (Reprinted by permission from *The Professional Practice of Architectural Working Drawings,* 3d Ed., © 2003 by John Wiley & Sons, Inc.)

Approach to Detailing

Before you hard-line draft a detail, you must understand its primary and secondary functions. Although functions vary, they may be categorized within a few divisions.

A. Structural—The intent of a detail may be to reveal the method of connection between two structural members or to show the transition between wood and steel members and the connective device to be used between them.

B. Architectural—The purpose of a detail may be to ensure that a particular architectural feature is explained, to maintain a certain aesthetic quality of a part of the building.

C. Environmental—A detail may reveal how to deal with environmental and natural forces, such as sun, rain, wind, snow, and light, as well as human-made problems of noise, pollution, and so on.

D. Human Needs—A detail may ensure that a particular human need is met. Stairs are a good example of this type of need, configured so as to allow a person to safely ascend or descend with the least amount of energy expended so as to avoid fatigue. This is done by formatting the proper angle of tread and riser. Special needs, such as those of elderly or physically impaired persons, are discussed in Chapter 3.

E. Connection—It is critical to detail a transition of one plane into another, for example, the connection between the wall and the floor, or between the wall and the roof or ceiling.

F. Material Limits—A detail may reveal the limits of the material with which you are dealing. You can drill a hole into a 2 × 6 floor joist, but how large a hole can you make before you weaken the member too much? The limits can be dimensioned or noted right in the detail.

G. Facilitation—In a tenant improvement drawing, a floor may be elevated to allow housing of computer cables. A detail can be drafted through this floor, showing the floor system support and the minimum clearances needed to accommodate the cables for maintenance.

Detailing Based on a Proper Sequence

Step 1. The drafter can accomplish the crucial **blockout** stage by blindly copying the freehand sketch provided. Although this approach may be the most expedient, it misses two very important points: The drafter will never catch errors in the sketch, and the drafter becomes a tracer rather than a significant and valuable employee of the firm. Quickly outline the functional constraints of the detail, and check to see that the sketch complies.

Step 2. Once you have laid out the most significant form, you can now draw its adjacent parts. For example, in drafting an exterior bearing footing for a wood floor system, do not draft the floor first and then add the footing; rather, draft the footing first as it is to be built.

Step 3. Add critical dimensioning.

Step 4. Strategically place notes so they clearly and easily convey the message.

Step 5. Designation of materials for the various pieces (wood, steel, earth, etc.) can be added at this point or at any of the previous stages.

Step 6. Profiling and **outlining** are almost synonymous. Darken the perimeter of the most important shape or shapes in the detail.

Step 7. Using the proper method described earlier in this book, add reference symbols, a title, and a scale so that each detail has an identifying "name" (title) and scale.

Shortcut

When details were drafted by hand, copies were often kept on file. A specific detail could then be copied, corrected by scissor drafting, recopied on vellum, and then put onto an adhesive that could be applied to the construction documents. Some offices may still follow this practice of working with details.

In offices that use computers, each detail produced in the architect's office can be archived and later retrieved when needed. These digital images can be changed to meet any new application needs.

Offices using computers and hand drafting prepared tracers with a minimal amount of information so that a drafter could later add new information to this so-called **bare bones detail**. This practice is still used in some offices, but it is best done electronically. These bare bones details are developed, filed, and later retrieved as a datum stage to be updated with new and pertinent information.

Sizing Details

If you are working with a 24″ × 36″ sheet of vellum similar to that formatted in Chapter 2, and you extend the tick marks to form a matrix for detail placement, you will discover that the space measures 4⅝″ high × 6½″ wide. These spaces can be doubled in both width and height, or in both directions, depending on the scale of the detail.

With the availability of word processing and CAD, the drawing zone has been further subdivided into the drawing area and the note or keynote area. See Figure 13.19. The detail placed on one side allows the noting (done by CAD, word processor, etc.) to be done with ease. The drafter finishes the detail by drawing the leaders, thus connecting the notes with the drawing. See Figure 13.20. A further refinement is the use of **keynoting**. This refers to the practice of giving each note a number or a letter. When the detail is drafted, the leaders will use the corresponding number or letter pertaining to the note. See Figure 13.21. This method can be used by a manual drafter or by CAD, expediting the drawing procedure.

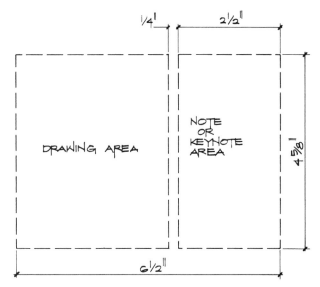

Figure 13.19 Detail format with noting area. (Reprinted by permission from *The Professional Practice of Architectural Working Drawings,* 3d Ed., © 2003 by John Wiley & Sons, Inc.)

■ FOOTING DETAIL

The exterior bearing footing for a residence is not unlike the freehand sketch found in Figure 13.9—but evolved. The difference between one footing and another can be so subtle that it takes a trained eye to

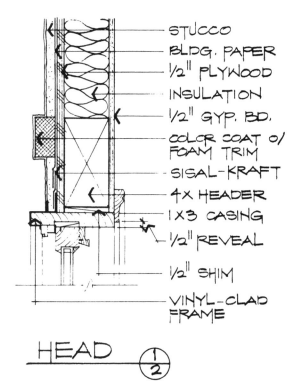

Figure 13.20 Window detail with noting format. (Reprinted by permission from *The Professional Practice of Architectural Working Drawings,* 3d Ed., © 2003 by John Wiley & Sons, Inc.)

distinguish them. As you compare the freehand detail with the hard-line detail shown in Figures 13.9 and 13.23 through 13.26, note the size difference at the bottom, the thickness of the foundation wall, the number of rebars, backfill, and sand versus gravel under the slab. These are two details that look alike but are really totally different in how they react to the various forces acting on them.

Before we hard-line the exterior bearing footing for the residence, let's look at four considerations for this type of footing.

A. *Configuration.* Most typically used is a two-pour, inverted "T" shape. Through the years, the industry has found this to be the best distributor of weight that uses the least amount of material. The inverted T distributes weight over a vast area. Notice how the weight from above is distributed on the soil in Figure 13.22A. Surrounding the example are dimensions: "X" is based on the weight of the structure and the ability of the soil to hold up this weight.

As a rule of thumb, the thickness should be, as the example shows, ½X. The depth of the footing, marked "A," again depends on the stability of the soil or the frost line, or even a requirement of building officials, as a minimum. The prevailing attitude is, however, that rather than use established maximums, soundness of construction should prevail. The amount of the stem of the inverted "T" that extends above the soil might be a matter of how high it should be to keep moisture from the first piece of wood to come in contact with the concrete or to prevent termite infestation.

B. *Soil.* The cost of a piece of property might depend mostly on the view it provides, its convenience to various major streets, its slope, and so on, but many clients overlook the condition and quality of the soil. If a property has loosely filled soil (not permitted in many areas), the depth of the footing may have to extend far beyond the fill to firm soil, making the foundation very expensive. Moreover, in a marshy area where the **bearing pressure** of the earth (weight that can be put onto the soil measured in pounds per square foot) is minimal, the type and shape of the foundation may dictate a prohibitively expensive system, making the property impractical if not completely unbuildable. See Figure 13.22B.

C. *Strength.* Concrete, an excellent material with regard to **compression** forces, is very brittle in tension. The load imposed from above puts the concrete in compression, which is its strength. However, the footing travels the length of a wall, and with expansive soil or irregular loading, forms a beam that is in tension. This beam will break or shatter along the

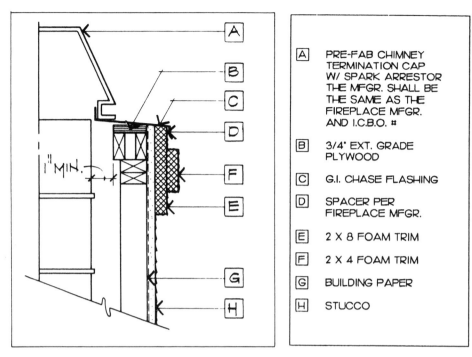

A	PRE-FAB CHIMNEY TERMINATION CAP W/ SPARK ARRESTOR THE MFGR. SHALL BE THE SAME AS THE FIREPLACE MFGR. AND I.C.B.O. #
B	3/4" EXT. GRADE PLYWOOD
C	G.I. CHASE FLASHING
D	SPACER PER FIREPLACE MFGR.
E	2 X 8 FOAM TRIM
F	2 X 4 FOAM TRIM
G	BUILDING PAPER
H	STUCCO

Figure 13.21 Chimney detail with keynoting format. (Reprinted by permission from *The Professional Practice of Architectural Working Drawings,* 3d Ed., © 2003 by John Wiley & Sons, Inc.)

top or bottom, depending on the forces at work—thus the introduction of reinforcing bars, which are strong in tension, like a rope or chain, but rather weak in compression. By combining the two materials, we impart strength in both tension and compression. See Figure 13.22C.

D. *Energy.* In this era of energy-efficient buildings, architects are paying extra attention to areas through which heat is lost. The movement of heat, as any physics major will tell you, is from hot to cold. In colder weather, we must heat structures using whatever natural resources are available: natural gas, petroleum products, or in some cases electricity. To keep it from leaving the structure, heat is contained by means of insulating floors, walls, and ceilings. Notice the various possible locations for insulation on the footing in Figure 13.22D.

There are numerous other factors to consider in designing a footing. Where should the plastic membrane be put (if one is to be used)? Between the slab and the sand? Below the sand? How is the thickness of the slab determined? Does it require reinforcing? Backfill is still another factor—how much? The list goes on and on, always depending on conditions at the proposed building site. The answers to these questions relate to strength, energy conservation as a reaction to soil, and/or to the selected building shape, as mentioned earlier.

Exterior Bearing Footing (Residence)

STAGE I (Figure 13.23). The grade line should be drawn first. This becomes the datum from which you establish all of the necessary vertical dimensions, such as the distance to be placed between the floor and the grade. The width of the footing (**bearing surface**) is the next item to be measured. Half this width is centered for the stem wall. Footing thickness and slab thickness are positioned, and finally the beginning of the stud above the stem wall is drawn to create the slot for the slab.

STAGE II (Figure 13.24). After checking the accuracy of the first stage, proceed to the inclusion of the adjacent parts: insulation, sand or gravel, sill, the stud with its sheathing, and the termination points of the detail, which will be turned into break lines at a later stage.

STAGE III (Figure 13.25). This stage is actually a combination of Stages 3 and 5, dimensioning and material designation. Be sure to use the correct designation of material for each of the seven or so different materials used here: plywood, batt insulation, rigid insulation, concrete, rebars, and so on.

STAGE IV (Figure 13.26). This is the final stage, which includes additional profiling and noting. To keep the noting consistent from detail to detail, many offices have a standard set of notes. The project manager may select the proper notes from this standard list and make them available to the drafter. In other

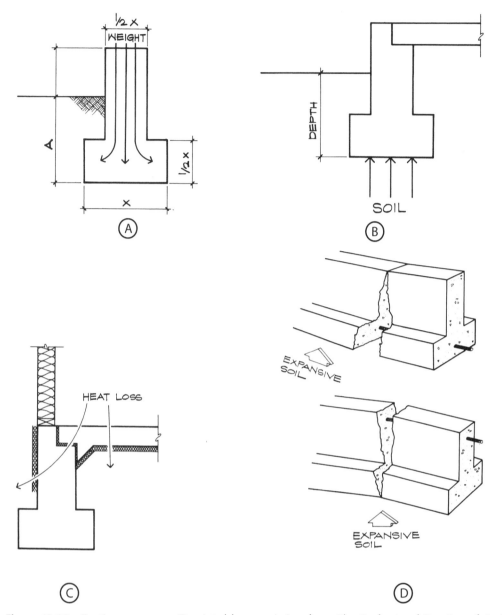

Figure 13.22 Footing concerns. (Reprinted by permission from *The Professional Practice of Architectural Working Drawings*, 3d Ed., © 2003 by John Wiley & Sons, Inc.)

offices, especially small offices, this practice may not be used at all; rather, the drafter is presumed to have the necessary training and ability to note a detail properly. Detailing on a CAD system is merely a matter of recalling the proper notes, which have been stored in the computer, and positioning them.

If the notes are word processed, the drafter merely prints the necessary notes onto an adhesive and applies them to the drawing in the form of a chart called *keynotes*. See Figure 13.21. This procedure can easily be adapted to the computer as well.

■ WINDOW DETAIL

Before drafting a window detail, the drafter should understand the action of the window's moving parts, its attributes, the installation procedure, and how to prepare the surrounding area before and after installation.

The window selected for our sample residence is an Atrium double-tilt window. See Figure 13.27. It was selected because it is not the typical double-hung, casement, or sliding window, and because of its special features.

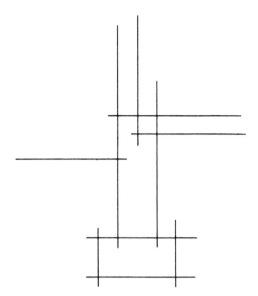

Figure 13.23 Stage I: Exterior bearing footing. (Reprinted by permission from *The Professional Practice of Architectural Working Drawings,* 3d Ed., © 2003 by John Wiley & Sons, Inc.)

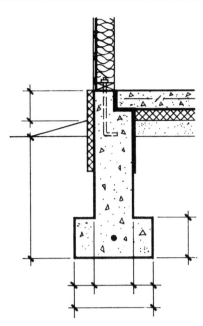

Figure 13.25 Stage III: Exterior bearing footing. (Reprinted by permission from *The Professional Practice of Architectural Working Drawings,* 3d Ed., © 2003 by John Wiley & Sons, Inc.)

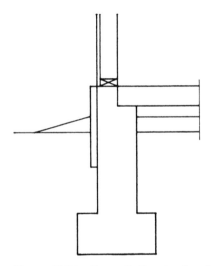

Figure 13.24 Stage II: Exterior bearing footing. (Reprinted by permission from *The Professional Practice of Architectural Working Drawings,* 3d Ed., © 2003 by John Wiley & Sons, Inc.)

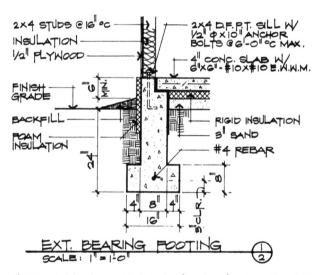

2X4 STUDS @ 16" OC
INSULATION
1/2" PLYWOOD
FINISH GRADE
BACKFILL
FOAM INSULATION
2X4 D.F. P.T. SILL W/ 1/2" Ø X 10" ANCHOR BOLTS @ 6'-0" OC MAX.
4" CONC. SLAB W/ 6"X6"-#10X#10 E.W.W.M.
RIGID INSULATION
3" SAND
#4 REBAR

EXT. BEARING FOOTING
SCALE: 1" = 1'-0"

Figure 13.26 Stage IV: Exterior bearing footing. (Reprinted by permission from *The Professional Practice of Architectural Working Drawings,* 3d Ed., © 2003 by John Wiley & Sons, Inc.)

Weatherproofing

By studying the installation method, the detailer can better emphasize certain features of the detail. As seen in the original photograph (Figure 13.27), there are fins around the perimeter that are used to nail the window in place. Therefore, the rough opening (the rough framed opening) must have enough clearance to accommodate the preconstructed window. In this case, the clearance will be ½″ both vertically and horizontally, compensating for any irregularity in the framing members and allowing the window to be placed into the rough opening perfectly level. The wood shim under the windowsill in this sketch functions as a leveling device while sealing the space between the rough sill and the finished sill of the window.

Before and after the fin of the window is nailed to the wall, a moisture/vapor barrier is placed around the

Figure 13.27 Atrium double-tilt window. (Courtesy of the Atrium Door & Window Company, a Division of Fojtasek Companies, Inc. Reprinted by permission from *The Professional Practice of Architectural Working Drawings,* 3d Ed., © 2003 by John Wiley & Sons, Inc.)

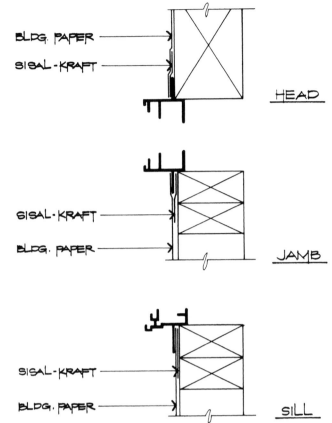

Figure 13.28 Placement of building paper around window. (Reprinted by permission from *The Professional Practice of Architectural Working Drawings,* 3d Ed., © 2003 by John Wiley & Sons, Inc.)

frame. The "Weatherproofing" section in Chapter 11 will acquaint you with the various materials used to waterproof windows and the reasons for the positioning of particular pieces of waterproofing material.

For the installation of this window, we use an asphalt-saturated kraft paper to cover the building and a secondary strip (a band of about 6"–8") of heavily saturated, heavyweight kraft-type paper called ***sisal-kraft.***

In Figure 13.28, note the positioning of the building paper and its secondary member, the sisal-kraft. Both sheets are placed under the fin on the jamb and both sheets over the fin on the head. This strategic placement acts to shed water and prevent its penetration. This method is unique to Zone C (see the map in Figure 11.45).

Raised Frame

For this residence, there will be a raised plaster frame around each window. Such frames, called **stucco mold** (affectionately called **stucco bumps**), can be produced in a number of ways. Two possible solutions are described here. The first is to use one or more pieces of wood to raise the surface, as seen in Figure 13.29. Notice how the building paper is carried completely around the wood (including the metal mesh, which is not shown).

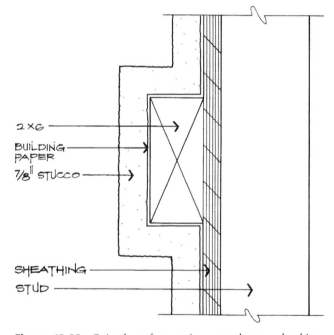

Figure 13.29 Raised surface using wood as a backing. (Reprinted by permission from *The Professional Practice of Architectural Working Drawings,* 3d Ed., © 2003 by John Wiley & Sons, Inc.)

The exterior plaster (stucco) follows the contour of the complete unit.

A second possible solution is the use of **Styrofoam**. See Figure 13.30. In this example, two pieces of foam have been placed over the first two coats of stucco, which are called the **scratch coat** and the **brown coat**. The final coat (called the **color coat**) is placed over the entire unit, completing the image as a whole. Notice the position of the building paper.

For this sample residence, the second method is used and a keystone is placed at the top of the raised frame, as can be seen in elevation. Figure 13.31 shows the placement of the building paper and the sisal-kraft (called **counterflashing**).

Rough Opening Size

Most manufacturers' brochures contain written descriptions of the window itself and its various features, the available stock sizes, suggested details depending on the context, and a drawing of the window at $3'' = 1'-0''$ scale. For example, a DW2030 is really $19\frac{1}{2}'' \times 29\frac{1}{2}''$. Manufacturer drawings can be used as a tracer for hand-drafted, AutoCAD, or Revit details. Drawings can be downloaded; it is best to download the configuration of the window itself. Do not blindly use any suggested solutions, as the courts have determined that the manufacturer is not responsible for its performance. Instead, use the manufacturer's suggested drawings as a basis on which to adjust the drawing to meet local codes and waterproofing/weatherproofing requirements. Be sure to adjust the manufacturer's window drawing to $3'' = 1'-0''$. See Figure 13.32.

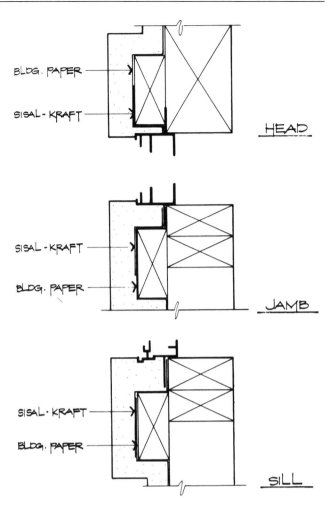

Figure 13.31 Raised frame of wood. (Reprinted by permission from *The Professional Practice of Architectural Working Drawings,* 3d Ed., © 2003 by John Wiley & Sons, Inc.)

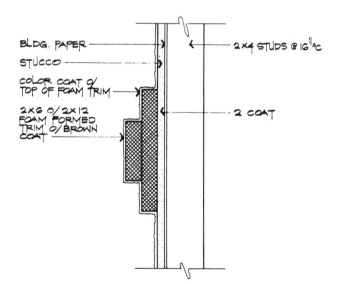

Figure 13.30 Raising a surface with foam. (Reprinted by permission from *The Professional Practice of Architectural Working Drawings,* 3d Ed., © 2003 by John Wiley & Sons, Inc.)

Window Detail (Residence)

Stage I (Figure 13.33) Actually, this is not a drawing stage, but rather a preparation stage. The $3'' = 1'-0''$ vertical section provided by the manufacturer's literature is downloaded to the computer. See Figure 13.32.

Stage II (Figure 13.34). The rough framing is drawn on the drawing of the window. Care must be taken in redrawing any important line that was inadvertently eliminated or has faded away. The fin is especially important. Finally, the rough opening is established.

Stage III (Figure 13.35). As we look at this detail, we should be able to see the lines of the jamb. To save time and for the sake of clarity, some offices do not put these lines into the detail. A true detail should include such lines, hence our choice to include them here. The interior and exterior wall coverings (skin) were drafted at this stage. Note the lining of the building felt over the fin for moisture control and the inclusion

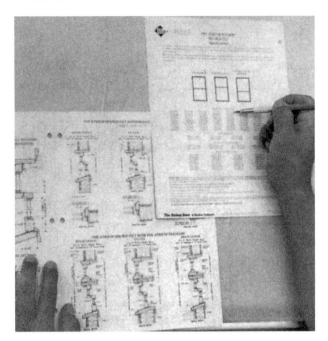

Figure 13.32   Rough opening sizes. (Reprinted by permission from *The Professional Practice of Architectural Working Drawings,* 3d Ed., © 2003 by John Wiley & Sons, Inc.)

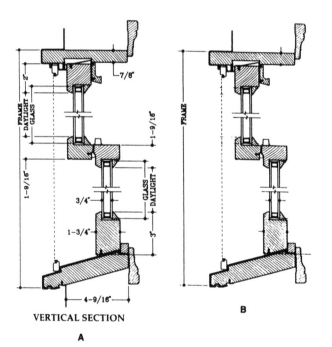

VERTICAL SECTION

A

B

Figure 13.33   3″ = 1'-0″ drawing by manufacturer. (Reprinted by permission from *The Professional Practice of Architectural Working Drawings,* 3d Ed., © 2003 by John Wiley & Sons, Inc.)

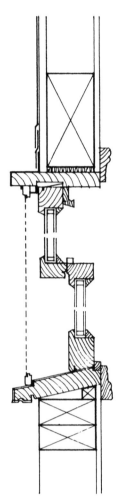

Figure 13.34   Laying out the rough frame. (Reprinted by permission from *The Professional Practice of Architectural Working Drawings,* 3d Ed., © 2003 by John Wiley & Sons, Inc.)

avoid long leaders. Be sure to create a margin for uniformity of appearance. The detail style is referred to as *freestyle,* with noting scattered around the perimeter. A better method would be to use the keynoting mentioned earlier in this chapter.

■ FIREPLACE

Fireplaces have gone through quite an evolution over the past century: from masonry fireplaces, which are still built, to metal; from fully vented fireplaces using chimneys to those that have no vent at all. Some varieties burn wood as fuel; others burn natural gas or, more recently, gelled alcohol. Wood-burning fireplaces are not allowed by some municipalities.

Fireplaces can be built to use remote control starters (much like those used for a television). They can also be constructed to recirculate warm air. Fireplaces can

of insulation below the header. Finally, the raised window frame is drafted.

Stage IV   (Figure 13.36). Noting and referencing complete the detail. The positioning of notes is critical for ease of reading. Do not crowd the detail, but also

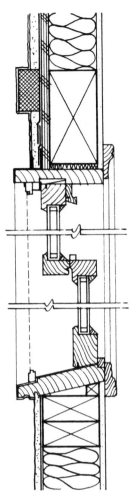

Figure 13.35 Applying the interior and exterior skin onto the wall surface. (Reprinted by permission from *The Professional Practice of Architectural Working Drawings*, 3d Ed., © 2003 by John Wiley & Sons, Inc.)

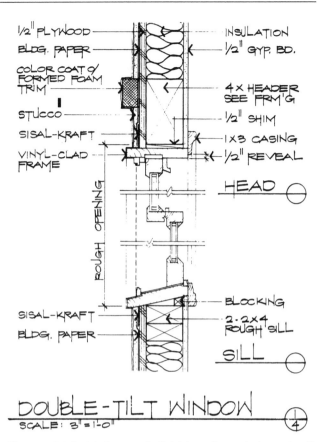

Figure 13.36 Noting and finishing the window detail. (Reprinted by permission from *The Professional Practice of Architectural Working Drawings*, 3d Ed., © 2003 by John Wiley & Sons, Inc.)

be made to look like fireplaces or designed to look like furniture. Portable fireplaces, which burn gelled alcohol, can be moved from room to room, much the way furniture is rearranged. When you move, you take the fireplace with you.

Many metal fireplaces are fitted with pockets for recirculating air. The air around the fire chamber is heated and redirected back into the room. You can even have a thermostat-controlled blower installed, which increases the movement of the warm air, thus achieving greater efficiency in heat circulation. This means that 20,000 to 75,000 Btu/hr of heat can be recaptured. See Figure 13.37.

For the sake of this discussion, fireplaces are categorized as follows:

Standard fireplace. The normal masonry units that are usually job-built and require the detailer to draft the

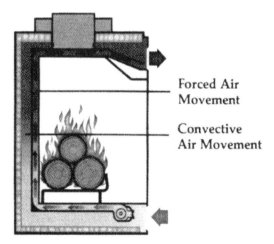

Figure 13.37 Heat circulation. (Courtesy of Majco Building Specialties, L.P. Reprinted by permission from *The Professional Practice of Architectural Working Drawings*, 3d Ed., © 2003 by John Wiley & Sons, Inc.)

Figure 13.39 Majestic wall-vented fireplace. (Courtesy of Majco Building Specialties, L.P. Reprinted by permission from *The Professional Practice of Architectural Working Drawings,* 3d Ed., © 2003 by John Wiley & Sons, Inc.)

Figure 13.38 Majestic heat-circulating fireplace. (Courtesy of Majco Building Specialties, L.P. Reprinted by permission from *The Professional Practice of Architectural Working Drawings,* 3d Ed., © 2003 by John Wiley & Sons, Inc.)

fireplace from the throat. Often built of concrete block, brick, or stone.

Prefabricated fireplaces. Built of steel, with the chimney built of double- or triple-wall units that snap together. A typical unit can be seen in Figures 13.37 and 13.38.

Direct-vented fireplaces. Built of steel and similar to the prefabricated fireplaces previously described, except that they are vented directly out an adjacent wall. See Figures 13.39 and 13.40. Note the uninterrupted windows surrounding the fireplace in the photograph.

Portable fireplaces. Made of metal and built much like an oven, so that the outer surface gets warm but not hot to the touch. Can be housed in a cabinet like a television set, and uses a clean-burning gelled alcohol.

Fireplace for a Residence

For a residence, the Majestic 42 unit was selected for its heat-circulating features. See Figure 13.38.

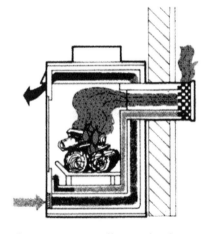

Figure 13.40 Wall-vented schematic. (Courtesy of Majco Building Specialties, L.P. Reprinted by permission from *The Professional Practice of Architectural Working Drawings,* 3d Ed., © 2003 by John Wiley & Sons, Inc.)

Much like the Atrium window discussed earlier, this fireplace has a metal fin (tab) around the perimeter of the front face that can be nailed to the surrounding framing. The metal fireplace must not come into contact with the framing around it. The manufacturer suggests a minimum clearance of about ½″, but the local codes should be checked.

The chimney is a triple-wall unit and does not necessarily go straight up through the ceiling and/or roof.

Bends of 30° can be incorporated as the chimney goes through the space provided. This space, called the **chimney chase**, allows the chimney to pierce the ceiling or roof at a convenient point, so as not to interrupt the plane of the roof at an intersection (such as a valley) or to bypass a beam or other structural member. See Figure 13.41. Straps are then used to stabilize the chimney to the adjacent framing members. See Figure 13.42. Note the inclusion of a recommended 2″ clearance space.

A firestop spacer should be used on top of the ceiling joist or on the underside of the roof joist when there is an attic space. See Figure 13.43.

The total area around the opening (**chase**) should be insulated even if the wall is an inside wall. If the fireplace is on a second floor or on a first floor constructed of wood, the space under the fireplace should also be insulated. In fact, it is always best to read the installation manual before detailing the framework around the structure. The detailer should not worry about how the smoke is drafted out of the fire chamber or the inner workings of the fireplace, because the fireplace engineering has already been done by the fireplace manufacturer's designers.

Framing. The walls around a prefabricated fireplace are framed in the same way as all other walls. Even the opening for the fireplace is framed in the same manner as other openings, such as doors, skylights, windows, and so on. See Figure 13.44.

The framing on a residence is unique because:

A. The fireplace is backed against a bearing wall.
B. The rafters of the main part of the roof will come down to the bearing wall.
C. The ceiling joists run perpendicular to the main rafters.

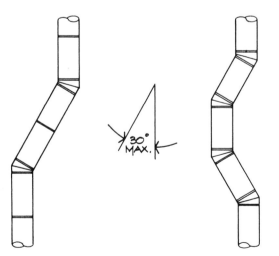

Figure 13.41 Bends in chimney section. (Reprinted by permission from *The Professional Practice of Architectural Working Drawings,* 3d Ed., © 2003 by John Wiley & Sons, Inc.)

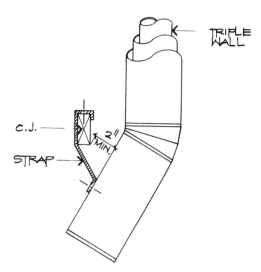

Figure 13.42 Chimney attached to adjacent members. (Reprinted by permission from *The Professional Practice of Architectural Working Drawings,* 3d Ed., © 2003 by John Wiley & Sons, Inc.)

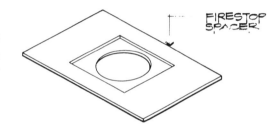

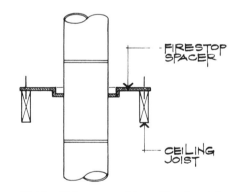

Figure 13.43 Chimney position. (Reprinted by permission from *The Professional Practice of Architectural Working Drawings,* 3d Ed., © 2003 by John Wiley & Sons, Inc.)

D. A California framed roof must also be reframed with an opening. *California frame* is a framing process in which the major zone (see Chapter 9) of a roof is completely framed first and joined by the minor zone. Each form is built completely into itself and later integrated with the other zones/forms.

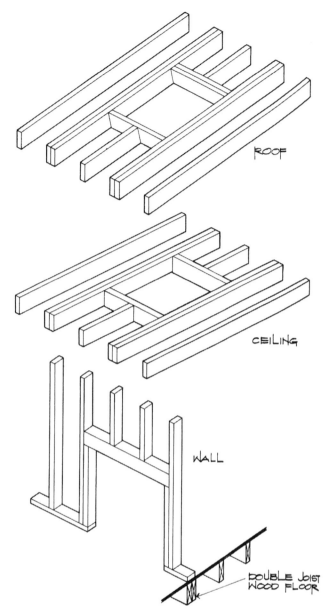

Figure 13.44 Framing an opening. (Reprinted by permission from *The Professional Practice of Architectural Working Drawings,* 3d Ed., © 2003 by John Wiley & Sons, Inc.)

E. The chimney will be contained inside a wood chase and capped with metal.

See Figure 13.45 for a model simulation of this area and Figure 13.46 for a full section of a fireplace.

Chimney above Roof. In most cases, a chimney must rise two feet higher than the highest part of the roof within a ten-foot radius. See Figure 13.47.

Chimney Chase. There are a number of ways of terminating the chimney above the roof. A round top termination, as seen in Figure 13.48, can be used to

Figure 13.45 Model simulation of the framing through the roof. (Reprinted by permission from *The Professional Practice of Architectural Working Drawings,* 3d Ed., © 2003 by John Wiley & Sons, Inc.)

"top it off," and the finish will be left in this state. A second possibility is to purchase a constructed metal chase to cover this metal termination. A third suggestion is to use a wood chase with a UL-listed constructed cap.

Development of the Residential Fireplace

A full section of the residential fireplace is developed in four stages.

STAGE I (Figure 13.49). Start with the context. Detail the plate line, floor line, wall, and roof outline. These lines establish the parameters within which the detailer can explore the framing members and place the prefabricated fireplace.

STAGE II (Figure 13.50). The ceiling joists and rafters are sized and positioned according to the framing plan. Because this is not a masonry fireplace, the drafter need not be concerned with a foundation. (For drafting full masonry fireplaces, read the chapter on fireplaces in the companion book, *The Professional Practice of Architectural Detailing.*)

Next, the fireplace is positioned in this cavity, with the minimum clearances required by code. At this stage, the drafter must be conversant with code restrictions as well as the method of installation. For example, it is important to detail how the flue is to be stabilized within the cavity, what kinds of firestops are required, and where they are positioned.

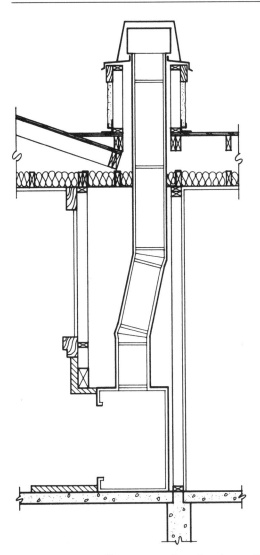

Figure 13.46 Full section of a fireplace. (Reprinted by permission from *The Professional Practice of Architectural Working Drawings,* 3d Ed., © 2003 by John Wiley & Sons, Inc.)

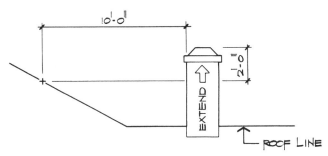

Figure 13.47 Chimney above roof. (Reprinted by permission from *The Professional Practice of Architectural Working Drawings,* 3d Ed., © 2003 by John Wiley & Sons, Inc.)

Manufacturers' literature includes installation instructions and standard manufactured pieces that are available to make such installation possible. The drafter should also check the project book to verify finish materials for the face of the fireplace and the hearth.

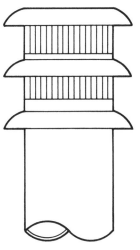

Figure 13.48 Round top termination. (Reprinted by permission from *The Professional Practice of Architectural Working Drawings,* 3d Ed., © 2003 by John Wiley & Sons, Inc.)

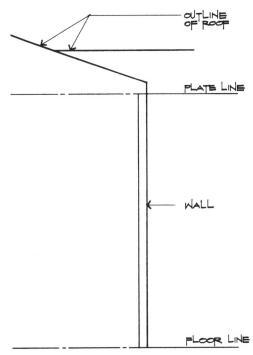

Figure 13.49 Stage I: Establishing the parameters of the fireplace location. (Reprinted by permission from *The Professional Practice of Architectural Working Drawings,* 3d Ed., © 2003 by John Wiley & Sons, Inc.)

STAGE III (Figure 13.51). Once the materials have been checked, material designations are included in the detail. Wood, insulation, concrete, and even the outside wall of the metal fireplace are shown. At this stage, sheet metal, such as for the cap, is drafted with a single heavy line.

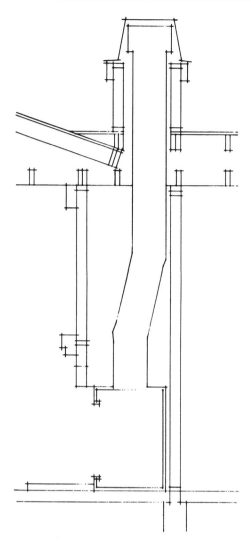

Figure 13.50 Stage II: Residential fireplace. (Reprinted by permission from *The Professional Practice of Architectural Working Drawings,* 3d Ed., © 2003 by John Wiley & Sons, Inc.)

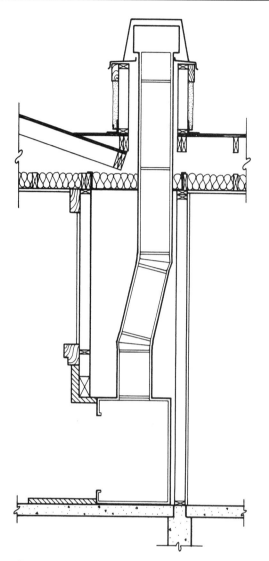

Figure 13.51 Stage III: Residential fireplace. (Reprinted by permission from *The Professional Practice of Architectural Working Drawings,* 3d Ed., © 2003 by John Wiley & Sons, Inc.)

STAGE IV (Figure 13.52). The detailer must be aware of a number of items on all details, as well as those that are unique to specific details, as is the case with a fireplace. Unlike the footing detail, which describes a structural part of a building, the fireplace detail is one for which a context already exists. The second factor that the detailer must identify and describe accurately is the prefabricated unit itself. Thus, the final stage must be dealt with much in the same fashion as the detail was developed.

First in the final sequence is identification of the context: the rafters, the ceiling joists, the floor, and the cell (surrounded with studs) within which the fireplace will be placed, including the housing for the chimney.

Next in this sequence is identification of the fireplace and the flue, in such a way that the outline of the fireplace is clear in relationship to the surrounding structure.

The building code and the manufacturer's installation directions will reveal certain clearances that must be maintained and dimensioned, and attachments and firestop spacers that must be identified. Merely positioning them is not sufficient.

Next, the decorative (**noncombustible**) portions that surround the opening—the chimney, the floor (**hearth**) and the wall plane of the fireplace, and the ceiling— should be described and dimensioned.

Finally, if there are portions within this drawing that should be enlarged and explored, reference bubbles or notes are included to direct the reader to these details. Although it may seem that this is referring a detail to a detail, it is really not. (See the chimney portion of Figure 13.47.) This drawing, as the title indicates, is

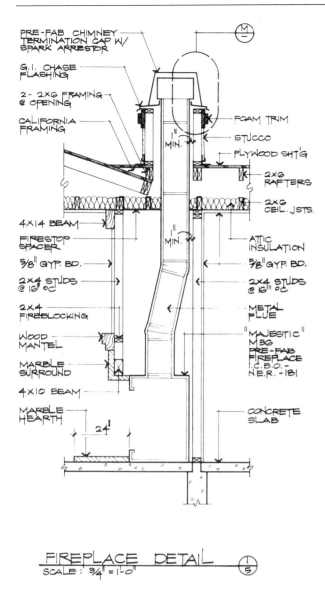

PRE-FAB CHIMNEY TERMINATION CAP W/ SPARK ARRESTOR

G.I. CHASE FLASHING

2 - 2x6 FRAMING @ OPENING

CALIFORNIA FRAMING

FOAM TRIM

STUCCO

PLYWOOD SHT'G

2x6 RAFTERS

2x6 CEIL. JSTS.

4x14 BEAM

FIRESTOP SPACER

ATTIC INSULATION

5/8" GYP. BD.

2x4 STUDS @ 16" oc

2x4 FIREBLOCKING

5/8" GYP. BD.

2x4 STUDS @ 16" oc

METAL FLUE

WOOD MANTEL

"MAJESTIC" M36 PRE-FAB FIREPLACE I.C.B.O. - N.E.R. -181

MARBLE SURROUND

4x10 BEAM

MARBLE HEARTH

24'

CONCRETE SLAB

FIREPLACE DETAIL
SCALE : 3/4" = 1'-0"

Figure 13.52 Stage IV: Half-section of fireplace. (Reprinted by permission from *The Professional Practice of Architectural Working Drawings*, 3d Ed., © 2003 by John Wiley & Sons, Inc.)

a *half-section*—a hybrid between a building section and a full-blown detail.

■ STAIR DESIGN AND VERTICAL LINKS

The stair design for any type of stairway will have to address the various physical and dimensional requirements while adhering to building code restrictions. The architect will need to have some basic information before designing the stairs and the accompanying stair details. The first information required is the computed height between the floor levels. Second, the designer needs the dimensional requirements for the width of the stairs, and the length of the stair run, to accommodate the number and width of the desired stair **treads**. After the floor-to-floor dimension is computed, this dimension will then become the basis for the number and height of the stair risers. An example of how this may be achieved is described mathematically as follows:

1. Floor to ceiling = 8'-0"
2. Ceiling thickness = 5/8"
3. Second-floor wood joist = 11¼"
4. Second-floor subfloor = ¾"

Therefore, the floor-to-floor dimension is 9'-0 5/8" or 108.625".

Desired riser height dimension = 6½" to 7"
Desired tread dimensions = 10½" (11" for commercial)

Riser Computation Example

Assume that there are 15 risers; therefore, 108.625" divided by 15 equals 7.28" + risers or 7⅜" risers. This does not meet current building code requirements. Try 16 risers: 108.625" divided by 16 equals 6.79" or 6¾" + risers, which does meet building code requirements. Most building codes require that a rise in every step be not less than 4" nor greater than 7".

Tread Computation Example

Prior to computing the number and size of the treads for the preceding riser example, it is recommended that the governing building code requirements for the minimum width of the tread size be verified. Most codes require the tread size to be not less than 11" as measured horizontally between the vertical planes of the furthermost projection of the adjacent treads.

As determined by the foregoing riser computation, the stair calls for sixteen 6¾" risers. For most stairway designs, the number of treads will be one less than the number of risers. Therefore, for the tread computation and code requirement, fifteen 11" treads will be used in this example. To compute the dimensional length of the stairway run using fifteen 11"-wide treads, it would mathematically equate to 15 × 11" or 165". Therefore, the critical dimension to satisfy the number of treads in feet and inches would be 165" divided by 12, which converts into a minimum space requirement of 13'-10".

Stair Width.   The desired or required stairway width will vary with the architect's design and the type of building that the stairway serves relative to the building code requirements. For most governing building codes, the required stairway width for commercial and public buildings must not be less than 44". In stairways serving residential structures or having an occupant load of less than 49, the stairway must not be less than 36″ in width.

Handrails. Handrail designs and their projection into the required stairway width are governed by existing building code requirements. The allowed distance is 3½″ from each side of a stairway. A three-dimensional drawing of an acceptable handrail design is shown in Figure 13.53. The height and tops of handrails and the handrail extensions must not be less than 34″ nor more than 38″ above the nosing of the treads and stairway landings.

Headroom. Another concern for a stairway designer is the minimum headroom clearance stipulated in most building codes. Generally, the headroom clearance must not be less than 6′-8″ or 6.67′ (verify with local code). This clearance is to be measured vertically from a place that is parallel and tangent to the stairway tread nosings. Figure 13.54 graphically depicts a minimum headroom clearance requirement for a stairway.

The foregoing information and examples illustrate the basic concerns in designing stairways for a specific structure and the spaces required to meet these concerns. For further information on stairway designs and the various materials from which they may be constructed, refer to the third edition of *The Professional Practice of Architectural Detailing* (John Wiley & Sons Inc.).

Guardrails. **Guardrails** are safety devices found on stairway landings, balconies, and decks where the height

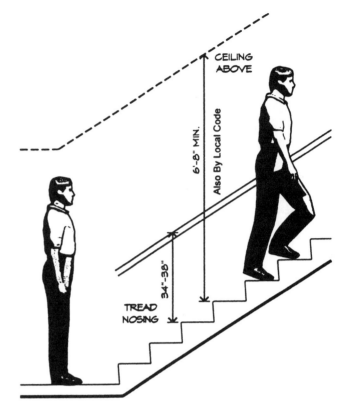

Figure 13.54   Headroom clearance.

of those elements is 30″ or more above the adjacent grade or floor below. The structural design to stabilize the supporting vertical members is predicated on a horizontal force, measured in pounds per linear foot, and must be calculated by a structural engineer. Allowable openings in the guardrail assembly, as required by most building codes, depend on the occupancy classification and use of the structure. For residential use, the maximum clear openings must not exceed 4″. For commercial and industrial structures, the maximum clear openings must not exceed 4″ and 42″ high. An example of a guardrail assembly is shown in a three-dimensional drawing in Figure 13.55.

The construction materials used for stairways include wood, steel, poured-in-place concrete, precast concrete, or a combination of any of these materials. Figures 13.56, 13.57, and 13.58 illustrate a partial floor plan for a three-story residence that incorporates a wood stairway construction at the different floor levels. The stairway designs vary from a straight run and landings to a partial radial shape.

Starting at the basement level, as shown in Figure 13.56, and knowing the established basement floor-to-floor dimension of 10′-6″, or 126″, the designer can calculate the number and height of the stairway risers. Starting from the basement floor-to-floor, using 7″-high risers, eighteen risers will be required. Therefore, when using

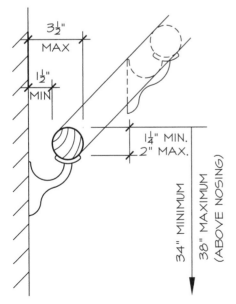

Figure 13.53   Handrail requirements.

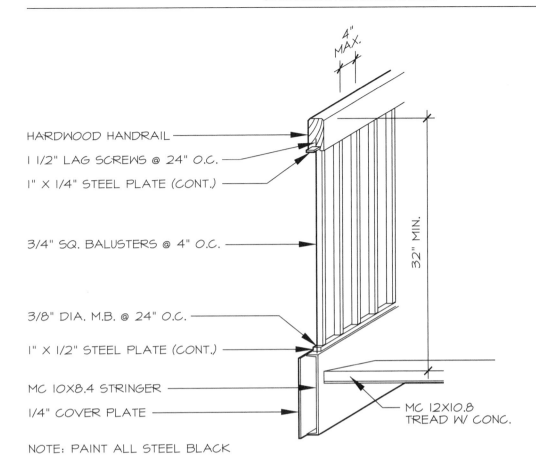

HARDWOOD HANDRAIL

1 1/2" LAG SCREWS @ 24" O.C.

1" X 1/4" STEEL PLATE (CONT.)

3/4" SQ. BALUSTERS @ 4" O.C.

3/8" DIA. M.B. @ 24" O.C.

1" X 1/2" STEEL PLATE (CONT.)

MC 10X8.4 STRINGER

1/4" COVER PLATE

4" MAX.

32" MIN.

MC 12X10.8 TREAD W/ CONC.

NOTE: PAINT ALL STEEL BLACK

Figure 13.55 Balustrade detail.

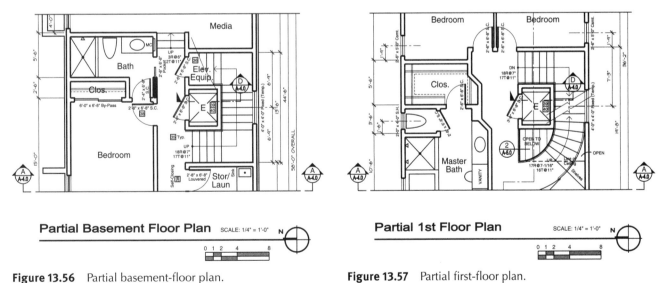

Partial Basement Floor Plan SCALE: 1/4" = 1'-0"

Figure 13.56 Partial basement-floor plan.

Partial 1st Floor Plan SCALE: 1/4" = 1'-0"

Figure 13.57 Partial first-floor plan.

11"-wide treads, seventeen risers will be required. The length of the space required for seventeen 11"-wide treads will be 15'-6" plus the width of the two stairway landings. The width of the landing is 42", as is the width of the stairway. The foregoing information is what was required to physically lay out this stairway design, which surrounds an elevator shaft enclosure.

The next step in this stairway design is to provide stair details as part of the project's working drawings. As shown in Figure 13.59, a section is cut at the bottom of

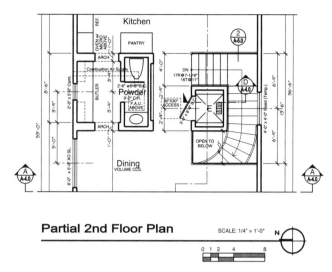

Partial 2nd Floor Plan   SCALE: 1/4" = 1'-0"

Figure 13.58   Partial second-floor plan.

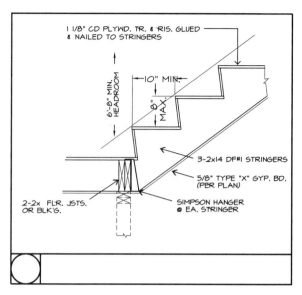

Figure 13.60   Stringers to landing.

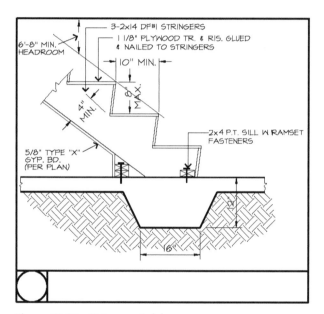

Figure 13.59   Stringers at slab.

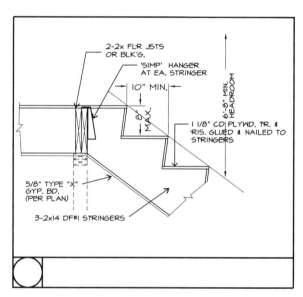

Figure 13.61   Stringers to second floor.

the stairway, showing how the stringers are anchored at the basement concrete floor. Another detail will show how the stringers occur at both landings (see Figure 13.60). The final detail, showing the method by which the stringers are attached to the floor joist, is illustrated in Figure 13.61.

As shown in Figure 13.57, the stairway access at the foyer has a partial radial curve in the design. An enlarged partial stair layout of this stairway segment is illustrated in Figure 13.62. This is done to show the inside and outer dimensions of a tread as a means for construction of the stairway, while illustrating the building code requirements

for the tread design. A three-dimensional detail is added to the working drawings for the purpose of clarity for this circular portion of the stairway design (see Figure 13.63).

Steel Stairway Details

Details of the steel stairway assembly used in the Madison Building are found in Chapter 17 of this book. This all-structural-steel building utilizes a steel-and-concrete stairway assembly.

Beginning at the ground-floor level, the steel stringers, fabricated from a standard steel channel, are attached

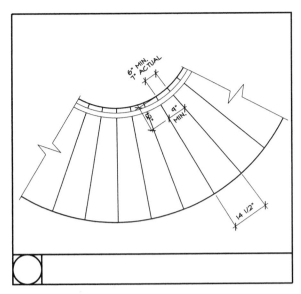

Figure 13.62   Partial stair plan.

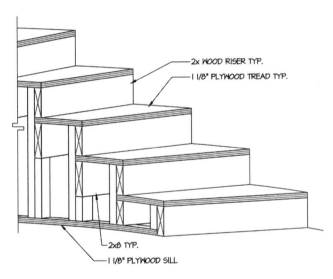

Winding Stair Framing
SCALE: 1"=1'-0"

Figure 13.63   Circular stair detail.

to the concrete floor with ¼″ steel plates and ½″ × 10″ anchor bolts. The typical tread design is a standard steel channel MC10 × 84 welded to the web of the channel stringer and filled with concrete. This detail assembly is illustrated in Figure 13.64.

The next connection detail is the stringer attachment at the intermediate landings and the support of the concrete at the landings, as shown in Figure 13.65. Note that the steel channel at the landing is used to support the steel stringers and the concrete at the landings. All connections are accomplished by assigned welds. The final detail for

the steel stairway assembly is shown for the various floor levels (see Figure 13.66). This detail illustrates a steel channel for the floor support and the support of the stringers. Steel angles are used for intermediate floor supports.

Concrete Stairs

Concrete stairways may be constructed in two ways. First, there are various precast concrete companies that manufacture different types of concrete stairs and will deliver and install them on the building site. Second, concrete stairways may be formed during construction of the building by incorporating the required steel reinforcing bars and then pouring the concrete in place. For many projects, a precast concrete stairway is desirable, because there is no cost of forming and subsequent form removal. When using a poured-in-place concrete stair, it is necessary to provide details, with the required steel reinforcing as part of the working drawings. A three-dimensional detail for a poured-in-place concrete stairway is depicted in Figure 13.67.

Composite Stairway Assembly

Another type of stairway uses a manufactured precast concrete, one-piece, closed tread and riser assembly. These precast units can be assembled with wood or steel stringers. This composite stairway requires architectural detailing, because it is necessary to size wood stringers for their span and the weight of the precast treads and risers and to show how they are attached to the supporting beams. A three-dimensional detail illustrating a precast tread and riser unit attached to wood stringers is shown in Figure 13.68.

■ MECHANICAL VERTICAL LINKS

The drawings for elevators of all types, and various lifting devices such as wheelchair lifts, chair lifts, and others, must include the detailing necessary to satisfy the installation requirements. An example of a residential-type electric elevator is shown in Figure 13.69. The planned area for the wall framing and the openings that surround the electric elevator car must adhere to all the clearances required by the elevator manufacturer. The planning must also include the required space designated by the manufacturer for the machine room equipment. This room is located adjacent to and under the stairway run. A three-dimensional drawing of the framed opening is shown in Figure 13.69. This particular elevator has a lift capacity of approximately 750 pounds.

A more detailed example of a manufacturer's requirements is shown in the plan view illustrated in Figure 13.70. This drawing, furnished by a specific

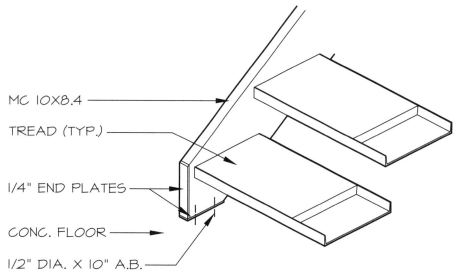

MC 10X8.4

TREAD (TYP.)

1/4" END PLATES

CONC. FLOOR

1/2" DIA. X 10" A.B.

Figure 13.64   Stringer to concrete.

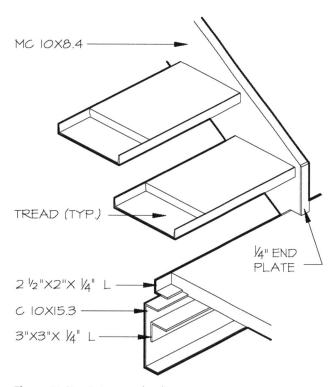

MC 10X8.4

TREAD (TYP.)

1/4" END PLATE

2 1/2"X2"X 1/4" L

C 10X15.3

3"X3"X 1/4" L

Figure 13.65   Stringer to landing.

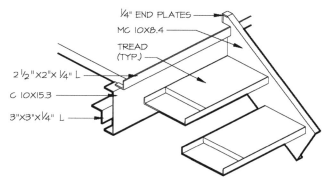

1/4" END PLATES

MC 10X8.4

TREAD (TYP.)

2 1/2"x2"x 1/4" L

C 10X15.3

3"x3"x1/4" L

Figure 13.66   Stringer to floor.

elevator manufacturer, shows the information an architect or designer will need to integrate into the working drawings. Note that the shaft dimension requirements, the clearances for this specific elevator, and the electrical supply must be shown in the working drawings. A section through the elevator shaft and machine room is shown in Figure 13.71. This drawing depicts the length of the vertical travel, the electrical supply location, and the required 8″-deep pit depression that is required for

cab clearance. The area and dimensions for the pit area must be shown accurately on the foundation plan of the working drawings.

To assist in planning access to the electric elevator, use the various car configurations available from the manufacturers. Examples of car configurations are illustrated in Figure 13.72. A photograph of a finished electric elevator installation is shown in Figure 13.73.

Another manufactured device used in the development of a vertical link is a stair lift. This unit is ideal for persons with walking disabilities or other physical limitations. Figure 13.74 depicts a plan view of the stair lift positions and the dimensional aspects of the unit as it projects into the stairway run. A photograph of a stair lift installation is shown in Figure 13.75.

For persons who rely on the use of a wheelchair for vertical access, the use of a vertical lift is desirable. As in addressing the dimensional requirements of an elevator, the architect or designer will need to provide the dimensions,

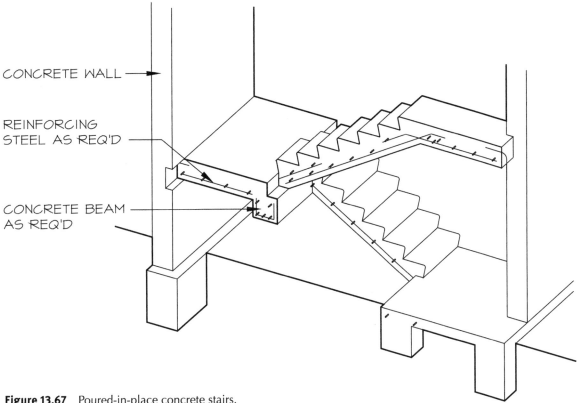

CONCRETE WALL

REINFORCING
STEEL AS REQ'D

CONCRETE BEAM
AS REQ'D

Figure 13.67 Poured-in-place concrete stairs.

clearances, and electrical supply information as stipulated by the manufacturer's specifications. An example of a platform plan, with its requirements for a vertical lift and the vertical travel dimensions, is depicted in Figures 13.76 and 13.77. A photograph of a finished vertical lift installation is illustrated in Figure 13.78. This vertical lift unit is constructed of fiberglass that is rust-free and has a nonskid surface. Such units are available in various colors. Their maximum load capacity is 750 pounds.

A vertical linking unit that is convenient for lifting groceries and other heavy items from one level to another is a home waiter, frequently referred to as a *dumbwaiter*.

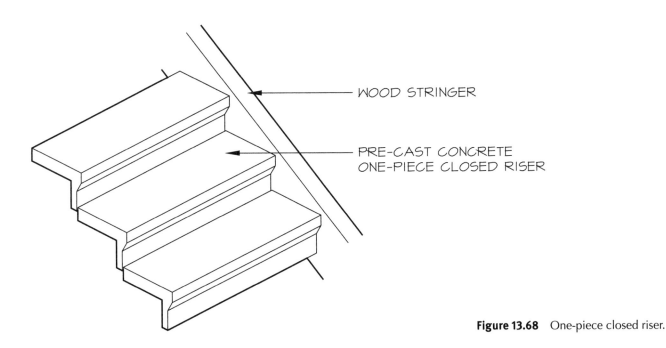

WOOD STRINGER

PRE-CAST CONCRETE
ONE-PIECE CLOSED RISER

Figure 13.68 One-piece closed riser.

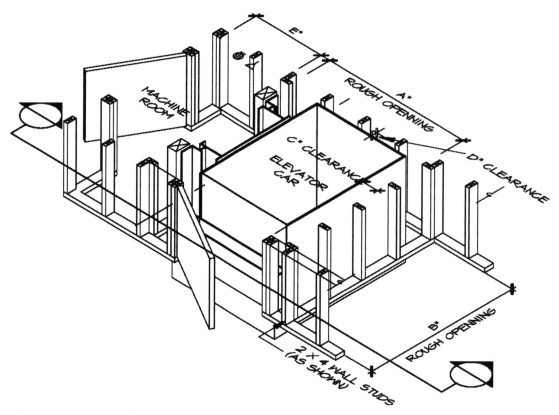

Figure 13.69   Framed elevator opening.

These units vary in shaft size and maximum load capacity. The space planning and layout requirements for dimensions and clearances will be delineated in the working drawings, as described for elevators and other lifting devices. A shaft plan illustrating dimensions and clearances for a two-landing home waiter installation is depicted in Figure 13.79. This particular unit is limited to a 75-pound lifting capacity. Figure 13.80 shows a section of this home waiter unit illustrating the vertical

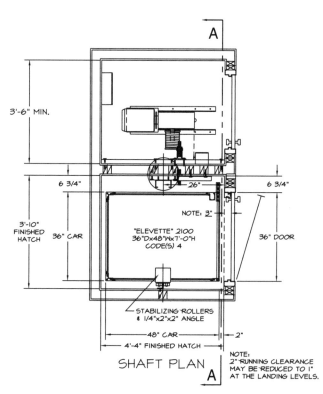

Figure 13.70   Shaft plan.

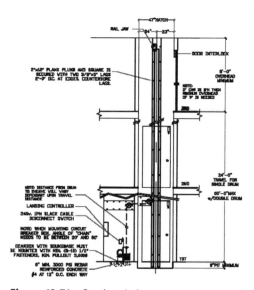

Figure 13.71   Section A-A.

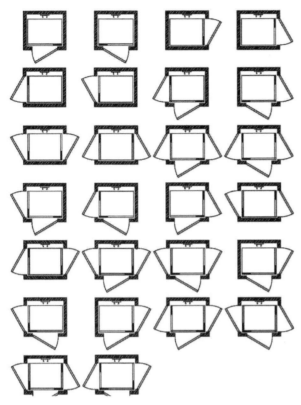

Figure 13.72   Car configurations.

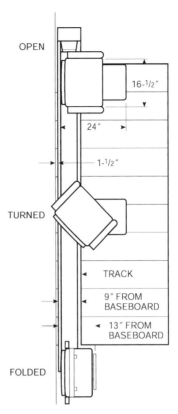

Figure 13.74   Stair lift diagram.

Figure 13.73   Elevette. (Courtesy Inclinator Co. of America.)

Figure 13.75   Stair lift. (Courtesy Inclinator Co. of America.)

travel dimensions, clearances, machine equipment room location, and the desired counter height. The vertical link units described here are but a few examples of lifting units that are found primarily in residential projects.

■ DETAILING IN BIM/REVIT

Detailing in Revit does not mean you throw away the details you have on file to be used as a template for your new buildings. You set up a sheet per your office standards and import finished details.

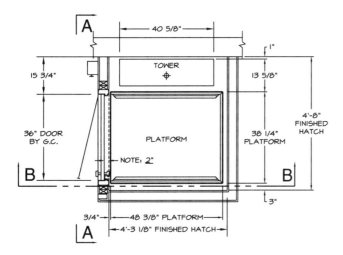

PLATFORM & TOWER

Figure 13.76   Vertical lift diagram.

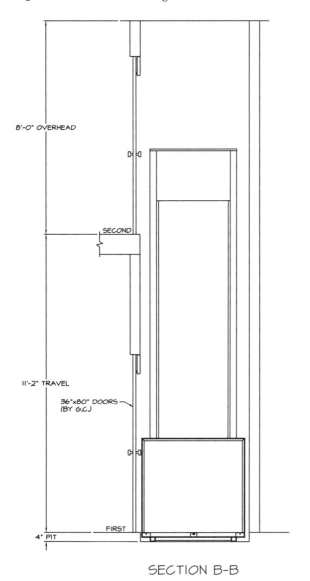

SECTION B-B

Figure 13.77   Section B-B.

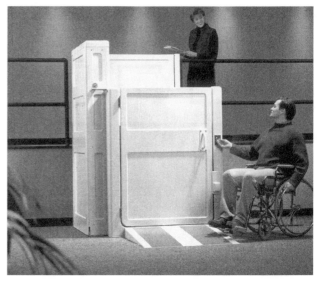

Figure 13.78   Spectralift. (Courtesy Inclinator Co. of America.)

Detailing on construction documents is usually done in 2-D. This is true of both hand-drafted details and computer-generated details done in AutoCAD. The good news is that Revit and AutoCAD are compatible. Therefore, if you have a CAD file of details, you can easily transfer them to Revit. Hand-drafted details can be scanned into the system.

Although we often talk about stock details, in practice we need to customize each detail to the special task to be performed in the current project and structure. Listed here are a few of the factors that must be addressed on every detail:

- Reaction to the specific soil condition
- Foundation and structure protection from moisture and frost
- Waterproofing elements in the structure such as windows, doors, and roofing
- Checking structural recommendations for seismic activity
- Local building requirements (and good judgment) for minimums and maximums
- Clarity for construction execution

■ TENANT IMPROVEMENT DETAILS

Tenant improvement is the work done for and by a client on leased space in an existing building, such as for a medical facility or a law office. The tenant improvement process is explained with specific details in Chapter 18. However, here we cover the evolution of typical details found in tenant improvement. The condition we use as a sample is a new wall built short of the existing ceiling to cover existing electrical, plumbing, and heating and

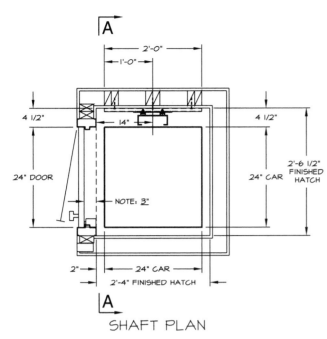

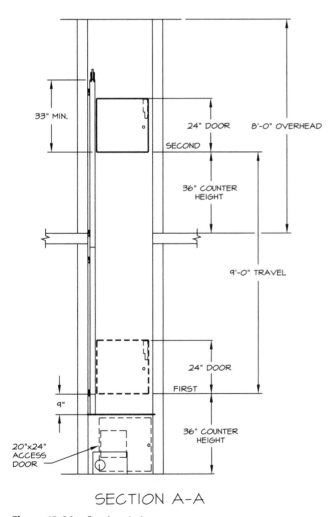

Figure 13.79 Shaft plan.

Figure 13.80 Section A-A.

air-conditioning ducts; this will include a detail of a wall that reaches the ceiling level of the existing building and a short wall (approximately 3′-0″ high) called a **pony wall**.

Partition Walls and Sections

In the development of the working drawings for a tenant improvement, it is necessary to provide sections for the various partition walls and other related wall assemblies. Initially in the drawing process for these partition walls, you block out the partition wall section and progressively delineate the various members required for completion of the detail. You then profile the completed detail with line quality that will make the drawing clear. Finally, you incorporate lettering, leader lines, and arrows in the detail. The progression of these partition wall sections is depicted in Figures 13.81, 13.82, and 13.83.

The drawing of partition wall section 3 in Figure 13.84 illustrates the condition where the partition wall terminates just above the suspended ceiling members. To stabilize this wall for lateral support, metal wall braces are attached to the top of the wall and the roof framing. This partition wall assembly occurs in the coffee bar and restroom areas.

Partition wall section 4 in Figure 13.84 indicates that the wall is to extend all the way to the roof framing in order to provide additional soundproofing between offices. This is achieved with sound-absorbing insulation board applied on the studs. Note that resilient clips are called for to provide greater soundproofing capability.

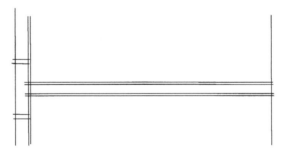

Figure 13.81 Preliminary wall section.

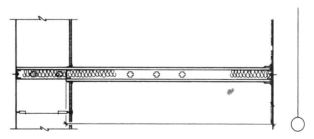

Figure 13.82 Preliminary wall section.

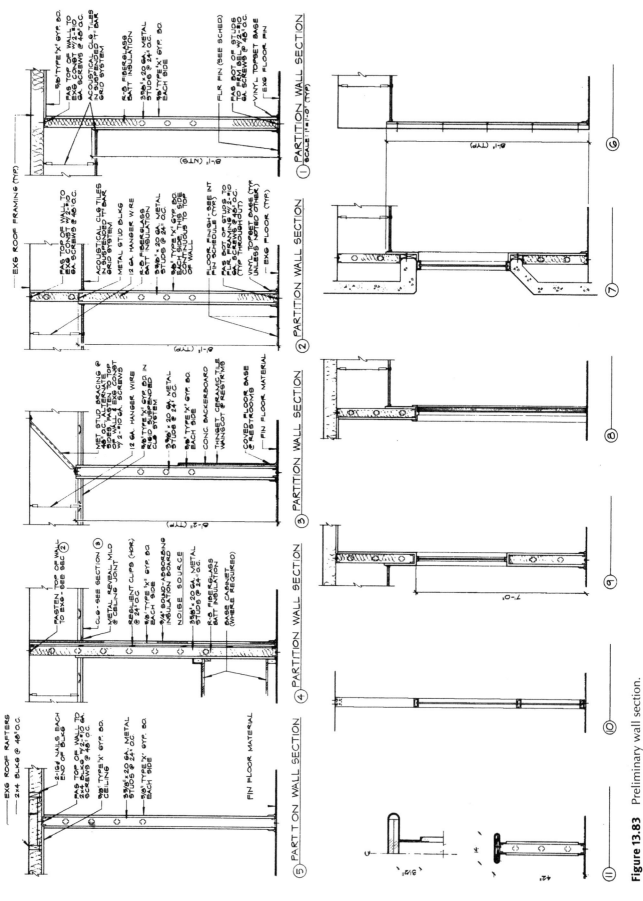

Figure 13.83 Preliminary wall section.

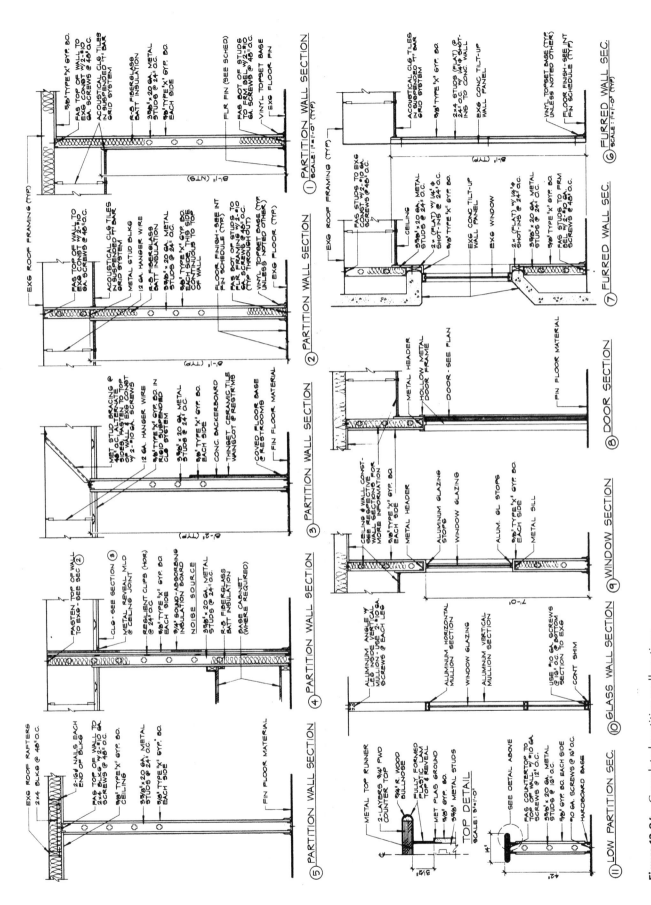

Figure 13.84 Completed partition wall sections.

The final partition section for this project is the low partition section 11 in Figure 13.84. First, this detail illustrates the height and width of the low partition and the various members that are required for this assembly. Because the low partition acts as a space divider, it also serves as a countertop.

Miscellaneous Wall Sections

Depending on the governing building code requirements and the tenant's use of the operating space, there may be various wall construction requirements. In the case where a non-load-bearing, one-hour fire-rated corridor is designed to include some glazing on the corridor walls, it will be necessary to satisfy a building code requirement that calls for a ¼"-thick (minimum) wire glass secured in steel frames. A detail for this condition is illustrated in Figure 13.85.

The internal walls between the "living" spaces for tenants may require that the walls be constructed to solve two conditions: One is to satisfy a one-hour fire-separation requirement, and the other is to provide a means of reducing or eliminating sound transmission between the tenant spaces. Figure 13.86 depicts the recommended non-load-bearing wall construction between living spaces to satisfy the fire and sound considerations.

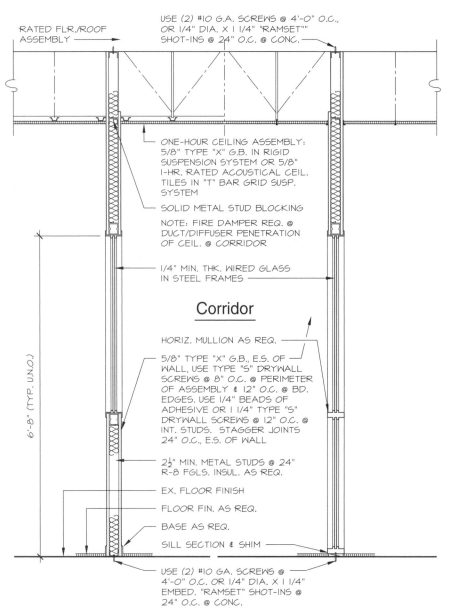

Figure 13.85   Glazed corridor wall (non-load-bearing).

Interior door designs will vary according to the desires of the tenant and the space plan designer. An example of an interior door design detail that includes a fixed matching panel above a door is shown in Figure 13.87. This detail is designed for a non-load-bearing wall and door condition.

When restrooms abut an office space or other area where people assemble, it is recommended that the dividing walls be constructed with sound insulation batts between the metal studs. Resilient clips are used to attach the gypsum board to the metal studs. This non-load-bearing wall section is illustrated in Figure 13.88.

In cases where one-hour fire-rated division walls are required to meet a building code requirement, the walls will be constructed from the tenant floor to the floor system above. The wall sections in Figure 13.89 illustrate the materials required to satisfy the construction of a one-hour non-load-bearing separation wall.

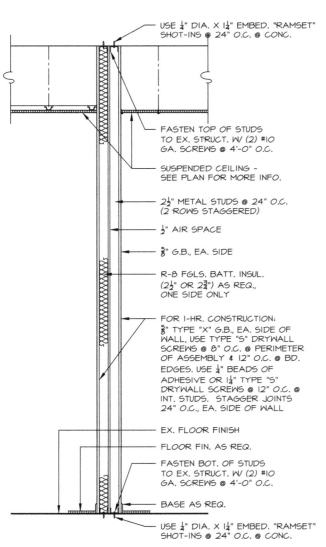

Figure 13.86 Fire and sound wall (non-load-bearing).

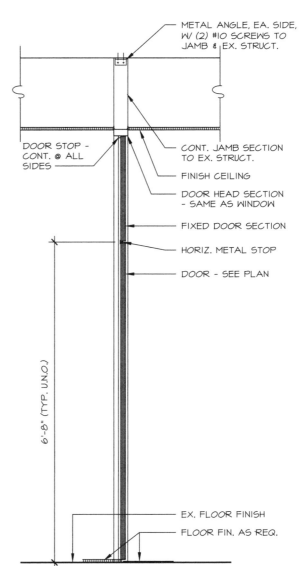

Figure 13.87 Interior door and fixed panel.

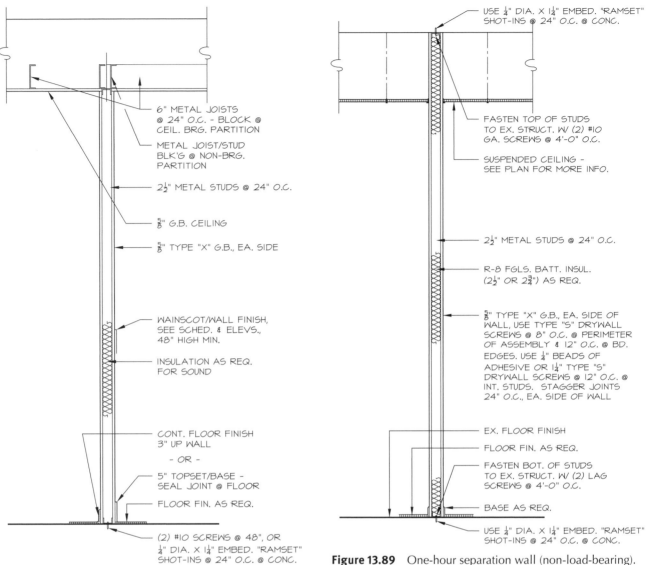

6" METAL JOISTS
@ 24" O.C. - BLOCK @
CEIL. BRG. PARTITION

METAL JOIST/STUD
BLK'G @ NON-BRG.
PARTITION

2½" METAL STUDS @ 24" O.C.

⅝" G.B. CEILING

⅝" TYPE "X" G.B., EA. SIDE

WAINSCOT/WALL FINISH,
SEE SCHED. & ELEVS.,
48" HIGH MIN.

INSULATION AS REQ.
FOR SOUND

CONT. FLOOR FINISH
3" UP WALL
- OR -

5" TOPSET/BASE -
SEAL JOINT @ FLOOR

FLOOR FIN. AS REQ.

(2) #10 SCREWS @ 48", OR
¼" DIA. X 1¼" EMBED. "RAMSET"
SHOT-INS @ 24" O.C. @ CONC.

Figure 13.88   Restroom partition (non-load-bearing).

USE ¼" DIA. X 1¼" EMBED. "RAMSET"
SHOT-INS @ 24" O.C. @ CONC.

FASTEN TOP OF STUDS
TO EX. STRUCT. W/ (2) #10
GA. SCREWS @ 4'-0" O.C.

SUSPENDED CEILING -
SEE PLAN FOR MORE INFO.

2½" METAL STUDS @ 24" O.C.

R-8 FGLS. BATT. INSUL.
(2½" OR 2¾") AS REQ.

⅝" TYPE "X" G.B., EA. SIDE OF
WALL, USE TYPE "S" DRYWALL
SCREWS @ 8" O.C. @ PERIMETER
OF ASSEMBLY & 12" O.C. @ BD.
EDGES. USE ¼" BEADS OF
ADHESIVE OR 1¼" TYPE "S"
DRYWALL SCREWS @ 12" O.C. @
INT. STUDS. STAGGER JOINTS
24" O.C., EA. SIDE OF WALL

EX. FLOOR FINISH

FLOOR FIN. AS REQ.

FASTEN BOT. OF STUDS
TO EX. STRUCT. W/ (2) LAG
SCREWS @ 4'-0" O.C.

BASE AS REQ.

USE ¼" DIA. X 1¼" EMBED. "RAMSET"
SHOT-INS @ 24" O.C. @ CONC.

Figure 13.89   One-hour separation wall (non-load-bearing).

P A R T

Case Studies

As you seek a job in an architectural office, you will see many examples of construction documents of work in progress. We cannot emulate this in a textbook, but we can show a few examples of actual construction documents. These are to be used as references, not to be copied. In addition to being a violation of copyright, copying will not achieve the results you want and need. Each project is unique: Among other things, codes differ, environmental conditions (such as soil conditions and proximity to salt-laden ocean air) differ, and so each structure will also differ.

There are five examples in this part:

Chapter 14—Construction Documents for a One-story, Conventional Wood-framed Residence

Chapter 15—Construction Documents for a Two-story, Wood-framed Residence with Basement

Chapter 16—Conceptual Design and Construction Documents for a Steel and Masonry Building (Theater)

Chapter 17—Madison Steel Building

Chapter 18—Tenant Improvements

chapter

14

CONSTRUCTION DOCUMENTS FOR A ONE-STORY, CONVENTIONAL WOOD-FRAMED RESIDENCE

■ CONCEPTUAL DESIGN

The Jadyn Residence

This chapter presents a hypothetical project, generated to provide a model illustration. The initial design and its subsequent changes are incorporated to illustrate the natural evolution of a design into a set of working drawings. Most of the changes are not based on design concepts or approaches, but rather to re-create typical, uncomplicated problems that might confront the beginning drafter.

Site Requirements

The design purpose is to create a home that has room for growth. The site is a typical city lot in Anytown, U.S.A. Because the zoning is R-1 (residential), the setbacks are 15'-0" in the front, 5'-0" on the sides, and 15'-0" at the rear. Water flows to the rear in the direction of the lot's slope, which is greater at the rear property line. This slope opens up to a city view to the rear of the lot. See Figure 14.1.

Client Requirements

Along with the bedroom and two baths, the client requested a family room and kitchen, oriented toward the view, and living room, nook, and formal dining room.

Most importantly, the structure had to be able to expand to accommodate a second-floor addition. See Chapter 15 for an in-depth treatment of this topic.

Initial Schematic Studies

Using what is commonly called **bubble diagramming**, room relationships were quickly established. See Figure 14.2. The bedroom, family room, and kitchen were oriented to the rear of the lot to take advantage of the view and avoid the street noise. With the prevailing wind coming from the northwest, each of these rooms will be well ventilated. The garage was positioned perpendicular to the street. Circulation is through the center of the structure, which serves as a spline or connector to all of the rooms.

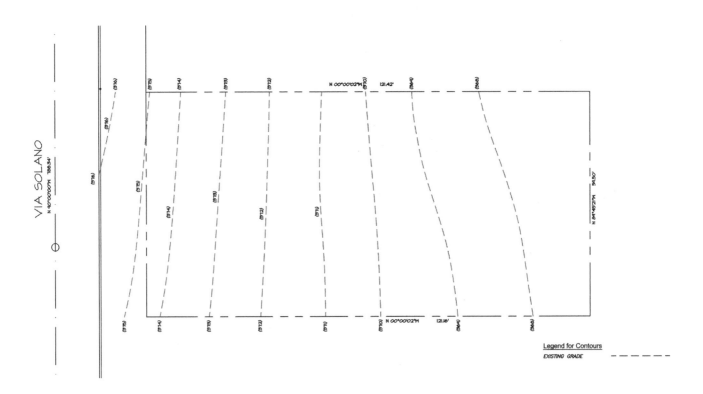

Topography Map
SCALE: 1/8" = 1'-0"

Figure 14.1 Jadyn residence site.

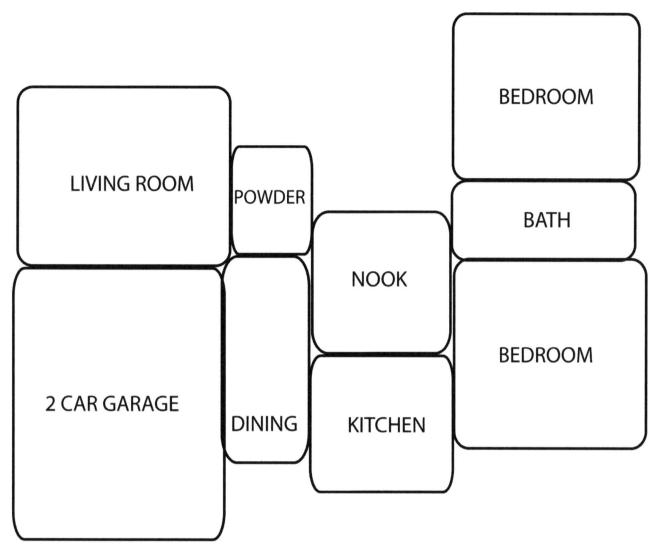

Figure 14.2 Bubble diagramming the Jadyn residence.

■ DESIGN AND SCHEMATIC DRAWINGS

The schematic drawings represent the culmination of many hours of designer-client decisions. The final changes chosen by the client are based on such things as financing, size of the structure, or projected number of users. Eventually, a final design decision is made and signed, and at that point becomes the final design proposal used by the architect to develop a set of construction drawings.

The architect develops preliminary drawings in response to the client's needs. These drawings provide the basis for the formulation and incorporation of changes and new ideas. Included for this example are a site plan (Figure 14.3), floor plan (Figure 14.4), and a couple of elevations (Figure 14.5).

If this set of drawings is approved, additional preliminary drawings are conceived, which may include a roof plan (Figure 14.6), a design section (Figure 14.7), and possibly a framing plan.

Client Changes

The preliminary floor plan plays a very important part in the development of a final configuration or shape of a structure. It gives the client time to look at and discuss some of the important family needs or to make major changes before the project progresses too far.

Client changes are an integral part of the design process: It is much more likely that the client will generate changes to a plan than it is to have a client fully accept the plan as first presented. It is also common for the client to order or request changes throughout the entire design process and even construction of the project.

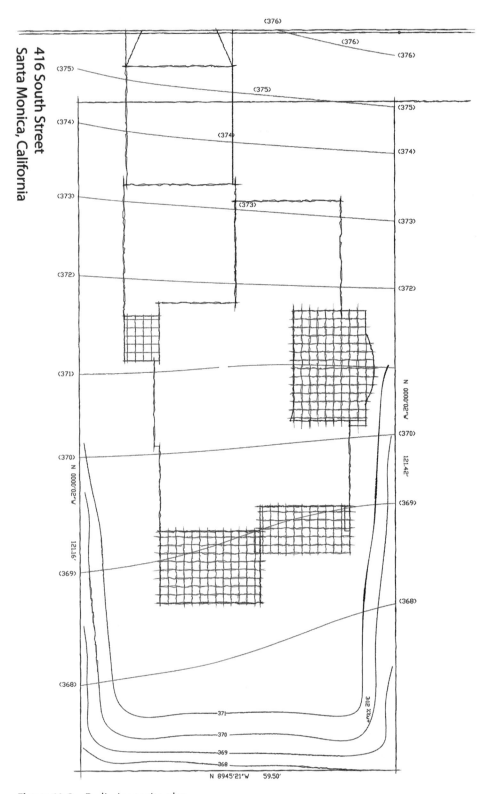

Figure 14.3 Preliminary site plan.

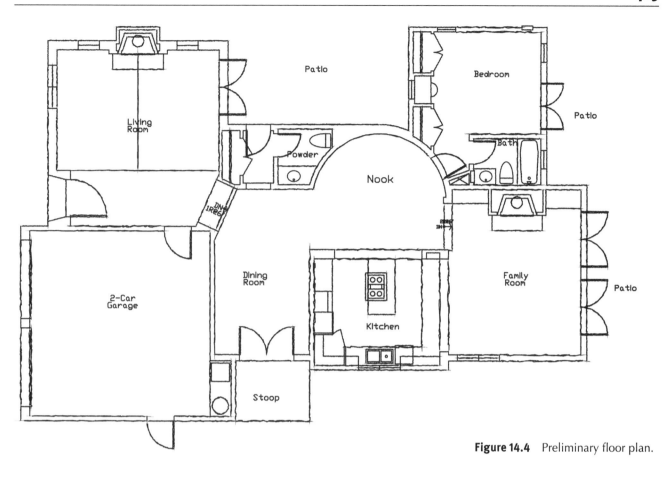

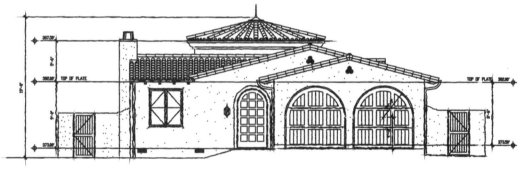

Figure 14.4 Preliminary floor plan.

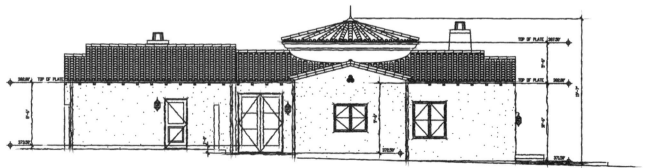

Figure 14.5 Preliminary elevations.

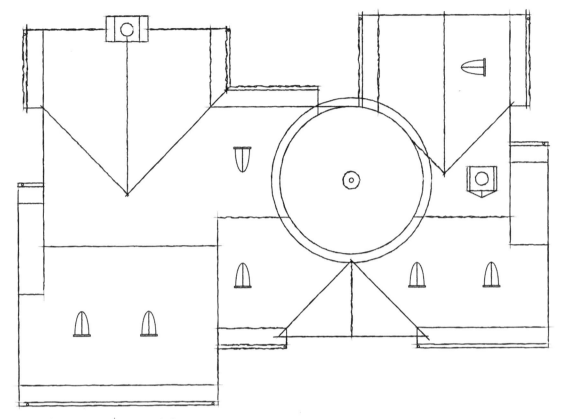

Figure 14.6 Preliminary roof plan.

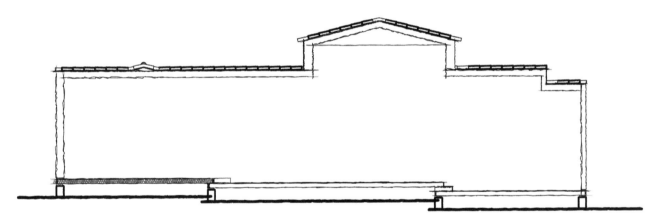

Figure 14.7 Preliminary building design section.

Model

For the sake of visualization, a model may be constructed over a copy of the preliminary floor plan. Because of the cost of model making, finished finite models are not always done, but simple massing models aid a client to visualize the project. The model can be built of foam-core board or museum board. Such a model allows the client to see the relationship of rooms in three dimensions and the positioning of furniture in relation to the walls.

Revit is another tool that allows visualization of a project. Though it may not help with specific room scales, it does create a definitive shape and mass of the future home.

With a more sophisticated computer model, the client can virtually will fly around or walk through the entire building.

Development of Elevations

The model helps the clients to visualize how the structure will look and to comprehend the preliminary exterior elevations, as seen in Figure 14.8. In this example, a simple series of rectangular shapes were extruded; the roof was then added and features delineated to establish a 3-D view or a schematic design.

■ EVOLUTION OF THE WORKING DRAWINGS

In Chapters 15 through 17, the case studies are tracked stage by stage within the confines of the specific topic. Examine each example for the specific type of construction. Here we cover a general pattern for evolution of the working drawings.

Other Preliminary Drawings

Other preliminary drawings may be done by the design and structural associates, making the CAD drafter's task easier. Such drawings might include a preliminary foundation plan, a revised preliminary building section and roof plans, and a revised framing system.

Cartoon of the Project

A **cartoon sheet** format, or **mock set** as it is called in some regions, is a reduced replica of the distribution of the drawings on each of the working drawing sheets, drawn on an 8½″ × 11″ sheet of paper. These can be accomplished by substituting rectangles in place of the actual drawings, as shown in Figures 14.9 and 14.10.

Procedure for Single or Multiple Working Drawing Sheets

After looking at the cartoon of each sheet, the project architect must determine how these working drawing sheets will evolve. Will a single drafter take on the responsibility for each single sheet, or will a number of drafters be working on it? Can parts of a single sheet be delegated to two or three individuals, drawn on separate sheets, and assembled? Once the project architect makes this decision, the drafters are selected and the drawing tasks are delegated.

Developing Construction Documents from a 3-D Model

A 3-D model, if one is generated, is rotated into the appropriate positions to obtain the roof plan and the corresponding elevations (see Figure 14.11). The 3-D model is sliced horizontally and vertically. The horizontal slice is used to produce the floor plan. If the roof half is rotated in the plan view, a reflected ceiling plan is produced. The vertical cut produces a view of the structure called a **building section**. For examples of the floor plan and building section, see Figure 14.12. A summary of the results of this exercise is shown in Figure 14.13.

The next step for the CAD drafter is to construct the structure as a 3-D model. See an example of such a section in Figure 14.14. Although this may seem like a lot of work at this stage, it really is not when you consider that the floor plan will be used as the base (datum) for the framing plan, electrical plans, mechanical plans, and foundation plans, as seen in Figure 14.15.

The sections can be enlarged to produce a base for partial sections and details, as shown in Figures 14.16 and 14.17, respectively. Taking a small portion of the model, a detail is blocked out and further data are provided to complete the detail. In this manner, the 3-D model becomes the datum, in essence, the glue that holds the entire set of drawings together.

■ SITE PLAN, VICINITY MAP, ROOF PLAN, AND NOTES

As stated earlier, the drawings can be done by a single individual or by two or more drafters. If two drafters are to work simultaneously, there must be a clear delegation of responsibilities, a format that allows such a procedure to work, and an understanding by the project manager as to the drafters' skills.

For an example of how this can be achieved, consider the following:

1. Site plan
2. Vicinity map
3. Roof plan
4. Energy notes (conservation plan)
5. Mandatory features and devices (required features for conservation)
6. Sheet index

The first three components will be done by one drafter and the remaining three by a second drafter. In fact, in some offices, an administrative assistant who is familiar with typing and word processing can receive additional training in drafting and forward the notes to a CAD drafter, who can then insert the notes in the proper position.

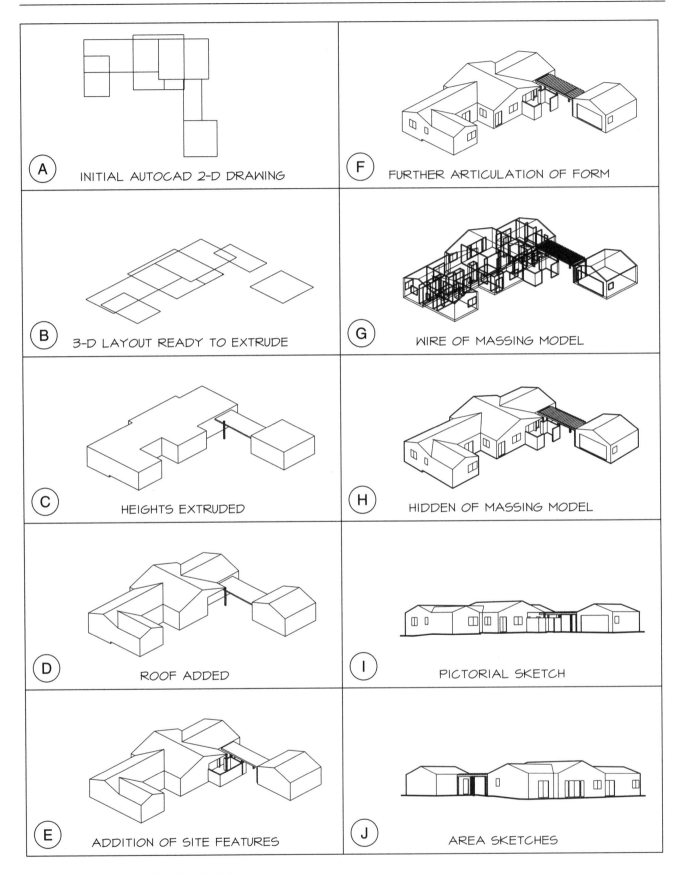

(A) INITIAL AUTOCAD 2-D DRAWING

(B) 3-D LAYOUT READY TO EXTRUDE

(C) HEIGHTS EXTRUDED

(D) ROOF ADDED

(E) ADDITION OF SITE FEATURES

(F) FURTHER ARTICULATION OF FORM

(G) WIRE OF MASSING MODEL

(H) HIDDEN OF MASSING MODEL

(I) PICTORIAL SKETCH

(J) AREA SKETCHES

Figure 14.8 Evolution of a 2-D to 3-D sketch.

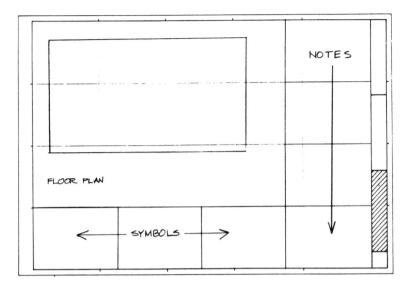

Figure 14.9   Cartoon of floor-plan sheet.

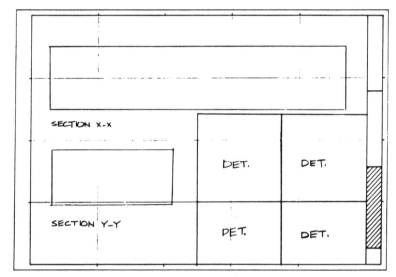

Figure 14.10   Cartoon of section sheet.

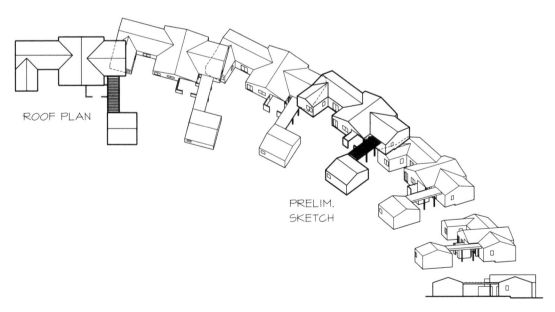

Figure 14.11   Rotation of massing model into ortho view.

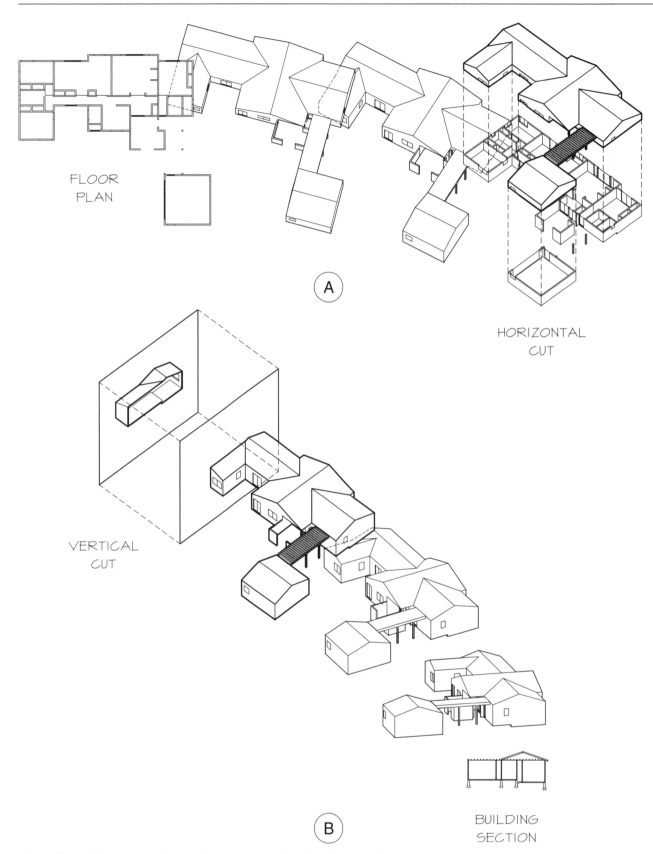

FLOOR
PLAN

A

HORIZONTAL
CUT

VERTICAL
CUT

B

BUILDING
SECTION

Figure 14.12 Horizontal and vertical sections through preliminary sketch.

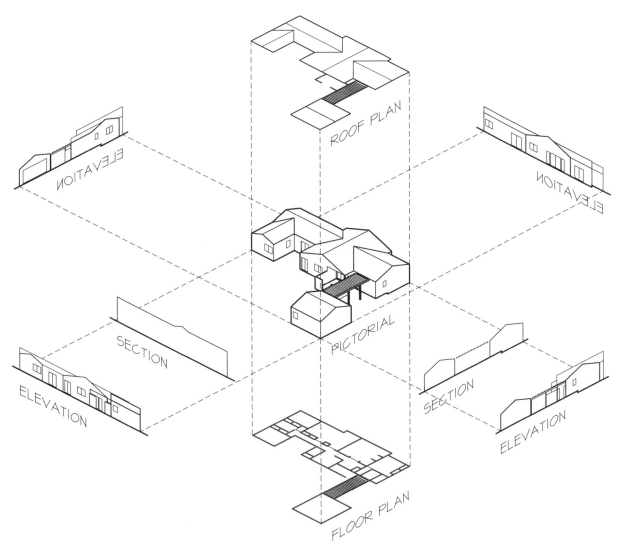

Figure 14.13 Evolution of construction documents.

If the office computers are networked and a third drafter is periodically available, this third drafter may be delegated the responsibility to draft only the vicinity map portion of the drawing. Thus, the entire site plan is done by multiple employees.

If the drawings are done by hand, each component part can be scissored and the parts assembled to form the entire sheet, including the notes. An engineering copier can then be used to make a single original on vellum.

■ JADYN RESIDENCE SITE PLAN

This drawing was sent to the client for approval and was included in the site plan, floor plan, and all other established drawings. As with all drawings, the site plan

data were provided on one layer, allowing the drafter to control the data drafted.

STAGE I   (Figure 14.18). After positioning the outline of the site on the sheet, the setbacks should be drawn. In this instance, they are 15'-0" in the front, 5'-0" on the side, and a minimum of 15'-0" at the rear. It appeared that the structure would not be very close to the rear property line. This drawing was drafted at a ¹/₈" scale.

STAGE II   (Figure 14.19). The next step was to locate and dimension the house and garage onto the site. Dimension lines were positioned to locate the structure from all sides of the property line. The sidewalk, parkway, and power pole were then drawn in, the driveway was positioned, and the textured concrete walks were inserted.

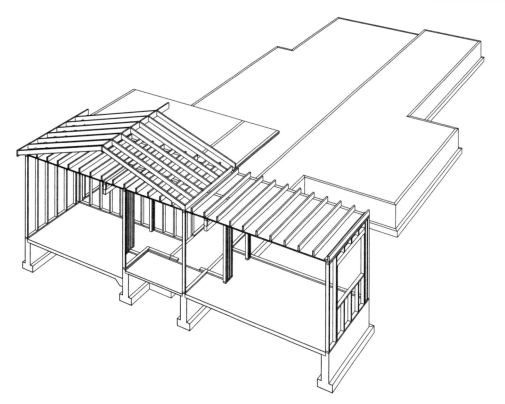

Figure 14.14 Incorporating the individual elements.

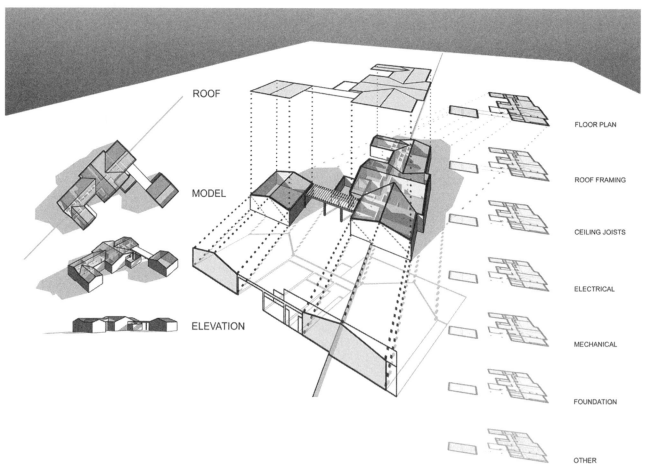

Figure 14.15 Floor plan as a base for other drawings.

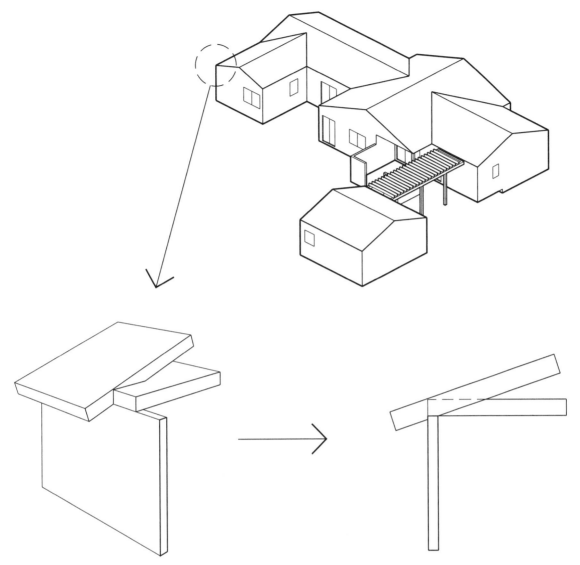

Figure 14.16 Isolating an area and detailing.

STAGE III (Figure 14.20). At this stage, existing trees were positioned, and dimensioning continued with the location dimensions of the driveway. Public utility lines, including sizing and noting, were next in the drawing order. Finally, the legal description and a description of the concrete-block wall, curb break, and all other notes (including the north arrow) were given. The title and scale were also included. Specific notes were added regarding city requirements, so the contractor could perform in compliance with regional regulations.

■ JADYN RESIDENCE FLOOR PLAN

The Jadyn residence floor plan was developed over several stages. The floor plan is by far the most important drawing in a set of working drawings, because it

sets the stage for all dimensions in terms of width and length.

The floor plan, Sheet A-101, can be done by two individuals. While one develops the floor plan, the other develops the construction notes, electrical and utility symbols, and abbreviations. Electrical and utility symbols and abbreviations—standard items in most offices—can be transferred into a drawing. Simply import the desired information, be it a set of construction notes, symbols, or an office standard that has been previously prepared.

To allow the floor-plan drafter to work at his or her own speed without interruptions, two separate drawings were made and later merged electronically.

The positioning of the abbreviations, notes, and symbols can be done in one stage but on multiple layers.

An intermediate stage is often reproduced several times using an electronic file and given to associates to

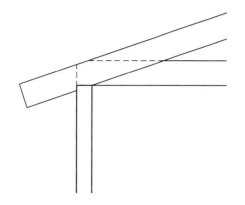

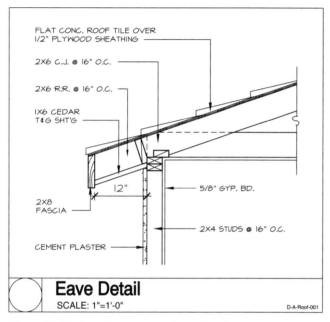

FLAT CONC. ROOF TILE OVER
1/2" PLYWOOD SHEATHING

2X6 C.J. @ 16" O.C.

2X6 R.R. @ 16" O.C.

1X6 CEDAR
T&G SHT'G

12"

5/8" GYP. BD.

2X8
FASCIA

2X4 STUDS @ 16" O.C.

CEMENT PLASTER

Eave Detail
SCALE: 1"=1'-0"

D-A-Roof-001

Figure 14.17 Isolating and creating a detail.

generate additional masters for framing plans, structural drawings, and/or separate electrical plans, to mention just a few. The format of this would be XREF in AutoCAD.

It would be most convenient to have a ¼" scale drawing as well as a ⅛" drawing of the floor plan. With CAD, you simply enter the scale factor and the scale is changed immediately.

STAGE I (Figure 14.21). The general shape of the structure is blocked out. The block-out is accomplished with a single line. The line that defines the perimeter is drawn with a solid line. This is the outside wall line, which allows the drafter to check outside overall dimensions to ensure proper positioning on the site. With CAD, this would establish the datum or base. In the case of a wood structure, grids are set at 1'-0" and snaps are set at 1" for stud line or face-of-stud dimensioning.

STAGE II (Figure 14.22). Into this single-lined floor plan, wall thickness is incorporated, starting with the outside perimeter. Next, lines are drawn defining the thickness of the interior walls. Openings in the wall (windows and doors) are located and positioned. The drafter must be sure to verify the minimum openings for the doors and the sizes of the windows; ADA requirements may dictate some of these measurements. Notice that jambs were left on both sides of the windows and doors to house the support for the beam and/or headers that will eventually be used.

STAGE III (Figure 14.23). Before commencing Stage III, the drafter should turn to the project book and glean all the specifics regarding appliances, plumbing fixtures, and fireplaces. This information is then translated into drawings, as shown. Windows have also been incorporated into the drawing. Sizes are found in the preliminary schedule based on the design and energy analysis.

STAGE IV (Figure 14.24). This stage is the most critical, because all of the dimensions are established at this time. A check print was made of Stage III, and the dimensions and their numerical values established. This was all done rapidly, but with great accuracy.

Based on this positioning of extension and dimension lines, totals are carefully checked to ensure that important walls or windows were not missed.

Cutting plane lines and their respective bubbles are drawn to refer the reader to the building section drawings.

A check print will be made at this stage, and dimensional corrections will be noted, as well as any other change or correction to be made. The project manager may even overlay the original over the foundation plan to discover any other errors or omissions.

STAGE V (Figure 14.25). After receiving **redlines**, or corrected drawings, from the project manager, it is a good idea to follow up on this check print with a procedure sheet of your own. This could be done by using the floor-plan checklist. Because this is a standard office form for all floor plans, not all items will apply. You can make this form a job-specific checklist by highlighting what you feel is critical information and/or having your immediate supervisor check the list for you. Armed with this new tool, you can proceed, with confidence, to draft the final stage of this most critical sheet.

Most of the notes can be reduced to four categories:
A. Identification of the rooms, appliances, and equipment
B. Identification of items that are in the contract and those that are to be provided by the owner
C. Positioning and location of structural members (some of which are inside walls)

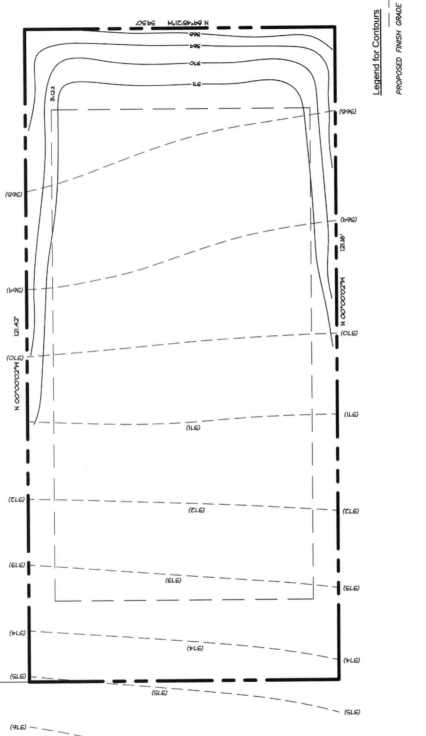

Figure 14.18 Stage I: Site plan.

Legend for Contours

PROPOSED FINISH GRADE

VIA SOLANO

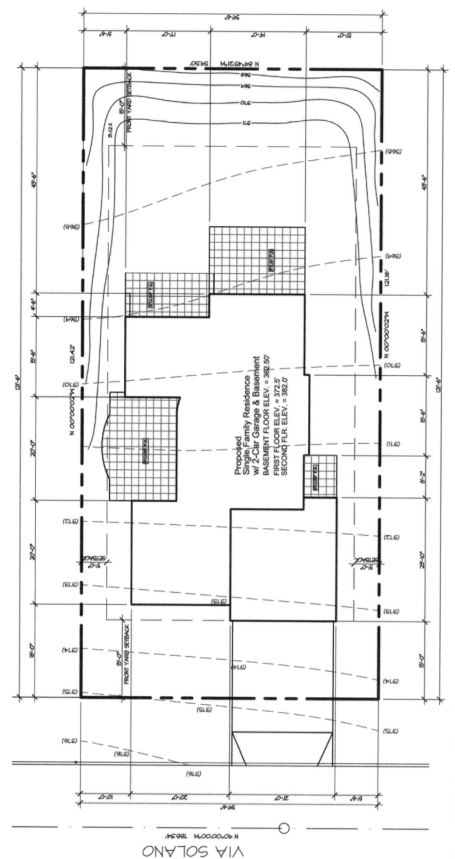

Figure 14.19 Stage II: Site plan.

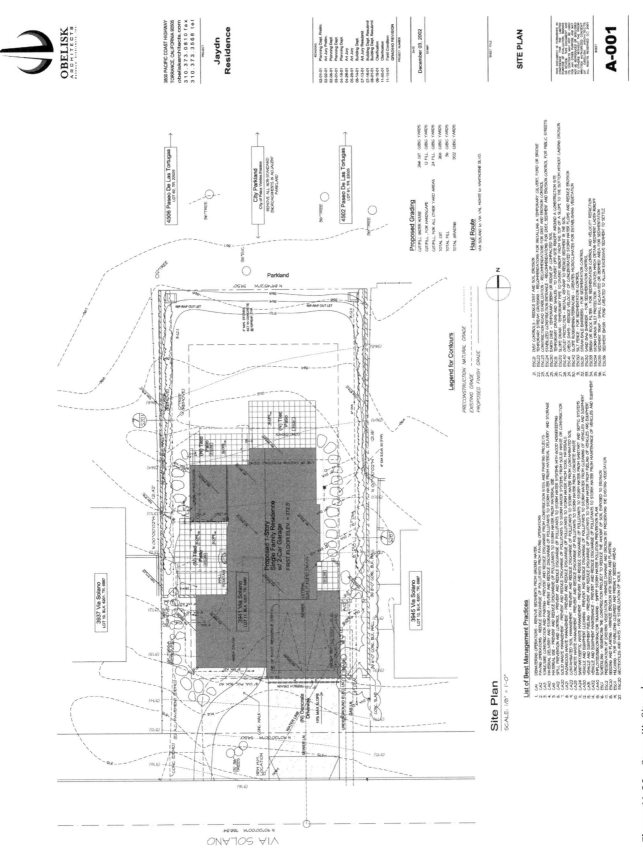

Figure 14.20 Stage III: Site plan.

477

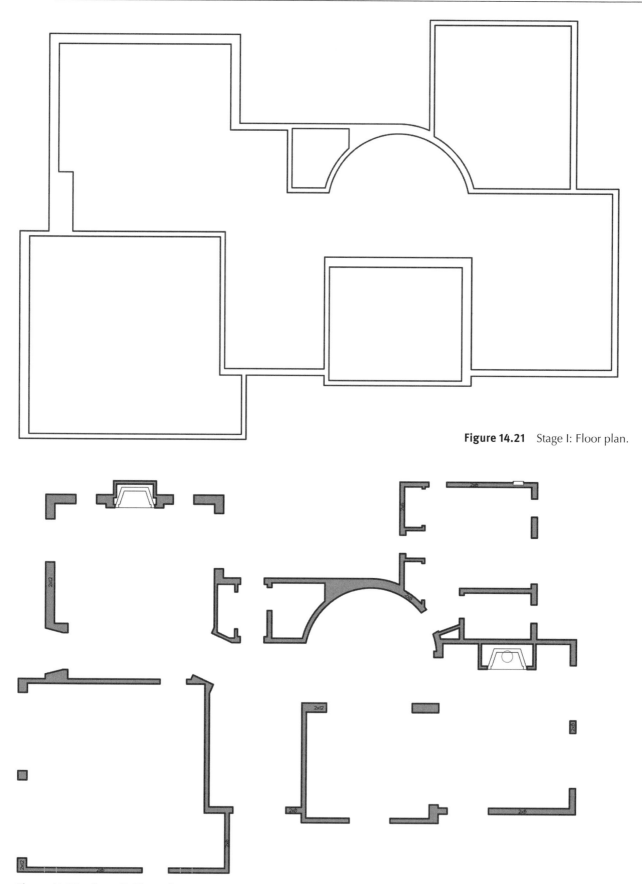

Figure 14.21 Stage I: Floor plan.

Figure 14.22 Stage II: Floor plan.

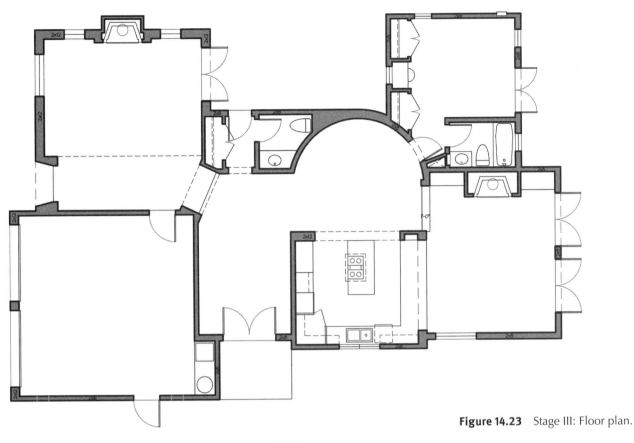

Figure 14.23 Stage III: Floor plan.

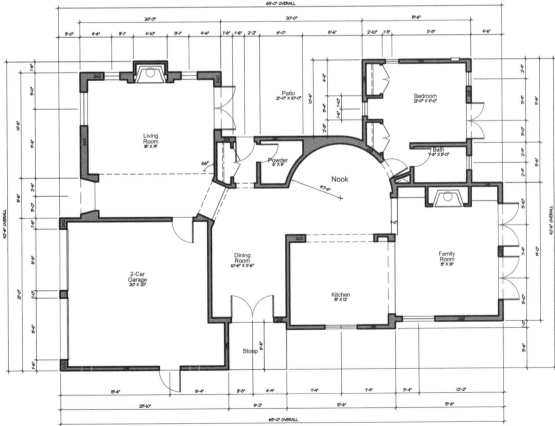

Figure 14.24 Stage IV: Floor plan.

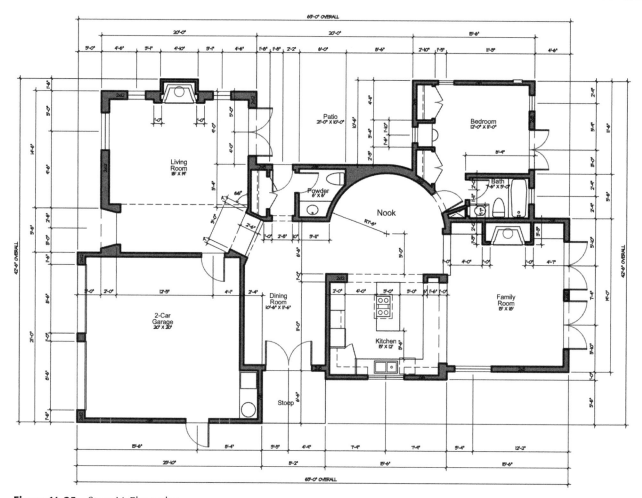

Figure 14.25 Stage V: Floor plan.

D. Special needs that may be established by codes, such as notes dealing with the forced air unit (FAU) and water heater (W/H).

STAGE VI (Figure 14.26). This is the culminating stage for the floor plan, where it all "comes together." The drawings at this stage incorporate the floor plan, construction notes, symbols, abbreviations, and, of course, the border and title blocks (not shown in Figure 14.26).

■ JADYN RESIDENCE ROOF PLAN

The roof plan can be superimposed on the site plan. When this is done, the building line and the roof outline are reversed, with the building line solid and the roof line dotted. On a true roof plan, the outline of a roof is a solid line.

STAGE I (Figure 14.27). The scale selected for the residence roof plan was $1/8'' = 1'-0''$. The outline of the building can be drawn by taking the first stage of the

floor plan, making a ½ reduction, and overlaying the roof.

STAGE II (Figure 14.28). The roof and building lines are darkened at this stage. Arrows are drawn to indicate the direction of the slope.

STAGE III (Figure 14.29). Skylight and chimney locations are the first to be drawn at this stage. Some architectural offices show plumbing vents that come through the roof, as a confirmation of their positions. Detail and section reference bubbles are next and, finally, noting is completed.

■ JADYN RESIDENCE BUILDING SECTIONS

Before a building section of any building is undertaken, it is essential to understand and comprehend the structural system at work and how the building will be assembled using this system. The drafter must be familiar with the walls, bearing footings, and their locations, and

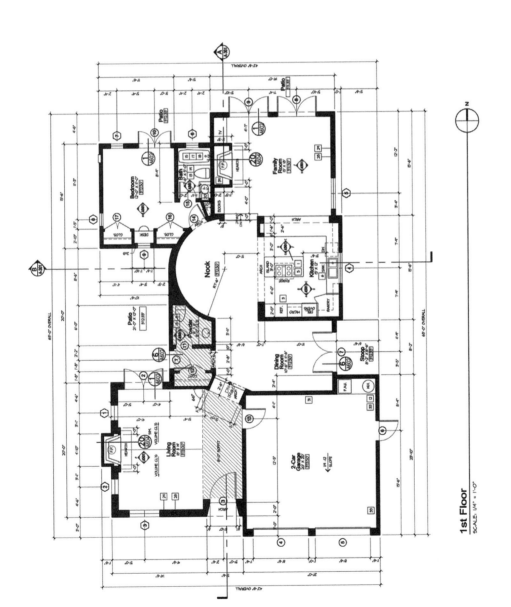

Figure 14.26 Stage VI: Floor plan.

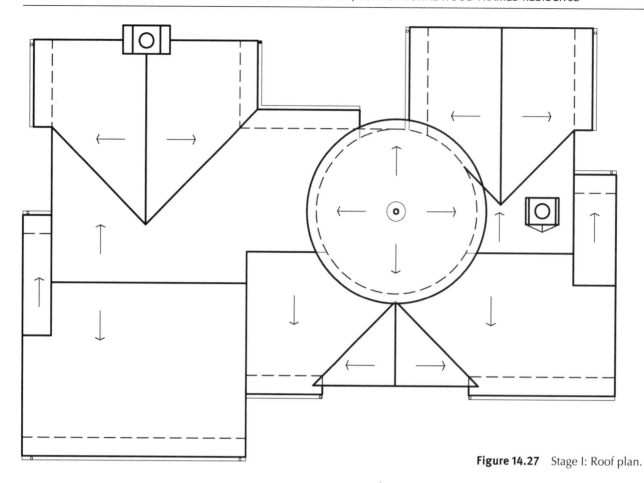

Figure 14.27 Stage I: Roof plan.

Figure 14.28 Stage II: Roof plan.

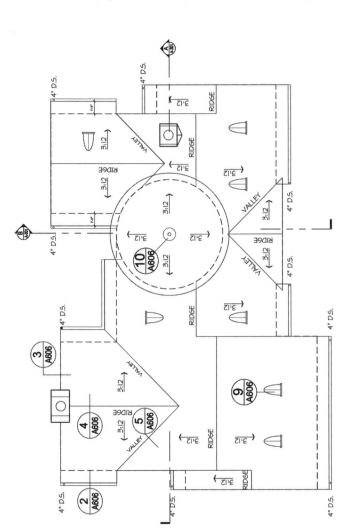

ROOF PLAN NOTES:

Roof Plan
SCALE: 1/4" = 1'-0"

Figure 14.29 Stage III: Roof plan.

with how the weight of the structure, starting at the roof, is distributed downward.

Initial Building Section Stages

STAGE I   (Figure 14.30). This stage establishes heights. As the floor plan controls the width and depth of the residence, the building sections control the heights. The floor line and plate line are the most critical from a building perspective. The Jadyn residence has three floor lines because of the change of level that occurs at the bearing wall located in the center of the structure. Many planning departments require that the top of the ridge be dimensioned, to make sure it does not obstruct views for neighbors; thus, this is often included in exterior elevations.

STAGE II   (Figure 14.31). The outline of the roof and the positioning of the bearing walls are incorporated at this stage.

STAGE III   (Figure 14.32). As seen in the drawing, the building section is receiving detail at the various intersections. The top and bottom plates, as well as the seat in the stem wall for the slab, are drafted.

STAGE IV   (Figure 14.33). This is a very critical stage, because it establishes all of the structural components, their position and direction, and even the direction in which the section was taken.

Note the inclusion of the material designation and the makeup of the foundation with its insulation and sand. Walls show drywall, and the ceiling reveals the direction of the ceiling joist.

Correction of Drawing Errors

At this point a check print is made. Using the check print, the project manager can redline errors, position dimensions, and make notes for a beginning drafter.

Errors can occur in any drawing; it is no different with a building section. Some errors are easy to correct, whereas others are a bit more difficult. Both types of errors are addressed here, and possible solutions are suggested.

Because a building section is the result of the foundation plan, roof plan, and roof framing systems used, the framing is checked and corrections clearly noted on the check print. Using a set of simple commands, most computers can be made to isolate a drawing and produce a mirror image of it.

Later Building Section Stages

STAGE V   (Figure 14.34). Having made all the necessary corrections at the previous stage, Stage V becomes very straightforward. Noting of the component parts and dimensioning become the most important tasks. All the parts should be identified. Material designations for insulation, roof material, and concrete are done at this stage, as well as referencing to reveal footing details and eave details.

Figure 14.30   Stage I: Building sections.

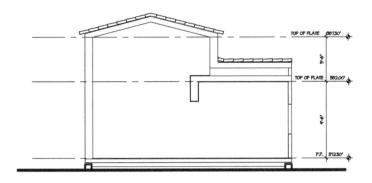

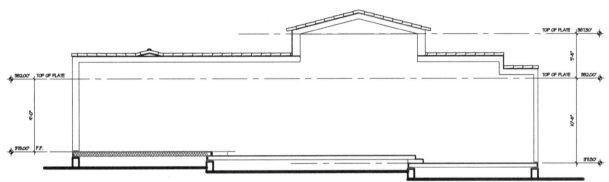

Figure 14.31   Stage II: Building sections.

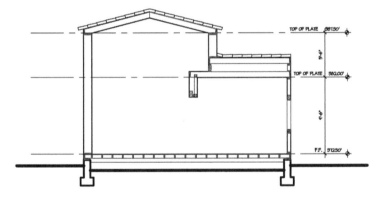

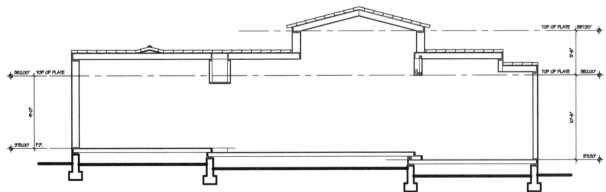

Figure 14.32   Stage III: Building sections.

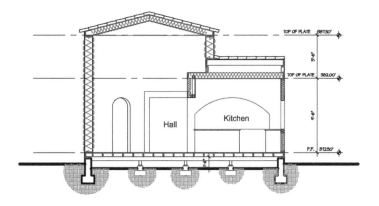

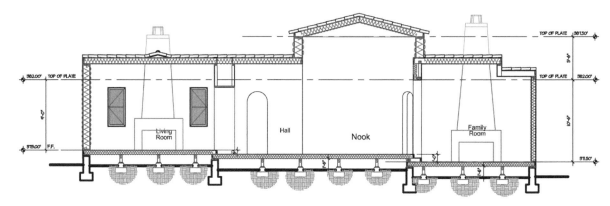

Figure 14.33 Stage IV: Building sections.

STAGE VI (Figure 14.35). This is not really a stage in the evolution of the building sections, but more of an assembly stage for the plot sheet. The final stages of the details and the building section are merged at this point and positioned onto the title block sheet in the final plotting.

■ JADYN RESIDENCE EXTERIOR ELEVATIONS

The exterior skin of the Jadyn residence will be cement plaster. A three-coat system will be used, which includes an initial "scratch" coat, a second "brown" coat, and a thin final coat (called a finished *color coat*). If Styrofoam is used to raise portions of the wall surface, two coats of plaster are placed first; then the foam and the final color coat are placed over the entire ensemble. The roof is gabled with vents in the gable end, which is called the *rake*.

Exterior Elevations

The drafter selected to do the exterior elevation is likely to be the same person who drafted the building section,

because both drawings reveal vertical dimensions and both use the same pitch development and ceiling heights.

STAGE I (Figure 14.36). The initial stage is to block out the vertical distances between the floor line and the plate line. This base can be taken from the section drawings. This plate layout is the base of the exterior elevations.

STAGE II (Figure 14.37). The basic shape is now drawn over the plate and floor line. The beginning and end points of the wall are constructed, and the pitch is measured from the intersection of these wall lines and the plate line. Once the pitch has been established and constructed in the section drawings, the drafter gives the roof thickness and obtains the roof thickness via the rafter size and the outline of the roof shape from the roof plan.

STAGE III (Figure 14.38). Window and door locations are obtained from the floor plan, and the openings are defined. Any exterior articulation is drafted at this stage.

STAGE IV (Figure 14.39). The material designation for the roof has been drawn. Next, the outline of the chimney was located, with the chimney extending 2'-0" above the highest point within a 10'-0" radius.

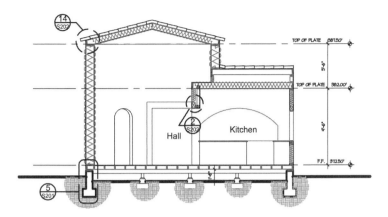

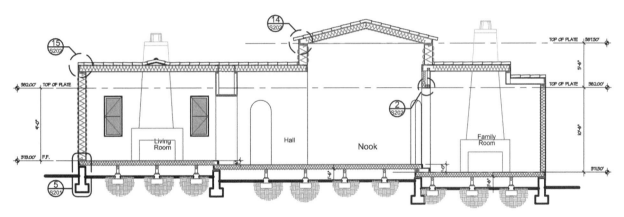

Figure 14.34 Stage V: Building sections.

The finished configurations of the windows and doors have also been drawn at this stage. This includes any changes requested by the client or the firm's design division.

STAGE V (Figure 14.40). This is the dimensioning, noting, and referencing stage. It is also the stage at which some items, required but held up for owner approval, are drawn. Notice the dimensioning procedure used on the exterior elevation. The floor-to-plate lines and roof pitch are expressed as a ratio; the chimney as minimum clearances.

STAGE VI (Figure 14.41). All parts of the exterior elevations are assembled and are combined onto the sheet along with the title block and border, which are standard to the specific architectural office.

Referencing

Referencing is the process of referring the plan user or reader to a section, a partial section, or an enlarged detail of a specific area. To accomplish this, the top half of

the reference bubble indicates the name of the detail, and the bottom number indicates the sheet on which the particular detail can be found. Sizes can be found on the schedule by numbers, letters, and symbols. You will typically see detail reference bubbles around all windows, doors, beam connections, and so on.

Noting

Whenever possible, noting is done outside the elevation within the right margin. However, you cannot fit all of the notes in one place without having to use long leaders pointing to the subject. Therefore, certain notes are made inside the elevation to reduce the length of the leaders. Good rules of thumb in regard to leaders are not to allow them to cross more than one object line, never cross a dimension line, and keep the leader length to a minimum.

Keynoting is used by many offices. This is a procedure of numbering and placing all of the notes on one side (usually the right). You then place a leader in the desired

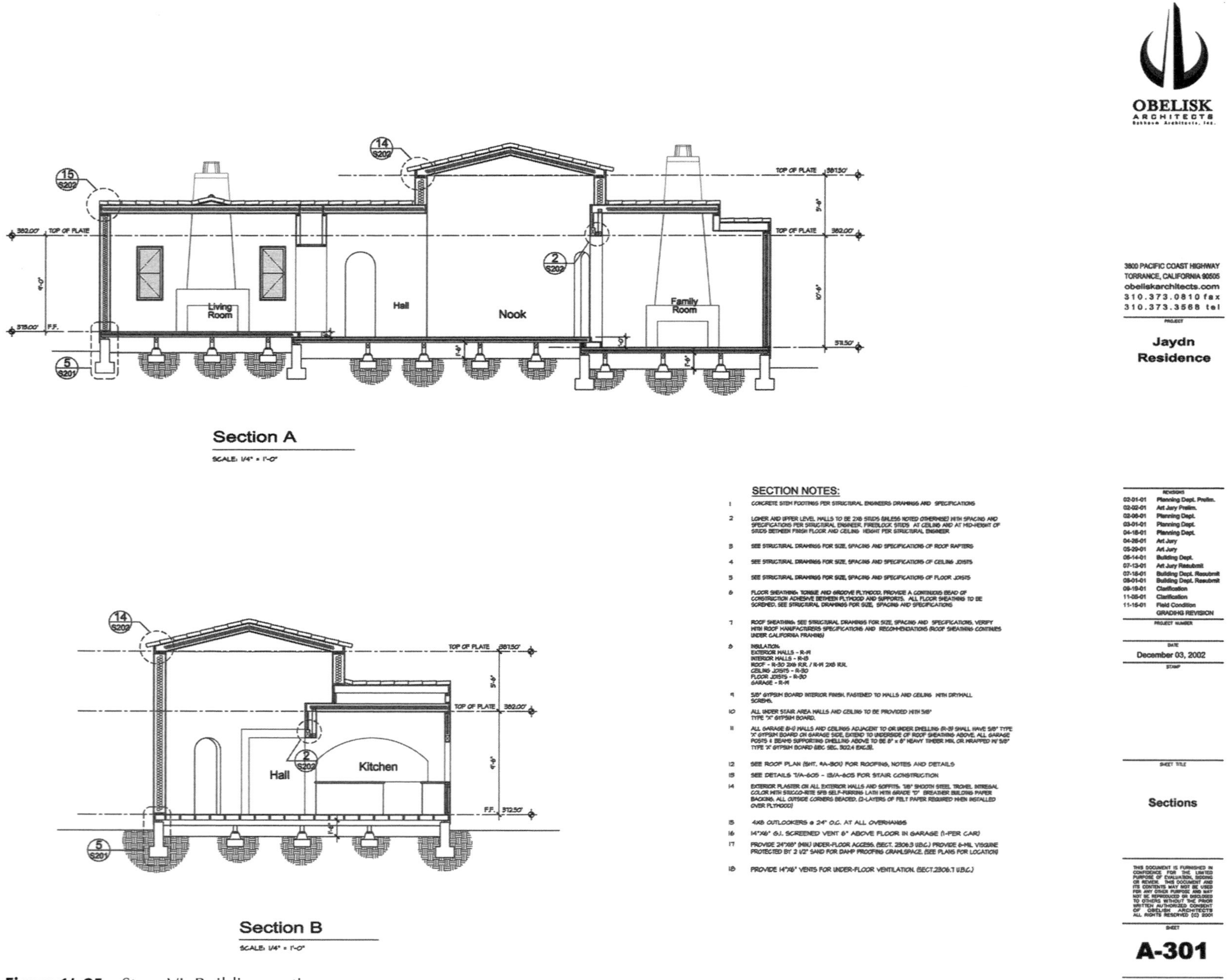

Section A

SCALE: 1/4" = 1'-0"

Section B

SCALE: 1/4" = 1'-0"

Figure 14.35 Stage VI: Building sections.

Figure 14.36 Stage I: Exterior elevations.

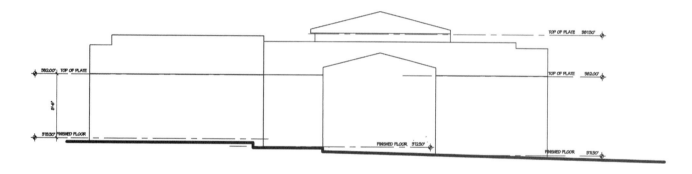

Figure 14.37 Stage II: Exterior elevations.

location. Rather than placing the note at the end of the leader, you use a reference bubble that refers to the correct note.

The advantage of keynoting is standardization of the notes. Keynoting also allows the drafter to make direct references to the specification numbers right on the notes. Numbering systems recommended by the American Institute of Architects are similar to the numbering system used by public libraries and can be incorporated in a keynotes area.

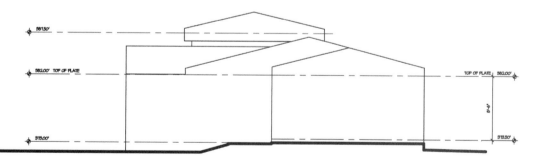

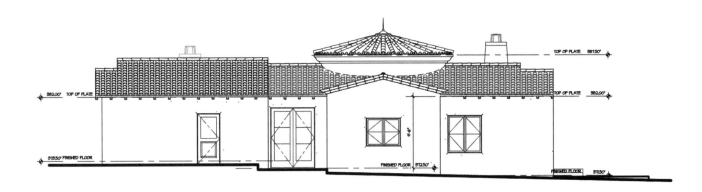

Figure 14.38 Stage III: Exterior elevations.

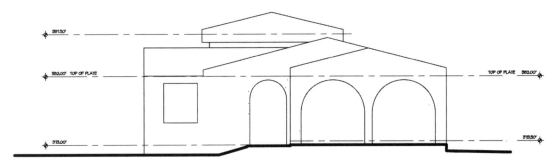

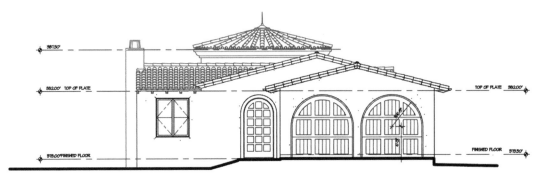

Figure 14.39 Stage IV: Exterior elevations.

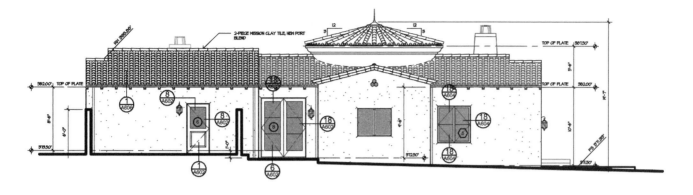

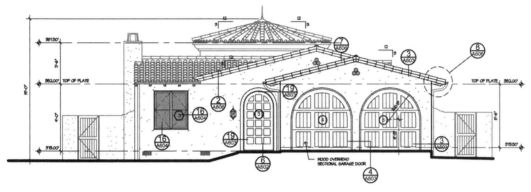

Figure 14.40   Stage V: Exterior elevations.

■ JADYN RESIDENCE FOUNDATION PLAN

Having considered the ingredients of a foundation plan and the graphic (drafted) translation of these forms, we next sequentially draft a foundation plan for the Jadyn residence. It will be developed as a raised foundation and a slab-on-grade system. Be sure to read Chapter 9 so that you understand the structural system by which the building is assembled; you will need to appreciate the location and position of bearing and non-bearing footings, posts and their pads, and the need for and location of shear walls.

The process begins with the positioning of the foundation plan, using the floor plan as a base. This is done to speed the drawing process, but more importantly, to ensure that the foundation does, in fact, sit under the floor plan and aligns with it.

The non-bearing walls are removed. Dotted lines represent the width of the footing. The exterior walls that extend into the building and become the interior walls must be checked for plate alignment. Refer to Chapter 9 for an explanation of this problem and its resolution.

Evolution of the Jadyn Residence Foundation Plan

For a more complex foundation design, a consultation from an engineer may be required, but in this example a foundation was laid out in four stages.

STAGE I   (Figure 14.42). After the wall line was placed in the correct position, a line was added on either side of these lines to represent the width of the footing. Next, the steps were positioned from the floor plan. In CAD, change the line type on the specific layer to hidden lines, using the office standards for layers.

STAGE II   (Figure 14.43). Dimension lines were introduced at this stage. The square forms represent the **piers,** which are the primary support for the girders. **Girders** support the floor joists, which in turn support the plywood floor the occupants walk on. These piers and girders are typically spaced in a grid of 6 to 7 feet center to center. In this stage, the grid is established and blocked out.

STAGE III   (Figure 14.44). Numerical values, noting, and referencing are done in that order. The bubbles refer the viewer to the details that will be on this sheet but are drawn on a separate page. Each large bubble with

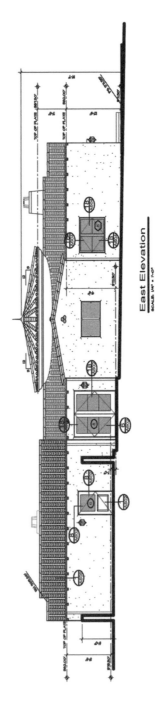

Figure 14.41 Stage VI: Exterior elevations.

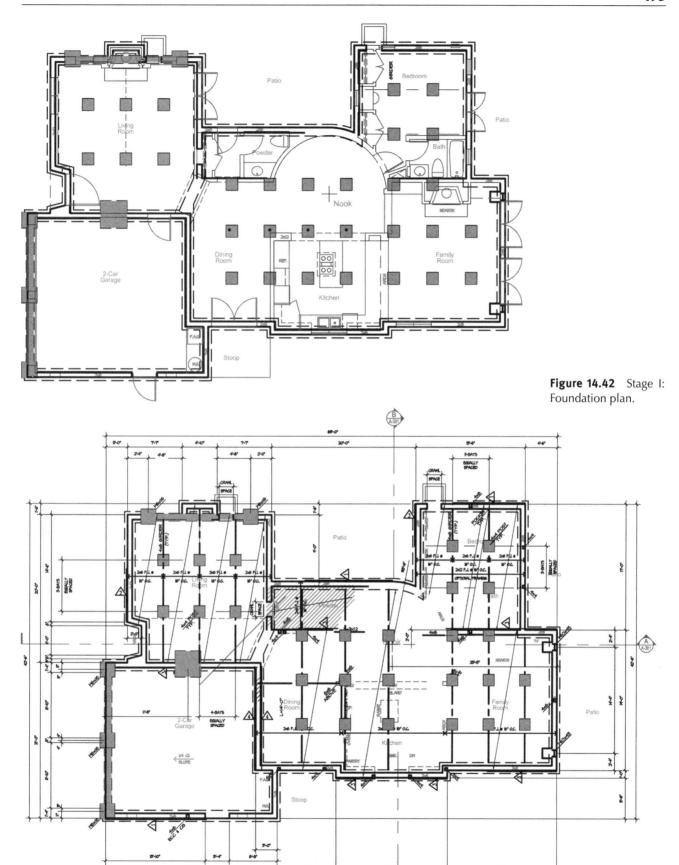

Figure 14.42 Stage I: Foundation plan.

Figure 14.43 Stage II: Foundation plan.

a triangle drawn around half of it refers the viewer to a building section.

If an area is to be depressed, a simple notation is sufficient. In this residence, we have four areas with depressed slabs and one major change of level. To ensure that the viewer reads the plans correctly, a half bubble, with the horizontal portion showing the high and low sides, is employed. It is cross-hatched so as to be noticeable.

In some offices, all of the symbols—depressed slab, detail reference, north arrow, and so on—are pasted. With a computer, a library of symbols can be produced in the office, recalled, and positioned as needed for any project.

STAGE IV (Figure 14.45). A final check is made of the set before it can be considered finished. To avoid massive changes at the end, great care must be taken at each stage.

Finally, the titles and scale are positioned, thus completing the foundation plan. Details and material notes are imported onto the sheet. See Figure 14.46

for the completed foundation plan of a slab-on-grade version.

■ FRAMING A RESIDENCE

In considering the Jadyn residence, let's examine the specific detail as well as the overall look. As in all structural analysis, we first describe the overall structure, starting with the top of the building and working downward.

The roof is a gable roof, built of rafter to form a triangle. The sides at the base of the triangle accept the weight of the roof (called the **dead load**) and the weight of movable objects (called the **live load**). Movable objects might be architectural décor, roofers walking about, and so on.

The main roof is completely sheathed. The sheathing in turn acts as a diaphragm to resist earthquakes, wind, or any other force acting upon this structure. In addition, the total wall surface will also be sheathed with plywood to resist any lateral forces acting upon the structure. This plywood wall membrane, along with other material, will

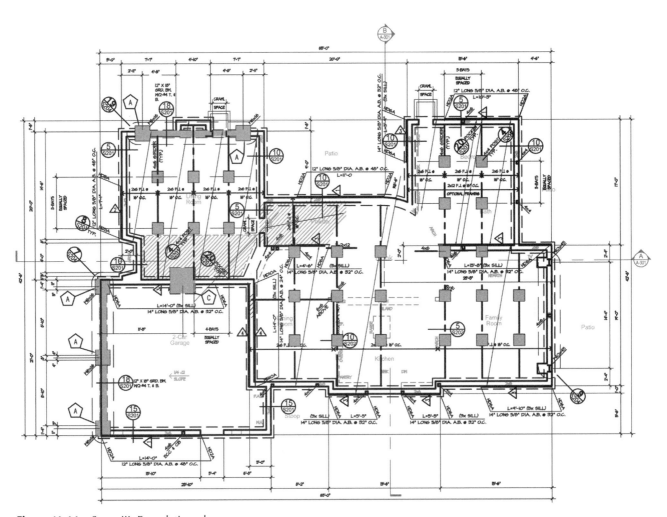

Figure 14.44 Stage III: Foundation plan.

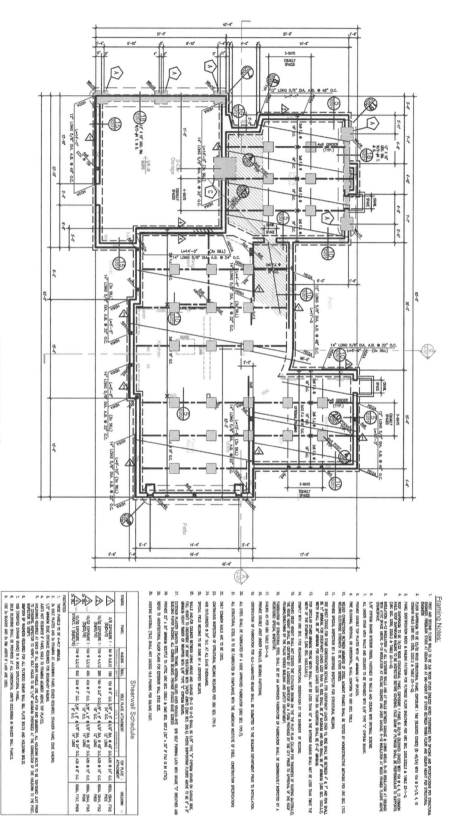

Figure 14.45 Stage IV: Foundation plan, raised wood.

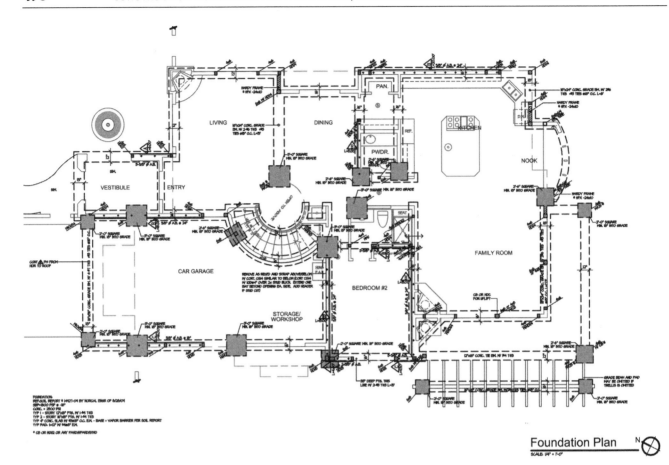

Figure 14.46   Stage IV: Foundation plan, slab-on-grade.

also work to prevent heat loss on cold days and heat gain on hot days.

A second way of holding up the roof by changing the direction of the ceiling joist is to turn the ridge into a beam. This beam is subsequently supported by a post and by a concrete pad that distributes this concentrated load over the ground. Figure 14.47 shows a model illustrating this method.

Next, consider the ceiling system. The ideal procedure is to install the ceiling joists in the same direction as the rafters, to complete the desired triangle. See Figure 14.48. The beginning, the end points, and the lap of other ceiling joists are well secured to form a solidly built triangle. Another solution is to use a wood truss system, as opposed to the conventional rafter/ceiling joist system.

In a wood truss, the rafter and ceiling joist as shown in Figure 14.48 are integrated as a total unit. Because of the way they are configured, the forces on trusses are distributed to the ends of the trusses and thus can span greater distances. They are prebuilt in the shop and delivered ready for erection. Light roof trusses (built of 2 × 4 and 2 × 6 members) are light enough that two framers can lift the units into place. Spaced at 16 to 24 inches on center,

these trusses can easily span between 20 and 30 feet, depending on exterior forces such as snow load, wind, earthquake, and so forth. Heavy timber trusses can span upward of 100 feet. Look at Figure 14.49 and compare the appearance of the structure with the previous illustration. The metal plates used to connect the various components are toothed fasteners. (A piece of metal is punched to form a projection like a tooth, and the whole plate is pressed into position by the truss manufacturer.)

The member perpendicular to the truss and on the top side is called a **purlin**. Purlins keep the trusses from toppling over like dominos.

The negative aspect to the use of trusses, if you can call it a negative, is the reduction of attic space.

To show alternative solutions and their implications, we ran the ceiling joist parallel to the ridge and perpendicular to the rafters. This shortens the span of the ceiling joists and runs them in the same direction, as required by the two roofs adjacent to the main roof. However, this causes two additional problems: We have not created a triangle, and we must find a way to hold up the ridge.

Within these bearing walls are openings. A header or lintel is used to distribute the weight of the ceiling and roof around the openings.

Figure 14.47   Ridge beam and its support.

Figure 14.48   Creating a structural triangle.

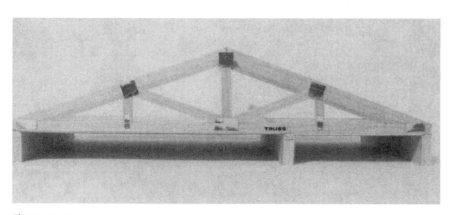

Figure 14.49   Truss system.

■ JADYN RESIDENCE ROOF FRAMING PLAN

As described at the beginning of this chapter, there are two ways of developing framing plans: superimposed and separate development. For the roof framing plan, the initial procedure is to print a copy of the floor plan, prior to the dimensioning stage, onto vellum. The roof framing plan is drawn onto this copy. With CAD, you simply use an earlier layer of the floor plan that does not show the notes and dimensions.

STAGE I (Figure 14.50). The outline of the floor plan and roof plan is imported and becomes the base sheet for this drawing. Be sure to pick a floor-plan stage that shows only the openings for the windows and doors and does not have the doors and windows drawn in. This allows you to show the beams and headers easily. Lighten the lines to allow for easy reading of the framing members. The roof plan is imported from the established roof plan as an XREF.

STAGE II (Figure 14.51). The ridge beams and the direction of the roof framing members are determined and indicated by arrows with only one head. The duration is indicated by arrow lines with a full head. If the design incorporates skylights or chimneys, these should be located as well. Ridge beams and beams over critical openings (in load-bearing walls) are placed.

Beams that support the roof framing members are shown and sized for the support of the roof system.

The window and door headers are included in the beam category. These are the shorter beams that support the roof over the window and door spans.

STAGE III (Figure 14.52). Bearing walls can be identified by the pouché of the walls; California frame areas are also indicated. If ceiling joists are to be included in the plan, this is the stage at which you would provide those data, usually indicated as the roof framing members are indicated and duration demonstrated with arrows.

STAGE IV (Figure 14.53). The roof framing plan is drawn in diagrammatic fashion and includes notations for the struts, California frame, ties, and so on. All headers and beams are checked and labeled. To eliminate the redundant task of labeling every beam or header, a special note can be included to identify all 4 × 4 or less. A legend identifying bearing and non-bearing walls is also included.

STAGE V (Figure 14.54). In the final stage, all the components that make up this set are merged onto a plot sheet for the roof framing plan.

■ JADYN RESIDENCE INTERIOR ELEVATIONS

Several examples of interior elevations are provided to show the basic progression of the drawings through various stages.

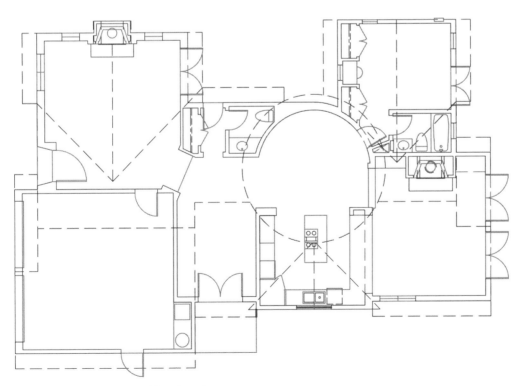

Figure 14.50 Stage I: Roof framing plan.

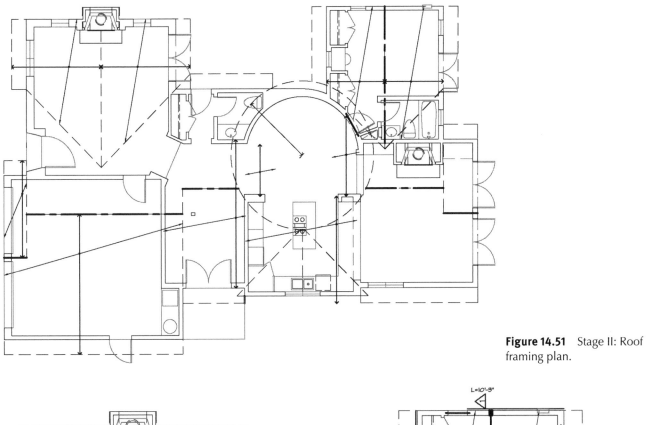

Figure 14.51 Stage II: Roof framing plan.

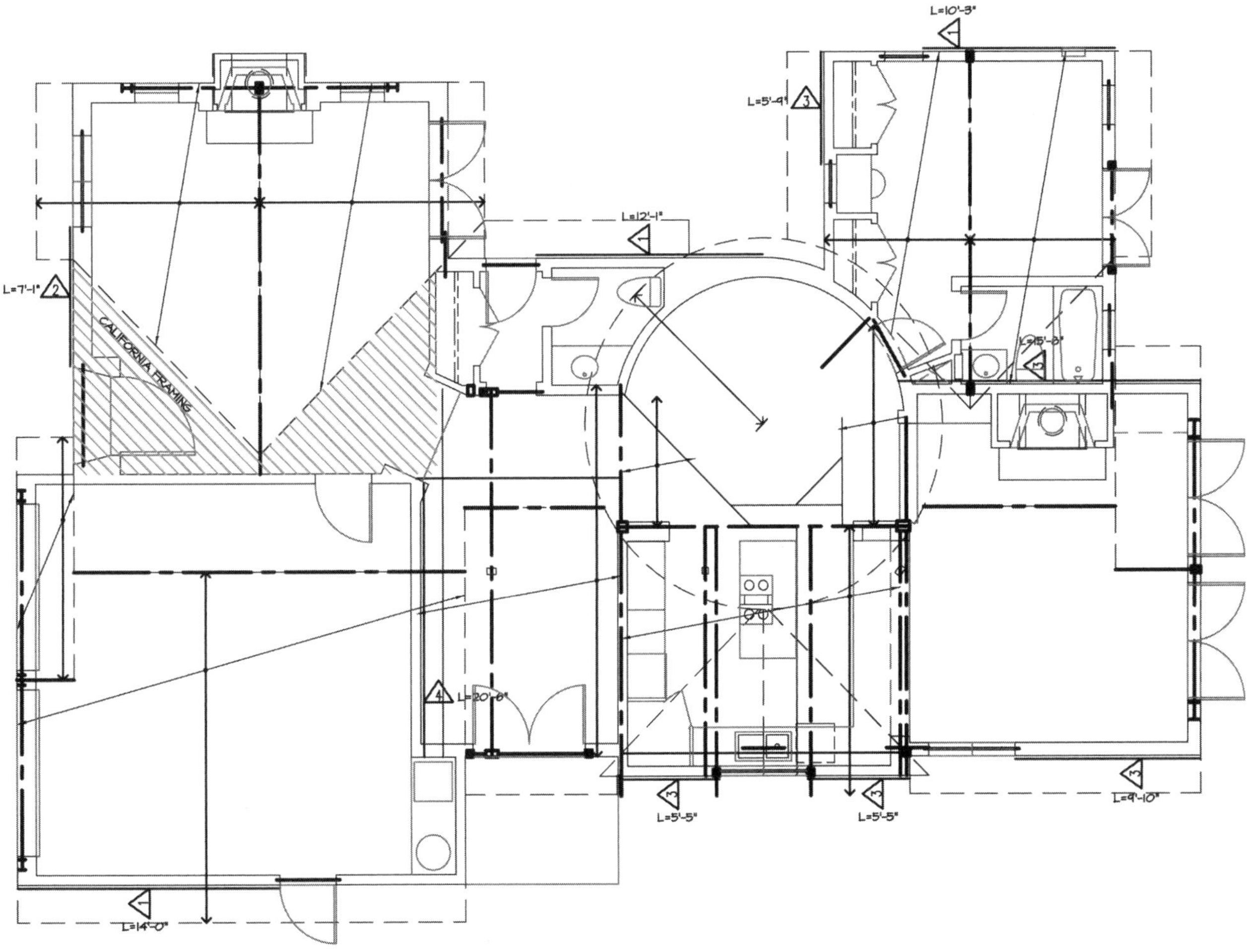

Figure 14.52 Stage III: Roof framing plan.

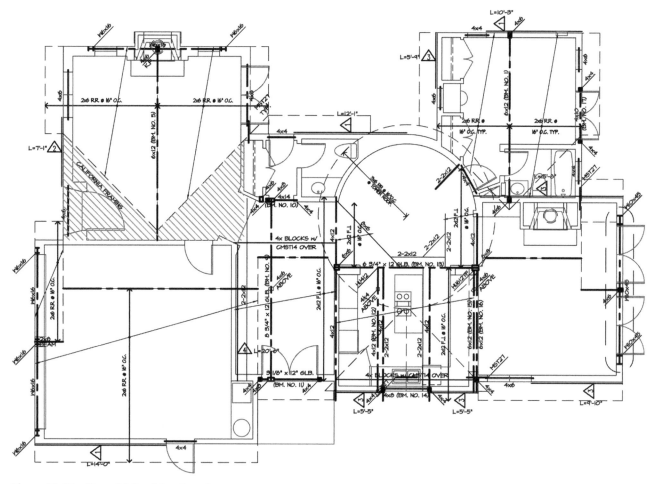

Figure 14.53 Stage IV: Roof framing plan.

STAGE I (Figure 14.55). This is the block-out stage. Before beginning this stage, the drafter should consult the project book to become familiar with the shapes and sizes of the various kitchen appliances, plumbing fixtures, cabinets, and washer and dryer. The drafter first lays out the ceiling line, the floor line, and the wall line.

STAGE II (Figure 14.56). Once the basic outline of the room is established, the doors and drawers are lightly outlined. If preconstructed cabinets are to be used, the distributor can usually help you draft the doors and drawers based on the available sizes. A catalog listing basic sizes may be available in the project book; basic available sizes are usually displayed on the backs of these catalogs. If the cabinets are to be custom built, the designer should simply follow common cabinet practices.

With the use of a template, plumbing fixtures and the surrounding areas are drawn. If the ceramic tile extends on the wall surface for only a couple of rows, this area is called a **splash**. If it extends the entire height of the wall, or at least to the height of a person, it is called a **wainscot**.

After the kitchen appliances, windows, and plumbing fixtures are placed, clearances are checked to see that they meet code requirements. For example, the water closet in one of the bathrooms is located between the tub and the cabinets. A 30″ minimum clearance is required here by most municipalities. There are similar requirements for the space between the upper and base cabinets.

STAGE III (Figure 14.57). All information about cabinet sizes and configuration, door swings, and shelves, as well as all necessary vertical dimensions, are included at this stage. Horizontal dimensions should be limited, as they are available from the floor plan.

STAGE IV (Figure 14.58). There are two ways to approach the final stage of a set of interior elevations. The first is to use a standardized office checklist. A second method is to develop one of your own, which should include the following:

    A. Call-outs for all surface materials, other than those that exist on the finish schedule.

    B. A description of all appliances, even those that are not on the surface facing the observer (for

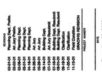

Figure 14.54 Stage V: Roof framing plan.

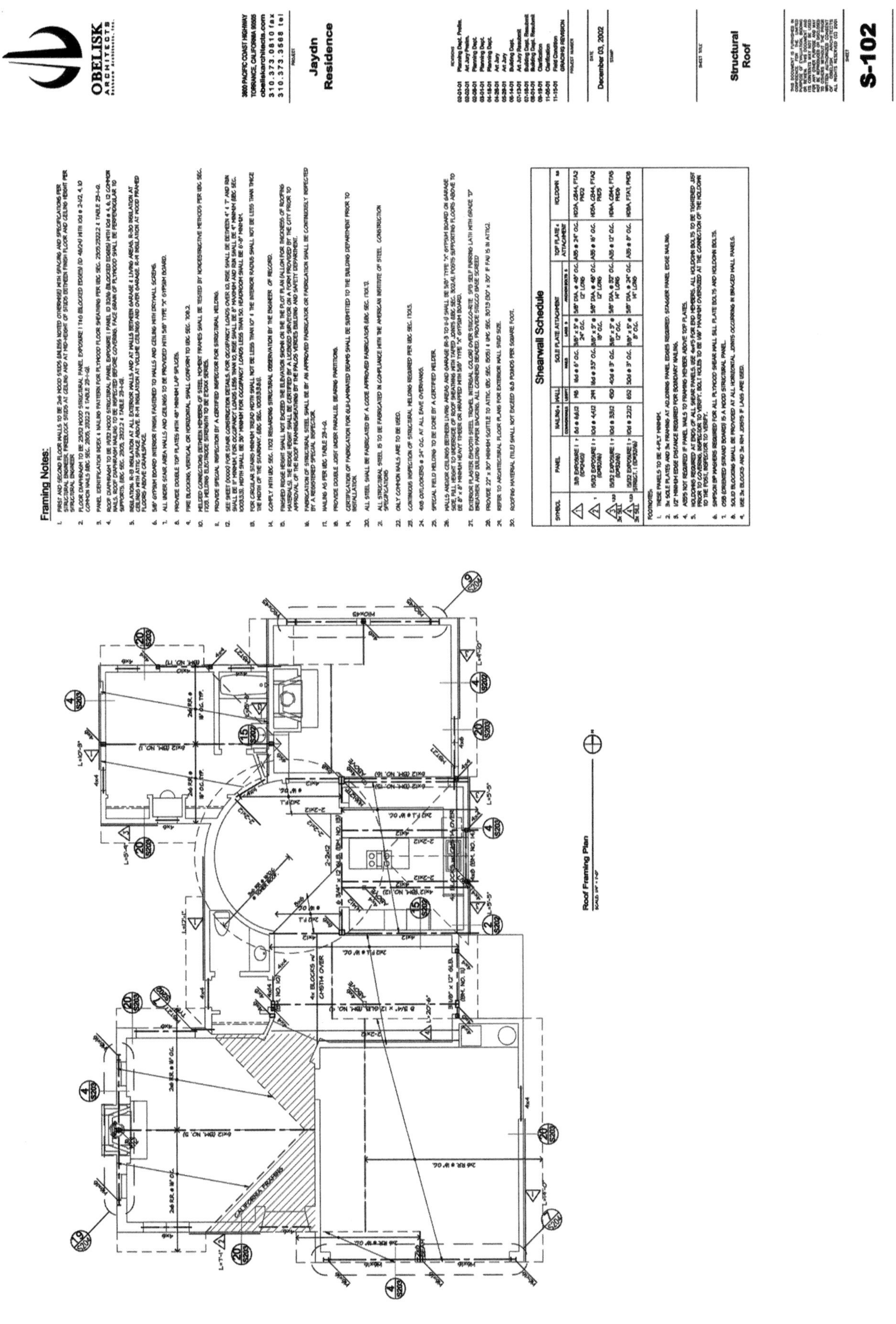

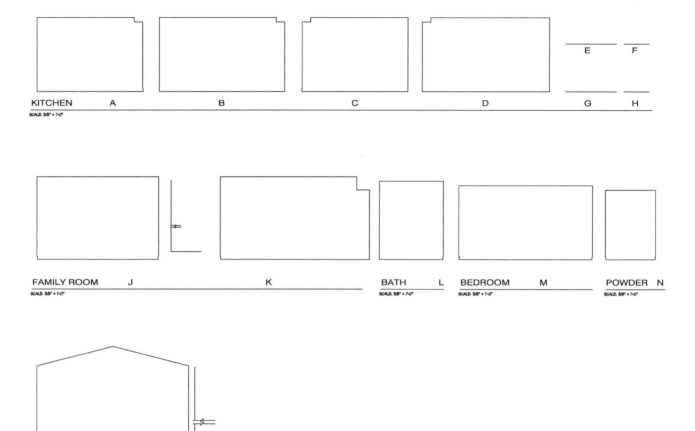

Figure 14.55   Stage I: Interior elevations.

example, sinks, garbage disposals, recessed medicine cabinets).

C. A description of nonstandard items.

D. The use of standard conventions to denote shelves, cabinet door swings, drawers, and so forth.

E. Any clearances that must be maintained. Refrigerator and oven/microwave are two good examples for this consideration.

Profiling also plays an important part in the final stage. Notice how heavy the lines are around the perimeter, so as to define the limits of the wall. Most other lines are drawn with a medium-dark line, except for objects that can be seen on the exterior elevation as well. This is why the window above the sink is drawn with a medium-light line.

To understand the position of a contractor who must build this interior, ask, "What will prevent me from building this kitchen or bathroom? What description, dimension, or clearance is missing?" Then note or dimension any missing elements.

■ SET CHECK

In-House Plan Checker

Every office has a plan checker. It may be the architect, the project manager, or the job captain. Along with checking the plans for the same types of items that a Department of Building and Safety might check for, this office person will check to see that the sheets coordinate with each other and have correctly included all of the client's needs and changes.

Dimensions (Horizontal)

Even if the dimensions have been checked for errors, in addition, the dimensions of one sheet are again checked against another. The floor-plan measurements are checked with the dimensions posted on the foundation plan to validate that this foundation will in fact set properly under the walls shown and dimensioned on the floor plan.

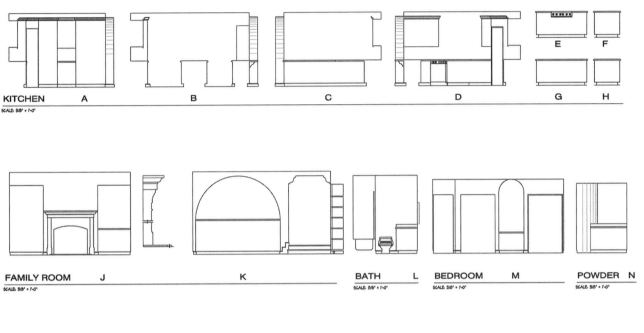

KITCHEN   A   B   C   D   E   F   G   H
SCALE: 3/8" = 1'-0"

FAMILY ROOM   J   K   BATH   L   BEDROOM   M   POWDER   N
SCALE: 3/8" = 1'-0"   SCALE: 3/8" = 1'-0"   SCALE: 3/8" = 1'-0"   SCALE: 3/8" = 1'-0"

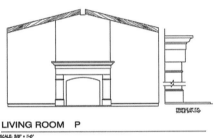

LIVING ROOM   P
SCALE: 3/8" = 1'-0"

Figure 14.56 Stage II: Interior elevations.

The side yards on the site plan are added to the overall width of the building, as expressed on the foundation plan or floor plan; two inches are added for the thickness of the skin of the building (stucco, in the case of this residence), and this total is checked against the size of the lot as expressed around the perimeter of the site in the form of metes and bounds. This check validates that the structure, with its measurements and setbacks, will in fact fit and can be situated correctly on the property.

If plan checks were done properly at the various stages, this final check becomes nothing more than a pro forma exercise. Nevertheless, it is important: An error not caught at this final stage can be extremely expensive to correct (or work around) once construction begins!

Remember, just because a dimension is given does not automatically mean that the component has been dimensioned properly. Merely sizing an object is of little value if the craftsperson does not know where to position the object (its location). The opposite is also true. A pier or a beam may be positioned (located), but if the craftsperson does not know its size, the information is of little use.

Dimensions (Vertical)

Because most of the main drawings included in this set are plans, it might appear that the horizontal distances are the main dimensions to check. Nothing could be further from the truth. Vertical dimensions should be checked throughout. With the floor plan as the main sheet for horizontal dimensions, the building section becomes the basis for most vertical dimensions. For example, anytime you extend a roof over an area, such as the entry, you should check the framing to see if there is enough space for a door and the header above the door. Head clearance above a stairwell should always be checked as well.

Whenever you pierce a horizontal plane or an angular plane—such as a roof, floor, or ceiling—with a skylight, stairwell, chimney, or some other such object, a section or partial section should be drawn to check for clearances.

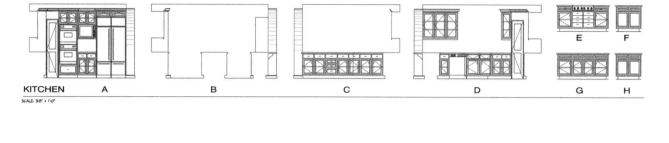

KITCHEN   A   B   C   D   E   F   G   H
SCALE: 3/8" = 1'-0"

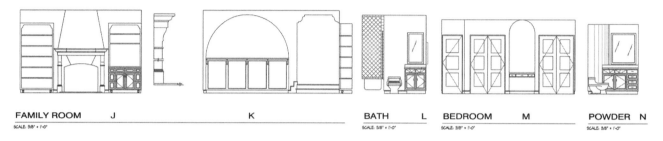

FAMILY ROOM   J   K   BATH   L   BEDROOM   M   POWDER   N
SCALE: 3/8" = 1'-0"   SCALE: 3/8" = 1'-0"   SCALE: 3/8" = 1'-0"   SCALE: 3/8" = 1'-0"

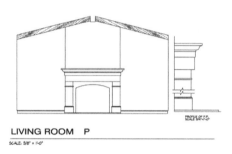

LIVING ROOM   P
SCALE: 3/8" = 1'-0"

PROFILE OF F.P.
SCALE 3/4"=1'-0"

Figure 14.57   Stage III: Interior elevations.

Cross-Referencing

A critical step is to check any cross-referencing. Especially if there is more than one drafter on a job, it is essential to see that all references to details actually refer to details that do in fact exist, and that the proper letter or number is included in each reference bubble. For example, the eave area of a building section may refer to an eave detail. The checker must be sure the detail name in the bubble, such as "D," is the same as that actually given to the detail. Remember, reference bubbles are divided in two. The upper half houses the name, and the lower half indicates the number of the sheet on which you can find this detail.

In addition, dimensional referencing must be checked. If a change in the drawings is made on one plan and the drafter does not have the advantage of using Revit, the drafter must follow through the entire set of drawings and confirm that the change was made throughout the set of drawings.

Plan Check and Correction

For the beginning drafter, it would be good practice to visit the local Department of Building and Safety to find out how personnel there check plans, or to obtain a set of simple plans that has gone through this process and study the list of corrections required by that particular municipality.

Some offices will provide you with a blank plan check correction list, which will allow you to determine and anticipate exactly what the plan checker will look for. This checklist will include specific notes that are required to be on the plans, without which a permit cannot be obtained.

Over the years, many offices have developed their own checklists, often referred to as a **punch list**. Familiarity with these forms and lists cannot help but make you a more conscientious and effective drafter.

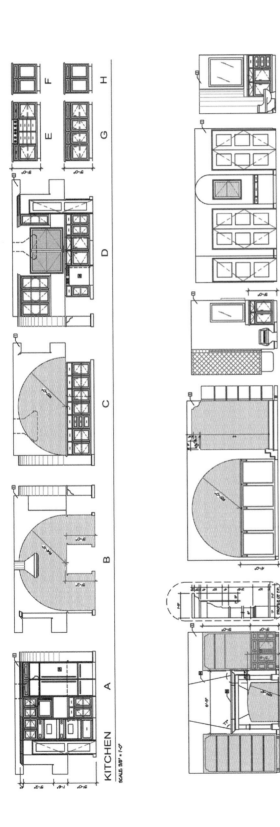

Figure 14.58 Stage IV: Interior elevations.

CONSTRUCTION DOCUMENTS FOR A TWO-STORY, WOOD-FRAMED RESIDENCE WITH BASEMENT

◼ SCHEMATIC DESIGN FOR BLU RESIDENCE

As you view this home, you will notice that the Blu residence first floor resembles the Jadyn residence. In fact, the Blu residence incorporated the first floor of the Jadyn residence and added a basement and second floor. The site location for this project was a home with a city view to the north. The site dimensions are approximately 60′ in width and 120′ in depth, adjacent to a public road. Figure 15.1 graphically illustrates the plan, showing its relationship to the view, access road, and compass direction.

Site Development Regulations

Site development regulations, enforced by the community's planning commission, covered building setback requirements, building height limit, parking requirements, and the allowable building coverage of the site. These are considered together with the site and floor-plan development.

Other regulatory agencies included a neighborhood compatibility review board and a state coastal commission. The neighborhood compatibility review board primarily dealt with the scale and massing, and the coastal commission task is to protect the coastline for the benefit of the general public. The architect dealt with the architectural design of the building, building colors and textures, and the landscaping plan, which were subject to review and approval by the state coastal commission.

After researching all the site development regulations and gathering the design data for our clients' needs, we started the conceptual design process.

Clients' Requirements

The clients, a young husband and wife with children, wanted to develop the site to its maximum potential. The site allowed a two-story residence with a maximum floor area of 2,900 square feet measured from the outside wall dimensions. Given these two factors, they wanted the following rooms: living room, dining room, kitchen, nook, study or family room, guest bath, mud room and laundry, and three bedrooms with two full bathrooms, a gym, and a wine room. They also wanted a two-car garage and shop area. These requirements are termed the **program**.

Initial Schematic Studies

Our initial schematic studies worked through the relationships among the rooms as well as room orientation on the site. Room orientation required that we locate the major rooms, such as the family room, kitchen, and master bedroom, so that they would face the ocean and capture a city view. The garage and entry had to be adjacent to the road for accessibility.

Because the site is small, and because the setback regulations further reduced the buildable area, we obviously needed to design a two-story building to meet the clients' requested number of rooms.

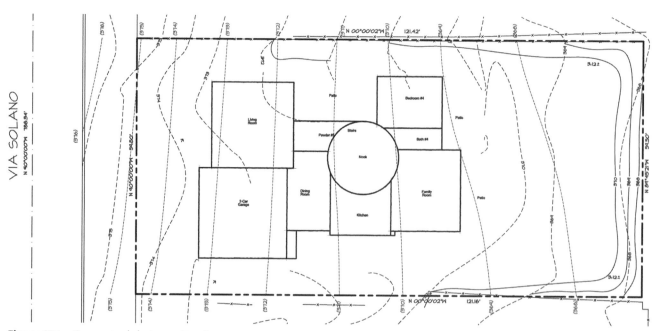

Figure 15.1   Conceptual design—site plan.

First Floor. Figure 15.2 shows a schematic study of the first-floor level. This figure also illustrates some early decisions we made: locating the entry court on the south side of the building; providing access to the city view from the kitchen, nook, and family room; locating the dining room and living room in an area that would allow access from the outside; and providing a basement area for the mechanical system, the wine storage area, and the gym.

Second Floor. We developed a schematic study for the second-floor level to show the desired location and relationships among the rooms, as well as a possible deck location. We wanted the master bedroom to have the best view in the home and also attempted to provide lots of natural light for all secondary bedrooms. See Figure 15.3.

Preliminary Blu Residence Floor Plans

Using the schematic studies as a basis for the various room locations, we developed scaled preliminary floor-plan drawings.

First Floor. The first-floor level, as Figure 15.4 shows, was planned to follow the site contour, which sloped to the north. Thus, we included floor transitions from the living room, dining room, and family room levels. Our choice of courtyards on the exterior areas was influenced by a light and entertainment areas protected from prevailing wind. At this stage, the scaled plan adhered to all the setback requirements and was within the allowable floor area established by the design review board. We did add floor area to the basement level to accommodate the balance between the board requirements and the clients' desires.

Second Floor. The second-floor preliminary plan, as Figure 15.5 shows, was basically an extension of the first-floor level. It provided a master bedroom with a city view and had a deck adjacent to the bedroom area. A portion of the hall, which provided the circulation to the various rooms, was opened to the nook below. This gave the nook a high ceiling and allowed both areas to have natural light from high windows called *clerestory windows*.

Roof and Exterior Elevation Studies

From these preliminary floor plans, we developed roof and exterior elevation studies to investigate any design problems that might require some minor floor-plan adjustments. We made these adjustments as we drew the floor plans for the construction documents.

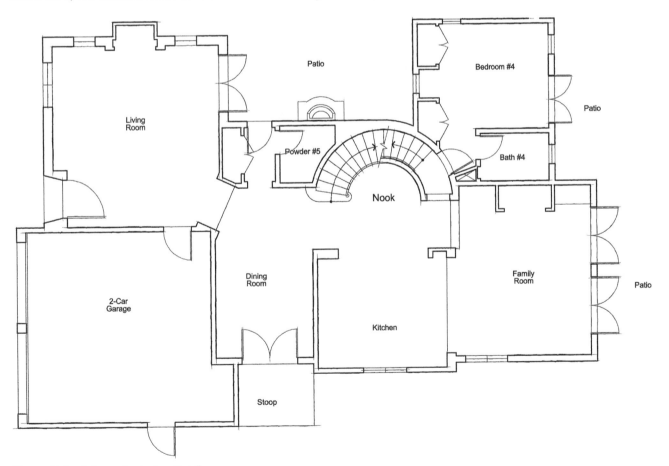

Figure 15.2 Schematic study—first floor.

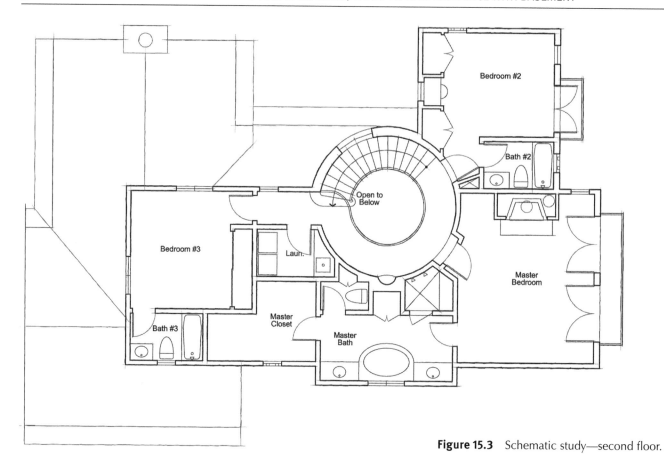

Figure 15.3 Schematic study—second floor.

Figure 15.4 First-floor preliminary plan.

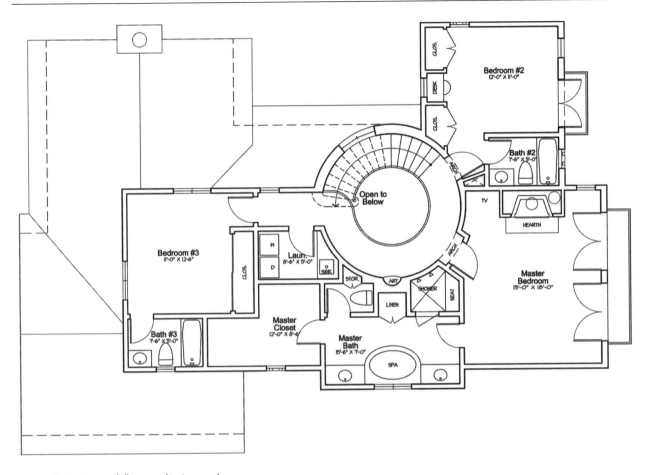

Figure 15.5 Second-floor preliminary plan.

Roof Design. The development of the exterior elevations started with the roof design. We decided to use a roof pitch of 3 in 12 to achieve a specific style of architecture: in this case, Spanish colonial revival. This style met the maximum height of building allowed by the design review board; it also determined the roof material. We selected two-piece mission tiles for the roof and cement plaster for the exterior walls. Because this style of architecture was established in the 1920s, we used wood windows and doors to stay authentic to the style. The glass, however, was double glazed throughout, to provide greater insulation during both the winter and summer months.

Exterior Elevations. The window designs combined fixed glass and operable sections as well as separate operable sections. Using the previously mentioned design criteria, we developed sketches of the exterior elevations. Figure 15.6 shows the four sides of this residence using these exterior materials and window elements.

After we completed these studies, we submitted them to the clients and to the various regulatory agencies. We incorporated their adjustments and refinements into the final drawing of the construction documents. Once the client approved the schematic design, we proceeded to the design development phase.

■ SITE PLAN

Stage I

The civil engineer provided the office with a digital copy of the topography, which became Stage I and the base sheet. The site was drawn full size in model space and positioned on the sheet for plotting.

Stage II

The second stage of the site plan (see Figure 15.7) can yield a combination site plan and roof plan. For our example, a solid outline of the shape of the residence is positioned on the site. We established the perimeter of the structure from both the ground-floor and upper-floor plans and placed it onto the topography map.

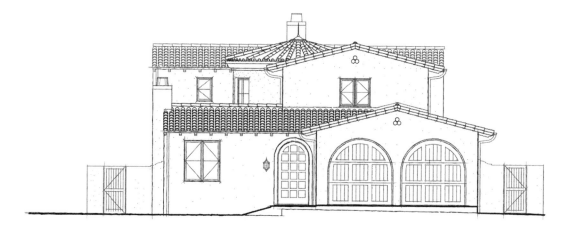

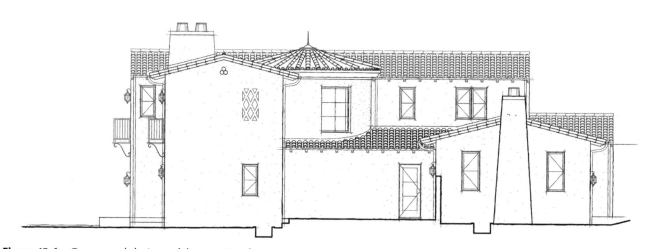

Figure 15.6 Conceptual designs of the exterior elevations.

Stage III

After confirming that the setbacks were correct and the size of the structure was acceptable in relationship to the site, we set the lines on the correct layer. See Figure 15.8. We next included the material designations for walks, driveways, and pavers.

There are various levels on the ground surface. A look at the final stage of the site plan (Figure 15.10) shows the different heights. The area adjacent to the family room is the lowest; the property slopes downward to the rear.

The **setbacks**—that is, the dimensions needed to locate the structure—were then added to the site plan.

Stage IV

All improvements were dimensioned next. These improvements were located from the property line or the building itself. The slope direction of the roof, the decks, and even such areas as the driveway were indicated by arrows and/or notes. See Figure 15.9.

Notes were next to be added, and we used broad general terms. Utilities were shown. The sewer line is typically marked with an "S," the gas line with a "G," and the water main with a "W." Often **hose bibb** locations (garden hose connections) as well as the various steps around the building are determined. The legal description of the property is included.

Figure 15.7 Stage II: Site plan.

Stage V

The final stage for the site plan sheet is shown in Figure 15.10. In the previous stage, we had nearly finished the site and roof plan. All that remained was the title, north arrow, and construction notes.

■ FIRST-FLOOR PLAN

Stage I

Stage I uses face of stud and face of walls as a base. Because the floor plan is the first construction document to be drawn, care must be taken to establish the correct base for the materials being used.

Stage II

Measurements are carefully taken from the preliminary floor plan, verified, and checked against the site plan. See Figure 15.11. The door jambs of the garage and

entry are enlarged to give the illusion of a thicker wall construction.

Stage III

At this stage, all equipment was placed in the kitchen and the bathrooms. See Figure 15.12. The stairs to the basement and to the upper level are shown. Most important are the level changes that are beginning to show between the living room and dining room and the dining room and family room, and the slight change between the garage and the house. Windows and doors around the perimeter were also located.

Stage IV

This is a critical step in the plan because it is the dimension line stage. This step also includes variations of line quality, because the dimension lines must be precise but must not detract from the main body of the drawing. Every wall and partition must be located and every door

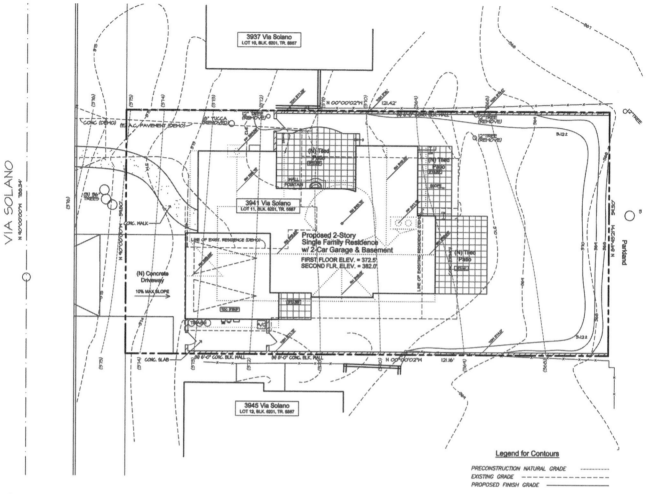

Figure 15.8   Stage III: Site plan.

and window must be sized. Door and window designations were also added at this stage. See Figure 15.13.

Stage V

Room titles were included on the floor plan in this stage. See Figure 15.14. Various pieces of equipment, such as the range, oven, and sink, were described, as were other parts of the structure such as closets, garage doors, lift counter for the bar, and so on. The titles are general and do not include the construction method, finish, or function. Naturally, the dimensions were checked again and corrections made as necessary.

Stage VI

Title, scale, and north arrow completed this sheet. The plan sheet was formatted, F.P. Notes were added, and the plan was plotted for client revisions. See Figure 15.15.

■ SECOND-FLOOR PLAN

Stage I

The first stage is, of course, that of establishing a base. What makes structures with multiple floors unique is the multitude of datum points. In the case of this two-story structure, we must consider a vertical datum as well as the normal horizontal ones. Along with wall alignment (load-carrying walls), we have stairs that link the two floors. The total rise and run of the stairway must be defined early in the development stage. The riser and tread design should be determined for a better understanding of the proportion of treads to risers and how they are detailed for different building materials. Duplicating the first-floor plan and making alterations ensures wall alignment where required. An alternative method is to XREF the first floor and create the second floor over it.

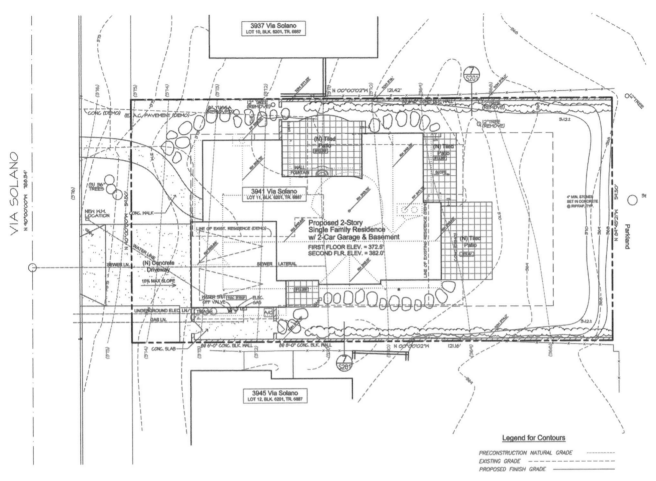

Figure 15.9 Stage IV: Site plan.

Stage II

The upper floor plan has many walls that align with the walls below on the ground floor. Therefore, a copy of the lower floor is made for the upper floor and shifted at an even offset (say, 100' in a direction). This allowed us to regain exact alignment if a wall was unintentionally removed. For example, say you were to remove the stairs from the upper floor plan so that the upper hall could be constructed. At any later point, you can copy the lower stair again and shift it by exactly the offset distance (in our example, 100') so that now it is perfectly registered.

Figure 15.16 shows the stage at which bathroom equipment, closet poles, stairs, and several windows were located.

Stage III

At this stage we added dimension lines to the floor plan. The dimension lines were not done initially right on this plan, but rather were done on a plot sheet, checked for accuracy, and corrected as required.

Stage IV

At Stage IV, we added dimensions, so these dimensions had to be checked against those on the lower-floor plan. It is always important to check walls that line up under one another. See Figure 15.17.

Stage V

We added notes at this stage, which included titles and necessary area descriptions. As with the ground-floor plan, the notes are general in nature and do not describe construction methods, workmanship, or installation requirements that are described in the specifications. However, on a smaller project like this one, the specifications can be included on the set of the construction documents. See Figure 15.18.

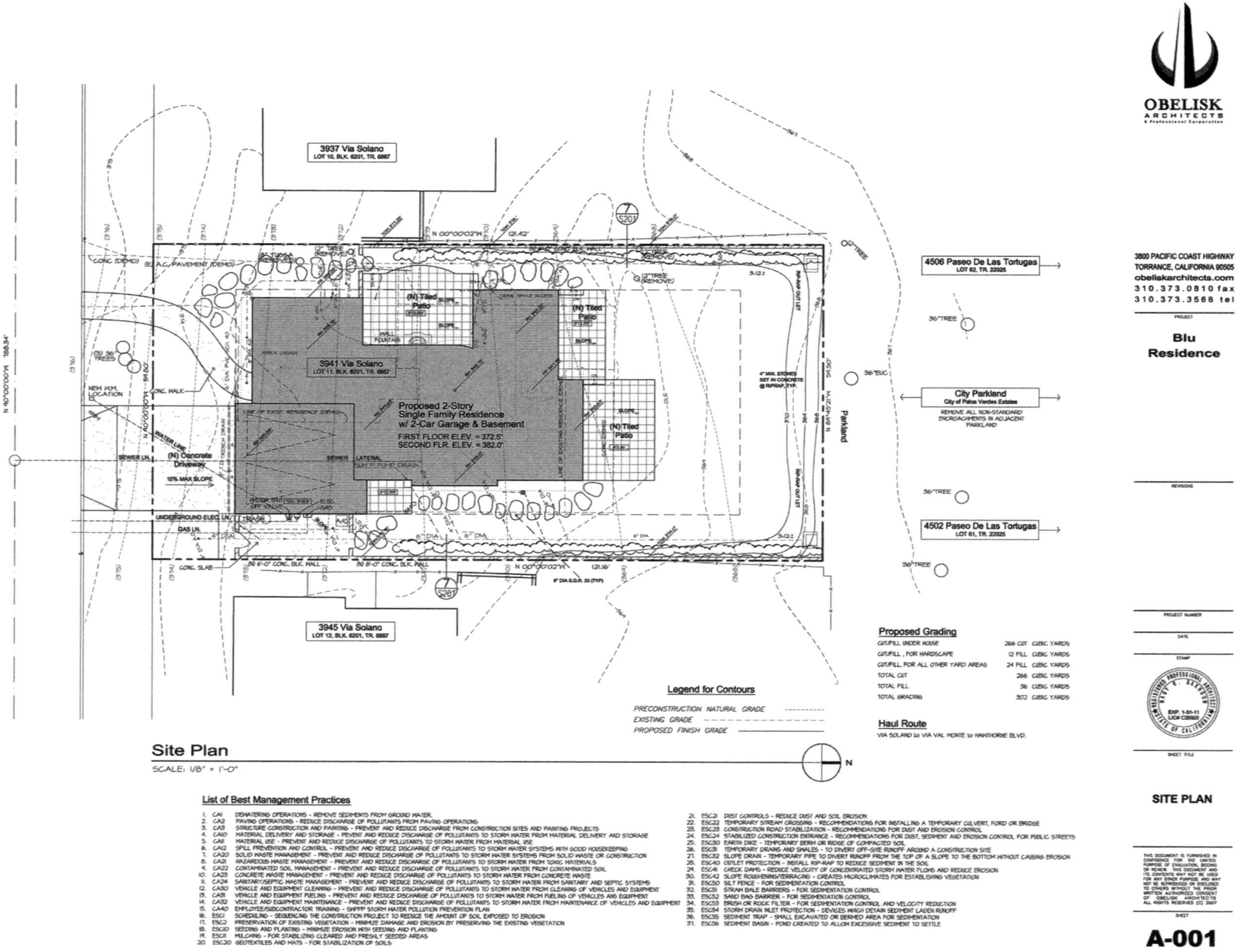

Figure 15.10 Stage V: Site plan.

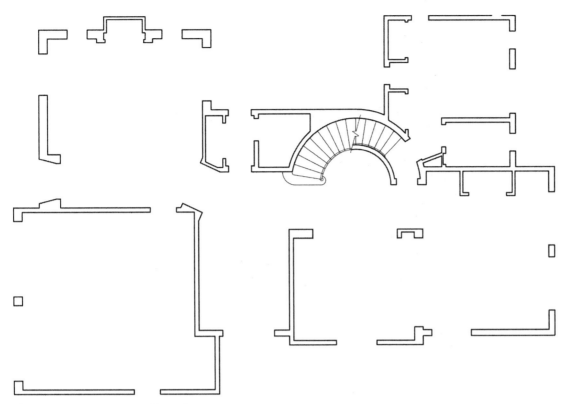

Figure 15.11 Stage II: First-floor plan.

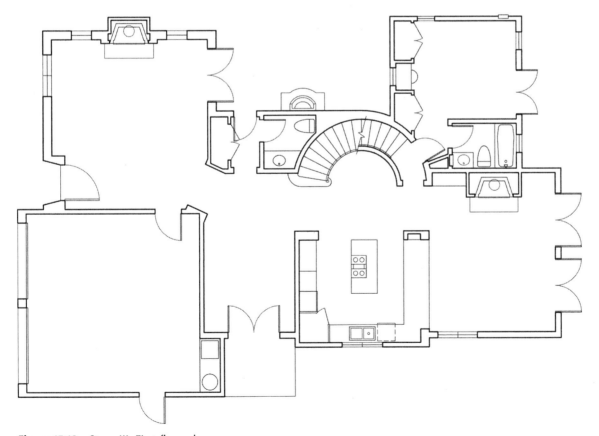

Figure 15.12 Stage III: First-floor plan.

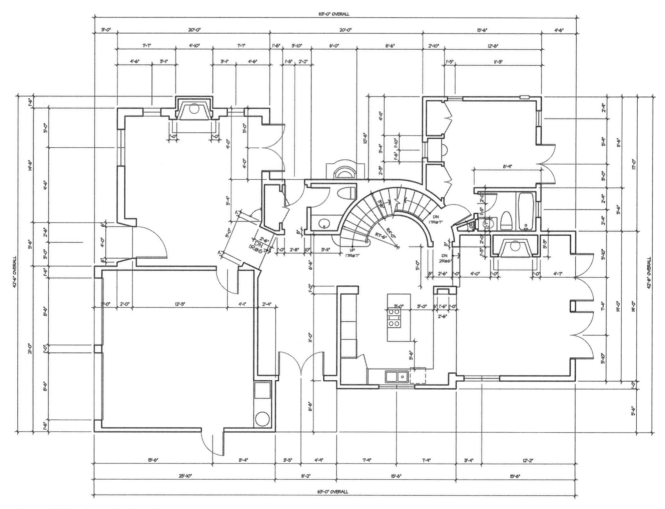

Figure 15.13   Stage IV: First-floor plan.

Stage VI

Title, scale, and north arrow completed this sheet. The plan sheet was formatted, F.P. Notes were added, and the plan was plotted for client revisions. See Figure 15.19.

■ ROOF PLAN

On a true roof plan, the outline of a roof is a solid line and the building line is a hidden line.

Stage I   (Figure 15.20). The scale selected for the residence roof plan was ⅛″ = 1′-0″. The scale can be enlarged if a roof system is more complex; ¼″ = 1′-0″ is also an acceptable scale.

Stage II   (Figure 15.21). The roof and building lines were darkened at this stage. Arrows were drawn to indicate the direction of the slope.

Stage III   (Figure 15.22). Skylight and chimney locations were the first to be located at this stage. Some architectural offices show plumbing vents that come through the roof, as a confirmation of their positions. Detail and section reference bubbles were next and, finally, noting was completed.

■ BLU RESIDENCE BUILDING SECTIONS

It is impossible to draw an accurate elevation without, at the very least, a partial section. It is this fact that makes the section a critical drawing to develop in order to establish accurate elevations.

Stage I

This stage sets the plans for the building section. See Figure 15.23. The base for the building section is threefold. It establishes measurements vertically from floor to floor and then to the plate line, as well as for the

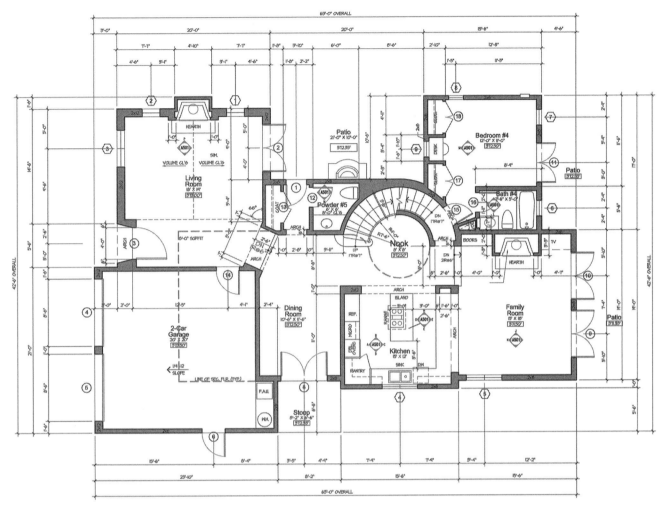

Figure 15.14 Stage V: First-floor plan.

horizontal measurements from wall to wall. The positioning of the stairs is critical at this stage. For the elevation, the building section base becomes its datum.

Stage II

With the datum established in Stage I, the building section is ready for roof shape, the precise location of the stairs, and the footing shape. See Figure 15.24. In fact, the building section of this drawing coordinates the first-floor plan (and basement) with the second-floor plan, and the roof plan with the preliminary details or structural decisions that have already been made.

Stage III

All interior and exterior walls were outlined using Western frame construction, and the locations of walls and guardrails were taken from the floor plan. See Figure 15.25.

The upper-floor level was definitely established, as were the various horizontal members. Specific sizes of these members were obtained from the structural engineer or architect.

Stage IV

All of the individual members were drafted at this stage. Of particular interest is the top of the roof. See Figure 15.22. Examine the second-floor plan (Figure 15.19) or the roof framing plan (Figure 15.44). These show where this actual section slice was taken. See Figure 15.26.

The material designations—earth, concrete block, concrete, and roof tile—were added at this stage.

Stage V

Vertical heights were established based on the type of framing chosen, heights required by local code, and client needs. We obtained basic framing member sizes and

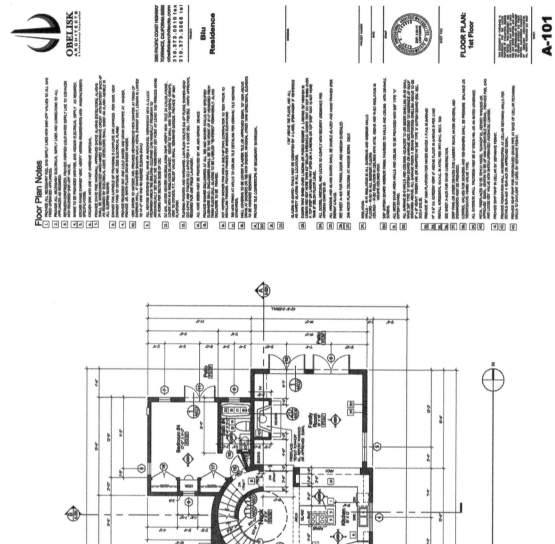

Figure 15.15 Stage VI: First-floor plan.

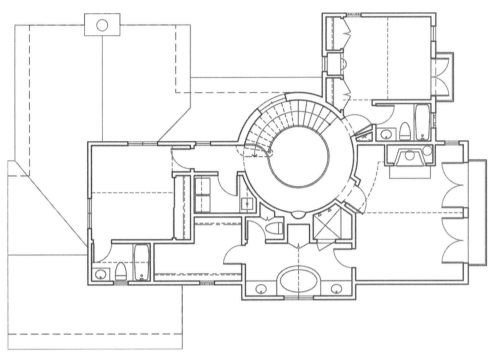

Figure 15.16 Stage II: Second-floor plan.

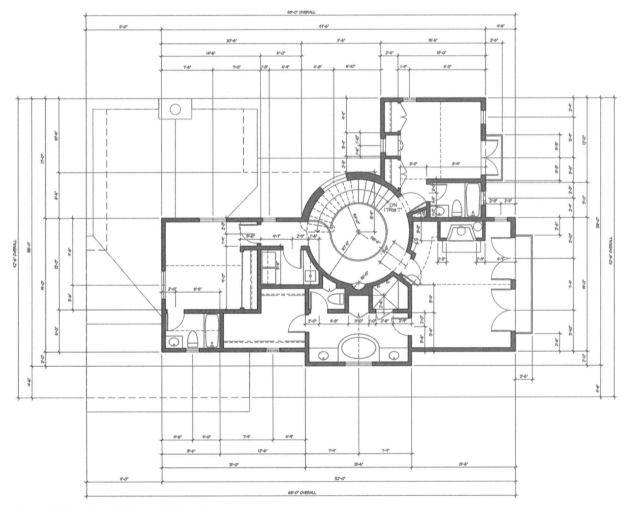

Figure 15.17 Stage IV: Second-floor plan.

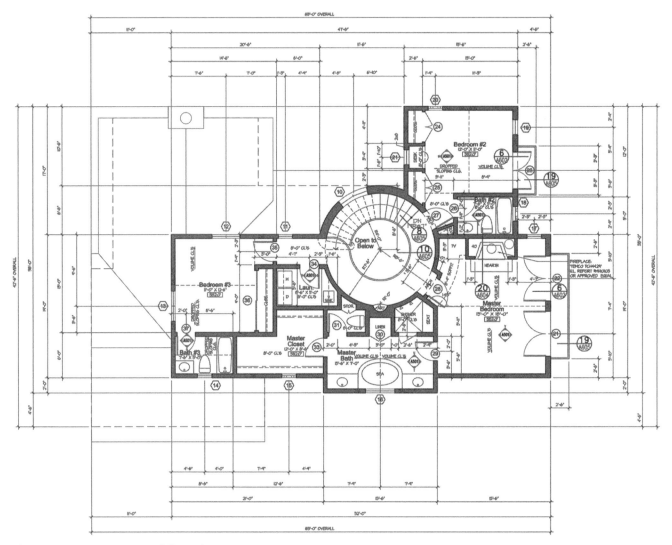

Figure 15.18   Stage V: Second-floor plan.

noted them from the structural engineering drawings. Detail references, room titles, drawing title, and scale finished this drawing. See Figure 15.27.

Stage VI

We combined the stages of dimensioning, noting, and setup of the plot sheet, thus making this the final stage. See Figure 15.28.

■ BLU RESIDENCE BUILDING ELEVATIONS

Exterior elevations directly correlate to building sections, as mentioned earlier. The roof pitch and its height must be established in section view for accurate depiction of the exterior elevations. If the pitch

and overhang are not drawn in section first, a partial section can establish the eave location relative to the correct height.

If the elevation drawings are not parametric with other drawings, as they are when the Revit program is used, it is ideal to limit the repetition of dimensions.

Stage I

Similar to the section Stage I, the plate heights established on the sections will aid the drafter in setting up the correct vertical dimensions for the elevation. If the section has been completed, an XREF or copy of the sections is a great shortcut for developing the elevations. See Figure 15.29.

Before starting the exterior elevations, you should always carefully study two drawings—the floor plans and building sections—and use the building sections as a

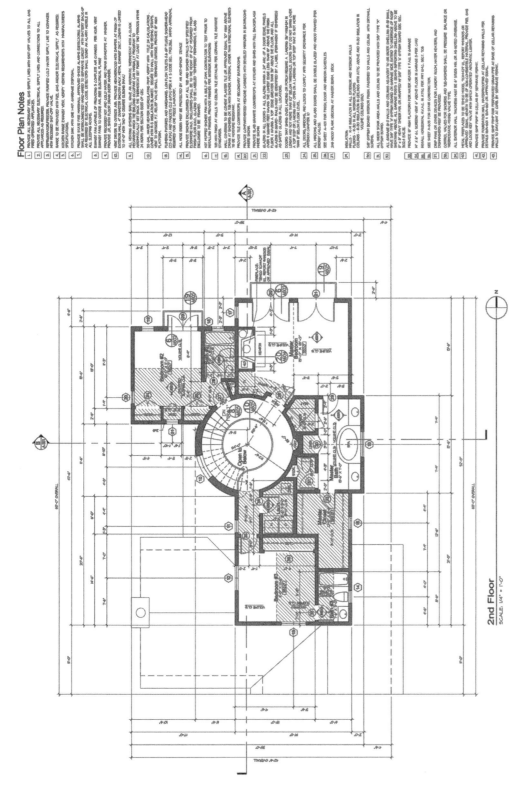

Floor Plan Notes

2nd Floor
SCALE: 1/4" = 1'-0"

Figure 15.19 Stage VI: Second-floor plan.

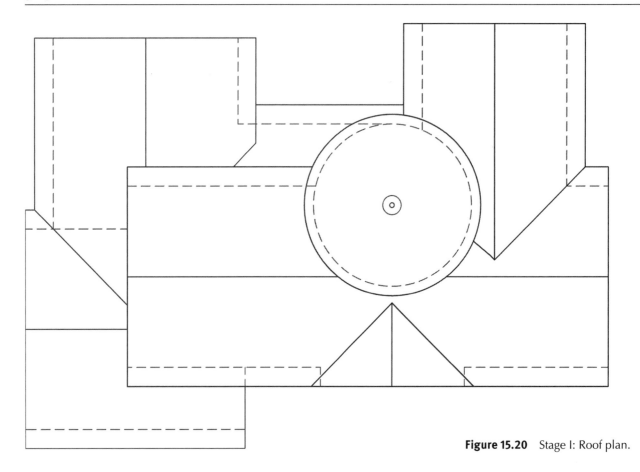

Figure 15.20 Stage I: Roof plan.

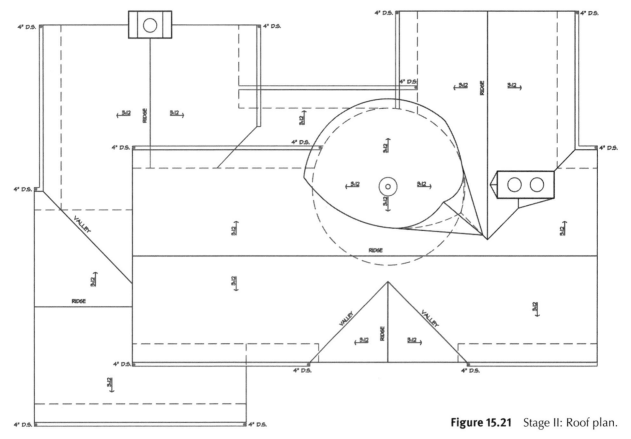

Figure 15.21 Stage II: Roof plan.

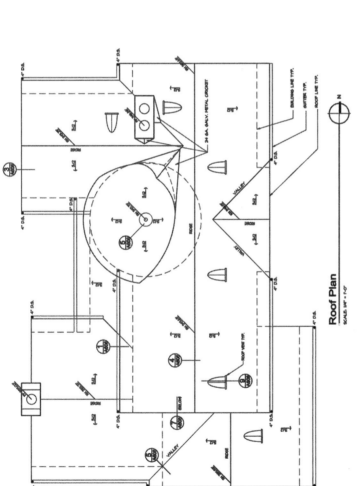

ROOF PLAN NOTES:

ROOF SLOPES:

1. ROOF SLOPES ARE SHOWN DIRECTLY ON ROOF PLAN DRAWING.
2. IN THE ABSENCE OF SLOPES SHOWN ON STRUCTURAL DRAWINGS OR ARCHITECTURAL DRAWINGS, ROOM CARPENTER SHALL PROVIDE REQUIRED SHIMMING BELOW ROOF SHEATHING TO ALLOW FOR PROPER SLOPE OF ROOF TO DRAIN.
3. NO OBSTACLE SHALL PREVENT WATER FLOW TOWARD DRAINS.

ROOF MATERIAL:

1. PITCHED ROOF TO BE CLASS "A" 1/8-TILE, TWO-PIECE MISSION TILE RUSTIC IMPORT BLEND (ZERO 1 BR-3529, 4200 BLS. PER SQUARE) INSTALLED OVER 30 LBS. FLAT NONFLAMMABLE FELT PER UBC TABLE 15-D-1.
2. THE HEADS OF ALL TILE SHALL BE NAILED.
3. THE NOSES OF ALL EAVE COURSE TILES SHALL BE FASTENED WITH APPROVED CLIPS.
4. ALL RAKE TILES SHALL BE NAILED WITH TWO NAILS.
5. THE NOSES OF ALL RIDGE, HIP AND RAKE TILES SHALL BE SET IN A BED OF APPROVED MORTAR.

WATERS AND ROOF DRAIN:

1. GUTTERS SHALL BE CONSTRUCTED OF 18 GA. COPPER WITH 1/4" EXPANSION JOINTS EVERY 50 FEET MAXIMUM.
2. GUTTERS SHALL SLOPE 1/8" PER FOOT TOWARD RAIN WATER LEADERS.
3. UNLESS SPECIFIED OTHERWISE, RAIN WATER LEADERS ARE EXPOSED AND LOCATION IS SHOWN ON ROOF PLAN.

ROOF PENETRATION:

1. VENTS AND ROOF STACKS SHALL PROJECT ABOVE ROOF BY THE MINIMUM DISTANCE REQUIRED BY APPLICABLE CODES AND SHALL BE LOCATED IN AREAS NOT VISIBLE FROM STREET.

MECHANICAL EQUIPMENT:

1. MECHANICAL EQUIPMENT INCLUDING CONDENSER UNITS WILL BE LOCATED ON CONCRETE PADS IN YARD. EXACT LOCATION OF EQUIPMENT TO BE COORDINATED ON SITE BY ARCHITECT M.O.

ATTIC VENTILATION:

ATTIC VENTILATION NOTES:

1. TOTAL ATTIC VENTILATION SHALL BE A MINIMUM OF 1/50 OF THE AREA TO BE VENTILATED OR 1/300 FOR MECH. VENTING.

Roof Plan
SCALE: 1/4" = 1'-0"

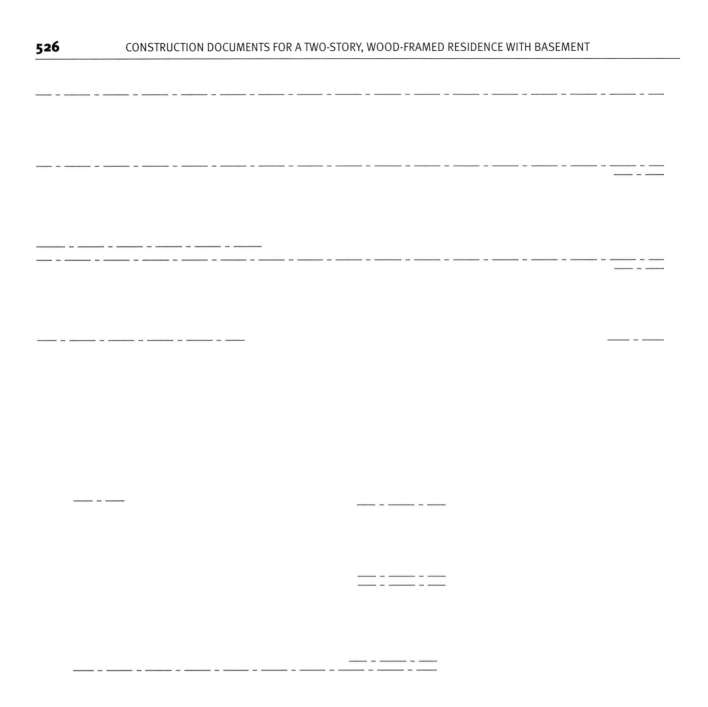

Figure 15.23   Stage I: Building section.

base. The floor plans give the width and length of the structure.

Stage II

The positioning of the walls and the roof are blocked out in this stage. If the sections are utilized, you will find that much of this work has already been completed for you. See Figure 15.30. This is the stage that gave the exterior elevation shape. The floor plan was used to locate exterior wall lines and windows, and the roof plan was used to help define the outline of the roof.

Stage III

The previous stages established all of the horizontal lines and most of the vertical lines. Stage III then produced all the parts, such as windows and doors and vertical steps, back within the body of the building. These vertical lines

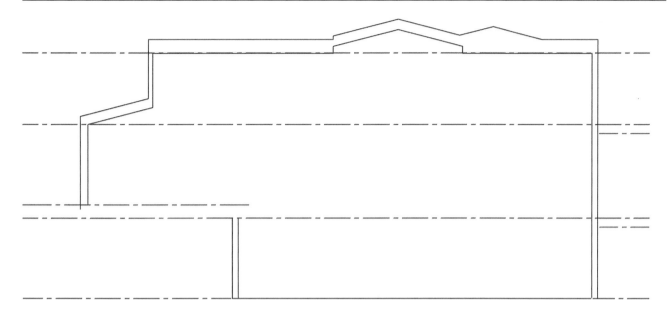

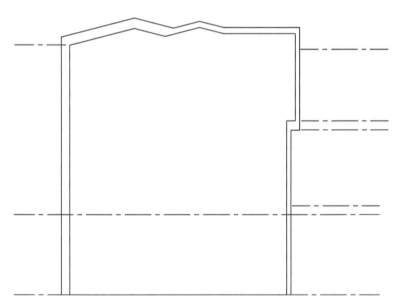

Figure 15.24 Stage II: Building section.

were obtained from the floor plans. Window and door shapes were confirmed from the manufacturer's literature and drawn accurately or imported as blocks. See Figure 15.31.

Stage IV

Material designations for the various finishes and materials for the roof and the surface of the wall were drafted.

See Figure 15.32. The wall material shown is cement plaster; the roof material is two-piece mission tiles.

Stage V

Vertical dimensions were referred to the building section or noted for the sake of clarity and to minimize duplication. See Figure 15.33. The hidden lines designating the swing of doors and windows were drafted, together with

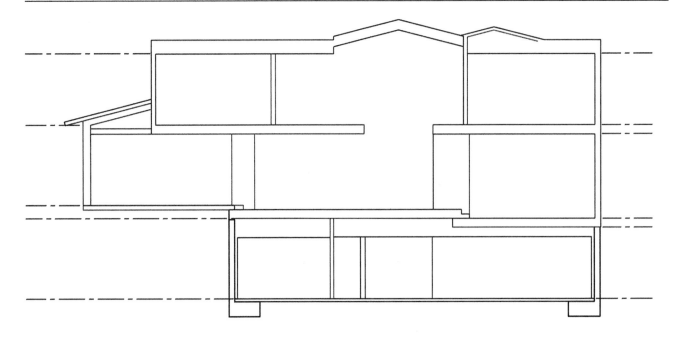

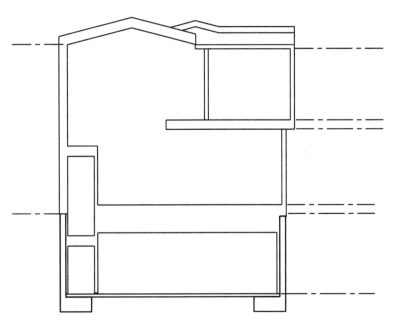

Figure 15.25 Stage III: Building section.

the divisions (called **lights**) in the french doors. Various notes were placed on the elevations to identify such items as the fascia, tiles, gate, and garage door.

Stage VI

The overall building height, from the lowest point of grade to the highest point of the roof, is critical dimen-

sional data. The drawing was located on a plot sheet and added notes and required information were provided for the completion of the building elevations. See Figure 15.34.

Call-outs are generic in nature and depend on the specifications for specific material, quality, size, and workmanship. For a small project like this, it is acceptable to include specifications with the plan notes.

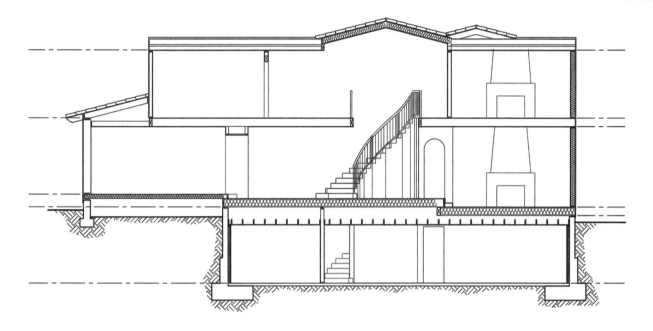

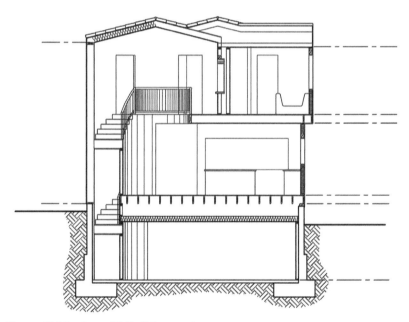

Figure 15.26 Stage IV: Building section.

■ FOUNDATION PLAN: SLAB AND RAISED WOOD

Two foundation plans are shown here: concrete slab for the basement area and a raised wood floor for the area that does not have a basement under it. The basement floor must be a slab, whereas the first-floor area that sits above the basement can be wood framed; the first floor may also be a slab in areas where the basement does not extend under the floor above.

Stage I

The computer-drafted base stage utilizes the floor plan, because it is usually laid out before the foundation plan and represents the area required to be supported. The

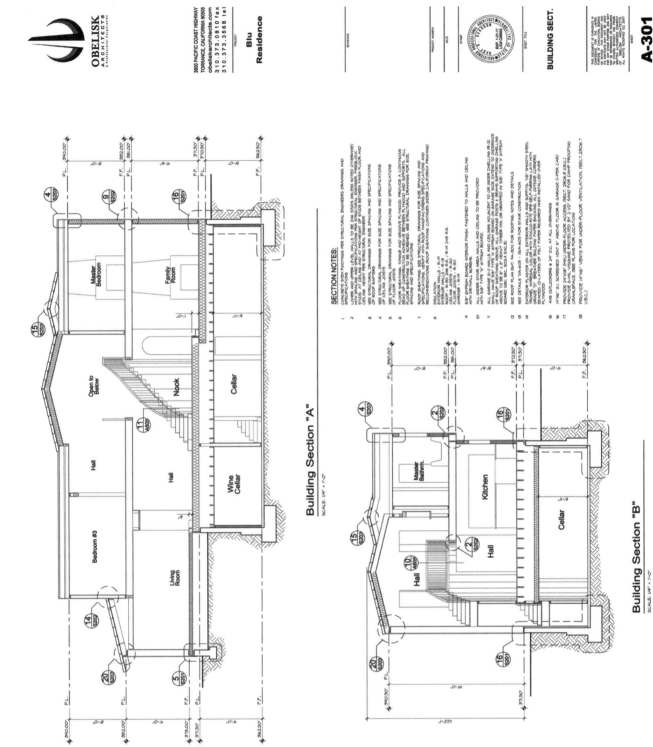

Building Section "A"

SCALE: 1/4" = 1'-0"

Building Section "B"

SCALE: 1/4" = 1'-0"

Figure 15.27 Stage V: Building section.

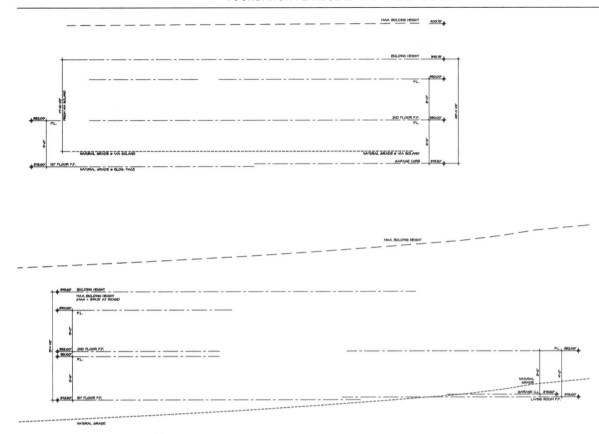

Figure 15.28 Stage VI: Building section.

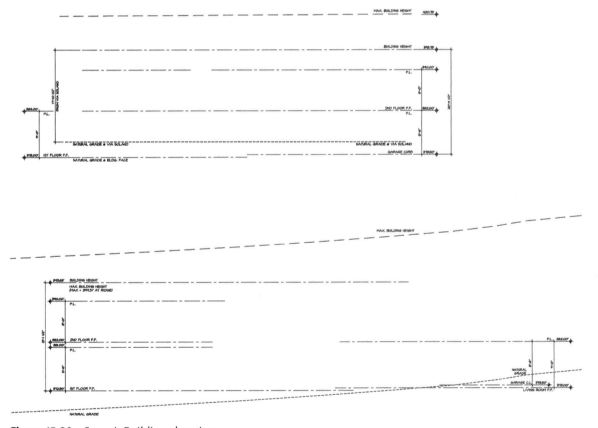

Figure 15.29 Stage I: Building elevations.

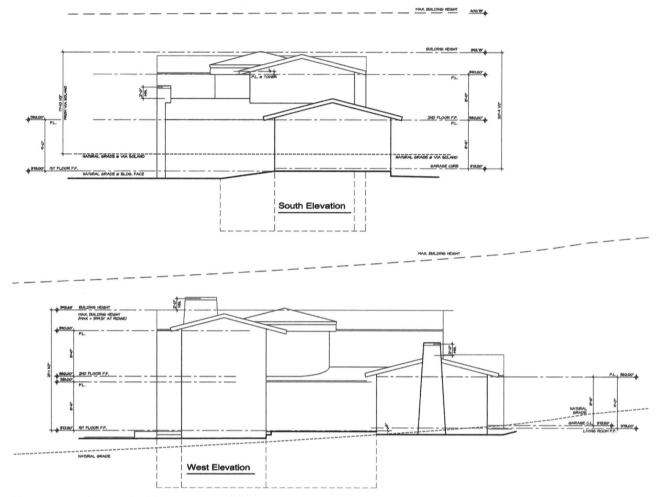

Figure 15.30   Stage II: Building section and elevations.

floor plan is XREFed into the structural set of drawings, so as to allow floor-plan changes to be updated simultaneously with the foundation. The determination of load-bearing walls is made in this stage.

Stage II

Figure 15.35 shows the layout stage. The basement retaining wall will hold back the soil for the basement level. The footing width has been dictated by the height of the retaining wall and soil bearing pressure.

The dotted and solid lines of the foundation plan show the shape or width of the footing and foundation walls. The double solid line around the perimeter of the garage represents a 6″ curb that extends above the grade far enough to keep the sill away from the soil level; this is called the **grade**.

The footing for the basement retaining wall is large because it is not restrained (not created like a rigid 3-D box) at the top and acts as a full cantilever. The dotted lines in the basement area represent the footing widths. The dotted lines do not extend into the area below the

hall between the garage and entry; because the leg of the footing is so large that the garage and entry overlap each other, they are treated as a solid mass. The garage is the only area that is a slab on the ground. The double lines around the edge represent the width of the 6″ wall.

Stage III

Figure 15.36 shows the beginning of the dimensioning stage for the foundation. Only a limited number of dimensions are required. Most dimensions are located on the floor plans.

The sizes for the various members in the building were obtained from the structural engineer's design plan. However, with this type of structure, this framing plan could have been done **in house** (by the drafting team in the office).

Stage IV

The material designations for such items as concrete, masonry, and insulation include the delineation of the

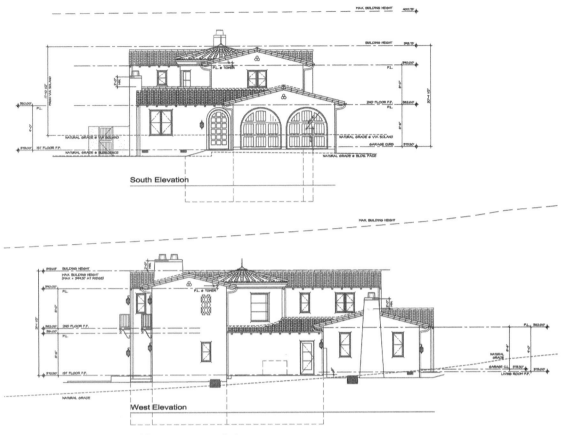

Figure 15.31   Stage III: Building section and elevations.

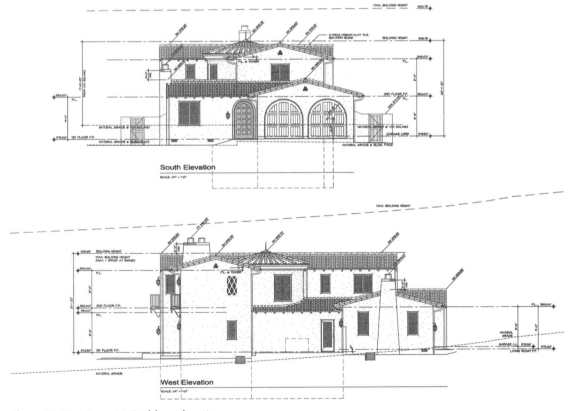

Figure 15.32   Stage IV: Building elevations.

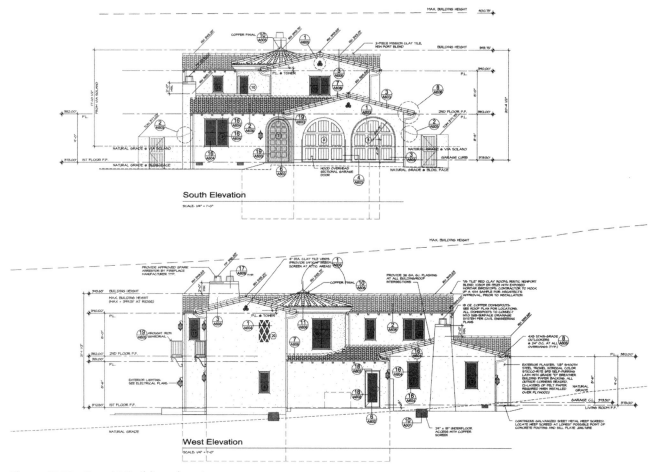

Figure 15.33 Stage V: Building elevations.

structural components, such as joists, studs, beams, and rafters. Detail reference bubbles are located, and the material designation is established. See Figure 15.37.

Stage V

This is the noting stage—the final stage. See Figure 15.38. Notes were added next. These notes take the form of descriptions of the slab, sizes of spread footings, or notes describing a part of the drafted foundation. Often the **material specifications** are included on this sheet (as might a schedule of shear tables including the structural values to resist wind or seismic activity). The title, scale, and north arrow finished this sheet.

■ BLU RESIDENCE FOUNDATION PLAN: RAISED WOOD

Understand that the Blu residence is not unique in having a wood foundation as well as a concrete slab foundation. Often garage floors are concrete while the homes

also have raised wood floor systems. What is unique is the way the basement plays a part in the equation.

In many of the following stages, steps will mimic those in the prior slab system. If the stages sound familiar, that is not by mistake. The process follows the same rules established earlier, although the drawing created for wood portions of the project will look different.

Stage I

Identify the load-bearing walls by using the early-stage drawing of the floor plan. The floor plan is XREFed into the structural set of drawings.

Stage II

The layout of the foundation plan was done after the floor plan had been finalized to the point where all exterior and interior walls had been established.

The square forms represent the **piers** which are the primary support for the girders. **Girders** support the floor joists, which in turn support the plywood floor that the

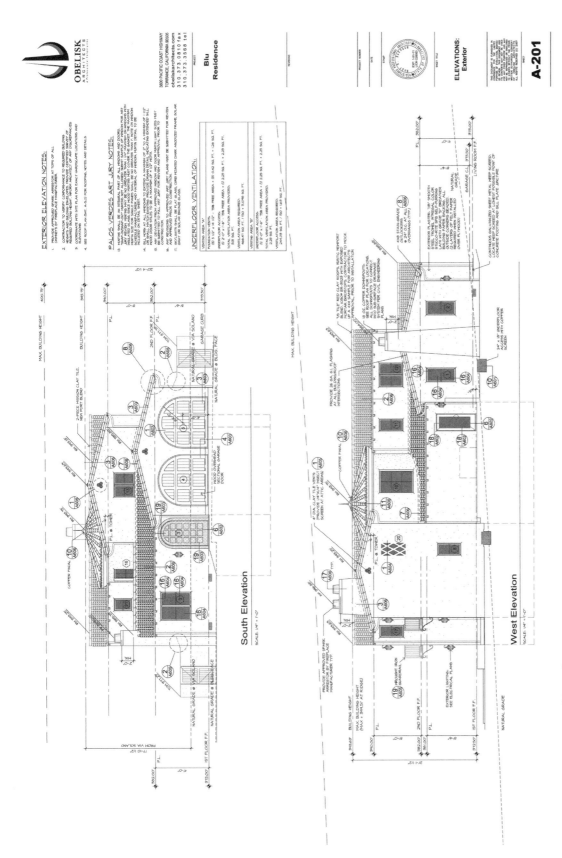

Figure 15.34 Stage VI: Building elevations.

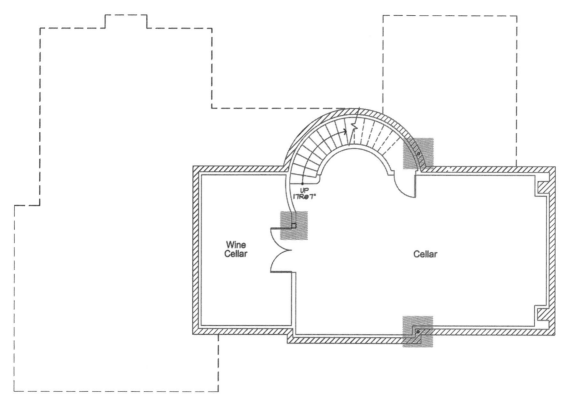

Figure 15.35   Stage II: Foundation plan (slab).

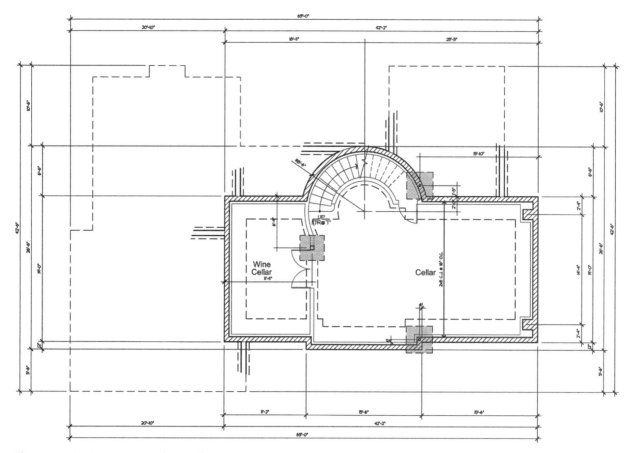

Figure 15.36   Stage III: Foundation plan.

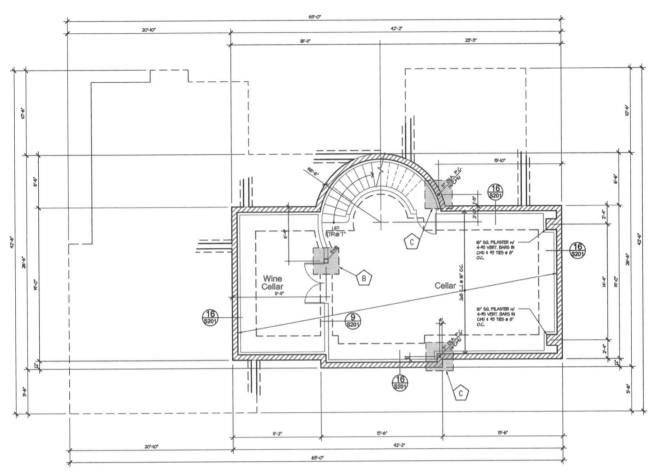

Figure 15.37   Stage IV: Foundation plan.

occupants walk on. These piers and girders are typically spaced in a grid of 6'–7' center to center. The closer to 6 the spacing is, the less **deflection**, or sag, will exist in the floor joists. In this stage, the grid is established and blocked out.

Stage III

The sizes for the various members in the building were obtained from the structural engineer's design plan. This stage shows the beginning of the dimensioning for the foundation and the call-out sizes for the lumber to be used.

The main difference between this stage and the previous stage was the inclusion of girders (floor beams to support floor joists). They are shown by a very dark centerline. Joists are shown by a dark line and arrows (half arrowheads); these show the size, spacing, and direction of the floor joists. See Figure 15.39.

Stage IV

The material designations for such items as concrete, masonry, and insulation were delineated. The structural

components, such as joists, studs, beams, and rafters, were drawn. Detail reference bubbles were located and materials were established.

Stage V

This is the noting stage—the final stage. See Figure 15.40. Reference bubble numbers, title, scale, and north arrow completed this drawing.

■ FRAMING PLAN

Stage I

Typically, we need to draft a framing plan over an XREF of the specific plan involved. This will usually determine the scale of the drawing. In this case, it was ¼″ = 1'-0″.

First- and Second-Floor Framing Plans.   There are two plans here: the first-floor plan showing the floor framing for the second floor, and the second-floor plan showing the roof framing.

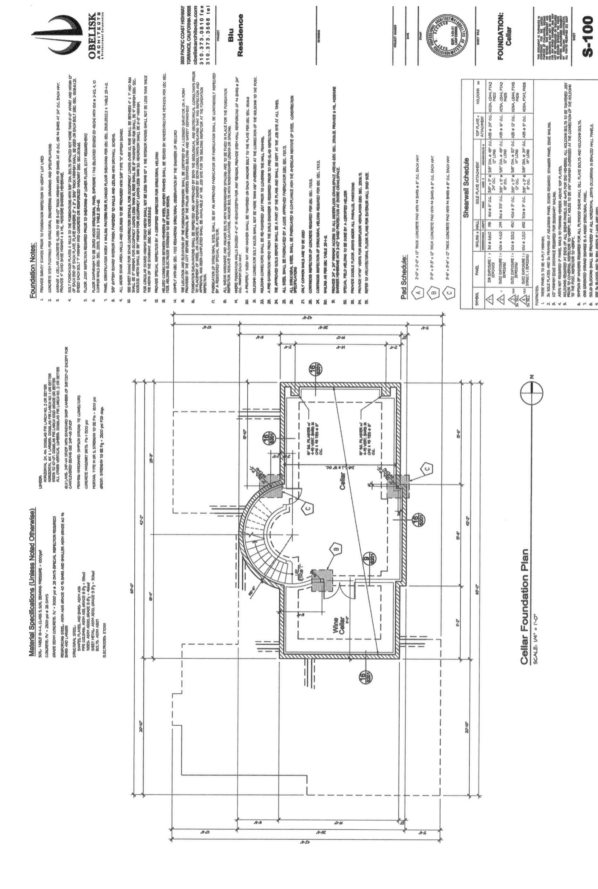

Figure 15.38 Stage IV: Foundation plan.

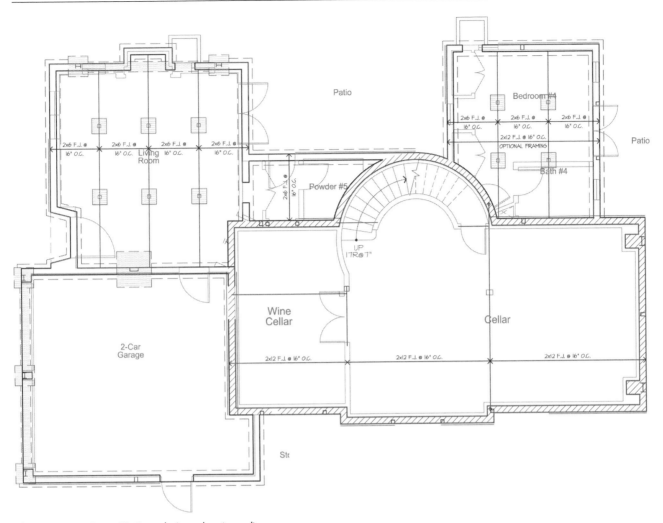

Figure 15.39   Stage III: Foundation plan (wood).

On these small framing plans, we decided to demonstrate the abbreviated method of showing the members, drafting all beams and headers but not all joists. The floor and ceiling joists are shown by a dimension-type line using a half arrowhead on each end. Beams and headers are shown over windows and doors as a centerline-type line. See Figure 15.41.

Second Floor with the Roof Framing Plan. On the roof framing plan, headers and beams are shown as centerlines, and the ridge, hip rafters, and valley members are drafted with solid lines. A hip rafter rests on the corner of the structure and is held in place by the forces from the rafters coming against it from either side. Rafters themselves are drafted with an arrow and duration arrow.

All exterior walls and interior bearing walls are drafted solid (i.e., using solid lines). All non-bearing walls are also located for reference.

If you look carefully, you can tell when a beam sits on a post or a post on a beam. If the beam sits on a post, you will see the line that simulates the beam drafted over the post. If the post sits on top of the beam, the lines of the beam stop short of the post or the post is noted as a king post. See Figure 15.42.

Stage II

First- and Second-Floor Framing Plans. To better understand the drawings in Figure 15.43, look at the final-stage framing plan with all the notations, material specifications, and schedules. This drawing provides all the information required for the contractor to construct the building. Studying the building section shown in Figure 15.28 will provide clarity to the plan view of the framing plans established here. See Figure 15.43.

Second Floor with the Roof Framing Plan. On the roof framing plan, provide all required notations, material specifications, and schedules, just as we have done for the first- and second-floor framing plans. See Figure 15.44 for the completed roof framing plan.

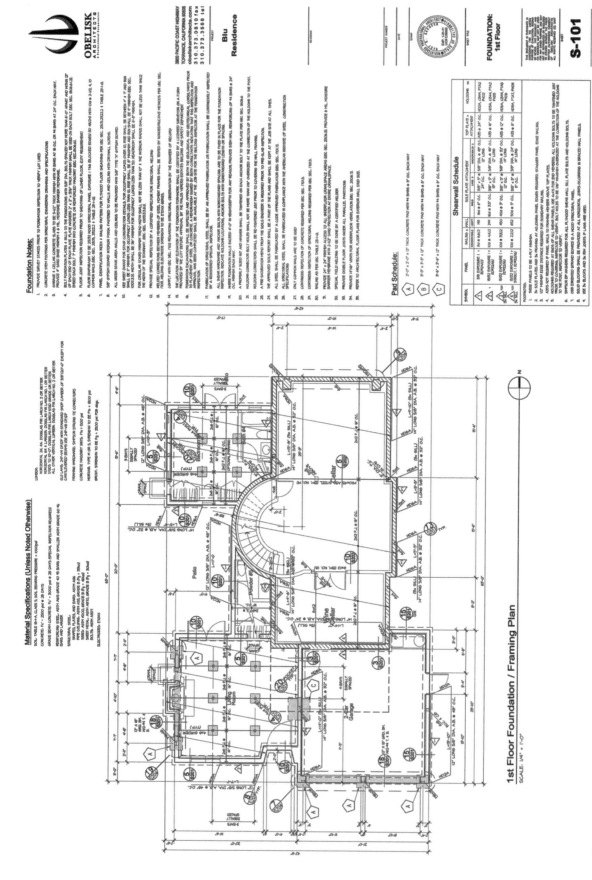

Figure 15.40 Stage V: Foundation plan.

SUPPORT DRAWINGS FOR BLU RESIDENCE

Although this chapter focuses on specific primary drawings, numerous sheets of drawings are required to complete the construction documents. Figure 15.45 is a title sheet. This sheet typically provides city notes, general notes, a vicinity map, abbreviations, and a symbols legend, as well as a sheet index and scope of work.

Many sheets are needed for a complete set of working drawings. Figure 15.46 represents a typical interior sheet for the Blu residence, and Figure 15.47 shows a typical detail sheet. A typical set of drawings for a residence like this could exceed eight sheets of details.

For more complex designs, an electrical layout drawing can be overlaid on an XREF of the floor plan. See Figure 15.48 for a sample electrical layout.

We have included a dozen sheets for this project, but more than another dozen were left out. It is not unusual for a cohesive, comprehensive set of drawings for construction to contain thirty or more sheets of construction documents. The more thorough the drawings are, the more clarity is provided for all the contractors and subcontractors who will build this unique prototype that we called the Blu residence.

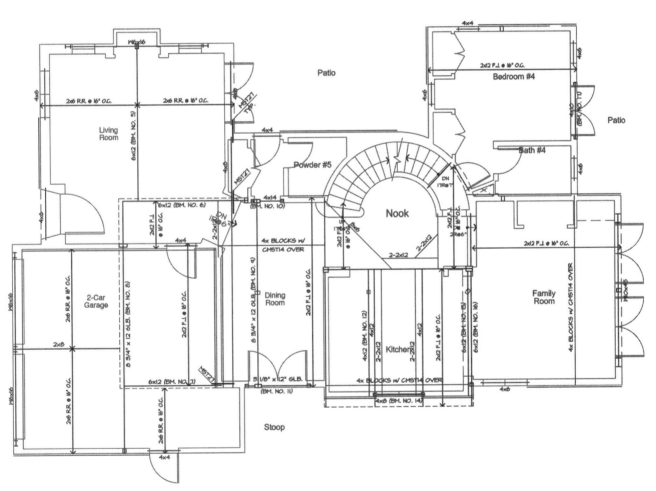

Figure 15.41 Stage I: Second-floor framing plan.

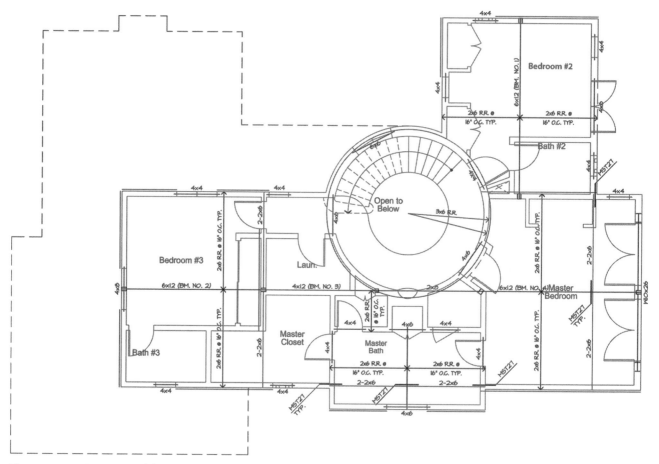

Figure 15.42   Stage I: Roof framing plan.

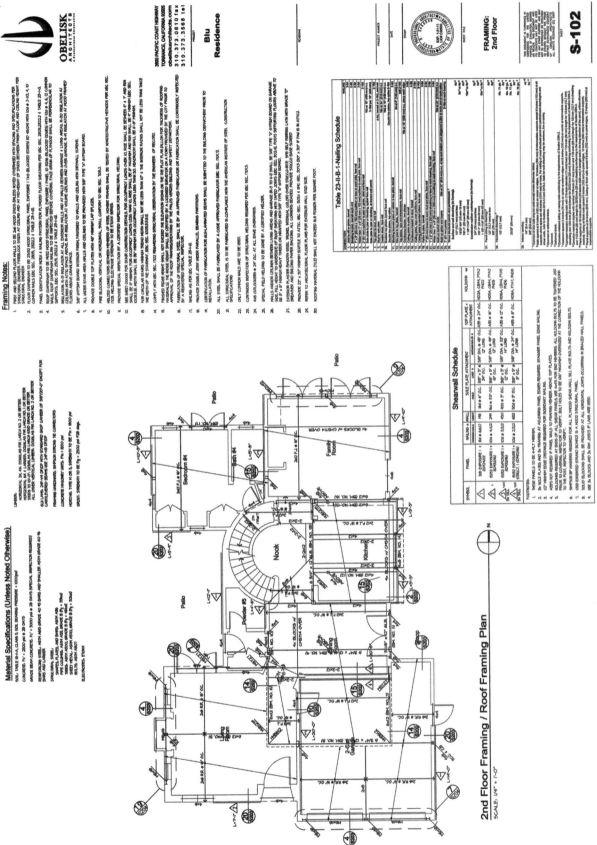

Figure 15.43 Stage II: Second-floor framing plan.

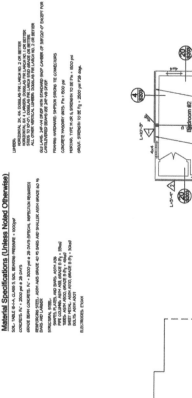

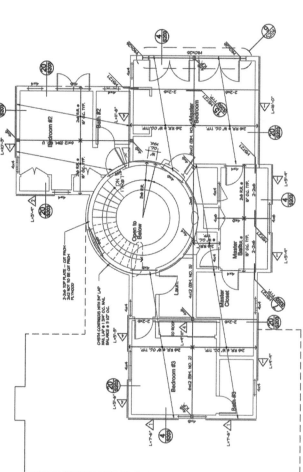

Roof Framing Plan
SCALE: 1/4" = 1'-0"

Figure 15.44 Stage II: Roof framing plan.

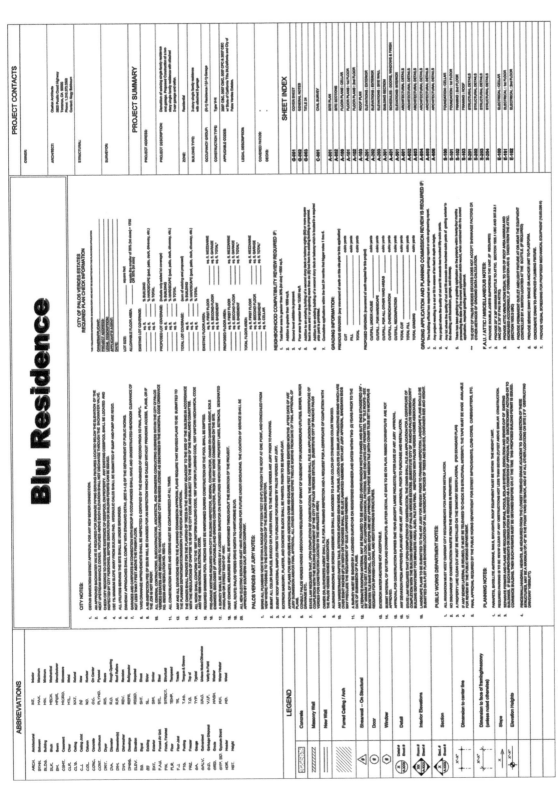

Figure 15.45 Title sheet.

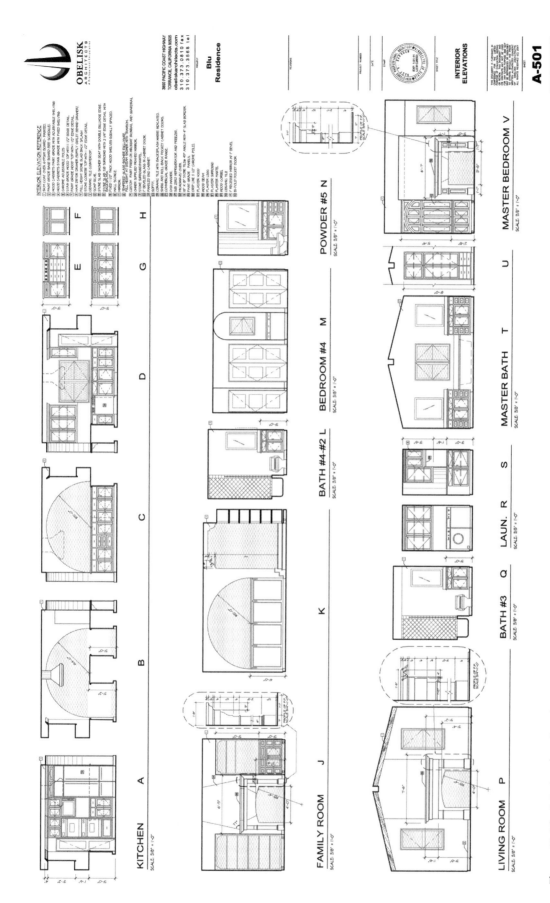

Figure 15.46 Interior elevation sheet.

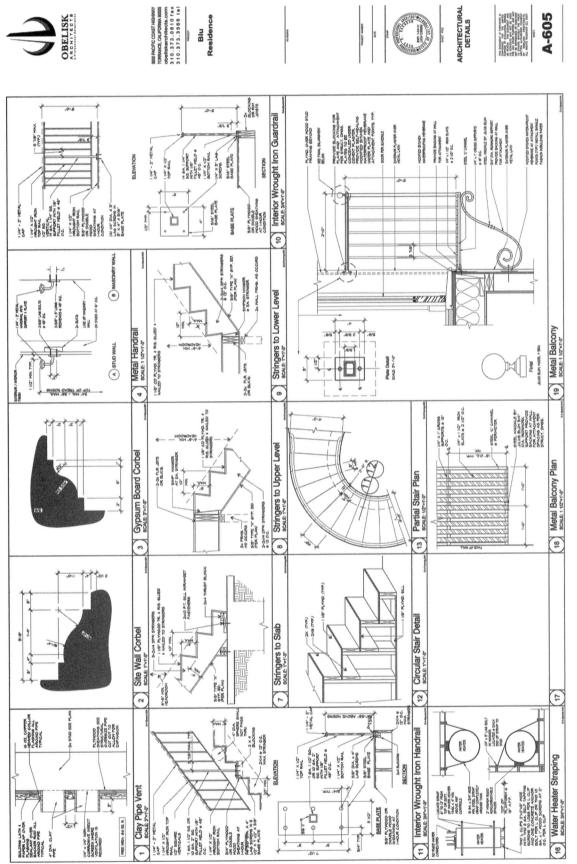

Figure 15.47 Detail sheet.

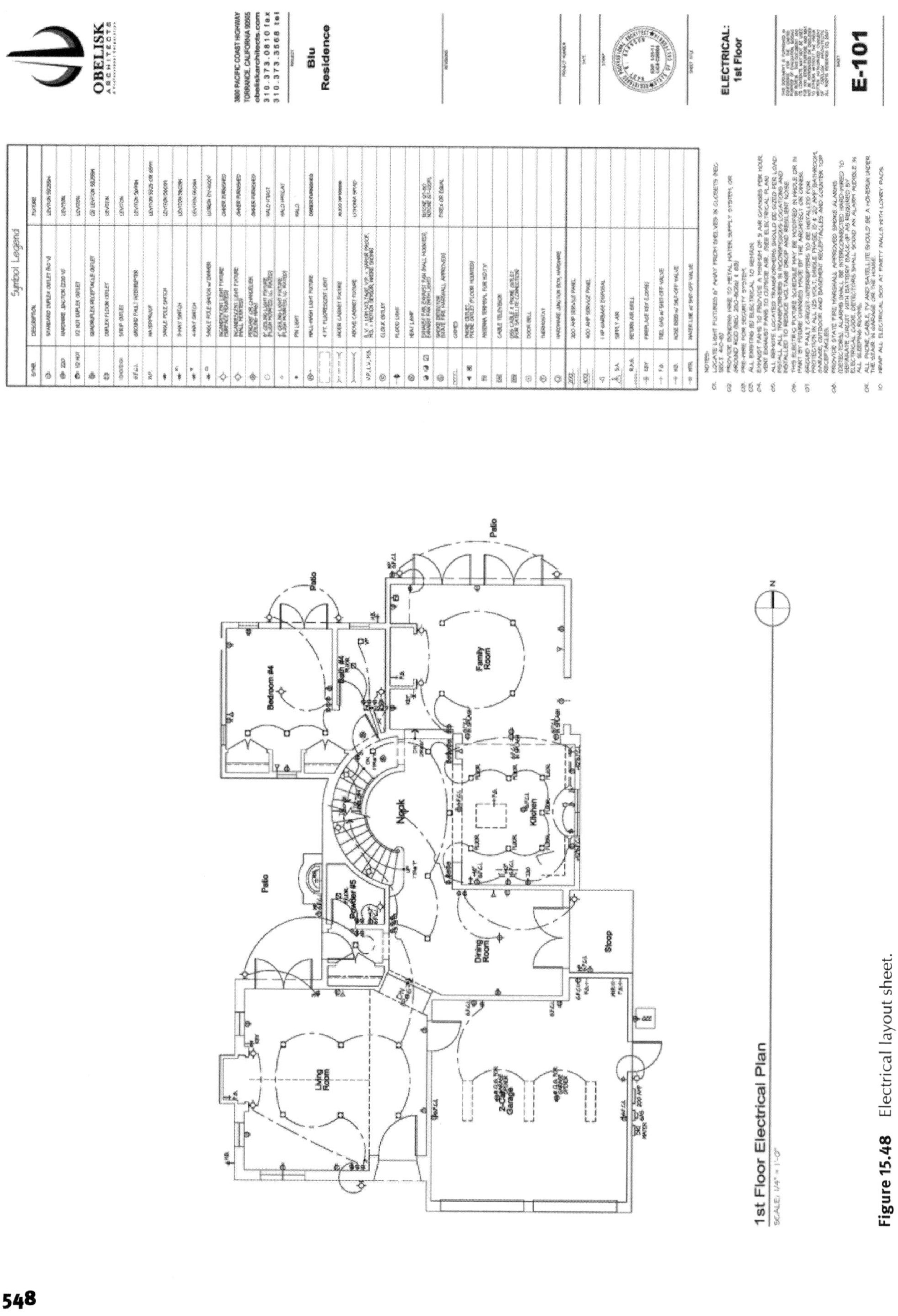

1st Floor Electrical Plan

SCALE: 1/4" = 1'-0"

Figure 15.48 Electrical layout sheet.

chapter

16

CONCEPTUAL DESIGN AND CONSTRUCTION DOCUMENTS FOR A STEEL AND MASONRY BUILDING (THEATER)

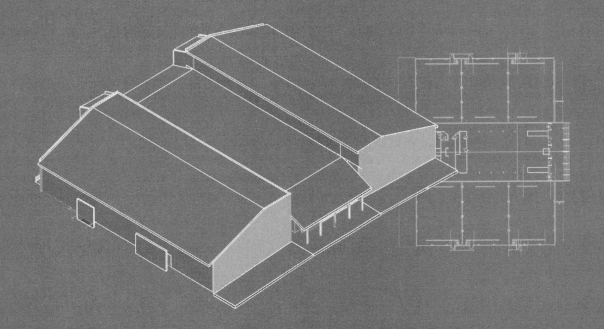

■ INTRODUCTION

Before you read this chapter, review the Revit section of Chapter 3, where much of this information has been covered in depth. This chapter is very abbreviated and is used only to demonstrate a set of reference drawings. For example, in the evolution of the elevations, working drawings are shown in stages for only one of the elevations; at the final stage, however, all forms are shown.

The method of designing a structure varies from office to office and from school to school. Since this textbook is concerned with working drawings, we will keep it simple.

While concepts are being developed, and ideas and research materials are being considered, designs are often drawn freehand and with sketches. These preliminary sketches can also be done on computer. With Revit, you can begin even at this stage to study masses, their relationship, and the effects of the sun on the structure. Of course, with Revit you must model the form (BIM) first and then take it to a high level later. The more information you include up front, the greater the reward and the easier the process. When you use Revit for a project, clients, contractors, architectural associates, and (naturally) the architect can spot and solve problems before they really become problems.

In this chapter and the next (Chapter 17), we will start with freehand design sketches and possibly a real model.

As expressed in the Revit section of Chapter 3, there is currently a fine line between design development and construction documents. This will change as each architectural firm adopts BIM. At that point, the contracts will be front loaded: When the design development is complete, the construction documents will almost be finished as well.

■ CONCEPTUAL DESIGN: SITE AND CLIENT REQUIREMENTS

The client required a theater building with six separate auditoriums of 200 seats each. The sloping site of approximately three acres also had stringent architectural restrictions.

The proposed structure, with six auditoriums, office, restrooms, and storage and food areas, required approximately 26,000 square feet. The seating area dictated the required onsite parking for 400 automobiles.

To satisfy fire requirements, the primary building materials selected were structural steel and concrete block. The concrete block was chosen because it also would provide an excellent sound barrier between the auditoriums and the lobby.

The initial concept provided for three auditoriums on each side of a central service core, which would contain the lobby, toilet facilities, food bar, and storage areas. The core would provide controlled circulation and access to the auditoriums, facilities, and required fire exits. Efficient arrangements for the 200 seats and fire code requirements governed the auditorium dimensions. The wall dimensions also had to be compatible with the concrete-block module. The upper-floor level would contain the projection rooms, the manager's office, an employee toilet, and additional storage rooms. The stair location for this upper area was also governed by fire department and building code design criteria.

■ DESIGN DEVELOPMENT PUNCH LIST

The punch list for this theater project was based on the site plan and the client requirements. It included notes on all sorts of matters, as well as design possibilities, ideas, and reminders.

- Walk the site with the client
- Egress and ingress only available from the west
- Best location on the site for parking on the south side
- Two traffic lanes at 90°
- Explore desirable areas for lobbies, exit stairs, utilities, and trash areas
- Establish locations of supporting steel columns
- Locate disability parking per ADA requirements
- Location of ice bank cooling system
- Second-floor load vs. required stairs, restrooms, and potential location for mechanical ducts
- Add third floor and revise square footage
- Verify exact position of steel columns in relationship to third floor
- Stairs for roof access
- Explore different types of windows and finishes
- Consult structural engineers early for:
  - Circular opening
  - Shear walls to relieve starkness of solid walls
  - Continuing curvilinear walls
  - Shape and mass of the sculptured concrete element around columns
- Explore and decide on exterior surface materials for curvilinear walls

■ INITIAL SCHEMATIC STUDIES

After programming the basic physical requirements for this proposed project, we began schematic site development.

Stage I

The irregularly shaped site had a west-to-east crossfall averaging 22' from the lowest to the highest grade. See Figure 16.1. Complicating the site further was a 25'-wide utility easement located near the center of the site. We could not build any of the structure in this easement.

Stage II

The initial schematic site study, shown in Figure 16.2, depicts the structure located north of the utility easement on the upper portion of the site. We thought this location would provide the most suitable parking layout for access to the theater, as well as a higher floor elevation for site drainage. The site entrance for automobiles is from the east property line only.

Stage III

After the schematic site development was completed, we designed the scaled preliminary first-floor plan

(Figure 16.3) and preliminary parking layouts. Client requirements determined the first-level floor plan. Parking layouts and automobile circulation were designed to be compatible with the natural topography of the site; we paralleled the parking stalls and driveways with the existing grades. We also terraced the parking levels. This reduced the amount of rough and finish grading to be done. Stairs, as well as ramps for disabled persons, were provided at the front of the theater.

Stage IV

From the scaled preliminary first-floor plan, we made overlay studies of the second floor. Correct projector port locations for each auditorium, and required exit locations, determined the second-floor design. Other spaces and their locations were more flexible. See Figure 16.4.

Stage V

Buildings in the area where this theater is located are subject to the jurisdiction of an architectural review

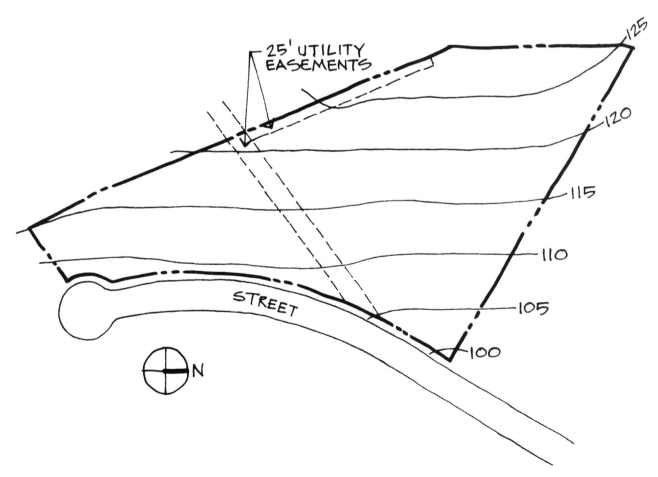

Figure 16.1 Preliminary site plan.

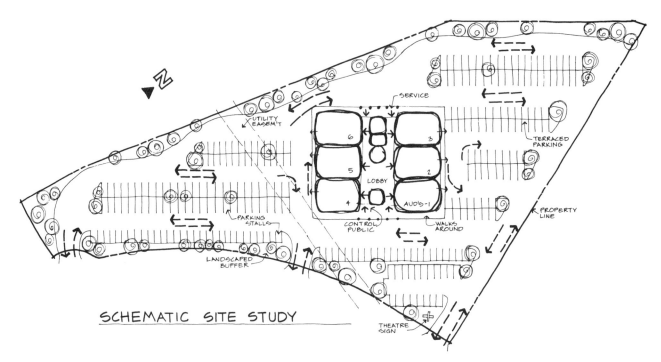

SCHEMATIC SITE STUDY

Figure 16.2   Schematic site study for theater.

committee, with written criteria dictating exterior appearances and materials. One of these restrictions stated that the roof must be of mission tile with a minimum pitch of 4 in 12. Another requirement was that all roof-mounted mechanical equipment must be shielded from view. By providing the required sloping roof planes over the auditoriums and the rear and front lobby access, we created a well that would screen the roof-mounted heating and ventilating equipment.

For aesthetic reasons, we decided to soften the facade of the building by breaking up the long exterior blank walls at the rear of the auditoriums. We added a heavy timber arbor to provide shadows on the blank walls. See Figure 16.5A. The arbor stain and general design were chosen to be compatible with the mission tile. To provide an acceptable finish, we covered the concrete block with a plaster finish. To enhance the exterior and further define the design elements, as well as to fulfill building department requirements, we added concrete columns in the colonnade. Instead of using three-dimensional drawings for presentation, a conceptual model was constructed, defining the general massing of the building as well as major architectural features. This model is shown in Figure 16.5B.

Design Development with Revit

Even in the development stage, BIM differs significantly from, say, AutoCAD. This may sound strange coming

from the authors of a drawing textbook, but with BIM you need to know more about the finished product than about drawing methods. For example, for this theater project, we needed to learn (to mention just a few items):

- What the client can supply, such as the proper slope of the stage, and other knowledge derived from years of building theaters
- Volume and size of the concession area
- Whether the client believes in video games (determines whether a game arcade becomes part of the theater)
- The local and regional building codes applicable to the proposed site
- All about cars:
  - Turn radius
  - Parking requirements
  - Ratio of compact vs. regular stalls
  - Aisles required between rows of cars
  - Parking required for disabled patrons
- Dedicated green space—minimum required and optimum
- Environmental concerns and elements to be designed in anticipation of the future

Of course, this is above and beyond the aesthetic building form, "normal" environmental concerns, concepts, essence, and so on that dictate the spirit and parti

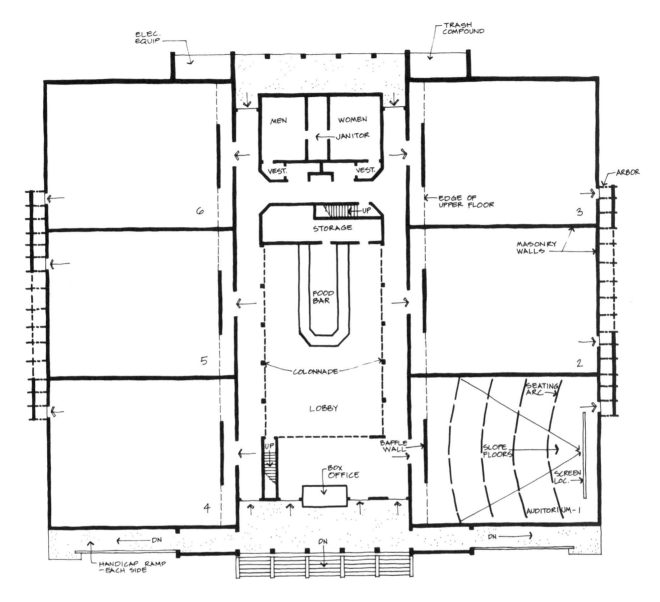

Figure 16.3 Preliminary ground-floor plan.

(essence in drawing form). The BIM in Figure 16.6 shows the beginning of the parametric (interrelated) model. Form the shape and remove the roof to produce pilasters, columns, the upper floor, and the lower floor, plus the section and interior elevations that are needed so they can be easily retrieved via the theater-project browser. See Figure 16.7.

3-D BIM Study: Before Working Drawings

As you finish the so-called initial schematic studies, you must put the information in a performance stage. Go to

Revit and build the 3-D image, solving each of the views you will need for the working drawings. Resolve the problem of the pilaster (widening of the block wall) and its connection with the roof. Do the same with the wall of the second floor and the roof, and the connection of the columns to the roof. This is when you will consult associates regarding conflicts of the paths for the structural work, mechanical (e.g., ductwork) installations, plumbing, and so on.

Resolve the easement (right-of-way for the electrical utility) that runs across the site. This is a very good time to cut the major and minor sections through the building and decide which interior elevations you will need

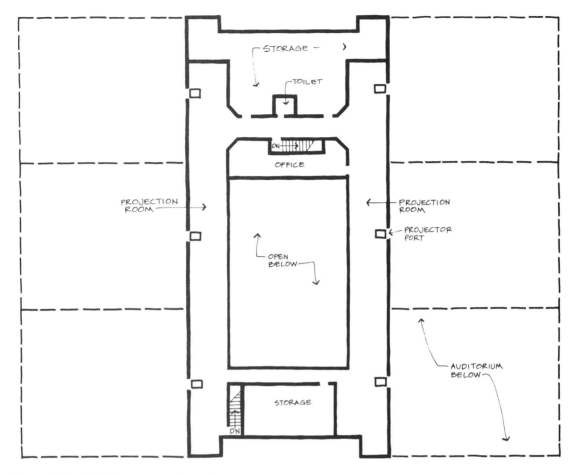

Figure 16.4   Preliminary upper-floor plan.

to show. Add the various engineering, mechanical, and lighting drawings, and you will have a project browser that is nearly a parametric modeler.

■ SITE PLAN

The primary purpose of the site plan was to locate the structure on the lot and indicate the proposed parking plan. Depending on its complexity, the site plan may or may not be combined with the grading plan. For this project, the grading plan, the site plan, and the paving plan were done separately. Figure 16.8 is an aerial photo of the completed project.

If you own an older version of Revit (say, 2010), you will probably do the site plan with AutoCAD. However, if you have Revit version 2012 or later, the total development of the site plan can be done to intersect with the other drawings. The development of the site plan begins with an abbreviated punch list (see the following) and then a series of drawings at different stages of evolution (see Figures 16.9 through 16.13). Check Figures 16.13A

and 16.13B to see the minute detail to which the grading plan is drawn.

Site Plan Punch List

- Metes and bounds, easements
- Building a site cross-section
- Limit of grading—cut and fill
- Movement of water through the site
- Utility plan, grading plan, landscape plan, irrigation plan
- Bearing pressure of soil
- Dimensioning principles of a site plan
- Property contours
- What the owner will provide, in drawing form
- How to execute a site plan using Revit
- Proper symbols and conventions for a site plan
- Abbreviations used on the site plans (e.g., "TC" means top of curb)

As you look at this punch list, (outline of the procedure for each stage), note that the punch list is an abbreviated list of things to look out for when drawing each step.

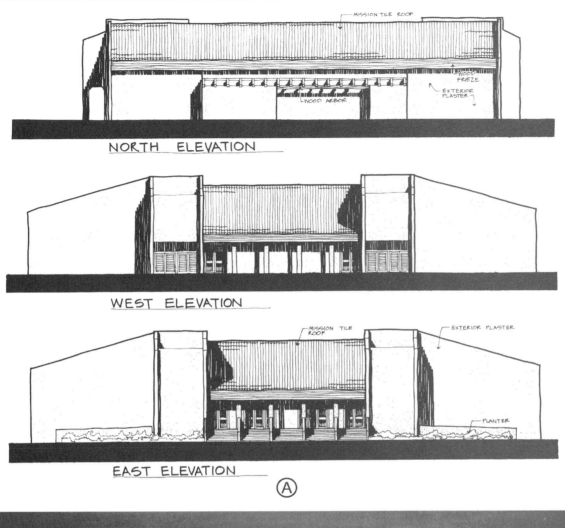

NORTH ELEVATION

WEST ELEVATION

EAST ELEVATION

(A)

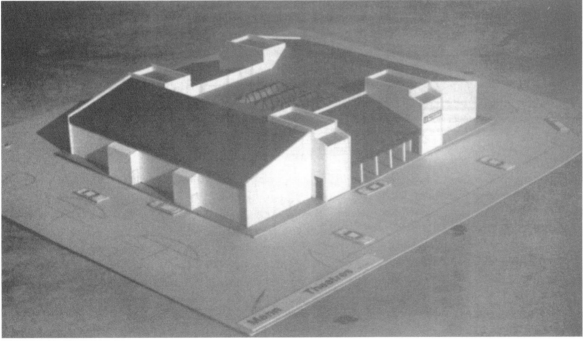

(B)

Figure 16.5 (A) Preliminary exterior elevations. (B) Conceptual model.

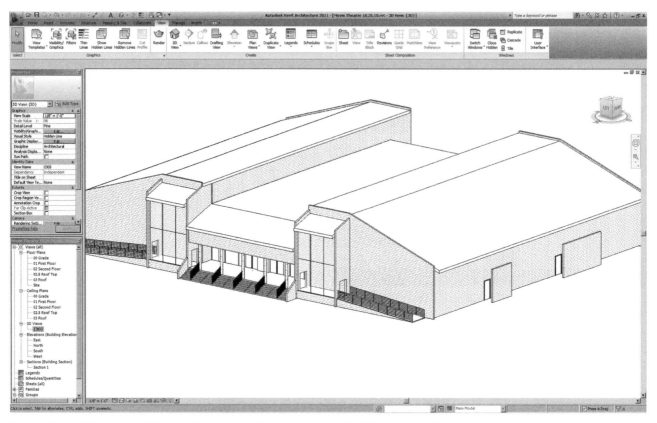

Figure 16.6   BIM model of theater. (Screenshots © Autodesk Inc. All Rights Reserved.)

■ FOUNDATION PLAN

The foundation plan was not originally a part of the Revit vocabulary. A new datum line must be set and the foundation portion of the theater must be drawn under the floor plan. The foundation plan is coordinated with the structural engineer and the soil engineer, thus producing a platform that will appropriately distribute the weight of the structure onto the site. The punch list will help you identify foundation concerns, while the photo reinforcement will assist you in understanding the needs of the craftspersons in the field.

Although pictures like this are generally not available when you are producing working drawings, we have included them so that beginners can see the actual architectural construction, and begin to consider the visualizations that must take place during the production of BIM and the subsequent working drawings.

Photo Reinforcement

- Illustration showing the detail necessary in a drawing to control water flow (Figure 16.13).
- Visualize the quantity of earth to be moved (Figure 16.14).

- Plan what to do with the excess soil (Figure 16.15).
- Stakes are used to control the grading process (Figure 16.16).
- Chalk lines guide the digging of the foundation and help locate the pilasters (periodic widening of the walls) that act as columns to support the support members above (Figures 16.17, 16.18, and 16.19).
- Visualize ramps for persons with disabilities (Figure 16.20).

Foundation Plan Punch List

- Converting shape into plan view
- Hidden lines for seating rake (slope for viewing)
- Detail call-out
- Referencing to engineering calculations and drawings
- Dimensioning (especially arcs for seating slope)
- Noting material designations: steel, masonry, and concrete
- Grade beams, shear wall, and spacing of framing anchors
- Block module
- Dowels
- How to incorporate and supervise structural engineering symbols to indicate size of footing (diagonal lines)

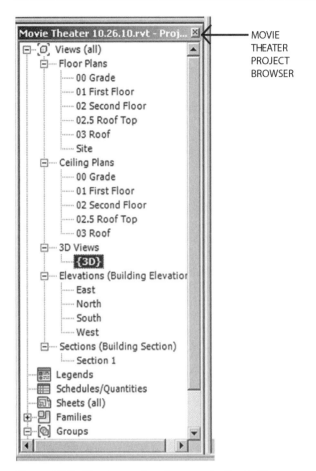

MOVIE
THEATER
PROJECT
BROWSER

Figure 16.7 Theater project browser in Revit. (Screen shots © Autodesk Inc. All Rights Reserved.)

Figure 16.8 Aerial photo of finished site. (William Boggs Aerial Photography. Reprinted with permission.)

- Identify venting
- How to deal with sheet size vs. size of structure
- Slab reinforcing
- Ramps for persons with disabilities

The various stages of the foundation plan drawings are shown in Figures 16.21 through 16.26.

Look at the punch list. Form an outline of the stages for the following drawing. This puch list is just a minimum list so the foundation chapter should be followed.

Since the building above the foundation is made of concrete block, the dimension is based on a block module. Figure 16.21 shows a chart using this module system using 18″ long and 4″ or 8″ tall blocks. If you do not adhere to these limits, you will have to cut the blocks and the integrity of the system of blocks will be ruined. Windows and door openings also follow this module.

■ GROUND-FLOOR PLAN

The floor plan (and the building section) is the base datum from which all other drawings are established. It is also the first preliminary drawing to be used in BIM.

It must be done comprehensively and adhere to all of the principles of drawing. When the model is done, the construction documents for the floor plan will be almost complete except for a few items that must be checked.

If you were working with AutoCAD, you would first set up grid and snap as shown in Figure 16.27. In Revit, this is started in the design development stage.

When the design development is finished and you wish to begin the floor plan (as a working drawing), you need only locate the project browser and download a nearly complete construction document of the floor plan (bottom left of your Revit screen; see Figure 16.28).

Floor Plan Punch List

- Find and plan the best way to develop a form on Revit.
- Keep walls aligned.
- Truly understand the block module and its impact on the location of selected windows and doors.
- Know how to integrate concrete block with steel and wood.
- Be able to draw correct material designations.
- Follow national and international standards.
- Accommodate persons who use wheelchairs; know how to differentiate between disabled ramps and planters.
- Compare radial lines of the foundation plan with those on the floor plan.
- Be able to draw a projection window and indicate its required projection angle.
- Develop special symbols (e.g., symbol for projector, in this theater project).
- Know how to space fire extinguishers; incorporate information regarding the concession stand and restrooms.

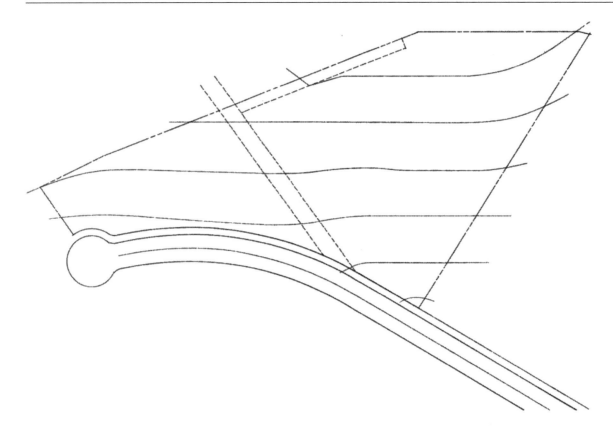

Figure 16.9   Stage I: Design development.

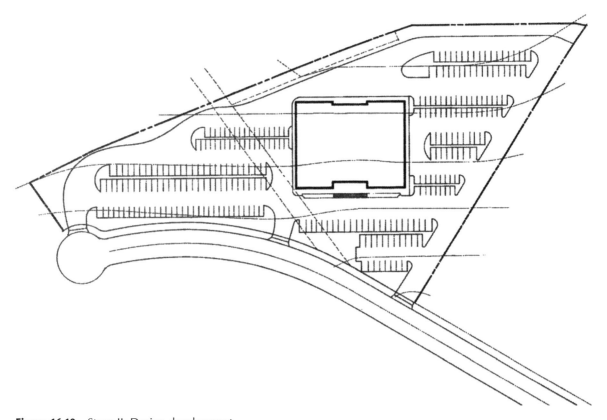

Figure 16.10   Stage II: Design development.

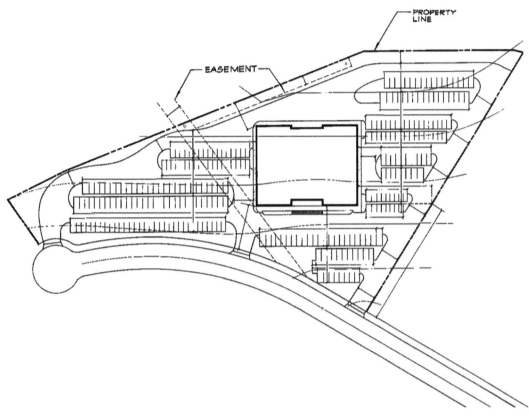

Figure 16.11 Stage III: Design development.

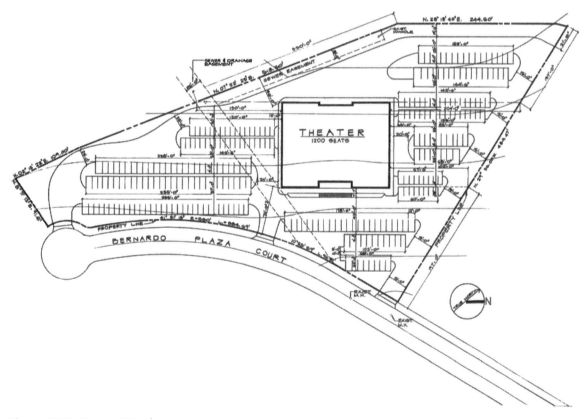

Figure 16.12 Stage I: Site plan.

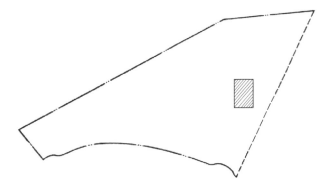

(A) Portion of grading plan to be enlarged.

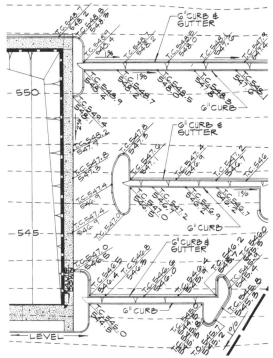

(B) Portion of grading plan enlarged.

Figure 16.13 Enlargement of site/grading plan to reveal water-flow control detail.

Photo Reinforcement

- Understand the order of how a masonry building is built: The foundation and walls are built first, then the walls for the interior floor are constructed, but much later (Figures 16.29 and 16.30).
- In this project, there are six separate theaters in the complex. The theaters have two floors between them. Figure 16.31 shows the initial appearance of the space for the central lobby.

- A second floor sits above; this floor provides space for the equipment and projectionists to show the movies, plus storage, an office, and an employee toilet/restroom. A hole in this floor reveals the concession stand below. (See Figures 16.32–16.40.)

■ PARTIAL FLOOR PLAN AND INTERIOR ELEVATIONS

The partial floor plan shown in Figures 16.41 and 16.42 includes the concession areas and restrooms. Only a few interior elevations are shown and described here.

This partial floor plan was drawn at twice the size of the first-floor plan. We took advantage of the computer's ability to instantly change the size of a drawing.

Punch List for Partial Floor Plan and Interior Elevations

- Show the plumbing fixtures, stairs, and drinking fountains.
- Do material designations for the interior elevations.
- Add any dimensions not shown on the major floor plan.
- Check dimensions against ADA requirements and verify accuracy.
- Check reference bubble for interior elevation against partial floor plan.

At this scale, we could also show the double wall for the plumbing. (See the wall with toilets.)

The four rectangles at the bottom of the drawing in Figure 16.43 represent columns. Two more columns appear to be located next to the walls, but they are actually inside the walls. They were included for visual continuity and have no structural implications.

The left half of the drawing was blocked out to receive the interior elevations, with one exception: the floor plan of the toilet on the upper-floor level located slightly left of center on the drawing. The rectangle to the right of the upper-floor toilet would become the interior elevation for that toilet, while the long rectangle at the bottom would become the interior elevation of the entry to the restrooms and telephone area. See Figure 16.44.

■ EXTERIOR ELEVATIONS

Elevations are predrawn in Revit; they do not have to be drawn from scratch, as with AutoCAD. When you use AutoCAD, the exterior elevations are some of the last working drawings you will do, mostly because they depend so heavily on the floor plan, roof plan, building sections, and so on.

Figure 16.14 Graded site without structure. (William Boggs Aerial Photography. Reprinted with permission.)

Figure 16.15 Grading the property.

Figure 16.16   Stakes placed by surveyor.

Figure 16.17   Chalk lines for foundation.

Figure 16.18   Chalked lines ready for trenching. (William Boggs Aerial Photography. Reprinted with permission.)

Figure 16.19 Trenched footings.

Design development of exterior elevations (depending on office practice) is done in four or more stages (see Figures 16.45, 16.46, 16.47, and 16.48). Elevations are usually done in ortho (2-D) as shown to maintain accuracy. Verify the elevations against your 3-D image, and then begin the working drawing images with the project browser (Figure 16.45).

There are only two or three stages in the development of working drawings, as seen in Figure 16.49. The last design development stage and the first stage of the final exterior elevations produce the other three exterior elevations. See Figure 16.50. The North elevation is identical to the South elevation, although you might title this differently (e.g., "North/South elevation") or add "South elevation similar."

Elevation Punch List

- Know the purpose of the drawings.
- Understand titling (NSEW).
- Know how to lay out each elevation.
- Verify the datums.
- Know how odd shapes are displayed.
- Redraw if something critical is drawn.
- Understand key plan, pivot point.
- Know how windows and doors are represented.
- Know how substructures are displayed (e.g., pilasters).
- Correctly make reference to schedules.

Figure 16.20 Columns to support upper floor and forms for the stairs adjacent to the disabled ramps.

BLOCK MODULE
(3/8" HORIZONTAL AND VERTICAL MORTAR JOINTS)

LENGTH	NO. 16" LONG BLOCKS	LENGTH	NO. 16" LONG BLOCKS	HEIGHT	NO. 4" HIGH BLOCKS	NO. 8" HIGH BLOCKS	HEIGHT	NO. 4" HIGH BLOCKS	NO. 8" HIGH BLOCKS
0'-8"	1/2	20'-8"	15 1/2	0'-4"	1		10'-4"	31	
1'-4"	1	21'-4"	16	0'-8"	2	1	10'-8"	32	16
2'-0"	1 1/2	22'-0"	16 1/2	1'-0"	3		11'-0"	33	
2'-8"	2	22'-8"	17	1'-4"	4	2	11'-4"	34	17
3'-4"	2 1/2	23'-4"	17 1/2	1'-8"	5		11'-8"	35	
4'-0"	3	24'-0"	18	2'-0"	6	3	12'-0"	36	18
4'-8"	3 1/2	24'-8"	18 1/2	2'-4"	7		12'-4"	37	
5'-4"	4	25'-4"	19	2'-8"	8	4	12'-8"	38	19
6'-0"	4 1/2	26'-0"	19 1/2	3'-0"	9		13'-0"	39	
6'-8"	5	26'-8"	20	3'-4"	10	5	13'-4"	40	20
7'-4"	5 1/2	27'-4"	20 1/2	3'-8"	11		13'-8"	41	
8'-0"	6	28'-0"	21	4'-0"	12	6	14'-0"	42	21
8'-8"	6 1/2	28'-8"	21 1/2	4'-4"	13		14'-4"	43	
9'-4"	7	29'-4"	22	4'-8"	14	7	14'-8"	44	22
10'-0"	7 1/2	30'-0"	22 1/2	5'-0"	15		15'-0"	45	
10'-8"	8	30'-8"	23	5'-4"	16	8	15'-4"	46	23
11'-4"	8 1/2	31'-4"	23 1/2	5'-8"	17		15'-8"	47	
12'-0"	9	32'-0"	24	6'-0"	18	9	16'-0"	48	24
12'-8"	9 1/2	32'-8"	24 1/2	6'-4"	19		16'-4"	49	
13'-4"	10	40'-0"	30	6'-8"	20	10	16'-8"	50	25
14'-0"	10 1/2	50'-0"	37 1/2	7'-0"	21		17'-0"	51	
14'-8"	11	60'-0"	45	7'-4"	22	11	17'-4"	52	26
15'-4"	11 1/2	70'-0"	52 1/2	7'-8"	23		17'-8"	53	
16'-0"	12	80'-0"	60	8'-0"	24	12	18'-0"	54	27
16'-8"	12 1/2	90'-0"	67 1/2	8'-4"	25		18'-4"	55	
17'-4"	13	100'-0"	75	8'-8"	26	13	18'-8"	56	28
18'-0"	13 1/2	200'-0"	150	9'-0"	27		19'-0"	57	
18'-8"	14	300'-0"	225	9'-4"	28	14	19'-4"	58	29
19'-4"	14 1/2	400'-0"	300	9'-8"	29		19'-8"	59	
20'-0"	15	500'-0"	375	10'-0"	30	15	20'-0"	60	30

Figure 16.21 Block module chart.

- Know how to display different materials.
- Avoid inserting unnecessary information.
- Make distinctions between steel, masonry, and wood.
- Do correct dimensioning.
- Account for waterproofing and condensation.
- Be able to do referencing and noting.
- Identify flashing.
- Accommodate requirements of local codes on elevations.

Photo Reinforcement

- The owner's and architect's vision (Figure 16.51)
- Rear of the building (Figure 16.52)

- How the theater front will look at the beginning (Figure 16.53)
- Close-up of the disability ramp (Figure 16.54)

■ BUILDING SECTIONS

In the case of building sections, the decision is when and why to create them, rather than what to create. See the discussion of building sections in Chapter 10.

The theater in this example was a fairly large building, and we needed to draw the section as large as possible (given the limitations of sheet size) to reveal how the building was to be assembled. We decided to break

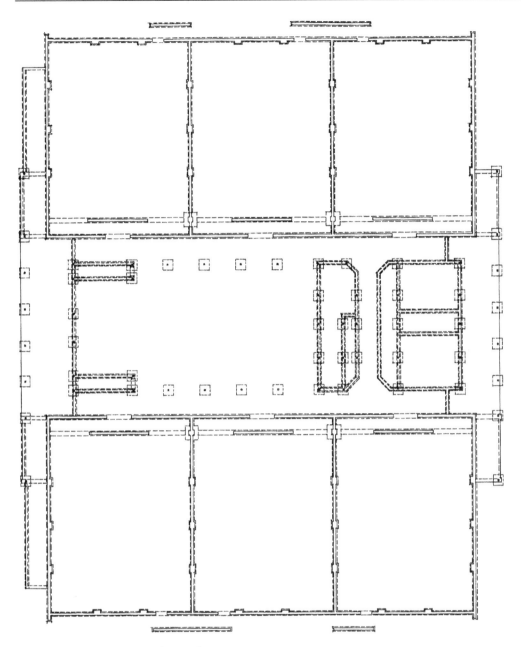

Figure 16.22 Stage I: Foundation plan.

out portions of the structure where information would have been repeated over and over. Thus, three portions were removed that contained **redundant** information. The term *redundant*, in this context, refers to areas that contain the same information for a long length. Most of the decisions about the structure must be solved at the design development stage, as the structural engineer verifies the sizes and forms of the support members.

Because the floor of each auditorium was sloped, we used two floor levels to describe the structure: level "A" for the top and level "B" for the bottom.

At the design development stage for the structure, the form is completed, windows and doors are positioned, and the roof configuration is shown, as are stairs, disability ramps, columns, and so on.

Building sections will not appear on the Revit project browser until the sections are selected and drawn.

Building Section Punch List

- Review, check, and include:
  - Type of foundation

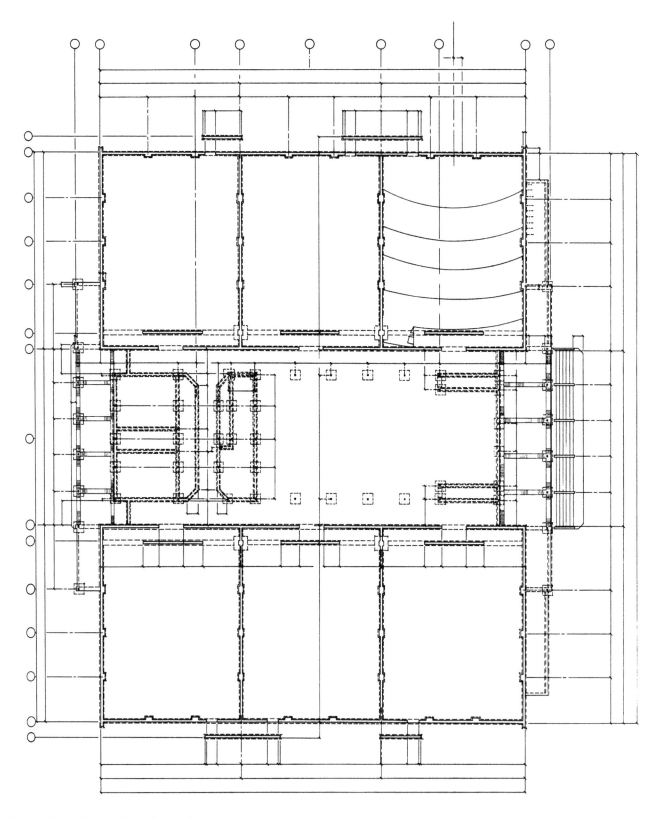

Figure 16.23 Stage II: Foundation plan.

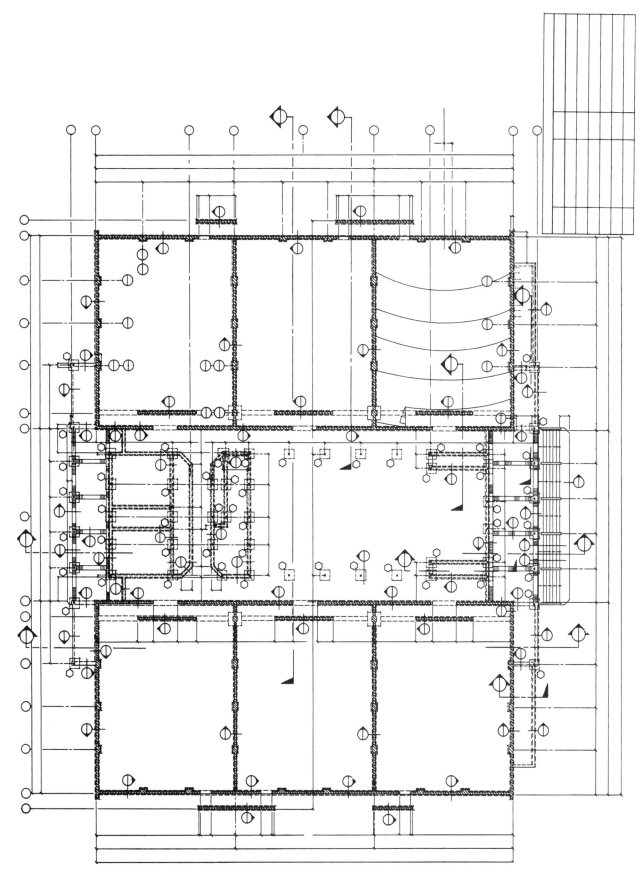

Figure 16.24 Stage III: Foundation plan.

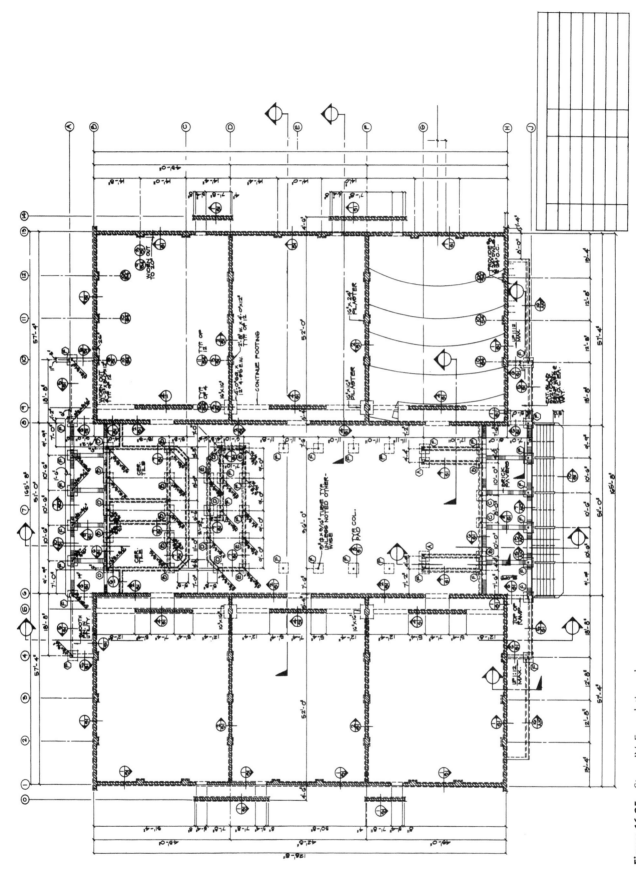

Figure 16.25 Stage IV: Foundation plan.

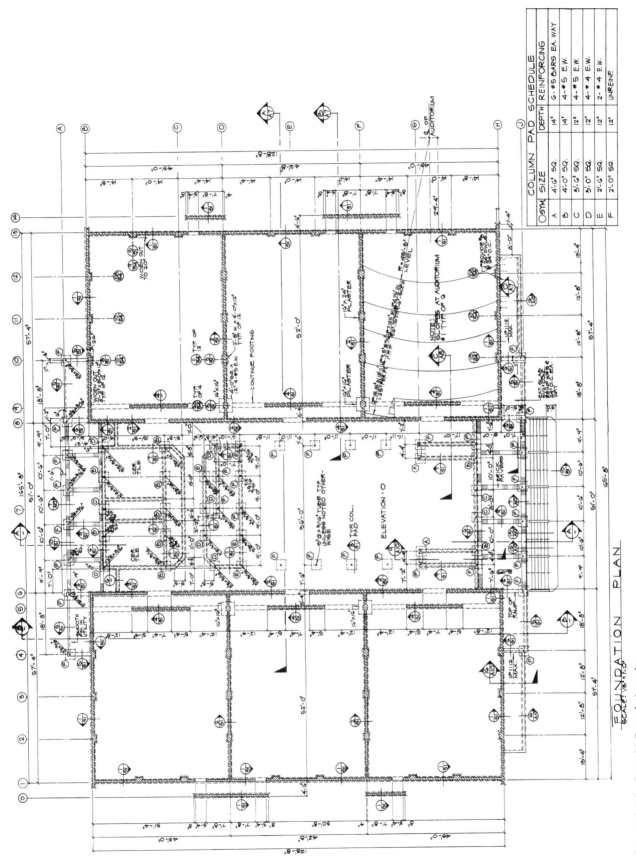

Figure 16.26 Stage V: Foundation plan.

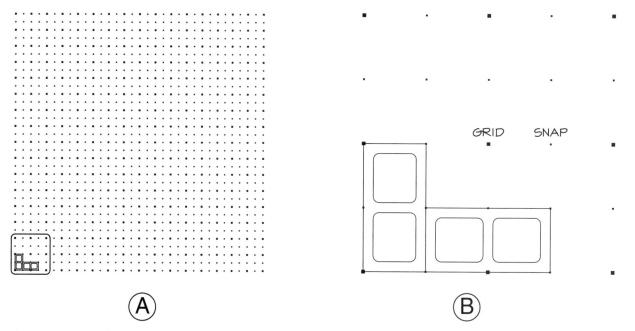

Figure 16.27 Grid and snap set to block module.

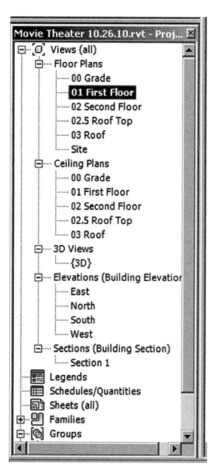

Figure 16.28 Floor plan from project browser in Revit. (Screenshots © Autodesk Inc. All Rights Reserved.)

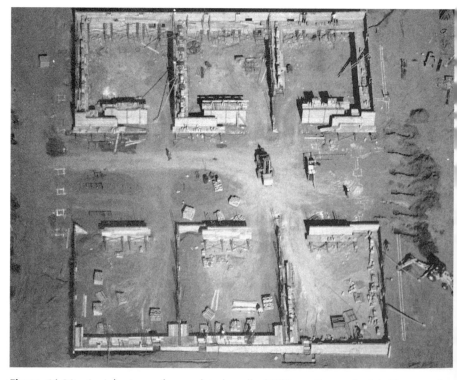

Figure 16.29 Aerial view of completed wall. (William Boggs Aerial Photography. Reprinted with permission.)

Figure 16.30   View of entry, lobby, and back of theater.

Figure 16.31   View looking toward lobby.

- Floor system
- Exterior and interior wall construction
- Beam and column sizes and their materials
- Plate and/or wall heights
- Floor elevations
- Floor members (size and spacing)
- Floor sheathing, material and size
- Ceiling members (size and spacing)
- Roof pitch

- Roof sheathing, material and size
- Insulation requirements
- Finished roof material
- Scale of drawing against finish sheet size
- Sections properly selected
- Detail reference
- Major datum established: floor to plate, plate to floor (if more than two stages)
- Proper noting, conventions, and symbols

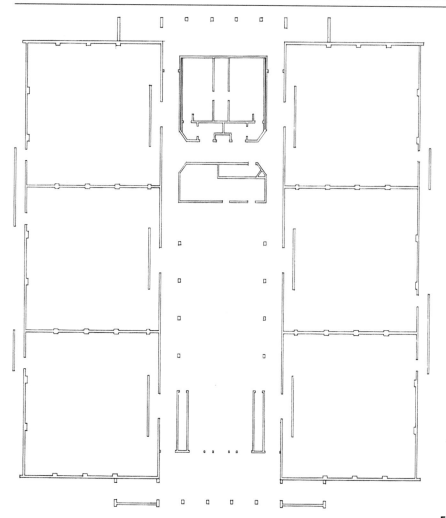

Figure 16.32 Stage I: Design development.

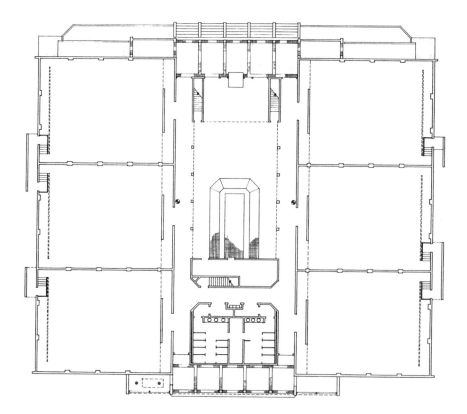

Figure 16.33 Stage II: Design development.

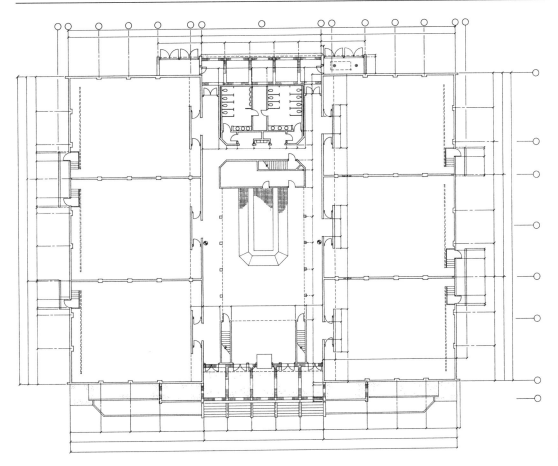

Figure 16.34 Stage I: Working drawing.

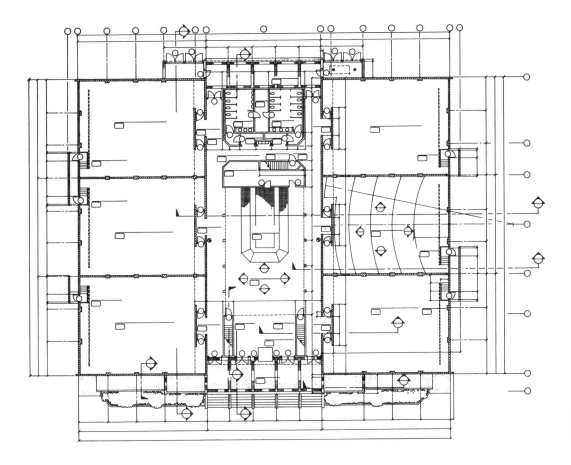

Figure 16.35 Stage II: Working drawing.

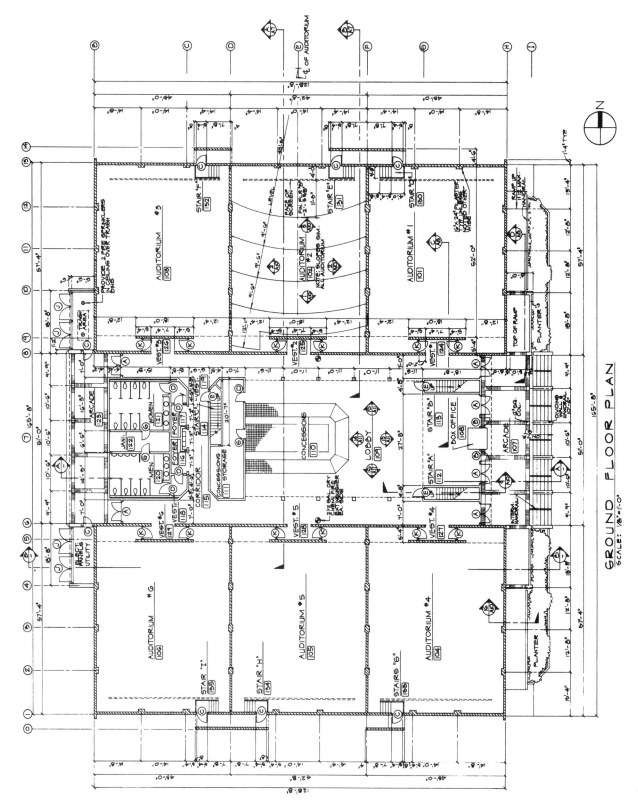

Figure 16.36 Stage III: Finished working drawing.

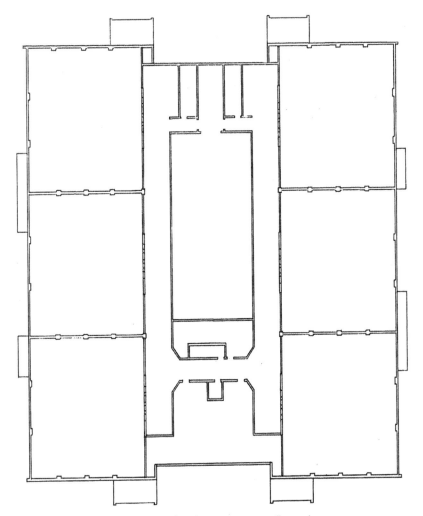

Figure 16.37 Stage I: Design development, upper-floor plan.

- Ridge height if required by local building codes
- Dimensions—do not repeat dimensions that appear on the floor plan
- Water drainage—roof
- Material designations
- Stair, elevators, escalators, lifts, ramps
- Partial sections as required
- Best use of dimensional reference system (if used)
- Suspended ceilings

Photo Reinforcement

See the drawings in Figures 16.55 through 16.58. Unique terms for the building sections of the theater included:
  - TB—top of beam
  - TSG—tapered steel girder

■ ROOF PLAN

The roof plan and the roof framing plan were executed at the same time, in conjunction with the structural engineer, during the 3-D modeling stage. As for the roof plan, one must first study the design development of the first-floor plan, the upper-floor plan, the elevations, and (most importantly) the sections. If you look at the photograph in Figure 16.59, you can identify the five major portions of the roof: the north, south, east, and west outer portions and the center. All portions of the roof must drain properly. The center roof portion is split in the center and each half slopes away from the ridge to form a gable-type roof. At each of the four corners, there is a small roof form and an adjacent small form. Each of these roofs must be drained. Had this area not been fitted with a reverse slope and saddle, the water would have rested in the flat areas of the roof.

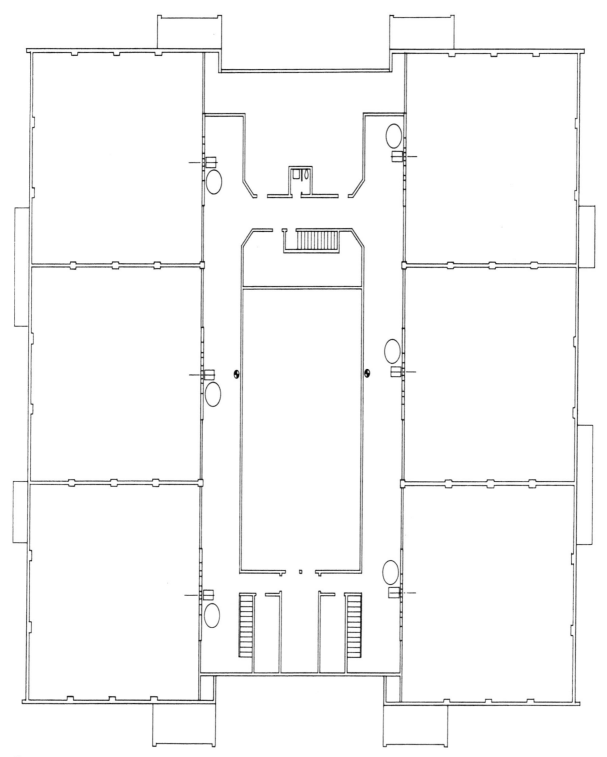

Figure 16.38 Stage II: Design development, upper-floor plan.

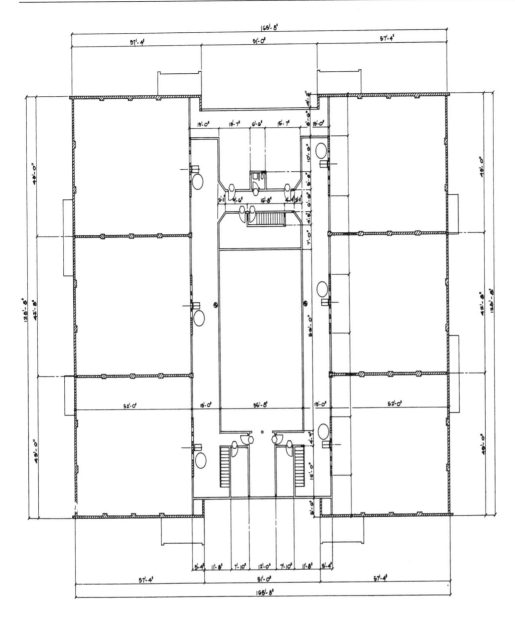

Figure 16.39 Stage I: Working drawing, upper-floor plan.

Roof Plan Punch List

- Understand planes and their geometry.
- Understand valleys and ridges.
- Know the correct designations of roof materials.
- Correctly specify framing, sheathing, waterproofing, and roof materials.
- Know how to drain water from a roof, using slope ratio, pitch, and direction of flow.
- Know where to incorporate flashing.
- Understand waterproofing requirements for openings in the roof.

Photo Reinforcement

- Aerial photograph of finished roof; this is what you must be able to visualize (Figure 16.59)
- Sketch of how to draw a roof (Figure 16.60); see also Figures 16.61-16.64

■ ROOF FRAMING PLAN

For a description of the parts of the roof framing plan, refer to the discussion in Chapter 9. This chapter describes the approach and method generally used to create the

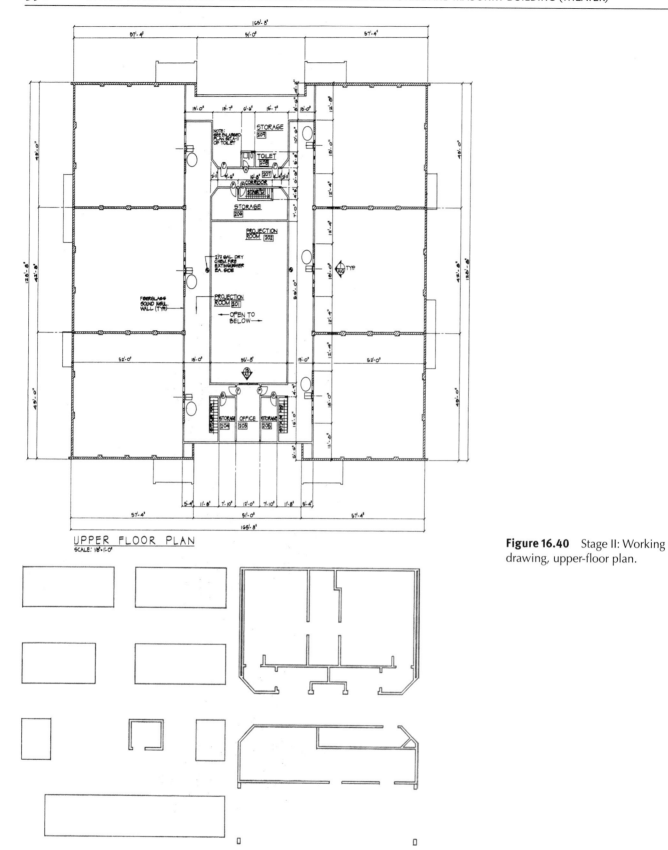

UPPER FLOOR PLAN
SCALE: 1/8"=1'-0"

Figure 16.40 Stage II: Working drawing, upper-floor plan.

Figure 16.41 Stage I: Design development—Partial floor plan and interior elevations.

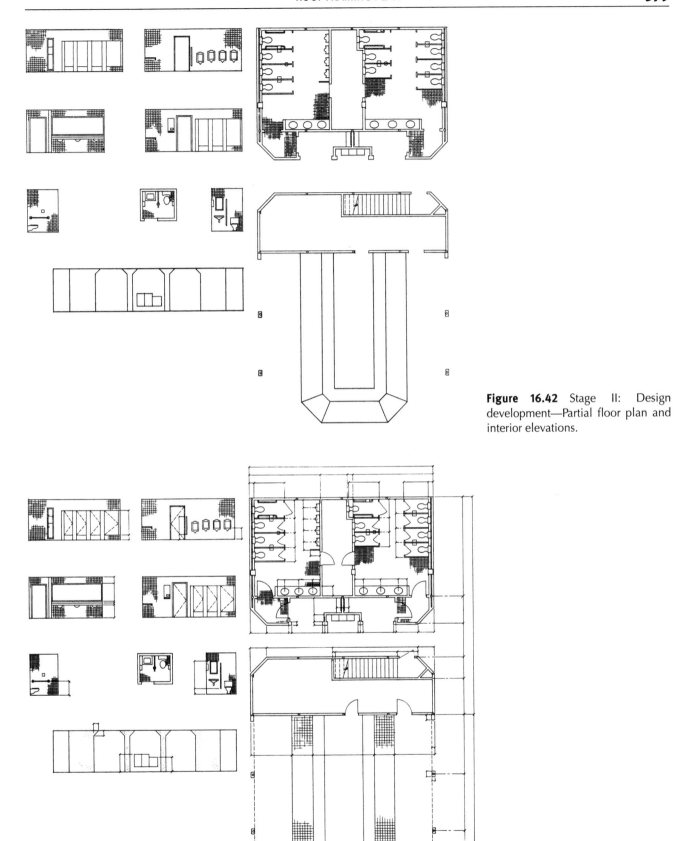

Figure 16.42 Stage II: Design development—Partial floor plan and interior elevations.

Figure 16.43 Stage I: Working drawing—Partial floor plan and interior elevations.

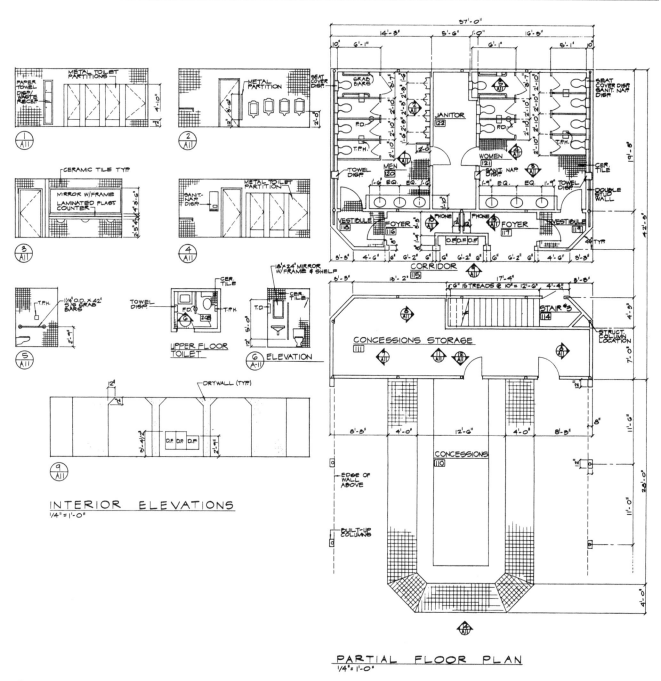

Figure 16.44 Stage II: Working drawing—Partial floor plan and interior elevations.

plan for the theater example. The model was developed as all of the critical decisions were made and executed (see Figure 16.65). The model and plan were sent to the structural engineer for information input (location of columns and beams, etc.). When the engineer returned the sketches, the information was added to the model (see Figure 16.66). The precise dimension lines were floor, ceiling, and top walls.

Roof Framing Plan Punch List

- Specific framing plan
- Tributary loads
- Floor framing
- Ceiling
- Roof framing
- Framing around openings for chimney, stairs, skylights

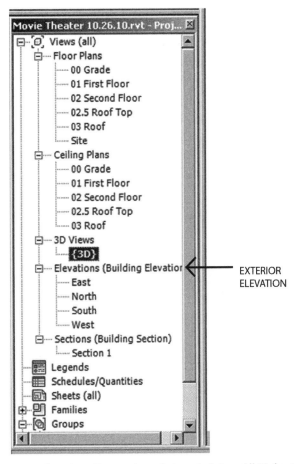

Figure 16.45 Project browser for exterior elevation. (Screenshots © Autodesk Inc. All Rights Reserved.)

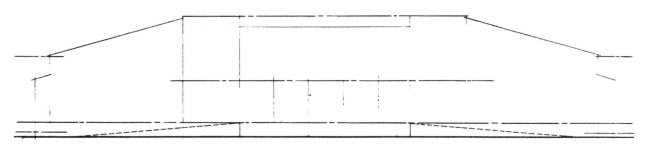

Figure 16.46 Stage I: Design development—Exterior elevations.

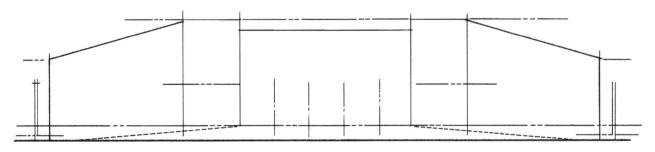

Figure 16.47 Stage II: Design development—Exterior elevations.

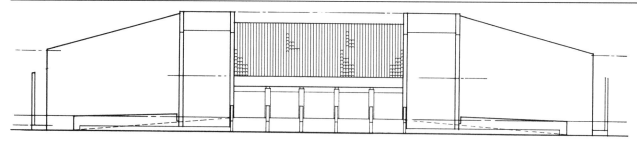

Figure 16.48 Stage III: Design development—Exterior elevations.

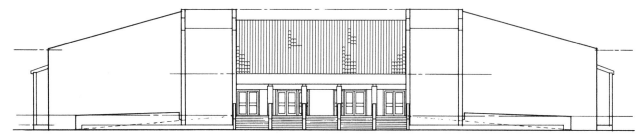

Figure 16.49 Stage I: Working drawing—Exterior elevations download from BIM.

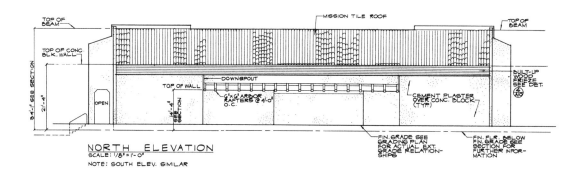

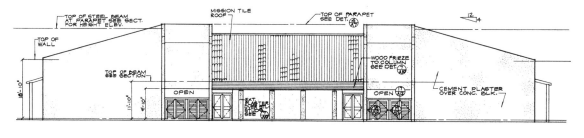

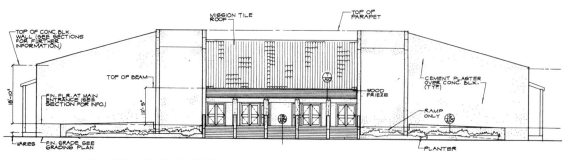

Figure 16.50 Final stage: Working drawing—Exterior elevations.

Figure 16.51 Front view of finished structure. (Photography: Kent Oppenheimer.)

Figure 16.52 Rear view of finished structure.

- Proper representation of beams, headers, girders, and the like
- Representation for roof sheathing
- Proper representation of ridges, valleys, and their size
- Beam with post over or under
- Structural post within a wall
- Representation of two framing systems on a single drawing
- Correct call-outs for steel members and wood members
- Proper designations for height of framing members
- Proper representation of double members

Figure 16.53   Front of theater. (William Boggs Aerial Photography. Reprinted with permission.)

Figure 16.54   Front of theater showing ramp for disabled persons. (William Boggs Aerial Photography. Reprinted with permission.)

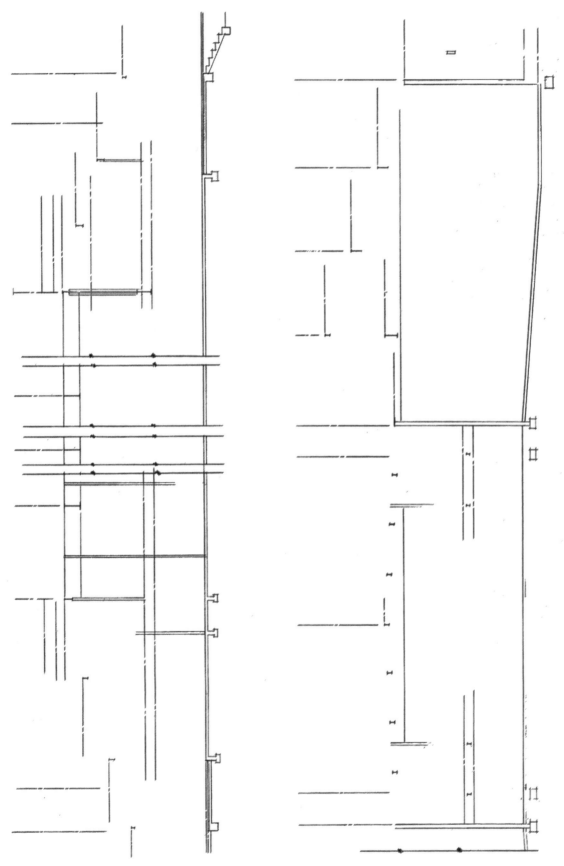

Figure 16.55   Stage I: Design development—Building sections.

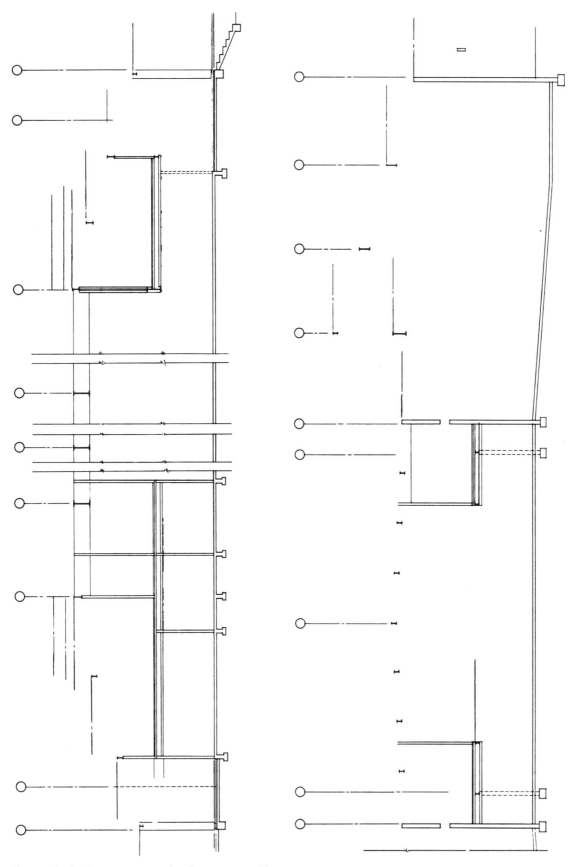

Figure 16.56 Stage II: Design development—Building sections.

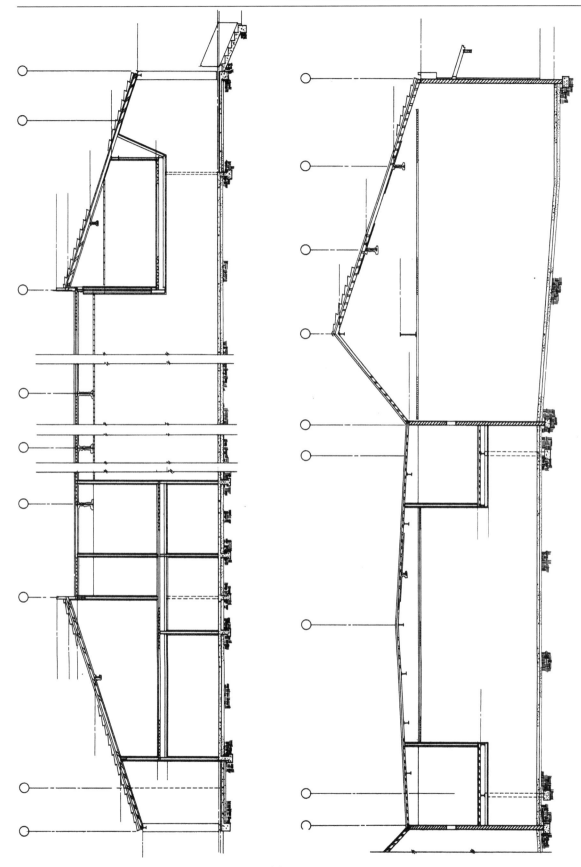

Figure 16.57 Stage III: Design development—Building sections.

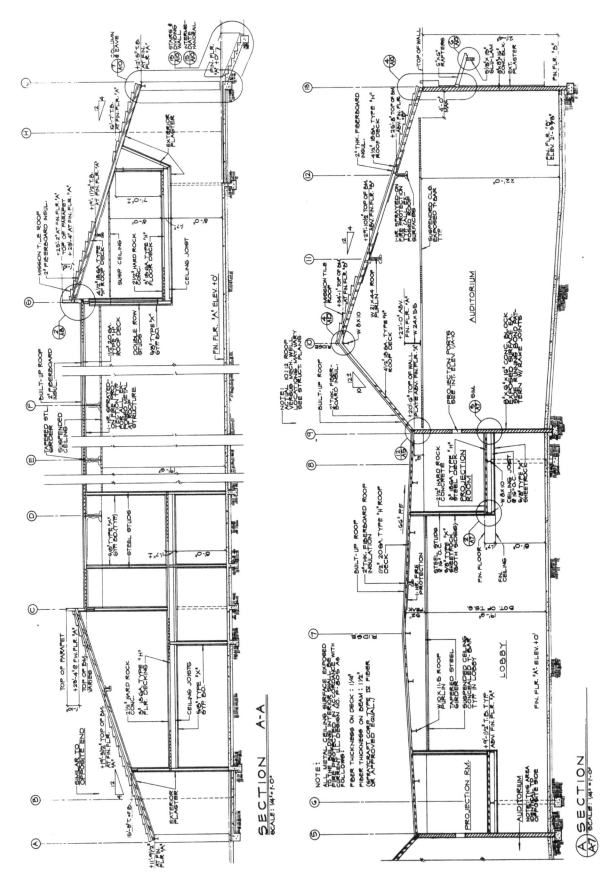

Figure 16.58 Final stage: Working drawing—Building sections.

Figure 16.59 Finished roof. (William Boggs Aerial Photography. Reprinted with permission.)

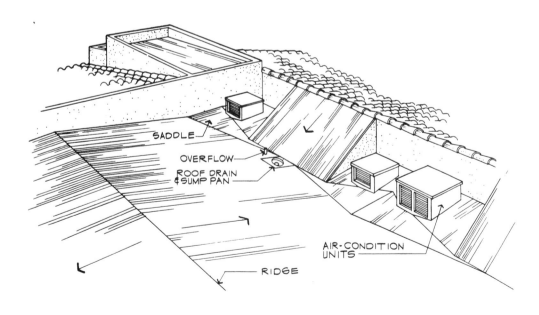

Figure 16.60 Corner of central portion of roof.

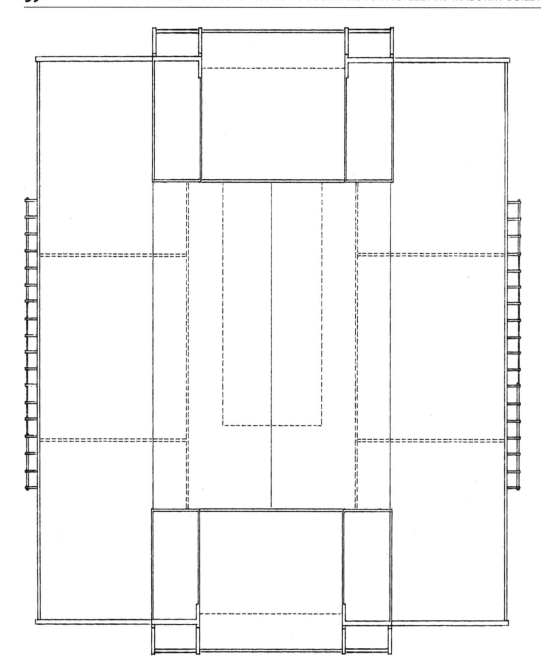

Figure 16.61 Stage I: Design development—Roof plan.

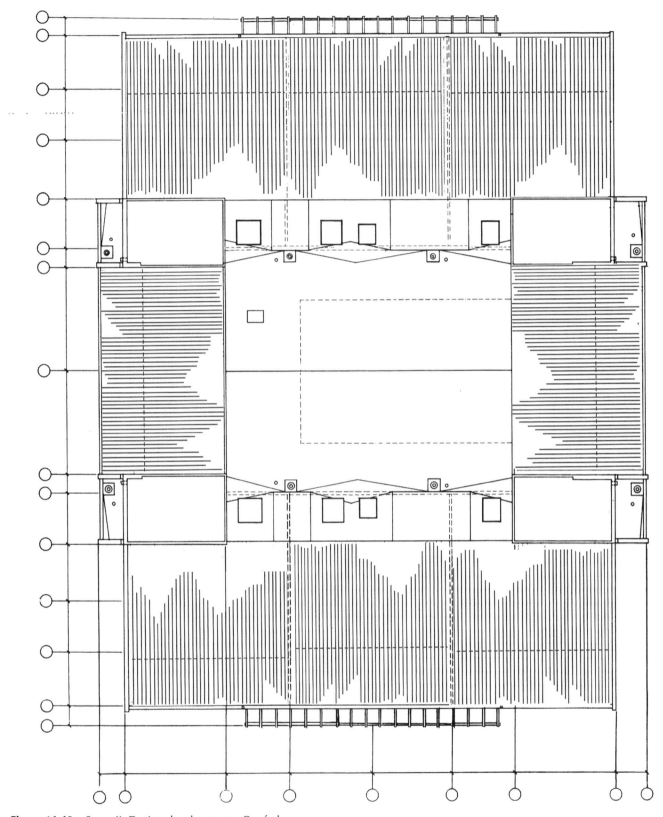

Figure 16.62 Stage II: Design development—Roof plan.

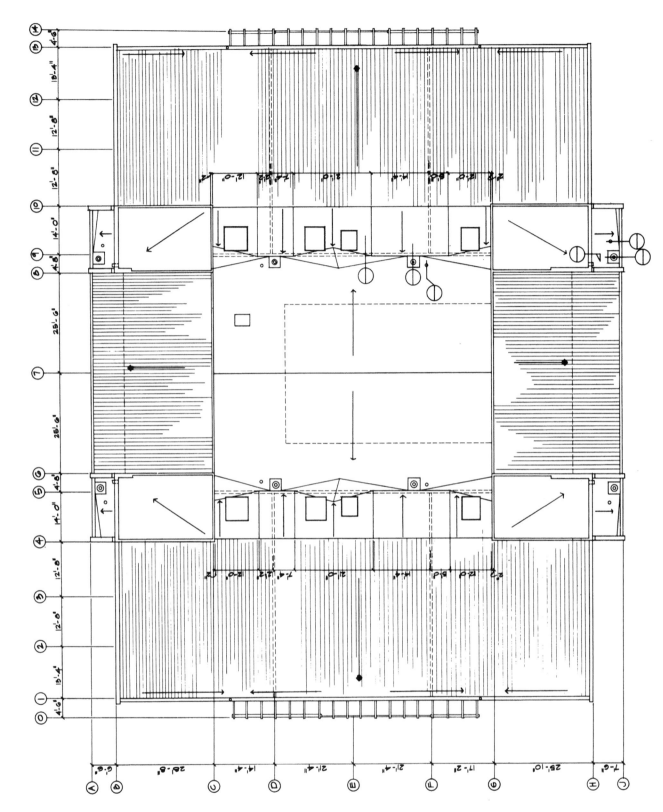

Figure 16.63 Stage III: Working drawings—Downloaded image of roof plan.

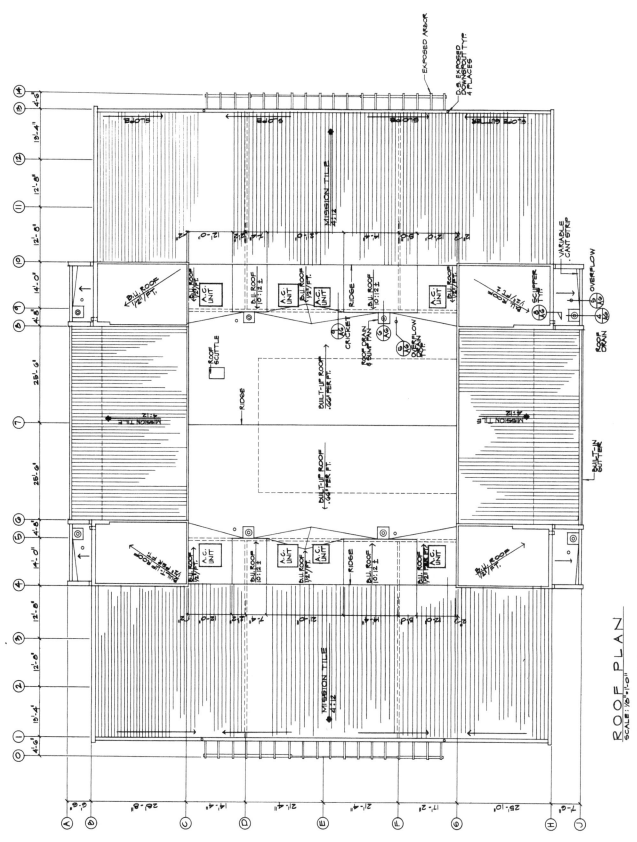

ROOF PLAN
SCALE: 1/8"=1'-0"

Figure 16.64 Final stage: Roof plan.

593

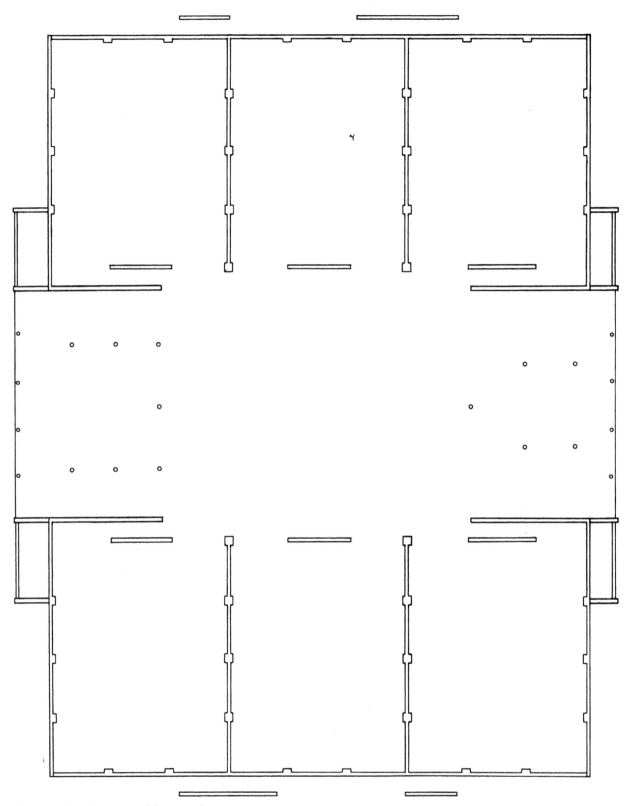

Figure 16.65   Stage I: Roof framing plan.

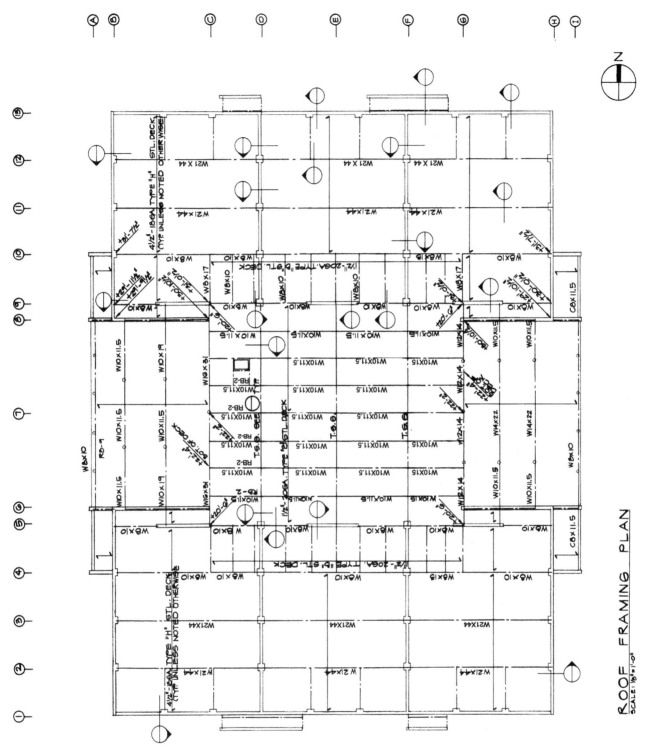

Figure 16.66 Roof framing plan: Transfer of information from structural engineer

595

chapter

17

MADISON STEEL BUILDING

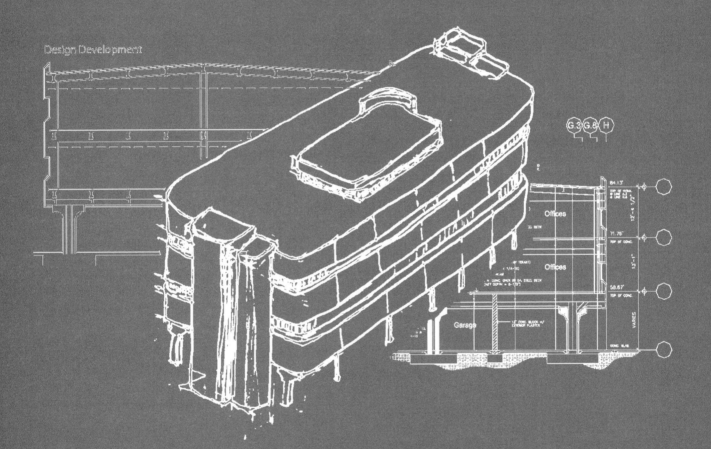

■ INTRODUCTION

A reminder: Before you read this chapter, review the Revit section of Chapter 3. In much the same manner as we approached Chapter 16, this chapter has been abbreviated and should be used as a reference only. Here we trace the evolution of only one elevation, until the final stage where all four exterior elevations will be shown.

The first set of drawings was designed freehand, and then the Revit model (BIM) was started. We will call this phase the design development stage; it was initially done in ortho (plan and elevations; see Figures 17.1, 17.2, 17.3, 17.4, and 17.5) and then section framing was done. The generic modeling feature was not used. The Revit drafting program is very specific in its choices of materials, sizes, and dimensions for location. This front-loads the task, so that what used to take five or six stages to produce the construction documents now takes one to three stages.

■ THE MADISON OFFICE BUILDING

The client, an insurance company, requested an architectural firm to design an office building, titled the Madison Office Building, with a gross floor area of approximately 33,000 square feet and adequate ground-level parking. The ground-level parking requirement dictated that the office areas be located on the second- and third-floor levels. The remaining ground-floor level would be used primarily for public access control and meeting existing building code requirements.

The long, rectangular-shaped property had one automotive access point on the west side. This dictated the parking design, as well as the locations of the supporting structural members, including the steel columns and shear wall.

After members of our firm walked around the site and studied the adjacent commercial developments, the initial schematic studies were begun. As stated, ingress and egress for automobile traffic was available only on the west end of the site. It was determined that parking stalls were best located adjacent to the south property line and with opposing parking stalls accessible from two traffic lanes.

Design Development Punch List

The following notes, reminders, and concerns went into a wide-ranging punch list, developed while walking around the site with the client:

- Egress and ingress only available from west.
- Best location on site for parking is on the west side.

- Two traffic lanes at 90° to the street and 90° parking.
- Explore desirable areas for lobbies, exit stairs, utilities, and trash areas.
- Establish locations of supporting columns to accommodate parking.
- Determine the best disabled parking location.
- Location of stairs, restrooms, and potential location for mechanical ducts.
- Add third floor and verify required square footage.
- Verify exact position of steel columns in relationship to third floor.
- Roof access for stairs.
- Explore different types of windows and finishes.
- Consult a structural engineer early for
  - Circular openings and lower height for offices
  - Shear walls to relieve starkness of solid walls
  - Continue curvilinear walls
  - Shape and mass of the sculptured concrete elements around columns
  - Potential location for chase (for air-conditioning ducts)
- Explore exterior surface materials for curvilinear walls.

Design Development

When the conceptual design is finished, the BIM drawing is started. See Figure 17.6. A Revit 3-D drawing is precise, with the proper materials and dimensions used. Eighty % of the knowledge needed to create a Revit image is about architecture (drawing knowledge is only 20% of the equation). Remember, Revit is parametric, so as you download the plan, elevation, section, or framing drawing and make changes, the changes are immediately reflected in the other drawings. However, changes in the first-floor plan will not appear in the second or third floor unless you program Revit to do so. For example, in this building the columns on the first floor must align with those on the second and third floors.

When you are using BIM and Revit, there are certain things you must know at various stages of the evolution of the structure:

- What additional requirements does the client have for the structure?
- How does the client imagine the facility might be divided?
- Building code and planning department requirements.
- All about cars
  - Turning radius
  - Parking requirements
  - Ratios of standard cars to compact, and number of disabled/handicapped spots
  - Are there to be dedicated greenspaces?
  - Impact of building/parking on major streets and freeway
  - Noise from freeway

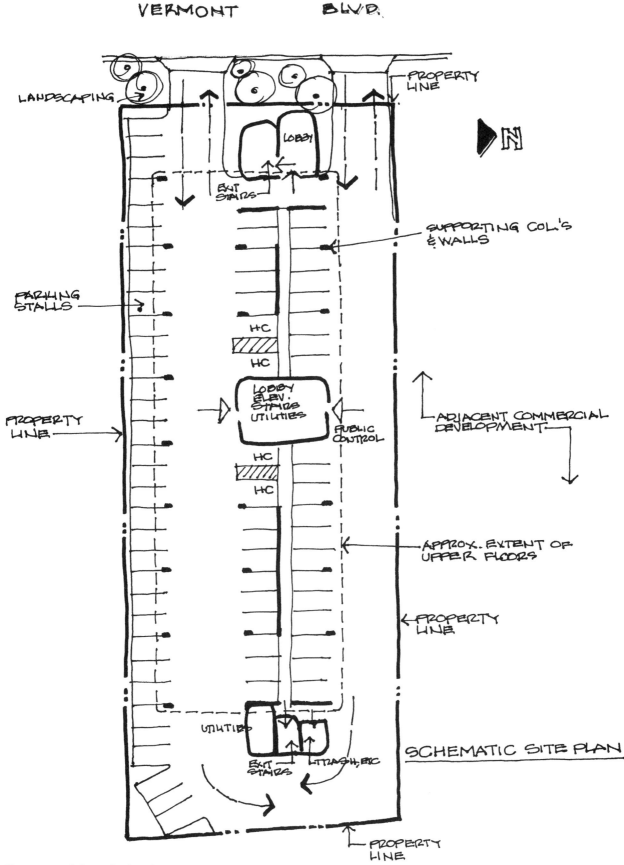

Figure 17.1 Schematic site plan.

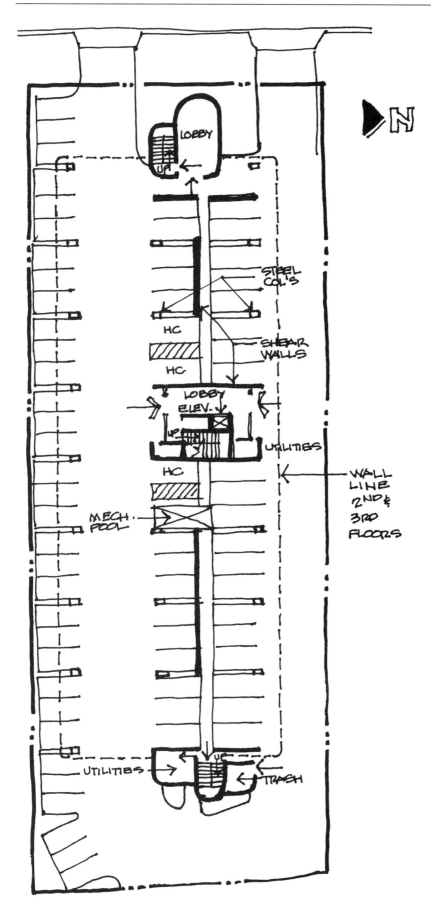

Figure 17.2   Preliminary ground-floor plan.

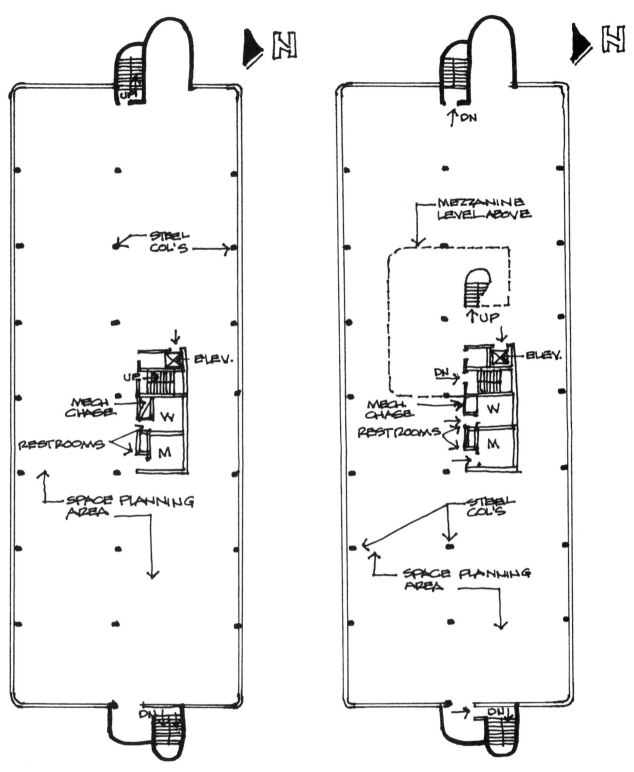

Figure 17.3 Preliminary second-floor plan.

Figure 17.4 Preliminary third-floor plan.

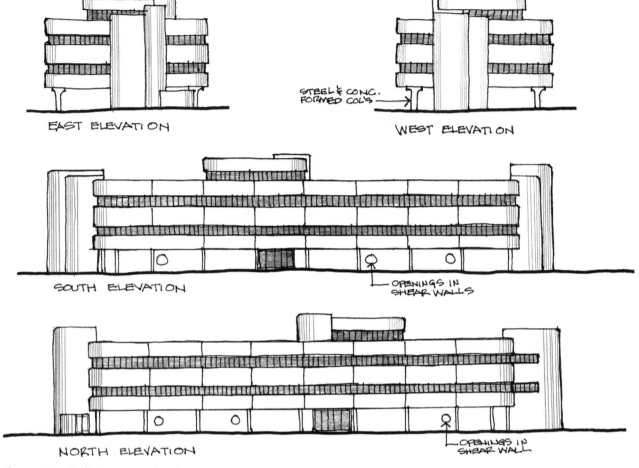

EAST ELEVATION

WEST ELEVATION

STEEL & CONC.
FORMED COL'S →

SOUTH ELEVATION

→ OPENINGS IN
SHEAR WALLS

NORTH ELEVATION

OPENINGS IN
SHEAR WALL

Figure 17.5 Preliminary exterior elevations.

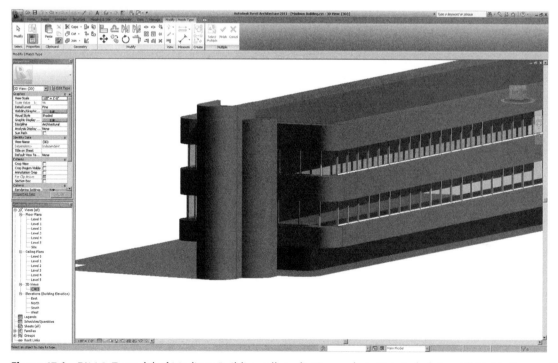

Figure 17.6 BIM 3-D model of Madison Building (all steel). (Screenshots © Autodesk Inc. All Rights Reserved.)

- Materials of construction. Because the building is above ground, can we use Styrofoam as an outside finish (built like a surfboard)?
- The more you know about architecture, the better the BIM.

Note: To follow the drawing evolution in this chapter, you must use Revit 2011 or later.

■ FLOOR-PLAN DESIGN DEVELOPMENT PHASE

Floor-Plan Design Development

- Precisely lay out parking, stairs, traffic lanes, disabled parking stalls, and spaces for public access.
- Parking to establish rhythm for structural columns.
- Base above on a basic matrix system called the "**dimensional reference system**" established for all structural members (Figure 17.7).
- Basic template for all other drawings established (Figure 17.8).
- Dimensional reference system use on template and basic matrix (Figure 17.9). For example, this tells viewers that there is an identifying wall located north of column "D."
- Elliptical wall incorporated into stairwell walls and lobby locations (Figures 17.9 and 17.10).

- "Ice bank" system (also referred to as *off-peak cooling system*) will be on matrix lines D and E as determined by architect and mechanical engineer. See Figure 17.10.

Floor-Plan Punch List

- Be sure to double-check matrix system with template.
- Keep walls and columns aligned.
- Designate materials properly.
- Follow national and international standards.
- Check dimensions for wheelchair users.
- Check elevator size for number of users.
- Show pavers and patterns used.
- Verify all dimensions with template.

Ground-Floor Punch List

- Verify reference symbols for building sections. This will make the section appear on the Revit project browser.
- Finalize the initial structure design with the structural engineer. This must be done early to reveal architectural/structural conflicts (e.g., columns and minimum parking dimensions; see Figures 17.11 and 17.12).
- Double-check:
  - Placement of notes
  - Disabled designations

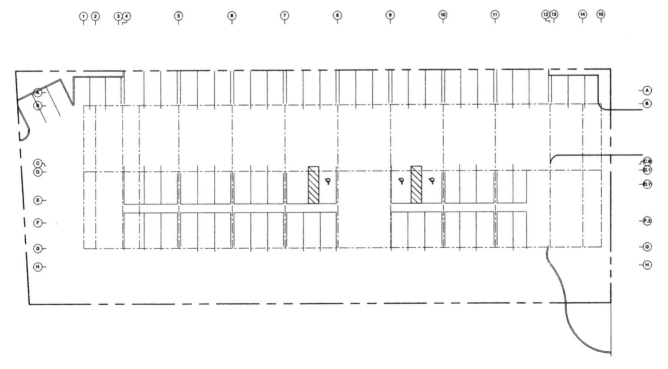

Figure 17.7 Stage I: Matrix system (design development).

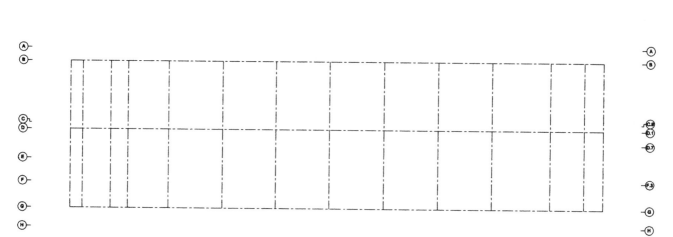

Figure 17.8 Stage II: Matrix template (design development).

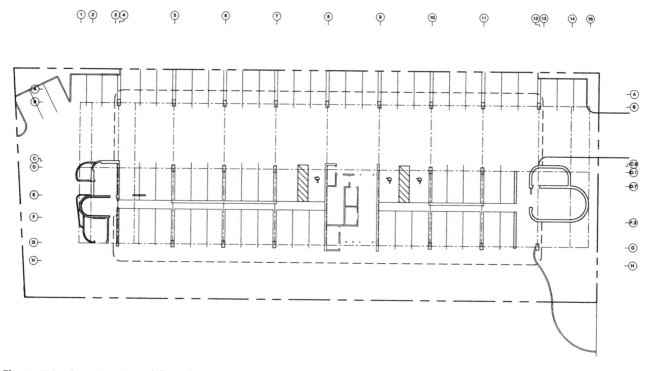

Figure 17.9 Stage III: Ground-floor design development.

- Steel and concrete column reference detail symbols
- Material call-outs
- Size and material for automobile wheel stops
- Trash area and access gate size
- Steel arbor members for open trellis above trash compound
- Method of showing floor pavers

- Shading of walls for clarity
- North arrow placement

Second-Floor Design Development Phase

- Update matrix (see Figure 17.13 and Figure 17.14) to show location of all columns and include external wall thickness.

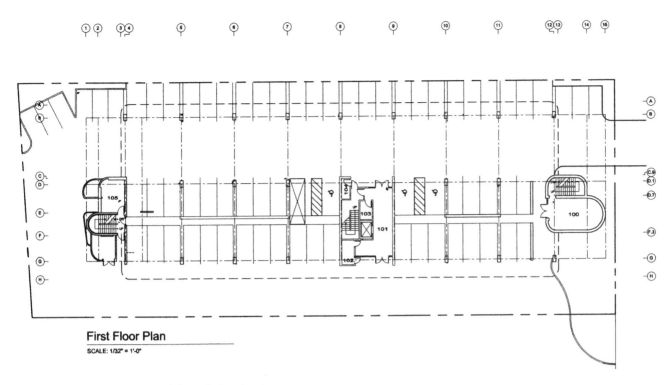

First Floor Plan
SCALE: 1/32" = 1'-0"

Figure 17.10 Stage IV: Ground-floor design development.

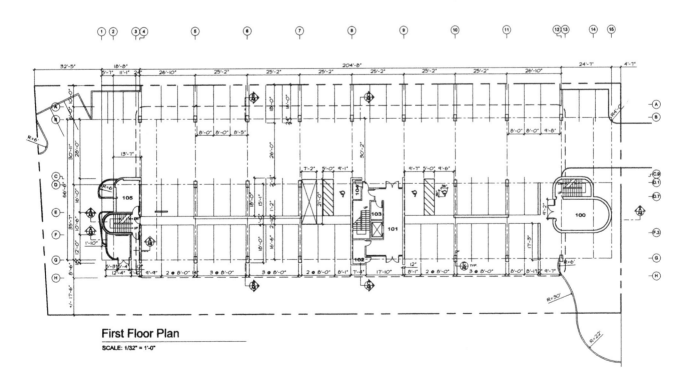

First Floor Plan
SCALE: 1/32" = 1'-0"

Figure 17.11 Stage I: Ground-floor working drawings.

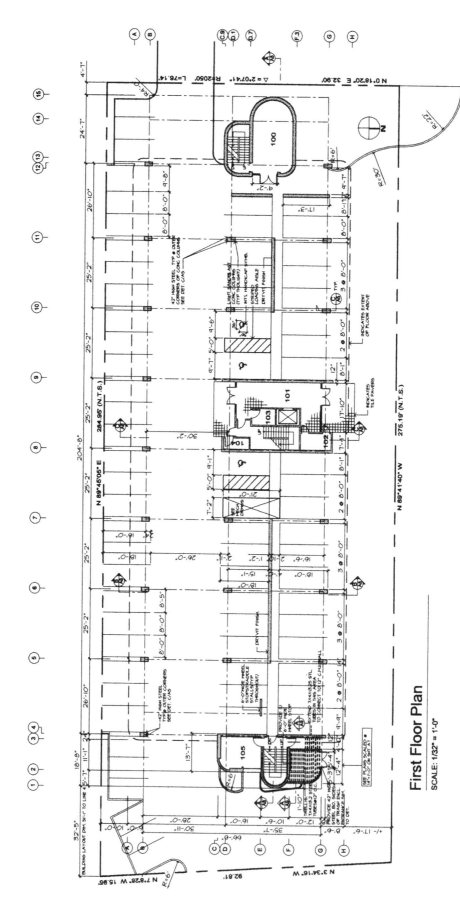

First Floor Plan

SCALE: 1/32" = 1'-0"

Figure 17.12 Stage II: Ground-floor working drawings.

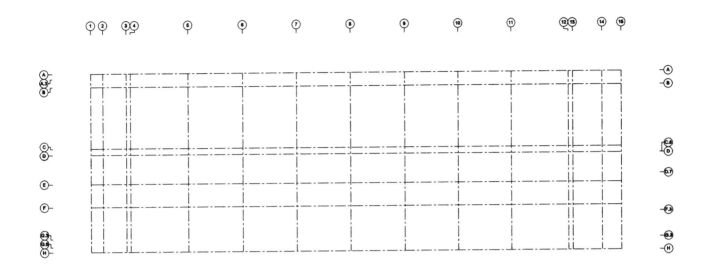

Figure 17.13   Stage I: Second-floor plan design development.

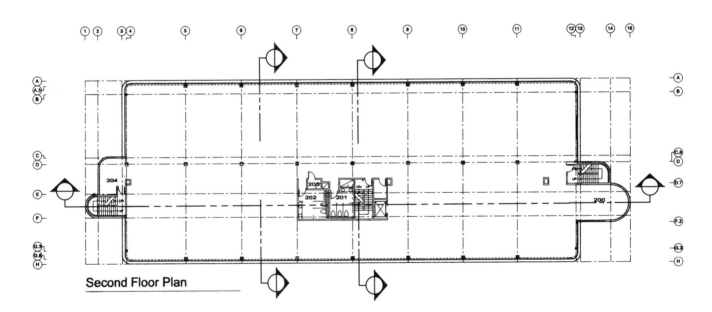

Second Floor Plan

Figure 17.14   Stage II: Second-floor plan design development.

- Locate columns.
- Locate stairshaft walls, restrooms, and stairs.
- Select areas for major and minor building sections.
- Toggle back and forth and watch if the sections will evolve; they are now on the Revit project browser!
- Evolve the sections and plan at the same time. These are the two most important drawings in a set of working drawings; from these two drawings, all the other drawings can be developed.

Second-Floor Punch List

- Locate structure cross-section and reference symbol for structural sections.
- Reference other potential details (such as steel columns and steel beam connections); locate reference bubble at the center supporting columns.
- Insert references for exterior windows and wall assembly.

- Detail symbols for steel columns at the exterior walls.
- Locate fire extinguisher cabinet and mechanical chase locations.

Second-Floor Working Drawings

Having finished the design development phase, proceed to the working drawings (Figures 17.15–17.17).

Third-Floor Design Development Phase

- A new template (based on the second-floor template) now includes interior wall D-5 and F-1 (Figure 17.18).
- Use the second floor as a punch list. Much of what happens on the second floor is repeated on the third floor (Figure 17.19).
- Add a stair, for access to mezzanine level accessible from the third floor.
- Check and draw men's and women's restrooms, elevators, vertical mechanical shafts required for air-conditioning ducts, and room numbering (for the schedule) into the Revit 3-D model (Figure 17.20).

Third-Floor Punch List

- Lay out and verify all dimensions and where they should be positioned; verify with second-floor plan.
- Detail symbols.
- Location of recessed fire extinguisher cabinets.
- Location of exit signs.
- Review larger-scaled drawing of the stairwell, lobby areas, and restrooms. These notes tell viewers where to find enlarged drawings.

Third-Floor Working Drawings

Having finished the third-floor development phase, proceed to the working drawings (Figures 17.21–17.23).

Exterior Elevation Design Development Phase

- Broken lines represent floor (yes, they can be changed). The marked elevations must be as close to finish heights as possible. This is the datum of elevations. For this example, only one of the four will be done, except on the final working drawing, where all four exterior elevations will be shown. See Figure 17.24.
- Draw ground level with a solid line. See Figure 17.25.
- Use solid lines for construction lines.
- Mass the structure, starting with the horizontal masses.
- Avoid square edges at the roof floor and wall masses; this will give the building a sculptural appearance. See Figure 17.26.
- Encase the steel columns in concrete.
- Utilize the fluid nature of concrete.

- Concrete-over-steel columns provide larger visual proportional mass.
- Begin to define the roof and window areas.
- Add window mullions, glass entry door, glazing in the lobby area, and the access gate at the trash area. See Figure 17.27.
- Consult structural engineer regarding round openings in shear walls.
- Shade glazed area and use vertical lines to simulate curved wall edges, corners of roof sections, and floor masses. See Figure 17.28.

Elevation (Working Drawings) Punch List

- One phase only. In Revit, the design development stage (as in almost all drawings) almost completes the stages of the exterior elevations and, as was said before, the more you know about architecture, the better you can complete the design development.
- All four elevations are shown here (see Figure 17.29).
- Notes are added, including the sizes of the stud members for the open trellis work at the trash area.
- Openings in masonry shear wall are shown and noted with size of the opening.
- All necessary details for the set are referenced (detail bubbles).
- Exterior wall and spandrel materials are designated.

Third-Floor Framing Plan Design Development Phase

- Recall the matrix layout shown in Figure 17.19 to locate columns and beams. Be sure to use the correct matrix for each floor.
- Deal with matrices 4 through 12 and A/3 through G/8 (Figure 17.30).
- Draw the exterior walls and include stairwells.
- If you can borrow the image from Figure 17.19, it will be a time saver and will add to the uniformity and continuity between floors.
- Send the drawing to the consulting structural engineer for use in developing engineering calculations and intermediate beam location.
- Put in required beams for stairwell and lobby.
- Show beams around elevator.
- Because this is an all-structural-steel building, intermediate structural members that span between north/south members receive corrugated steel decking with a hard-rock concrete topping. See Figure 17.31.

Third-Floor Framing Plan (Working Drawings) Punch List

- Draw in dimensions according to the structural engineer's work.

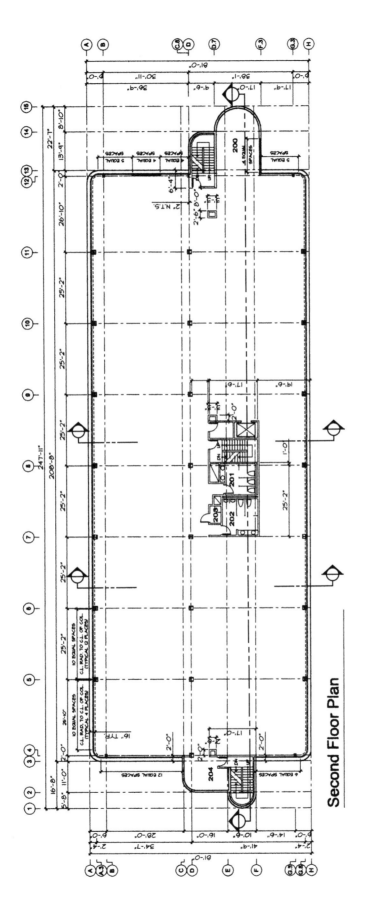

Figure 17.15 Stage I: Second-floor plan working drawings.

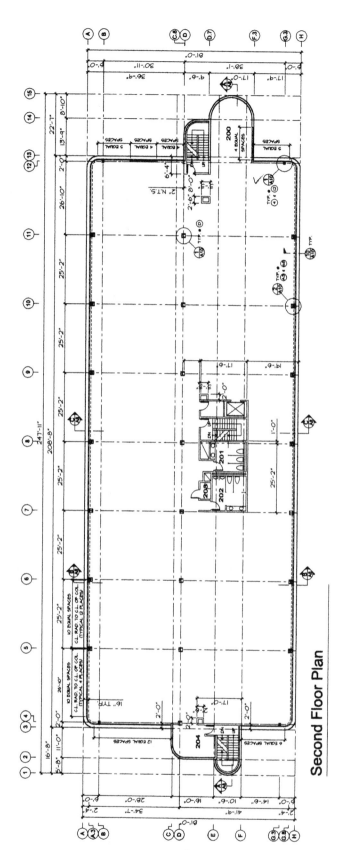

Second Floor Plan

Figure 17.16 Stage II: Second-floor plan working drawings.

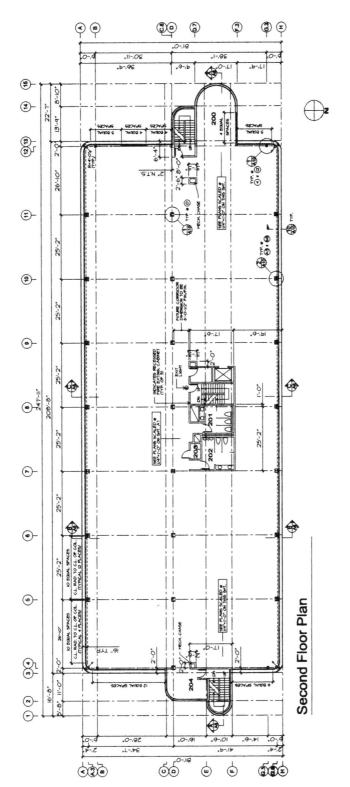

Figure 17.17 Stage III: Second-floor plan working drawings.

611

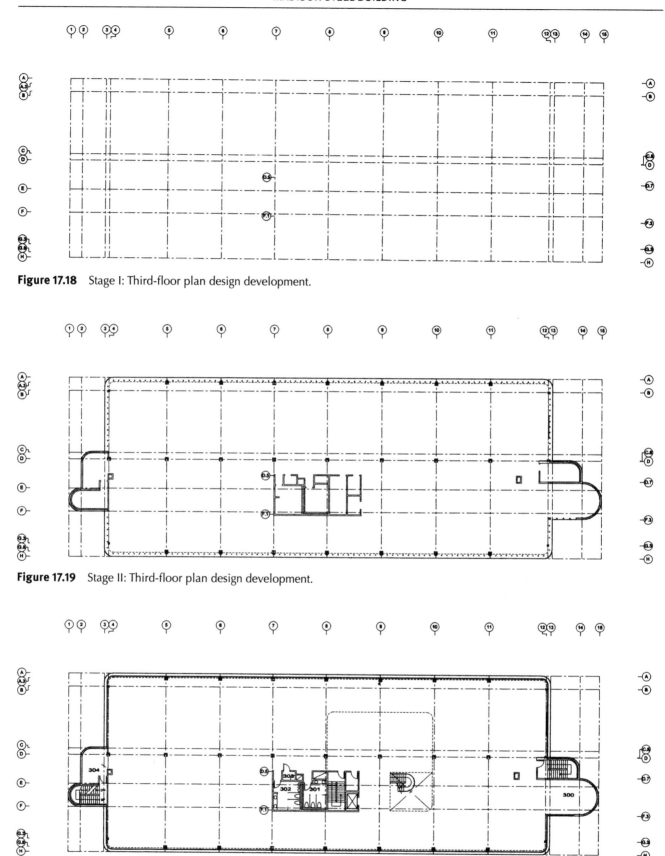

Figure 17.18 Stage I: Third-floor plan design development.

Figure 17.19 Stage II: Third-floor plan design development.

Third Floor Plan

Figure 17.20 Stage III: Third-floor plan design development.

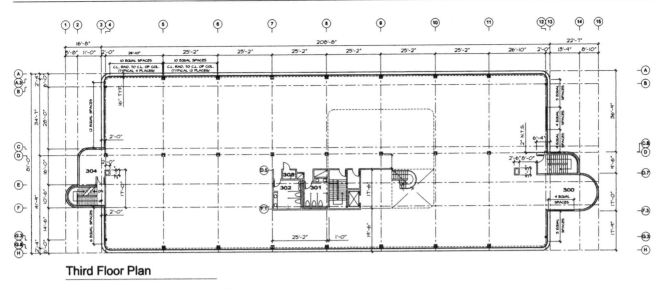

Figure 17.21 Stage I: Third-floor plan working drawings.

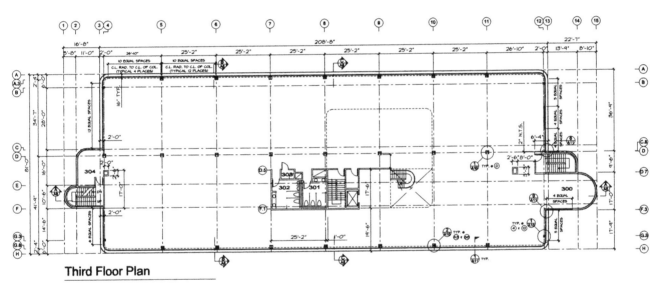

Figure 17.22 Stage II: Third-floor plan working drawings.

- Check dimension values; this is critical to maintaining structural simplicity.
- Indicate notes, referencing, and detail reference in the elevation area.
- Include various structure detail reference bubbles (Figure 17.32).
- Include beam and steel column sizes (Figure 17.33).
- Add general notes defining thickness of concrete floor filling and the gauge of corrugated steel decking substance between matrix lines 6 and 7, as well as stairwell areas.
- Include legend (Figure 17.34).

B.F. and M.F. are defined as lateral forces, such as earthquake or strong wind, and are resized by mo-ment connections, found at steel beam and column connections.

> T.S.—top of steel
> B.F.—braced frame
> M.F.—moment frame

- M.F. show on north/south walls.
- B.F. is noted on materials 4 and 12.

Building Section Design Development Phase

- Check with plans to see the correct direction of sections.
- Establish height and align column and beam locations.

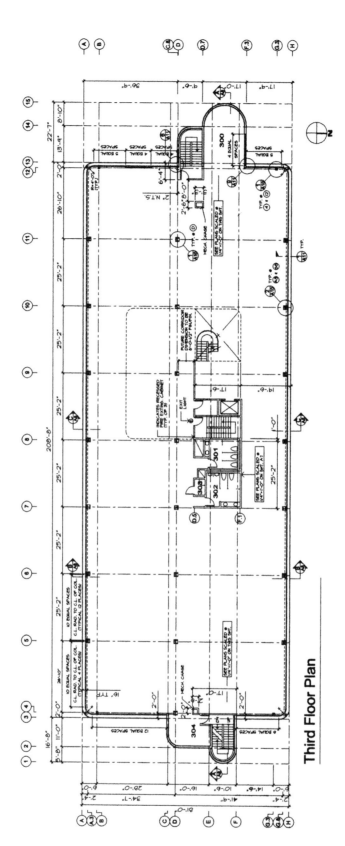

Figure 17.23 Stage III: Third-floor plan working drawings.

Figure 17.24 Stage I: Exterior elevation design development.

Figure 17.25 Stage II: Exterior elevation design development.

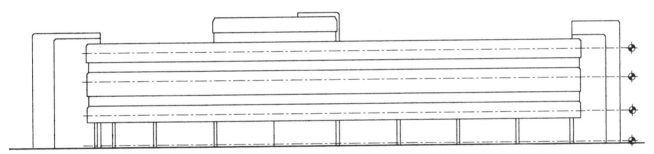

Figure 17.26 Stage III: Exterior elevation design development.

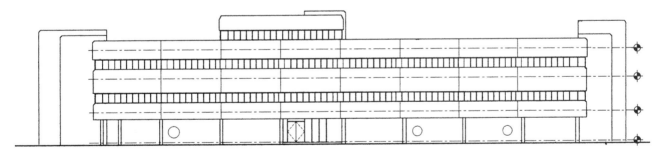

Figure 17.27 Stage IV: Exterior elevation design development.

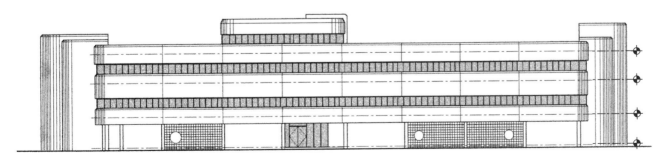

Figure 17.28 Stage V: Exterior elevation design development.

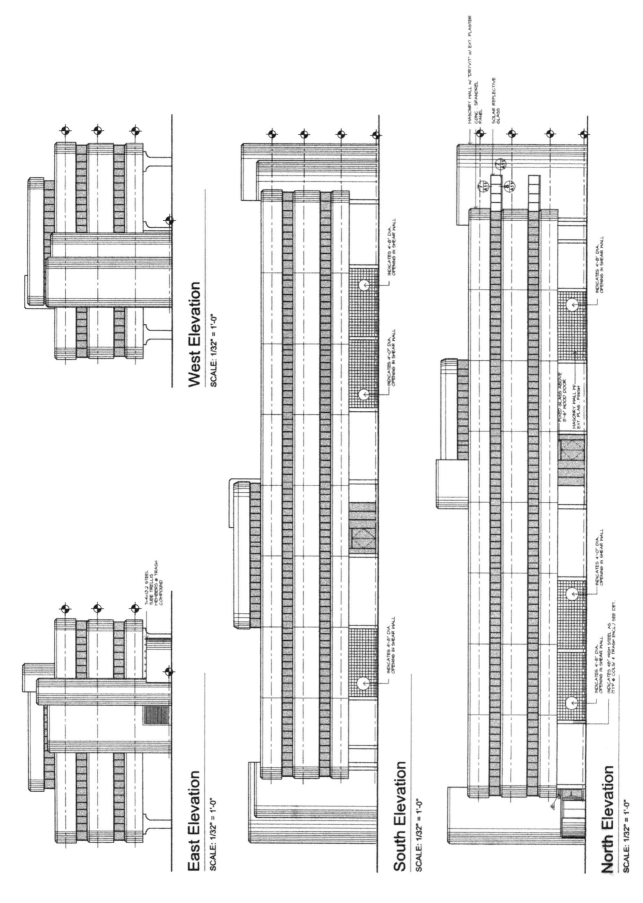

East Elevation

SCALE: 1/32" = 1'-0"

West Elevation

SCALE: 1/32" = 1'-0"

South Elevation

SCALE: 1/32" = 1'-0"

North Elevation

SCALE: 1/32" = 1'-0"

Figure 17.29 Final stage: Exterior elevations working drawings.

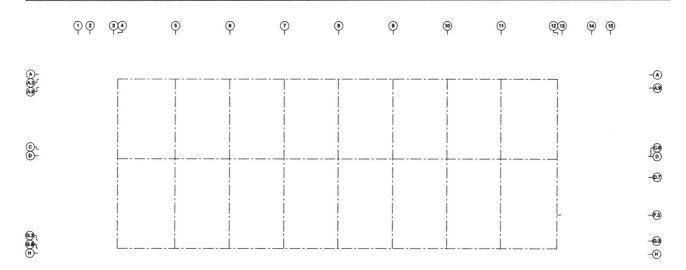

Third Floor Framing Plan

Figure 17.30 Stage I: Third-floor framing plan design development.

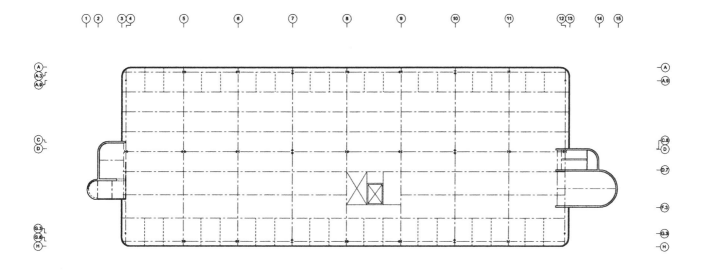

Third Floor Framing Plan

Figure 17.31 Stage II: Third-floor framing plan design development.

- Establish matrix for this drawing.
- Use broken lines for horizontal floor and ceiling levels and column and beam locations.
- Double-check with structural engineer to determine necessary clearances and heights required to facilitate various structural members. See Figures 17.35 and 17.36.
- Under the direction of the structural engineer, draw steel supporting members for roof and second- and third-floor framing members.

- Draw a broken line for finished floor just above the steel floor members. This allows space for decking material and concrete topping. See Figure 17.37.
- The details (shown later in this chapter) must be done at this stage.
- These details are incorporated into the building section.
- The building section taken on matrix line 6 is now profiled.

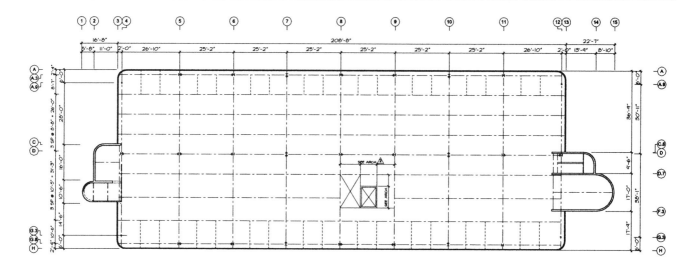

Third Floor Framing Plan

Figure 17.32 Stage I: Third-floor framing plan working drawings.

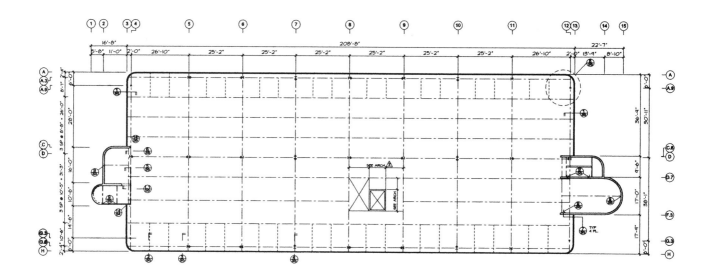

Third Floor Framing Plan

Figure 17.33 Stage II: Third-floor framing plan working drawings.

• Window bands around the building have been recessed; this helps define the fenestration.

• The exterior has been covered in Styrofoam; a detail of the exterior is shown later in Figure 17.41.

Building Section Working Drawings Punch List

• For clarity and ease of reading, the matrix and numbers and letters were kept large; so were the bubbles containing references. Note how this was solved by offsetting the matrix lines below the call-outs (Figure 17.38).

• The top of the concrete floor level elevation and the top of the roof insulation are located adjacent to the parapet wall.

• Spaces have been designated for offices and garage use (Figure 17.39).

• A broken line designates the extent of the suspended ceiling.

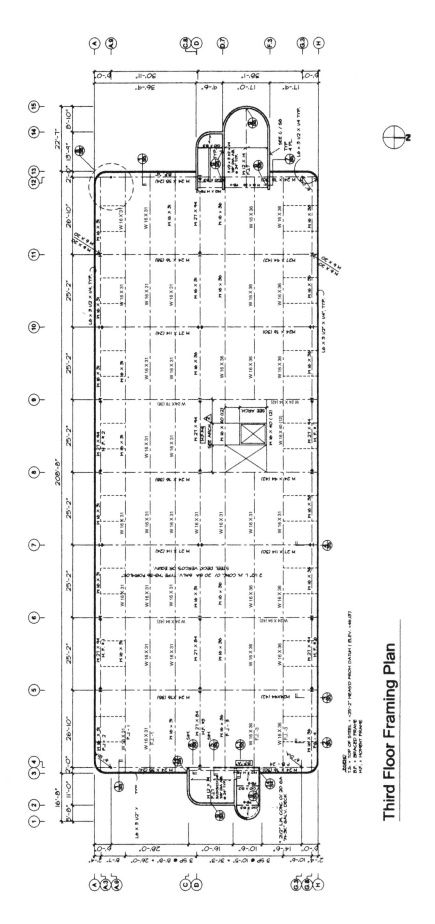

Third Floor Framing Plan

Figure 17.34 Stage VI: Third-floor framing plan working drawings.

619

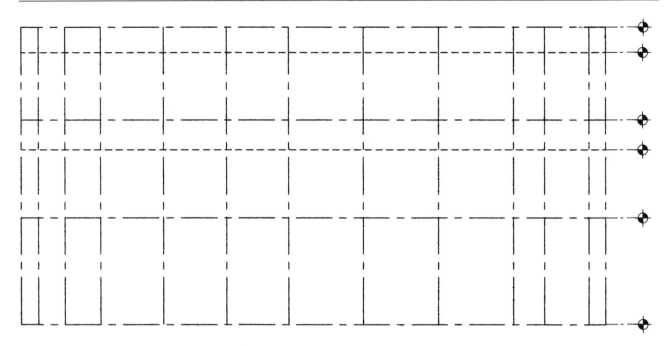

Figure 17.35 Stage I: Building section B-B design development.

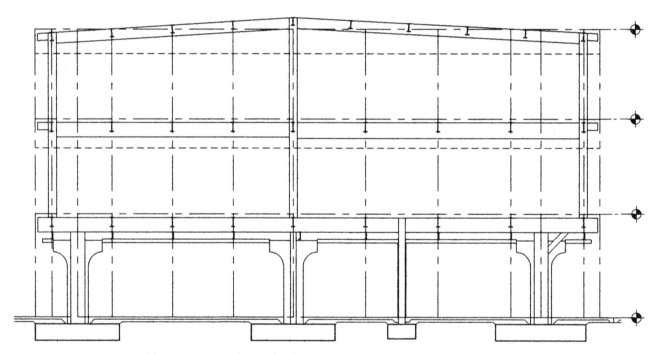

Figure 17.36 Stage II: Building section B-B design development.

- The steel roof and supporting floor beams are defined. The size and weight of these members will be designated on the framing plans.
- The depth of the concrete floor topping and the gauge of the corrugated steel decking have been noted.

- Detail references for items requiring a one-hour fire-rated assembly have been noted for the supporting columns and the ground-floor ceiling.
- The concrete-block shear wall is cross-hatched for definition, and the height of this wall is shown.

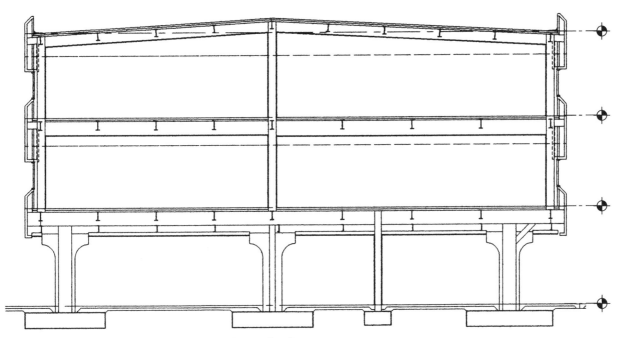

Figure 17.37 Stage III: Building section B-B design development.

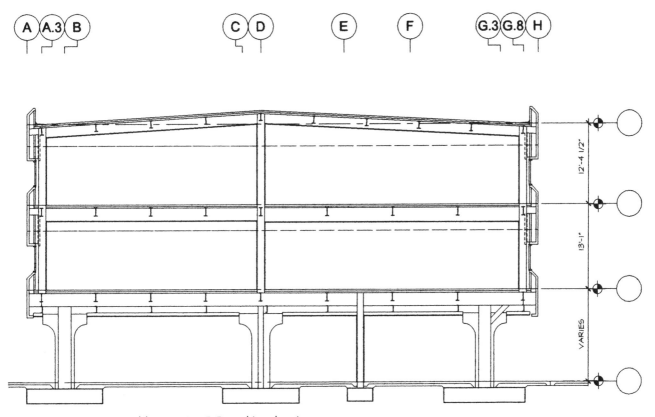

Figure 17.38 Stage I: Building section B-B working drawings.

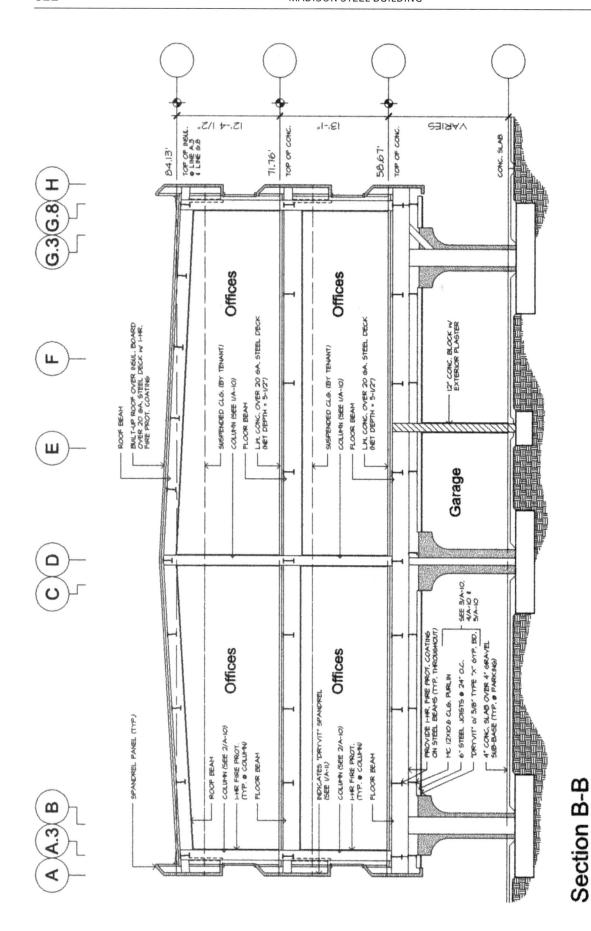

Section B-B

Figure 17.39 Stage II: Building section B-B working drawings.

- The types of roofing and insulation materials are indicated, and the steel decking and fire protection requirements are noted.
- The size of the steel ceiling joists and their spacing are noted for the ground-floor ceiling.
- The thickness of the ground-floor concrete and its substrate is noted.
- The concrete shape encasing the steel columns at the ground-floor level has been shaded for clarity.
- The graphic designation for earth has been indicated for reasons of clarity.

- To understand how the beams and columns were attached, see Figures 17.40 and 17.41.
- Slope of parking is noted to drain water from this open area; the dimension is listed as "varies" (see Figure 17.42).
- For the concrete-covered columns, see Figure 17.42.
- Finally, the designation of the building section title has been lettered in, along with the scale of the drawing.

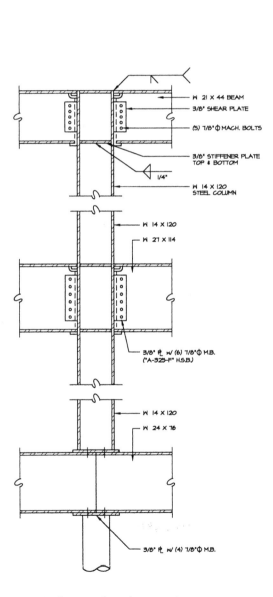

Figure 17.40 Structural steel connections.

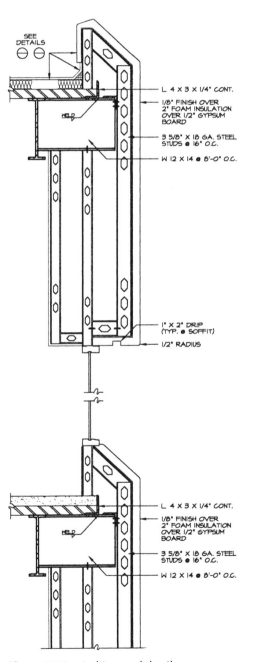

Figure 17.41 Architectural details.

Details Necessary Early in Design Development

Figure 17.41 shows a structural detail for a series of steel connections involving steel roof beams and steel floor beams and engineered assembly members for them.

Once the structural engineer and the architect have finalized the member sizes for the structural skeleton, the architectural detailing may commence. These details—and there will be many—will be predicated on the sizes and connections of the steel framing members. An example of an architectural detail that has been designed and detailed for the assembly of the exterior wall members and their attachment to the steel frame is shown in Figure 17.41. These members incorporate the use of light steel framing members, gypsum board, and 2″ foam insulation board.

As was previously mentioned, the steel columns at the ground-floor level are to be encased in concrete and formed to give a desirable architectural appearance. The concrete encasement will also provide the necessary fire protection around the steel columns. This column detail is shown in Figure 17.42 and is applicable along matrix lines 4 through 12 and along lines B, D, and G. Note that the roof drainage pipe lines are concealed within the composite column, with their termination occurring 3″

above the parking floor level. As mentioned earlier, the vertical dimension line titled "Varies" is so designated because of the change of floor levels in the parking floor for the purpose of providing proper water drainage.

Figure 17.43 is a pictorial view of the composite steel and concrete column found along the aforementioned intersecting matrix lines. Note that a portion of the spread concrete footing has been removed for the purpose of showing the concrete floor slab connection. Generally, the concrete spread footings are found to be symmetrical.

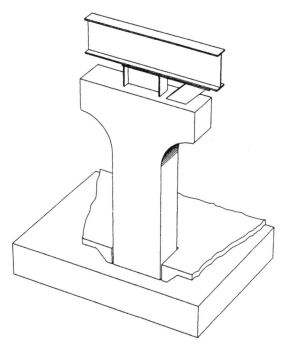

Figure 17.43 Pictorial view of composite steel and concrete column.

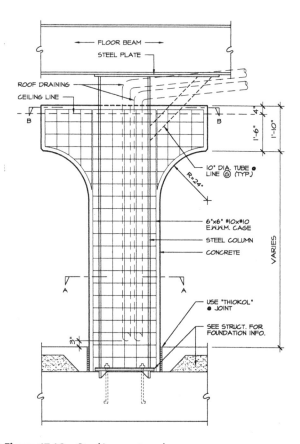

Figure 17.42 Steel/concrete column.

Figure 17.44 Formwork for concrete spread footing at steel columns.

Figure 17.44 is a photograph showing the formwork set in preparation of pouring concrete for a spread footing, similar to that in Figure 17.42.

The use of structural steel members and light steel framing members for the construction of various types of buildings is highly desirable and reduces the use of wood as a structural entity.

■ SUMMARY

The order in which the drawings in this chapter appear was based on how they would be submitted to the building department, not the order in which they were drawn. Many required drawings were not shown; our intention was only to show the reader the process of producing drawings in Revit.

Each office operates differently. For example, in 2011 many offices were using a combination of Revit and AutoCAD based on the education and skills of their employees. For some time to come, details will probably be done on AutoCAD, because of the wealth of details on file in that program and the detail templates that have begun to appear in architectural offices in the past ten or so years.

We hope our message has gotten across: To fully use Revit, you must have a wealth of architectural knowledge, be able to think three-dimensionally, and be able to create multiple drawings at one time. A floor plan cannot be done in this 3-D world without the elevations, building sections, roof plan, framing plans, and certain details.

18

TENANT IMPROVEMENTS

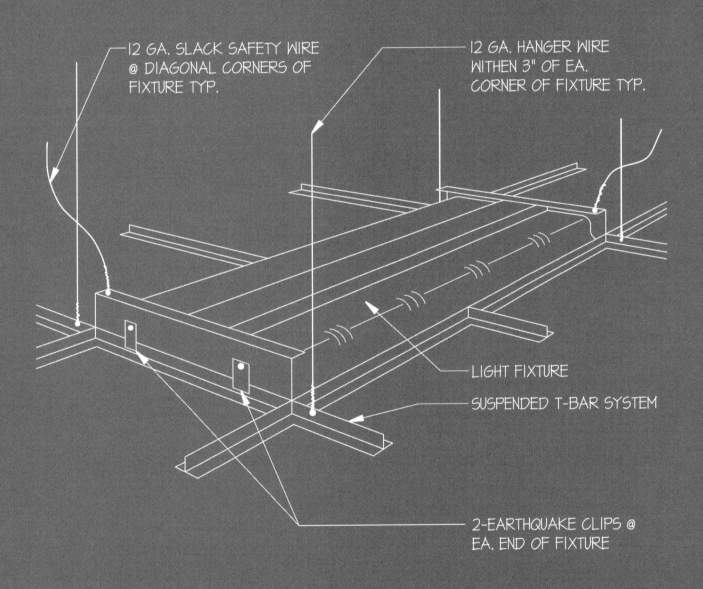

12 GA. SLACK SAFETY WIRE @ DIAGONAL CORNERS OF FIXTURE TYP.

12 GA. HANGER WIRE WITHEN 3" OF EA. CORNER OF FIXTURE TYP.

LIGHT FIXTURE

SUSPENDED T-BAR SYSTEM

2-EARTHQUAKE CLIPS @ EA. END OF FIXTURE

■ TENANT IMPROVEMENT INTRODUCTION

Unlike other building described in this book, **tenant improvement** (also called **space planning**) is not about how to draw construction documents for a structure; rather, it is about the planning of nonresidential buildings. The building is directly built and the interior space is leased, rented, or sold for occupancy as a condominium (that is, shared space owned by a group). This will be demonstrated by the use of two existing office buildings.

Building A, which has a large, undeveloped, open space with nonrequired travel and exit corridors yet to be constructed, will illustrate the necessary design procedures to satisfy corridor and exit travel to an existing lobby and two stairwells. Construction assemblies for exit corridor walls will be detailed to satisfy specific building code requirements.

Three tenant suite spaces will be illustrated as an example of the partial development for a large floor area. Exit requirements for these three spaces will be discussed, with an example of a tenant separation-wall assembly that will be constructed between the various suites. Building A and its illustrations provide an example of open space planning for tenant suites, required exiting, and wall construction requirements. Working drawings for the tenant suites are not illustrated.

Building B will demonstrate the entire procedure for developing an undeveloped floor area into a suite for a specific tenant. This procedure will include drawings for the assigned floor area reflecting the tenant's requirements for the function of its business. At the end of this chapter, these drawings will be finalized into working drawings, with explanations of the various stages necessary to complete the drawings for construction and bidding purposes.

The **improvement** of a space, in most cases, is defined as the construction of the interior walls, doors, windows, ceilings, movable partitions, and specialty items that may be required for the function of the tenant's daily tasks. Improvements also include cabinetry, hardware, plumbing fixtures, finished floors, carpeting, and finished painting. Such improvement usually includes supplementary heating, ventilating, and air-conditioning systems, sized and installed for a designated space or area.

Internal planning deals with the task areas enclosed within the walls by various construction assemblies. The tenant—that is, the user—will provide the necessary design criteria for the designer to plan the various task areas. Design criteria may include such information as room use, room sizes, and toilet facilities; electrical, telephone, and equipment locations; special lighting requirements; and desired floor, wall, and ceiling finishes.

In most cases, the designer or drafter will plan within a designated area of an existing structure, although they may plan an entire floor area. Generally, designated areas are found in multitenant buildings and vary in square footage. It should be noted that tenant improvement may also entail redeveloping an existing constructed space. This situation requires that the room dimensions, lighting fixtures, structural components, equipment locations, and existing electrical and mechanical locations be verified before the preliminary design process begins.

■ EXISTING BUILDINGS

It is imperative that the first step in drafting a set of construction documents for a tenant improvement project be production of a drawing called **as built**. This drawing features the dimensions of the structure as it stands; hence the name "as built."

Often the original set of construction documents is available to the tenant improvement drafter, but the parameters of the inside of the structure must be re-measured. The reason is that a structure is rarely built to the precise size shown on the original drawing.

The as-built drawing becomes the datum or base for the entire set of construction documents from this point on, whether drawn by hand or on the computer. If the original set of documents is available, the as-built drawing is derived by making the necessary corrections on the existing drawings: moving walls, column locations, and so forth.

■ EXISTING FLOOR LEVEL— BUILDING A

With a given floor plan for an existing three-story undeveloped structure, we can explore potential floor areas for tenant use. Figure 18.1 illustrates the second-floor level of this building. As illustrated, the existing stairwells, men's and women's toilet facilities, elevator shaft, telephone room, and janitor's room have been constructed according to building code requirements. The first prerequisite is to establish a corridor that satisfies all exit requirements of the governing building and fire codes.

Exit Corridors

Figure 18.2 shows a pictorial with a corridor that satisfies code relative to width and location. The walls and ceiling construction of the corridor must meet the requirements for a one-hour fire-rated assembly. A detailed construction section of this assembly is depicted in Figure 18.3. Metal studs are illustrated; however, wood studs may be used if they meet the governing fire code requirements. It should be noted that most building codes require exit doors into the corridor to have a 20-minute fire-rated

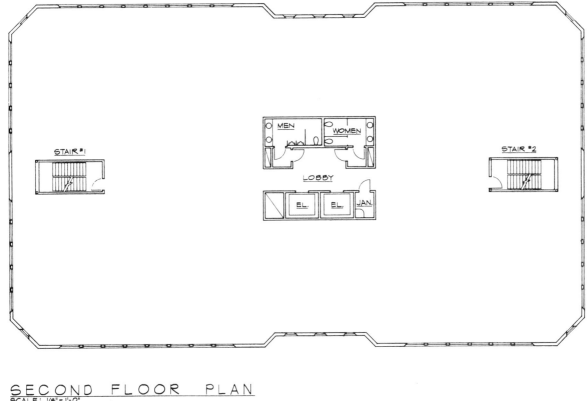

SECOND FLOOR PLAN
SCALE: 1/8"= 1'-0"

Figure 18.1 Existing undeveloped floor.

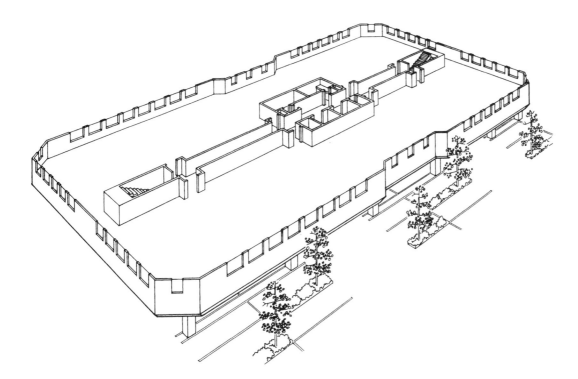

Figure 18.2 Pictorial view of corridor.

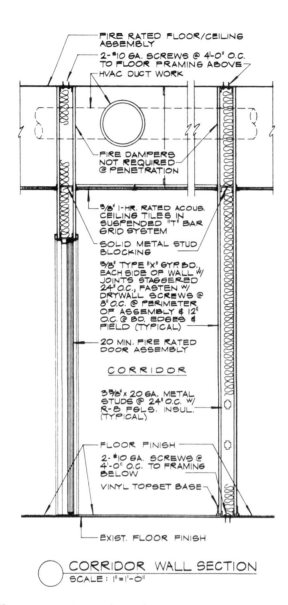

FIRE RATED FLOOR/CEILING ASSEMBLY

2-#10 GA. SCREWS @ 4'-0" O.C. TO FLOOR FRAMING ABOVE

HVAC DUCT WORK

FIRE DAMPERS NOT REQUIRED @ PENETRATION

5/8" 1-HR. RATED ACOUS. CEILING TILES IN SUSPENDED "T" BAR GRID SYSTEM

SOLID METAL STUD BLOCKING

5/8" TYPE "X" GYP.BD. EACH SIDE OF WALL W/ JOINTS STAGGERED 24" O.C., FASTEN W/ DRYWALL SCREWS @ 8" O.C. @ PERIMETER OF ASSEMBLY & 12" O.C. @ BD. EDGES & FIELD (TYPICAL)

20 MIN. FIRE RATED DOOR ASSEMBLY

CORRIDOR

3 5/8" x 20 GA. METAL STUDS @ 24" O.C. W/ R-8 FGLS. INSUL. (TYPICAL)

FLOOR FINISH

2-#10 GA. SCREWS @ 4'-0" O.C. TO FRAMING BELOW

VINYL TOPSET BASE

EXIST. FLOOR FINISH

CORRIDOR WALL SECTION
SCALE: 1" = 1'-0"

Figure 18.3   Fire-rated corridor construction.

assembly, as designated in the corridor section in Figure 18.3. As described earlier, it is essential that you verify the dimensions by re-measuring the structure. Even if you have the original drawings of the structure, you must verify its size, window and door locations, stairs, elevator location, and even the corridor locations. You will always discover that changes in size and location of existing walls occurred during construction.

Tenant Areas

After an exit corridor that will be used by various tenants on this floor is established, designated areas or floor areas required to satisfy the particular users' space require-

ments may now be formulated. In dealing with a tenant's area requirements, the designer must adhere to building code criteria relative to the number of exits required for a specific area.

An example of required exiting is depicted in Figure 18.4, which shows that Suite A has a floor area of 3,200 square feet. Because of this suite's area and occupant load, the building code requires two exit doors to the corridor. According to the code, these two doors must be separated by a distance of one-half the length of the diagonal dimension of this area. See Figure 18.4. Figure 18.5 illustrates this condition pictorially. This code requirement will be a primary factor in the internal planning of this suite. As shown in Figure 18.6, the floor area of Suite C is less than 1,600 square feet; thus, according to the building code, this suite requires only one exit to the common corridor. It should be noted that additional toilet facilities may be required by the building code authorities, predicated on the number of employees occupying the particular suites. This would be a planning factor for the tenant improvement design.

Tenant Separation Wall

When there are numerous tenants on a given floor level, local building department authorities and building codes may require a one-hour fire-rated wall assembly between each tenant area and the next. Figure 18.7 illustrates a non-load-bearing, one-hour fire-rated wall assembly incorporating metal studs and gypsum board. A **non-load-bearing wall** is one that does not support ceiling or floor weight from above or any other weight factors distributed to this wall. Wall insulation is shown as a means to decrease noise transmission between the various tenants.

The construction techniques for a wall assembly used within a specific suite may vary. Figure 18.8 illustrates an example of a wall partition section used in offices for tenant improvements. Note that this wall partition extends to the roof framing in order to reduce the sound transmission between the various rooms and halls, and maintains a secure office condition.

Building A has been used to illustrate the basic procedures and requirements for potential suite developments within a large, existing, undeveloped floor space. Building B, in contrast, will illustrate the procedures implemented in an architect's office for a tenant improvement design and the completion of working drawings.

■ DEVELOPMENT OF WORKING DRAWINGS—BUILDING B

As discussed earlier, internal suite planning is developed from the tenant's criteria that satisfy the needs for its business function.

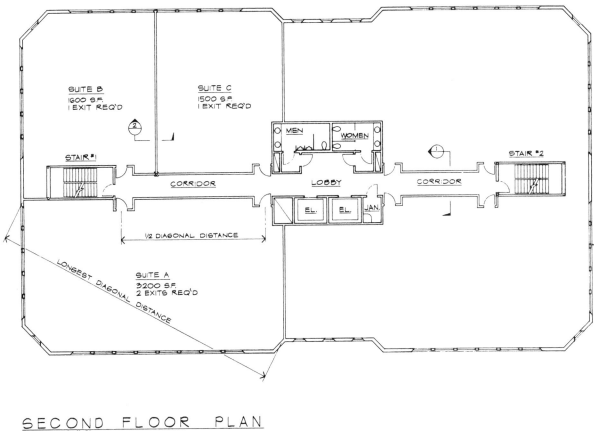

SECOND FLOOR PLAN
SCALE: 1/8" = 1'-0"

Figure 18.4 Suites A, B, and C.

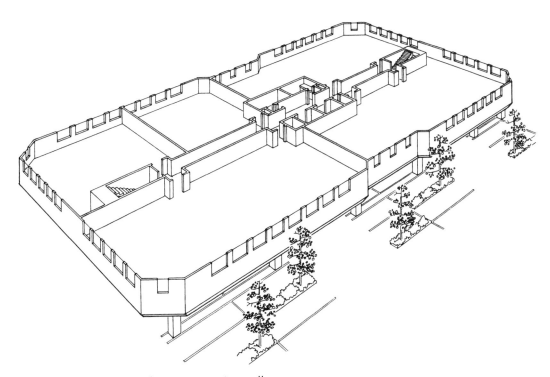

Figure 18.5 Pictorial view of tenant separation walls.

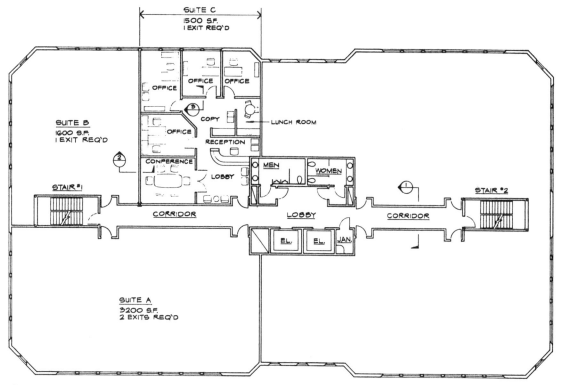

Figure 18.6 Floor plan—Suite C.

In planning a given undeveloped space on the second floor of an existing office building, the designer will visit the space and verify the structural components, such as columns and beam heights. The designer and staff will take measurements to verify existing inside area dimensions, column locations, window sizes, and the spacing of window mullions. In some cases, mechanical, electrical, and/or plumbing components, such as exhaust ducts, roof drainage pipes, and water lines for domestic and mechanical use, may be located in this undeveloped space. If so, they should be plotted on the initial plan layout.

Figure 18.9 shows the undeveloped floor plan of an existing second-floor level of a two-story office building. The process of making working drawings for the improvement of Suite 201 starts with the tenant requirements and verification of the existing space and conditions. Note the existing steel columns, stairs, mechanical shafts, roof drain lines, windows, and window mullion locations.

Planning of Task Areas

The tenant for this designated space deals with graphic communications and has provided the designer with a list of the various rooms needed, their preferred sizes,

their use(s), and their relationships to each other. This communication between client and architect becomes the program for the project.

Schematic Study

The rooms specified by the tenant include a reception area, three offices, a conference room, a large studio accommodating numerous drawing boards, a small studio for airbrush media, a copy room, and a storage room. The tenant also desired a coffee area with cabinets and sink and a service area for cleanup of art implements. The location of walls and rough plumbing for the restrooms already exist; therefore, these rooms require only finishing.

Given the preceding information dealing with specific task areas, schematic studies can now begin in order to show tentative room locations and their relationship to one another. Figure 18.10 illustrates a conceptual floor plan in schematic form, which will be used in discussing the various areas and their locations with the tenant.

Following this procedure, a preliminary floor plan will be developed to scale, including suggested locations for the required furniture. This drawing may be done in freehand, as is shown in Figure 18.11.

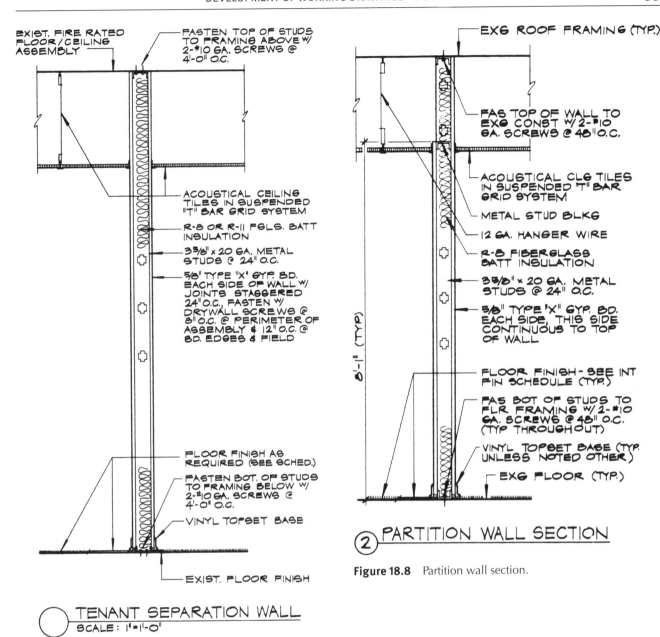

Figure 18.7   Tenant separation wall.

Figure 18.8   Partition wall section.

Upon the tenant's acceptance of the preliminary plan, a plan is created to show the required room locations and sizes (see Figure 18.12). Note that the division walls between the offices, adjacent to the exterior wall with windows and mullions, are located to intersect at the window mullions and concrete column locations. This eliminates the problem of a division wall butting into a glass area, which obviously would be undesirable.

The location of existing structural columns presents planning obstacles in relation to various spaces. It would be desirable to conceal a column within a division wall wherever possible. Note in Figure 18.12 that some of the existing steel pipe columns have been incorporated into various wall locations.

Interior Partition Wall Construction

Now that the locations of walls, doors, and windows have been established, details for the construction of these components will be designed as a part of the working drawings for this tenant improvement project.

For the sake of clarity, it is recommended that existing walls and new walls be delineated differently. For example, the existing walls can be drawn with two separate lines, and new walls with two lines pouchéd or hatched,

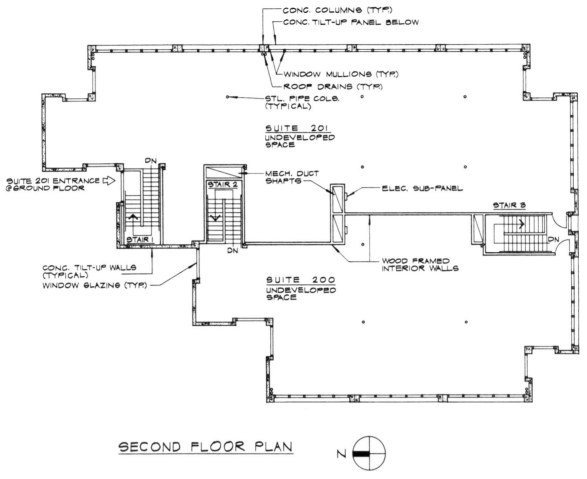

SECOND FLOOR PLAN

N

Figure 18.9 Undeveloped floor area plan—Building B.

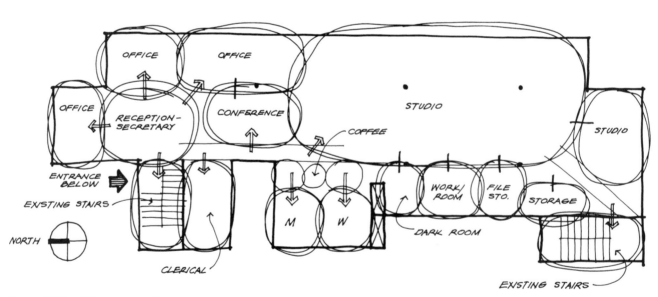

Figure 18.10 Schematic study.

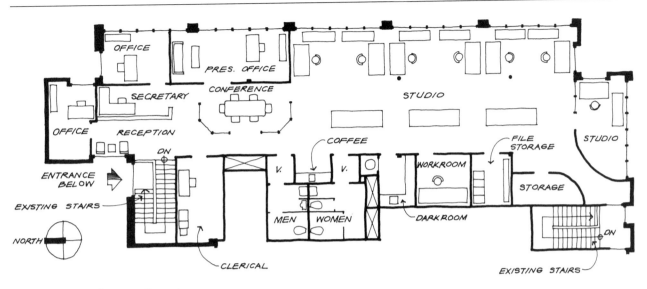

Figure 18.11 Preliminary floor plan.

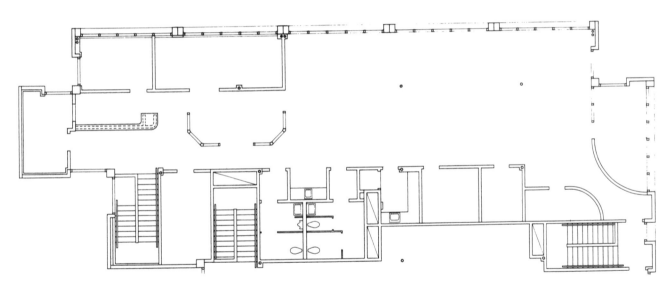

Figure 18.12 Wall development plan.

so that viewers can distinguish between them. Wall symbols can be used for reference. Note the wall shading and wall symbols in Figure 18.13. The main structural consideration in detailing non-bearing interior walls is to provide lateral stability. For this assembly, the wall will be braced with metal struts in compression from the top of the wall to the existing structural members above, as shown in Figure 18.14. A metal strut used for lateral wall support is shown in the photograph in Figure 18.15. This wall assembly uses steel studs for the wall structure; however, wood studs are also used for partition wall assemblies. A photograph of steel stud framing members is shown in Figure 18.16. The finish ceiling members will terminate at each wall parti-

tion, because the use of this wall assembly dictates that walls be constructed before the ceiling is finished. This method provides more design flexibility for the ceiling and lighting layout, which is illustrated and discussed later in regard to the design and layout of the ceiling plan. Figure 18.14 illustrates a suspended ceiling, which is assembled with 12-gauge hanger wires and metal runners supporting the finish ceiling material. In regions of the country where there is earthquake activity, the suspended ceiling areas are braced to minimize lateral movement. One method is shown in Figure 18.14, where 12-gauge wire at a 45° angle is assembled in a grid pattern, providing lateral stability for the suspended ceiling.

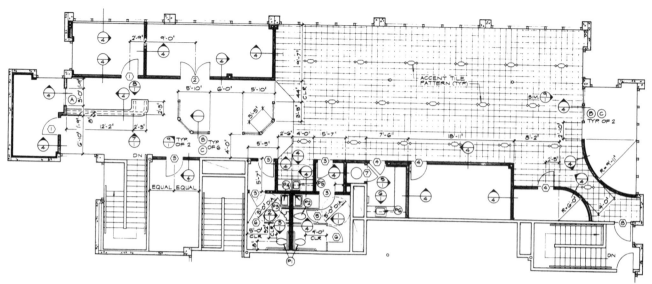

Figure 18.13 Wall shading and wall symbols.

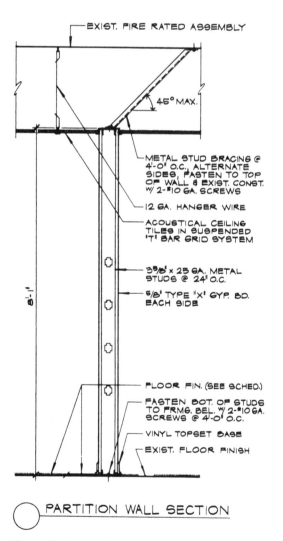

EXIST. FIRE RATED ASSEMBLY

45° MAX.

METAL STUD BRACING @ 4'-0" O.C., ALTERNATE SIDES, FASTEN TO TOP OF WALL & EXIST. CONST. W/ 2-#10 GA. SCREWS

12 GA. HANGER WIRE

ACOUSTICAL CEILING TILES IN SUSPENDED 'T' BAR GRID SYSTEM

3⅝' x 25 GA. METAL STUDS @ 24" O.C.

⅝' TYPE "X" GYP. BD. EACH SIDE

FLOOR FIN. (SEE SCHED.)

FASTEN BOT. OF STUDS TO FRMG. BEL. W/ 2-#10 GA. SCREWS @ 4'-0" O.C.

VINYL TOPSET BASE

EXIST. FLOOR FINISH

8'-1"

PARTITION WALL SECTION

Figure 18.14 Non-bearing partition wall.

Figure 18.15 Stabilizing strut. (Reprinted by permission from *The Professional Practice of Architectural Working Drawings*, 3d Ed., © 2003 by John Wiley & Sons, Inc.)

In cases where the ceiling is installed prior to the construction of the wall partitions, a similar method for stabilizing the wall, as shown in Figure 18.17, will be incorporated into the wall assembly. For the working drawings of this tenant improvement project, though, the wall section illustrated in Figure 18.14 will be used.

In tenant improvements projects, it often happens that the tenant or user will require additional soundproofing methods for the wall construction that separates specific areas. Figure 18.18 illustrates a separation wall terminating at the roof or floor system of an existing structure. This method helps to reduce the transmission of sound from one area to another through the ceiling and plenum areas. A **plenum** *area*, a space used primarily for the location of mechanical ducts and equipment, is

Figure 18.16 Wall framing—steel studs. (Reprinted by permission from *The Professional Practice of Architectural Working Drawings,* 3d Ed., © 2003 by John Wiley & Sons, Inc.)

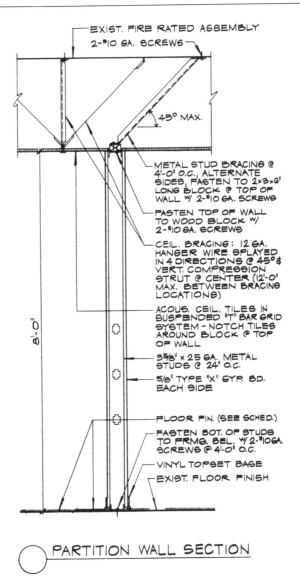

PARTITION WALL SECTION

Figure 18.17 Non-bearing partition wall.

usually located above the finished ceiling. Figure 18.19 is a photograph of a small mechanical unit in the plenum area, which will distribute warm and cold air to the various tenant areas. It was decided that the studio would not have a finished ceiling so that the mechanical ducting for the heating, cooling, and ventilation could be exposed (shown later in the ceiling plan). In this case, the wall partitions will be detailed to extend to, and be secured at, the roof rafters (illustrated in Figure 18.20). Note that where the walls and rafters are not adjacent to each other, 2 × 4 blocking at 4'-0" o.c. is installed to stabilize the wall laterally.

Often, as in this project, a mechanical equipment room is required to enclose a mechanical unit that will provide cooling, heating, and ventilating for a particular suite only. However, because of the noise produced by certain mechanical units, it is good practice to detail the walls of the mechanical room in such a way that the noise of the motors is minimized. A detail of one such

wall is shown in Figure 18.21. Note that sound-absorbing board is installed on the inside of the mechanical room.

Existing Wall Furring

In projects where there are existing unfinished concrete or masonry walls, it will be desirable to furr out these walls in order to provide for electrical and telephone service and to develop a finished wall surface. **Furring** is adding a new inner wall to the main wall behind. Figure 18.22 illustrates a wall section where 1½" metal furring studs have been attached to the existing unfinished concrete wall surface. In this detail, 5/8"-thick, type "X" gypsum wallboard has been selected for the interior wall finish.

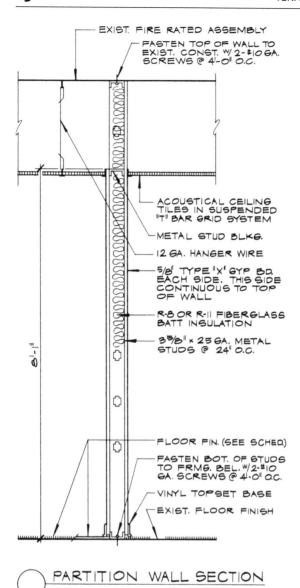

EXIST. FIRE RATED ASSEMBLY

FASTEN TOP OF WALL TO EXIST. CONST. W/ 2-#10 GA. SCREWS @ 4'-0" O.C.

ACOUSTICAL CEILING TILES IN SUSPENDED "T" BAR GRID SYSTEM

METAL STUD BLKG.

12 GA. HANGER WIRE

5/8" TYPE "X" GYP BD. EACH SIDE. THIS SIDE CONTINUOUS TO TOP OF WALL

R-8 OR R-11 FIBERGLASS BATT INSULATION

3 5/8" x 25 GA. METAL STUDS @ 24" O.C.

FLOOR FIN. (SEE SCHED.)

FASTEN BOT. OF STUDS TO FRMG. BEL. W/ 2-#10 GA. SCREWS @ 4'-0" O.C.

VINYL TOPSET BASE

EXIST. FLOOR FINISH

8'-1"

PARTITION WALL SECTION

Figure 18.18 Sound deterrent partition wall.

Figure 18.19 Mechanical unit. (Reprinted by permission from *The Professional Practice of Architectural Working Drawings,* 3d Ed., © 2003 by John Wiley & Sons, Inc.)

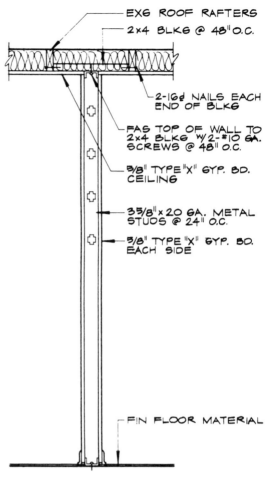

EX6 ROOF RAFTERS

2x4 BLKG @ 48" O.C.

2-16d NAILS EACH END OF BLKG

FAS TOP OF WALL TO 2x4 BLKG W/ 2-#10 GA. SCREWS @ 48" O.C.

5/8" TYPE "X" GYP. BD. CEILING

3 5/8" x 20 GA. METAL STUDS @ 24" O.C.

5/8" TYPE "X" GYP. BD. EACH SIDE

FIN FLOOR MATERIAL

Figure 18.20 Wall section.

Interior Glass Wall Partition

The tenant requested the use of glass wall partitioning to partially enclose the conference room area. The use of glass and metal frames for wall partitions still requires horizontal stability, as is necessary for other types of wall partitions. A section through this glass wall partition is shown in Figure 18.23. Note that all glazing will be tempered glass, as required by building codes and for the safety of the user.

Low Wall Partition

A low wall, called a **pony wall**, and a countertop are provided to separate the reception area from the secretarial area. This 42"-high wall will be attached to the adjacent wall and anchored at the base, as indicated in Figure 18.24. The stability of a low wall is most critical at the base; therefore, the method of assembly will be determined by the structural components of the existing structure.

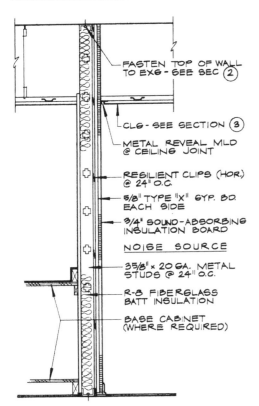

FASTEN TOP OF WALL TO EXG - SEE SEC ②

CLG - SEE SECTION ③

METAL REVEAL MLD @ CEILING JOINT

RESILIENT CLIPS (HOR.) @ 24" O.C.

5/8" TYPE "X" GYP. BD. EACH SIDE

3/4" SOUND-ABSORBING INSULATION BOARD

<u>NOISE SOURCE</u>

35/8" x 20 GA. METAL STUDS @ 24" O.C.

R-8 FIBERGLASS BATT INSULATION

BASE CABINET (WHERE REQUIRED)

Figure 18.21   Sound wall section.

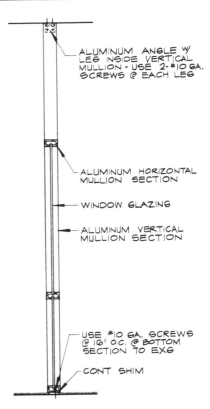

ALUMINUM ANGLE W/ LEG INSIDE VERTICAL MULLION - USE 2-#10 GA. SCREWS @ EACH LEG

ALUMINUM HORIZONTAL MULLION SECTION

WINDOW GLAZING

ALUMINUM VERTICAL MULLION SECTION

USE #10 GA. SCREWS @ 16" O.C. @ BOTTOM SECTION TO EXG

CONT SHIM

Figure 18.23   Glass wall partition.

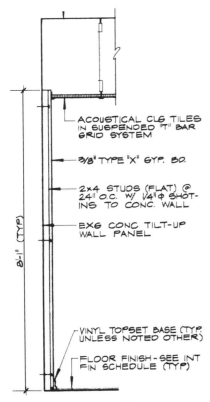

ACOUSTICAL CLG TILES IN SUSPENDED "T" BAR GRID SYSTEM

3/8" TYPE "X" GYP. BD.

2x4 STUDS (FLAT) @ 24" O.C. W/ 1/4"∅ SHOT-INS TO CONC. WALL

EXG CONC TILT-UP WALL PANEL

8'-1" (TYP)

VINYL TOPSET BASE (TYP UNLESS NOTED OTHER)

FLOOR FINISH - SEE INT FIN SCHEDULE (TYP)

Figure 18.22   Existing wall furring.

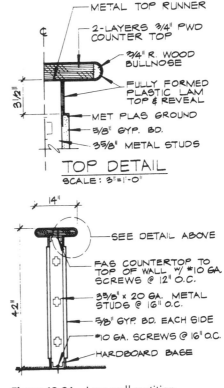

METAL TOP RUNNER

2-LAYERS 3/4" PWD COUNTER TOP

3/4" R. WOOD BULLNOSE

FULLY FORMED PLASTIC LAM TOP & REVEAL

MET PLAS GROUND

5/8" GYP. BD.

35/8" METAL STUDS

3 1/2"

TOP DETAIL
SCALE: 3"=1'-0"

14"

SEE DETAIL ABOVE

FAS COUNTERTOP TO TOP OF WALL W/ #10 GA. SCREWS @ 12" O.C.

35/8" x 20 GA. METAL STUDS @ 16" O.C.

5/8" GYP. BD. EACH SIDE

#10 GA. SCREWS @ 16" O.C.

HARDBOARD BASE

4'-2"

Figure 18.24   Low wall partition.

Interior Door and Window Assemblies

The door and window assemblies will be detailed to illustrate to the contractor the type of headers over the openings and the types of door and window frames that have been selected. The stabilization at the tops of these assemblies will be identical or similar to the stabilization for the wall partitions. Figure 18.25 depicts the use of a metal header over the door opening, incorporating the use of a hollow metal door frame. The manufacturer and type of metal door frame will be called out on the door schedule.

Wall partitions that incorporate windows will be detailed to delineate the type of header, window frame material, and the construction of the wall portion in the assembly. The interior window located between office 3 and the secretarial area is detailed in a wall section illustrated in Figure 18.26.

The sizes, thickness, and types of doors and windows will be stipulated on the door and window schedules (illustrated later in this chapter). It should be noted that upon completion of the detailing for the various partition walls and door and window

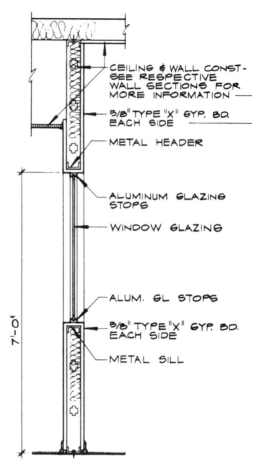

Figure 18.26   Interior window and wall section.

assemblies, these details will be referenced on the floor plan, using circles and numbers as a means of identification.

Electrical and Communication Plan

After the locations of partition walls, doors, windows, and furniture have been established, the architect or space planner, consulting with the tenant, may now proceed to develop an electrical and communication plan. The electrical portion of this plan will consist of the location of convenient electrical outlets installed approximately 12" above the floor, unless noted otherwise by a dimension at the outlet. The communication installation will comprise telephone jacks, a connection for the facsimile (fax) equipment, and a rough-in electrical service for the tenant's computer hardware. An electrical and communication plan prepared for this tenant of Building B is illustrated in Figure 18.27. It should be noted that, on some projects, the electrical and communication design may be so complex that separate plans must be provided and delineated for clarity.

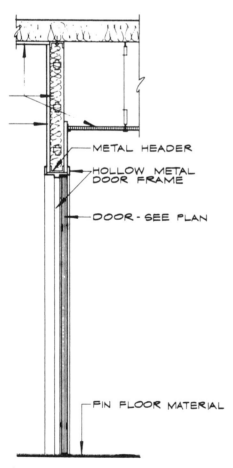

Figure 18.25   Interior door—wall section.

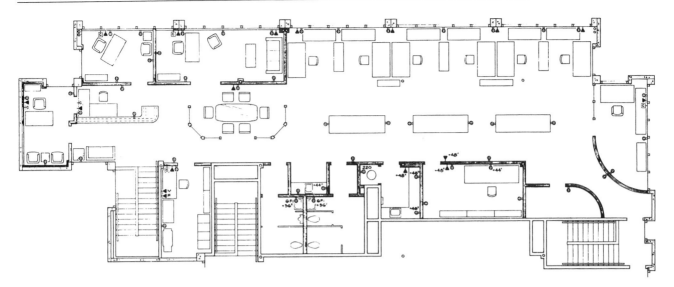

Figure 18.27   Electrical and communication plan.

Ceiling Plan

A ceiling plan that includes the height of the ceiling will be drawn to delineate the following: location of ceiling lighting fixtures, symbolized for reference to the lighting fixture schedule; suspended ceiling design; the type of system to be specified; and other types of ceiling finishes. Switch locations for the various lighting fixtures will also be shown on this plan.

For this project, it was decided that a suspended ceiling system with recessed lighting fixtures would be specified for offices 1, 2, and 3. As mentioned earlier and detailed in Figure 18.14, the walls will be installed first, thus providing the designer with greater design flexibility for the layout of the suspended ceiling grid system and the location of lighting fixtures. To illustrate the design flexibility of this wall installation method, the ceiling plan shown in Figure 18.28 shows the suspended ceiling and lighting fixtures to be symmetrical within the offices, thereby creating a more pleasing ceiling design and lighting fixture location. Mechanical ducts for heating and cooling these offices will be installed and concealed above the suspended ceiling system. Note that the walls are drawn with two lines only, as there are no wall openings at the ceiling level.

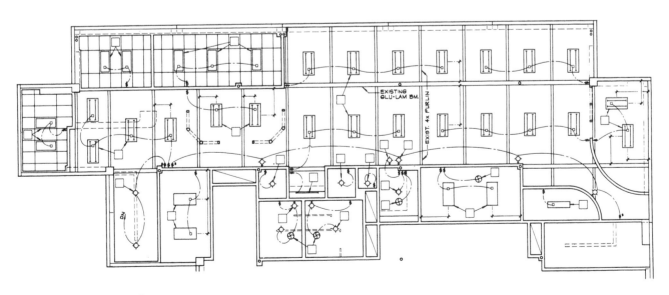

Figure 18.28   Ceiling plan.

At the request of the tenant, the remaining rooms and task areas will not have a suspended ceiling system; rather, gypsum wallboard will be attached directly to the existing structural roof members, with the gypsum board being finished and painted. For wall reference, see Figure 18.20.

The ceiling finish and location selected allow the mechanical ducts to be exposed and painted. These round mechanical ducts, when exposed and painted, will provide a decor compatible with the artwork and graphic design produced by this tenant. On the ceiling plan, as depicted in Figure 18.28, the designer has shown the desired location of the mechanical ducts and supply registers. The consulting mechanical engineer will specify, in the mechanical drawings, the sizes of the ducts, type of supply registers, and type of equipment to be used.

As previously mentioned, the lighting fixtures will be given a reference symbol that will also be on the electrical fixture schedule. That schedule will provide a description of the fixtures, including the manufacturer and model numbers. Designation of the finished ceiling material may be shown on the ceiling plan for convenience; in any case, these finishes will be designated on the interior finish schedule. Electrical and interior finish schedules, as well as other schedules, are discussed and illustrated later in this chapter.

Interior Elevations and Schedules

Interior elevations and schedules are usually included in the construction documents but were eliminated here, because their creation would follow the same procedures as those found in Chapters 11 and 12. They are also shown in their entirety in the construction documents evolution discussion to follow in this chapter.

■ WORKING DRAWINGS

The following paragraphs describe the working drawings at various stages of the development for the tenant improvement project in Building B.

Floor Plan

STAGE I (Figure 18.29). At a larger scale, the draftsperson lightly blocked out all the existing exterior and interior walls for the area identified as Suite 201. This drawing included existing windows, structural columns, roof drain leaders, stairwells, and mechanical shafts. Also included in this first-stage drawing was the initial site plan layout.

STAGE II (Figure 18.30). After the required room locations and their sizes were determined from the schematic drawings, wall locations were established with their accompanying dimension lines only. All the existing and new walls were darkened for future clarity. Doors and their swing directions were added, along with wheelchair clearances in the men's and women's restrooms. The various interior elevations were lightly blocked out, and the site plan—illustrating the exact location of Suite 201 in this existing structure—was finalized.

STAGE III (Figure 18.31). At this stage of the floor plan, all the wall partitions were dimensioned, and the new walls were darkened solid to distinguish them from the existing walls. Note that in the reference room, next to the darkroom, a wall was eliminated to provide more space for equipment. See Stage II. Door symbols and their numbers have been incorporated, along with plumbing fixture symbols and their accompanying designations. Also included are reference bubbles for the various wall sections with their designated numbers and locations. Interior elevation reference symbols have been added and will later be located on their respective wall elevations. Symbols for glass sizes are shown at the various glass partition locations. At this stage of the floor plan, the specified tile floor and accent pattern locations are delineated in the studio area. The lines on the interior elevations are darkened and profiled for clarity with material designations, cabinet door swings, incorporating the various dimension lines.

STAGE IV (Figure 18.32). This is the final stage for the floor plan, interior elevations, and site plan. A wall legend is included on the floor plan, illustrating the various wall conditions. All final notes and room designations have been lettered, and the designated wall detail numbers have been placed in the various reference bubbles. Lettering and dimensioning on the interior elevations are finalized at this stage, along with the titling and reference numbering for various wall elevations as they relate to the floor plan. Final notes are lettered on the site plan, and titles are provided for the site plan and floor plan. The scales used for various drawings are now lettered and located below the drawing titles.

Furnishing, Electrical, and Communication Plan

STAGE I (Figure 18.33). The initial step for this stage was to draft a floor plan incorporating the exterior walls, interior partitions, plumbing fixtures, and cabinet locations. Note that door swings and their directions are not delineated. In many offices, this stage may be a reproduction of an earlier floor-plan stage, or may be XREFed.

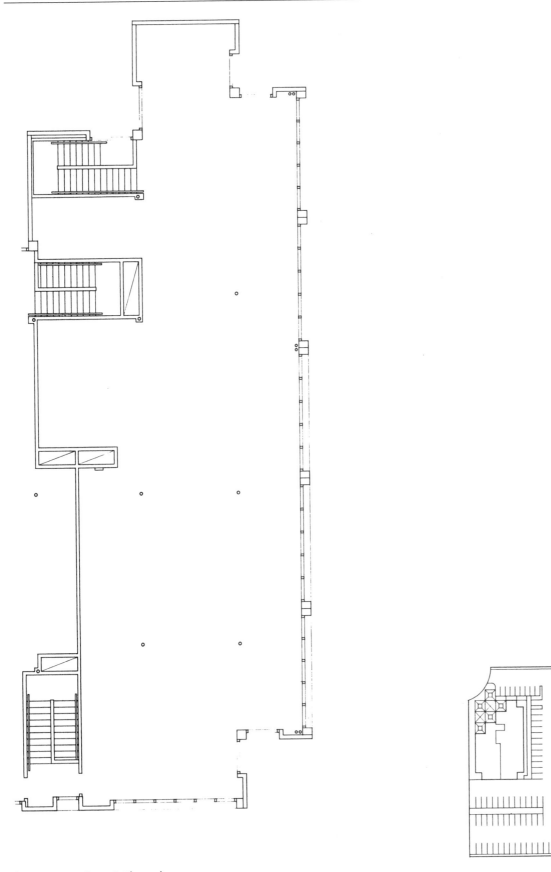

Figure 18.29 Stage I: Floor plan.

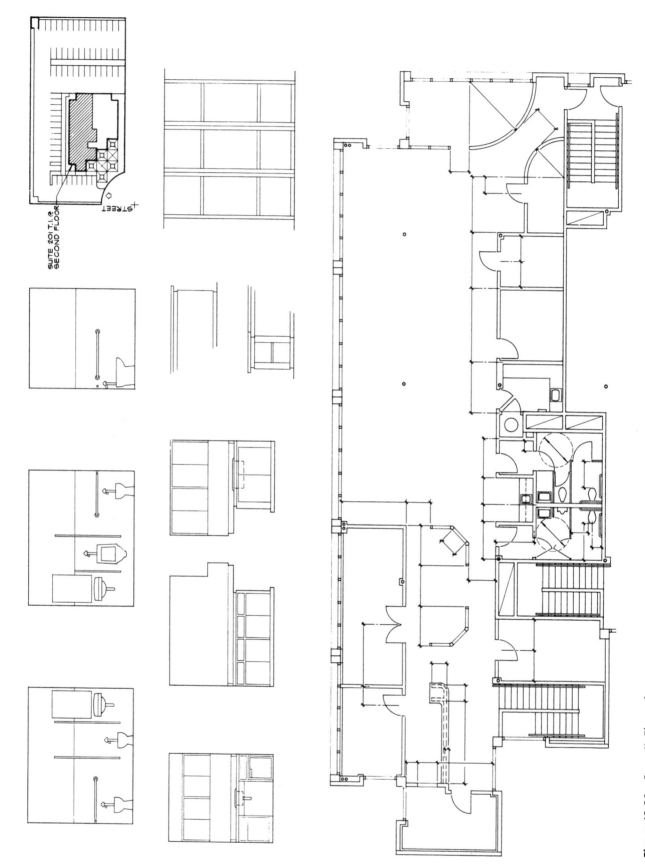

644

Figure 18.30 Stage II: Floor plan.

SUITE 201 T.I. @
SECOND FLOOR

STREET

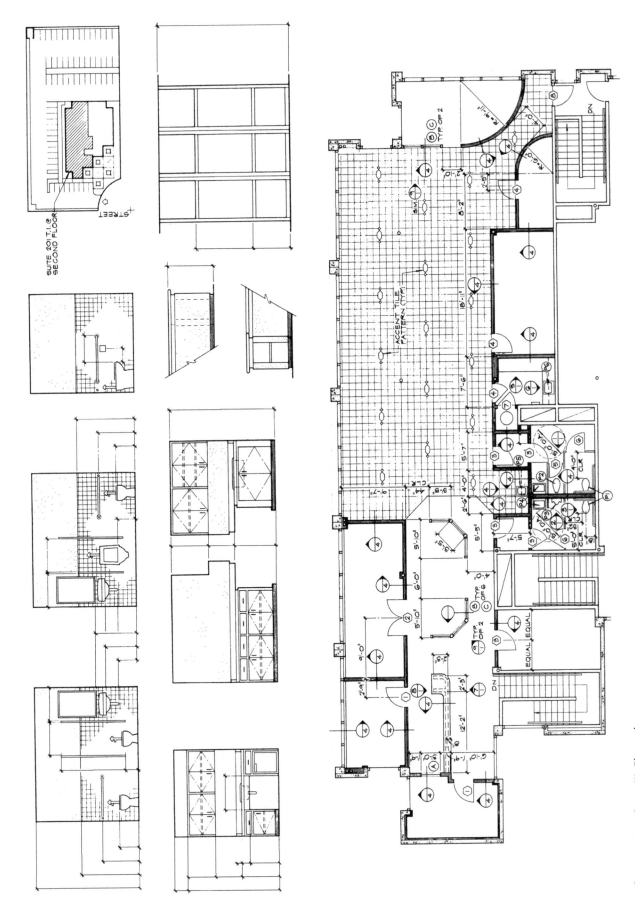

Figure 18.31 Stage III: Floor plan.

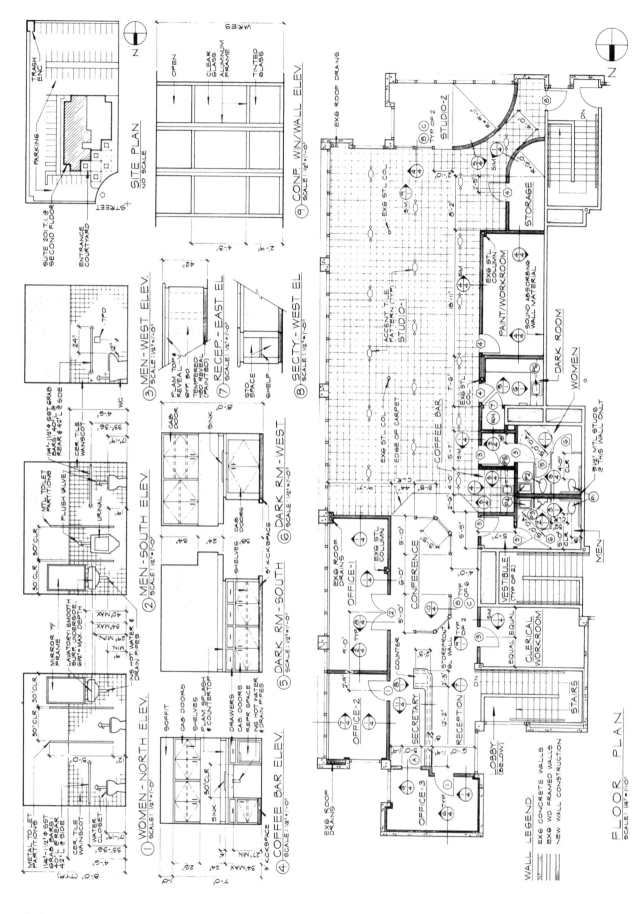

Figure 18.32 Stage IV: Floor plan.

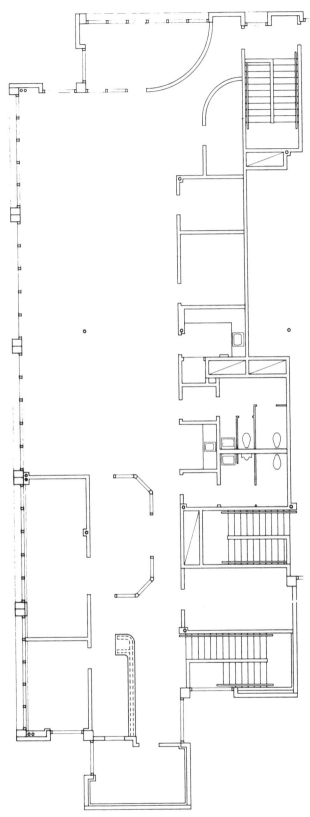

Figure 18.33 Stage I: Electrical plan—furnishing layout.

STAGE II (Figure 18.34). The first concern at this stage was to lay out all the required furniture necessary for the function of the tenant's business. With the furniture locations established, electrical, telephone, and facsimile outlets can now be located as required by the tenant. Also included at this stage is a furnishing schedule, which may be completed at a later stage or may be xrefed.

STAGE III (Figure 18.35). To complete the electrical plan and furnishing layout, symbols for furniture identification are located accordingly and lettered for reference on the furnishing schedule. Final notes are provided for electrical outlet locations, as well as for the various furnishing items that will be supplied by the tenant. The furnishing schedule is now complete, as it provides symbol designations, sizes, and manufacturers' equipment designations. A legend is drawn and completed for the identification of electrical symbols, such as for the type of outlets and switches. General construction notes covering the various construction phases are included with this drawing.

Ceiling Plan

STAGE I (Figure 18.36). At this stage, the exterior and interior walls are lightly blocked out, illustrating the walls as they appear at the ceiling level.

STAGE II (Figure 18.37). The exterior and interior walls are darkened to provide greater clarity at this stage. The three office areas that will have a suspended ceiling system have been delineated to illustrate the grid pattern, lighting fixture location, and their identification symbols. Also shown are the light switches for the various lighting fixtures. All the surface-mounted lighting fixtures, exhaust fans, and accompanying switches for the various fixtures are completed in this stage. Fixture symbols are now located for the identification of the various electrical fixtures. (The symbols will be completed at a later stage.) Finally, schedules for the doors, electrical fixtures, plumbing fixtures, and room finishes are drawn in preparation for listing the various sizes, materials, and manufacturers' identification numbers.

STAGE III (Figure 18.38). The final stage of the ceiling plan includes lettering all the lighting fixture symbols and locating the heating supply air ducts and diffusers. Dimensioning of some of the various lighting fixtures has now been completed, as have the final notes and the title of the drawing. The scale designation and ceiling heights are called out.

The various schedules that were blocked out in Stage II are now completed, providing all necessary information and symbol identification.

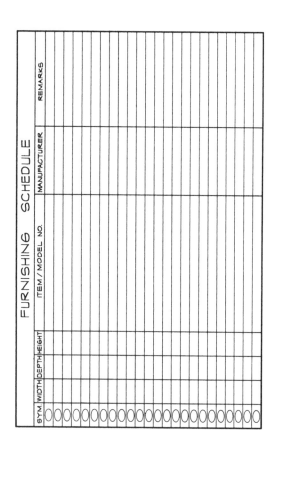

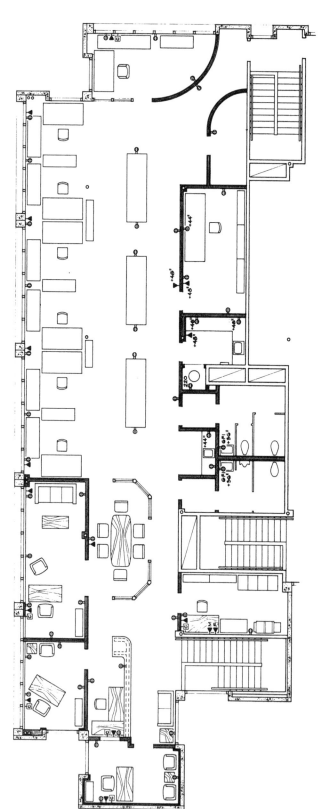

Figure 18.34 Stage II: Electrical plan—furnishing layout.

SYMBOL LEGEND

SYM.	DESCRIPTION
(telephone)	TELEPHONE OUTLET, F=FAX M=MODEM
HB	COMPUTER NETWORK JUNCTION
=O	DUPLEX OUTLET
=O GFI	w/ GROUND FAULT INTERRUPTER
=O 220	220 VOLT OUTLET
$	SINGLE POLE TOGGLE SWITCH
$3	3-WAY SWITCH
EXIT	EXIT SIGN (BATTERY)

FURNISHING SCHEDULE

SYM.	WIDTH	DEPTH	HEIGHT	ITEM / MODEL NO.	MANUFACTURER	REMARKS
F1	60"	30"	29"	EXECUTIVE DESK	FURNITURE INC.	ROSEWOOD
F2	"	"	"	SECRETARIAL DESK	"	TEAK
F3	"	24"	26"	FREESTANDING TYPING TABLE	"	"
F4	90"	35"	28"	CONFERENCE TABLE	"	ROSEWOOD
F5	48"	24"	29"	WORKTABLE	"	BLACK PLAM TOP
F6	29"	26"	40"	HI-BACK DESK CHAIR	"	ROSEWOOD TRIM
F7	22"	24"	32"	ARMCHAIR	"	BLACK
F8	18"	20"	30"	SECRETARIAL CHAIR	"	ROSEWOOD
F9	22"	24"	31"	SIDECHAIR	"	COFFEE
F10	80"	32"	26"	3-SEAT SOFA	"	"
F11	62"	"	"	2- "	"	
F12	48"	21"	17"	COFFEE TABLE	"	ROSEWOOD
F13	18"	18"	19"	SQUARE TABLE	"	TEAK
F14	24"	24"	"	"	"	ROSEWOOD
F15	48"	13"	72"	BOOKCAGE	"	
F16	36"	"	"	"	"	
F17	72"	37 1/2"	57"	DRAFTING/WORK TABLE	ARCHSTATION INC.	BLACK
F18	72"	24"	29"	FOLDING TABLE	FURNITURE INC.	BLACK PLAM TOP
F19	60"	21"	"	3-DRAWER REF DESK	N/A	CUSTOM-SEE DRAWING
F20	96"	24"	29"	FOLDING TABLE	FURNITURE INC.	BLACK PLAM TOP
F21	72"	13"	60"	BOOKCASE	"	WHITE MELAMINE
F22	48"	"	"	"	"	
F23	19"	21"	44 1/2"	VARIABLE HT DRAFTING CHAIR	ARCHSTATION INC.	BLACK
F24	23"	26"	"	ARMCHAIR	"	"

GENERAL CONSTRUCTION NOTES

1. The contractor and all sub-contractors shall verify all dimensions and conditions at the site, and shall notify the Architect of any discrepancy.
2. All architectural, mechanical, plumbing and electrical requirements must be coordinated before the contractor proceeds with construction.
3. In all cases where a conflict may occur such as between items covered by specifications and notes on the drawings, or between general notes and specific details, the Architect shall be notified and he will interpret the intent of the contract documents.
4. Details noted as typical shall apply in all cases unless specifically shown or noted otherwise.
5. Where no specific detail is shown, the framing or construction shall be identical or similar to that indicated for like cases of construction on this project.
6. In no case shall working dimensions be scaled from plans, sections or details on the drawings.
7. Workmanship and materials shall conform to the requirements of the current edition of the Uniform Building Code.
8. All fire rated walls shall use fire rated gypsum board and be fire-taped.
9. All Plumbing, Electrical, and Mechanical installations shall comply with their respective governing codes.
10. All legal exits shall be operable the from inside without the use of a key, special knowledge or effort.
11. Metal studs by "Metal Studs Inc." (or approved equivalent), ICBO #0000. See details and sections for more information.
12. Suspended Ceiling System by "Gypsum Ceilings Inc." (or approved equivalent), ICBO #0000. Installation shall be per Ch. 47 of the UBC & the following requirements:

   A. Lateral support provided by 4- #12ga wires splayed in 4 directions at 90° apart. Connect wires to the main runner within 2" of the crossrunner & to the structure above at an angle not exceeding 45° from the plane of the ceiling. These lateral support points shall be at 12'-0" o.c. (max) in each direction, with the first point within 4' of the wall.

   B. Provide vertical compression struts at the center of the lateral support points described above in item "A". Compression struts may be of metal stud material.

   C. Discontinuous ends of main runners and crossrunners shall be vertically supported within 8" of the discontinuous end.

   D. Lighting fixtures and air diffusers shall be supported directly by wires to the structure above.

ELECTRICAL PLAN / FURNISHING LAYOUT
SCALE: 1/4"=1'-0"

Figure 18.35 Stage III: Electrical plan—furnishing layout.

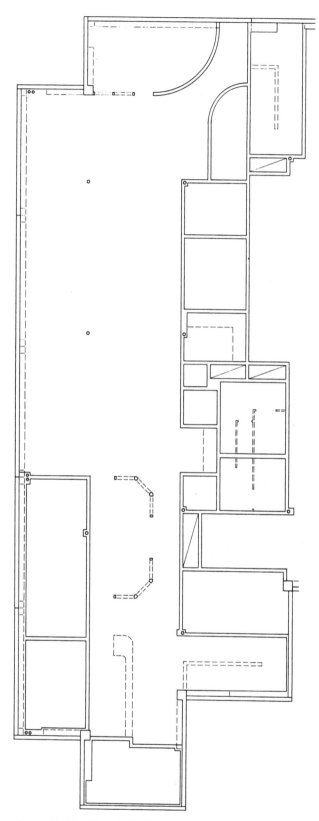

Figure 18.36 Stage I: Ceiling plan.

Tenant Improvement and Revit

Presently, most tenant improvement work is done on AutoCAD, not on Revit. This is because the buildings being used by tenants have already been built, in most cases using designs drafted in AutoCAD. We are in a transitional period, and of the structures currently being built, only a small portion of them are designed and drawn in Revit. Thus, the drawings must still be verified in size and shape and drawn over. A multistory building occupancy might be drawn in Revit because of the complexity of re-routing plumbing, air conditioning, heating, and so on. However, this calls for a new version of Revit, as the existing program is not yet designed to catch conflicts as these functions are re-routed. It is hoped that by 2013 or 2014 the changeover will begin.

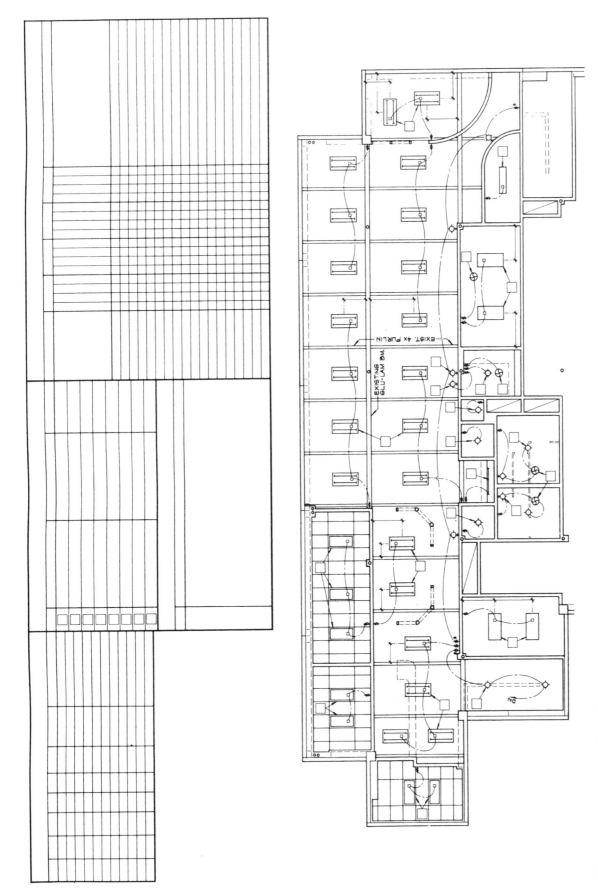

Figure 18.37 Stage II: Ceiling plan.

EXIST. 4x PURLIN

EXISTING
GLU-LAM BM.

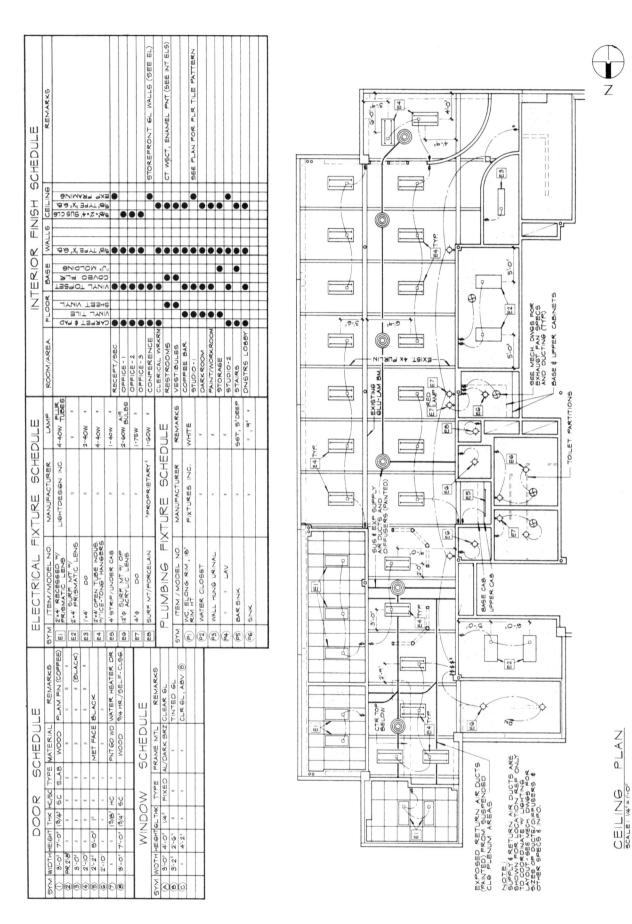

CEILING PLAN
SCALE: 1/4" = 1'-0"

Figure 18.38 Stage III: Ceiling plan.

INDEX

Abbreviations, 31, 37, 187
Academy of the Sciences, 80
Accessibility, 13, 80, 84, 86–87, 89, 268, 508
ADA, *see* Americans with Disabilities Act
Adjustable triangle, 45, 356
Adli residence, 70, 278, 284, 361, 366–369
Administration department, 4
AIA, *see* American Institute of Architects
AIA Architectural Graphics Standards, 7, 31, 80, 126–127, 131, 143
American Institute of Architects (AIA), 7, 31–32, 49, 80, 95, 285, 387, 489
Americans with Disabilities Act (ADA), 13, 80, 85, 87, 89, 91, 108, 268
American Wood Preservers Association, 125
Anchor bolt, 38, 299–300, 304, 309–310, 409, 412–413, 423
Anthropometrics, 86
Appliances:
    list of, 281
    schedules for, 194–195
    symbols for, 396, 400
Appliqué, 27, 30
Apprenticeship, 5
Architects: 4–5, 7, 9, 12–13, 35, 80, 91–92, 103–105, 109, 117, 119, 129, 131, 145, 161, 163, 169, 180, 225, 227, 352, 390, 422, 448, 463, 508, 550, 632, 640
    landscape, 12, 93, 246
    project, 5, 95, 467
    state, 393
Architect/Client relationship, 7
Architectural details, 5, 30, 44, 422–424, 426, 447, 624
    definition of, 422
    examples of, 422–428
    fireplaces, 439–441
    footing detail, 20, 288, 291, 294, 297, 303, 428–431, 442
    hard-lining of, 428
    insulation, 110–115, 136, 140, 157, 159–160, 185, 274, 291, 431
    rough opening size for, 261, 263, 433, 435–436
    sizing details, 429–430
    stairways, 443–448
    window detail, 430, 432–433, 435, 437, 448
Architectural drafting, 26–27, 35, 448
Architectural Graphics Standards, 7, 31, 80, 126–127, 131, 143, 448
Architectural lettering, 20–24, 280, 304
Architectural office, 4–15
    and architect/client relationship, 7–10
        construction, observation of, 12–13
        schematic designs/reviews, 7–12
    building codes, 13–14
        exit requirements, 13, 628
        influence on BIM, 14
        influence on design, 13
        nailing schedule, 309, 337, 356
    and computer–aided drafting, 5–78
        DXF vs. DWG formats, 53, 78
        layering, 49–50, 55–56, 62, 66, 68, 70, 205
        lettering size, 30, 65
        paper, 60–61, 67, 69
        paper vs. virtual space, 50, 52, 59–60, 65, 73

pen settings, 65, 68
    scale of drawings, 30
    vector vs. raster drawings, 52
    X-referencing, 50, 52, 54
design department, 4–5
energy codes, 13
initial preparation phase, procedure during, 178, 213
organization, 5
production department, 4–5
professional organizations, involvement in, 7
resources on,
    computer resources, 6
    manufacturers' literature, 7
    retail sources, 7
    standards, 49–50
Architectural profiling, 20
Architectural standards and techniques, 18
Architecture, sustainable, 89, 91, 103, 106, 108–132
Architecture Registration Exam (ARE), 5
Arrowheads, 19, 105, 276, 295, 308, 537
"As-built" drawings, 628–630
Attic, 116, 309, 324, 327, 337, 385
    ventilation system for, 324
Axial plane, 35
Axial reference plane, 99, 200, 263–264, 306, 337

Bailey residence, 237–239, 300, 348–349
Balloon framing, 142–143
Base, 52, 55, 60, 65, 74–75, 120
Basement floor plan (foundation plans), 153, 297–298, 304, 377
Batt insulation, 112–113, 431
Beams, 33, 140, 148, 151–152, 155, 164–165, 170, 295, 299, 327–328, 331–333, 337–338, 393, 498, 539, 608, 620
Bearing, 20, 25, 29, 99, 103, 130, 136, 140, 154, 156, 166, 205, 207, 222–223, 228, 288–295, 299–300, 304, 327, 337–338, 422–423, 429–431, 433, 456–458, 484, 498, 630
Berm, 131
Bidding and negotiating, 12
Bio-filter, 242
Bituminous saturated felts, 386
"B" leads, 48
Bloom energy source, 132–133
Blu residence (case study), 507–548
Bolts in concrete, 38, 423
Boring log, 227
Boundary control plane, 35
Braces, let-in, 377, 380, 384–385
Break lines, 18, 356, 369, 431
Brick pavers, 304
Bubble diagramming, 462–463
Building codes, 13–14, 80, 86, 95, 103, 115, 117–119, 136, 142, 157–159, 179–182, 443–444, 456–457, 630
    design, influence on, 13
    exit requirements, 13, 628
    influence on building information modeling (BIM), 14
    nailing schedule, 309, 337, 356
Building location on site, 13, 227, 247, 250
Building materials and systems, 136
Building occupancy, 13, 136, 650

Building sections, 5, 30, 44, 55, 71, 95, 102, 167, 173–174, 190, 347–361
    defined, 348
    design section, 354–355
    drafting of, 348, 356
        concrete, 353
        and pitch, 348, 356
    examples of, 348, 350–354, 360–363
    full sections, 352
    number of, 350
    partial sections, 349, 352, 357
    plate height, 348
    stages, 359–360
    steel structures, 358
    types of, 351–352
    wall sections, 351–352
Building use, 13

Cabinets, 391–397, 502
CAD, *see* Computer-aided drafting
Caisson, concrete, 299, 304–306
Call-outs, 23, 25, 37–38, 92, 169, 247, 276, 289–291, 293, 295, 308–309, 327, 333–334, 352, 355, 360
Cartooning (sheet formatting), 49, 68
    computer cartooning, 190
Case studies, *see* Jaydn Residence; Blu Residence; Madison Steel Building; Mann Theater; Tenant improvements
Caissons, 299, 304–306
Catch basin, 242
Ceiling plan, 52, 63, 332, 476, 635, 637, 641–642, 647, 650–652
Central control unit (CCU), 272, 279
Centralized controller, 271
Checklists, 277, 390, 504
    exterior and interior elevations, 384
    floor plans, 281
    foundation plans, 310
    framing, 337
    Revit, 283, 285
    roof framing, 580
    section, 353
    site and grading plans, 250
Children, planning for, 80, 393, 508
Chimney, 327, 329, 431, 436, 438–442, 486–487
Circle templates, 44
Clay Residence, 199, 205
Client(s): 4, 12, 27, 188, 246, 258–266
    requirements of, 508
Clip compass, 45
Code nailing schedule, 309, 337, 356
Codes, *see* Building codes
Colinita residence, 279
Column pad schedule, 297
Columns, 35–36, 44, 306, 332–338
    concrete, 152, 165, 169, 563, 624
    elevation heights of, 65
    pilasters, 295
    steel, 62, 99, 109, 169–171, 173–174, 205, 278, 297, 303, 341, 353, 428, 607–608, 624
    wood, 293, 299
Combined-material:
    symbols, 275
Commercial building, 250, 305, 384, 409

Communication plan, 640–642
Compass, 44–45, 222–223, 227–228, 323
Composite drafting, 27, 55
Composite stairway assemblies, 447
Composite systems, 136, 159
Computer(s), 18, 20, 27–28, 55
    advantages for, 73–74
    for CAD, 49, 75, 402
    cartooning, 190–191
    designing, 188
    disadvantages of, 72–73
    drafting with, 49
    and electrical, 271
    floor plans on, 277–278
    interior elevations on, 395
    and metrics, 40
    model, 197
    roof plan on, 327
    site and grading plans on,
        227–228
    tracking drawings on, 69, 188
Computer-aided drafting (CAD), 18, 20, 27, 41,
        49, 53–55
    advantage of using, 73–74
    disadvantages of using, 72–73
    future of, 75
    and office standards, 49
        DXF vs. DWG formats, 53
        layering, 51–52, 62
        paper, 55
        paper vs. virtual space, 59
        pen settings, 65
        scale factor, 61
        vector vs. raster drawings, 52–53
        X-referencing, 54
    schedules, 409–411
    sizing of, 28
Computer cartooning, 68
Concrete, 166–167, 264
    bolts in, 308
    grade beam, 109
    graphic symbol, 31
    footing/foundation, 111, 136, 138, 288
    pads, 297, 303
    poured in place:
        tilt up, 153–154
        stairs, 449
    precast, 152–154
        floor systems using, 151
        roof system using, 155
    reinforcing, 293, 303
    structure, 119–122, 151
    slab, 149–151, 288–289
Concrete block, 31, 157–158, 174–175, 181,
        259–261, 275, 295, 298, 306, 352,
        374–375, 377, 382, 438, 550. See also
        Concrete masonry units (CMU)
Concrete columns, 119, 151–152, 263–264, 295,
        552, 604, 624
Concrete floor systems, 149, 151
    above-grade, 151
    at ground-floor level, 299, 557, 603
    on-grade, 192, 300, 304, 491, 494, 496
    precast prestressed concrete, 152–153
    slab floors, 288, 290
        call-out, 289–291
        curbs, 289, 300
        footings, 169, 288, 295, 345
        foundation plans, 26, 102, 186, 288–293,
            299–300
        reinforcing (steel), 149, 151–155, 157–158,
            288–291, 293, 297, 306, 409
        sloping concrete areas, 290

Concrete masonry units (CMU), 112–113,
        158, 174–175, 181, 342, 382. See also
        Concrete block
Concrete pads, 262, 264, 297–299, 303
    and steel columns, 109, 174, 624
Concrete roof systems, 153–155
Concrete stairways, 446–447
Concrete wall systems, 153–154
    precast concrete walls, 154
    tilt-up wall panels, 153
Condensation, 95, 385–386, 564
Construction administration, 12–13
Construction documents (CD), 4, 7, 12, 18, 20,
        30, 49–50, 54, 62, 73, 89–90, 93, 95,
        103–104, 106
    guidelines for preparation of, 178–215
    transition from design development to, 9–12
Consultants, 5, 12–13, 35, 180, 182, 352
Contour lines, 225, 230
Controls (accessibility), 86–87, 91–92
Conversion rules (in drafting), 37
Coordinates, 67, 222
Copiers, paper, 26–27, 48
Cost estimators, 12
Counterflashing, 386
Coving, 394
Cross-hatching, 20, 289, 295, 494, 620
Cross-reference, 62, 66, 186, 200, 391, 413
Cross-referencing, 52, 54–55, 186, 504
Cross-sections, 26, 41–43, 225–228, 239–241,
        243, 328, 348, 352, 554, 607
Curbs, 86–90, 230
    driveway and , 250–251
    ramps, curb, 84–85
    site and grading plans, 242
Cut and fill procedures, 233–234

Datum base, 188–190
Daylight grade elevation, 234
Dead load, 136, 494
Decorative doors, 265
Delivery methods, 78, 208–215
Denn Engineers, 244–245
Design(s):
    building code influence on, 13
    building information modeling (BIM), 14–15
    energy code influence on, 13
    preliminary, 27, 68, 93, 230, 628
    sketches, 44
Design department, 4
Design development (DD), 9–10, 608, 615–616
Design section, 352, 354–356, 361
Details, 2, 93–95, 104, 180, 550–552, 598, 603,
        608, 624. See also Architectural details
Deterioration of materials, 108, 120
Diazo process, 30, 48, 55
Dimensioning, 20, 31, 63, 165, 171, 174, 261,
        283, 484
    columns, 264
    doors and windows, 259, 264
    exterior elevations, 258, 487
    interior elevations, 258–259
    masonry, 261
    plans, 186, 230, 265, 332
    steel, 262, 264
Dimensional reference system, 33–35, 188,
        236–264, 275, 280, 305–306, 348, 575,
        603
Disabilities, planning for persons with, 13, 80
    interior elevations, 84–85
    ramp, 87, 89, 241
Dividers, 44–45, 391
Document numbering systems, 197

Doors:
    accessibility of, 86
    cabinet, 392–394
    codes, 268
    dimensioning, 261
    details, 184–185
    dotted lines on, 377
    elevations, 372
    exterior, 268, 374
    in floor plans, 268
    handle, 87
    head/jamb, 117, 261
    height, 163, 174, 181–182
    hinged, 265
    interior, 268, 457
    masonry, 261
    panel, 265, 404
    schedules for, 258, 369, 372, 404–405,
        416
    types of, 265, 267
    reference, 258
    Revit, 92
    swing, 86, 91, 118, 265, 356, 374, 397
    thresholds, 87
    weather-stripped, 111
    width, 182
Doorways, accessibility of, 86
Dots, drafting, 44
Dotted lines, 19, 146, 250, 289, 377, 380,
        391–392, 491, 532
Double-action doors, 265, 267
Downspouts, 121–122, 250, 384
Drafting, 18, 44
    architectural, 26
    of building sections, 356
        and pitch, 356
    composite, 27
    computer, see CAD; Computer-aided drafting
    conversion, 37–38
    equipment for, 44–45
        basic equipment, 45
        erasers and erasing shields,
            27, 45
        lead holders, 44–45, 48–49
        pencils, 44–45, 48
        scale, 45
        supplemental equipment, 45
        tape, 44, 47
        triangles, 45
    of exterior elevations, 383–384
    freehand, 27
    of interior elevations (examples), 394–395
    manual, 27–28
    mechanical, 23–30
    photography, 27
    reproduction methods, 27
    rules, 178
    scissors, 27
Drainage, 108, 120–121, 232–233, 241–243,
        245–246, 250, 290, 380, 424, 551. See
        also Grading and drainage
Drawing(s), see specific type of drawing (e.g.,
        Floor plans)
Drawing exchange format (DXF), 53
Drinking fountains (accessibility), 84, 87–88,
        393, 560
Driveways, 9, 71, 230, 235–236, 239, 241–242,
        250–251, 289, 310, 471, 512
Drywells, 112
Dumbwaiters, 449
Dusting brush, 45
DWG format, 53, 56
DXF, see Drawing exchange format

Eaves, 71, 115–116, 121, 145, 147, 163, 193, 326, 356, 369, 424, 427, 484
Egress requirements, *see* Exit requirements
Electrical and utility symbols, 268, 270, 473
  letter symbols, 270
  number symbols, 270
Electrical plan (tenant improvements), 26, 54–56, 71, 186, 276–277, 647
Electrical rating, 276
Electric erasers, 45–46
Elevations, 9, 15, 20–22, 26, 56, 66, 71, 89, 95, 99, 102
  daylight grade, 234
  exterior, *see* Exterior elevations
  floor, 231, 348, 384, 571
  interior, *see* Interior elevations
Elevators, 445, 447–448, 450, 452, 603
Energy codes, 13
Energy conservation, 110–111, 108, 165, 185
Engineers, 8, 11
Engineered lumber, 140, 142, 144, 342
  floor framing, 141
  floor joists, 140–142
  roof systems, 148–149
  sheathing panels, 144, 147
English equivalents, 37
English system, 37, 41–42, 105
Envelope, energy, 110–111, 116
Environmental concerns:
  deterioration of materials, 108
  drainage, 121–122
  fire, 116–117, 119, 630
  frost, 108, 123, 125–127
  lateral influences, 109
  smoke, 116–119
  snow, 108, 115
  sound and noise, 112–113, 131
  and sustainable architecture, 108
  temperature, 116, 119, 128–129, 385
  termites, 108, 125–126
  underground gases, 123
  water table, 108, 123, 125
Equipment:
  for drafting, 44–49
    basic equipment, 44–45
    erasers and erasing shields, 45–46
    lead holders, 44–45, 48–49
    lead pointers, 45, 49
    pencils, 45, 48–49
    scale, 46
    tape, 28, 44
    triangles, 46
  mechanical, 23, 46
Eraser drafting, 45
Erasers, 45, 46
Erasing shields, 46
Ergonomics, 88
Exit corridors, 14, 628, 630
Exit requirements, 13, 628
Expansion joint, 119–120, 250, 310
Exterior dimensioning, 258
Exterior elevations, 163, 165, 171, 366–390, 486, 489–493, 511–512, 531–535, 581–582
  BIM/Revit, 389–391
  cartooning, 191
  checklist, 384
  dimensional layout, drafting by, 367, 384
  direct projection, drafting by, 366
  doors and windows on, 375
  drafting of, 383–384
    hidden lines, use of, 384
    material, designation of, 392
  masonry structures, 174

pivot point, 375
  for post and beam systems, 165–167
  purpose of, 366
  scale for, 369
Exterior finishes, 192–193
Exterior walls (foundation plans), 290, 292

Face frame (of cabinet), 392
Face of stud (F.O.S.), 162, 206, 257, 278, 282, 304, 474, 513
Fibrous filler, 113
Fill (soil) procedures, 233, 242
Films, transparent/translucent, 26, 47
Finishes:
  exterior, 192–193
  interior, 192–194
Finish grading, 250, 384
Finish schedules, 15
  interior, 406, 415
  wall, 408
Fire, 120
  environmental concern, 113–116
Fire and smoke, 116
Fire blocking, 117
Fireplaces, 289, 436
  architectural details, 439–441
  chimney, 440
  framing, 338
  masonry, 289
  remote, 436
  types of, 438
Fire-rated wall assemblies, 13, 630
Firm, architectural, *see* Architectural office
Fixed windows, 373
Flashing, 138, 384, 386
"F" leads, 48
Floors and floor systems, 136–141
  concrete floor systems, 149–152
    above-grade, 151
    on-grade, 149
  precast prestressed concrete, 155
  steel, 155
  steel reinforcing of concrete, 155
  wood, *see* Wood floors and wood floor systems
Floor elevation (grading plan), 231–233
Floor framing, 337–339, 343, 537, 539, 608
  above masonry, 342
  conventional floor, 330
  with engineered lumber, 342
Floor joists, *see* Joists
Floor plans, 2, 53–285, 478–481, 517–523. *See also* Foundation plans
  checklist for, 281
  on computer, 277–278, 281
  datum, 203
  design development, 603
  dimensioning, 260, 265
  doors in plan view, 268
  electrical and utility symbols in, 270
  furniture plan, 279
  masonry structures, 174, 259, 262–263
  materials, 275
  punch list, 557, 560
  Revit, 95, 280–281
  scale, 30
  steel structures, 169, 263–264, 607–614
  tenant improvements, 632, 642–646
  troubleshooting, 285–286
  two-story building, 170
  types of, 254
  windows, 261
  wood frame structure, 165

Floralis Generica, 107, 129
Flush doors, 265, 393
Flush overlay doors, 393
Folding doors, 267
Fome-Core board, 112
Footings, *see also* Foundation plans, 95, 111, 288–317, 377, 563, 624
  caisson, 304–306
  checklisk, 310
  concrete slab floor, 149–150
  design, 288
  details, 20, 184, 288, 422–426, 433
  pier/spread, 409, 413
  stepped, 290, 380–381
  wood floor, 136, 140, 291
Formatting, 44, 53, 59, 190, 442, 449
F.O.S., *see* Face of stud
Foundation plans, 26, 41–44, 287–317, 491–496, 536–540
  basement floor plan, 297
  checklist for, 310
  concrete slab floor, 307
  conventions, 300
  examples of, 311–312
    masonry walls, building with, 295
    steel columns, 297, 303
  Revit, 102, 556–570
  sloping concrete, 290
  types of, 288
  water table, 125
  wood floor, 136–140, 291
Foundations:
  hidden lines on, 19
  section, 288–289
Frames, window, 640
Framing:
  balloon, 142
  conventional wood stud, 162, 164–165
  engineered lumber, 342–343
  floor, 330, 337–338, 342
  post and beam, 142
  roof, *see* Roof framing
  western, 142, 144, 519
Freehand drawing, 27, 423–424
French curve, 45
Frost, 123, 126
Frost line, 123, 126
Full sections, 344, 352
Furniture plan, 277–229
Furring, 159, 637, 639

Gable roof, 102, 323–326, 384, 494
Galvanized, 120, 145, 156–160, 426
Garage, 9, 235
Gases, underground, 108
Geology maps, 225, 227
Geothermal, 128
GFI (ground fault interrupt), 269
Givens residence, 228, 249, 297, 345, 350, 363
Glass wall partition, interior, 638–639
Grab bars, 84, 87, 393
Grade elevations, 225, 230–236, 242, 250
Grading, finish, 225, 231
Grading plans, *see* Site and grading plans
Graphic symbols, 31, 187
Green architecture, 91, 107–112
Grid pattern (steel columns), 263, 265, 356, 358, 635, 647
Ground fault interrupt (GFI), 269
Grouping dimensions, 31
Guardrails, 444, 519
Gutters, 121, 193, 222, 384, 413

Hand drafting, 44, 93, 190, 429
Handrails, 85, 160, 427
    composite, 161
    for stairways, 444
Hard conversion, 38, 41
Hard drive, 65
Hard-lining, 428
Hardscape, 246
"HB" leads, 48
Headers, 53, 308, 327–328, 331–332, 337–338
Headroom clearance (stairways), 444
Heating, 111
Heating, Ventilation, and Air Conditioning
        (HVAC), 6, 171, 344, 628
Height, 86–89
    building, 13, 163
    human, 81, 86–89
    lettering, 18, 30, 55, 65
    plate, 348, 380
Hidden lines, 19, 46, 95, 205, 295, 304
Hinged doors, 265, 377, 384
Hip rafters, 312, 333, 539
Hip roof, 163, 311, 321, 323, 326
"H" leads, 48
Hollow-core, 404
Horizontal control plane, 33
Horizontal section, 26, 188
Human concerns, 80–106
Human considerations, 80
Human resources, 4–5
HVAC, see Heating, Ventilation, and Air
        Conditioning

IDP, see Intern Development Program
Insulation:
    building, 108, 110–115, 484
    environmental, 108
    footing, 111
    rigid, 115
    and snow, 115
    sound, 112–113, 457
Interior dimensioning, 181, 257
Interior elevations, 366, 390–402
    on computer, 395
    dimensions of, 394
    dotted lines, use of, 392
    evolution of set of, 396
    examples, 399–401
    information shown on, 391
    intersections, wall and floor, 394–395
    materials for, 392
    naming of, 391
    purpose and content of, 390–391
    Revit, 389–390, 397
    scale for use with, 391–392
    sources of measurement for, 391
    titles assigned to, 391
Interior finishes, 192, 194, 406
Interior walls:
    partitions, 170
Internal load-bearing foundation, 136
Intern Development Program (IDP), 5
Internet, 6–7, 10, 70, 80, 105, 223
Interrelationship of drawings, 186
Intersections:
    of two walls, 257–260
    of wall and floor, 356, 394–395,
Internship, 5
Irrigation plan, 222, 246, 249
Isolation, 113

Jacks, 250, 640
Jadyn Residence (case study), 461–505

Jamb, 20, 117, 261, 406, 423, 434–435
James Orland, CE, 331, 335–336, 345
Job numbers, 195–196
Jobsite, 151–152, 173, 299
Joists:
    ceiling, 66, 71, 112, 308–309, 359, 439–440,
        442, 496, 498
    engineered floor, 141–142
    floor, 136, 138, 140, 142, 192, 292–293, 331,
        491
    sawn lumber, 113, 164
Joints, 119–120, 181–182, 282
Journeyman, 69–70
Junior drafter, 5, 28, 69
Jurisdiction, 221, 236, 551

Katnik residence, 277, 362
Keynotes, 197, 422
Key plans, 167, 276–277, 285, 370–372, 374
Kitchen, 10, 394–396
Kizirian plans, 244–245, 251, 280

Landscape architects, 12, 93, 246
Landscape plan, 222, 246, 248
Latitude, 129, 130
Lateral design, 114–115
Lavatory, 89–91, 393
Layering (CAD), 49–50, 55, 62, 66, 68, 70, 205
Layers of production drawings, 199
Leadership in Energy and Environmental Design
        (LEED), 6, 12, 78, 91–92, 103, 106
Lead holders, 45, 48–49
Lead pointers, 45, 48–49
Lead types, 48
LeBeau residence, 57, 77
LEED, see Leadership in Energy and
        Environmental Design
Legal description of project, 192, 195, 220, 473,
        512
Legend, 197, 230, 268, 274, 308, 498, 647
Let-in braces, 380, 384
Lettering, 18, 20–21, 23–25, 30, 50, 65–66
Lettering size, 30, 50, 65, 280
Light steel framing, 136, 157, 161, 169,
        624–625
Lines, 18–20. See also Dotted lines
    arrowheads, 19, 105, 276, 295, 308
    dark, 18, 20, 26
    hidden, see Hidden lines
    light, 18–20, 389
    material designation, 20
    medium, 18, 502
    weights of, 18–20
Live load, 494
Load-bearing foundation, 136
Load-bearing walls, 99, 136, 156, 166, 200, 292,
        498, 534
Lobby, 394, 608
Location dimensions, 31, 33, 250, 372, 473
Location on site, 598
Location plan, 222
Longitude, 129
Longitudinal section, 26
Lot lines, 222–223, 225, 247
Lumber:
    engineered, see Engineered lumber
    sawn, 145
Lumber joists, see Joists

Madison Steel Building (case study), 597–625
Mann Theater Building (case study), 549–595
Manual drafting, 18, 23, 27–28, 44, 59, 62, 78
Manufacturers' literature, 7, 179

Masonry, 174–175, 259–267, 295, 382,
        549–595. See also Concrete
    block module, 564
    doors and windows, 261
    floor framing above, 342
    modular and nonmodular, 40, 181
    sound, 113
    and steel, 264, 267, 382
    and wood, 263
Masonry structures, 378, 382
    chalking, 297, 301
Masonry veneer, 158–159, 193
Masonry wall systems, 157–158
MasterFormat, 6
Materials, 31, 135–176, 444
    analysis of, 181–182
    composite, 161
    concrete, 149–152, 170
    fire, 116
    masonry, 158–159, 174–176
    precast, 152–154
    for roof, 144–146
        combined, 274–275
        steel, 156
        wood, 162, 333
    in section,
    specifications, 192
Materials and Specifications, 10
Material designations, 392
Mechanical drafting, 23, 30, 46, 366
Mechanical equipment, 45, 182–183, 382, 552,
        637
Mechanical lettering, 23
Metal baffle, 113
Metes and bounds, 222
Metric scale, 39, 45
Metric system, 35
    actual vs. nominal size, 37
    computers, 40–41
    conversion rules, 37
    drawing sheet size, 39
    English equivalents, 37
    modules, 40
    notation method, 35
    possible sizes, 40
    scales, metric, 38
    scaling factor,
    unit change
Military Specification, 105
Mock set, 467
Modular units, 158, 174–175, 181–182
Module, 181
Moisture protection, 6, 138
Moment frame, 109
Monitor, computer, 109, 613

NAAB, see National Architecture Accrediting
        Board
Nailing schedule, 309, 337, 356
National Architecture Accrediting Board
        (NAAB), 5
National Council of Architectural Registration
        Board (NCARB), 5
Net sizing, 25
Networked computers, 4, 54, 75
Neutral zone, 35–36, 188
N.I.C., see Not in the contract
Noise (as environmental concern), 112, 221
Nominal size, 25
Notation method, 35
Notes/noting, 30, 55, 89, 375
    keynotes, 197, 422
Not in the contract (N.I.C.), 392

Numbering systems, document, 197
Number symbols (floor plans), 268

Observation, 7, 12–13, 337
Occupancy, building, 13, 136, 180, 444
Odd-shaped plans, 369
Office, architectural, *see* Architectural office
Office building, 598–599, 601
Offsets, 225, 259–260, 295, 304, 311, 368, 423–424, 618
One-story residence. *see* Jadyn residence (case study)
Oriented Strand Board (OSB), 109, 142, 144, 148, 157
Orientations, 8–9, 68, 95, 103, 220, 228–231, 366–367
Original drawings:
  rolling, 47
  saving, 65
OSB, *see* Oriented Strand Board
Outline, 19–20, 62, 66, 103, 278, 312, 392–397
Overlay drafting, 27

Panel doors, 265, 372
Panels, wood, 109
Parallel bar, 48
Parking stalls, 84, 551, 598, 603
Partial sections, 344, 352, 467, 575
Partitions, 640, 642
Paste-up drafting, 27, 55
Peninsula Community Church, 246, 248–249
Pen settings (CAD), 65, 68
Permafrost, 127
Photo-drafting, 27, 55
Photography, 27
Photo mechanical transfer (PMT), 27
Pier footing schedules, 409, 413
Pilasters, 35
Pitch, 115
Pivot points, 95, 370–373, 375
Plain paper copiers, 26–30
Planes, 33–35, 52
Planes of reference, 33
Plank-and-beam system, 144–147
Planking, 138–140, 145, 147, 164–165
Planning strategy, 186–187
Plan north, 366
Plans, *see specific types of plans* (e.g., Floor plans)
Plan templates, 45, 356
Plant list, 246
Plastic, 6, 44–45, 159–160, 290, 293
Plates:
  height of, 163, 349, 353, 380
  top, 163, 353, 356, 368, 380
Platform framing, 142, 144
Plat maps, 222–223, 225, 227
PLC, *see* Power Line Carrier
Plenum area, 171, 173, 382, 636–637
Plot plan, 26, 222, 225
Plumbing facility requirements, 87
Plumbing fixtures, 56
  schedules, 95
  symbols, 273
PMT (photo mechanical transfer), 27
Point of beginning (P.O.B.), 223–224
Point of view, 178–179
Polar coordinates, 222
Post and beam framing, 143
Post hold-down (concrete slab floor), 289, 293, 299
Pouché, 56, 66
Power line carrier (PLC), 271

Precast concrete:
  floor systems using, 154, 166
  roof systems using, 154–155, 168
  wall systems using, 154–155, 166–168
Predrawn schedules, 414
Preliminary designs/reviews, 27, 68, 93, 230, 628
Preliminary drawings, 5, 9, 182, 463, 467, 557
Preservatives, wood, 125–126
Prestressed concrete, precast, 152–153
Processor, computer, 271, 429
Production department, 4–5
Production drawings, 106, 199
Professional organizations, involvement in, 7
Profiling, 20
Programming, 4, 186, 550
Programming, project, 180
Project architect, 5, 95, 198, 386, 467
Project book, 191–192, 396, 441, 474, 500
Project programming, 180
Proportional dividers, 45
Public buildings, accessibility of, 80–89, 164, 443
Punch list, 13, 390, 550, 554–557

Radio frequency, 271
Rafters, hip, 333, 539
Rainfall, 9, 121, 126
Ramps, 84–85, 93, 181, 447, 557
Raster drawings (CAD), 52
Redline, 4, 474
Reference bubbles, 33, 51, 266, 275, 280, 306, 371, 386, 391–392
Referencing, 50–55, 165, 290, 374, 386, 487
Regional considerations, 183–185
Regulations, 13, 84, 87, 182, 263, 508
Reinforcing, 149–158, 297, 310, 431, 447
Reinhardt, C. W., 23
Reprodrafting, 27, 55
Reproduction methods, 26–29, 48, 208
Request for Information (RFI), 13
Resources, 4–6, 68, 112, 431
Restroom facilities, 88
Retail sources, 7
Reviews, 5, 7, 9–10
Revit, 10, 15, 79–106, 280–281, 550
  case study, 597–625
  design development, 552–553
  detailing, 451–452
  exterior elevations, 389
  floor plans, 280–285
  interior elevations, 397
  schedules, 411–413
    doors, 419
    windows, 419
  site plans, 228–231, 554
  tenant improvement, 650
Revit checklist, 283, 285
Revolving doors, 268
Rigid frame, 109
Rigid insulation, 111
Riprap, 122–123, 241–242
Risers, 276, 423–424, 429, 443–445, 447, 449
Rolling original drawings, 47
Rolling ruler, 45
Roofs and roof systems, 136, 144–149, 153–157, 311, 318–346
Roof drainage, 121–122, 624, 624
Roof framing, 102, 148, 308, 318–346, 498–501, 539–544
  design, 320
  hip roof, 323–327
  light steel roof, 157
  materials for, 333

decking, 157
  steel, 157, 340
  wood, 142, 144–145, 346,
  wood and steel combined, 335–336
  skylight, 328
Roof plans, 311, 319–330, 446, 482–483, 524–525, 592–593
Room finish schedules, 15, 406, 408–409
Room manual, 49
Rough opening, 261, 263, 433, 435–436
Rounding off, 38, 41, 278
Royal Truck Stop, 262–263

Sawn lumber floor joist, 136. *See also* Joists
Sawn lumber roof systems, 147
Scale(s), 27–30
  of drawings, 30, 571
  metric, 39–41
  triangle, 46
Scaling factor, 41, 61, 67, 191, 474
Schedules:
  appliance, 95, 276, 408
  door, 369, 404, 410, 416, 640
  interior finish, *see* Finish schedules
  plumbing fixture, *see* Plumbing fixtures, schedule
  window, 372–374, 404–405, 409, 413, 415, 417
Schematic Design (SD), 7
Scissors drafting, 27, 55, 429
Sculptured doors, 265
Scuppers, 102
Sections, 347–363. *See also* Building sections
Separation wall, 118, 457–458, 630–633
Setbacks, 9, 13–14, 195, 220, 225
Shear wall, 95, 109, 153, 183, 300, 304, 309, 405, 408, 412
Shear wall finish schedule, 408
Sheathing panels, 144, 148
Sheet number, 467
Sheet size, 30, 39, 49–50, 60
Shelving (accessibility), 86
Shoe, 394
Shop drawings, 12, 353
Shot-ins, 291
Shweiri residence, 8–12
Siding, wood, 117, 193, 374–375, 384
Sills, 126, 128, 258, 406, 423, 433
Sisal-Kraft, 343
Site and grading plans, 5, 219–251. *See also* Grading plans
Site analysis, 220
Site improvement plan, 247–249
Site slope, 234, 239
Size:
  lettering, 30, 50, 65, 280
  net/nominal, 25
Size dimensions, 25
Sizing:
  net/nominal, 25
Sizing details, 429
Sketches/sketching, 44
Skylight attic, 102, 112, 272, 324, 326–328
Slab floors, concrete, *see* Concrete floor systems
Sliding doors, 19, 267
Smoke, 118
Snow, 115
Soffit, 195
Soft conversion, 38, 41
Soils, 5, 12, 149, 184, 225–227
Soils map, 225
Solar, 129
Solar plotting, 130

Solatube, 112
Solid core (SC), 404
Solstice, 131–132
Sound (as environmental concern), 112, 117
Space planning, *see* Tenant improvements (case study)
Split-level residence, floor plans for, 254
Spread footing schedules, 95, 409, 413
Stair lifts, 448, 451
Stairways, 14, 118, 443–448, 514
    composite stairway assemblies, 447
    computations, 443
    details of, 446–447
    guardrails for, 444–446
    handrails for, 444
    headroom clearance with, 444
    steel stairways, 446–447
    width of, 443–444
Standards (office), 17–78
    abbreviations, 31
    dimensioning, 25, 31
    for drafting, 26
    hand drawing, 44
    graphic, 31, 32
    graphic symbols, 32
    layering, 62
    lettering, 20–24, 30
    lettering size, 30
    lines, 18–19
    materials, 31
    materials in section, 31
    military specification, 105
    metrics, 35–43
    office, 30, 49–50
    pen settings, 65
    and procedure, 186
    Revit, 84, 102
    scale of drawings, 30
    sheet size, 30
    scale of drawings, 55
    size of sheets, 30
    and techniques, 18
    X-referencing, 54–55
Standardized sheets, 27
Standard titles, 50, 65
Steel, 109, 156, 169–174, 262–265, 335–338
    columns, 62, 99, 109, 169–171, 262–265, 297
    decking roof system, 157
    framing, 157
    reinforcing of concrete, 152
    roof framing system, light, 157
    sections, 353, 358, 382
    stairways, 446–447
    structures, 305, 359, 382, 424
    studs, 155–156, 160, 262–263, 271, 274
    stud wall framing system, 156
Steel and masonry building, *see* Mann Theater Building (case study)
Stem wall, 291, 295, 304, 431
Stepped footing, 366, 380–381, 384
Stories, number of, 13
Straightedge, parallel, 24, 45–46
Structural system, selection of, 182–183, 191
Stucco, 374
Stud framing system, 162–163, 169
Studs:
    steel, 156–157
    wood, 140–144, 162
Styrofoam, 435, 486
Sump pit, 123
Sun, 129, 135
Sustainable architecture, 112–113
Swale, 242

Sweet's Catalog File, 265, 268
Symbols:
    doors and windows, 405
    floor plan, 270

Tabulated schedules, 404–406
Tape, 27–28
Task areas, planning of, 628, 632
Task numbers, 196
Temperature, 48, 115, 123, 125
Templates, 44–45, 105, 273
Tenant improvements (case study), 627–652
    "as-built" drawings, 628
    details, 452–453
    partition walls and sections, 633
    Revit, 650
    working drawings, 642
Termites, 125, 127
Theater (case study), 549–595
3-D models, 75, 96–97, 101, 188, 197, 199, 387, 467
Thompson residence, 350
Thresholds, 84, 87
Tilt-up wall panels, 153–154
Title references, 391
Titles, 30, 50, 62
    standard, 50, 65, 69
Toilet, 89–91
Tongue-and-groove planking, 138–140, 145, 164–165
Topography map, 225–226, 228, 241
Top plates, 356, 368, 380
Top view, 26, 197
Translucent films, 26, 47
Treads, 276, 443–447
Trenching, 297–299, 309, 562
Triangles, 24, 45–46, 49
Triangle scale, 46
Trombe wall, 111
Trough drains, 122
Trusses, 145, 148, 336–337, 496
T-square, 46
Two-hour area separation wall, 118
Two-pour system (concrete slab floors), 149, 291
Two story residence, *see* Blu residence (case study)

Underground gases, 108, 123
Underwriters laboratory (UL), 116
Unit change, 37
Urinal, 84, 87
Utility plan, 22, 245, 554
Utility symbols, *see* Electrical and utility symbols

Vector drawings, 52
Vellum, 24–28
Veneer, masonry, 158–159, 193
Ventilation system, attic, 326
Ventilators, 119
Vertical axis wind turbine (VAWT), 126
Vertical control dimension, 35–36
Vertical control plane, 33
Vertical lifts, 448–449, 452
Vertical links, 421–452. *See also* Stairways
Vicinity map, 222
Virtual space, 50, 52, 59–60, 73

Wall assemblies, fire-rated, 13, 422, 453, 635
Wall finish schedule, shear, 408
Walls and wall systems:
    concrete walls, 153
        precast concrete walls, 154
        tilt-up wall panels, 153

masonry walls, 157, 159
    wood walls, 142, 162
Wall sections, 351–353
Water closet, 84, 87, 90–91
Water heater, 281
Waterproofing, 123, 386
Water table, 108, 123, 125
Weatherproofing, 385, 433–434
Western (platform) framing, 142–144
Wheelchairs, 85–86
Wheelchair lifts, 447
Wind, 126
Windows, 372
    detail, 53, 430, 432, 434–437
    dimensioning, 258–260
    and doors, 261
    dotted lines on, 377
    duel glazed, 111
    finished opening, 261
    fixed, 373–374
    flashing, 112
    head, 20, 423, 434
    in plan view, 268
    jamb, 20, 423, 434
    number symbols, 268
    rough opening, 261, 435
    schedules, 405, 414–415, 417–418
    sill, 433
    symbols, 269, 405–406
    tenant improvements, 640
    types of, 376–377
Wiring, electrical, 271
Wood:
    building sections, drawings of, 163–165
    deterioration, 120
    engineered, 140
    floor system, 136, 291, 529
    foundation, 295, 299
    framing, 255, 333, 335, 380
    material, 162–163
    pressure-treated, 125–126
    post and beam, 142, 164
    for roof framing, 144–145, 147–148
    siding, 374
    stair, 444, 447
    truss, 145
    wall, 142
Wood floors and wood floor systems, 136–141
Wood frame structures, 255, 380, 382
Wood residence (case study), *see* Blu or Jadyn Residence
Wood roof systems, 144–148
Wood siding, 144, 374–375, 377
Wood wall systems, 142
    balloon framing, 143
    engineered lumber sheathing, 144
    planking, 145
    post and beam framing, 143
    western (platform) framing, 142
Word processing, 429, 467
Working drawings, 5–6, 59, 68, 70, 75, 89, 95, 102, 104–105, 132, 163, 165–167, 169, 187–190, 195, 197, 200, 222, 254, 276, 446–448, 450, 463, 467, 473, 541, 550, 553, 556–557, 560, 563, 628, 630, 632–633, 636, 642
Working drawings punch list, 608, 618

X-referencing (X-ref), 50, 52, 54

Zoom-in, 28, 59, 69, 75